MW01091932

Teacher Guidebook Level C

A Reason For Spelling® Teacher Guidebook - Level C

ISBN#0-936785-30-6

Published by The Concerned Group, Inc.
PO Box 1000, 700 East Granite, Siloam Springs, Arkansas 72761

Publisher: Russ L. Potter, II • Senior Editor: Bill Morelan
Copy Editors: Mary Alice Hill, Edward Sutherland • Story Editor: Tricia Schnell
Project Director: Lauren Aloha • Proofreader: Rachel Kulp, Becky Kinzey
Layout Director: Preston Toombs

Created by MOE Studio, Inc.
Authors: Rebecca Burton, Eva Hill, Leah Knowlton, Kay Sutherland
Black and White Illustrations: James McCullough • Colorization: Mark Decker
Design and Layout: Greg Hauth • Project Leader: Greg Sutherland

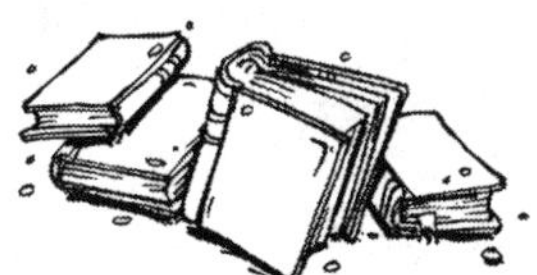

For more information about ***A Reason For Spelling,® A Reason For Handwriting,® A Reason For Science,®*** and ***A Reason For Guided Reading,®*** write to the address above or call (479) 549-9000

www.AReasonFor.com

Contents:

Acknowledgments:

Field Test Participants:

Virginia Allen, East Rockaway, New York • Mrs. Christine Baker, Belleville, Pennsylvania • Judy M. Banks, Carmichael, California • Darya Birch, San Clemente, California • Mari Anne Burns, Baton Rouge, Louisiana • Karen Dafflitto, St. Louis, Missouri • Kristen J. Dorsett, Prescott, Arizona • Ms. Laura Guerrera, East Rockaway, New York • Mrs. Anne Gutierrez, San Antonio, Texas • Jeanette O. Kappel, Winstead, Minnesota • Sharon K. Kobilka, San Antonio, Texas • Connie Kozitza, Winsted, Minnesota • Vivian I. Sawyer, Carmichael, California • Harold W. Souther, San Antonio, Texas • Cleo F. Staples, Auburn, California • Suezy Tucker, Auburn, California • Martha Woodbury, Los Angeles, California

Special thanks to:

Dr. Larry Burton, Dr. Carol Campbell, Dr. Lee Netherton, Melvin Northrup, Phyllis Paytee, Dr. Linda Romig

Placement Tests

In order to evaluate readiness and accurately meet individual student need, a simple placement test is recommended at the beginning of each school year.

Step 1: *Administer the test*

ay) Number your paper from one to twenty. I will say the word once, use the word in a sentence, then say the word again. Write a word beside each number on your paper.

(Allow ample time and carefully monitor progress.)

Step 2: *Evaluate the corrected tests using the following criteria:*

If the student correctly spells 17 to 20 words:
- Assign the student to Level C program
- Encourage the student to work independently
- Select and assign several Other Word Forms to spell and test

If the student correctly spells 8 to 16 words:
- Assign the student to Level C program
- Allow opportunities to work independently
- Offer Other Word Forms activities

If the student correctly spells 0 to 7 words:
- Administer Level B placement test
- Based on results, you may choose to:
  a) Assign student to Level B worktext and offer Other Word Form activities, or
  b) Assign student to Level C worktext, without optional activities

Placement Test Level C

1.	began	We **began** to eat.
2.	hello	The children said **hello** to us.
3.	north	We traveled **north.**
4.	place	This **place** is pretty.
5.	broke	The window **broke** in the storm.
6.	sudden	The **sudden** noise scared us.
7.	belong	This does not **belong** to me.
8.	rush	He was in a **rush** to get home.
9.	sight	That was a funny **sight.**
10.	cage	My bird is in a **cage.**
11.	seventh	I was the **seventh** in line.
12.	track	She ran around the **track.**
13.	paper	My **paper** is torn.
14.	busy	Dad's new job keeps him **busy.**
15.	smile	She has a cheerful **smile.**
16.	open	He left the door **open.**
17.	song	That new **song** is fun to sing.
18.	mouth	My braces make my **mouth** sore.
19.	apart	I can't tell the twins **apart.**
20.	able	I will be **able** to go with them.

Placement Test Level B

1.	hat	I bought a new **hat.**
2.	men	The **men** are working hard.
3.	into	The frog jumped **into** the pond.
4.	box	We have a **box** of toys.
5.	must	They **must** be tired.
6.	late	She will be **late** for school.
7.	keep	I **keep** wishing it was my birthday.
8.	hope	I **hope** you turned in your paper.
9.	today	**Today** is my birthday.
10.	car	The **car** is shiny and clean.
11.	like	I **like** to play outside.
12.	bird	The **bird** hops across the yard.
13.	books	He has some **books** to read.
14.	food	This **food** is very good.
15.	round	The world is **round.**
16.	toy	The **toy** is for him.
17.	dish	The **dish** has fruit in it.
18.	back	Let's come **back** tomorrow.
19.	think	I **think** this is a fun game.
20.	done	If the food is **done,** we can eat.

Day One

Literature Connection - Each week begins with a Scripture verse, followed by a theme story that develops the principles found in that verse. Topic and description are provided to inform the teacher of story content. Some teachers may choose to use this theme story for the Monday morning devotional. (A dramatized CD version of the story is also available.)

Discussion Time *(optional)* - Discussion questions follow each story, giving the teacher the opportunity to evaluate student understanding, and to encourage students to apply the values found in the Scripture to their own lives.

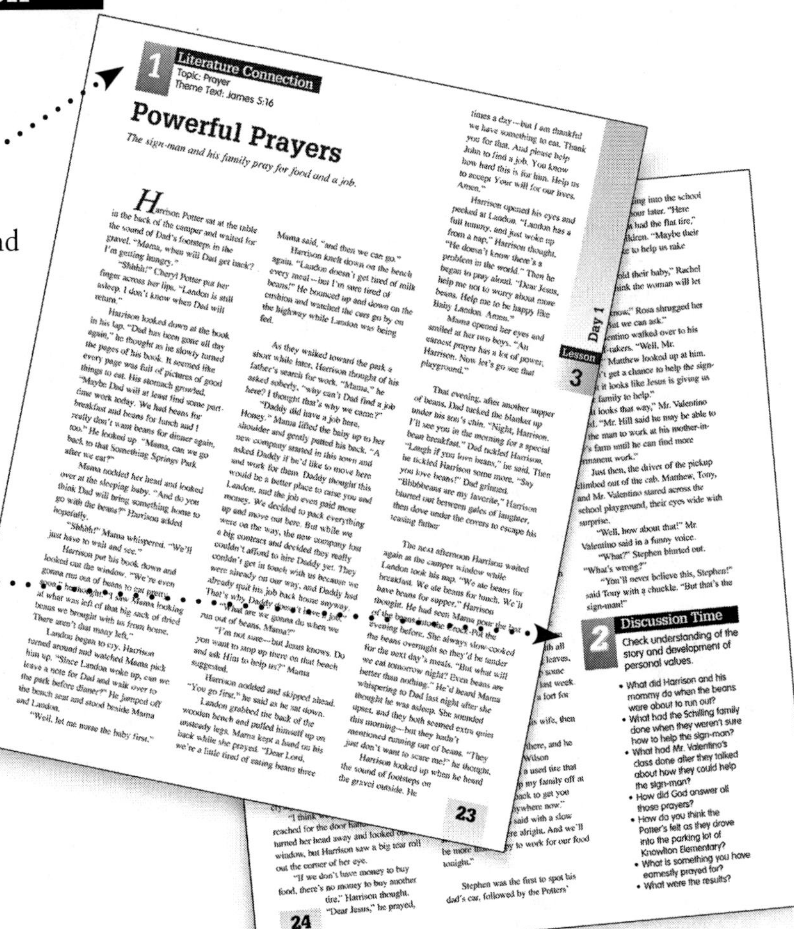
1 Literature Connection
Topic: Prayer
Theme Text: James 5:16

Powerful Prayers

The sign-man and his family pray for food and a job.

2 Discussion Time
Check understanding of the story and development of personal values.

- What did Harrison and his mommy do when the beans were about to run out?
- What had the Schilling family done when they weren't sure how to help the sign-man?
- What had Mr. Valentino's class done after they talked about how they could help the sign-man?
- How did God answer all those prayers?
- How do you think the Potter's felt as they drove into the parking lot of Knowlton Elementary?
- What is something you have earnestly prayed for?
- What were the results?

Lesson 3 Day 1

23

24

Day One (cont.)

Preview - The test—study—test sequence begins with this pre-test which primarily uses sentences related to the story. Research has shown that immediate correction by the student—under teacher supervision—is one of the best ways to learn to spell.

Customize Your List *(notepaper graphic)* - An opportunity is provided to test additional words of the teacher's choice.

Say *(bubble graphic)* - Instructions to the students that are to be read aloud by the teacher are marked with the Say symbol for easy identification.

Take a Minute *(clock graphic)* - Simple instructions are provided for committing to memory the Scripture verses upon which the stories are based.

Progress Chart *(chart graphic)* - Students may record their Preview scores for later comparison against their Posttest scores.

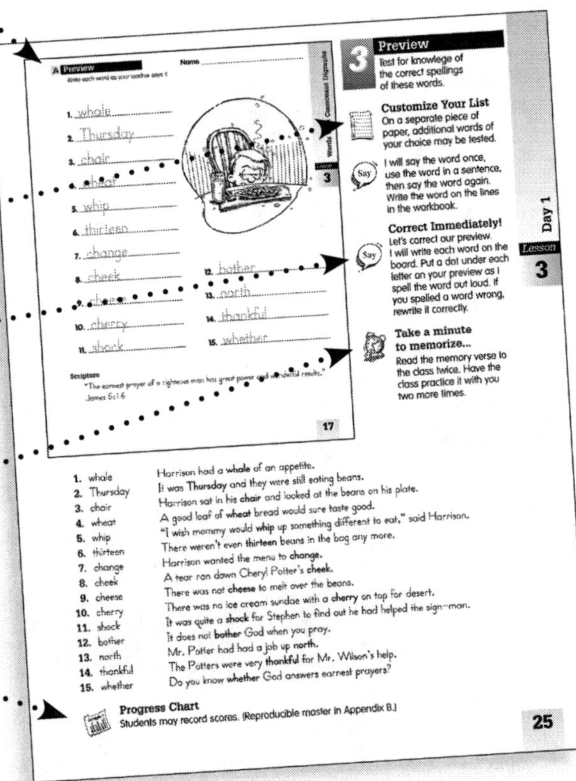
3 Preview
Test for knowledge of the correct spellings of these words.

Customize Your List
On a separate piece of paper, additional words of your choice may be tested.

I will say the word once, use the word in a sentence, then say the word again. Write the word on the lines in the workbook.

Correct Immediately!
Let's correct our preview. I will write each word on the board. Put a dot under each letter on your preview as I spell the word out loud. If you spelled a word wrong, rewrite it correctly.

Take a minute to memorize...
Read the memory verse to the class twice. Have the class practice it with you two more times.

Lesson 3 Day 1

1. whale — Harrison had a **whale** of an appetite.
2. Thursday — It was **Thursday** and they were still eating beans.
3. chair — Harrison sat in his **chair** and looked at the beans on his plate.
4. wheat — A good loaf of **wheat** bread would sure taste good.
5. whip — "I wish mommy would **whip** up something different to eat," said Harrison.
6. thirteen — There weren't even **thirteen** beans in the bag any more.
7. change — Harrison wanted the menu to **change**.
8. cheek — A tear ran down Cheryl Potter's **cheek**.
9. cheese — There was not **cheese** to melt over the beans.
10. cherry — There was no ice cream sundae with a **cherry** on top for desert.
11. shock — It was quite a **shock** for Stephen to find out he had helped the sign-man.
12. bother — It does not **bother** God when you pray.
13. north — Mr. Potter had had a job up **north**.
14. thankful — The Potters were very **thankful** for Mr. Wilson's help.
15. whether — Do you know **whether** God answers earnest prayers?

Progress Chart
Students may record scores. (Reproducible master in Appendix B.)

17

25

Day One (cont.)

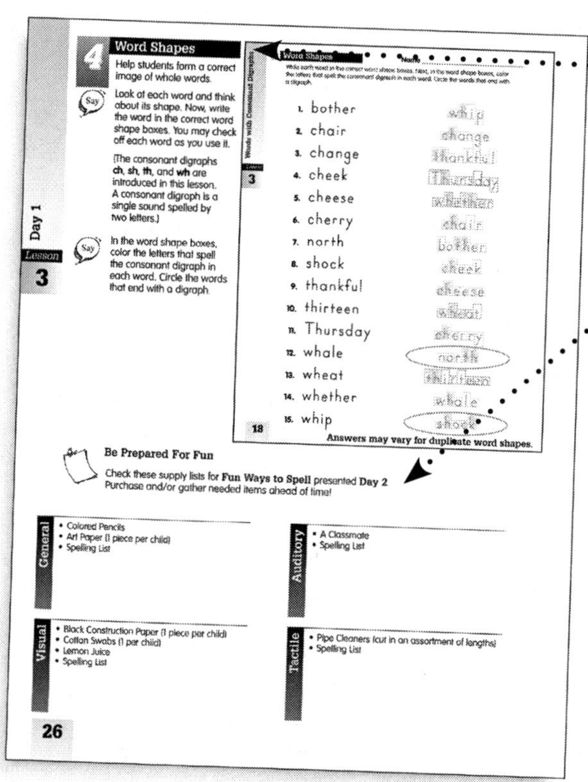

4 Word Shapes

Help students form a correct image of whole words.

Say: Look at each word and think about its shape. Now, write the word in the correct word shape boxes. You may check off each word as you use it.

(The consonant digraphs **ch**, **sh**, **th**, and **wh** are introduced in this lesson. A consonant digraph is a single sound spelled by two letters.)

Say: In the word shape boxes, color the letters that spell the consonant digraph in each word. Circle the words that end with a digraph.

Day 1 Lesson 3

1. bother
2. chair
3. change
4. cheek
5. cheese
6. cherry
7. north
8. shock
9. thankful
10. thirteen
11. Thursday
12. whale
13. wheat
14. whether
15. whip

Answers may vary for duplicate word shapes.

Be Prepared For Fun

Check these supply lists for **Fun Ways to Spell** presented **Day 2**. Purchase and/or gather needed items ahead of time!

General
- Colored Pencils
- Art Paper (1 piece per child)
- Spelling List

Auditory
- A Classmate
- Spelling List

Visual
- Black Construction Paper (1 piece per child)
- Cotton Swabs (1 per child)
- Lemon Juice
- Spelling List

Tactile
- Pipe Cleaners (cut in an assortment of lengths)
- Spelling List

26

Word Shapes - The use of "Shape Boxes" is a research-based method that helps students form a correct visual image of each spelling word. An additional exercise is provided to enhance student identification of spelling patterns and thus strengthen phonemic awareness.

Be Prepared for Fun *(list graphic)* - For teacher convenience, a weekly supply list is provided for "Fun Ways to Spell" on Day 1. Supplies for the "General" activity are readily available in most classrooms. Other categories may require minimal extra planning.

Day Two

Hide & Seek - Another research-proven method of spelling instruction, Hide & Seek, is highly effective for dealing with multiple intelligences and varying learning styles.

Other Word Forms *(optional)* - A variety of activities allow students to become familiar with other forms of the week's spelling words.

Fun Ways to Spell - Four options are offered each week. In addition to a "General" activity, "Auditory," "Tactile," and "Visual" options are provided for students with different learning styles. Suggestions are also given for adapting these activities to various classroom settings.

Introduction

Level

C

Day Three

Language Arts Activity - Research studies show that meaningful, practical use of spelling words helps students become more familiar with the words they are studying. The weekly "Working with Words" activity is designed to offer practice in this area.

Take a Minute - Reminders to commit Scripture verses to memory are provided periodically.

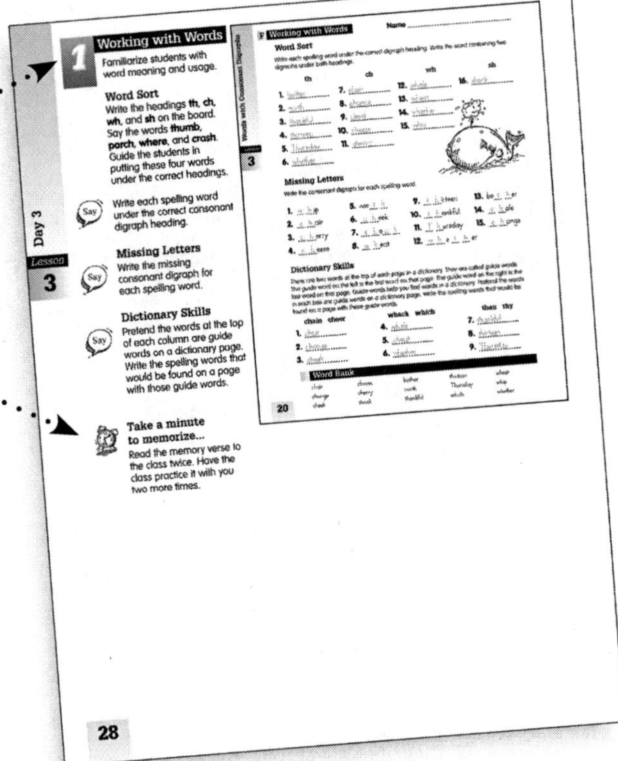

Day 3

Lesson 3

1 Working with Words

Familiarize students with word meaning and usage.

Word Sort

Write the headings **th, ch, wh,** and **sh** on the board. Say the words **thumb, porch, where,** and **crash**. Guide the students in putting these four words under the correct headings.

Say: Write each spelling word under the correct consonant digraph heading.

Missing Letters

Say: Write the missing consonant digraph for each spelling word.

Dictionary Skills

Say: Pretend the words at the top of each column are guide words on a dictionary page. Write the spelling words that would be found on a page with those guide words.

Take a minute to memorize...

Read the memory verse to the class twice. Have the class practice it with you two more times.

Working with Words — Name

Word Sort

Missing Letters

Dictionary Skills

Word Bank

20

28

Day Four

Dictation - Students write dictated words to complete sentences. This strengthens their word usage and context skills. Previously taught spelling words are also included in this activity, providing maintenance of spelling skills.

Proofreading - Proofreading allows students to become familiar with the format of standardized tests as they mark misspelled words. Proofreading is also a critical skill that can be incorporated in students' own writing.

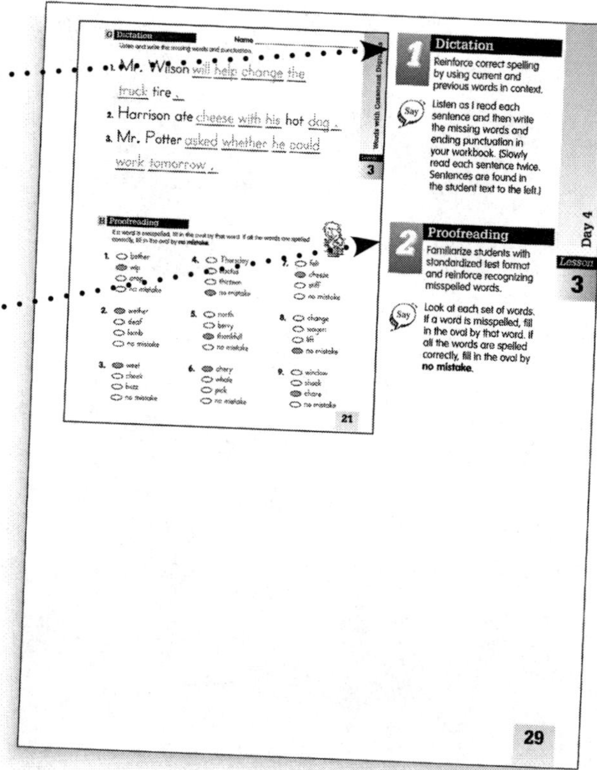

G Dictation — Name

1. Mr. Wilson will help change the truck tire.
2. Harrison ate cheese with his hot dog.
3. Mr. Potter asked whether he could work tomorrow.

H Proofreading

21

Day 4

Lesson 3

1 Dictation

Reinforce correct spelling by using current and previous words in context.

Say: Listen as I read each sentence and then write the missing words and ending punctuation in your workbook. (Slowly read each sentence twice. Sentences are found in the student text to the left.)

2 Proofreading

Familiarize students with standardized test format and reinforce recognizing misspelled words.

Say: Look at each set of words. If a word is misspelled, fill in the oval by that word. If all the words are spelled correctly, fill in the oval by **no mistake**.

29

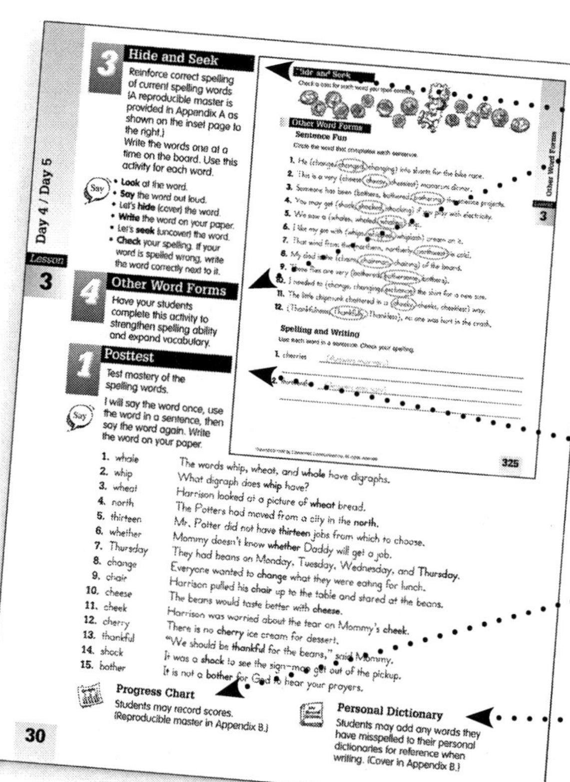

Day 4 / Day 5

Lesson 3

3 Hide and Seek

Reinforce correct spelling of current spelling words. (A reproducible master is provided in Appendix A as shown on the inset page to the right.)

Write the words one at a time on the board. Use this activity for each word.

Say
- **Look** at the word.
- **Say** the word out loud.
- Let's **hide** (cover) the word.
- **Write** the word on your paper.
- Let's **seek** (uncover) the word.
- **Check** your spelling. If your word is spelled wrong, write the word correctly next to it.

4 Other Word Forms

Have your students complete this activity to strengthen spelling ability and expand vocabulary.

1 Posttest

Test mastery of the spelling words.

Say: I will say the word once, use the word in a sentence, then say the word again. Write the word on your paper.

1. whale — The words whip, wheat, and **whole** have digraphs.
2. whip — What digraph does **whip** have?
3. wheat — Harrison looked at a picture of **wheat** bread.
4. north — The Potters had moved from a city in the **north.**
5. thirteen — Mr. Potter did not have **thirteen** jobs from which to choose.
6. whether — Mommy doesn't know **whether** Daddy will get a job.
7. Thursday — They had beans on Monday, Tuesday, Wednesday, and **Thursday.**
8. change — Everyone wanted to **change** what they were eating for lunch.
9. chair — Harrison pulled his **chair** up to the table and stared at the beans.
10. cheese — The beans would taste better with **cheese.**
11. cheek — Harrison was worried about the tear on Mommy's **cheek.**
12. cherry — There is no **cherry** ice cream for dessert.
13. thankful — "We should be **thankful** for the beans," said Mommy.
14. shock — It was a **shock** to see the sign-man get out of the pickup.
15. bother — It is not a **bother** for God to hear your prayers.

Progress Chart
Students may record scores. (Reproducible master in Appendix B.)

Personal Dictionary
Students may add any words they have misspelled to their personal dictionaries for reference when writing. (Cover in Appendix B.)

30

(Inset page:)

Hide and Seek

Other Word Forms

Sentence Fun

Spelling and Writing

325

Day Four (cont.)

Hide & Seek/Other Word Forms *(optional)* - These activities provide additional opportunity for students to practice other forms of their spelling words. (Note: These pages are not in the Student Worktext. A reproducible master for each week is provided in Appendix A.)

Day Five

Posttest - The test—study—test sequence of learning is completed with the posttest. Again, most sentences relate to the theme story.

Progress Chart *(chart graphic)* - Students may now record their posttest scores to evaluate their weekly progress.

Personal Dictionary *(dictionary graphic)* - Students may add any words they have misspelled to their personal dictionaries. Each student may refer to his/her custom dictionary while journaling or during other writing activities.

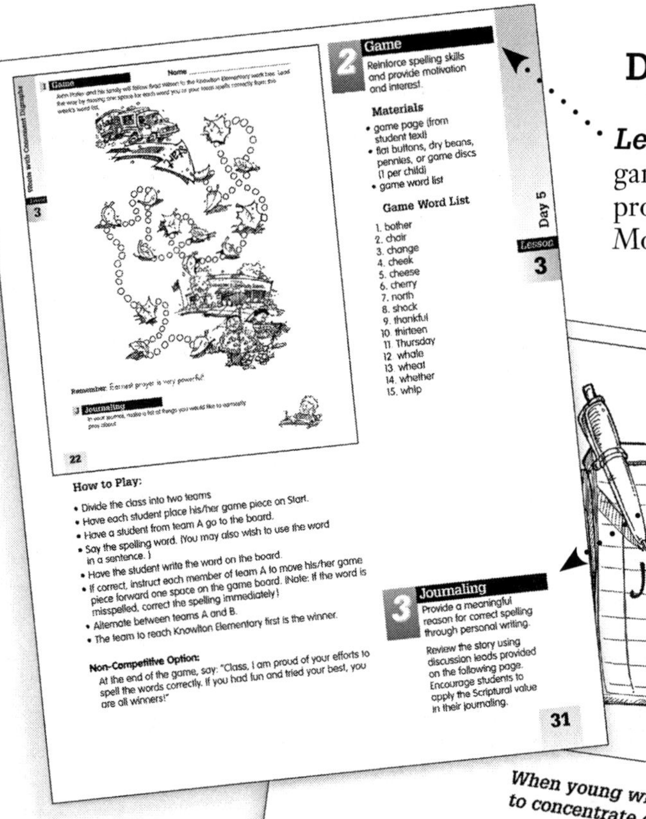

Remember: Earnest prayer is very powerful!

22

2 Game

Reinforce spelling skills and provide motivation and interest.

Materials
- game page (from student text)
- flat buttons, dry beans, pennies, or game discs (1 per child)
- game word list

Game Word List
1. bother
2. chair
3. change
4. cheek
5. cheese
6. cherry
7. north
8. shock
9. thankful
10. thirteen
11. Thursday
12. whale
13. wheat
14. whether
15. whip

Day 5

Lesson 3

How to Play:
- Divide the class into two teams
- Have each student place his/her game piece on Start.
- Have a student from team A go to the board.
- Say the spelling word. (You may also wish to use the word in a sentence.)
- Have the student write the word on the board.
- If correct, instruct each member of team A to move his/her game piece forward one space on the game board. (Note: If the word is misspelled, correct the spelling immediately!)
- Alternate between teams A and B.
- The team to reach Knowlton Elementary first is the winner.

Non-Competitive Option:
At the end of the game, say: "Class, I am proud of your efforts to spell the words correctly. If you had fun and tried your best, you are all winners!"

3 Journaling

Provide a meaningful reason for correct spelling through personal writing.

Review the story using discussion leads provided on the following page. Encourage students to apply the Scriptural value in their journaling.

31

Day Five (cont.)

Learning Game *(optional)* - The weekly "board game" may be used to reinforce spelling skills and produce motivation and interest in good spelling. Most games can be played multiple times.

My Journal

Journal Entry - The underlying goal of spelling instruction is to create better writers! This weekly journaling activity allows students to apply their spelling skills in a meaningful way, while encouraging them to make the featured value their own. Guided discussion questions are provided to assist in reviewing the value taught by the story.

When young writers are free to concentrate on what they want to say rather than mechanics, their thoughts can flow more freely.*

Thought for the Week - Quotes from the comprehensive spelling research provide helpful insights for the teacher.

32

*Wilde, Sandra. 1990. A Proposal for a New Spelling Curriculum. The Elementary School Journal, Vol. 90, No. 3, January: 275-289

Introduction

Level C

Research Basis

A Reason For Spelling® emphasizes a balance between spelling skills, application, and student enjoyment. In short, it is designed to be both meaningful and fun! Each level promotes successful classroom practices while incorporating the following research findings:

Research Findings:	Application:
Daily Practice. A daily period of teacher-directed spelling activities based on meaningful content greatly enhances student proficiency in spelling.	Daily lessons in ***A Reason For Spelling***® provide systematic development of spelling skills with a focus on Scripture verses and values.
Spelling Lists. The most productive spelling lists feature developmentally-appropriate words of highest frequency in writing.	Through daily lessons, challenge words, and other word forms, ***A Reason For Spelling***® focuses on the high frequency words children and adults use in daily writing.
Test—Study—Test. Effective educational programs are built on the learning model of "Test—Study—Test."	***A Reason For Spelling***® follows a weekly pretest/posttest format, and also includes a cumulative review for each unit.
Accurate Feedback. Pretest and proofreading results are crucial in helping students identify words that require their special attention.	Regular pretests and proofreading activities in ***A Reason For Spelling***® help students identify words requiring their special attention.
Visual Imaging. Learning to spell a word involves forming a correct visual image of the whole word, rather than visualizing syllables or parts.	Every lesson in ***A Reason For Spelling***® features word-shape grids to help students form a correct visual image of each spelling word.
Study Procedures. The most effective word-study procedures involve visual, auditory, and tactile modalities.	***A Reason For Spelling***® uses the "look, say, hide, write, seek, check" method as a primary teaching tool.
Learning Games. Well-designed games motivate student interest and lead to spelling independence.	***A Reason For Spelling***® includes a wide variety of spelling games at each instructional level.
Self-Correction. Student focus, accomplished through such activities as self-correction of pretests, is an essential strategy for spelling mastery at every grade and ability level.	Teacher directed self-correction of pretests and reviews is encouraged throughout ***A Reason For Spelling***®.
Regular Application. Frequent opportunities to use spelling words in everyday writing contribute significantly to the maintenance of spelling ability.	***A Reason For Spelling***® provides opportunities for journaling in each lesson to promote the use of assigned spelling words in personal writing.

Research Bibliography

Cohen, Leo A. 1969. *Evaluating Structural Analysis Methods Used in Spelling Books.* Doctoral Thesis, Boston University.

Davis, Zephaniah T. 1987. Upper Grades Spelling Instruction: What Difference Does It Make? *English Journal*, March: 100-101.

Dolch, E.W. 1936. A Basic Sight Vocabulary. *The Elementary School Journal*, Vol. 36: 456-460.

Downing, John, Robert M. Coughlin and Gene Rich. 1986. Children's Invented Spellings in the Classroom. *The Elementary School Journal*, Vol. 86, No. 3, January: 295-303.

Fiderer, Adele. 1995. *Practical Assessments for Literature-Based Reading Classrooms.* New York: Scholastic Professional Books.

Fitzsimmons, Robert J., and Bradley M. Loomer. 1980. *Spelling: The Research Basis.* Iowa City: The University of Iowa.

Gardner, Howard.1993. *Multiple Intelligences: The Theory in Practice.* New York: Basic-Books.

Gentry, J. Richard. 1997. *My Kid Can't Spell.* Portsmouth, NH: Heinemann Educational Books.

Gentry, J. Richard and Jean Wallace Gillet. 1993. *Teaching Kids to Spell.* Portsmouth, NH:Heinemann Educational Books.

Gentry, J. Richard. 1985. You Can Analyze Developmental Spelling-And Here's How To Do It! *Early Years K-8*, May:1-4.

Goswami, Usha. 1991. Learning about Spelling Sequences: The Role of Onsets and Rimes in Analogies in Reading. *Child Development*, 62, 1110-1123.

Graves, Donald H.1977. Research Update: Spelling Texts and Structural Analysis Methods. *Language Arts 54* January: 86-90.

Harp, Bill. 1988. When the Principal Asks, "Why Are Your Kids Giving Each Other Spelling Tests?" *Reading Teacher*, Vol. 41, No. 7, March: 702-704.

Hoffman, Stevie and Nancy Knipping. 1988. Spelling Revisited: The Child's Way. *Childhood Education*, June: 284-287.

Horn, Ernest.1926. *A Basic Writing Vocabulary: 10,000 Frequently Used Words in Writing.* Monograph First Series, No. 4. Iowa City: The University of Iowa.

Horn, Thomas. 1946. *The Effect of the Corrected Test on Learning to Spell.* Master's Thesis, The University of Iowa.

Horsky, Gregory Alexander. 1974. *A Study of the Perception of Letters and Basic Sight Vocabulary Words of Fourth and Fifth Grade Children.* Doctoral Thesis, The University of Iowa.

Lacey, Cheryl. 1994. *Moving On In Spelling.* Jefferson City, Missouri: Scholastic.

Lutz, Elaine. 1986. ERIC/RCS Report: Invented Spelling and Spelling Development. *Language Arts*, Vol. 63, No. 7, November: 742-744.

Marino, Jacqueline L. 1978. *Children's Use of Phonetic, Graphemic, and Morphophonemic Cues in a Spelling Task.* Doctoral Thesis, State University of New York at Albany.

Morris, Darrell, Laurie Nelson and Jan Perney. 1986. Exploring the Concept of 'Spelling Instructional Level' Through the Analysis of Error-Types. *The Elementary School Journal*, Vol. 87, No. 2, 195-197.

Nicholson, Tom and Sumner Schachter. 1979. Spelling Skill and Teaching Practice-Putting Them Back Together Again. *Language Arts*, Vol. 56, No. 7, October: 804-809.

Rothman, Barbara. 1997. *Practical Phonics Strategies to Build Beginning Reading and Writing Skills.* Medina, Washington: Institute for Educational Development.

Scott, Jill E. 1994. Spelling for Readers and Writers. *The Reading Teacher*, Vol. 48, No. 2, October: 188-190.

Simmons, Janice L. 1978. *The Relationship Between an Instructional Level in Spelling and the Instructional Level in Reading Among Elementary School Children.* Doctoral Thesis, University of Northern Colorado.

Templeton, Shane. 1986. Synthesis of Research on the Learning and Teaching of Spelling. *Educational Leadership*, March: 73-78.

Tireman, L.S. 1927. *The Value of Marking Hard Spots in Spelling.* Doctoral Thesis, University of Iowa.

Toch, Thomas. 1992. Nu Waz for Kidz tu Lern Rdn, Rtn. *U.S. News & World Report*, September 14: 75-76.

Wagstaff, Janiel M. *Phonics That Work! New Strategies for the Reading/Writing Classroom.* Jefferson City, Missouri: Scholastic.

Watson, Alan J. 1988. Developmental Spelling: A Word Categorizing Instructional Experiment. *Journal of Educational Research*, Vol. 82, No. 2, November/December: 82-88.

Webster's New *American Dictionary.* 1995. New York: Merriam-Webster Inc.

Wilde, Sandra. 1990. A Proposal for a New Spelling Curriculum. *The Elementary School Journal*, Vol. 90, No. 3, January: 275-289.

English Second Language (ESL)

Effective teachers are always sensitive to the special spelling challenges faced by ESL students. While it is not practical to provide specific guidelines for every situation where the teacher may encounter students with limited English proficiency, the following general guidelines for two of the most prominent cultural groups (Asian & Hispanic) may prove helpful.

alphabet — Many Asian languages have a significantly different kind of alphabet and students may need considerable practice recognizing English letters and sounds.

vowels — Some Asian languages do not have certain English vowel sounds. Speakers often substitute other sounds. Spanish vowels have a single sound: *a* as in *ball*, *e* as in *eight*, *i* as in *ski*, *o* as in *over*, *u* as in *rule*. The Spanish *a* is spelled *e*, *e* is spelled *i* or *y*, and *i* is often spelled *ai* or *ay*.

ô — The variety of *ô* spellings may cause some problems for Spanish-speaking students.

ü, ů — The *ů* sound does not occur in Spanish, and may cause problems.

ou — This sound is spelled *au* in Spanish.

r — This sound does not exist in Spanish. Many Asian languages do not have words ending with *r*.

b, d, h, j — Spanish and Asian speakers often confuse the sounds of *b / d* and *h / j*

ge, gi, j — In Spanish, *ge*, *gi*, and *j* most closely resemble the English *h*.

l, f — Many Asian languages do not have these sounds.

k, q — The letter *k* does not exist in Spanish, but the sound k is spelled with either *c* or *qu*. The letter *q* always occurs with *ue* or *ui*.

p, g — In most Asian languages, the consonants *p* and g do not exist.

v — In Spanish, the letter *v* is pronounced *b*.

w — There are no Spanish-originated words with the letter *w*.

y — In Spanish, *y* is spelled *ll*.

x, z — In Spanish, *x* is never used in the final position. There is no letter or sound for *z*.

ch, sh — The Spanish language does not have the sound *sh*. Spellers often substitute *ch*. Many Asian languages do not contain *sh* or *ch*.

wh, th — The initial *wh* and *th* sounds do not exist in most Spanish and some Asian languages. The Spanish *d*, however, is sometimes pronounced almost like the *th*.

kn — This sound may be difficult for both Spanish and Asian spellers.

s clusters — Spanish clusters that begin with *s* are always preceded by the vowels *a* or *e*. The most common clusters that will cause problems are *sc*, *sk*, *sl*, *sm*, *sn*, *sp*, *sq*, *st*, and *sw*. Many of these do not occur in Asian languages.

pl, fl, tr, fr, dr — These sounds are used in Spanish, but may not be present in some Asian languages.

ng, nk, nt, nd — Many Asian languages don't have *ng*, *nk*, *nt*, or *nd*. Spanish doesn't include the *ng* ending.

silent letters — The only silent letter in Spanish is *h*. Silent consonants such as those in *mb*, *lk*, and *gh* do not occur in Spanish or Asian languages.

double consonants — The only double consonants in Spanish are *cc*, *ll*, and *rr*.

ed — In Spanish, the suffix *ed* is pronounced aid. This can be very confusing, especially when the *ed* has the soft *t* sound as in *dropped*.

plurals — Spanish rules for adding plurals are: For words ending in a vowel, add *s*. For words ending in a consonant, add *es*. This may cause confusion both in pronunciation and spelling of English words.

contractions — Only two contractions are used in Spanish: *a el* becomes *al*, and *de el* becomes *del*. Apostrophes do not exist.

syllables — Many Asian languages consist entirely of one and two syllable words. Thus, many longer English words are often confusing.

Spelling Generalizations

In the English language, spelling cannot be taught primarily by rules or generalizations. It's a complex language that has evolved from many other languages and therefore contains many irregularities. There are exceptions to almost all spelling rules.

Research, however, indicates that some generalizations are of value in teaching children to spell. These generalizations have few exceptions and apply to a large number of words. Familiarity with these spelling rules can be helpful to many learners. In addition, generalizations that deal with adding suffixes to words can be quite valuable in expanding a student's ability to spell other word forms.

The following generalizations may prove to be helpful:

- The letter *q* is always followed by *u*.
- Every syllable contains a vowel. *Y* can also serve as a vowel.
- Words that end in silent *e*:
  ... drop the *e* when adding a suffix beginning with a vowel. (live, living)
  ... keep the *e* when adding a suffix beginning with a consonant. (time, timely)
- Words that end in *y*:
  ... are not changed when adding suffixes if the *y* is preceded by a vowel. (say, saying)
  ... change the *y* to *i* when adding suffixes if the *y* is preceded by a consonant, unless the suffix begins with *i*. (try, tried, trying)
- When *ei* or *ie* are used in a word, the *i* usually comes before the *e* except when they make the /ā/ sound, or follow after a *c*. (believe, eight, ceiling)
- Words ending in one consonant preceded by a single vowel usually double the final consonant when adding a suffix beginning with a vowel. (begin, beginning)
- Words ending with the sounds made by *x*, *s*, *sh*, and *ch* add the suffix *es* to form plurals. (mix, mixes)
- Proper nouns and most proper adjectives begin with capital letters.

Multiple Intelligences

In recognition of the multiple intelligences theory, ***A Reason For Spelling***® provides activities to meet the varied needs of your students. (See "Fun Ways to Spell," and "Hide & Seek.")

Scripture Translation

Each weekly lesson in ***A Reason For Spelling***® begins with a Scripture verse. This is followed by a contemporary theme story designed to bring out key values found in the verse.

Teachers are strongly encouraged to introduce each lesson by reading the "Theme Text" aloud (or have a student read the verse aloud to the class). This helps set the stage for the principles and values students will be focusing on that week.

Scripture verses used in ***A Reason For Spelling***® are similar in most translations, allowing teachers to use the Scripture translation their school prefers, without affecting academic content.

Personal Spelling Dictionary

A great way to encourage students' spelling awareness is to help them develop and maintain their own Personal Spelling Dictionary at their desk to refer to when writing. This can be either a spiral-bound or loose-leaf notebook with a few pages designated for each letter of the alphabet. Throughout the school year, encourage students to constantly add words to their Personal Spelling Dictionary, not only from spelling class, but from other classes as well. These should include words a student finds difficult to spell, as well as words of particular interest. (Reproducible cover in Appendix B.)

Word Walls

Another excellent method of promoting spelling awareness in your classroom is to create a word wall. This wall (often a large bulletin board) contains commonly used words and words of special interest to your class. The classroom word wall becomes a permanent reference list that students may refer to as they read and write.

Words may be arranged in a variety of ways. Some examples include traditional alphabetical order; groups (such as math words, weather words, color words); or by the targeted vowel. For example:

A	E	I	O	U
gate	eaten	bit	horn	fun
tar	dread	like	dog	fur
cat	her	tonight		bubble

Some words could even have picture or context clues added. Sample words from word families being studied, or interesting words students want to know how to spell are added throughout the year. Students should be reminded not to simply copy the words from the wall, but to look at the word needed, then write it from memory—or write the word they are having difficulty with, then check it against the word wall.

Games can be played using the word wall as well.

- Rhyming Words: Ask students to find a word that "begins with G and rhymes with rod."
- Sentence Sense: Write the letter l on the board, then say "Look for a word that begins with an l and fits this sentence: I _ _ _ _ Jesus."
- Chant & Clap: Chant the spelling words, clapping for each vowel or consonant.
- Dictate & Write: Dictate a sentence for students to write using words found only on the wall.
- Read My Mind:

Say: I am thinking of one of the words on the wall. It has ______ letters. It begins with _____ . The vowel is ______. It fits in this sentence: _________________.

Flip Folders

The Flip Folder is a great way for students to use the research-based, time-tested "Look—Hide—Write—Seek—Check" method to learn spelling words. They may do this activity on their own or with a partner.

On the front of a standard file folder, make two cuts to create three flaps (see diagram below). On a separate piece of paper, have students make three columns, then write the words they need to study in the first column. Now have students slide the paper into the folder so that the words are under the first flap.

- Open Flap 1 and ***Look*** at the first word.
- Now ***Hide*** the word by closing the flap.
- Open Flap 2 and ***Write*** the word in the middle column.
- Open Flaps 1 & 2 and ***Seek*** the word to ***Check*** your spelling. If the word is misspelled. . .
- Open Flap 3 and ***Write*** the word correctly in the third column.

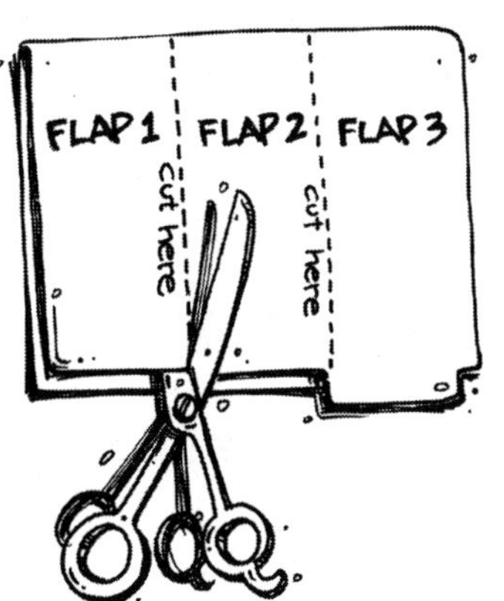

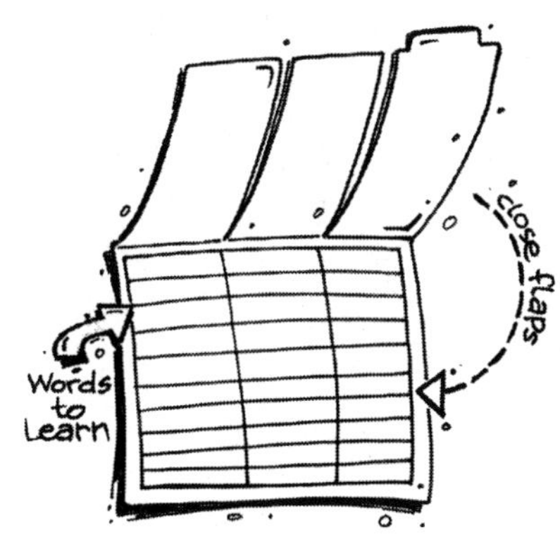

Temporary Spelling/Journaling

The goal of ***A Reason For Spelling***® is to create proficient and self-reliant spellers and writers. By combining inventive spelling (through journaling) with formal spelling instruction, an excellent environment is created for students to develop into expert spellers. (Reproducible Journal cover in Appendix B.)

As children learn to spell, they go through several stages. The move from one stage to another is gradual even though students may spell from more than one stage at one time. Just as a toddler who is talking in complete sentences doesn't suddenly regress to babbling, so students tend to remain relatively stable within and between stages. Recognized stages of spelling development include:

Precognitive Stage: Children use symbols from the alphabet for writing words, but letters are random and do not correspond to sound. (eagle = dfbrt; eighty = acbp)

Semiphonetic Stage: Children understand and consistently represent sounds with letters. Spellings are often abbreviated representing only the initial and/or final sounds. (eagle = e; eighty = a)

Phonetic Stage: Students in this stage spell words like they sound. The speller perceives and represents every sound in a word, though spellings may be unconventional. (eagle = egl; eighty = aty)

Transitional Stage: Students think about how words appear visually. Spelling patterns are apparent. Spellings exhibit customs of English spelling such as vowels in every syllable, correct e-marker and vowel digraph patterns, inflectional endings, and frequent English letter sequences. (eagle = egul; eighty = eightee)

Conventional Stage: This stage develops over years of word study and writing. Correct spelling has different instructional levels. Correct spelling for a group of words that can be spelled by the average third grader would be "third grade level correct" spelling. (eagle = eagle; eighty = eighty)

An effective way to help students transition through the stages is to edit their first drafts, then talk with them about corrections. Discuss why changes are necessary. Encourage students to rewrite journal entries so others can read them easily. Display student work whenever possible. Teach students that invented spelling makes it easier for the writer, but that revision to standard spelling is a courtesy to the reader.

Word Lists

Word lists in ***A Reason For Spelling***® are based on frequency of use in student and adult writing; frequency of use in reading materials; spelling difficulty; and grade level familiarity.

Studies used in the development of these lists include: *Dolch Basic Sight Vocabulary* (a list of 220 high frequency words); *The American Heritage Word Frequency Book* (a study of word frequency in print materials for grades three through nine); Starter Words (the 190 most frequently used words in children's writing, school materials, and adult print materials); and *A Basic Vocabulary of Elementary School Children*.

These standard references were extensively cross-checked with other respected studies (Gates; Horn; Greene & Loomer; Harris & Jacobson). It is significant to note that very few differences were found among these sources.

For teacher convenience, lesson numbers follow each word, and challenge words are indicated by a star.

Level-B

above-5
add-1
again-2☆
air-15
along-27☆
also-23
always-23
another-28
any-17
apple-1☆
arm-14
around-21
ask-1
asked-1☆
baby-17
back-27
bake-7
balloon-20☆
band-26
barn-14
bath-1☆
be-8
bear-15
because-3☆
been-3
before-22☆
begin-3
bell-29
below-11☆
bend-26
beside-15☆
best-2
better-29
between-8☆
Bible-9☆
bird-16
birthday-13☆
blind-26
block-27☆
blow-11
boat-10
books-19
both-28
bow-21
box-4
boys-22
break-7☆
bring-27
brother-28☆
bubble-5☆
buy-9
cake-7
called-23☆
came-7
camp-1
candy-26
car-14
card-14
care-15☆
child-9☆
children-23
circle-16
city-17☆
clean-8
clock-27
cloud-21☆
cold-10
color-16
could-19
count-21
cow-21
crown-21☆
cry-9
dark-14
dear-19
different-29☆
digit-3
dinner-29☆
dish-25
does-5
don't-10☆
done-5
door-22
dot-4
draw-23
dress-29
drop-4
dry-9
duck-27
each-23
ear-19
east-8
easy-17☆
end-26
enjoy-22
even-8
ever-2
every-17
eye-15
family-17
far-14
farm-14
fast-1
father-28☆
find-26
fine-15
finish-25
fire-15
first-16
fish-25
flower-21☆
fly-9
food-20
forgot-4☆
form-22
found-21
friend-26☆
frog-4
full-19
funny-29
game-7
gate-7
gave-7
give-3
gone-4
grade-7
grand-26
grass-29
great-7☆
grow-11
guess-29
gym-3☆
hang-27
hard-14
hat-1
have-1
he's-8
head-2
hear-19
heard-16☆
heart-14☆
help-2
here-19
high-9☆
hold-10
holy-17
home-10
hope-10
horse-22
house-21
I'm-9
important-22☆
index-26☆
Indian-26
into-3
its-3
Jesus-8☆
job-4☆
jump-5
just-5
keep-8
kid-3
kind-26
knew-20☆
know-11
large-14☆
last-1
late-7
left-2
leg-2
letter-29☆
light-9
like-15
line-15
live-3
looked-19☆
Lord-22
lost-4
lot-4
low-11
lunch-23☆
map-1
men-2
might-9
milk-27
mitten-29
most-10
mowing-11☆
must-5
name-7
nest-2
never-2☆
new-20
next-2
night-9
noise-22
none-5
noon-20
number-5
obey-7☆
odd-4
often-4
old-10
once-5☆
only-17
orange-22
other-28
over-10☆
own-11
page-7
paint-13
part-14
party-14☆
pay-13
penny-17
people-8
plan-1
plays-13
pond-26
praise-13☆
pray-13
pull-29
purple-16
quit-3
rabbit-29
rain-13
read-8
ready-17
right-9
road-10
roll-10
room-20
round-21
row-11
say-13
second-26☆
sentence-2
set-2
shelf-25☆
shoe-25
shoes-25☆
shop-25
short-25☆
should-25
show-25
shut-25
sick-27
sing-27
sister-3
sleep-8☆
slow-11
small-23
snow-11
snowman-11☆
soft-4
something-27☆
sometimes-5☆
soon-20
sound-21
south-21
stay-13
stayed-13☆
still-29
stood-19☆
store-22
story-17
study-17☆
such-23
sum-5
talk-27
than-1
thank-28
their-15
these-28
thick-28
thin-28
think-28
third-16☆
those-28
thought-28
through-20☆
throw-11
tie-9
today-13
together-28☆
told-10
tomorrow-4☆
too-20
took-19
tooth-20
tow-11
toy-22
train-13
tree-8
truck-27
under-16
until-3☆
use-20
very-17
voice-22☆
vowel-21
walk-23
want-23
wanted-23☆
wash-25
water-16
way-13
we'll-8
were-16
what-5
where-15
which-23
while-15☆
who-20
wish-25
wood-19
word-16
work-16
world-16☆
would-19
write-15
wrote-10☆
yard-14
year-19☆
zoo-20

Level-C

able-27
address-8
afraid-16
ago-20
airport-23
alarm-25
allow-22
alone-20
amount-22
angel-13
angry-17
answer-1
anyhow-22
apart-25
April-27
argue-25
army-25
artist-25
asleep-14
August-21
aunt-9
autumn-21
awake-16
bark-25
began-1
behind-9
belong-9
berry-1
bicycle-19
body-1
boot-31
boss-14
bother-3
bottle-27
bought-21
bread-5
bright-11
broke-5
brook-29
brought-21
bump-9
burn-28
bushes-29
busy-17
butter-8
buzz-2
cactus-2
cage-13
candle-27
careful-15
carry-17
cattle-27
caught-11
cause-21
center-26
certain-14
chair-3
chalk-11
change-3
charge-25
cheek-3
cheese-3
cherry-3
chest-1
chill-1
choose-31
circus-14
classroom-8
clay-4
close-4
cloth-4
clothes-11
clown-22
collar-2
cookie-29
copy-15
corner-23
course-23
cover-15
crash-10
crayon-5
creek-17
crop-2
cross-5
crowd-22
date-16
daughter-21
deaf-2
December-26
deep-17
die-19
dirt-28
dollar-26
doubt-22
drank-9
drew-31
driver-26
drown-22
eagle-27
early-28
earn-28
earth-10
edge-13
eight-16
February-17
felt-2
field-17
fight-19
flag-4
flame-4
flash-4
flew-31
float-20
floor-23
follow-20
football-29
forget-26
fork-15
fort-23
fought-21
fourth-23
fresh-10
Friday-19
front-1
fruit-31
gas-14
gift-1
giraffe-13
glass-4
glove-4
goes-20
gold-20
good-bye-29
grab-5
grandfather-9
grandmother-9
gray-5
ground-22
group-31
half-11
hall-21
hammer-26
handle-27
happen-8
hatch-10
heavy-17
held-1
hello-2
herd-28
honey-17
hood-29
hook-29
horn-23
hour-22
huge-13
hurry-28
husband-9
ink-9
January-13
jar-13
jealous-13
jolly-13
judge-13
jug-13
juice-13
July-13
June-13
kept-15
key-15
kick-10
knee-11
knot-11
ladder-8
lady-16
lamb-2
later-26
lay-16
learn-28
leave-17
less-14
lesson-8
lie-19
life-19
lift-1
list-1
loose-31
loud-22
made-16
mail-16
March-25
mark-25
market-25

marry-17
match-10
meal-17
mean-17
merry-8
metal-27
middle-27
million-8
mirror-26
Monday-9
moon-31
mouse-22
mouth-22
nearby-19
neck-10
needle-27
neighbor-11
neighborhood-29
north-3
notebook-29
November-26
October-15
open-20
order-23
owe-20
pants-2
paper-16
park-25
pass-14
paw-21
person-28
pick-1
place-4
plain-4
plane-16
plant-4
please-4
plow-22
plus-4
pool-31
poor-23
porch-10
pour-23
power-22
prayer-5
price-5
prize-5
proud-5
pulley-29
puppy-1
push-29
queen-15
quick-15
quiet-15
quilt-15
quite-15
race-14
rack-15
rage-13
rake-15
ranch-10
raw-21
really-8
remember-26
return-28
ripe-19
river-26
rode-20
rope-20
rubber-8
ruler-31
rush-10
sack-10
saddle-27
sail-16
salt-21
sandwich-10
sang-9
Saturday-28
save-14
score-23
scrap-7
scratch-7
scream-7
screen-7
scrub-7
search-28
sell-14
September-28
serve-28
seventh-14
sew-20
shade-16
shampoo-31
shark-25
sharp-25
shock-3
shook-29
shout-22
shown-20
shy-19
sidewalk-11
sight-11
sign-19
silver-26
since-14
skate-5
skin-5
skip-5
sleeve-4
slice-4
smart-25
smell-8
smile-19
smooth-31
soap-14
song-21
sore-23
sorry-14
spell-5
spend-5
splash-10
spoke-20
sport-23
spread-7
spring-7
sprinkle-27
squirrel-27
stamp-9
start-25
stiff-2
storm-23
straight-7
strange-7
straw-7
stream-7
street-7
string-7
strong-7
sudden-8
sugar-26
suit-31
summer-26
Sunday-2
sunny-8
supper-8
sweet-14
switch-10
table-16
taught-21
teacher-10
team-17
telephone-20
test-1
thankful-3
thirteen-3
thirty-28
though-11
threw-7
thumb-11
Thursday-3
tight-19
tiny-19
toast-20
track-15
travel-27
truth-31
Tuesday-31
turtle-27
twelve-2
twenty-17
unhappy-8
upon-21
visit-1
wagon-2
wait-16
wall-21
Wednesday-11
weigh-16
west-2
whale-3
wheat-3
whether-3
whip-3
whole-11
wild-19
wind-9
window-2
wing-9
wipe-19
wolf-29
woman-29
wonder-26
wool-29
wore-23
worse-28
wrap-11
young-9

Level-D

accept-2
across-14
against-3
agree-4
ahead-3
alike-5
all right-16
almost-16
aloud-15
alphabet-13
already-16
although-11
among-10
annoy-21
anyway-29
anywhere-26
apartment-10
appear-27
applause-16
appointment-21
April Fools' Day-31
Arbor Day-31
arrest-2
arrow-2
attic-2
author-16
avenue-7
avoid-21
awful-16
backyard-29
bandage-2
barber-17
bare-26
barnyard-17
bathroom-29
bathtub-29
battle-23
beard-27
beast-14
beautiful-7
became-4
bedroom-29
bedspread-29
behave-4
believe-4
belt-10
bent-10
birth-19
blade-8
blank-10
blanket-8
blood-1
bloom-7
bluff-13
bomb-11
bounce-15
branch-1
brand-1
breakfast-3
bridge-8
broom-7
built-3
bulldozer-20
bulletin-20
burst-19
butcher-20
button-25
cabbage-2
cane-4
cape-4
capture-22
cardboard-17
carnival-17
carpet-17
cart-17
castle-23
cave-4
cellar-14
cereal-27
champion-25
chance-14
cheer-27
chef-13
chicken-25
chief-4
choice-21
chose-5
Christmas-31
citizen-14
clear-8
climb-11
clue-7
coach-5
collect-2
Columbus Day-31
comb-11
comfort-3
common-25
compare-26
cord-16
cotton-25
cough-13
couldn't-28
county-15
couple-3
cousin-3
crack-8
craft-13
cream-8
crooked-20
crow-5
crust-10
cure-20
curious-20
curl-19
curtain-25
curve-19
dairy-26
damage-2
danger-22
dare-26
dead-3
decide-14
deer-27
delight-11
depend-2
dessert-19
destroy-21
dew-7
didn't-28
disappear-27
disappoint-21
dive-5
dock-1
dollhouse-15
donor-22
dragon-25
dream-8
drift-13
drum-8
due-7
dumb-11
during-20
dust-1
Easter-31
either-22
elephant-13
else-14
employ-21
enjoyment-21
enough-13
enter-22
everybody-29
evil-23
except-2
exciting-14
fail-4
fair-26
false-16
famous-14
fare-26
farmer-17
farther-17
fault-16
favor-22
fear-27
feather-22
fence-14
festival-23
fierce-27
final-23
finger-22
fireplace-29
firm-19
fist-1
flock-1
flour-8
flow-8
flute-7
fog-16
folks-11
footprint-20
forest-16
forward-10
fountain-25
freight-4
frost-10
frown-15
fry-8
fully-20
furious-20
furniture-19
further-19
garbage-17
garden-17
gear-27
general-23
gentle-23
germ-19
glance-14
glare-26
glue-7
goodness-20
government-10
gown-15
graph-13
grave-8
groan-8
Groundhog Day-31
growl-5
guard-10
hadn't-28
hair-26
Halloween-31
handful-20
Hanukkah-31
hardly-17
hare-26
harm-17
harsh-17
haul-16
hawk-16
he'd-28
he'll-28
here's-28
herself-29
hollow-5
homemade-29
homework-29
honor-22
hospital-23
however-15
human-7
humor-22
hung-1
I'd-28
Independence Day-31
instead-3
iron-5
it'll-28
jelly-4
joint-21
jungle-23
kitchen-25
knife-11
knob-11
label-23
Labor Day-31
laid-4
laugh-13
lazy-4
lead-3
lean-4
least-4
leather-3
legend-10
lemon-25
level-23
limb-11
lion-25
listen-25
loaf-13
lonely-5
loyal-21
marbles-17
Martin Luther King Day-31
May Day-31
meant-3
measure-3
Memorial Day-31
merchant-10
mild-10
model-23
moist-21
moment-10
motor-22
movement-7
movie-7
mustard-2
nature-22
near-27
neither-22
New Year's Day-31
newspaper-29
nothing-2
notice-5
noun-15
nurse-19
oak-5
object-2
offer-16
office-13
oily-21
orphan-13
ought-11
outdoors-15
oven-25
overalls-29
overlook-20
owl-15
owner-22
package-2
Passover-31
past-1
pasture-22
pause-16
peace-14
pear-26
pebble-1
perfect-19
period-27
photograph-13
picture-22
pile-5
pine-5
plank-8
plastic-2
playground-29
pleasant-3
plural-20
point-21
police-14
pollute-7
possible-23
pound-15
powder-15
practice-2
Presidents' Day-31
press-14
pretend-10
public-2
puddle-23
pumpkin-2
pure-20
purpose-19
quarrel-16
railroad-29
rather-22
rear-27
reason-25
recess-14
reign-11
rejoice-21
remind-10
repair-26
reply-5
reptile-1
rescue-7
ribbon-25
ridge-1
robin-25
roof-7
rose-5
rough-13
royalty-21
ruin-25
sauce-16
scarce-26
scare-26
scarf-17
scene-14
science-14
scout-15
secret-4
self-1
several-23
share-26
she'll-28
she's-28
shove-1
simple-23
sincerely-27
sink-1
sir-19
siren-25
skirt-19
slippery-9
smash-9
smoke-8
snap-8
somewhere-29
son-14
soybean-21
spark-17
speak-8
spear-27
spill-9
spirit-9
split-9
spray-9
stare-26
starve-17
station-4
steady-9
steer-27
stew-8
stool-9
stout-15
stove-5
strap-9
stretch-9
strike-9
stroke-9
struck-9
stuff-13
style-9
sunshine-29
supply-5
sure-20
sweat-3
swept-1
swift-13
tear-27
Thanksgiving-31
there's-28
they'd-28
thorough-11
thoughtful-11
thread-9
thrill-9
throat-9
tied-5
tiger-5
topsoil-21
total-23
touch-1
tough-13
tourist-20
toward-16
tower-15
tray-4
trouble-3
trout-15
true-9
trust-1
tune-7
turkey-19
uncle-23
underground-15
understand-10
unknown-11
upstairs-26
usual-7
Valentine's Day-31
visitor-22
voyage-21
we've-28
wealth-3
wear-26
weary-27
weird-27
weren't-28
what's-28
where's-28
who's-28
whom-7
whose-11
within-29
wooden-20
worry-19
worst-19
worth-19
wouldn't-28
wreath-11
wren-11
wrong-10
yarn-17
yesterday-3

Curriculum Objectives

Introduction

Level

C

Literature Connection
To increase comprehension and vocabulary development through a value-based story.

Discussion Time
To check understanding of the story and encourage personal value development.

Pretest
To test for knowledge of correct spellings of current spelling words.

Word Shapes
To help students form a correct visual image of whole words and to help students recognize common spelling patterns.

Hide & Seek
To reinforce correct spelling of current spelling words.

Other Word Forms
To strengthen spelling ability and expand vocabulary.

Fun Ways to Spell
To reinforce correct spelling of current words with activities that appeal to varying learning styles.

Dictation
To reinforce using current and previous spelling words in context.

Proofreading
To reinforce recognition of misspelled words, and to familiarize students with standardized test format.

Language Arts Activity
To familiarize students with word meaning and usage.

Posttest
To test mastery of the current spelling words.

Learning Game
To reinforce correct spelling of test words.

Challenge Activities
To provide more advanced spellers with the opportunity to master more difficult words.

Journaling
To provide a meaningful reason for correct spelling through personal writing.

Unit Tests
To test mastery of the correct spelling of the words from each unit.

Action Game
To provide a fun way to review spelling words from the previous unit.

Certificate
To provide opportunity for parents or guardians to encourage and assess their child's progress.

Parent Letter
To provide the parent or guardian with the spelling word lists for the next unit.

Phonics Units *(Levels A and B only)*
To provide a supplement for promoting phonemic awareness, and a review of basic phonic skills.

Common Spelling Patterns

The following list of sounds and spelling patterns will help you easily identify words with similar patterns.

Sounds	Sample Words	Sounds	Sample Words
a	**a**sk, h**a**t	ō	**o**ld, b**oa**t, h**oe**, gl**o**b**e**, bl**ow**
ā	**a**pron, l**a**t**e**, m**ai**l, pl**ay**	ô	t**a**lk, c**au**se, dr**aw**, s**o**ft, th**ough**t
ä	f**a**ther, p**ar**t, h**ear**t	ôr	st**or**y, m**ore**, w**ar**d, f**our**
âr	aw**are**, f**air**, b**ear**, th**ere**	oi	p**oi**nt, b**oy**
b	**b**erry, a**b**le, scru**b**	ou	ab**ou**t, pl**ow**
ch	**ch**eese, bun**ch**, la**tch**, na**tu**re	p	**p**lan, re**p**ly, sna**p**, su**pp**ly
d	**d**og, la**dd**er	r	**r**an, me**rr**y, mo**r**e, **wr**ite
e	b**e**d, h**ea**vy, s**ai**d	s	**s**ay, gue**ss**, **sc**ent, pri**c**e, **c**ity
ē	sh**e**, h**ea**t, fr**ee**, ni**e**ce, k**ey**	sh	**sh**ip, ca**sh**, mi**ss**ion, ma**ch**ine, spe**ci**al, vaca**ti**on
f	**f**ish, loa**f**, o**ff**, enou**gh**, pro**ph**et	t	**t**en, pu**t**, bu**tt**er, creas**ed**
g	**g**ive, for**g**ot, shru**g**	th	**th**in, e**th**nic, wi**th**
h	**h**as, any**h**ow, **wh**ole	t̲h̲	**th**em, wor**th**y, smoo**th**
wh	**wh**ine, **wh**ich	u	c**u**p, d**o**ne, wh**a**t, y**ou**ng
i	d**i**g, g**y**m	ū	h**u**man, y**ou**, n**ew**, t**u**n**e**
ī	f**i**nd, p**ie**, m**i**c**e**, tr**y**	ü	cl**ue**, d**o**, s**oo**n, fr**ui**t
îr	cl**ear**, d**eer**, pi**er**ce, c**er**eal, h**ere**	u̇	t**oo**k, sh**ou**ld, p**u**sh
j	**j**ust, en**j**oy, **g**erm, hu**ge**, bu**dge**	ûr	**ear**n, st**er**n, f**ir**st, w**or**k, Th**ur**sday
k	**k**eep, hoo**k**, sti**ck**, s**ch**ool, **c**an	v	**v**isit, a**v**oid, arri**ve**
l	**l**eft, Ju**l**y, hau**l**, fu**ll**y, te**ll**	w	**w**ash, drive**w**ay
m	**m**eal, cal**m**, cli**mb**, co**mm**on, hy**mn**	y	**y**oung, famil**i**ar
n	**n**ice, fu**n**, tu**nn**el, **kn**ow	z	la**z**y, ja**zz**, pri**z**e, rai**s**e, rein**s**, e**x**ample
ng	alo**ng**, bri**ng**i**ng**, thi**n**k	zh	mea**s**ure, ero**s**ion
o	n**o**t, p**o**nd, w**a**tch	ə	**a**bove, wat**e**r, anim**a**l, gall**o**n, thankf**u**l

Spelling
Blue

Letter

Provide the parent or guardian with the spelling word lists for the first unit.

Show your parents or guardian this letter that lists your spelling words for the first unit. Put it where you will remember to practice the words together.

Dear Parent,

We are about to begin our first spelling unit containing five weekly lessons. A set of fifteen words will be studied each week. All the words will be reviewed in the sixth week. Values based on the Scriptures listed below will be taught in each lesson.

Lesson 1	Lesson 2	Lesson 3	Lesson 4	Lesson 5
answer	buzz	bother	clay	bread
began	cactus	chair	close	broke
berry	collar	change	cloth	crayon
body	crop	cheek	flag	cross
chest	deaf	cheese	flame	grab
chill	felt	cherry	flash	gray
gift	hello	north	glass	prayer
held	lamb	shock	glove	price
lift	pants	thankful	place	prize
list	stiff	thirteen	plain	proud
Monday	Sunday	Thursday	plant	skate
pick	twelve	whale	please	skin
puppy	wagon	wheat	plus	skip
test	west	whether	sleeve	spell
visit	window	whip	slice	spend
Ephesians 5:16	Ephesians 5:20	James 5:16	Philippians 3:1	Ephesians 1:4

Have each student remove this letter from his or her worktext prior to beginning Lesson 1.

1 Literature Connection
Topic: Doing good
Theme Text: Ephesians 5:16

The Sign of Opportunity

Matthew sees a man by the roadside holding a sign that says, "Will Work for Food." Does the man really need help or not?

Mrs. Schilling pulled out of Knowlton Elementary School and headed toward home.

"Ah we almost home?" Emily lisped, leaning forward against her seat belt.

"You were with Mom when she brought us to school this morning, Em." Matthew smiled at his little sister—who wasn't so little anymore. "Everything looks different from this direction, though, doesn't it, Sis?"

"There's the grocery store we shop at, Em." Mom pointed out her window toward the huge store. "We'll be home in about 15 minutes."

"How much is 15 minutes?" Emily asked.

"By the time we get home, you'd be about halfway through your Zacchaeus video—if we started it right now." Elizabeth Schilling smiled as she flipped the blinker to switch lanes.

"Can we staht it white now? Can we? Can we?"

"We don't have your Zacchaeus video with us, Em," Mom said. "You were watching it at home right before we left to pick up the boys."

"Is 15 minutes to the paht wheah Zacchaeus climbs the twee?" Emily persisted.

Matthew pulled a video from the box on the Suburban's floor, then slid it into the player between the front seats. "Fifteen minutes is where Jesus heals Bartimaeus the beggar in your *Miracles of Jesus* video, Em," he said. "I'll start that one for you instead."

"Mom! Matthew!" Alex shouted suddenly. "Look at that poor man! He has a sign that says, 'Will Work for Food.'" Alex pointed out his window. "We should feed him, Mom. He looks like he needs clothes, too!"

"His clothes look like they're too big," Matthew said as they got closer.

Mom drove past the sign-man without a word. "Stop! Stop!" the boys shouted frantically.

"I'm not sure that would be such a good idea, guys." Mom frowned as she turned off the highway onto the blacktop county road. "Sometimes people make signs like that because they want you to feel sorry for them. They just want you to give them money. They don't really want to work for anything."

"Help the blind! Please help the blind!" Bartimaeus pleaded from the TV. Emily watched as the people ignored him on their way to see Jesus.

"How do you know who really needs help then?" Matthew turned to watch the sign-man through the back window.

"Well," Mom said thoughtfully, "I think there's always work for people who really want to work."

"But what if he's tried and can't find anything?" Alex strained in his seat belt to keep the man in view.

"Jesus, Son of David, have mercy on me!" Emily's eyes were glued to the screen as blind Bartimaeus groped for his walking stick and tried to stand in the closely-packed crowd. "Jesus, have mercy on me!"

Mom signaled for another turn. "Some people even pretend to be crippled or blind so people will feel sorry for them and give them money," she added. "Anyway, I don't think it's safe for me to pick up a strange man." She glanced over her shoulder at the boys with a "this-conversation-is-over" look and turned up the radio.

No one said anything else until they pulled into their driveway. "Jesus would help him," Emily said suddenly, as the video finished with Jesus healing blind Bart's eyes.

Later that evening the Schilling family gathered in the boys' room for worship.

"It's my tun to pick the stowy!" Emily handed Mom a brightly-colored picture book. "I want the Zacchaeus one." Emily snuggled onto her daddy's lap as Mom thumbed through the pages looking for the story.

"We read Zacchaeus last time it was your turn to pick, Em," Alex moaned.

"Let's sing first!" Emily jumped out of her daddy's lap and started the verse of her favorite song. "Zacchaeus was a wee little man." She bent over and pretended to measure just how short Zacchaeus was. "A wee little man was he. He climbed up in a sycamoah twee for the Laud he wanted to see. And as the Savio walked that way..."

The family watched with interest as Emily continued to do the motions with the song. She pretended to climb a tree, then walked her two fingers up her arm. She shaded her eyes as she finished. "And as the Savio passed that way He looked up in the twee. And he said, 'Zacchaeus, you come down.'" Emily pointed her index finger at her watching family. "Sing!" she said. The family joined her and sang. "For I'm going to your house today. For I'm going to your house today."

Emily clapped her hands and climbed back up onto Daddy's lap. Her eyes were riveted to the pages as Mom read. Everyone else watched the changing expressions of anticipation, excitement, and contentment on Em's face. She was special to them all and they were glad she was happy.

"Why did no one like Zacchaeus?" Mom asked as she closed the book.

"He was a tax collector!" Matthew said.

"Why was that a problem?" Dad turned to look at Matthew.

Emily scrunched her

Story (continued)

face into a frown. "He cheated!"

"Why would Jesus want to go home with a cheater who didn't work for his money?" Mom touched the end of Emily's nose.

"Jesus loves us even when we make bad choices," Matthew explained.

"Maybe he wanted to change," Alex suggested.

"No one wants a cheater to work for them," Matthew said.

Dad raised his eyebrows. "What if he just wanted people to think he was changing so he could cheat them even more?"

Emily pointed up. "Jesus loves evwyone!"

"I think the sign-man is a lot like Zacchaeus," Matthew said thoughtfully. "Nobody likes him. No one wants to eat with him, either. They think that he's a bad man and they just drive on past him."

"Who is this sign-man, Matthew?" Dad looked over at his oldest son.

"We saw him on the way home," Alex interrupted. "He was standing beside the road with a sign that said, 'Will Work for Food.'" Alex crawled onto his Dad's lap.

"Did you see him when you came home, too?"

Dad shook his head. "No, I didn't see anyone like that on the way home today."

"Good." Emily put her hands on her hips. "Maybe somr one took him home fowah suppah."

"Our Scripture verse this morning at school was something like, 'Make the most of every chance you have for doing good.'" Matthew looked into his father's eyes. "Doesn't that mean we should help this guy, Dad?"

As Dad hesitated, Mom looked around her boys' comfortable room. Toys filled the cubicles in the corner. The handsome twin beds had clean, matching sheets. Through the closet door she could glimpse rods full of attractive, well-made clothes—even the dirty clothes hamper was packed with them! Her three precious children were freshly bathed and ready for bed after a big supper of potato soup and blueberry muffins.

"No one really goes hungry in our little town, do they Thomas?" Mom reached out and straightened one of Emily's curls. "People can get food stamps and welfare money. . . and most churches have assistance programs. I don't think I've ever known anyone around here who's ever had to go without food."

Dad shrugged. "I really don't know, Elizabeth," he said. "I know there are some people who are willing to work for a while, but as soon as they get money, they buy alcohol or drugs. Since no one works well when they're drunk or high, they usually lose their jobs. But we don't really know anything about this 'sign-man' as you call him." Dad paused. "Maybe he'll be there tomorrow. Right now, though, we can pray for the sign-man, and Jesus might give us an idea of how we could help him."

The family reverently bowed their heads. Then Dad asked an all-knowing God to help them find what the sign-man needed most.

(to be continued)

2 Discussion Time

Check understanding of the story and development of personal values.

- What do you think Mrs. Schilling could have done for the sign-man when she saw him on the way home from school? Why?
- What do you think the Schilling family should do for the sign-man if they see him again?
- Why do you think Paul told the Ephesians to "Make the most of every opportunity you have for doing good"?
- Tell about a time when your family had an opportunity to help someone.
- How do you feel when you have done something good for someone?
- How did the people you helped feel?

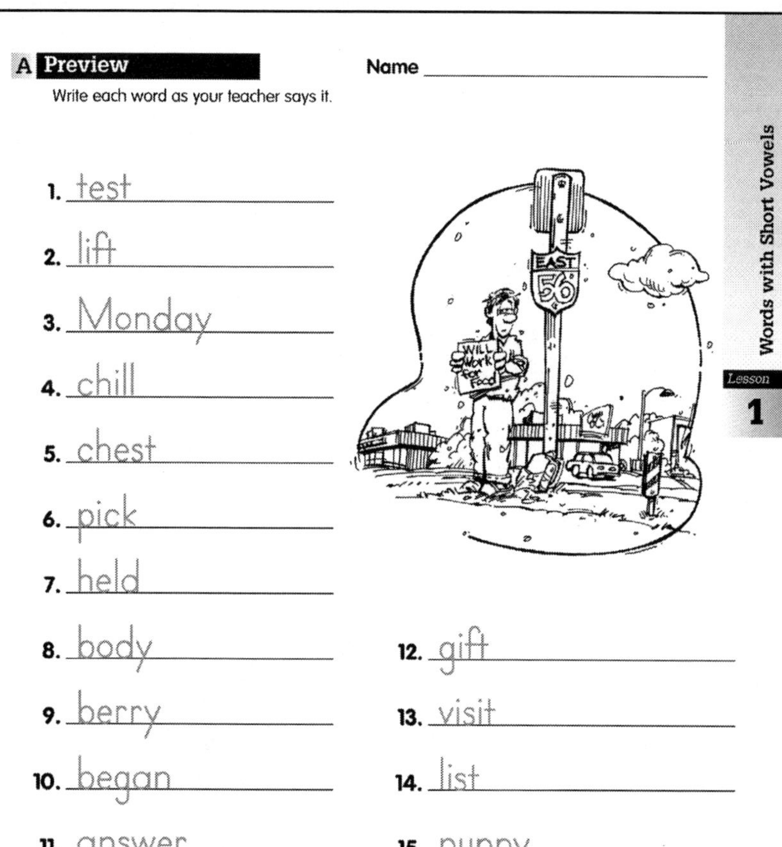

A Preview
Name
Write each word as your teacher says it.
1. test
2. lift
3. Monday
4. chill
5. chest
6. pick
7. held
8. body
9. berry
10. began
11. answer
12. gift
13. visit
14. list
15. puppy
EAST
56
WILL Work for Food
Words with Short Vowels
Lesson 1
Scripture
Ephesians 5:16
5

3 Preview

Test for knowledge of the correct spellings of these words.

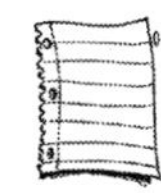

Customize Your List
On a separate piece of paper, additional words of your choice may be tested.

I will say the word once, use the word in a sentence, then say the word again. Write the word on the lines in the worktext.

Correct Immediately!
Let's correct our preview. I will write each word on the board. Put a dot under each letter on your preview as I spell the word out loud. If you spelled a word wrong, rewrite it correctly.

Take a minute to memorize...
Read the memory verse to the class twice. Have the class practice it with you two more times.

1.	test	This isn't a **test**, but a preview to see what you already know.
2.	lift	Please **lift** this box of videos into the car for me.
3.	Monday	The Schillings were on their way home from school **Monday** afternoon.
4.	chill	There was no **chill** in the air.
5.	chest	The sign-man had a sign in front of his **chest.**
6.	pick	It is not safe to **pick** up a stranger.
7.	held	The man **held** the sign in his hand.
8.	body	Your **body** needs food.
9.	berry	What kind of **berry** muffins did the Schillings eat for supper?
10.	began	The Schillings **began** worship by singing, "Zacchaeus was a Wee Little Man."
11.	answer	Mr. Schilling did not have an **answer** for all their questions.
12.	gift	The **gift** of helping someone will bring a blessing to you.
13.	visit	A **visit** to a nursing home might do you good.
14.	list	Make a **list** of the good things you could do.
15.	puppy	The Schillings do not have a **puppy.**

Progress Chart
Students may record scores. (Reproducible master in Appendix B.)

Day 1

Lesson 1

4 Word Shapes

Help students form a correct image of whole words.

Look at each word and think about its shape. Now, write the word in the correct word shape boxes. You may check off each word as you use it.

(Short vowels are usually found in syllables in which a vowel is immediately preceded and followed by a consonant, consonant cluster, or digraph.)

In the word shape boxes, color the letter that spells the short vowel sound in each word. Circle the words that have two syllables.

Words with Short Vowels — Lesson 1

B Word Shapes Name ____________________

Write each word in the correct word shape boxes. Next, in the word shape boxes, color the letter or letters that spells the short vowel sound in each word. Circle the words that have two syllables.

Word	Answer
1. answer	(puppy)
2. began	(visit)
3. berry	held
4. body	test
5. chest	pick
6. chill	list
7. gift	lift
8. held	gift
9. lift	(Monday)
10. list	chill
11. Monday	chest
12. pick	(answer)
13. puppy	(began)
14. test	(berry)
15. visit	(body)

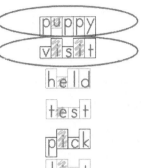

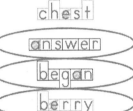

6

Answers may vary for duplicate word shapes.

Be Prepared For Fun

Check these supply lists for **Fun Ways to Spell** presented **Day 2**. Purchase and/or gather needed items ahead of time!

General

- Pencil
- 3 x 5 Cards (15 per child)
- Spelling List

Auditory

- Rhythm Instruments (two wooden spoons, two pan lids, maracas)
- Spelling List

Visual

- Sidewalk Chalk
- Spelling List

Tactile

- Play Dough
- Spelling List

C Hide and Seek

Name ____________________

Place an **X** on a coin for each word you spell correctly.

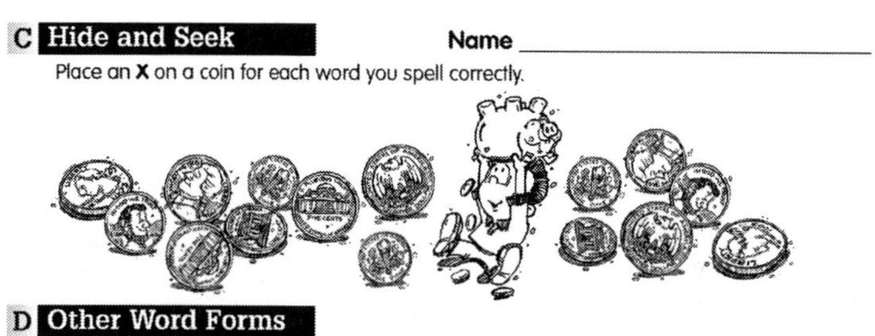

D Other Word Forms

Using the words below, follow the instructions given by your teacher.

answerable	bodies	hold	listlessness	tested
answering	bodily	holding	enlisted	testing
begin	chillier	holds	picked	tests
beginner	chilliest	lifted	pickier	visitation
beginning	chilliness	lifting	pickiest	visited
begun	chilly	listing	picking	visiting
berries	gifted	listless	puppies	visitor

E Fun Ways to Spell

Initial the box of each activity you finish.

1.

Spell your words with puzzles.

3.

Spell your words in rhythm.

2.

Spell your words with sidewalk chalk.

4.

Spell your words with play dough.

1 Hide and Seek

Reinforce correct spelling of current spelling words.

Write the words one at a time on the board. Use this activity for each word.

- **Look** at the word.
- **Say** the word out loud.
- Let's **hide** (cover) the word.
- **Write** the word on your paper.
- Let's **seek** (uncover) the word.
- **Check** your spelling. If your word is spelled wrong, write the word correctly next to it.

2 Other Word Forms

This activity is optional. Have students find and circle the Other Word Forms that are antonyms of the following:

hotter
the end
releasing

3 Fun Ways to Spell

Four activities are provided. Use one, two, three, or all of the activities. Have students initial the box for each activity they complete.

Options:

- assign activities to students according to their learning styles
- set up the activities in learning centers for the class to do throughout the day
- divide the class into four groups and assign one activity per group
- do one activity per day

General

To spell your words with puzzles...
- Write each word on a card.
- Cut each card into thirds using a straight cut.
- Mix your puzzle pieces.
- Put the puzzles together.
- Check your spelling.

Auditory

To spell your words in rhythm...
- Look at a word on your spelling list.
- Close your eyes.
- Play your rhythm instruments softly while you whisper the spelling of the word.
- Open your eyes and check your spelling.

Visual

To spell your words with sidewalk chalk...
- Write each of your spelling words on the sidewalk (ball court or playground).
- Check your spelling.

Tactile

To spell your words with play dough...
- Roll pieces of play dough into ropes.
- Use the ropes to make the letters of each word.
- Put them in the right order to spell each word.
- Check your spelling.

Day 3

Lesson 1

1 Working with Words

Familiarize students with word meaning and usage.

Sentence Fun

At the top of your page, choose the spelling word that best completes each sentence and write it on the line.

ABC Order

Write the words **wagon**, **with**, **window**, and **west** on the board. Explain to the students that when words begin with the same letter, they need to look at the second letter in each word to put the words in alphabetical order. If the first two letters are the same, look at the third letter. Guide the students in putting these four words in alphabetical order.

Look at each set of words. Write them in alphabetical order on the lines.

Take a minute to memorize...

Read the memory verse to the class twice. Have the class practice it with you two more times.

Words with Short Vowels

Lesson 1

F Working with Words Name ____________________

Sentence Fun

Write the correct spelling word on the line to complete each sentence.

1. On Monday, Mom parked at the school.
2. She did not pick up the sign-man.
3. The sign he held said, "Will Work for Food."
4. Mom tried to answer the boy's questions.
5. Soon, my dad began to pray for the sign-man.
6. Jesus went to visit Zacchaeus.

ABC Order

Dictionary words are listed in alphabetical order. Words beginning with **a** come first, then words beginning with **b**, and so on. It is simple to find a word in the dictionary if you know about alphabetical order. Write the words from each group in alphabetical order.

test puppy list

1. list 2. puppy 3. test

When words begin with the same letter, look at the second letter to put the words in alphabetical order. Write the words in alphabetical order.

gift berry body

4. berry 5. body 6. gift

If the first two letters are the same, look at the third letter. Write the words in alphabetical order.

chill chest lift

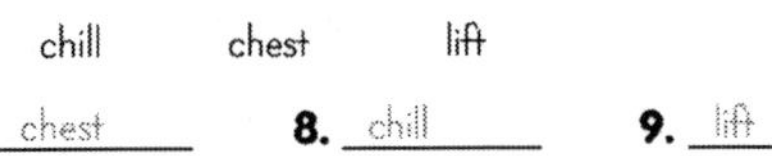

7. chest 8. chill 9. lift

Word Bank

answer	held	list	body	chill
began	test	pick	Monday	chest
berry	gift	visit	puppy	lift

8

G Dictation

Name ____________

Listen and write the missing words and punctuation.

1. Mom will pick up the boys from school on Monday .
2. Please write each answer on your test .
3. The sign he held said ," Will Work for Food ."

H Proofreading

If a word is misspelled, fill in the oval by that word. If all the words are spelled correctly, fill in the oval by **no mistake**.

1.	4.	7.
○ red	● bary	● monday
● anser	○ ten	○ began
○ list	○ lift	○ list
○ no mistake	○ no mistake	○ no mistake

2.	5.	8.
○ bus	● pik	○ held
○ held	○ gift	○ man
● pupy	○ God	○ fun
○ no mistake	○ no mistake	● no mistake

3.	6.	9.
○ lad	○ chest	● bodie
● chil	○ run	○ test
○ tan	● vizit	○ pot
○ no mistake	○ no mistake	○ no mistake

Words with Short Vowels

Lesson 1

9

1 Dictation

Reinforce correct spelling by using current and previous words in context.

Listen as I read each sentence and then write the missing words and ending punctuation in your worktext. (Slowly read each sentence twice. Sentences are found in the student text to the left.)

2 Proofreading

Familiarize students with standardized test format and reinforce recognizing misspelled words.

Look at each set of words. If a word is misspelled, fill in the oval by that word. If all the words are spelled correctly, fill in the oval by **no mistake**.

3 Hide and Seek

Reinforce correct spelling of current spelling words. (A reproducible master is provided in Appendix A as shown on the inset page to the right.)

Write the words one at a time on the board. Use this activity for each word.

- **Look** at the word.
- **Say** the word out loud.
- Let's **hide** (cover) the word.
- **Write** the word on your paper.
- Let's **seek** (uncover) the word.
- **Check** your spelling. If your word is spelled wrong, write the word correctly next to it.

4 Other Word Forms

Have your students complete this activity to strengthen spelling ability and expand vocabulary.

1 Posttest

Test mastery of the spelling words.

I will say the word once, use the word in a sentence, then say the word again. Write the word on your paper.

Check a coin for each word you spell correctly.

Other Word Forms

Sentence Fun

Write the word that completes each sentence.

1. When the telephone rings, she ___answers___ it. — answering / answers
2. After swimming all day, he felt ___chilly___. — chilling / chilly
3. Sal and her mom picked ___berries___ on the hill. — berries / berrying
4. Tom ___lifted___ his head when he heard the noise. — lifted / lifting
5. Meg ___listed___ things she wanted. — enlisted / listed
6. It is hard to tell which cat is the ___pickiest___. — pickiest / picking
7. The ___visiting___ speaker told good stories. — visiting / visited
8. The ___bodies___ of the race cars were built strong. — bodily / bodies
9. We will be ___tested___ over five chapters in math. — tests / tested
10. My little sister is ___beginning___ school this year. — begun / beginning
11. The glass I was ___holding___ slipped from my hands. — holds / holding
12. The ___puppies___ have fluffy fur and curly tails. — puppy / puppies
13. People are ___gifted___ in many different ways. — gifts / gifted
14. When I got to school, class had ___begun___. — begun / begin
15. The air is ___chillier___ than it was yesterday. — chillier / chilliest
16. My cousin came as a ___visitor___ to our class. — visited / visitor
17. We had trouble ___lifting___ the rocks. — lifting / lifts
18. ___Picking___ strawberries with a friend is fun. — picked / picking
19. Several kids brought ___gifts___ to the party. — gifted / gifts
20. We ___visited___ the zoo for our field trip. — visited / visiting

Other Word Forms — Lesson 1

327

1.	lift	Please **lift** the TV over the front seat.
2.	pick	Emily wanted to **pick** a video.
3.	Monday	The Schillings were on their way home **Monday** afternoon.
4.	began	The story of Bartimaeus **began** with him begging by the gate.
5.	answer	Jesus knows the **answer** to every problem.
6.	chest	Matthew's **chest** felt tight when he saw the sign-man.
7.	body	Your **body** needs a balanced diet every day.
8.	berry	The **berry** muffins are everyone's favorite.
9.	chill	We will **chill** the drinks in the refrigerator.
10.	gift	The **gift** of kindness is always welcome.
11.	held	Dad **held** Emily on his lap.
12.	list	Make a **list** of people you could help.
13.	puppy	You can help the **puppy** who is at the humane society.
14.	visit	Take the opportunity to **visit** someone in the hospital.
15.	test	Did you study hard for the final **test**?

Progress Chart

Students may record scores. (Reproducible master in Appendix B.)

Personal Dictionary

Students may add any words they have misspelled to their personal dictionaries for reference when writing. (Cover in Appendix B.)

I **Game** Name ______________________

Matthew and Alex want to ask God what the sign-man needs. Lead the way by moving one space for each word you or your team spells correctly from this week's word list.

Remember: Don't pass up a chance to do what Jesus would do.

J **Journaling**

Our text this week says to make the most of every opportunity for doing good. In your journal, make a list of people you can help.

2 Game

Reinforce spelling skills and provide motivation and interest.

Materials

- game page (from student text)
- flat buttons, dry beans, pennies, or game discs (1 per child)
- game word list

Game Word List

1. answer
2. began
3. berry
4. body
5. chest
6. chill
7. gift
8. held
9. lift
10. list
11. Monday
12. pick
13. puppy
14. test
15. visit

How to Play:

- Divide the class into two teams.
- Have each student place his/her game piece on Start.
- Have a student from team A go to the board.
- Say the spelling word. (You may also wish to use the word in a sentence.)
- Have the student write the word on the board.
- If correct, instruct each member of team A to move his/her game piece forward one space on the game board. (Note: If the word is misspelled, correct the spelling immediately.)
- Alternate between teams A and B.
- The team to reach the sign-man first is the winner.

Non-Competitive Option:

At the end of the game, say: "Class, I am proud of your efforts to spell the words correctly. If you had fun and tried your best, you are all winners!"

3 Journaling

Provide a meaningful reason for correct spelling through personal writing.

Review the story using discussion leads provided on the following page. Encourage students to apply the Scriptural value in their journaling.

Journaling (continued)

- Why do you think the sign-man was standing beside the road? (Brainstorm and list students' responses on the board.)
- Why did Mrs. Schilling not want to stop and help the sign-man? (She thinks: He really doesn't want to work. He just can't find a job he likes. He might be pretending. It's not safe.)
- What did Blind Bart want Jesus to do? (Give him some money.)
- What did Jesus do for Blind Bart? (Healed his eyes.)
- Our text this week says to make the most of every opportunity for doing good. Make a list in your journal of people you can help.

Day 5

Lesson 1

Take a minute to memorize...
Have the class say the memory verse with you once.

"A baby learns to talk by talking. A child learns to spell by spelling."*

*Wilde, Sandra. 1990. A Proposal for a New Spelling Curriculum. The Elementary School Journal, Vol. 90, No. 3, January: 275-289.

1 **Literature Connection**
Topic: Thankfulness
Theme Text: Ephesians 5:20

Thankful for Differences

Mr. Valentino's students learn about how Jesus healed ten lepers. Since Jesus helped needy people, should they help the sign-man?

"Stephen! Stephen!" Matthew walked across the classroom toward his friend. "Did you see that man Friday on the way home from school?"

"What man?" Stephen took the library books out of his backpack and stuffed them into his desk.

"The one with the sign. He was by the highway right before you turn to go to my house."

"My house is the other way, Matthew. What man are you talking about?"

"There was this man in baggy clothes. He was holding a sign that read, 'Will Work for Food' when we came home from school Friday."

Tony plunked his handwriting worktext on his desk beside Stephen and Matthew. "Well, he was still there when we drove by after my piano lesson," he said. "I tried to get Grandma Miller to stop, but she said, 'Tony-O, you never know about people like that.'"

"He was gone by the time Dad came home from work. Emily thinks someone invited him home for supper." Matthew said. "He wasn't there this morning either, so maybe she was right."

"I finished my handwriting border sheet before breakfast this morning." Tony opened his worktext and tore out the finished page. "It says, 'Make the most of every opportunity you have for doing good.' I wonder why Grandma Miller wouldn't stop?"

"Mom says that he may just want us to feel sorry for him. She thinks he could get a job if he looked for one rather than begging beside the road. I don't know why, but she thinks it might not be safe to help him." Matthew took his lunch from his backpack and headed toward the shelf where lunches were kept. "Dad says the sign-man might be an alcoholic or druggie that can't keep a job."

"Yeah, and if we gave him money he might buy alcohol instead of food." Tony placed his border sheet in the basket marked "handwriting."

"Well, alcohol can sure change people!" Matthew sat down at his desk as the bell rang. "It really messed up my cousin Victoria. I guess drugs can do the same thing."

The children all took their seats as Mr. Valentino stepped to the front of the classroom. "This morning I'd like to start our day by talking about how Jesus treated people and how they felt about what He did."

He began to walk slowly around the classroom. "When Jesus was alive there was a horrible disease called leprosy. It wasn't understood very well. It was kind of like AIDS is today—because there was no cure, and people were scared they might catch it and die from it. People in Jesus' time didn't understand about germs and how they're spread, so people who got leprosy had no idea where it came from. Patchy sores would appear on their bodies, then become oozy, runny, and repulsive. As time went on, the victim's nose, ear lobes, fingertips, and toes started to get numb. Soon the numbness spread, and some people even became paralyzed. Often the disease left people deformed and ugly."

Mr. Valentino stopped to adjust a mini-blind to keep the sun out of Beth's eyes. "Worse than the disease itself," he continued, "was that lepers were outcasts. Once a person noticed a patchy spot on their skin they were declared unclean by the priest and forced to leave their jobs, homes, family, and friends to roam around the countryside—alone except for other lepers. It was even sadder because the Jews believed leprosy was a punishment from God for something really awful the leper had done!"

He paused. "Sometimes the symptoms would go away just as mysteriously as they had come. Perhaps a lot of different skin problems were thought to be leprosy at first. If the patches cleared up, then the priest could declare a leper clean and send him home to friends and family." Mr. Valentino smiled at the children's serious faces.

"Now at the beginning of His ministry Jesus was healing and teaching in towns all over Galilee. Word of His healing power reached even the banished lepers. Crowds always surrounded Jesus and this was a problem for lepers who were not supposed to get near healthy people. One day a desperate leper came to Jesus on the outskirts of a village. The crowd parted, making a wide path for him as he made his way to Jesus. When he reached Him the leper knelt down in front of Jesus and said, 'I know that You can heal me if You will.'"

"Jesus looked at the man and understood how much he was suffering." Mr. Valentino stopped by Matthew's desk and put a hand on his shoulder. "The crowd that stood around Jesus and the bold leper gasped as Jesus reached out and touched the leper with His hands." He turned to face Matthew, put his other hand on his shoulder, and looked directly into his eyes. "Then Jesus said, 'I am willing. Be clean!' Immediately the leprosy left the man and he was cured."

Matthew smiled as Mr. Valentino continued his story. "Another day on His way to Jerusalem, Jesus walked along the border between Galilee and Samaria. As He neared a village ten lepers came out to meet Him. They stopped before getting too close and yelled, 'Master, have mercy on us.' Jesus saw how horrible their leprosy was and told them to go on into the village and show themselves to the priest. One of them, a hated Samaritan, also

Story (continued)

went to the priest. The lepers rushed ahead of Jesus toward the local synagogue, but before they got there, their leprosy had vanished!"

Mr. Valentino wiggled his fingers. "The Samaritan felt the tingle of feeling return to his fingers, and he felt the warm dirt between his toes, and he looked down at the healthy, pink skin of his arms—he probably even reached up to feel the tip of his nose!" Mr. Valentino rubbed the end of his own nose with a grin as he continued the story.

"Without hesitating, the Samaritan whirled around and rushed back through the throng of people coming into the village with Jesus. The people scrambled to get out of his way. When he got to Jesus, he fell on his knees, bowed to the ground, and thanked Him for what He had done. Jesus said to him, 'Weren't there ten of you healed? Where are the other nine? Get up and be on your way; your faith in Me is what made it possible for Me to heal you.'"

Mr. Valentino walked to the board and wrote Ephesians 5:20. "Always give thanks for everything to our God and Father in the name of our Lord Jesus Christ," he said as he printed the text on the board. "Why do you think Jesus touched the first leper instead of just sending him to the priest like he did the ten?" The room was silent.

"How do you think the leper felt as Jesus touched him?" Mr. Valentino persisted.

"He might not have been touched for a long time," Matthew suggested. "He was probably surprised."

"Good, Matthew. How do you think the disciples felt when they saw the hated Samaritan coming back through the crowd toward Jesus?"

Setsuko slowly raised her hand. Mr. Valentino nodded in her direction. "Angry?" Setsuko asked.

Mr. Valentino nodded his approval. "I agree with you, Setsuko. The Jews didn't want the healthy Samaritans around, so a Samaritan with leprosy was really someone to stay away from! How do you think Jesus felt when He saw the Samaritan returning?"

Sarah looked down at her hands. "Happy?" she said hesitantly.

"Yes, Sarah. I think Jesus was also delighted about the chance He had to teach His disciples about caring for all people—not just ones that were like them."

Mr. Valentino then saw Tony's waving hand. "Yes, Tony?"

"Mr. Valentino, did you see the sign-man Friday beside the road?"

"Yes, Tony, I saw the man with the sign. And I've thought a lot about him over the weekend. God gives each of us the gift of being able to make choices. Some people make choices that are not good. Sometimes it's best to let people live with the choices they've made for a while so they can learn to make better ones next time. But I keep wondering if the sign-man really needed help, and maybe I missed the opportunity of doing good like we talked about last week in spelling."

"What sign-man?" Rachel asked.

Stephen looked back at Rachel. "There was a man beside the road Friday afternoon waving a sign around that read 'Will Work for Food.'"

"We saw him too," Daniel said. "My dad said he may just want money so he can buy drugs or something. He said that if we stopped to help him he might try to rob us."

"That must be why Mom said it wouldn't be safe for us to pick him up," Matthew added.

Tony looked at the words written on the board. "Always give thanks for everything to our God and Father in the name of our Lord Jesus Christ," he whispered. "I bet the sign-man wishes he had something to thank God for."

"Mr. Valentino," Kristin asked in a troubled voice, "how do you know if people really need help?"

Mr. Valentino thought for a moment before he answered. "I'm not sure there's an easy answer to that question, Kristin. Perhaps God is using our sign-man to teach us an important lesson about people who are different from us—just like he used the thankful Samaritan leper so long ago." He paused. "Let's ask God for wisdom on how to deal with this problem." The class bowed their heads as Mr. Valentino asked God to help them know what to do about the sign-man.

(to be continued)

2 Discussion Time

Check understanding of the story and development of personal values.

- How was the tenth leper different from the other nine?
- How is the sign-man different from the students in Mr. Valentino's class? (Brainstorm. Make a list on the board.)
- How did Jesus treat the outcasts of His time?
- How should you treat someone who is different from you?
- How do you think the class could safely help someone like the sign-man?

A Preview Name ______________

Write each word as your teacher says it.

1. wagon
2. Sunday
3. twelve
4. buzz
5. window
6. cactus
7. pants
8. stiff
9. collar
10. deaf
11. felt
12. hello
13. west
14. lamb
15. crop

Words with Short Vowels

Lesson 2

Scripture
Ephesians 5:20

11

3 Preview

Test for knowledge of the correct spellings of these words.

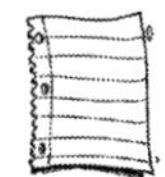

Customize Your List

On a separate piece of paper, additional words of your choice may be tested.

I will say the word once, use the word in a sentence, then say the word again. Write the word on the lines in the worktext.

Correct Immediately!

Let's correct our preview. I will write each word on the board. Put a dot under each letter on your preview as I spell the word out loud. If you spelled a word wrong, rewrite it correctly.

Take a minute to memorize...

Read the memory verse to the class twice. Have the class practice it with you two more times.

Day 1

Lesson 2

1.	wagon	Jesus did not ride in a **wagon** pulled by oxen.
2.	Sunday	Jesus started walking to the next village early **Sunday** morning.
3.	twelve	The **twelve** disciples walked from village to village with Jesus.
4.	buzz	The **buzz** of excited voices could be heard far away.
5.	window	She watched the crowd around Jesus from her **window.**
6.	cactus	There was no **cactus** growing in Jerusalem.
7.	pants	Men did not wear **pants** in Jerusalem when Jesus was here.
8.	stiff	The lepers' robes were **stiff** with dirt and grime.
9.	collar	There was no **collar** on the men's robes.
10.	deaf	Some lepers went **deaf** and couldn't hear any more.
11.	felt	The lepers **felt** very alone and isolated.
12.	hello	The Jews could not believe that Jesus would even say **hello** to a leper.
13.	west	Jesus walked **west** toward the next village.
14.	lamb	The **lamb** played in the pasture beside the road where Jesus walked.
15.	crop	The barley **crop** was growing on the other side of the road.

Progress Chart

Students may record scores. (Reproducible master in Appendix B.)

4 Word Shapes

Help students form a correct image of whole words.

Look at each word and think about its shape. Now, write the word in the correct word shape boxes. You may check off each word as you use it.

(Short vowels are usually found in syllables in which a vowel is immediately preceded and followed by a consonant, consonant cluster, or digraph.)

In the word shape boxes, color the letter or letters that spell the short vowel sound in each word. Circle the words that have two syllables.

Words with Short Vowels — Lesson 2

B Word Shapes Name ______________________

Write each word in the correct word shape boxes. Next, in the word shape boxes, color the letter or letters that spell the short vowel sound in each word. Circle the words that have two syllables.

Word	Answer
1. buzz	hello (circled)
2. cactus	window (circled)
3. collar	twelve
4. crop	stiff
5. deaf	buzz
6. felt	cactus (circled)
7. hello	wagon (circled)
8. lamb	west
9. pants	collar (circled)
10. stiff	crop
11. Sunday	deaf
12. twelve	felt
13. wagon	lamb
14. west	pants
15. window	Sunday (circled)

12

Answers may vary for duplicate word shapes.

Be Prepared For Fun

Check these supply lists for **Fun Ways to Spell** presented **Day 2**. Purchase and/or gather needed items ahead of time!

General
- Chalk or Whiteboard Marker
- Chalkboard or Whiteboard (could be individual boards for each child)
- Spelling List

Auditory
- Box to Store Letters
- a, b, c, c, d, e, e, f, f, g, h, i, l, l, m, n, o, p, r, S, s, t, u, v, w, w, y, z, z (written on seasonal shapes like schoolhouses or books)
- Spelling List

Visual
- Glitter Glue
- Art Paper (2 or 3 pieces per child)
- Spelling List

Tactile
- Thick Pile Carpet Squares
- Spelling List

C Hide and Seek Name ____________________

Place an **X** on a coin for each word you spell correctly.

D Other Word Forms

Using the words below, follow the instructions given by your teacher.

buzzed	cropping	feelingly	twelfth
buzzes	crops	hellos	wagons
buzzing	deafen	lambs	westerly
cacti	deafening	panting	western
collared	deafness	stiffens	westward
cropped	feel	stiffly	windowless
cropper	feeling	stiffness	windows

E Fun Ways to Spell

Initial the box of each activity you finish.

1. 

Spell your words with chalk.

3. 

Spell your words out of the letter box.

2. 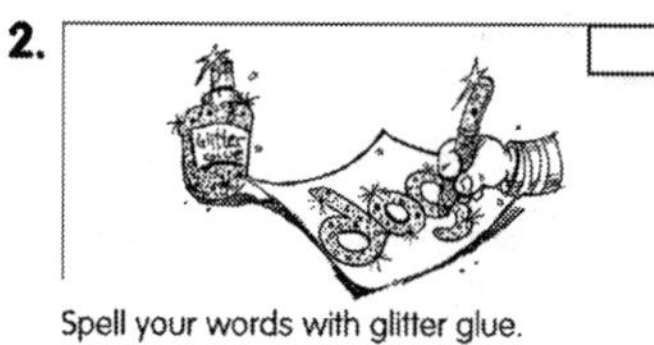

Spell your words with glitter glue.

4. 

Spell your words on carpet.

Words with Short Vowels — Lesson 2

13

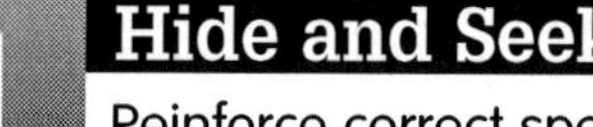

1 Hide and Seek

Reinforce correct spelling of current spelling words.

Write the words one at a time on the board. Use this activity for each word.

- **Look** at the word.
- **Say** the word out loud.
- Let's **hide** (cover) the word.
- **Write** the word on your paper.
- Let's **seek** (uncover) the word.
- **Check** your spelling. If your word is spelled wrong, write the word correctly next to it.

2 Other Word Forms

This activity is optional. Have students write original sentences using these Other Word Forms:

westward
lambs
windowless
cropped

3 Fun Ways to Spell

Four activities are provided. Use one, two, three, or all of the activities. Have students initial the box for each activity they complete.

Options:

- assign activities to students according to their learning styles
- set up the activities in learning centers for the class to do throughout the day
- divide the class into four groups and assign one activity per group
- do one activity per day

General

To spell your words with chalk…
- Put your spelling list on your desk.
- Look at a word; then, walk to the chalkboard (or whiteboard).
- Write your spelling word on the chalkboard (or whiteboard).
- Return to your desk.
- Check your spelling.

Auditory

To spell your words out of the letter box...
- Spell a word from your list by putting the letters in the right order.
- Check your spelling.
- Spell your word out loud.

Visual

To spell your words with glitter glue…
- Write each of your spelling words on your paper.
- Check your spelling.

Tactile

To spell your words on carpet...
- Use your fingertip to write a spelling word on the carpet.
- Check your spelling.
- Smooth the word out with your hand and write another.

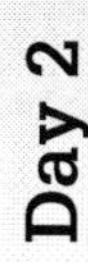

2

1 Working with Words

Familiarize students with word meaning and usage.

Complete the Story

Write this incomplete sentence on the board:
Mary had a little __.
Have a volunteer complete the sentence.

Use each spelling word once to complete the story.

Take a minute to memorize...

Read the memory verse to the class twice. Have the class practice it with you two more times.

F Working with Words Name ______________

Complete the Story

Matthew enjoyed the stories in his reading book about the settlers. Use each spelling word once to complete this story.

A covered **1.** wagon bounced along the trail. It was 1860 and the Smiths were headed **2.** west to California. They hoped to find some land to raise sheep, **3.** lamb s, and **4.** crop s. The family had been traveling since **5.** Sunday night. Their legs felt **6.** stiff and hard to move. Their dresses and **7.** pants were covered with dust.

"Pa," Ma called. "Tell Billy to come here."

Pa suddenly realized Billy was missing! Right beside the **8.** cactus was their **9.** twelve -year-old son. They **10.** felt scared. Pa and Ma had heard the **11.** buzz of rattlesnakes, but Billy wouldn't hear them. He was **12.** deaf.

"When did you last see Billy?" Pa asked.

"The last time we stopped, he ran off to look for rocks. I thought he got back in the wagon with you."

"I should have paid more attention," Pa sighed and ran his finger around his **13.** collar. He jumped from the wagon and grabbed his rifle.

"Wait for me," Ma cried. "I'm coming with you."

They shaded their eyes and looked around. Suddenly, they heard a voice call, "**14.** Hello." Ma and Pa whirled around, and there was Billy, perched on the back of the wagon. With relief they hugged him as Ma exclaimed, "Next time, I'll look out the back **15.** window before I panic!"

Word Bank

buzz	crop	hello	stiff	wagon
cactus	deaf	lamb	Sunday	west
collar	felt	pants	twelve	window

G Dictation Name ____________

Listen and write the missing words and punctuation.

1. The sign-man wore baggy pants.
2. His body felt stiff from standing all day.
3. Jesus was happy to heal the deaf man.

Words with Short Vowels

Lesson 2

H Proofreading

If a word is misspelled, fill in the oval by that word. If all the words are spelled correctly, fill in the oval by **no mistake**.

1. ○ twelve ○ gift ● buz ○ no mistake
2. ○ west ● caktus ○ puppy ○ no mistake
3. ○ collar ○ felt ○ berry ● no mistake
4. ● krop ○ wagon ○ chill ○ no mistake
5. ○ body ● def ○ window ○ no mistake
6. ○ window ○ hello ○ test ● no mistake
7. ○ visit ○ pants ● lamm ○ no mistake
8. ○ stiff ○ answer ○ Monday ● no mistake
9. ● Sundy ○ chest ○ pick ○ no mistake

15

1 Dictation

Reinforce correct spelling by using current and previous words in context.

Listen as I read each sentence and then write the missing words and ending punctuation in your worktext. (Slowly read each sentence twice. Sentences are found in the student text to the left.)

2 Proofreading

Familiarize students with standardized test format and reinforce recognizing misspelled words.

Look at each set of words. If a word is misspelled, fill in the oval by that word. If all the words are spelled correctly, fill in the oval by **no mistake**.

3 Hide and Seek

Reinforce correct spelling of current spelling words. (A reproducible master is provided in Appendix A as shown on the inset page to the right.)

Write the words one at a time on the board. Use this activity for each word.

- **Look** at the word.
- **Say** the word out loud.
- Let's **hide** (cover) the word.
- **Write** the word on your paper.
- Let's **seek** (uncover) the word.
- **Check** your spelling. If your word is spelled wrong, write the word correctly next to it.

4 Other Word Forms

Have your students complete this activity to strengthen spelling ability and expand vocabulary.

1 Posttest

Test mastery of the spelling words.

I will say the word once, use the word in a sentence, then say the word again. Write the word on your paper.

Hide and Seek

Check a coin for each word you spell correctly.

Other Word Forms

Clues

Use the clues to write the words.

1. glass to let light in — windows
2. baby sheep — lambs
3. what a bee does — buzzes
4. wheat, rice, corn — crops
5. not eastern — western
6. loud noise — deafening
7. after eleventh — twelfth
8. desert plants — cacti
9. breathing hard — panting
10. rigidly — stiffly

Hidden Words

Use the word bank to help you find and circle each of the words in the puzzle.

a	t	w	e	l	f	t	h	l	a	m	b	s
e	w	i	n	c	r	o	p	s	i	b	u	t
p	a	n	t	e	d	c	a	c	t	i	z	i
a	g	d	e	a	f	e	n	i	n	g	z	f
w	o	o	z	w	e	s	t	e	r	n	e	f
e	l	w	z	s	e	d	i	b	e	f	s	l
l	y	s	f	s	l	c	n	c	d	g	h	y
f	h	e	g	m	w	a	g	o	n	s	i	l

Word Bank

buzzes	crops	feel	panted	stiffly	wagons	windows
cacti	deafening	lambs	panting	twelfth	western	

1. cactus — There is no **cactus** growing there.
2. crop — The **crop** of barley was not yet harvested.
3. buzz — There was a noisy **buzz** of flies around the lepers' sores.
4. stiff — The bandages around the sores were **stiff** and dirty.
5. felt — The lepers **felt** Jesus would help them.
6. collar — There was no **collar** on his robe.
7. pants — Many Israeli men wear **pants** today.
8. deaf — The people seemed **deaf** to the teachings of Jesus.
9. window — The lepers anxiously watched for Jesus from the shack's **window.**
10. hello — The lepers were not greeted with a warm **hello.**
11. twelve — There were **twelve** disciples.
12. Sunday — It was **Sunday** when Jesus walked to the next village.
13. wagon — The **wagon** was loaded with sheaves of harvested barley.
14. lamb — The **lamb** stood beside its mother in the green pasture.
15. west — The sun slowly set in the **west.**

Progress Chart

Students may record scores. (Reproducible master in Appendix B.)

Personal Dictionary

Students may add any words they have misspelled to their personal dictionaries for reference when writing. (Cover in Appendix B.)

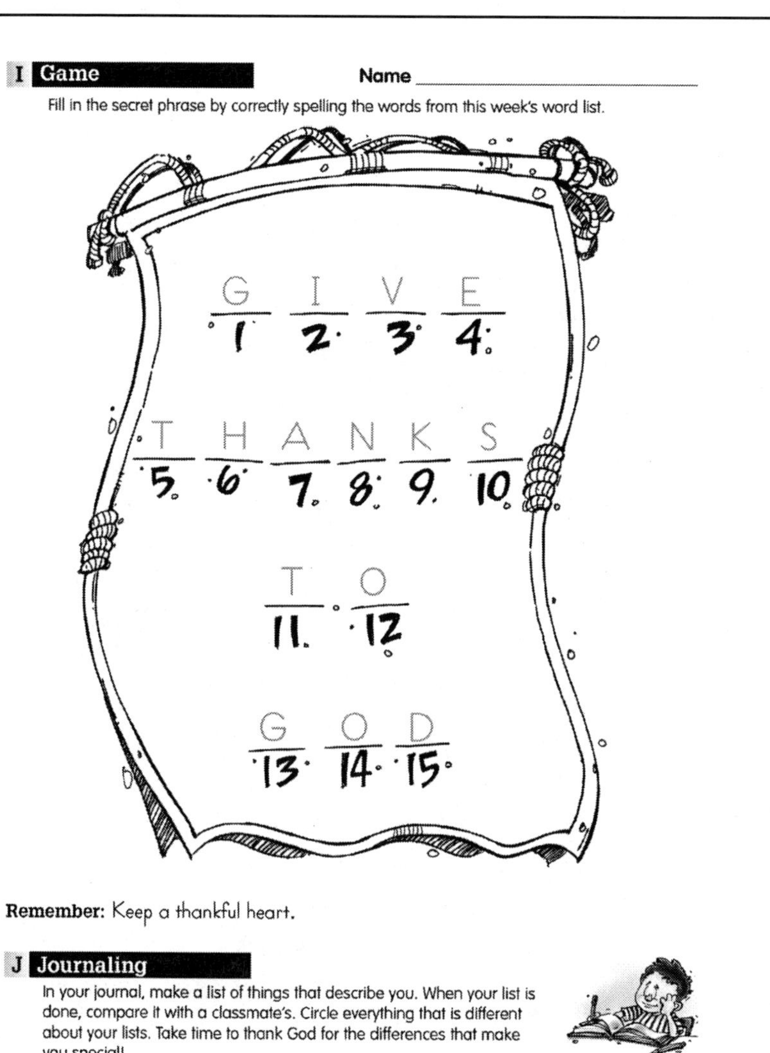

Words with Short Vowels

Lesson 2

I Game Name ____________

Fill in the secret phrase by correctly spelling the words from this week's word list.

Remember: Keep a thankful heart.

J Journaling

In your journal, make a list of things that describe you. When your list is done, compare it with a classmate's. Circle everything that is different about your lists. Take time to thank God for the differences that make you special!

16

2 Game

Reinforce spelling skills and provide motivation and interest.

Materials

- game page (from student text)
- pencils (1 per child)
- game word list

Game Word List

Team A	Team B
1. buzz (G)	1. pants (G)
2. cactus (I)	2. stiff (I)
3. collar (V)	3. Sunday (V)
4. crop (E)	4. twelve (E)
5. deaf (T)	5. wagon (T)
6. felt (H)	6. west (H)
7. hello (A)	7. window(A)
8. lamb (N)	8. buzz (N)
9. pants (K)	9. cactus (K)
10. stiff (S)	10. collar (S)
11. Sunday (T)	11. crop (T)
12. twelve (O)	12. deaf (O)
13. wagon (G)	13. felt (G)
14. west (O)	14. hello (O)
15. window (D)	15. lamb (D)

How to Play:

- Divide the class into two teams.
- Have a student from team A choose a number from 1 to 15.
- Say the word that matches that number from the team's word list. (You may also wish to use the word in a sentence.)
- Have the student write the word on the board.
- If correct, have each member of team A write the given letter in the matching space on his/her game page.
- Alternate between teams A and B having the students choose a number of a blank space.
- The team to complete the secret phrase first is the winner.

Non-Competitive Option:

At the end of the game, say: "Class, I am proud of your efforts to spell the words correctly. If you had fun and tried your best, you are all winners!"

3 Journaling

Provide a meaningful reason for correct spelling through personal writing.

Review the story using discussion leads provided on the following page. Encourage students to apply the Scriptural value in their journaling.

Day 5

Lesson

2

Journaling (continued)

- Raise your hand if you think you are really good at addition.
- Now, stand beside your desk if you think you are good at sports.
- Sit down if you enjoy reading.
- Put your thumb up if you have handwriting that is neat and easy to read.
- Pat your head if you often don't miss any on your Spelling tests.
- Raise your hand if you can think of one thing about yourself that is different from everyone else in the room. (Write responses on the board.)
- In your journal, make a list of things that describe you. Your list might include things like: I do well in math. I'm neat. I'm a good friend. I draw well. When your list is done, compare it with a classmate's. Circle everything that is different about your lists. Take time to thank God for the differences that make you special!

Take a minute to memorize...
Have the class say the memory verses from lessons 1 and 2 with you.

"A major need for inventive spellers is to have someone answer their questions and correct their mistakes."*

*Lutz, Elaine. 1986. ERIC/RCS Report: Invented Spelling and Spelling Development. Language Arts, Vol. 63, No. 7, November: 742-744.

Powerful Prayers

The sign-man and his family pray for food and a job.

Harrison Potter sat at the table in the back of the camper and waited for the sound of Dad's footsteps in the gravel. "Mama, when will Dad get back? I'm getting hungry."

"Shhhh!" Cheryl Potter put her finger across her lips. "Landon is still asleep. I don't know when Dad will return."

Harrison looked down at the book in his lap. "Dad has been gone all day again," he thought as he slowly turned the pages of his book. It seemed like every page was full of pictures of good things to eat. His stomach growled. "Maybe Dad will at least find some part-time work today. We had beans for breakfast and beans for lunch and I really don't want beans for dinner again, too." He looked up. "Mama, can we go back to that Something Springs Park after we eat?"

Mama nodded her head and looked over at the sleeping baby. "And do you think Dad will bring something home to go with the beans?" Harrison added hopefully.

"Shhhh!" Mama whispered. "We'll just have to wait and see."

Harrison put his book down and looked out the window. "We're even gonna run out of beans to eat pretty soon," he thought. "I saw Mama looking at what was left of that big sack of dried beans we brought with us from home. There aren't that many left."

Landon began to cry. Harrison turned around and watched Mama pick him up. "Since Landon woke up, can we leave a note for Dad and walk over to the park before dinner?" He jumped off the bench seat and stood beside Mama and Landon.

"Well, let me nurse the baby first," Mama said, "and then we can go."

Harrison knelt down on the bench again. "Landon doesn't get tired of milk every meal—but I'm sure tired of beans!" He bounced up and down on the cushion and watched the cars go by on the highway while Landon was being fed.

As they walked toward the park a short while later, Harrison thought of his father's search for work. "Mama," he asked soberly, "why can't Dad find a job here? I thought that's why we came?"

"Daddy did have a job here, Honey." Mama lifted the baby up to her shoulder and gently patted his back. "A new company started in this town and asked Daddy if he'd like to move here and work for them. Daddy thought this would be a better place to raise you and Landon, and the job even paid more money. We decided to pack everything up and move out here. But while we were on the way, the new company lost a big contract and decided they really couldn't afford to hire Daddy yet. They couldn't get in touch with us because we were already on our way, and Daddy had already quit his job back home anyway. That's why Daddy doesn't have a job."

"What are we gonna do when we run out of beans, Mama?"

"I'm not sure—but Jesus knows. Do you want to stop up there on that bench and ask Him to help us?" Mama suggested.

Harrison nodded and skipped ahead. "You go first," he said as he sat down.

Landon grabbed the back of the wooden bench and pulled himself up on unsteady legs. Mama kept a hand on his back while she prayed. "Dear Lord, we're a little tired of eating beans three times a day—but I am thankful we have something to eat. Thank you for that. And please help John to find a job. You know how hard this is for him. Help us to accept Your will for our lives. Amen."

Harrison opened his eyes and peeked at Landon. "Landon has a full tummy, and just woke up from a nap," Harrison thought. "He doesn't know there's a problem in the world." Then he began to pray aloud. "Dear Jesus, help me not to worry about more beans. Help me to be happy like Baby Landon. Amen."

Mama opened her eyes and smiled at her two boys. "An earnest prayer has a lot of power, Harrison. Now let's go see that playground."

That evening, after another supper of beans, Dad tucked the blanket up under his son's chin. "Night, Harrison. I'll see you in the morning for a special bean breakfast." Dad tickled Harrison. "Laugh if you love beans," he said. Then he tickled Harrison some more. "Say you love beans!" Dad grinned. "Bbbbbeans are my favorite," Harrison blurted out between gales of laughter, then dove under the covers to escape his teasing father.

The next afternoon Harrison waited again at the camper window while Landon took his nap. "We ate beans for breakfast. We ate beans for lunch. We'll have beans for supper," Harrison thought. He had seen Mama pour the last of the beans into the Crock-Pot® the evening before. She always slow-cooked the beans overnight so they'd be tender for the next day's meals. "But what will we eat tomorrow night? Even beans are better than nothing." He'd heard Mama whispering to Dad last night after she thought he was asleep. She sounded upset, and they both seemed extra quiet this morning—but they hadn't mentioned running out of beans. "They just don't want to scare me!" he thought.

Harrison looked up when he heard the sound of footsteps on the gravel outside. He

Story (continued)

jumped up and pushed open the camper door. "Dad! You're back early!" He greeted his Dad with a big bear hug.

"Would you go get the map off the front seat of the pickup, Son?" Dad rumpled Harrison's hair absently as his son took the keys from his outstretched hand. When Harrison returned with the map, Mama was burping Landon. She looked solemn as Dad said, "I'll get the trailer hooked up to the pickup while you change Landon."

Dad climbed out of the back of the camper and Harrison went along to help him with the hookup routine.

"Here's the map, Dad. Where are we going? Did you find a new job? Did they pay you yet? What are we going to eat for breakfast?"

"I don't know the answers to all those questions, Son." Dad took the map from Harrison and put it in his jacket pocket. "Mama and I thought we'd drive to the outskirts of town and see if there are any help-wanted signs in the windows of the small businesses and fast food places out that way."

Soon the Potters headed out of town in their pickup truck, their possessions bouncing along in the trailer behind. Harrison and Landon were buckled in securely between them. Suddenly, there was a large BANG! Dad struggled to control the pickup as it jerked violently to the right. His elbow hit Landon's car seat, and the baby started to cry. Dad braked hard and fought the lurching truck to the shoulder of the road.

"What happened, John?" Mama reached over Harrison to comfort the crying baby.

"I think we just had a blowout." Dad reached for the door handle. Mama turned her head away and looked out her window, but Harrison saw a big tear roll out the corner of her eye.

"If we don't have money to buy food, there's no money to buy another tire," Harrison thought. "Dear Jesus," he prayed, "My mamma is sad. Help us to get money for food and a tire. Amen."

John Potter's shoulders slumped as he unhooked the trailer from the pickup. A car whizzed by, then slowed down and turned around. It came back and stopped across from him on the other side of the highway. John looked up to see a big man get out and approach him. "Hi. I'm Brad Wilson," the man said. "Do you have everything you need, sir?"

John stood up and wiped the sweat off his forehead. "As a matter of fact, I don't!" He frowned and stepped back from the hitch. "My name's Potter. And frankly, I don't have a spare tire, I don't have food to feed my wife and two boys up there in the pickup, I don't have any money to buy food, and I don't have a job or any hope of getting one in the near future." John sighed as the words just rushed out, then suddenly embarrassed, he looked at the ground.

Mr. Wilson wanted to help, but realized the stranger didn't want a handout—all he seemed to have left was his dignity and pride. Mr. Wilson sent up a silent prayer for wisdom, then excused himself, and ran back across the highway for a hurried conversation with his wife and Stephen. When he came back, Mr. Potter was standing by the pickup window talking to his family.

"Would you like to come to the school work bee with us?" Mr. Wilson asked. "We're having hot dogs with all the fixings after we finish raking leaves, planting bulbs, and chopping up some trees that fell in that big storm last week. Some of us are even building a fort for the kids."

John Potter looked at his wife, then nodded his head.

"Mr. Hataski will be there, and he owns a gas station," Mr. Wilson continued. "I bet he has a used tire that will fit this rig. I'll drop my family off at school, then be right back to get you fixed up. Don't go anywhere now."

"Thanks," John said with a slow smile. "We'll be here alright. And we'll be more than happy to work for our food tonight."

Stephen was the first to spot his dad's car, followed by the Potters' pickup and trailer coming into the school parking lot about an hour later. "Here comes the family that had the flat tire," he told the other children. "Maybe their little boy would like to help us rake leaves!"

"I want to hold their baby," Rachel said. "Do you think the woman will let me?"

"I don't know," Rosa shrugged her shoulders. "But we can ask."

Mr. Valentino walked over to his excited leaf-rakers. "Well, Mr. Valentino," Matthew looked up at him. "We didn't get a chance to help the sign-man, but it looks like Jesus is giving us another family to help."

"It looks that way," Mr. Valentino smiled. "Mr. Hill said he may be able to hire the man to work at his mother-in-law's farm until he can find more permanent work."

Just then, the driver of the pickup climbed out of the cab. Matthew, Tony, and Mr. Valentino stared across the school playground, their eyes wide with surprise.

"Well, how about that!" Mr. Valentino said in a funny voice.

"What?" Stephen blurted out. "What's wrong?"

"You'll never believe this, Stephen!" said Tony with a chuckle. "But that's the sign-man!"

2 Discussion Time

Check understanding of the story and development of personal values.

- What did Harrison and his mommy do when the beans were about to run out?
- What had the Schilling family done when they weren't sure how to help the sign-man?
- What had Mr. Valentino's class done after they talked about how they could help the sign-man?
- How did God answer all those prayers?
- How do you think the Potter's felt as they drove into the parking lot of Knowlton Elementary?
- What is something you have earnestly prayed for?
- What were the results?

A Preview Name ______________________

Write each word as your teacher says it.

1. whale
2. Thursday
3. chair
4. wheat
5. whip
6. thirteen
7. change
8. cheek
9. cheese
10. cherry
11. shock
12. bother
13. north
14. thankful
15. whether

Words with Consonant Digraphs

Lesson 3

Scripture
James 5:16

17

3 Preview

Test for knowledge of the correct spellings of these words.

Customize Your List

On a separate piece of paper, additional words of your choice may be tested.

I will say the word once, use the word in a sentence, then say the word again. Write the word on the lines in the worktext.

Correct Immediately!

Let's correct our preview. I will write each word on the board. Put a dot under each letter on your preview as I spell the word out loud. If you spelled a word wrong, rewrite it correctly.

Take a minute to memorize...

Read the memory verse to the class twice. Have the class practice it with you two more times.

Day 1 Lesson 3

1.	whale	Harrison had a **whale** of an appetite.
2.	Thursday	It was **Thursday** and they were still eating beans.
3.	chair	Harrison sat in his **chair** and looked at the beans on his plate.
4.	wheat	A good loaf of **wheat** bread would sure taste good.
5.	whip	"I wish mommy would **whip** up something different to eat," said Harrison.
6.	thirteen	There weren't even **thirteen** beans in the bag any more.
7.	change	Harrison wanted the menu to **change.**
8.	cheek	A tear ran down Cheryl Potter's **cheek.**
9.	cheese	There was not **cheese** to melt over the beans.
10.	cherry	There was no ice cream sundae with a **cherry** on top for desert.
11.	shock	It was quite a **shock** for Stephen to find out he had helped the sign-man.
12.	bother	It does not **bother** God when you pray.
13.	north	A cold **north** wind was blowing.
14.	thankful	The Potters were very **thankful** for Mr. Wilson's help.
15.	whether	Do you know **whether** God answers earnest prayers?

Progress Chart

Students may record scores. (Reproducible master in Appendix B.)

4 Word Shapes

Help students form a correct image of whole words.

Look at each word and think about its shape. Now, write the word in the correct word shape boxes. You may check off each word as you use it.

(The consonant digraphs **ch**, **sh**, **th**, and **wh** are introduced in this lesson. A consonant digraph is a single sound spelled by two letters.)

In the word shape boxes, color the letters that spell the consonant digraph in each word. Circle the words that end with a digraph.

Words with Consonant Digraphs — Lesson 3

B Word Shapes Name ____________

Write each word in the correct word shape boxes. Next, in the word shape boxes, color the letters that spell the consonant digraph or digraphs in each word. Circle the words that end with a digraph.

1. bother	whip
2. chair	change
3. change	thankful
4. cheek	Thursday
5. cheese	whether
6. cherry	chair
7. north	bother
8. shock	cheek
9. thankful	cheese
10. thirteen	wheat
11. Thursday	cherry
12. whale	(north)
13. wheat	thirteen
14. whether	whale
15. whip	(shock)

18

Answers may vary for duplicate word shapes.

Be Prepared For Fun

Check these supply lists for **Fun Ways to Spell** presented **Day 2**. Purchase and/or gather needed items ahead of time!

General
- Colored Pencils
- Art Paper (1 piece per child)
- Spelling List

Auditory
- A Classmate
- Spelling List

Visual
- Black Construction Paper (1 piece per child)
- Cotton Swabs (1 per child)
- Lemon Juice
- Spelling List

Tactile
- Pipe Cleaners (cut in an assortment of lengths)
- Spelling List

C Hide and Seek

Name ______________________

Place an **X** on a coin for each word you spell correctly.

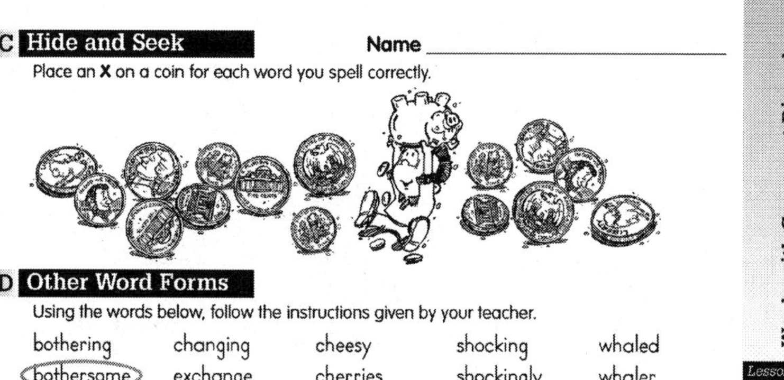

D Other Word Forms

Using the words below, follow the instructions given by your teacher.

bothering	changing	cheesy	shocking	whaled
bothersome	exchange	cherries	shockingly	whaler
chaired	cheekier	northerly	thankfully	whales
chairman	cheekiest	northern	thankfulness	whaling
changeable	cheekily	northward	thankless	whipped
changed	cheeky	shocked	thirteenth	whipping

E Fun Ways to Spell

Initial the box of each activity you finish.

1. 

Spell your words with pictures.

3. 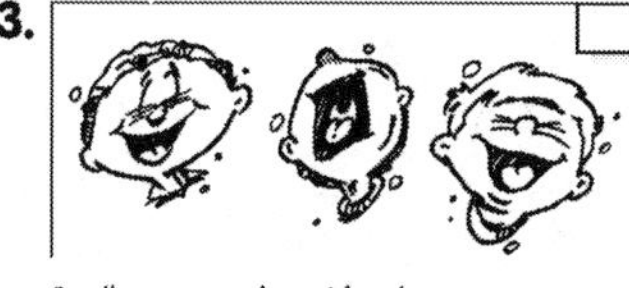

Spell your words out loud.

2. 

Spell your words with lemon juice.

4. 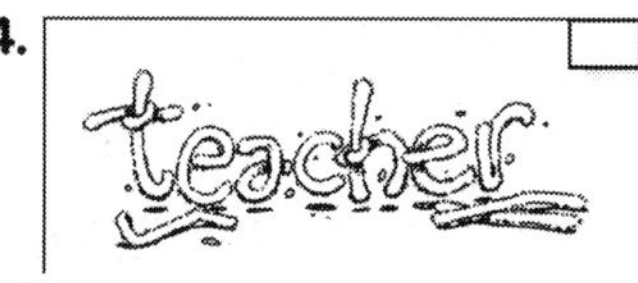

Spell your words with pipe cleaners.

Words with Consonant Digraphs

Lesson 3

19

1 Hide and Seek

Reinforce correct spelling of current spelling words.

Write the words one at a time on the board. Use this activity for each word.

- **Look** at the word.
- **Say** the word out loud.
- Let's **hide** (cover) the word.
- **Write** the word on your paper.
- Let's **seek** (uncover) the word.
- **Check** your spelling. If your word is spelled wrong, write the word correctly next to it.

2 Other Word Forms

This activity is optional. Have students find and circle the Other Word Forms that are synonyms of the following:

surprised
annoying
gratefulness

3 Fun Ways to Spell

Four activities are provided. Use one, two, three, or all of the activities. Have students initial the box for each activity they complete.

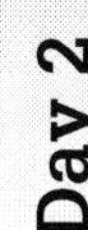

Day 2

Lesson 3

Options:

- assign activities to students according to their learning styles
- set up the activities in learning centers for the class to do throughout the day
- divide the class into four groups and assign one activity per group
- do one activity per day

General

To spell your words with pictures...

- Choose several words from your spelling list and draw pictures that illustrate the meanings of those words.
- Write the correct spelling word beside each picture.
- Check your spelling.

Auditory

To spell your words out loud...

- Have a classmate read a spelling word from the list.
- Say a sentence with that spelling word to your classmate.
- Spell the spelling word you used in that sentence to your classmate.
- Ask your classmate to check your spelling.
- Do this with each word on your word list.

Visual

To spell your words with lemon juice...

- Dipping a cotton swab in lemon juice, write each of your spelling words on black construction paper.
- Check your spelling before your writing disappears!

Tactile

To spell your words with pipe cleaners...

- Choose a word from your spelling list.
- It may be a favorite word or a word you have trouble remembering how to spell.
- Shape the pipe cleaner to spell that word.

1 Working with Words

Familiarize students with word meaning and usage.

Word Sort

Write the headings **th**, **ch**, **wh**, and **sh** on the board. Say the words **thumb**, **porch**, **where**, and **crash**. Guide the students in putting these four words under the correct headings.

Write each spelling word under the correct consonant digraph heading.

Missing Letters

Write the missing consonant digraph for each spelling word.

Dictionary Skills

Pretend the words at the top of each column are guide words on a dictionary page. Write the spelling words that would be found on a page with those guide words.

Take a minute to memorize...

Read the memory verse to the class twice. Have the class practice it with you two more times.

Words with Consonant Digraphs — Lesson 3

F Working with Words

Name ____________________

Word Sort

Write each spelling word under the correct digraph heading. If a word fits under two headings, write it under both.

th	ch	wh	sh
1. bother	7. chair	12. whale	16. shock
2. north	8. change	13. wheat	
3. thankful	9. cheek	14. whether	
4. thirteen	10. cheese	15. whip	
5. Thursday	11. cherry		
6. whether			

Missing Letters

Write the consonant digraph for each spelling word.

1. w h ip	5. nor t h	9. t h irteen	13. bo t h er
2. c h air	6. c h eek	10. t h ankful	14. w h ale
3. c h erry	7. s h o c k	11. T h ursday	15. c h ange
4. c h eese	8. w h eat	12. w h e t h er	

Dictionary Skills

There are two words at the top of each page in a dictionary. They are called guide words. The guide word on the left is the first word on that page. The guide word on the right is the last word on that page. Guide words help you find words in a dictionary. Pretend the boldface words below are guide words on a dictionary page. Write the spelling words that would be found on a page with these guide words.

chain cheer	**whack which**	**than thy**
1. chair	4. whale	7. thankful
2. change	5. wheat	8. thirteen
3. cheek	6. whether	9. Thursday

Word Bank

bother	cheek	north	thirteen	wheat
chair	cheese	shock	Thursday	whether
change	cherry	thankful	whale	whip

20

G Dictation

Name ______________________

Listen and write the missing words and punctuation.

1. Mr. Wilson will help change the truck tire .
2. Harrison ate cheese with his hot dog .
3. Mr. Potter asked whether he could work on Thursday .

H Proofreading

If a word is misspelled, fill in the oval by that word. If all the words are spelled correctly, fill in the oval by **no mistake**.

1. ○ bother ● wip ○ crop ○ no mistake

2. ● wether ○ deaf ○ lamb ○ no mistake

3. ● weet ○ cheek ○ buzz ○ no mistake

4. ○ Thursday ○ cactus ○ thirteen ● no mistake

5. ○ north ○ berry ● thankfull ○ no mistake

6. ● chery ○ whale ○ pick ○ no mistake

7. ○ felt ● cheeze ○ stiff ○ no mistake

8. ○ change ○ wagon ○ lift ● no mistake

9. ○ window ○ shock ● chare ○ no mistake

21

Words with Consonant Digraphs — Lesson 3

1 Dictation

Reinforce correct spelling by using current and previous words in context.

Listen as I read each sentence and then write the missing words and ending punctuation in your worktext. (Slowly read each sentence twice. Sentences are found in the student text to the left.)

2 Proofreading

Familiarize students with standardized test format and reinforce recognizing misspelled words.

Look at each set of words. If a word is misspelled, fill in the oval by that word. If all the words are spelled correctly, fill in the oval by **no mistake**.

3 Hide and Seek

Reinforce correct spelling of current spelling words. (A reproducible master is provided in Appendix A as shown on the inset page to the right.)
Write the words one at a time on the board. Use this activity for each word.

- **Look** at the word.
- **Say** the word out loud.
- Let's **hide** (cover) the word.
- **Write** the word on your paper.
- Let's **seek** (uncover) the word.
- **Check** your spelling. If your word is spelled wrong, write the word correctly next to it.

4 Other Word Forms

Have your students complete this activity to strengthen spelling ability and expand vocabulary.

Hide and Seek

Check a coin for each word you spell correctly.

Other Word Forms

Sentence Fun

Circle the word that completes each sentence.

1. He (change, (changed), changing) into shorts for the bike race.
2. This is a very (cheese, (cheesy), cheesiest) macaroni dinner.
3. Someone has been (bothers, bothered, (bothering)) the science projects.
4. You may get (shock, (shocked), shocking) if you play with electricity.
5. We saw a (whales, whaled, (whaling)) ship.
6. I like my pie with (whips, (whipped), whiplash) cream on it.
7. That wind from the (northern, northerly, (northwest)) is cold.
8. My dad is the (chairs, (chairman), chairing) of the board.
9. These flies are very (bothered, (bothersome), bothers).
10. I needed to (change, changing, (exchange)) the shirt for a new size.
11. The little chipmunk chattered in a ((cheeky), cheeks, cheekiest) way.
12. (Thankfulness, (Thankfully), Thankless), no one was hurt in the crash.

Spelling and Writing

Use each word in a sentence. Check your spelling.

1. cherries (Answers may vary)
2. thirteenth (Answers may vary)

Other Word Forms — Lesson 3

329

1 Posttest

Test mastery of the spelling words.

I will say the word once, use the word in a sentence, then say the word again. Write the word on your paper.

1. whale	The words whip, wheat, and **whale** have digraphs.
2. whip	What digraph does **whip** have?
3. wheat	Harrison looked at a picture of **wheat** bread.
4. north	Mr. Potter was driving **north** when the tire went flat.
5. thirteen	Mr. Potter did not have **thirteen** jobs from which to choose.
6. whether	Mommy doesn't know **whether** Daddy will get a job.
7. Thursday	They had beans on Monday, Tuesday, Wednesday, and **Thursday**.
8. change	Everyone wanted to **change** what they were eating for lunch.
9. chair	Harrison pulled his **chair** up to the table and stared at the beans.
10. cheese	The beans would taste better with **cheese**.
11. cheek	Harrison was worried about the tear on Mommy's **cheek**.
12. cherry	There is no **cherry** ice cream for dessert.
13. thankful	"We should be **thankful** for the beans," said Mommy.
14. shock	It was a **shock** to see the sign–man get out of the pickup.
15. bother	It is not a **bother** for God to hear your prayers.

Progress Chart

Students may record scores. (Reproducible master in Appendix B.)

Personal Dictionary

Students may add any words they have misspelled to their personal dictionaries for reference when writing. (Cover in Appendix B.)

Words with Consonant Digraphs

Lesson 3

I Game Name ______________________

John Potter and his family will follow Brad Wilson to the Knowlton Elementary work bee. Lead the way by moving one space for each word you or your team spells correctly from this week's word list.

Remember: Earnest prayer is very powerful!

J Journaling

In your journal, make a list of things you would like to earnestly pray about.

22

2 Game

Reinforce spelling skills and provide motivation and interest.

Materials

- game page (from student text)
- flat buttons, dry beans, pennies, or game discs (1 per child)
- game word list

Game Word List

1. bother
2. chair
3. change
4. cheek
5. cheese
6. cherry
7. north
8. shock
9. thankful
10. thirteen
11. Thursday
12. whale
13. wheat
14. whether
15. whip

How to Play:

- Divide the class into two teams.
- Have each student place his/her game piece on Start.
- Have a student from team A go to the board.
- Say the spelling word. (You may also wish to use the word in a sentence.)
- Have the student write the word on the board.
- If correct, instruct each member of team A to move his/her game piece forward one space on the game board. (Note: If the word is misspelled, correct the spelling immediately.)
- Alternate between teams A and B.
- The team to reach Knowlton Elementary first is the winner.

Non-Competitive Option:

At the end of the game, say: "Class, I am proud of your efforts to spell the words correctly. If you had fun and tried your best, you are all winners!"

3 Journaling

Provide a meaningful reason for correct spelling through personal writing.

Review the story using discussion leads provided on the following page. Encourage students to apply the Scriptural value in their journaling.

Day 5

Lesson 3

Journaling (continued)

- What does **earnestly** mean? (serious, grave, purposeful, sincere, determined, important)
- For what did the Potter family earnestly pray? (Food and a job for Dad.)
- Our text says, "The earnest prayer of a righteous man has great power and wonderful results." What were the wonderful results of the Potters' prayers? (They had food for supper and at least a temporary job.)
- Make a list of things in your journal about which you would like to earnestly pray.

Take a minute to memorize...
Have the class say the memory verses from lessons 1, 2, and 3 with you.

"When young writers are free to concentrate on what they want to say rather than mechanics, their thoughts can flow more freely."*

*Wilde, Sandra. 1990. A Proposal for a New Spelling Curriculum. The Elementary School Journal, Vol. 90, No. 3, January: 275-289.

1 **Literature Connection**
Topic: Being glad in the Lord
Theme Text: Philippians 3:1

Flu Shots & Fleas

When Kristin and Christopher have to go get flu shots, they learn that you can be glad in any situation if you trust in God.

Kristin chased the last few pieces of cereal around her bowl as she glanced at the glowing, green numbers on the microwave clock. Seven-thirty. Almost time to leave for school. She sighed and scooped a spoonful of milk with one little "O" shaped piece of cereal floating on top. "I'm not really hungry, Mom. Can I leave the rest of this?"

Mrs. Wright looked up from helping four-year-old Cory peel a banana. "There are only a few spoonfuls left. You need to finish your breakfast."

"I don't feel so good." Kristin slid her spoon around and around the bowl, soggy little "O's" bobbing along. "Maybe I should stay home today."

Mrs. Wright glanced at her daughter's slumped shoulders and gloomy expression. Her forehead wrinkled with concern as she reached across the table and laid a hand lightly on Kristin's forehead. "You don't feel too warm," she said. "I don't think you have a fever."

Christopher carried his empty cereal bowl to the sink. "She just wants to get out of going to the doctor today! She's a 'fraidy cat about getting shots!" He held up his spoon. "I bet the needle will be this long!"

"Shut up, Christopher!" Kristin glowered at her twin. "You don't like shots any more than I do."

"That's enough, both of you." When Mom sounded like that, the twins knew they'd better watch it. "Now, all of you get your teeth brushed quickly. We need to leave for school in five minutes." The twins and their younger sister, Cathy, left the table quietly, but Kristin stuck her tongue out at Christopher as she passed him in the hall.

They were almost to school when Mom reminded them about the doctor appointment. "Don't forget, it's at two-fifteen. That means I'll pick you up at one-forty-five. I've already talked to both your teachers, but give them these notes to remind them."

"Do we all have to go?" Kristin tried again to get out of it. "After all, Cory is the only one who needs to go for a regular check-up and booster vaccinations. The rest of us have had all that."

Mrs. Wright turned into the school drive and stopped before turning to look at Kristin. "Yes, Sweety," she said gently. "You all have to go. As I explained before, the doctors and nurses are concerned about a particularly serious type of flu this season. It's very hard on children or elderly people. Your dad and I want to keep you as safe and healthy as we can, and these flu shots will help do that." Mom handed Cathy and the twins each an envelope with their teacher's name on the front. "I'll see you this afternoon."

Cathy skipped off and Christopher waited on the curb for Tommy who was just arriving. Kristin started to walk slowly toward the school. "Kristin," Mom called through the car window. "It won't be that bad, Sweety. Just don't worry about it, okay?"

"Okay." Kristin watched as the green station wagon pulled away from the curb. She didn't even smile when she spotted Cory making fish faces against the back seat window.

But Kristin did worry, and the day went much too fast. She looked at the large, round clock on the classroom wall. Ten o'clock. It seemed only minutes later when she looked again. Eleven fifty! It was less than two hours until they had to leave for the doctor's office! Kristin looked around the room. Christopher caught her eye and held up his pencil. With a big grin he pretended he was a doctor giving his book a shot with the pencil. "You creep!" Kristin mouthed as she glared at him.

She turned back to the unfinished handwriting on her desk. "I hate getting shots!" Kristin mumbled under her breath. "They're scary and they hurt! I probably wouldn't get sick with that old flu anyway." Thoughts churned through her head as she wrote. "I don't think being sick a few days and staying in bed would be as bad as having to get a shot!" SNAP. Kristin stared at the broken off point of her pencil and the dark black mark on her handwriting sheet. She read what she'd written. "Whatever happens, dear friends, be glad i— "

"Whatever happens?" Kristin thought. "Even having to get a shot?"

At one-forty-five Kristin, Christopher, and Cathy climbed into the car for the trip to the doctor's office. "Mom, do I still have to get a shot?" Kristin asked desperately. "I'll wash my hands a lot and be really careful so I won't get sick. Please? I hate shots!"

"I realize that, Kristin. I don't think anyone likes shots." Mom checked for cars out the back window and changed lanes. "But sometimes we need to be thankful even for things we don't like. Before there were shots, or immunizations, many people died from illnesses we don't worry about today. Shots may hurt for a moment, but that's much better than hurting for a long time or even dying."

It was quiet in the car for a few moments. Mom broke the silence with a question. "Many years ago there was a war called World War II. Do you remember hearing about it?"

"Yes." Christopher answered. The girls nodded their heads. "Isn't that the war when a lot of people who weren't even soldiers were killed because of who they were?"

Story (continued)

"That's right, Son." Mrs. Wright sighed. "Many Jewish people were put in prison camps or killed. It was a bad time for this world. Some people tried to help. Onc lady, named Corrie Ten Boom, was caught helping. She was put in a prison camp, too. She managed to get a little copy of the Scriptures into the camp even though the guards were taking away everything that people had. It was very, very hard for the prisoners in the camps. There was hardly anything to eat, rags for clothes, and only wood bunks covered with straw. They were crowded, hungry, cold, and many were sick. The guards were mean to them. And there were fleas in the building she was in. Lots and lots of fleas biting them, and nothing they could do about it." Mom paused as she turned the car onto another road.

"What happened?" Cathy demanded. "What did the lady do?"

"She thanked God for the fleas!" Mom chuckled at the surprise on the four children's faces.

"That's crazy!" Christopher shook his head.

"She knew the Scriptures say to give thanks to God in all circumstances," Mom explained, "So she did just that. She didn't find out until later that the fleas really were something to be thankful for."

"What?" Christopher frowned as Mrs. Wright pulled into a parking space in front of the doctor's office. "How could anyone be thankful for fleas?"

"Well, she read the Scriptures to the others in that particular building in the prison camp. Hearing about God and His love helped them a lot. The guards would go into the other buildings and take away anything they found. But the guards never came into her building to search, or to stop them from worshiping. Can you guess why?"

"The fleas!" The children answered at the same time.

"That's right." Mom dropped the keys into her purse. "The guards didn't want to get fleas all over them. Those fleas kept the people in that building free of the guards so they could read the Scriptures." Mom opened her car door and then turned back. "I know getting a shot won't be fun, but it's not as bad as having fleas bite you all the time. It will be over quickly and will help to keep you healthy. So let's practice being glad and thankful in all things!"

Even Christopher looked a little scared when they entered the doctor's office, but he went first. When it was Kristin's turn she stared hard at a picture on the wall as she felt the nurse rub her skin with alcohol. "Dear God, help me be brave and still. Help it not to hurt too bad and be over quick." And it was.

That evening the twins sat at the kitchen table finishing their homework. Kristin erased the black mark her broken pencil had left on her handwriting paper, and then carefully finished the verse. "Mom, listen to this." Mrs. Wright turned from the cheese sandwiches she was grilling for supper. "Whatever happens, dear friends. . ." Kristin read, ". . .be glad in the Lord. That's like the story you told us today about being glad for fleas, isn't it?"

"And glad for shots!" Christopher grinned across the table as he held up his pencil like a syringe.

Kristin grinned back. "I'm glad to be done with shots for awhile!" Mom laughed as she turned back to the stove to finish supper.

A few minutes later, the Wright family sat around the table with bowed heads. Dad asked God's blessing on them and the food they were about to eat. And Kristin added her own silent prayer.

"Thank you, God, for helping me be still when I got my flu shot today. And help me to always be glad in You, no matter what happens!"

2 Discussion Time

Check understanding of the story and development of personal values.

- Why did Kristin say she might be getting sick?
- What kind of shot was Kristin getting, and why did she need it?
- What did Christopher do to make Kristin feel worse?
- What story did the twins' mother tell them?
- What did the lady who was put in a prison camp for helping others thank God for?
- How did the horrible fleas turn out to really be something for which to be thankful?
- Why do you think our Scripture says that whatever happens, we should be glad in the Lord?

A Preview Name ____________

Write each word as your teacher says it.

1. plant
2. clay
3. plain
4. slice
5. close
6. flag
7. please
8. flame
9. plus
10. flash
11. glass
12. place
13. glove
14. sleeve
15. cloth

Scripture

Philippians 3:1

Words with Consonant Clusters

Lesson 4

23

3 Preview

Test for knowledge of the correct spellings of these words.

Customize Your List

On a separate piece of paper, additional words of your choice may be tested.

I will say the word once, use the word in a sentence, then say the word again. Write the word on the lines in the worktext.

Correct Immediately!

Let's correct our preview. I will write each word on the board. Put a dot under each letter on your preview as I spell the word out loud. If you spelled a word wrong, rewrite it correctly.

Take a minute to memorize...

Read the memory verse to the class twice. Have the class practice it with you two more times.

Day 1

Lesson 4

1.	plant	Not a single **plant** grew inside the prison.
2.	clay	The **clay** turned to thick mud when it rained.
3.	plain	The women slept on **plain** wooden boards covered with straw.
4.	slice	They had only one **slice** of bread and a little soup to eat.
5.	close	All the prisoners gathered **close** to hear the Scriptures.
6.	flag	The stars on our **flag** stand for the fifty states in our nation.
7.	please	We should say "**please**" whenever we ask for something.
8.	flame	Mrs. Wright turned the **flame** down on the stove burner.
9.	plus	Christopher pretended a pencil was a syringe, **plus** other things.
10.	flash	Quick as a **flash**, Kristin stuck her tongue out at Christopher.
11.	glass	Cory made fish faces against the window **glass** in the car.
12.	place	Mother pulled into a parking **place** at the doctor's office.
13.	glove	The doctor slipped his hand into a new **glove.**
14.	sleeve	The nurse asked Christopher to roll up his **sleeve** for the shot.
15.	cloth	The nurse rubbed Kristin's arm with alcohol on a small **cloth.**

Progress Chart

Students may record scores. (Reproducible master in Appendix B.)

4 Word Shapes

Help students form a correct image of whole words.

Look at each word and think about its shape. Now, write the word in the correct word shape boxes. You may check off each word as you use it.

(The initial clusters **cl**, **fl**, **gl**, **pl**, and **sl** are introduced in this lesson. Unlike a digraph, in which two letters combine to form a single sound, the letters that make up a consonant cluster keep their sounds when pronounced in words. These clusters are often found at the beginning of words.)

In the word shape boxes, color the letters that spell the consonant cluster in each word. Circle the words that begin with a consonant cluster and end with a digraph.

Words with Consonant Clusters — Lesson 4

B Word Shapes Name ____________________

Write each word in the correct word shape boxes. Next, in the word shape boxes, color the letters that spell the consonant cluster in each word. Circle the words that begin with a consonant cluster and end with a digraph.

	Word	Answer
1.	clay	plain
2.	close	flash (circled)
3.	cloth	glass
4.	flag	please
5.	flame	plant
6.	flash	plus
7.	glass	flag
8.	glove	sleeve
9.	place	clay
10.	plain	close
11.	plant	glove
12.	please	cloth (circled)
13.	plus	slice
14.	sleeve	flame
15.	slice	place

24

Answers may vary for duplicate word shapes.

Be Prepared For Fun

Check these supply lists for **Fun Ways to Spell** presented **Day 2**. Purchase and/or gather needed items ahead of time!

General
- A Classmate
- Spelling List

Auditory
- Voice Recorder
- Spelling List

Visual
- a, c, e, e, e, f, g, h, i, l, m, n, o, p, s, s, t, u, v, y (written on upside-down cups)
- Spelling List

Tactile
- Art Paper (2 or 3 sheets per child)
- Magazines
- Glue Sticks
- Scissors
- Spelling List

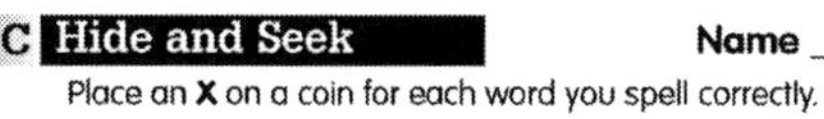

C Hide and Seek **Name** ______________________

Place an **X** on a coin for each word you spell correctly.

D Other Word Forms

Using the words below, follow the instructions given by your teacher.

closed	clothing	glassful	plainness	sleeves
closely	cloths	glassy	planted	sliced
closeness	flagged	gloved	planter	slices
closer	flagging	placed	planting	slicing
closest	flames	placement	pleased	
closing	flaming	places	pleasing	
clothe	flashing	placing	pleasingly	
clothed	flashy	plainly	sleeveless	

E Fun Ways to Spell

Initial the box of each activity you finish.

1. 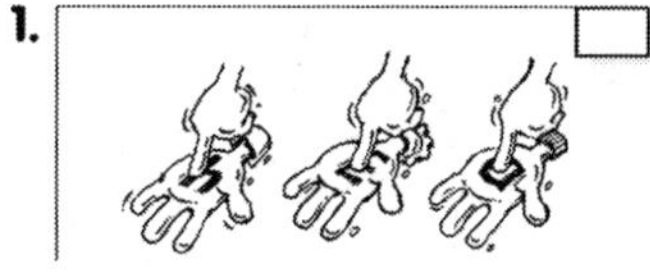

Spell your words in your classmate's hand.

3. 

Spell your words using a tape recorder.

2. 

Spell your words with paper cups.

4. 

Spell your words with magazine clippings.

Words with Consonant Clusters

Lesson 4

1 Hide and Seek

Reinforce correct spelling of current spelling words.

Write the words one at a time on the board. Use this activity for each word.

Say

- **Look** at the word.
- **Say** the word out loud.
- Let's **hide** (cover) the word.
- **Write** the word on your paper.
- Let's **seek** (uncover) the word.
- **Check** your spelling. If your word is spelled wrong, write the word correctly next to it.

2 Other Word Forms

This activity is optional. Have students unscramble these letters to write Other Word Forms:

liapnyl	(plainly)
escild	(sliced)
gggafiln	(flagging)
lsasufgl	(glassful)

3 Fun Ways to Spell

Four activities are provided. Use one, two, three, or all of the activities. Have students initial the box for each activity they complete.

Day 2

Lesson 4

Options:

- assign activities to students according to their learning styles
- set up the activities in learning centers for the class to do throughout the day
- divide the class into four groups and assign one activity per group
- do one activity per day

General

To spell your words in your classmate's hand...
- Have your classmate sit next to you and hold his (or her) palm open in front of and facing both of you.
- Use your fingertip to write a spelling word in the palm of your classmate's hand.
- Have your classmate say each letter as you write it and then say the word you spelled.
- Next, have your classmate write a word in your palm.

Auditory

To spell your words using a voice recorder...
- Record yourself as you say and spell each word on your spelling list.
- Listen to your recording and check your spelling.

Visual

To spell your words with paper cups...
- Spell a word from your list by putting the cups in the right order.
- Check your spelling.

Tactile

To spell your words with magazine clippings...
- Cut the letters you need from old magazines.
- Glue the letters to your paper in the correct order.

Day 3

Lesson 4

1 Working with Words

Familiarize students with word meaning and usage.

Rhyming Words

Say the words **sheep** and **leap**. Ask students if these words rhyme. Write the words on the board. Explain to the students that, although the words are spelled differently, they still rhyme because **ee** and **ea** are both ways to spell the sound of **/ē/**.

At the top of your page, write the spelling word that rhymes with the given word. Remember, a word may rhyme even when the spelling is different.

Clues

Read each clue. Find the spelling word that is a synonym and write it on the line. Remember, a synonym is a word that means the same or almost the same as another word.

Dictionary Skills

At the bottom of your page, draw a line to the correct meaning for each **dictionary entry** below.

Take a minute to memorize...

Read the memory verse to the class twice. Have the class practice it with you two more times.

Words with Consonant Clusters — Lesson 4

F Working with Words   Name ____________

Rhyming Words

Write the spelling word that rhymes with the words below.

1. spice slice	6. sneeze please	11. class glass
2. play clay	7. space place	12. clash flash
3. grain plain	8. grieve sleeve	13. brag flag
4. broth cloth	9. shove glove	14. rose close
5. slant plant	10. blame flame	15. truss plus

Clues

Write the spelling word that matches each clue.

1. shut close	7. satisfy please	13. add plus
2. mitten glove	8. fragile glass	14. shrub plant
3. fabric cloth	9. fire flame	15. jacket sleeve
4. gleam flash	10. cut slice	
5. simple plain	11. banner flag	
6. area place	12. play dough clay	

Dictionary Skills

The words listed and explained in a dictionary are called entry words. A dictionary tells what words mean and how they are used. Draw a line to the correct meaning for each dictionary entry below.

1. close — space for a person or thing
2. slice — to shut
3. place — to make glad
4. please — a thin flat piece cut from something

Word Bank

clay	flag	glass	plain	plus
close	flame	glove	plant	sleeve
cloth	flash	place	please	slice

26

G Dictation

Name ___________

Listen and write the missing words and punctuation.

1. Kristin placed the glass on the window sill.
2. Please roll up your sleeve for your shot.
3. Miss ten Boom's guard would not come close to them.

H Proofreading

If a word is misspelled, fill in the oval by that word. If all the words are spelled correctly, fill in the oval by **no mistake**.

1.	4.	7.
cloth	glass	plain
cherry	plant	chair
klay (filled)	thankful	hello
no mistake	no mistake (filled)	no mistake (filled)

2.	5.	8.
wheat	gluv (filled)	change
klose (filled)	plus	pleaze (filled)
flash	Sunday	twelve
no mistake	no mistake	no mistake

3.	6.	9.
flaem (filled)	whip	sleave (filled)
flag	plase (filled)	west
whether	slice	pants
no mistake	no mistake	no mistake

27

Words with Consonant Clusters

Lesson 4

1 Dictation

Reinforce correct spelling by using current and previous words in context.

Listen as I read each sentence and then write the missing words and ending punctuation in your worktext. (Slowly read each sentence twice. Sentences are found in the student text to the left.)

2 Proofreading

Familiarize students with standardized test format and reinforce recognizing misspelled words.

Look at each set of words. If a word is misspelled, fill in the oval by that word. If all the words are spelled correctly, fill in the oval by **no mistake**.

Day 4

Lesson 4

Day 4 / Day 5

Lesson 4

3 Hide and Seek

Reinforce correct spelling of current spelling words. (A reproducible master is provided in Appendix A as shown on the inset page to the right.)

Write the words one at a time on the board. Use this activity for each word.

- **Look** at the word.
- **Say** the word out loud.
- Let's **hide** (cover) the word.
- **Write** the word on your paper.
- Let's **seek** (uncover) the word.
- **Check** your spelling. If your word is spelled wrong, write the word correctly next to it.

4 Other Word Forms

Have your students complete this activity to strengthen spelling ability and expand vocabulary.

1 Posttest

Test mastery of the spelling words.

I will say the word once, use the word in a sentence, then say the word again. Write the word on your paper.

Other Word Forms — Lesson 4

Hide and Seek

Check a coin for each word you spell correctly.

Other Word Forms

Prefixes and Suffixes

Choose the correct prefix or suffix to make a new word. Write the new word on the line.

1. flame + (ly, s) = flames
2. glass + (y, ness) = glassy
3. flag + (ly, s) = flags
4. close + (less, ly) = closely
5. place + (s, ness) = places
6. sleeve + (less, ing) = sleeveless
7. flash + (ness, ing) = flashing
8. slice + (ly, s) = slices
9. plain + (ing, s) = plains
10. (ex, im) + plant = implant
11. (dis, de) + close = disclose
12. (re, pre) + place = replace
13. (in, dis) + please = displease
14. (dis, ex) + plain = explain

Rhyming Words

Write the Other Word Form that rhymes with each word below.

1. tagged flagged
2. sassy glassy
3. claiming flaming
4. dragging flagging
5. splashing flashing
6. sneezed pleased
7. hosing closing
8. leaves sleeves
9. canter planter
10. basement placement
11. shoved gloved
12. slanted planted
13. dozed closed
14. freezing pleasing
15. icing slicing
16. vainly plainly

Word Bank

closed	flagging	glassy	plainly	pleased	slicing
closing	flaming	gloved	planted	pleasing	
flagged	flashing	placement	planter	sleeves	

330

1. plus — The women were hungry and sick, **plus** very cold.
2. flame — They didn't have even a small **flame** for warmth.
3. clay — The floor was hard **clay**.
4. cloth — There were holes in the **cloth** of the prisoners' dresses.
5. place — There were many, many fleas in that **place**.
6. flag — Our **flag** represents the freedom we enjoy in the United States of America.
7. glass — Kristin drank a **glass** of orange juice at breakfast.
8. slice — Christopher put strawberry jam on his **slice** of toast.
9. plain — Kristin likes her toast **plain**.
10. please — "Mom, do I have to get a shot?" Kristin asked. "**Please**? I hate shots!"
11. close — It was **close** to time to leave for the doctor's office.
12. plant — Kristin didn't notice the flowering **plant** in the doctor's waiting room.
13. glove — The nurse wore a latex **glove** on each hand.
14. sleeve — Kristin rolled up her **sleeve** so the nurse could give the flu shot.
15. flash — The shot was over in a **flash**.

Progress Chart

Students may record scores. (Reproducible master in Appendix B.)

Personal Dictionary

Students may add any words they have misspelled to their personal dictionaries for reference when writing. (Cover in Appendix B.)

I **Game** Name ____________________

Christopher and Kristin need to get shots today. Lead the way to the doctor's office by moving one space for each word you or your team spells correctly from this week's word list.

Remember: God wants us to find happiness in Him no matter what!

J **Journaling**

In your journal, write about some times when it might be hard to be glad. Then write a prayer asking God's help to always be glad in Him.

28

Words with Consonant Clusters Lesson 4

2 Game

Reinforce spelling skills and provide motivation and interest.

Materials

- game page (from student text)
- flat buttons, dry beans, pennies, or game discs (1 per child)
- game word list

Game Word List

1. clay
2. close
3. cloth
4. flag
5. flame
6. flash
7. glass
8. glove
9. place
10. plain
11. plant
12. please
13. plus
14. sleeve
15. slice

How to Play:

- Divide the class into two teams.
- Have each student place his/her game piece on Start.
- Have a student from team A go to the board.
- Say the spelling word. (You may also wish to use the word in a sentence.)
- Have the student write the word on the board.
- If correct, instruct each member of team A to move his/her game piece forward one space on the game board. (Note: If the word is misspelled, correct the spelling immediately.)
- Alternate between teams A and B.
- The team to reach the doctor's office first is the winner.

Non-Competitive Option:

At the end of the game, say: "Class, I am proud of your efforts to spell the words correctly. If you had fun and tried your best, you are all winners!"

3 Journaling

Provide a meaningful reason for correct spelling through personal writing.

Review the story using discussion leads provided on the following page. Encourage students to apply the Scriptural value in their journaling.

Journaling (continued)

- Why was the lady in Mrs. Wright's story put into prison? (She helped Jewish people during World War II.)
- What was the prison camp like? (Very crowded, dirty, poor food, etc.)
- Why did the lady thank God for the fleas? (Because she knew the Scriptures tell us to be thankful in all circumstances.)
- How did the lady help the other prisoners? (She had a copy of the Scriptures. Reading it to the other prisoners helped them learn about God's love and encouraged them to be kinder to each other.)
- Why didn't the guards take away her copy of the Scriptures like they took everything else? (The guards wouldn't come in their building because of all the fleas.)
- Why should we, like the lady in prison camp, be glad in the Lord no matter what happens? (Because God can take care of us in any circumstances.)
- How do you feel when you have to go to the doctor to get a shot?
- Can you think of some other times when it might be hard to be glad? Write in your journal about these times. Then, write a prayer asking God to help you always be glad in Him.

Take a minute to memorize...

Have the class say the memory verses from lessons 1, 2, 3, and 4 with you.

"Invented spelling is not a failure to spell the conventional way but a step on the road to reaching it."*

*Wilde, Sandra. 1992. You kan red this! Portsmouth, NH: Heinemann.

Our Very Own

Rachel learns about belonging when she finds out her step-mother is expecting a baby.

Rachel ran across the grass in front of Knowlton Elementary and jumped into the waiting van. "Father, what took you so long? Helen is never late picking us up after school."

Thirteen-year-old Rebecca walked down the sidewalk with Natalie, the youngest member of the family. Natalie looked around as Rebecca helped her into the van. "Where's Mommy?" she said. "I have a note for her."

Rachel's step-sister Vanessa climbed into the van behind Natalie. "Mommy's not here?" She put her backpack on the floor between her feet.

"Mommy's at home. She's tired, so I offered to come pick you up from school. Sorry I'm late. I got a phone call right as I was leaving the office." Father tuned around and watched Rebecca fasten Natalie's seat belt. "How was kindergarten today, Natalie?"

"Darby is going to have babies. Miss Robeson said so." Natalie unzipped her backpack and started pulling papers out. "Can I give you the note for Mommy?"

Father nodded as he pulled away from the curb and headed back into town. "When will Mrs. Darby have her twins?"

"Not twins. Miss Robeson says she's going to have four or five babies!" Natalie pulled out a rock, a long piece of string, and a couple of Barbie dolls from her backpack.

"Four or five?" Father's eyebrows shot up in surprise. "Who is this Mrs. Darby, Natalie?"

"Oh, you probably haven't seen her yet." Natalie turned the backpack upside down and shook the remaining contents out onto the seat beside her. "Miss Robeson bought her last week, but she didn't buy her husband."

Rebecca laughed. "Darby is their hamster, Father—not a lady."

Mr. Jacobson smiled. "You had me worried there for a minute. Our family has four children, but you didn't all come at the same time. I can't imagine bringing four babies home from the hospital at once."

A few minutes later Father turned into the grocery store parking lot. "What are we doing here?" Rachel frowned. "Helen usually gets the groceries. I want to get home and call Tony before supper. He wants to ride bikes in the park."

"I don't think you'll be able to do that today, Rachel. After we pick up a few things at the grocery store I need to run a couple of other errands. I have to mail this package for Mom and then stop by the office for a few minutes. Then I think we'll eat at Taco Bell®."

"Taco Bell®!" Vanessa shouted. "Can I get a kid's meal?"

"I want one, too," Natalie chimed in.

"Taco Bell® and kid's meals coming up," Father smiled.

Later that evening Father went into Rachel and Rebecca's room to tell them goodnight. "See you in the morning," he said and turned out the light.

"Hey!" Rachel sat up in bed. "I thought Helen was going to read us another chapter from *Little House on the Prairie*."

"She's too tired, Rachel," Father said. "I'll do it. Call Vanessa and Natalie while I ask Mom where she put the book."

"The book's right here, Father." Rebecca picked up the book and handed it to Mr. Jacobson.

"Vanessa! Natalie!" Rachel bellowed from her twin bed next to Rebecca's. "Time to hear *Little House on the Prairie*. Father's reading in our room tonight!"

"I could have hollered for them, Rachel," Father said with a sigh. "Mommy is resting. Go find Vanessa and Natalie and quietly tell them to come in here for the story."

Rachel crawled out from beneath the covers. "Is Helen sick?"

"No, just tired." Father reached over and fluffed Rachel's pillow as he watched her leave the room. "I wonder if Rachel will ever call Helen 'Mommy,'" he thought. "Helen and I have been married for over two years now. Rachel and Helen had some hard times in the past, but things have seemed to be better recently."

He looked over at his oldest daughter Rebecca, who was thumbing through the pages of the book, pausing to look at the pictures. "Rebecca remembers more about her mother's fight with cancer than Rachel, yet Rachel has had a much more difficult time adjusting to Catherine's death."

"Here we are Father!" Vanessa bounced into the room, bringing her father back to reality. "Now you can read to us!"

The next morning Rachel surveyed the choices on the breakfast table. "Why are we having cold cereal?" She frowned. "We usually have waffles on Wednesdays."

"Yeah. Mommy said she would make me blueberry ones." Natalie began to look through the cereal boxes for her favorite.

"Well, I made breakfast this time. I'm not too good at waffles, so it's either cold cereal this morning or cold cereal."

"What a choice!" Rebecca laughed. "I think I'll have cold cereal."

"Where's Helen?" Rachel asked. "Is she sick?"

"She's just very tired, girls. I just wanted to let her sleep a little extra this morning."

Story (continued)

"Who is going to take us to school?" Vanessa poured her milk on her cereal.

Rebecca looked at the kitchen counter. "And where are the lunches?"

"Lunches?" Mr. Jacobson scratched his head. "Well, I forgot about those. How about I bring you something from Taco Bell®? What time do you guys eat?"

"We had Taco Bell® last night," Vanessa complained.

"Well," Father bowed at the waist like a very proper waiter. "Today for lunch we have burritos or burritos." He turned to Rebecca. "What will you have, Miss?"

Rebecca smiled. "I think I'll have a burrito minus onions plus green sauce and sour cream."

"I don't want any red sauce," Natalie said.

"I want tomatoes and guacamole added to mine." Rachel took the milk jug from Vanessa and poured some milk on her cereal.

"I want just beans and cheese." Vanessa picked up her spoon.

"And I think I need my day planner to write down your lunch order!" Father laughed. "But let's thank the Lord for this meal we're about to eat first."

Later that afternoon the four Jacobson sisters waited on the front steps of Knowlton Elementary watching for the family's dark green van. Rachel stood up and kicked at a lone leaf that was blowing across the steps. Vanessa knelt down in front of Natalie and zipped her coat up under her chin.

"I wonder where Mommy is? She's late again today," Vanessa said.

"Do you think she's sick like our Mommy was before she died?" Rachel looked up at Rebecca for reassurance.

"She's just been tired for a few days, Rachel. Maybe she has the flu or something." Rebecca pulled Natalie onto her lap.

"Father said she wasn't sick. Remember at breakfast?" Vanessa took her backpack off and set it on the steps beside her.

"Well, something is wrong with her. She never skips reading to us at night." Rachel walked slowly toward the curb. "Come on, there's the van coming around the corner," she called over her shoulder.

"Look! Mommy isn't driving. Daddy's with her today," Natalie said.

Rachel and Rebecca exchanged glances. "I think you are right, Rachel. Something is definitely wrong. Father is doing all the things that Mom usually does." Rebecca stood up and headed toward the van.

Father pulled up to the curb and hopped out to open the door for the four girls. When everyone was settled, it grew quiet in the van. Father looked over at his wife and smiled lovingly. "Well, shall we tell them now or later?"

"Tell us what?" the four girls chorused.

"We're about to become a family of seven!" Father turned around so he could look at the girls' faces. "Your mother and I were not going to tell you until she was further along, but she is so tired and sleepy all the time, it's hard to keep it a secret without letting you worry."

"Seven babies?" Natalie looked over at Rebecca with big eyes. "Just like Darby!"

"Just one more baby," the older girl laughed. "We have six in our family counting Father and Mom. A baby would make our family grow to seven like Father said."

"Seven! What made you think I might have seven babies, Natalie?" Mother leaned her head back, closed her eyes and groaned.

"Oh, the kindergartners' hamster had seven babies last night." Vanessa explained.

"Now we'll have a baby at home, too!" Natalie leaned forward in her seat. "Will it come next week?"

"People babies take nine months to be born, Nat." Rebecca looked over at the little girl and smiled, then turned back toward the adults. "When is our baby due?"

"About the time school is out," Helen answered.

"A baby!" Rachel thought quietly to herself. "Babies are so cute. I hope it's a boy. Our family keeps changing. First we lose Mommy. Then we get Helen. Helen brings Vanessa and Natalie with her. Then we all leave Dallas and move here. And now we're going to get a baby."

As the van rolled toward home, she looked out the window and saw a group of children playing on the new equipment in Mason Springs Park. Then she glanced down at the handwriting sheet in her lap. "Long ago, even before He made the world, God chose us to be His very own." She thought about her family and the families of her friends. Some families choose to be together; some choose to split up—like Tony's. Some kids were born into a family, and some had parents choose to adopt them.

"Mr. Valentino said that God chose to love us before we were even born," Rachel mused. Suddenly, she looked at Helen, who gave her a tired smile. "This baby will be all of ours!" she said. "Because he's yours and Father's he won't have a step-mother or step-father. And we won't be step-sisters to him." She paused, then continued with a big smile. "This baby will be our very own!"

2 Discussion Time

Check understanding of the story and development of personal values.

- What happened to Rachel's biological mother?
- What did Rachel's step-mother stop doing that worried Rachel?
- Rachel has been angry at her step-mother in the past. What happens in this story to help you know that Rachel is starting to really love and appreciate her step-mother?
- How do you think Rachel feels when she finds out her step-mother is pregnant and not sick with a disease?
- How does Rachel feel about their unborn baby?
- When did God choose us to be his very own?

A Preview Name ____________

Write each word as your teacher says it.

1. spell
2. bread
3. broke
4. crayon
5. grab
6. price
7. prayer
8. prize
9. proud
10. skin
11. spend
12. skate
13. skip
14. gray
15. cross

Words with Consonant Clusters

Lesson 5

Scripture

Ephesians 1:4

29

3 Preview

Test for knowledge of the correct spellings of these words.

Day 1

Lesson 5

Customize Your List

On a separate piece of paper, additional words of your choice may be tested.

I will say the word once, use the word in a sentence, then say the word again. Write the word on the lines in the worktext.

Correct Immediately!

Let's correct our preview. I will write each word on the board. Put a dot under each letter on your preview as I spell the word out loud. If you spelled a word wrong, rewrite it correctly.

Take a minute to memorize...

Read the memory verse to the class twice. Have the class practice it with you two more times.

1.	spell	Be sure to **spell** all these words correctly.
2.	bread	The Jacobsons did not have **bread** for lunch.
3.	broke	The zipper **broke** on Natalie's backpack.
4.	crayon	A **crayon** fell out of Natalie's backpack onto the seat.
5.	grab	Father suggested they just **grab** something to eat at Taco Bell®.
6.	price	The **price** is right for a meal at Taco Bell®.
7.	prayer	The Jacobsons said a **prayer** before they ate.
8.	prize	There was a **prize** in the kid's meal at the restaurant.
9.	proud	Mr. Jacobson is **proud** of his family.
10.	skin	Mother's **skin** looked pale.
11.	spend	Mr. Jacobson doesn't usually **spend** so much time with his girls.
12.	skate	They did not **skate** at the roller rink with Mother.
13.	skip	Mother never likes to **skip** reading to the girls.
14.	gray	Mother's face looked **gray**.
15.	cross	Jesus died on the **cross** for us.

Progress Chart

Students may record scores. (Reproducible master in Appendix B.)

Day 1

Lesson

5

4 Word Shapes

Help students form a correct image of whole words.

Look at each word and think about its shape. Now, write the word in the correct word shape boxes. You may check off each word as you use it.

(The initial clusters **br**, **cr**, **gr**, **pr**, **sk**, and **sp** are introduced in this lesson. These clusters are often found at the beginning of words or after prefixes.)

In the word shape boxes, color the letters that spell the consonant cluster in each word. Circle the word that has two syllables.

Words with Consonant Clusters — Lesson 5

B Word Shapes Name ______________________

Write each word in the correct word shape boxes. Next, in the word shape boxes, color the letters that spell the consonant cluster in each word. Circle the word that has two syllables.

Word	Word shape
1. bread	skip
2. broke	spend
3. crayon	proud
4. cross	bread
5. grab	broke
6. gray	crayon (circled)
7. prayer	gray
8. price	grab
9. prize	cross
10. proud	skate
11. skate	price
12. skin	skin
13. skip	prize
14. spell	spell
15. spend	prayer

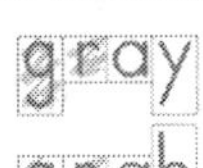

30

Answers may vary for duplicate word shapes.

Be Prepared For Fun

Check these supply lists for **Fun Ways to Spell** presented **Day 2**. Purchase and/or gather needed items ahead of time!

General
- Markers
- Art Paper (2 or 3 sheets per child)
- Spelling List

Auditory
- Spelling List

Visual
- Letter Tiles a, b, c, d, e, g, i, k, l, l, n, o, p, r, r, s, s, t, u, y, z
- Spelling List

Tactile
- Paint Bags (tempera paint in plastic, resealable bags secured at top with heavy tape-1 per child)
- Spelling List

C Hide and Seek Name ______________________

Place an **X** on a coin for each word you spell correctly.

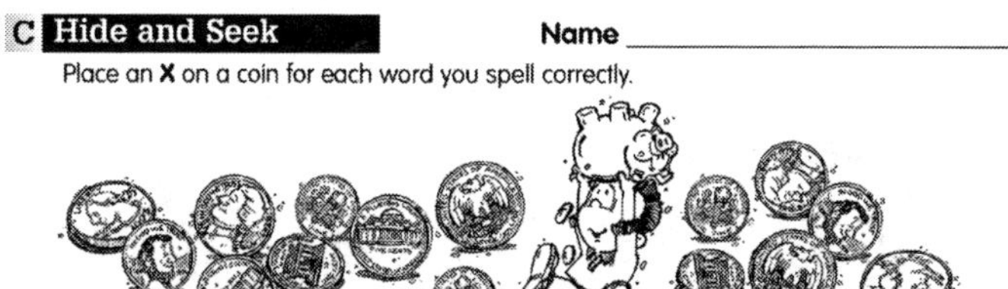

D Other Word Forms

Using the words below, follow the instructions given by your teacher.

breaded	crossword	priceless	skinned	spelling
break	grabbed	pricing	skinning	spender
breakable	grabbing	prized	skinny	spending
breaking	grayish	prizing	skipped	spent
broken	grayness	proudly	skipping	
crossed	prayerful	skater	skips	
crossing	prayerfully	skates	spelled	
crosswise	priced	skating	speller	

E Fun Ways to Spell

Initial the box of each activity you finish.

1\.

Spell your words with markers.

3\.

Spell your words while snapping.

2\.

Spell your words with letter tiles.

4\.

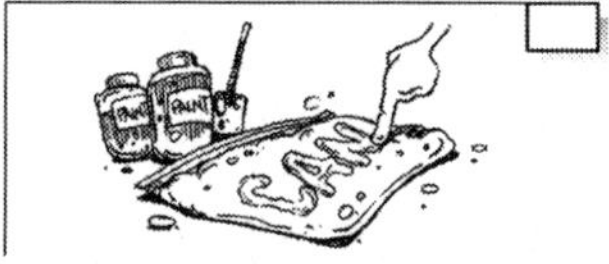

Spell your words with paint.

Words with Consonant Clusters

Lesson 5

31

1 Hide and Seek

Reinforce correct spelling of current spelling words.

Write the words one at a time on the board. Use this activity for each word.

- **Look** at the word.
- **Say** the word out loud.
- Let's **hide** (cover) the word.
- **Write** the word on your paper.
- Let's **seek** (uncover) the word.
- **Check** your spelling. If your word is spelled wrong, write the word correctly next to it.

Day 2

Lesson 5

2 Other Word Forms

This activity is optional. Have students write variations of this sentence using these Other Word Forms:

Heather can skip rope for a long time.

skipped, skipping, skips

3 Fun Ways to Spell

Four activities are provided. Use one, two, three, or all of the activities. Have students initial the box for each activity they complete.

Options:

- assign activities to students according to their learning styles
- set up the activities in learning centers for the class to do throughout the day
- divide the class into four groups and assign one activity per group
- do one activity per day

General

To spell your words with markers...
- Write a spelling word in thick, fat letters.
- Use other colored markers to decorate each letter with dots, flowers, stripes, etc.

Auditory

To spell your words while snapping...
- Look at a word on your spelling list.
- Close your eyes.
- Snap your fingers softly while you whisper the spelling of the word.
- Open your eyes and check your spelling.

Visual

To spell your words with letter tiles...
- Spell a word from your list by putting the tiles in the right order.
- Check your spelling.

Tactile

To spell your words with paint...
- Use your finger to write a spelling word on the paint bag.
- Check your spelling.
- Smooth out the paint and write another word.

1 Working with Words

Familiarize students with word meaning and usage.

Secret Words

Draw four boxes vertically on the board. Explain to the students that an acrostic is an arrangement of words in which some of the letters, taken in order, spell a word or phrase. Give the students these clues:

1. **something with ink that you write with** (Write the word **pen** across so **p** is in the first box.)
2. **the number before five** (Write the word **four** across so **r** is in the second box.)
3. **piece of cloth hung on a pole as a symbol of our country** (Write the word **flag** across so **a** is in the third box.)
4. **the color of a banana** (Write **yellow** across so **y** is in the fourth box.)

Ask students what word they see going down in the four boxes. **(pray)**

The boxed letters in the acrostic complete a phrase from the Scripture verse for this week. Use the clues to write the words in the puzzle; then, write the boxed letters on the lines to find the secret phrase.

Take a minute to memorize...

Read the memory verse to the class twice. Have the class practice it with you two more times.

Words with Consonant Clusters — Lesson 5

F Working with Words Name ______________

Secret Words

Use the clues to write the words in the puzzle. Then write the boxed letters on the lines below to find the words from this week's Scripture.

1. G r a y
2. c r o s s
3. b r e a d
4. c r a y o n
5. b r o k e
6. s p e l l
7. p r a y e r
8. p r o u d
9. s p e n d
10. s k a t e
11. g r a b
12. p r i c e
13. s k i p
14. s k i n

1. The skies are cloudy and __.
2. Jesus died on a __.
3. __ is used to make sandwiches.
4. You can color with a __.
5. The glass fell and __.
6. I learn to__words so I can write.
7. We talk to God in __.
8. Mom is __ of me.
9. I like to __time with Dad.
10. I fell a lot when I learned to __.
11. It is not polite to __food.
12. Mom got a lot of spinach for a good __.
13. I had to __ school when I was sick.
14. When I fell, I scraped the __ on my knee.

G o d c h o s e u s t o b e H i s

Word Bank

bread	cross	prayer	proud	skip
broke	grab	price	skate	spell
crayon	gray	prize	skin	spend

32

G Dictation

Name ____________________

Listen and write the missing words and punctuation.

1. A new baby will make her proud .
2. The children will close their eyes for prayer .
3. Dad put a slice of cheese on the bread .

H Proofreading

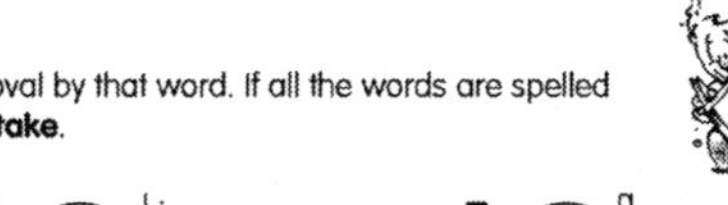

If a word is misspelled, fill in the oval by that word. If all the words are spelled correctly, fill in the oval by **no mistake**.

1. ○ bread ○ grab ○ sleeve ● no mistake	**4.** ○ skin ○ clay ● kross ○ no mistake	**7.** ○ flame ○ glove ● prise ○ no mistake
2. ○ price ● brocke ○ please ○ no mistake	**5.** ○ spell ● grae ○ close ○ no mistake	**8.** ○ list ○ body ● prowd ○ no mistake
3. ● craeon ○ skate ○ cheese ○ no mistake	**6.** ● praer ○ spend ○ place ○ no mistake	**9.** ○ skip ○ collar ○ bother ● no mistake

Words with Consonant Clusters

Lesson 5

33

1 Dictation

Reinforce correct spelling by using current and previous words in context.

Listen as I read each sentence and then write the missing words and ending punctuation in your worktext. (Slowly read each sentence twice. Sentences are found in the student text to the left.)

2 Proofreading

Familiarize students with standardized test format and reinforce recognizing misspelled words.

Look at each set of words. If a word is misspelled, fill in the oval by that word. If all the words are spelled correctly, fill in the oval by **no mistake**.

3 Hide and Seek

Reinforce correct spelling of current spelling words. (A reproducible master is provided in Appendix A as shown on the inset page to the right.)
Write the words one at a time on the board. Use this activity for each word.

- **Look** at the word.
- **Say** the word out loud.
- Let's **hide** (cover) the word.
- **Write** the word on your paper.
- Let's **seek** (uncover) the word.
- **Check** your spelling. If your word is spelled wrong, write the word correctly next to it.

4 Other Word Forms

Have your students complete this activity to strengthen spelling ability and expand vocabulary.

1 Posttest

Test mastery of the spelling words.

I will say the word once, use the word in a sentence, then say the word again. Write the word on your paper.

Hide and Seek

Check a coin for each word you spell correctly.

Other Word Forms

Hidden Words

Use the word bank to help you find and circle each of the words in the puzzle.

r	e	d	n	e	s	p	s	t	n	e	p	s
p	p	i	k	s	k	i	p	p	e	n	n	d
g	r	a	b	b	i	n	g	s	k	i	g	e
g	r	a	y	r	n	i	s	h	p	r	s	l
i	z	s	p	e	n	d	i	n	g	e	p	l
d	c	p	r	a	y	e	r	f	u	l	l	y
b	r	e	a	k	s	k	a	t	d	y	i	e
r	o	l	y	i	c	r	c	o	s	s	k	p
e	s	l	e	n	i	p	r	o	u	d	l	y
a	s	i	r	g	s	k	a	t	i	n	g	s
d	i	n	f	i	n	g	y	c	r	a	s	r
e	n	g	u	n	b	r	o	k	e	n	s	e
d	g	s	l	b	r	e	n	g	n	i	p	l
c	r	o	s	s	r	e	s	m	n	t	e	l

Word Bank

breaded	breaking	crossing	prayerful	proudly	skinny	spending
breaks	crayons	grabbing	prayerfully	skating	spelling	unbroken

331

1. spell — Please **spell** every word right.
2. gray — The van seats were **gray** leather.
3. cross — Father is not **cross** with the girls.
4. broke — Mr. Jacobson didn't know the zipper **broke**.
5. crayon — Natalie drew a picture using a red **crayon**.
6. grab — Let's **grab** something to eat at Taco Bell® again.
7. bread — They ate tortillas instead of **bread** at Taco Bell®.
8. price — The **price** of a taco is reasonable.
9. prize — Natalie likes the **prize** in her kid's meal.
10. proud — Father is **proud** that they will be having a new baby.
11. prayer — They said a **prayer** for the unborn baby.
12. skate — Mother was too tired to watch the girls roller **skate**.
13. skin — Helen Jacobson's **skin** is pale.
14. skip — Father was going to **skip** reading *Little House on the Prairie*.
15. spend — Mr. Jacobson will probably **spend** more time with his girls.

Progress Chart

Students may record scores. (Reproducible master in Appendix B.)

Personal Dictionary

Students may add any words they have misspelled to their personal dictionaries for reference when writing. (Cover in Appendix B.)

2 Game

Reinforce spelling skills and provide motivation and interest.

Materials

- game page (from student text)
- puzzle pieces (reproducible master in Appendix B, page 356)
- crayons
- scissors (1 per child)
- glue sticks (1 per child)
- game word list

Game Word List

1. bread
2. broke
3. crayon
4. cross
5. grab
6. gray
7. prayer
8. price
9. prize
10. proud
11. skate
12. skin
13. skip
14. spell
15. spend

Lesson 5

I Game Name ____________________

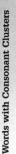

Glue on a piece of the puzzle-picture for each word you or your team spells correctly from this week's word list.

Remember: God has always loved you!

J Journaling

In your journal, write about your family. Talk about the family who lives in your home. Write about how often you see family members like your grandparents, aunts, uncles, and cousins.

34

How to Play:

- Have the students color the puzzle picture, then carefully cut the picture apart along the dotted lines.
- Divide the class into two teams.
- Have a student from team A go to the board.
- Say the spelling word. (You may also wish to use the word in a sentence.)
- Have the student write the word on the board.
- If correct, instruct each member of team A to glue on one piece of his/her puzzle picture. (Note: If the word is misspelled, correct the spelling immediately.)
- Alternate between teams A and B.
- The team to complete its puzzle pictures first is the winner.

Non-Competitive Option:

At the end of the game, say: "Class, I am proud of your efforts to spell the words correctly. If you had fun and tried your best, you are all winners!"

3 Journaling

Provide a meaningful reason for correct spelling through personal writing.

Review the story using discussion leads provided on the following page. Encourage students to apply the Scriptural value in their journaling.

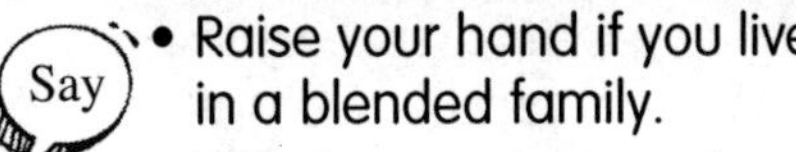
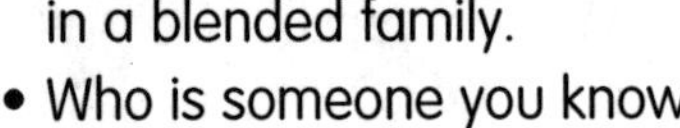

Journaling (continued)

Say

- Raise your hand if you live in a blended family.
- Who is someone you know that is adopted.
- Stand up if you live with your biological mom and dad.
- Pat your head if you are living with someone other than your mom or dad.
- Every family could get better at being a good family, but every family is special. What is your favorite thing about your very own family?
- Whose family do we all belong to? (God's)
- Write in your journal about your family. Talk about the family who lives in your home. Talk about how often you see family members like your grandparents, aunts, uncles, and cousins.

Take a minute to memorize...
Have the class say the memory verses from lessons 1, 2, 3, 4, and 5 with you.

"Spelling is a gradual process that develops through trial and error, and the best way to teach spelling is to give students freedom to take risks in their writing."*

*Scott, Jill E. 1994. Spelling for Readers and Writers. The Reading Teacher, Vol. 48, No. 2, October: 188-190.

1

Literature Connection

Topic: God's love for us
Theme Text: Ephesians 1:11

Gifts Beneath the Tree

When Rosa begins taking care of some tiny baby squirrels, she learns more about how much God cares for us.

"Dad! Dad! Come quick!" Mr. Vasquez heard the call through the open window beyond his desk. He quickly punched the save button on his computer and jumped up. His chair rolled back across the hardwood floor as he hurried outside.

"Dad! Dad! Come here!" Following the urgent voices, Mr. Vasquez rounded the corner of the house and ran toward the barnyard. "Hurry!"

Maria and Rosa knelt on the grass looking at something. Carlos stood behind them holding Barkley and Digby firmly by their collars. It was all the thirteen-year-old could do to hang on to the big dogs as they barked and jumped and tried to jerk away. Ten-year-old Maria was the first to spot their father coming. "Look, Dad!" she cried. "Isn't he adorable?"

"Are you kids all right?" Dad glanced at each child to make sure they were okay.

"We're fine, Dad." Carlos almost shouted to be heard over the barking dogs. "But I'm not sure he is."

"Who's he?" Dad relaxed and ran a hand across his forehead. "And what's so adorable?" Rosa pointed with one finger. A small reddish gob of fluff lay stretched out on the ground. It lifted a tiny head and stared fearlessly at Dad with shiny, black eyes.

"Well." Dad chuckled. "How do you do, little fellow?" He reached out and gently scooped the tiny creature up in one hand. "Are there any others around?" He slid the baby gently into his shirt pocket and turned to gaze carefully about on the grass.

"I don't think so." Rosa bounced up and began searching under the big pine tree. "Barkley and Digby found this one, but I don't think they hurt him. We were right here and caught them before they could bite him. What is he, Dad? Isn't he a baby squirrel?"

"A chickaree, actually." Dad cupped his hand over the pocket where the baby rested. "An American red squirrel. Probably about three weeks old."

"What's he doing out on the ground instead of in the tree?" Maria walked around the pine, still watching carefully.

"Something must have happened to his mother." Dad shook his head. "Baby squirrels usually stay put in their nests, but if they get too hungry, they sometimes venture out to look for food. This little guy looks pretty weak. We'll have to see what we can do about that." Dad started back toward the house and Rosa skipped along beside him. "Maria," he called back, "why don't you help Carlos tie the dogs up for a while. We'll keep watch in case any of this fellow's brothers or sisters show up."

"What do we feed him? Where will we put him? What shall we name him?" Rosa wondered aloud. "I wonder what happened to his mother? Do we have to keep him warm? Can he stay in my room?" Dad just grinned as the questions kept on coming. "Why is he called a chickaree? Isn't he a pretty red color?"

Rosa opened the back door for Dad. "Do you want answers to all those questions right now," Dad laughed, "or can we just answer them as we go along?"

"Just one for now," Rosa closed the door behind them. "Can we keep him?"

Dad gently took the tiny little squirrel out of his pocket and cradled it in his hand. "I don't think we have a choice, Rosita. We're all he has right now." The tiny squirrel began an awkward crawl up Dad's arm and let out a surprisingly loud cry of hunger just as Maria and Carlos came in.

"Wow!" Carlos flopped into a kitchen chair. "We'd better feed him—and fast!"

That was the last anyone sat still for a while. Carlos brought in the dogs' traveling kennel and cleaned it up. Maria emptied a cardboard box and filled it with layers of cotton, forming a nice warm bed. Rosa found an eyedropper while Dad warmed some milk. Then they all gathered around to watch as Dad held the eyedropper of milk up to the frantic little fellow's mouth.

At first he struggled to get away, not recognizing the dropper as the answer to his hunger. As soon as he tasted a little of the milk, however, he grabbed the eyedropper with his little front feet. It took six droppers full before he quit drinking. By then he was almost as wide as he was long. Dad set him gently in the nest box and the baby squirrel curled into a warm corner for a well-deserved nap.

"Well, now!" Dad sighed as he sank into a chair. "He should start feeling pretty chipper after that warm meal and a good rest."

"Chipper!" Rosa exclaimed. "That's perfect! You just named him, Dad. Chipper the chickaree." Rosa turned to her brother and sister. "Don't you think that's a good name?"

"I think it's fine." Carlos stood and stretched his back after peering into the squirrel kennel. "I also think it's our turn for supper."

Dad glanced out the window. Daylight was gone and just a few streaks of purplish pink lingered in the sky. "I'll get something together for supper while you run out and feed the dogs. And don't forget to check around the big pine for more baby squirrels."

The kids disappeared out the back door, and quickly had another surprise when Chipper's sister appeared at the base of the big tree. Maria and Rosa fed her while Carlos finished the chores and Dad fixed

Story Continued

supper. She quickly earned the name "Nipper" when she tried to sample fingers as well as milk!

After supper, Dad read a story. "Now I know it's not bedtime yet, but I suggest we call it a night." He lay the book on the lamp table. "We're in for a long night, and I think we ought to take turns."

"What are you talking about, Dad?" Rosa climbed onto his knee.

"Chipper and Nipper are going to wake up every two to three hours and want to be fed. They're young enough to still need meals frequently. If we take turns, then each of us will probably only have to get up once." He looked around at the excited faces. "Does everyone know exactly how to warm the milk and feed them?" Eager nods answered his question, and the family's adventure began.

After several nights of warming sweetened milk and feeding the demanding little chickarees several droppers full, the Vasquez children almost knew how to do it in their sleep! It wasn't easy, but the children decided the mischievous little balls of fur were worth it. Although they checked for a few days, no other baby chickarees showed up in the barnyard. Barkley and Digby were excited to finally be released.

The little chickarees obviously knew they were squirrels. They grew fast and climbed everything in the house. They chewed on twigs placed in their kennel. They gathered bits and pieces and made their own little play nests. The night feedings lasted only about two weeks until Nipper and Chipper decided they were ready for "real" food. They devoured peanuts, bread crusts, cabbage, and carrots as well as buds and grasses. It wasn't uncommon to find peanuts stored in very strange places.

Chipper couldn't have been sweeter. He spent most of his time in someone's pocket or nestled on a shoulder. He often slept on someone's pillow and hid his best peanuts in their hair.

Nipper seemed to think that people were okay at a distance, but she had better things to do than be held. Her little black eyes were constantly watching for trouble to get into.

The two chickarees enjoyed Rosa's eighth birthday almost as much as she did. There were ribbons to play in and packages to unwrap before the birthday girl got a chance. Nipper even sampled the birthday cake before anyone else. Chipper almost got thrown away when he took a nap in one of the empty gift boxes under some crumpled wrapping paper. Rosa took a whole roll of film with the camera that her dad gave her for her birthday—and most of those pictures had feisty little red chickarees in them. The squirrels were now a part of the family.

"Dad! Dad!" Mr. Vasquez rose from his desk and went to look out the window. "Dad, come quick! Look at this!" Shaking his head he jabbed the save button on his computer and went to see what was happening this time.

In the backyard, a very confused-looking Digby sat perfectly still while Nipper scolded him from her perch on the back of a nearby lawn chair. Barkley was barking furiously, but keeping his distance from the little red creature. Chipper stared at the noisy dogs from his place on Carlos shoulder. "She just ran out the door and I thought the dogs would get her—but I think they're afraid of her!" Carlos laughed. Nipper flipped her tail in the air with the rapid jerks that are a squirrel's way of threatening. She told the dogs just what she thought of them in squirrel talk, chattering for all she was worth.

Dad put an arm around each of his daughters as they stood watching the dogs and squirrels get acquainted. "Are they worth it, you guys? Are they worth getting up all hours of the night, cleaning up their messes, and finding peanuts all over the place?"

"Of course!" Rosa answered immediately.

"Absolutely." Carlos agreed.

"What makes them worth all that work and nuisance?" Dad asked.

Maria looked up at her dad. "It's because we enjoy having them around and because we love them."

Dad smiled. "So they're worth the sacrifice of sleep and time because we love and enjoy them?" He nodded thoughtfully. "In a way it reminds me of Christ's tremendous sacrifice for us. Christ even gave up His life for us. And because He loves us so much, He wants us to spend time with Him every day." He paused. "How does that make you feel?"

"It makes me love Him even more!" said Rosa.

Carlos and Maria nodded in agreement. "That's right!" said Dad. And while Chipper dozed and Nipper scolded, he pulled them all close in a big hug.

2 Discussion Time

Check understanding of the story and development of personal values.

- Why did the children call Mr. Vasquez to come quickly?
- What did Rosa's dad tell them red squirrels were called? (chickarees)
- How many chickarees did the family find?
- What did they name the baby squirrels, and why did they choose those names?
- What did they have to do to take care of the little chickarees?
- Did the children want the squirrels even though it was a lot of work and trouble taking care of them? Why?
- Who loves us even when we're not easy to love?

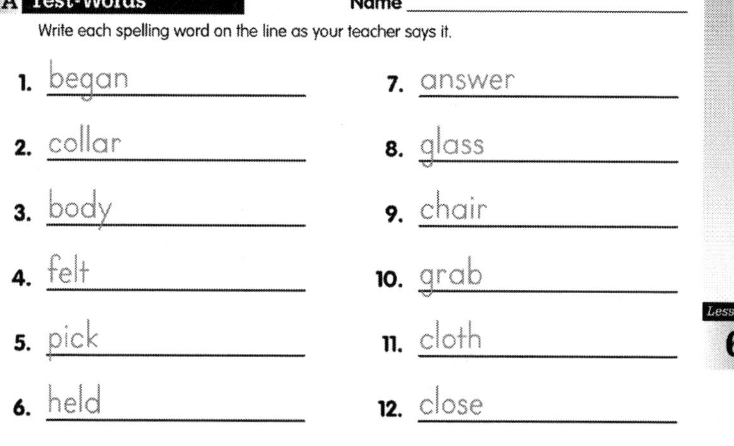

A Test-Words Name ____________

Write each spelling word on the line as your teacher says it.

1.	began	7.	answer
2.	collar	8.	glass
3.	body	9.	chair
4.	felt	10.	grab
5.	pick	11.	cloth
6.	held	12.	close

Review Lesson 6

B Test-Sentences

Write the sentences on the lines below, correcting each misspelled word, as well as all capitalization and punctuation errors. There are two misspelled words in each sentence.

the def boy could not hear the buz of the timer

1. The deaf boy could not hear the buzz of the timer.

Please plaice the gluv back in the drawer?

2. Please place the glove back in the drawer.

the doughnuts had cream cheeze and cherrie fillings,

3. The doughnuts had cream cheese and cherry fillings.

35

3 Test-Words

Test for knowledge of the correct spellings of these words.

I will say the word once, use the word in a sentence, then say the word again. Write the word on the lines in your worktext.

1. began	Rosa and Maria **began** calling for their dad.
2. collar	Carlos held tightly to Digby's **collar** until his dad came.
3. body	The tiny chickaree's **body** was covered with red fur.
4. felt	The children **felt** sorry for the tiny creature.
5. pick	"Gently **pick** up the chickaree," said Dad.
6. held	Maria **held** the chickaree carefully.
7. answer	The dropper was the **answer** to the animal's hunger.
8. glass	Dad poured the warm milk into a **glass**.
9. chair	Dad sat in a **chair** while he fed the chickaree.
10. grab	Chipper will **grab** the dropper with his little feet.
11. cloth	Dad put a soft **cloth** inside the kennel.
12. close	The kids were careful to **close** the door to the kennel.

4 Test-Sentences

Reinforce recognizing misspelled words.

Read each sentence carefully. Write the sentences on the lines in your worktext, correcting each misspelled word, as well as all capitalization and punctuation errors. There are two misspelled words in each sentence.

Take a minute to memorize...

Read the memory verse to the class twice. Have the class practice it with you two more times.

Day 2

Review 6

1 Test-Dictation

Reinforce correct spelling by using current and previous words in context.

Listen as I read each sentence. Then write the missing words and ending punctuation in your worktext. (Slowly read each sentence twice. Sentences are found in the student text to the right. The words **flag**, **flame**, **clay**, and **price** are found in this unit.)

2 Test-Proofreading

Familiarize students with standardized test format and reinforce recognizing misspelled words.

Look at each set of words. If a word is misspelled, fill in the oval by that word. If all the words are spelled correctly, fill in the oval by **no mistake**.

Review Lesson 6

C Test-Dictation

Name ____________

Listen and write the missing words and punctuation.

1. I will say the pledge to the flag .
2. The candle flame was very bright .
3. We can make a snake out of clay .
4. Write the price in red on each sticker .

D Test-Proofreading

If a word is misspelled, fill in the oval by that word. If all the words are spelled correctly, fill in the oval by **no mistake**.

1. ○ Monday ○ deaf ○ body ● no mistake
2. ○ hello ○ north ● cactis ○ no mistake
3. ● wip ○ thankful ○ please ○ no mistake
4. ○ slice ○ whale ○ spend ● no mistake
5. ○ glove ● spel ○ berry ○ no mistake
6. ● krop ○ shock ○ cheese ○ no mistake
7. ○ lamb ○ prayer ○ wheat ● no mistake
8. ○ west ○ chair ● chanje ○ no mistake
9. ○ north ○ plus ○ cross ● no mistake

36

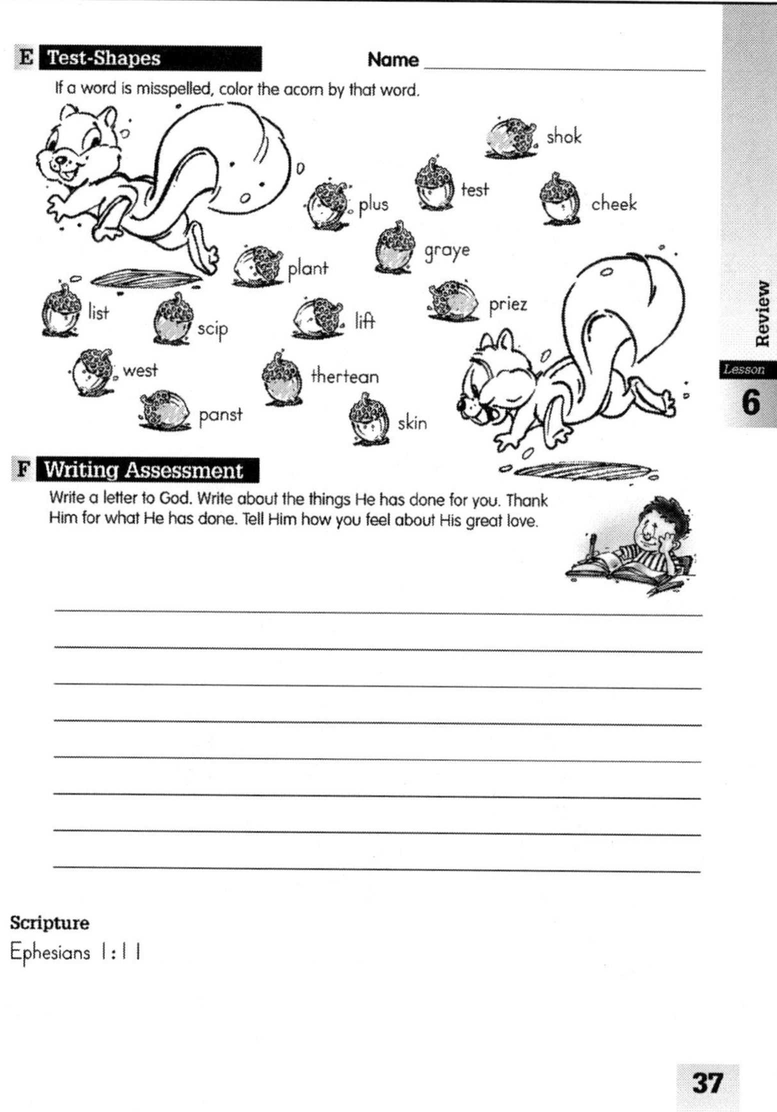

E Test-Shapes Name ________________

If a word is misspelled, color the acorn by that word.

shok
plus
test
cheek
graye
plant
priez
list
scip
lift
west
thertean
panst
skin

F Writing Assessment

Write a letter to God. Write about the things He has done for you. Thank Him for what He has done. Tell Him how you feel about His great love.

____

____

____

____

____

____

____

____

Scripture

Ephesians 1:11

Review

Lesson 6

37

1 Test-Shapes

Test mastery of words in this unit.

If a word is misspelled, color the object by that word.

2 Writing Assessment

Assess student's spelling, grammar, and composition skills through personal writing.

- Why did Dad think the baby squirrels were on the ground? (Something must have happened to their mother.)
- Why did the chickarees have to be fed every two or three hours? (That's how often their mother would have fed them. All little babies need to eat very often, even during the night.)
- Besides needing to be fed so often, how were the baby squirrels a nuisance? (They climbed, chewed, were noisy, and left nuts scattered all over the place.)
- Have you ever taken care of a baby animal or an injured animal that required a lot of work?
- The Scripture verse we studied this week says, "Because of what Christ has done we have become gifts to God that he delights in." What has Christ done for us? (Died to redeem us. Also, answered our prayers, helped us make right choices, forgave us, etc.)
- Write a letter to God. Write about the things He has done for you. Thank Him for what He has done. Tell Him how you feel about His great love.

"Inventive spelling refers to young children's attempts to use their best judgment about spelling."*

*Lutz, Elaine. 1986. ERIC/RCS Report: Invented Spelling and Spelling Development. Language Arts, Vol. 63, No. 7, November: 742-744.

Day 4

Review

6

1 Test-Sentences

Reinforce recognizing misspelled words.

Read each sentence carefully. Write the sentences on the lines in your worktext, correcting each misspelled word, as well as all capitalization and punctuation errors. There are two misspelled words in each sentence.

Review Lesson 6

G Test-Sentences Name ______________

Write the sentences on the lines below, correcting each misspelled word, as well as all capitalization and punctuation errors. There are two misspelled words in each sentence.

i'd like a weet roll, pleeze

1. I'd like a wheat roll, please.

On thersday we can vizit the farm.

2. On Thursday we can visit the farm.

Mom and dad gave us a pupie for a gitf

3. Mom and Dad gave us a puppy for a gift.

H Test-Words

Write each spelling word on the line as your teacher says it.

1. Sunday
2. chest
3. bread
4. proud
5. thankful
6. broke
7. crayon
8. flash
9. window
10. sleeve
11. twelve
12. spend

38

2 Test-Words

Test for knowledge of the correct spellings of these words.

I will say the word once, use the word in a sentence, then say the word again. Write the word on the lines in your worktext.

1. Sunday	By the next **Sunday,** the chickarees could eat foods like cabbage and peanuts.
2. chest	Chipper crawled up Carlos' **chest** and into his pocket.
3. bread	Nipper and Chipper liked **bread** crusts.
4. proud	Rosa, Maria, and Carlos were **proud** of Chipper and Nipper.
5. thankful	They were **thankful** for their new pets.
6. broke	The chickarees **broke** the tiny twigs to build a little nest.
7. crayon	Nipper gnawed on a purple **crayon.**
8. flash	Nipper looks like a **flash** of red light when she runs!
9. window	The chickarees scolded the dogs through the **window.**
10. sleeve	Chipper stuck his nose up Rosa's **sleeve.**
11. twelve	Nipper hid **twelve** peanuts in one day.
12. spend	Chipper can **spend** the night on Carlos' pillow.

I **Test-Editing** Name ____________

If a word is spelled correctly, fill in the oval under **Correct**. If the word is misspelled, fill in the oval under **Incorrect**, and spell the word correctly on the blank.

	Correct	Incorrect	
1. berry	●	○	________
2. chill	●	○	________
3. kross	○	●	cross
4. helo	○	●	hello
5. plian	○	●	plain
6. skate	●	○	________
7. stif	○	●	stiff
8. wether	○	●	whether
9. bother	●	○	________
10. prayer	●	○	________
11. wagun	○	●	wagon
12. whale	●	○	________

Review Lesson 6

39

3 Test-Editing

Reinforce recognizing and correcting misspelled words.

4 Action Game

Reinforce spelling skills and provide motivation and interest.

Materials

- 5 large squares of paper marked **O**
- 5 large squares of paper marked **X**
- 9 chairs

How to Play:

- Divide the class into two teams: **X**'s and **O**'s.
- Place nine chairs in the front of the room in three rows of three. The chairs will form a tic-tac-toe grid.
- Alternate between the two teams giving any word tested on days 1 through 4.
- If a student spells a word correctly, give him an **X** or **O** square to hold depending on which team he represents.
- Continue playing until all the words tested have been reviewed and/or the tic-tac-toe game in progress has been completed.

1 Game

Reinforce spelling skills and provide motivation and interest.

Materials

- game page (from student text)
- flat buttons, dry beans, pennies, or game discs (1 per child)
- game word list

Game Word List

Check off each word lightly in pencil as it is used.

Red (5 points)

1. lift
2. list
3. test
4. pants
5. west
6. plant
7. skip
8. skin
9. spell
10. plus
11. crop

Blue (10 points)

1. cheek
2. shook
3. thirteen
4. gray
5. prize
6. Monday
7. cactus
8. whip
9. slice
10. lamb
11. change

Yellow (15 points)

1. answering
2. puppies
3. buzzes
4. skater
5. picking
6. visitor
7. western
8. clothing
9. skipping
10. thankfully
11. pleased

Review Lesson 6

J Game   Name ____________________

Score points for each review word or Other Word Form you or your team spells correctly.

Remember: God is pleased with us for Jesus' sake.

40

How to Play:

- Divide the class into two teams.
- Have each student place his/her game piece on Start.
- Inform the students of the following point system:
  Red list words = **5** points, **Blue** list words = **10** points
  Yellow list words = **15** points (these are Other Word Forms)
- Have a student from team A choose a color: red, blue, or yellow.
- Say a word from the correct color list. (You may also wish to use the word in a sentence.)
- Have the student write the word on the board.
- If correct, ask each member of team A to move his/her game piece forward (to the right and up, counter clockwise) to the corresponding color in the first section. Record the score. If the word is misspelled, have each member of that team move his/her game piece to the "sad face" in the first section.
- Alternate between teams A and B.
- The team with the highest score at the end of three rounds is the winner. (A round begins and ends at Start.)

Non-Competitive Option:

At the end of the game, say: "Class, I am proud of your efforts to spell the words correctly. If you had fun and tried your best, you are all winners!"

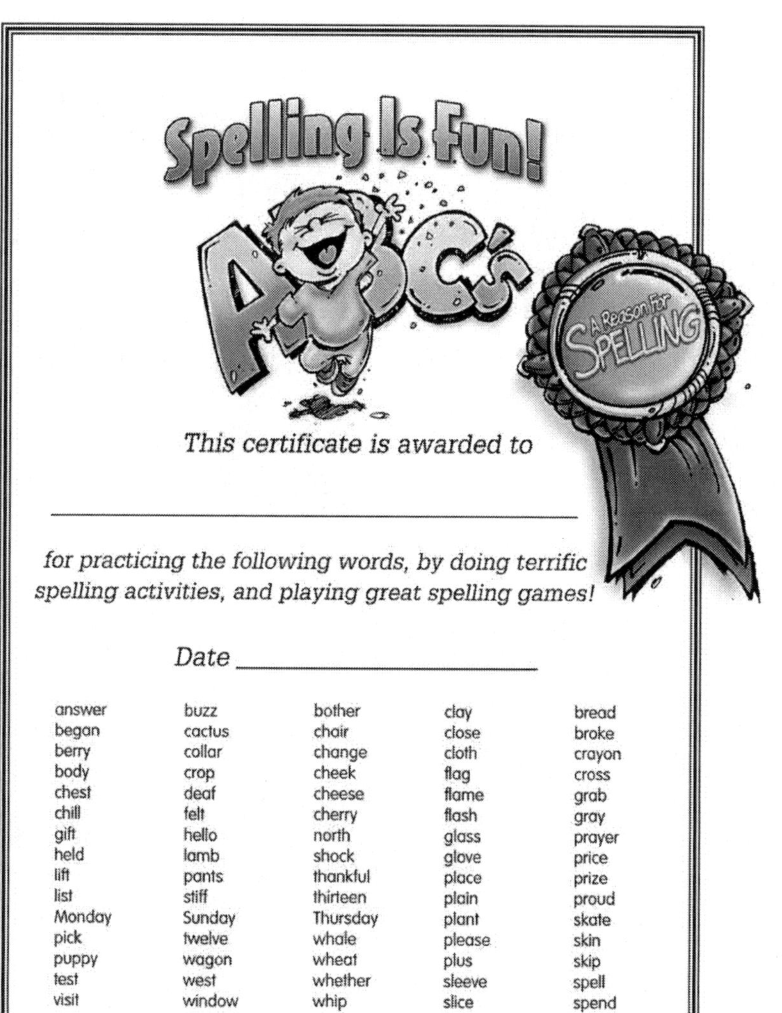

Spelling Is Fun!

A Reason for Spelling

This certificate is awarded to

____

for practicing the following words, by doing terrific spelling activities, and playing great spelling games!

Date ______________________

answer	buzz	bother	clay	bread
began	cactus	chair	close	broke
berry	collar	change	cloth	crayon
body	crop	cheek	flag	cross
chest	deaf	cheese	flame	grab
chill	felt	cherry	flash	gray
gift	hello	north	glass	prayer
held	lamb	shock	glove	price
lift	pants	thankful	place	prize
list	stiff	thirteen	plain	proud
Monday	Sunday	Thursday	plant	skate
pick	twelve	whale	please	skin
puppy	wagon	wheat	plus	skip
test	west	whether	sleeve	spell
visit	window	whip	slice	spend

2 Certificate

Provide an opportunity for parents or guardians to encourage and assess their child's progress.

- Write your name on the first line.
- Write the date on the next line.
- Be sure to show your parents or guardian all the words you've practiced spelling.

Take a minute to memorize...
Have the class say the memory verses from lessons 1, 2, 3, 4, 5, and 6 with you.

3 Letter

Provide the parent or guardian with the spelling word lists for the next unit.

Say Show your parents or guardian this letter that lists your spelling words for the next unit. Put it where you will remember to practice the words together.

Dear Parent,

We are about to begin a new spelling unit containing five weekly lessons. A set of fifteen words will be studied each week. All the words will be reviewed in the sixth week. Values based on the Scriptures listed below will be taught in each lesson.

Lesson 7	Lesson 8	Lesson 9	Lesson 10	Lesson 11
scrap	address	aunt	crash	bright
scratch	butter	behind	earth	caught
scream	classroom	belong	fresh	chalk
screen	happen	bump	hatch	clothes
scrub	ladder	drank	kick	half
spread	lesson	front	match	knee
spring	merry	grandfather	neck	knot
straight	million	grandmother	porch	neighbor
strange	really	husband	ranch	sidewalk
straw	rubber	ink	rush	sight
stream	smell	sang	sack	though
street	sudden	stamp	sandwich	thumb
string	sunny	wind	splash	Wednesday
strong	supper	wing	switch	whole
threw	unhappy	young	teacher	wrap
1 Peter 3:10	Ephesians 5:2	Philippians 4:4,5	1 Peter 4:8	1 Peter 4:10

1 **Literature Connection**
Topic: Lying
Theme Text: 1 Peter 3:10

Ice Cream Challenge

Tommy learns that lying can make you miserable!

"Hey, Tommy! Wait up!" Tommy turned at the sound of his best friend's shout. James ran up the sidewalk, his orange jacket flapping behind him like giant butterfly wings. "Are you gonna take Mr. Valentino's challenge?" He skidded to a halt just before running into Tommy. "Isn't it great? I can't decide between a cherry cheesecake or a chocolate-vanilla brownie super-duper sundae." James hardly paused for breath as the boys walked down the sidewalk. "Whichever, I'm sure I want nuts on the top and a cherry. My mom can't stand those candied cherries, so I always get hers. They're g-o-o-o-d! Can you believe Mr. Valentino's going to give us a coupon for a large sundae at the Ice Cream Castle?" James rubbed his hand in a circle on his stomach and smacked his lips. "Yummy, yummy to my tummy!"

"Don't forget the challenge part." Tommy kicked a pebble along the sidewalk in front of him. "We've got to read a bunch of books to get that coupon. That'll take a lot of time."

"Ah, no problem." James held up the battered blue backpack he carried in one hand. "I'm taking two books home today to get started with. I figure if I read some every day it won't be that hard to do. You want one of 'em?"

"Nah. I've got a book at home that Dad gave me about Babe Ruth and some other baseball heroes. I think I'll start with that." Tommy opened the back door of his mother's car. "Maybe we can trade books in a week or so, okay?"

"Sure. See ya tomorrow!" James called back over his shoulder as he walked on toward his ride.

"Yoo hoo! Troublesome Tommy! Where are you?" Tommy ignored his older sister Lisa's call and wriggled into a more comfortable position on his bed. He bent his knees to prop up his book and read, "Though many players have tried, none of them have come close to beating Joe DiMaggio's record. That amazing record of hits in 56 straight games remains unbeaten in baseball history. The year was 1941. . ."

"Tommy the Terror!" Lisa called again.

"Yeah, Lisa," Tommy answered half-heartedly just as Lisa came into his room. "What do you want?"

"Come on, Tommy, let's go outside." Lisa waved her hand toward the window. "Look, the weather is perfect today—sunny and not too cold."

"I've got to read this, Lisa." Tommy held up the book.

"But Tommy, the weather man said it may be rainy and cold tomorrow. You can read the book then." Lisa grabbed his arm and tugged. "Come on! It's a perfect day for roller blading!" She pulled again and he tumbled off the bed.

"All right, all right! I'm coming." Tommy grinned and followed Lisa into the hall. "I'll race you to the Mitchell's mailbox!" He challenged at the top of the stairs.

"You're on!" Lisa's short strawberry-blonde hair bobbed as she bounced down the stairs.

"Here, Tommy." James plunked a stack of three books on Tommy's desk the next week. "Ready to trade? This one's the best of all. You should start with it." James pulled a book out of the stack. The cover of the book showed a picture of a deep-sea diver swimming near a big shark. "It's about this scientist who studies all kinds of sharks. He was even attacked one time. It's an awesome story!"

"Great!" Tommy looked at the other books in the stack. "I'll bring some to you tomorrow."

"That book looks interesting." Stephen stopped by Tommy's desk. "Can I read it after you, Tommy?"

"Sure." Tommy stacked the books neatly on the corner of his desk.

"I've read two books since Mr. Valentino gave us the challenge." Stephen leaned against the edge of Tommy's desk. "How many have you guys read?"

"I've read these three." James ran a finger along the back of the stack of books.

"I, uh. . ." Tommy began, but just then Mr. Valentino called the class to order.

"Don't forget to make time for reading!" Mr. Valentino reminded the children as they settled at their desks. He walked briskly across the front of the classroom and pointed to the calendar. "It's been seven days since we began the reading challenge. I'm hoping that every one of my students will choose to earn a sundae. Or two or three! I know all of you can do it!"

Tommy sighed. James and Stephen were both ahead of him. The book about baseball heroes was really interesting, but he hadn't quite finished the last chapter about Hank Aaron. "I'll read a bunch this week," Tommy promised himself.

One morning a few weeks later James met Tommy at the classroom door. "I did it!" Tommy blinked when James waved a small piece of hot pink paper in his face. "Look at this, Tommy, my coupon for a free large sundae at the Ice Cream Castle! Wanna go together? You're about ready to get a coupon, aren't you?"

"Well, um, not quite." Tommy walked over and stuffed his notebook in his desk.

"Oh, okay," James followed him. "Did you like

Story (continued)

that book about the diver? I've got another one about some guys who study storms. They follow them around in an airplane!"

"An airplane?" Christopher joined the boys at Tommy's desk. "Can I borrow it?" Christopher grinned and pulled a familiar-looking slip of hot pink paper out of his pocket. "I've earned my first sundae, but I want to start reading to earn another one."

"Sure. It's in my desk. Do you wanna go to the Ice Cream Castle together?" James and Christopher headed over to James' desk to get the book. Tommy slumped in his seat. He really wanted to go with them to get their sundaes. Tommy sighed and turned his attention to Mr. Valentino as class began. But all morning he kept remembering that James and Christopher were going to the Ice Cream Castle.

Tommy stared at the math paper on his desk, but his mind was on anything but math problems. "I did finish my baseball heroes book and I've read most of the others." Tommy turned his pencil around and around in his hand. "I'm pretty close to finishing the number of pages Mr. Valentino said we had to read for each sundae. Maybe I should just say I've read enough. Then I can go with James and Christopher. I know I can finish reading the rest later, but it would be a lot more fun to go with my friends than by myself. Oh, I don't know what I should do. . ."

But at lunch time Tommy made the choice almost without thinking. "Mr. Valentino, I'm ready to write down the stuff I've read," he blurted out. He didn't feel so good inside when Mr. Valentino clapped him on the back with a big smile. He felt even worse a few minutes later after Mr. Valentino read over the list Tommy printed and said, "Tommy, I'm proud of you! You've been trying very hard in order to get this much reading done. Good job, young man."

Christopher and James were thrilled. "My mom or dad can probably take us tonight." James hopped around the other two boys at recess, his orange jacket billowing behind him. "I'll ask and call you after you talk to your parents. Ice Cream Castle, here we come!"

"YIPPEEE!" Christopher yelled and Tommy echoed it weakly.

That evening, Christopher chose a double fudge sundae, Tommy got a strawberry shortcake sundae, and James finally decided on a cherry cheesecake sundae with lots of nuts and an extra cherry on top. The boys laughed and clowned around, but for some reason, Tommy's sundae didn't taste quite as yummy as he had thought it would. He just didn't feel right inside.

And the bad feeling wouldn't go away. Tommy didn't sleep very well that night. He flipped and flopped in his bed, and the ice cream lay heavy in his stomach. He kept thinking about Mr. Valentino's broad smile and remembering his words, "I'm proud of you." Tommy didn't feel very proud. By morning he knew he had to do something to get rid of the horrible feeling.

Tommy waited until he saw a chance to talk to Mr. Valentino without a bunch of other kids around. He walked up to his teacher's desk, feeling like dozens of butterflies were flapping away in his stomach. Mr. Valentino's dark eyes rested on Tommy's face as he sputtered through the whole story. He told how he'd lied so he could get his sundae when his best friend did, even though he wasn't really finished with the reading. And he told how he'd felt so awful. Tommy finished with a whispered, "I'm sorry." Mr. Valentino didn't say anything for a moment and the butterfly wings beat even harder in Tommy's stomach.

Finally Mr. Valentino reached over and squeezed Tommy's shoulder. His familiar broad smile returned. "I'm glad you told me, Tommy, and I forgive you. But I'm not surprised you felt bad and didn't enjoy your sundae!" He chuckled. "The Scriptures say that lying makes us unhappy. Check out 1 Peter 3:10. It's in your handwriting book, and it's this week's verse." He gave Tommy another squeeze. "Read that Scripture and remember the ice cream you couldn't enjoy. Let that help you choose not to lie ever again."

Lisa popped into Tommy's room that afternoon. "Yoo hoo! Terrible Tommy! Let's go roller blading!"

Tommy stuck his finger in the book he was reading and looked up. "Can't," he replied. "I've gotta finish this reading."

"I thought you were already finished with all that. Didn't you go get your sundae last night?" Lisa plopped down beside her brother on the bed.

"Well. . ." Tommy hesitated, then told Lisa the whole story. "So, you see," Tommy shrugged, "I've got to finish it now."

Lisa stood and walked slowly to the door. Then, just before she disappeared into the hall, she turned. "Keep up the good work—Terrific Tommy," she said with a smile.

"That Scripture verse sure was true!" Tommy thought. "Lying made me feel terrible, but now that I've told the truth, I feel much better!" He grinned down at his book, and once more began to read.

2 Discussion Time

Check understanding of the story and development of personal values.

- What challenge did Mr. Valentino give his students?
- What kinds of books do you like to read?
- Was Tommy a fast reader? What makes you think that?
- What lie did Tommy tell his teacher?
- Why do you think Tommy told the lie?
- Did Tommy enjoy his ice cream sundae? Why or why not?
- Why do you think the Scripture says you must not lie if you want a happy and good life?

A Preview Name ____________

Write each word as your teacher says it.

1. spring
2. threw
3. scream
4. scrap
5. scratch
6. strong
7. screen
8. strange
9. straw
10. stream
11. street
12. spread
13. straight
14. scrub
15. string

Scripture
I Peter 3:10

Words with Consonant Clusters

Lesson 7

43

3 Preview

Test for knowledge of the correct spellings of these words.

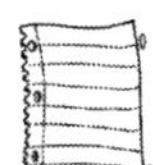

Customize Your List

On a separate piece of paper, additional words of your choice may be tested.

I will say the word once, use the word in a sentence, then say the word again. Write the word on the lines in the worktext.

Correct Immediately!

Let's correct our preview. I will write each word on the board. Put a dot under each letter on your preview as I spell the word out loud. If you spelled a word wrong, rewrite it correctly.

Take a minute to memorize...

Read the memory verse to the class twice. Have the class practice it with you two more times.

Day 1

Lesson 7

1.	spring	Baseball season begins in the **spring**.
2.	threw	Joe DiMaggio could hit almost any ball a pitcher **threw** to him.
3.	scream	Baseball fans **scream** wildly when a player hits a home run.
4.	scrap	Tommy stuck a **scrap** of paper in the book to mark his place.
5.	scratch	Sharks can smell blood from even a tiny **scratch**.
6.	strong	Some types of sharks have very **strong** jaws and many teeth.
7.	screen	Divers sometimes use a metal **screen** for protection from sharks.
8.	strange	When a storm is blowing in, the sky looks **strange**.
9.	straw	Powerful winds blow **straw** and dust into the air.
10.	stream	Rain will begin to **stream** down the windows very soon.
11.	street	The Ice Cream Castle is on the next **street**.
12.	spread	The dish tipped and melted ice cream **spread** across the table.
13.	straight	It ran **straight** to the edge and dripped on Tommy's clothes.
14.	scrub	Mom will have to **scrub** to get out that stain.
15.	string	Telling one lie often starts a **string** of lies.

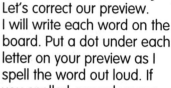

Progress Chart

Students may record scores. (Reproducible master in Appendix B.)

4 Word Shapes

Help students form a correct image of whole words.

Look at each word and think about its shape. Now, write the word in the correct word shape boxes. You may check off each word as you use it.

(In many words, a consonant cluster is made up of three letters. The third letter is usually **r**.)

In the word shape boxes, color the letters that spell the beginning consonant cluster in each word. Circle the word that does not begin with **/s/**.

Words with Consonant Clusters

Lesson 7

B Word Shapes Name ________________

Write each word in the correct word shape boxes. Next, in the word shape boxes, color the letters that spell the beginning consonant cluster in each word. Circle the word that does not begin with **/s/**.

	Word	Answer
1.	scrap	spring
2.	scratch	strange
3.	scream	screen
4.	screen	scrub
5.	scrub	stream
6.	spread	scream
7.	spring	straight
8.	straight	street
9.	strange	threw (circled)
10.	straw	string
11.	stream	strong
12.	street	scrap
13.	string	scratch
14.	strong	spread
15.	threw	straw

44

Answers may vary for duplicate word shapes.

Be Prepared For Fun

Check these supply lists for **Fun Ways to Spell** presented **Day 2**.
Purchase and/or gather needed items ahead of time!

General
- Pencil
- 3 x 5 Cards (15 per child)
- Scissors
- Spelling List

Auditory
- Rhythm Instruments (two wooden spoons, two pan lids, maracas)
- Spelling List

Visual
- Sidewalk Chalk
- Spelling List

Tactile
- Play Dough
- Spelling List

C Hide and Seek Name ____________________

Place an **X** on a coin for each word you spell correctly.

D Other Word Forms

Using the words below, follow the instructions given by your teacher.

scrapped	screening	springs	strangest	strung
scrapping	scrubbed	springy	streamer	(stronger)
scraps	scrubber	sprung	streamlined	strongest
scratched	scrubbing	straighten	streams	strongly
scratches	scrubby	straightening	streets	throw
scratchy	spreader	straightway	stringed	throwing
screamed	spreading	strangely	stringier	thrown
(screaming)	sprang	strangeness	stringing	
screams	springing	(stranger)	stringy	

E Fun Ways to Spell

Initial the box of each activity you finish.

1. 

Spell your words with puzzles.

3. 
Spell your words in rhythm.

2. 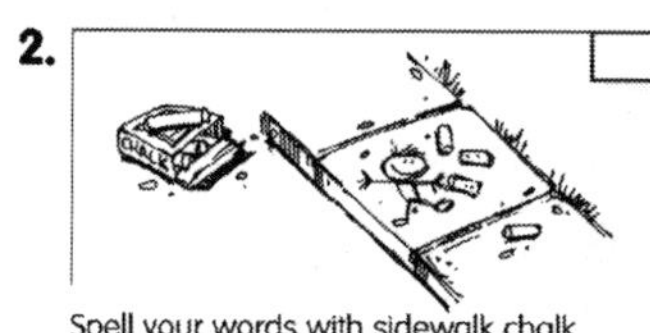

Spell your words with sidewalk chalk.

4. 

Spell your words with play dough.

Words with Consonant Clusters — Lesson 7

45

1 Hide and Seek

Reinforce correct spelling of current spelling words.

Write the words one at a time on the board. Use this activity for each word.

- **Look** at the word.
- **Say** the word out loud.
- Let's **hide** (cover) the word.
- **Write** the word on your paper.
- Let's **seek** (uncover) the word.
- **Check** your spelling. If your word is spelled wrong, write the word correctly next to it.

2 Other Word Forms

This activity is optional. Have students find and circle the Other Word Forms that are antonyms of the following:

weaker
friend
whispering

3 Fun Ways to Spell

Four activities are provided. Use one, two, three, or all of the activities. Have students initial the box for each activity they complete.

Options:

- assign activities to students according to their learning styles
- set up the activities in learning centers for the class to do throughout the day
- divide the class into four groups and assign one activity per group
- do one activity per day

General

To spell your words with puzzles...
- Write each word on a card.
- Cut each card into thirds using a straight cut.
- Mix your puzzle pieces.
- Put the puzzles together.
- Check your spelling.

Auditory

To spell your words in rhythm...
- Look at a word on your spelling list.
- Close your eyes.
- Play your rhythm instruments softly while you whisper the spelling of the word.
- Open your eyes and check your spelling.

Visual

To spell your words with sidewalk chalk...
- Write each of your spelling words on the sidewalk (ball court or playground).
- Check your spelling.

Tactile

To spell your words with play dough...
- Roll pieces of play dough into ropes.
- Use the ropes to make the letters of each word.
- Put them in the right order to spell each word.
- Check your spelling.

1 Working with Words

Familiarize students with word meaning and usage.

Spelling Clues

Recognizing that many words are made up of common letter patterns and/or smaller words can help students spell better. Write **sentence** on the board. Have a volunteer circle the smaller word **ten**, and the common letter pattern of **en**, which is used twice. Now, write the word **consonant**. Have a volunteer circle the smaller words **on** and **ant**.

Find the spelling word that contains the smaller word and write it on the line.

Missing Letters

Write the consonant cluster for each spelling word.

Take a minute to memorize...

Read the memory verse to the class twice. Have the class practice it with you two more times.

F Working with Words — Name ____________________

Spelling Clues

Write the correct spelling word on the line.

1. The little word **on** is in what bigger word? 1. strong
2. The little word **rat** is in what bigger word? 2. scratch
3. The little word **range** is in what bigger word? 3. strange
4. The little word **rap** is in what bigger word? 4. scrap
5. The little word **tree** is in what bigger word? 5. street
6. The little word **rub** is in what bigger word? 6. scrub
7. The little word **raw** is in what bigger word? 7. straw
8. The little word **read** is in what bigger word? 8. spread
9. The little word **ring** is in what bigger words? 9. spring, string
10. Write the words in which /ē/ is spelled **ee**. 10. screen, street
11. Write the words in which /ē/ is spelled **ea**. 11. scream, stream
12. Write the word in which /e/ is spelled **ea**. 12. spread

Missing Letters

Write the consonant cluster for each spelling word.

1. s c r een	5. s t r eam	9. s t r ing
2. s t r eet	6. s t r aw	10. s t r aight
3. s p r ead	7. t h r ew	11. s t r ange
4. s c r eam	8. s p r ing	12. s t r ong

Word Bank

scrap	screen	spring	straw	string
scratch	scrub	straight	stream	strong
scream	spread	strange	street	threw

Words with Consonant Clusters

Lesson 7

G Dictation

Name ____________________

Listen and write the missing words and punctuation.

1. Tommy's prize was a strawberry shortcake sundae.
2. Tommy felt strange after he told a lie.
3. He threw the ball straight to first base.

H Proofreading

If a word is misspelled, fill in the oval by that word. If all the words are spelled correctly, fill in the oval by **no mistake**.

1.	4.	7.
● scrach	○ spread	● stranj
○ straw	○ street	○ scrub
○ broke	○ prize	○ glass
○ no mistake	● no mistake	○ no mistake

2.	5.	8.
○ gray	● strate	○ north
○ proud	○ spring	● thrue
● screem	○ flag	○ held
○ no mistake	○ no mistake	○ no mistake

3.	6.	9.
○ prayer	○ string	● stong
○ cross	● streem	○ plain
○ skate	○ scrap	○ plus
● no mistake	○ no mistake	○ no mistake

47

1 Dictation

Reinforce correct spelling by using current and previous words in context.

Listen as I read each sentence and then write the missing words and ending punctuation in your worktext. (Slowly read each sentence twice. Sentences are found in the student text to the left.)

2 Proofreading

Familiarize students with standardized test format and reinforce recognizing misspelled words.

Look at each set of words. If a word is misspelled, fill in the oval by that word. If all the words are spelled correctly, fill in the oval by **no mistake**.

3 Hide and Seek

Reinforce correct spelling of current spelling words. (A reproducible master is provided in Appendix A as shown on the inset page to the right.)
Write the words one at a time on the board. Use this activity for each word.

- **Look** at the word.
- **Say** the word out loud.
- Let's **hide** (cover) the word.
- **Write** the word on your paper.
- Let's **seek** (uncover) the word.
- **Check** your spelling. If your word is spelled wrong, write the word correctly next to it.

4 Other Word Forms

Have your students complete this activity to strengthen spelling ability and expand vocabulary.

1 Posttest

Test mastery of the spelling words.

I will say the word once, use the word in a sentence, then say the word again. Write the word on your paper.

Other Word Forms — Lesson 7

Hide and Seek

Check a coin for each word you spell correctly.

Other Word Forms

Code Words

Use the code to write each Other Word Form.

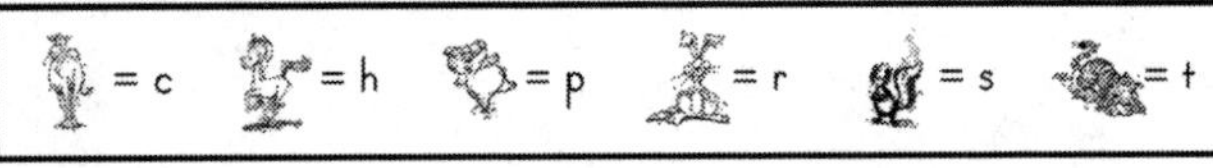

1. eamlined — streamlined
2. eening — screening
3. eading — spreading
4. atched — scratched
5. eams — screams
6. ung — strung
7. onger — stronger
8. ung — sprung
9. angest — strangest
10. ubber — scrubber
11. owing — throwing

332

1.	spread	James' orange jacket **spread** out behind him like butterfly wings.
2.	scratch	The scientist got more than a **scratch** when a shark attacked him.
3.	strong	Joe DiMaggio was a **strong** ball player with an amazing batting record.
4.	string	His **string** of hits in 56 straight games remains unbeaten today.
5.	threw	The pitcher **threw** an inside fast ball to Joe DiMaggio.
6.	scrub	A **scrub** is a baseball player who plays only when the best are unable to play.
7.	screen	Fresh air blew through the window **screen.**
8.	spring	The book said many storms happen in the **spring.**
9.	straight	The picture in the book showed a plane flying **straight** into gray clouds.
10.	street	Lisa wanted to roller blade down the **street.**
11.	straw	Lisa's hair is almost **straw** colored.
12.	strange	Tommy felt very **strange** inside when he lied to Mr. Valentino.
13.	scream	The word **scream** rhymes with ice cream.
14.	stream	The **stream** of melted ice cream ran down the side of the dish.
15.	scrap	James licked the last **scrap** of ice cream out of his dish.

Progress Chart

Students may record scores. (Reproducible master in Appendix B.)

Personal Dictionary

Students may add any words they have misspelled to their personal dictionaries for reference when writing. (Cover in Appendix B.)

I Game Name ________________

Tommy needs to tell Mr. Valentino the truth. Lead the way by moving one space for each word you or your team spells correctly from this week's word list.

Today's Lesson:

Start

Remember: You cannot be happy and be a liar.

J Journaling

In your journal, write about a time when you were tempted to lie. If you didn't lie, tell how you chose to be truthful. If you did tell a lie, tell how you felt about lying. (If you haven't made your lie right, ask God to help you do that, so you can be truly happy.)

48

2 Game

Reinforce spelling skills and provide motivation and interest.

Materials

- game page (from student text)
- flat buttons, dry beans, pennies, or game discs (1 per child)
- game word list

Game Word List

1. scrap
2. scratch
3. scream
4. screen
5. scrub
6. spread
7. spring
8. straight
9. strange
10. straw
11. stream
12. street
13. string
14. strong
15. threw

How to Play:

- Divide the class into two teams.
- Have each student place his/her game piece on Start.
- Have a student from team A go to the board.
- Say the spelling word. (You may also wish to use the word in a sentence.)
- Have the student write the word on the board.
- If correct, instruct each member of team A to move his/her game piece forward one space on the game board. (Note: If the word is misspelled, correct the spelling immediately.)
- Alternate between teams A and B.
- The team to reach Mr. Valentino first is the winner.

Non-Competitive Option:

At the end of the game, say: "Class, I am proud of your efforts to spell the words correctly. If you had fun and tried your best, you are all winners!"

3 Journaling

Provide a meaningful reason for correct spelling through personal writing.

Review the story using discussion leads provided on the following page. Encourage students to apply the Scriptural value in their journaling.

Journaling (continued)

- In our story this week, Tommy found out that lying doesn't bring happiness. What did Tommy lie about and why? (He told Mr. Valentino he had read the number of pages he was supposed to even though he hadn't. He wanted to get a coupon for an ice cream sundae so he could go to the ice cream shop with James and Christopher.)
- Is it ever okay to lie? (No. The Scriptures say to guard your lips from telling lies.)
- Have you ever lied about something?
- How did you feel inside after you lied?
- What did Tommy do to make his lie right? (He told Mr. Valentino that he had lied and said he was sorry. He read the pages he hadn't really read before then.)
- In your journal, write about a time when you were tempted to lie. If you didn't lie, tell how you chose not to be dishonest. If you did tell a lie, tell how you felt about lying.
  (If you haven't made your lie right, ask God to help you do that, so you can be truly happy.)

Take a minute to memorize...
Have the class say the memory verse with you once.

"When students invent spellings, they are thinking and learning about words."*

*Scott, Jill E. 1994. Spelling for Readers and Writers. The Reading Teacher, Vol. 48, No. 2, October: 188-190.

1 **Literature Connection**
Topic: Love for others
Theme Text: Ephesians 5:2

Difficult Daniel

Tommy and James try to love Daniel like God loves him.

"Okay, class." Mr. Valentino turned his back to write another math problem on the board. "Raise your hand if you can tell me how to. . ."

"YEEOW!" Kristin's scream startled everyone. Mr. Valentino jumped and dropped the marker in his hand. "Raising your hand might be a better way to get my attention, Kristin," he joked as he turned around. "I think that scream scared at least five years off my life. What seems to be the problem?"

"Daniel!" Red-faced Kristin pointed a finger at the boy seated in the desk behind her. "He pulled my hair. Hard!"

"Daniel, " Mr. Valentino was suddenly serious. "We'll talk at recess time. In the meantime let's remember our classroom rules." The teacher picked up his marker and turned everyone's attention back to math. "Now, Rachel, can you tell me how to find the answer to this problem?"

A few minutes later the room was fairly quiet as the students started their math assignment. Mr. Valentino walked from desk to desk answering questions and giving encouragement. Suddenly Matthew's hand shot up and waved frantically in the air. When Mr. Valentino got to his desk, Matthew forgot to be quiet. "He took my pencil!" Matthew thumped his hand on his desk. "It was lying right here and Daniel just walked by and grabbed it!" All eyes turned toward the corner of the room where Daniel stood at the pencil sharpener.

"Thank you, Matthew. I'll take care of it." The students settled back into their work, Mr. Valentino had a quiet talk with Daniel at the back of the room.

At recess time, Tony's suggestion to play "capture the flag" caught on quickly. Soon two teams were formed and the game was underway. The teams were pretty even and although lots of attempts were made to capture the flags, they remained safe. Tommy's heart pounded and his breath made white clouds in the cold air as he charged after Daniel. Just before Daniel reached the line of "prisoners," Tommy grabbed solidly at Daniel's arm through the cool leather of his jacket.

"Caught you!" Tommy cried.

"You did not!" Daniel started back toward his own side. "Come on, Stephen." He waved his hand at the "prisoner" at the front of the line. "Tommy wasn't even close. I freed you."

Stephen looked uncertainly around and then followed Daniel back to their team's side. Tommy stood there for a minute with his mouth gaping until he heard Beth screaming at him to catch Rachel before she freed someone else.

"Do you want a piece of my cookie?" The normal buzz of children's voices filled the room at lunch time that day. "Yuck! Carrot sticks again!" "Do you like pimento cheese sandwiches?" "My juice is already gone and I'm thirsty!" Suddenly, Beth sounded upset. "Mr. Valentino!" She held up a small package. "Look at my chips! Someone smashed every one of them!"

Mr. Valentino picked up the bag. "Anyone know how these chips were smashed?"

"Um, I saw Daniel at Beth's desk while she was gone to wash her hands," Setsuko spoke quietly, "but I couldn't see what he was doing."

Mr. Valentino laid the battered bag back on Beth's desk and sighed. "Daniel, come to my desk for a moment, please."

After lunch recess Mr. Valentino always read to them for a while. Students could draw, color, or just sit and listen as long as they were quiet. Tommy often liked to draw, but today he stretched out on the floor and lay his head on his jacket. Soon he was caught up in the story of Eeny, Meeny, Miney, Mo and Still-Mo. Mr. Valentino had begun the book by Sam Campbell just a couple days ago. The antics of the little squirrels entertained everyone. Laughter rippled across the room as Mr. Valentino read about Still-Mo's battle with a peanut tied to a rubber band.

Tommy glanced Daniel's way and the laughter died in his throat. Daniel was sitting on the floor writing something . . . on the bottom of his desk! Tommy sat up and looked around. No one else was paying any attention to Daniel. Mr. Valentino glanced up occasionally from the book he was reading, but he couldn't really see what Daniel was doing. Tommy stuck his leg across the aisle and poked Daniel's foot. When Daniel looked up at him, Tommy frowned and shook his head. Daniel just grinned, and finished what he was writing anyway.

That afternoon the class had a special treat. Rosa's dad brought Chipper and Nipper to visit. Nipper wasn't at all happy to see so many people. She scolded everyone from the safety of the small cage the chickarees had traveled to the school in. Chipper, however, enjoyed himself thoroughly. He sat on shoulders and burrowed through desks. He played with pencils and left peanut shells and pecan pieces everywhere. Matthew's glasses fascinated him and he loved burrowing under Kristin's wavy hair.

Rosa told her classmates how they had rescued and raised the twin chickarees. "Do any of you have questions about Chipper and Nipper?" she asked.

"Ch-ch-ch-ch-ch-ch-CHK!" Nipper screeched from the cage.

"Mr. Valentino!" Sarah forgot to raise her hand for once. "Daniel just poked Nipper

Story (continued)

with his ruler when he walked by on his way to the trash can."

Rosa rushed back to check on the frightened chickaree. Daniel's classmates glared at him as he returned to his desk.

"He's so mean!" Kristin muttered to no one in particular. Mr. Vasquez located Chipper in Tony's jacket hood and took the red squirrels home while Mr. Valentino got the class focused on their next activity. As Tommy left that afternoon he noticed that Daniel had to stay after school to talk to Mr. Valentino.

At recess a few days later a group of the kids decided to play baseball. Daniel was the last person to be chosen and he ended up on Tommy's team. He was last up to bat, but he hit a solid grounder. Beth ran up on the ball, picked it up, and threw it to James on first base.

"Got it!" James waved the ball inside his glove in the air. "You're out!"

"I am not!" Daniel shoved James. "I got to this base before the ball got here!"

"No way!" James stepped back on the base. "Didn't I catch this ball before Daniel touched base, Tommy?" James turned to the captain of Daniel's team.

"Yeah. You're out, Daniel." Tommy shrugged. "The ball got there first."

"No fair!" Daniel shoved James so hard that he fell. "You guys just don't like me." He stalked away from the field.

"Hey!" Tommy yelled after him. "What's wrong with you? Of course no one likes you to act like this! Kristin's right—you're mean to everyone!"

Later that evening Tommy snuggled under his covers as his mom rubbed his back. "Mom, what makes someone be mean to everyone?"

Mrs. Rawson rubbed for a moment in silence and then answered slowly, "If you're thinking about your friend, Daniel, I think it's probably because his mom and dad are having a lot of problems right now. They're talking about getting a divorce. I'm sure it's hard for Daniel to hear them argue and fight, but it's probably even harder for him to think of his family splitting apart. Be kind to him, Son." Tommy's mother brushed a kiss across his forehead. "I love you." She ruffled his hair and left the room quietly.

Tommy thought how awful it would be if his parents shouted at each other. He drifted to sleep feeling very sorry for Daniel.

"Setsuko, would you please read the verse that we're going to practice writing today?" Mr. Valentino asked during handwriting class the next day.

"'Be full of love for others, following the example of Christ who loved you.' Ephesians 5:2," Setsuko read.

"What do you think that means?" Mr. Valentino walked back and forth in front of the room. "Any ideas? Anyone? Tommy?"

Tommy looked down at his handwriting book. "Well, uh, I guess it means that we should love everyone because God loves us."

"Good." Mr. Valentino nodded. "Setsuko, do you have a comment?"

"Doesn't it mean that we have to be kind to others even when they're mean to us. I mean, isn't that what 'following the example of Christ' is talking about?" Setsuko bit her lip.

"Egg-zaca-tully!" A broad grin spread across Mr. Valentino's face. "Do you remember what Christ did when people did mean things to Him? When the soldiers shoved him down and even hit him? Nothing. He just loved them." Mr. Valentino spread his hands and shrugged his shoulders. "That's a pretty hard thing to do, isn't it? But we can love even the meanest person with God helping us." He paused. "Now, you've got a lot of l's in the verse today. Make sure you make them look the same and slant them all at the same angle as the rest of your letters, especially watching the h's and f's."

"Daniel might not be the meanest person, but he sure has been a pain to everyone lately," Tommy thought as he carefully wrote the f and two l's for the word "full." "I wasn't very kind at recess yesterday. God, help me to love him like You do even when he's really mean." Tommy glanced at James and their eyes met. He could tell James was thinking pretty much the same thing.

And they tried. The two friends tried to not get mad when Daniel did mean things to them and tried to include him in games and to be friendly to him. But it wasn't easy! They had to ask God for a whole lot of help. Daniel just seemed to get meaner every day.

After school one day, James waited nearby while Tommy packed his math homework into his backpack. Mr. Valentino crossed the empty room to Tommy's desk. "Boys, I just wanted to let you know that I've noticed how hard you've been trying to live up to the verse we talked about last week. I know it's not easy trying to be Daniel's friend right now. But I also know that you're making a bigger difference in his life than you can even guess. Daniel's having a really hard time right now and having you guys stick with him is very important. Will you pray with me now?" The boys nodded and all three bowed their heads as Mr. Valentino asked God to give the three of them His kind of love—especially for Daniel.

2 Discussion Time

Check understanding of the story and development of personal values.

- What were some of the things Daniel did that were wrong?
- Do you think Daniel would be very easy to love?
- Why did Tommy's mother think Daniel might be acting like that?
- How did Tommy and James follow Christ's example?
- Do you think Tommy's, James', and Mr. Valentino's friendship and love would help Daniel?
- How can you follow Christ's example every day in our classroom?

A Preview Name ____________________

Write each word as your teacher says it.

1. million
2. address
3. sudden
4. really
5. classroom
6. merry
7. rubber
8. ladder
9. supper
10. smell
11. butter
12. sunny
13. unhappy
14. lesson
15. happen

Words with Double Consonants

Lesson 8

Scripture
Ephesians 5:2

3 Preview

Test for knowledge of the correct spellings of these words.

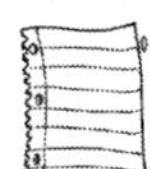

Customize Your List

On a separate piece of paper, additional words of your choice may be tested.

I will say the word once, use the word in a sentence, then say the word again. Write the word on the lines in the worktext.

Correct Immediately!

Let's correct our preview. I will write each word on the board. Put a dot under each letter on your preview as I spell the word out loud. If you spelled a word wrong, rewrite it correctly.

Take a minute to memorize...

Read the memory verse to the class twice. Have the class practice it with you two more times.

1.	million	One **million** is a very big number.
2.	address	Do you know your **address**?
3.	sudden	Kristin's **sudden** scream startled everyone.
4.	really	She was **really** upset because Daniel pulled her hair.
5.	classroom	The **classroom** was still while Mr. Valentino read a story.
6.	merry	The **merry** story kept their attention.
7.	rubber	It was about a squirrel trying to get a peanut tied to a **rubber** band.
8.	ladder	Chipper climbed up Matthew's arm, just like he was climbing a **ladder**.
9.	supper	Squirrels like to eat nuts for breakfast, lunch, and **supper**.
10.	smell	Beth's chips **smell** very good.
11.	butter	Setsuko has peanut **butter** cookies in her lunch.
12.	sunny	It is fun to play outside on **sunny** days.
13.	unhappy	Daniel was **unhappy** that he got out before reaching first base.
14.	lesson	Daniel needs to learn a **lesson**.
15.	happen	Good things **happen** when we ask God to help us love other people.

Progress Chart

Students may record scores. (Reproducible master in Appendix B.)

Day 1

Lesson 8

4 Word Shapes

Help students form a correct image of whole words.

Look at each word and think about its shape. Now, write the word in the correct word shape boxes. You may check off each word as you use it.

(In many words, a short vowel sound is followed by a double consonant. Occasionally a long vowel sound precedes a double consonant.)

In the word shape boxes, color the double consonant in each word.

Words with Double Consonants — Lesson 8

B Word Shapes Name ______________________

Write each word in the correct word shape boxes. Next, in the word shape boxes, color the double consonant in each word.

	Word	Word shape answer
1.	address	smell
2.	butter	sunny
3.	classroom	butter
4.	happen	merry
5.	ladder	classroom
6.	lesson	rubber
7.	merry	sudden
8.	million	unhappy
9.	really	supper
10.	rubber	ladder
11.	smell	lesson
12.	sudden	million
13.	sunny	address
14.	supper	happen
15.	unhappy	really

50

Answers may vary for duplicate word shapes.

Be Prepared For Fun

Check these supply lists for **Fun Ways to Spell** presented **Day 2**. Purchase and/or gather needed items ahead of time!

General
- Chalk or Whiteboard Marker
- Chalkboard or Whiteboard (could be individual boards for each child)
- Spelling List

Auditory
- Box to Store Letters
- a, b, b, c, d, d, e, h, i, i, l, l, m, n, n, o, o, p, p, r, r, s, s, t, t, u, y (written on seasonal shapes like pumpkins or leaves)
- Spelling List

Visual
- Glitter Glue
- Art Paper (2 or 3 pieces per child)
- Spelling List

Tactile
- Thick Pile Carpet Squares
- Spelling List

C Hide and Seek Name ____________________

Place an **X** on a coin for each word you spell correctly.

D Other Word Forms

Using the words below, follow the instructions given by your teacher.

addresses	happy	millionth	sunnier
addressing	ladders	rubberize	sunniest
buttery	lessons	rubbery	unhappily
classrooms	merrier	smelled	unhappiness
happened	merriest	smelling	
happening	merrily	smelly	
happier	millionaire	suddenly	
happiness	millions	suddenness	

E Fun Ways to Spell

Initial the box of each activity you finish.

1. 

Spell your words with chalk.

3. 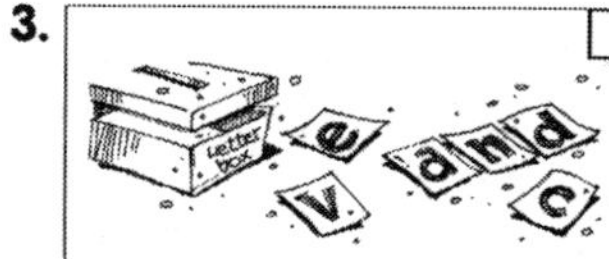

Spell your words out of the letter box.

2. 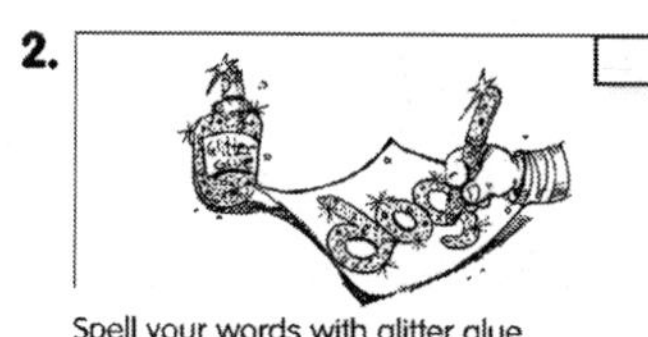
Spell your words with glitter glue.

4. 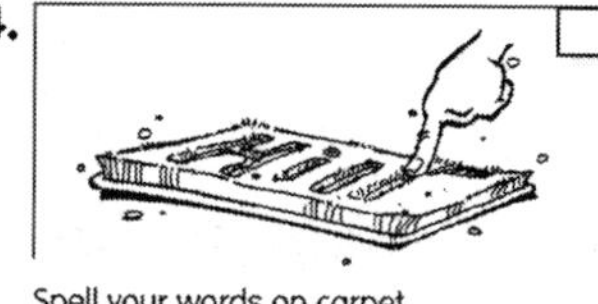
Spell your words on carpet.

Words with Double Consonants

Lesson 8

51

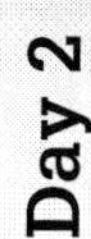

8

1 Hide and Seek

Reinforce correct spelling of current spelling words.

Write the words one at a time on the board. Use this activity for each word.

- **Look** at the word.
- **Say** the word out loud.
- Let's **hide** (cover) the word.
- **Write** the word on your paper.
- Let's **seek** (uncover) the word.
- **Check** your spelling. If your word is spelled wrong, write the word correctly next to it.

2 Other Word Forms

This activity is optional. Have students write original sentences using these Other Word Forms:

suddenly
ladders
buttery
sunniest

3 Fun Ways to Spell

Four activities are provided. Use one, two, three, or all of the activities. Have students initial the box for each activity they complete.

Options:

- assign activities to students according to their learning styles
- set up the activities in learning centers for the class to do throughout the day
- divide the class into four groups and assign one activity per group
- do one activity per day

General

To spell your words with chalk...
- Put your spelling list on your desk.
- Look at a word; then, walk to the chalkboard (or whiteboard).
- Write your spelling word on the chalkboard (or whiteboard).
- Return to your desk.
- Check your spelling.

Auditory

To spell your words out of the letter box...
- Spell a word from your list by putting the letters in the right order.
- Check your spelling.
- Spell your word out loud.

Visual

To spell your words with glitter glue...
- Write each of your spelling words on your paper.
- Check your spelling.

Tactile

To spell your words on carpet...
- Use your fingertip to write a spelling word on the carpet.
- Check your spelling.
- Smooth the word out with your hand and write another.

1 Working with Words

Familiarize students with word meaning and usage.

Syllables

Tell students that the words listed and explained in a dictionary are called **entry words** and that an entry word in the dictionary is often divided into syllables. Write the words **middle**, **squirrel**, **apple**, and **saddle** on the board. Explain that these are examples of entry words. Have a volunteer put a dot between the syllables.

Look at the first three items on your page and write how many syllables each word has. Now, write each spelling word on the line, putting a dot between the syllables.

Take a minute to memorize...

Read the memory verse to the class twice. Have the class practice it with you two more times.

Words with Double Consonants — Lesson 8

F Working with Words Name ____________

Syllables

An entry word in the dictionary is often divided into syllables.

> syl•la•ble [sil'ə'bəl] n. A unit of sound in a word. A syllable contains a vowel and possibly one or more consonants.

These are examples of entry words. Count how many syllables each word has and write the number on the line.

1. col•lar 2 **2.** cloth 1 **3.** Sat•ur•day 3

Find each of the words below in the dictionary. Write them in syllables, putting a dot between the syllables.

1. address ad•dress
2. happen hap•pen
3. lesson les•son
4. million mil•lion
5. sudden sud•den
6. supper sup•per
7. butter but•ter
8. ladder lad•der
9. merry mer•ry
10. rubber rub•ber
11. sunny sun•ny
12. really real•ly

What pattern did you notice when these words were divided into syllables?

13. (They were divided between the double consonant. Answers may vary.)

Write the word that has three syllables, putting a dot between the syllables.

14. unhappy un•hap•py

Write the spelling word that has only one syllable.

15. smell

Word Bank

address	happen	merry	rubber	sunny
butter	ladder	million	smell	supper
classroom	lesson	really	sudden	unhappy

52

G Dictation Name ______________

Listen and write the missing words and punctuation.

1. Her sudden scream sent a shock across the classroom .
2. Daniel was really unhappy and cross on Thursday .
3. The nurse held a rubber glove in his hand .

Words with Double Consonants

Lesson 8

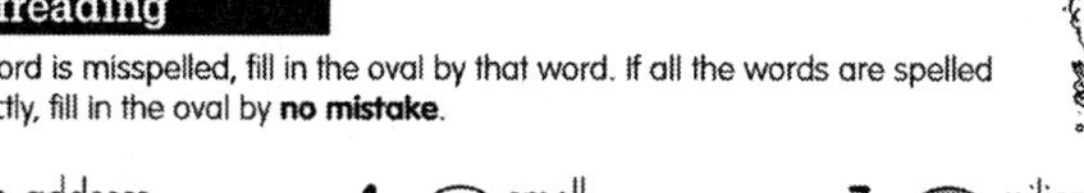

H Proofreading

If a word is misspelled, fill in the oval by that word. If all the words are spelled correctly, fill in the oval by **no mistake**.

1. ○ address ○ butter ○ scratch ● no mistake
2. ● clasroom ○ sunny ○ spell ○ no mistake
3. ● happin ○ screen ○ threw ○ no mistake
4. ○ smell ○ skin ● laddir ○ no mistake
5. ○ skip ● lessun ○ straight ○ no mistake
6. ○ supper ○ rubber ● merrie ○ no mistake
7. ● milion ○ stream ○ strong ○ no mistake
8. ○ unhappy ○ grab ● realy ○ no mistake
9. ● suddin ○ Thursday ○ slice ○ no mistake

53

1 Dictation

Reinforce correct spelling by using current and previous words in context.

Listen as I read each sentence and then write the missing words and ending punctuation in your worktext. (Slowly read each sentence twice. Sentences are found in the student text to the left.)

2 Proofreading

Familiarize students with standardized test format and reinforce recognizing misspelled words.

Look at each set of words. If a word is misspelled, fill in the oval by that word. If all the words are spelled correctly, fill in the oval by **no mistake**.

Day 4

Lesson 8

3 Hide and Seek

Reinforce correct spelling of current spelling words. (A reproducible master is provided in Appendix A as shown on the inset page to the right.)
Write the words one at a time on the board. Use this activity for each word.

- **Look** at the word.
- **Say** the word out loud.
- Let's **hide** (cover) the word.
- **Write** the word on your paper.
- Let's **seek** (uncover) the word.
- **Check** your spelling. If your word is spelled wrong, write the word correctly next to it.

4 Other Word Forms

Have your students complete this activity to strengthen spelling ability and expand vocabulary.

1 Posttest

Test mastery of the spelling words.

I will say the word once, use the word in a sentence, then say the word again. Write the word on your paper.

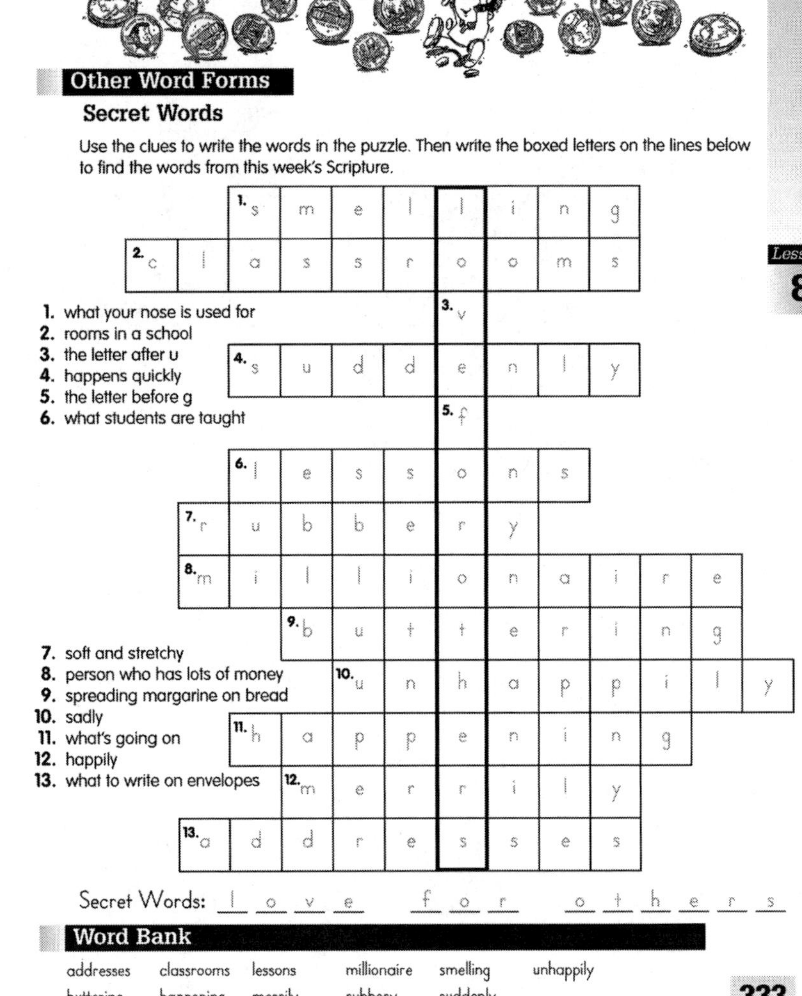

Hide and Seek

Check a coin for each word you spell correctly.

Other Word Forms

Secret Words

Use the clues to write the words in the puzzle. Then write the boxed letters on the lines below to find the words from this week's Scripture.

1. what your nose is used for — smelling
2. rooms in a school — classrooms
3. the letter after u — v
4. happens quickly — suddenly
5. the letter before g — f
6. what students are taught — lessons
7. soft and stretchy — rubbery
8. person who has lots of money — millionaire
9. spreading margarine on bread — buttering
10. sadly — unhappily
11. what's going on — happening
12. happily — merrily
13. what to write on envelopes — addresses

Secret Words: l o v e f o r o t h e r s

Word Bank

addresses	classrooms	lessons	millionaire	smelling	unhappily
buttering	happening	merrily	rubbery	suddenly	

Other Word Forms — Lesson 8 — 333

1.	unhappy	Matthew was very **unhappy** that Daniel took his pencil.
2.	ladder	Someone knocked over the **ladder**.
3.	classroom	Mr. Valentino talked quietly with Daniel at the back of the **classroom**.
4.	sunny	It was **sunny**, but cool, at recess that morning.
5.	merry	The children began a **merry** game of "capture the flag."
6.	rubber	The **rubber** soles of Tommy's shoes thumped as he chased Daniel.
7.	butter	James has a peanut **butter** and jelly sandwich for lunch.
8.	smell	Can you **smell** the apple in my lunch?
9.	million	Beth's chips were smashed into a **million** tiny pieces.
10.	sudden	All of a **sudden**, Nipper screeched "Ch-ch-ch-ch-ch-ch-CHK!"
11.	really	Daniel was **really** mean to poke the little squirrel with his ruler.
12.	happen	No one knew what might **happen** next.
13.	address	Daniel's **address** is 258 Stoneridge Court.
14.	supper	Tommy talked to his mom about Daniel after **supper**.
15.	lesson	What **lesson** did Tommy learn from Ephesians?

Progress Chart

Students may record scores. (Reproducible master in Appendix B.)

Personal Dictionary

Students may add any words they have misspelled to their personal dictionaries for reference when writing. (Cover in Appendix B.)

Words with Double Consonants

Lesson 8

I Game

Name ______________________

James and Tommy want to follow Jesus' example and treat Daniel with love. Lead the way by moving one space for each word you or your team spells correctly from this week's word list.

Remember: When you love others, you are following in Jesus' steps.

J Journaling

In your journal, write at least six ways you can follow Christ's example of kindness, here in our classroom.

54

2 Game

Reinforce spelling skills and provide motivation and interest.

Materials

- game page (from student text)
- flat buttons, dry beans, pennies, or game discs (1 per child)
- game word list

Game Word List

1. address
2. butter
3. classroom
4. happen
5. ladder
6. lesson
7. merry
8. million
9. really
10. rubber
11. smell
12. sudden
13. sunny
14. supper
15. unhappy

How to Play:

- Divide the class into two teams.
- Have each student place his/her game piece on Start.
- Have a student from team A go to the board.
- Say the spelling word. (You may also wish to use the word in a sentence.)
- Have the student write the word on the board.
- If correct, instruct each member of team A to move his/her game piece forward one space on the game board. (Note: If the word is misspelled, correct the spelling immediately.)
- Alternate between teams A and B.
- The team to reach Daniel first is the winner.

Non-Competitive Option:

At the end of the game, say: "Class, I am proud of your efforts to spell the words correctly. If you had fun and tried your best, you are all winners!"

3 Journaling

Provide a meaningful reason for correct spelling through personal writing.

Review the story using discussion leads provided on the following page. Encourage students to apply the Scriptural value in their journaling.

Journaling (continued)

- Daniel's actions in our story this week made it hard for Tommy to be his friend. How do you feel when a classmate cheats or is mean to you? (Angry, etc.)
- How did Christ act when people were mean to Him and hurt Him? (He forgave them and loved them anyway.)
- Are there sometimes reasons why people act mean? Explain. (Yes. Sometimes bad things happen to people that make them afraid or worried, and they act mean because of those feelings.)
- Is it okay to act mean if you have a reason? (No. Never.)
- How can we truly follow the example of Christ? (By treating everyone with kindness, even those who are unkind to us.)
- In your journal, write at least six ways that you can follow Christ's example of kindness here in our classroom.

Take a minute to memorize...
Have the class say the memory verses from lessons 7 and 8 with you.

"Spelling is more than rote memorization and drill."*

*Read, Charles, and Richard Hodges. 1982. "Spelling." In Encyclopedia of Educational Research, edited by H. Mitzel. 5th ed. New York: Macmillan.

Day 5
Lesson 8

1 **Literature Connection**

Topic: Being glad in the Lord
Theme Text: Philippians 4:4,5

Joyful Expedition

Beth finds something to be glad about, even when her family is in a car wreck.

"Dad's home! Dad's home!" Luke jumped off the couch and ran into the laundry room where Mom was taking a load of warm clothes out of the dryer. "Dad's home! Can we go now?"

Mrs. Hill put the fresh-smelling clothes on top of the dryer and turned to look at the excited face of her six-year-old son. "I need to fold these clothes before they get wrinkled. Run tell Beth we're about ready to go."

"Beth!" Luke ran up the stairs two at a time. "Beth, Dad's home! Let's go!"

Beth put down her book about Daniel Boone. "Okay. I'm coming."

"Hurry up, Beth, this will be fun." Luke handed Beth her leather boots, then stuffed the book into her backpack.

"What's so much fun about looking for a new car?" Beth carefully tied her bootlaces. "I like our old car just fine."

"You didn't like it last week when we were stuck beside the road because that alter-radar thing went out." Luke hopped over and looked out the window.

"Alternator," Beth giggled. "The alternator quit charging the battery and the car didn't have electricity anymore."

"Whatever!" Luke watched Dad get out of the car and walk into the house. "Dad says we can't trust the old car anymore. The windshield wipers quit last time it was raining. The thing that pumps the gas to the motor was broken two times. The tires are crooked. And the trans-missionary is messing up too."

"Transmission, Luke. It's not shifting smoothly." Beth corrected calmly as she picked up her backpack.

"Well, if you don't like looking at new cars you can always read your book about expositions," he said heading for the stairs.

"Expeditions," Beth laughed. "My book is about the great explorer, Daniel Boone, and the expeditions he led blazing the westward trail." She chuckled softly as she followed her younger brother downstairs.

"Just hurry! The rest of us want a new car!" he shot back.

Fifteen minutes later the Hill family piled out of their aging Oldsmobile at the nearest car dealership. Dad smiled at his wife. "Well, Janette, what do you want to look at first?"

"Look at this one, Beth!" Luke called, standing beside a Suburban. "We could each bring a friend when we go somewhere and still have lots of room for our stuff."

Dad walked over to the big red Suburban and opened the driver's side door. "I don't think we want to spend that much on a car, Luke. Look at this price tag." Dad lifted his son up so they could read the numbers together on the piece of paper glued to the window.

Beth ignored them and stopped to take a closer look at a Blazer. "I like this one." Beth ran her hand along the shiny blue paint of the door. "I'll bet Daniel Boone would drive a Blazer if he lived today. He liked to blaze trails."

Mother put her arm around Beth and smiled. "I don't think Daniel Boone would be as concerned about where to put his wife and kids on an expedition to find better hunting grounds."

Beth laughed and crawled into the back seat. "Oh, look. Here's a light you can turn on so you could read after dark, and it wouldn't bother the driver."

Luke came over and peeked inside the door on the other side. He pointed between the two front seats. "A TV-VCR would fit there. Then we could watch movies like Matthew and Alex do."

Dad climbed into the front seat and checked out the CD player and stereo system. "Think you could get used to this, Janette?" he asked his wife.

A salesperson walked up behind Dad. "Would you like to take it for a test drive?" He handed Dad a set of keys. "It has full-time all-wheel drive and an automatic transmission. The engine is a . . ."

"This is great, Luke." Beth patted the seat. "Look behind the seat at all that space for our stuff. This would be fun on a trip." The two children settled themselves in the Blazer's back seat for a quick test drive around town.

A few minutes later Dad returned to the car lot and asked, "Well, what do you think, Janette? Would you like to drive one of these?"

"I don't know. I didn't get to drive it, Ken," Janette Hill joked. "Seriously, I would like to look around some more. This is just our first stop. There isn't an air bag on the passenger side of this one. Those back seats don't look too comfortable, either. Every car dealer in town has a different sports utility vehicle. I looked up consumer reports on the Internet before you got home. They recommended the Explorer, the 4Runner and the Pathfinder. I think we should look at those."

By supper time the Hill family had looked at a 4Runner and a Pathfinder. "Let's eat and then go to the next dealership. I want to test drive the Explorer before we call it a day." Dad pulled into the Burger Barn parking lot and stopped the car.

"The 4Runner was a little too hard to get in and out of—I'd hate to climb that big step in a dress." Mom opened the restaurant door for Luke and Beth.

"But it gets such good gas mileage." Dad steered them toward a table. "It's lively too. That Blazer didn't accelerate nearly as well."

"The Pathfinder's ride was very smooth," Mom

Story (continued)

pointed out. "And the back seats of the Blazer won't be nearly as comfortable as the kids get older. It didn't have the quietest ride, either, and it doesn't seem to be as big."

The Hill family continued shopping for cars every afternoon the rest of the week. When things got slow, Beth pulled out her book and explored the west with Daniel Boone. Sometimes while her parents were talking to a salesperson, she would entertain Luke by reading aloud stories of the mountaineer. Besides going to dealerships, they also checked the Internet, and compared prices between dealers. Each vehicle came with what seemed like an infinite choice of options. By now, even Beth was getting excited about the purchase.

A week later during recess, Beth was playing four square with her friends. "I think Mom and Dad are going to get our new car today," Beth announced, aiming the four-square ball toward Katelynn's square.

"What did you decide to buy?" Katelynn bounced the ball back to Beth.

"I think the big green one. I can't keep all the names straight." Beth stretched to reach the ball in the corner of her square. "The ones we like best are all Daniel Boone names."

"Daniel Boone?" Katelynn watched Sarah pass the ball to Beth's square.

"Explorer, Pathfinder, Expedition, 4Runner, Mountaineer, and Blazer," Beth explained. "Dad wants something big enough to pull Grandma's horse trailer. His pickup has a hard time when it's loaded with all four horses." Beth missed the ball and ran across the playground after it. "I think that's why he'll get the big green one. We can put an extra seat in it. Your whole family could ride somewhere with us. I can hardly wait until school is out." Beth gave the ball to Sarah and moved to the last square.

When the bell rang at 3:00 o'clock, Beth grabbed her backpack and headed for the door.

Katelynn was right behind. "Look! They got the big green one. It's the one called the Expedition! Come on, I'll show you where the extra seat goes."

Katelynn and Beth ran out to the new green vehicle. The two girls crawled inside to look at everything. When Mr. Hatasaki came to see what Katelynn was doing, Mr. Hill got out and lifted the hood to show him the engine. Mom turned on the CD player and everyone oohed and ahhed at the lovely sound that filled the interior.

Katelynn's mom popped her head in the door. "It even smells new," Mrs. Hatasaki smiled. Luke brought Alex to see the TV-VCR and to try out the remote. Alex's mom came over to get him, and jumped when Mr. Hill demonstrated the alarm system.

After everyone had admired the new vehicle, the Hill family climbed in their seats and headed home. Beth saw Tony and Stephen in Grandma Miller's car and waved excitedly. The boys didn't recognize the Hill family in the new vehicle at first. But when Tony caught sight of Beth, he said something to Stephen, pointed, then waved back.

BANG! Beth screamed and was thrown to the left. Her head hit the window with a crack. Luke crashed into her shoulder as the new Ford skidded sideways across the intersection. The music from the CD player stopped. Beth sat up and looked into the front seats. "Mom! Mom, what happened?"

Dad unbuckled his seat belt and turned around. "Everyone okay?" he asked. "That red pickup decided not to stop for the light."

Beth looked at the red paint scar on the shiny new green of their crumpled hood. Everyone climbed out and stood on the curb. Mom and Dad knelt down in front of Beth and Luke and looked them over carefully. "Do you guys hurt anywhere?" Mom asked. The children shook their heads and continued to stare at the ruined Expedition.

"I'm glad we didn't trade in the Olds," Dad said looking at the damage. "At least you'll have something to drive tomorrow, Janette."

Beth shuddered, then laughed. "I don't think Daniel Boone would have liked this Expedition! It wasn't very long, and he liked to take long trips."

Mom smiled and gave her a hug. "I'm glad you can laugh, Beth," Mom said as Dad walked over to talk to the driver of the pickup and the police officer who had just arrived.

"We're all okay and that's the most important thing."

The next morning Katelynn met Beth at their classroom door. "Why didn't your mom bring you in your new Expedition? Did your dad take it?"

"No, it can't even be driven anymore. Our first Expedition didn't last very long," Beth joked.

Katelynn's eyebrows shot up and her eyes got wide. "Your Expedition is wrecked? And you're laughing?"

"Oh, Katelynn, our old car can last a little longer." Beth laughed and picked up her Daniel Boone book. "Besides nobody got hurt, just the cars. My mom says that 's what's really important. We'll probably get another Expedition—and maybe the next one will last longer."

Katelynn giggled and her eyes wandered to the board where Mr. Valentino had written the week's spelling Scripture. "Always be full of joy in the Lord; I say it again, rejoice! Remember that the Lord is coming soon." She turned to Beth. "Well, we can sure rejoice that only the Expedition got hurt!" Katelynn smiled, then gave her friend a hug.

2 Discussion Time

Check understanding of the story and development of personal values.

- How do you feel when you get something new?
- What did Beth want to show Katelynn about their new Expedition?
- What did the other family members want their friends to see?
- How do you feel when things don't go well?
- What is the worst thing that has ever happened to your family?
- Is it easy to always be full of joy in the Lord?

A Preview Name ______________________

Write each word as your teacher says it.

1. husband
2. grandfather
3. grandmother
4. belong
5. front
6. sang
7. stamp
8. ink
9. wind
10. bump
11. behind
12. drank
13. young
14. aunt
15. wing

Scripture
Philippians 4:4,5

Words with Consonant Clusters — Lesson 9

55

3 Preview

Test for knowledge of the correct spellings of these words.

Customize Your List

On a separate piece of paper, additional words of your choice may be tested.

I will say the word once, use the word in a sentence, then say the word again. Write the word on the lines in the worktext.

Correct Immediately!

Let's correct our preview. I will write each word on the board. Put a dot under each letter on your preview as I spell the word out loud. If you spelled a word wrong, rewrite it correctly.

Take a minute to memorize...

Read the memory verse to the class twice. Have the class practice it with you two more times.

Day 1 — Lesson 9

1.	husband	Janette Hill's **husband** test drove a Blazer.
2.	grandfather	Beth's **grandfather** had died the year before.
3.	grandmother	Sometimes Beth's **grandmother** needed her horses taken to the vet.
4.	belong	Beth was excited about "the big green one" that would **belong** to them.
5.	front	The Hills picked up their kids in **front** of Knowlton Elementary.
6.	sang	The group they listened to on the new CD player **sang** well.
7.	stamp	The new Expedition had everyone's **stamp** of approval.
8.	ink	The **ink** on the contract was barely dry before the Expedition was totaled.
9.	wind	The **wind** carried the smell of the smoking engines away.
10.	bump	The Expedition hit more than a **bump.**
11.	behind	No one hit the Expedition from **behind.**
12.	drank	The driver of the red pickup **drank** too much alcohol.
13.	young	The **young** driver in the red pickup looked scared.
14.	aunt	Beth's **aunt** couldn't believe it when she heard about the wreck.
15.	wing	Mr. Hill leaned back in his big **wing** chair and sighed.

Progress Chart

Students may record scores. (Reproducible master in Appendix B.)

4 Word Shapes

Help students form a correct image of whole words.

Look at each word and think about its shape. Now, write the word in the correct word shape boxes. You may check off each word as you use it.

(In many words, a consonant cluster starts with **m** or **n**. These clusters are never at the beginning of a word. They represent a nasal sound, so spellers may tend to leave out the **m** or **n**.)

In the word shape boxes, color the consonant cluster with **m** or **n** in each word. Circle the words that have more than one consonant cluster.

Words with Consonant Clusters — Lesson 9

B Word Shapes Name ____________

Write each word in the correct word shape boxes. Next, in the word shape boxes, color the consonant cluster with **m** or **n** in each word. Circle the words that have more than one consonant cluster.

Word	Answer
1. aunt	ink
2. behind	(front)
3. belong	young
4. bump	sang
5. drank	bump
6. front	belong
7. grandfather	aunt
8. grandmother	(grandfather)
9. husband	wing
10. ink	(stamp)
11. sang	wind
12. stamp	behind
13. wind	husband
14. wing	(drank)
15. young	(grandmother)

56

Answers may vary for duplicate word shapes.

Day 1 Lesson 9

Be Prepared For Fun

Check these supply lists for **Fun Ways to Spell** presented **Day 2**. Purchase and/or gather needed items ahead of time!

General
- Colored Pencils
- Art Paper (1 piece per child)
- Spelling List

Auditory
- A Classmate
- Spelling List

Visual
- Black Construction Paper (1 piece per child)
- Cotton Swabs (1 per child)
- Lemon Juice
- Spelling List

Tactile
- Pipe Cleaners (cut in an assortment of lengths)
- Spelling List

Words with Consonant Clusters

Lesson 9

C Hide and Seek Name ____________________

Place an **X** on a coin for each word you spell correctly.

D Other Word Forms

Using the words below, follow the instructions given by your teacher.

aunts	drink	stamped	winging
belongings	drunk	stamping	wings
belongs	inking	stamps	younger
bumped	inky	winded	youngest
bumpily	sing	winding	youngster
bumping	singing	windy	
bumpy	songs	winged	

E Fun Ways to Spell

Initial the box of each activity you finish.

1. 

Spell your words with pictures.

3. 
Spell your words out loud.

2. 

Spell your words with lemon juice.

4. 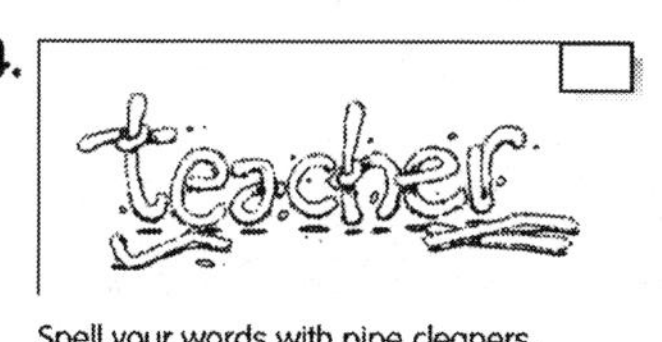

Spell your words with pipe cleaners.

57

1 Hide and Seek

Reinforce correct spelling of current spelling words.

Write the words one at a time on the board. Use this activity for each word.

Say

- **Look** at the word.
- **Say** the word out loud.
- Let's **hide** (cover) the word.
- **Write** the word on your paper.
- Let's **seek** (uncover) the word.
- **Check** your spelling. If your word is spelled wrong, write the word correctly next to it.

Day 2

Lesson 9

2 Other Word Forms

This activity is optional. Have students find and circle the Other Word Forms that are synonyms of the following:

rugged
vocalizing
my mom's sisters

3 Fun Ways to Spell

Four activities are provided. Use one, two, three, or all of the activities. Have students initial the box for each activity they complete.

Options:

- assign activities to students according to their learning styles
- set up the activities in learning centers for the class to do throughout the day
- divide the class into four groups and assign one activity per group
- do one activity per day

General

To spell your words with pictures...
- Choose several words from your spelling list and draw pictures that illustrate the meanings of those words.
- Write the correct spelling word beside each picture.
- Check your spelling.

Auditory

To spell your words out loud...
- Have a classmate read a spelling word from the list.
- Say a sentence with that spelling word to your classmate.
- Spell the spelling word you used in that sentence to your classmate.
- Ask your classmate to check your spelling.
- Do this with each word on your word list.

Visual

To spell your words with lemon juice...
- Dipping a cotton swab in lemon juice, write each of your spelling words on black construction paper.
- Check your spelling before your writing disappears!

Tactile

To spell your words with pipe cleaners...
- Choose a word from your spelling list.
- It may be a favorite word or a word you have trouble remembering how to spell.
- Shape the pipe cleaner to spell that word.

Lesson 9
Day 3

1 Working with Words

Familiarize students with word meaning and usage.

Spelling Clues

Complete the top of your page by reading each spelling clue.

Proofing

Write this sentence on the board: **My teecher is the clasroom**. Ask the students to find the misspelled words. Demonstrate the mark used in proofreading to show that a word is misspelled. Now, ask students if any words are missing. Draw the proofreading mark used to show that a word is missing.

You will be using proofer's marks to show the errors in the paragraph at the bottom of your page. After proofing, write the misspelled words correctly on the lines.

Take a minute to memorize...

Read the memory verse to the class twice. Have the class practice it with you two more times.

Words with Consonant Clusters — Lesson 9

F Working with Words Name ____________

Spelling Clues

Write the spelling words that contain the cluster **mp**.

1. bump 2. stamp

Write the spelling words that contain the cluster **nd**.

3. behind 4. husband
5. grandfather 6. wind
7. grandmother

Write the spelling words that contain the cluster **ng**.

8. belong 9. wing
10. sang 11. young

Proofing

Use proofreader's marks to show the errors in the paragraph below. Write the seven misspelled words correctly on the lines.

◯ word is misspelled	^ word or words missing

When my ant Ida was a girl, she lived her granfather and grandmoter. She often found yung animals that had been hurt, and brought them home care for. One day she found a bird with a broken wimg. She knew it did not truly beloung to her, but she cared for it gently until had healed. She then took it back to the woods beehind the barn and set it free.

1. aunt 4. young 6. belong
2. grandfather 5. wing 7. behind
3. grandmother

Word Bank

aunt	bump	grandfather	ink	wind
behind	drank	grandmother	sang	wing
belong	front	husband	stamp	young

58

G Dictation Name ____________

Listen and write the missing words and punctuation.

1. Beth sat in the front seat with her grandmother .
2. Beth screamed when her head bumped the window .
3. My aunt sang as she helped the young boy .

H Proofreading

If a word is misspelled, fill in the oval by that word. If all the words are spelled correctly, fill in the oval by **no mistake**.

1. ○ belong ○ aunt ○ ladder ● no mistake
2. ● bihind ○ wing ○ really ○ no mistake
3. ○ merry ● drakn ○ strange ○ no mistake
4. ○ bump ○ classroom ● granfather ○ no mistake
5. ● granmother ○ ink ○ lesson ○ no mistake
6. ○ sang ● huzband ○ million ○ no mistake
7. ○ sudden ○ supper ● frunt ○ no mistake
8. ● stanp ○ wind ○ street ○ no mistake
9. ○ happen ● yung ○ rubber ○ no mistake

Words with Consonant Clusters — Lesson 9

59

1 Dictation

Reinforce correct spelling by using current and previous words in context.

Listen as I read each sentence and then write the missing words and ending punctuation in your worktext. (Slowly read each sentence twice. Sentences are found in the student text to the left.)

2 Proofreading

Familiarize students with standardized test format and reinforce recognizing misspelled words.

Look at each set of words. If a word is misspelled, fill in the oval by that word. If all the words are spelled correctly, fill in the oval by **no mistake**.

Day 4 / Day 5

Lesson **9**

3 Hide and Seek

Reinforce correct spelling of current spelling words. (A reproducible master is provided in Appendix A as shown on the inset page to the right.)
Write the words one at a time on the board. Use this activity for each word.

- **Look** at the word.
- **Say** the word out loud.
- Let's **hide** (cover) the word.
- **Write** the word on your paper.
- Let's **seek** (uncover) the word.
- **Check** your spelling. If your word is spelled wrong, write the word correctly next to it.

4 Other Word Forms

Have your students complete this activity to strengthen spelling ability and expand vocabulary.

1 Posttest

Test mastery of the spelling words.

I will say the word once, use the word in a sentence, then say the word again. Write the word on your paper.

Other Word Forms — Lesson 9

Hide and Seek

Check a coin for each word you spell correctly.

Other Word Forms

Scrambled Words

Use the sentence clues to help you unscramble the words. Write the unscrambled word in the sentence.

lobseng	**1.** The kitten belongs to my aunts.
ginigsn	**2.** Tommy is singing at the top of his voice.
iwngdni	**3.** Grandmother is winding her yarn into a ball.
snorft	**4.** The fronts of the cabinets are scratched.
egonury	**5.** Meg is younger than her sister.
bdempu	**6.** When it was dark, I bumped my head.
kirnd	**7.** I am so hot, I need a drink.
psastm	**8.** Tony played with the stamps and got inky.
swing	**9.** The little bird tried its wings.
ymbup	**10.** This road is rough and bumpy.
strongyue	**11.** Grandpa tells stories about when he was a youngster.
tadspem	**12.** Beth was cold and stamped her feet to warm them.
idwyn	**13.** On a windy day, my hat blew away.

Code Words

Use the code to write each Other Word Form.

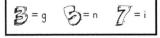

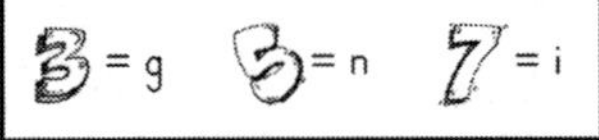

1. w 7 5 3 7 5 3 winging

2. belo 5 3 7 5 3 s belongings

334

1.	grandfather	Beth's **grandfather** had loved horses.
2.	grandmother	The children's **grandmother** needs a way to get the horses to the vet.
3.	wing	Mr. Hill leaned back in his **wing** chair and said, "Let's get the green one."
4.	husband	Janette Hill and her **husband** Ken spent a lot of time choosing the Expedition.
5.	belong	That new green Expedition will **belong** to the Hill's.
6.	front	Mom and Dad picked up their children in **front** of the school.
7.	ink	The **ink** dried quickly on the check, and they went to pick up the kids.
8.	sang	Beth **sang** for joy as she skipped toward the new, green Expedition.
9.	bump	Beth and Luke didn't even have a **bump**.
10.	stamp	Luke started to **stamp** his foot in frustration.
11.	behind	The red pickup did not come from **behind**.
12.	wind	The warm **wind** carried the smell of gasoline and burning oil.
13.	young	The **young** man in the pickup was shaking with fear.
14.	drank	He **drank** more alcohol than was legal.
15.	aunt	The children's **aunt** was shocked at the sad story of the drunk driver and the wreck.

Progress Chart

Students may record scores. (Reproducible master in Appendix B.)

Personal Dictionary

Students may add any words they have misspelled to their personal dictionaries for reference when writing. (Cover in Appendix B.)

I Game Name ____________________

Go along with the Hill family as they shop for a new vehicle. Move one space for each word you or your team spells correctly from this week's word list.

Remember: Be happy and full of joy!

J Journaling

Write a paragraph about all the things you can rejoice about.

Game

Reinforce spelling skills and provide motivation and interest.

Materials

- game page (from student text)
- flat buttons, dry beans, pennies, or game discs (1 per child)
- game word list

Game Word List

1. aunt
2. behind
3. belong
4. bump
5. drank
6. front
7. grandfather
8. grandmother
9. husband
10. ink
11. sang
12. stamp
13. wind
14. wing
15. young

How to Play:

- Divide the class into two teams.
- Have each student place his/her game piece on Start.
- Have a student from team A go to the board.
- Say the spelling word. (You may also wish to use the word in a sentence.)
- Have the student write the word on the board.
- If correct, instruct each member of team A to move his/her game piece forward one space on the game board. (Note: If the word is misspelled, correct the spelling immediately.)
- Alternate between teams A and B.
- The team to reach the car lot first is the winner.

Non-Competitive Option:

At the end of the game, say: "Class, I am proud of your efforts to spell the words correctly. If you had fun and tried your best, you are all winners!"

3 Journaling

Provide a meaningful reason for correct spelling through personal writing.

Review the story using discussion leads provided on the following page. Encourage students to apply the Scriptural value in their journaling.

Journaling (continued)

- At the end of our story this week, why was Katelynn so surprised Beth was happy? (The brand-new Expedition had been wrecked.)
- What reason did Beth have to be thankful? (Just the Expedition got hurt—no people.)
- Even when things aren't going well, we can rejoice. What does our memory verse tell us to remember? ("Always be full of joy in the Lord; I say it again, rejoice!... Remember that the Lord is coming soon.")
- Write a paragraph about all the things you can rejoice about.

Take a minute to memorize...
Have the class say the memory verses from lessons 7, 8, and 9 with you.

"The kinds of errors that achieving children make change systematically, and each new stage reflects a logical step toward mastery of our complex spelling system."*

*Henderson, Edmund, 1985. Teaching Spelling. Boston" Houghton Mifflin Company.

Day 5

Lesson 9

1 **Literature Connection**
Topic: Love for others
Theme Text: 1 Peter 4:8

Love Finds a Way

Tommy's loving response to Daniel's meanness makes a difference in Daniel.

"Mr. Valentino, this tape player won't work." Kristin stood by her teacher's desk and held out one of the cassette players from the listening center. "I tried several different headsets and different cassette tapes, but the player still won't work."

"Let's see, Kristin." Mr. Valentino turned the machine over to take out the batteries and something rattled inside. "Hmmm. Sounds like something's broken in there." He shook it lightly and it rattled again. "Maybe someone dropped it. We'll have to make do without it for now." Mr. Valentino laid the cassette player on his desk with a thoughtful expression.

"Um, Mr. Valentino?" Kristin was still standing there. "Three of the tapes are torn up, too."

"What?" Mr. Valentino looked back quickly.

"I, umm. . .three of the tapes at the listening center are torn up," Kristin repeated. "I just found them that way," she was quick to say. "I didn't do it."

Mr. Valentino rubbed his hand across the back of his neck. "It's okay, Kristin. Thanks for letting me know." Mr. Valentino gave her a reassuring smile. "Would you put those messed up tapes on my desk with the recorder, please?"

"Yes, sir," Kristin said.

Just then, Setsuko walked up. "Mr. Valentino, this book has some pages torn out." She held it out to her teacher, who flipped it open in his hands. Several pages near the end had been ripped out. "I just checked it out from the school library yesterday." Setsuko looked miserable. "I'm sure it was okay then, but when I took it out of my desk today, it was all torn up." She sniffled and a tear made its way down her face. "I didn't do it, really I didn't."

Mr. Valentino gave her a gentle pat on the back. "Don't worry about it, Setsuko. We'll deal with it." As Setsuko returned to her seat, Mr. Valentino placed the torn book on the growing pile on his desk, then let his gaze sweep slowly around the room.

At recess James cornered Tommy. "Have you noticed how all kinds of things in our classroom are getting ruined lately?" he questioned. "The pencil sharpener disappeared, the globe is broken off its base, there's a hole in the wall, the hanging ivy plant got knocked down—and now the tape player and tapes, and Setsuko's library book!" James ticked each item off on his fingers as he talked. "Something's going on!"

Tommy nodded, as he watched his classmates playing in the cold air. "We'd probably better stick closer to Daniel," he muttered.

"You think Daniel's behind all this?" James asked, then answered his own question with a nod. "Sure. That makes sense. He seems more angry every day." The friends stood in silence for a moment. Then James asked, "Okay, what's the plan?"

The two boys stayed close to Daniel over the next few days. They played what he played at recess. They watched when he went to the pencil sharpener or the trash can. Wherever he went, either Tommy or James went also. They tried to cheer him up when he was upset and calm him down when he got angry.

Then one morning Christopher Wright appeared at Tommy's elbow as he bent over the drinking fountain in the hallway of Knowlton Elementary School. "Did you see it when you came in?"

"See what?" Tommy wiped the soft sleeve of his green plaid flannel shirt across his dripping mouth as he stood and stared at Christopher.

"The vandalism," Christopher almost whispered. "Someone sprayed black paint all over the school sign. Didn't you notice?"

"No, I rode my bike today and Mom drove right behind me. I was really concentrating to make sure I did everything right so she'd let me ride again." Tommy walked back down the hall to peer out the glass doors. Sure enough, black paint covered much of the brick and metal sign. Groups of students clustered here and there, talking in hushed tones about the vandalism. "Wow!" Tommy shook his head. "Oh, wow!"

"Yeah," Christopher agreed as the boys moved out of the way to let some older kids into the building. "I don't think anyone knows who did it. Why would someone want to, anyway?"

"Who knows?" Tommy shook his head as the two boys entered their classroom.

At noon recess a few days later, Tommy rushed outdoors with the rest of the kids. Soon he was enjoying a great game of catch with Stephen. Stephen threw a really high, long ball and Tommy rushed backward to catch it. Just as it smacked into his glove, he noticed Daniel disappearing around the side of the school building. "Be back in a minute!" He threw a fastball back to Stephen and then followed Daniel.

Tommy rounded the corner of the building, but didn't see Daniel anywhere. He decided to go on into the front of the school. Maybe Daniel had gone around to go into the office that way. But there was no one in the front of the school, either. Tommy glanced around before turning toward the front door. Then he stopped and stared. His bike! He walked slowly over to the rack. Thick army green paint covered the bike, still dripping over the bike's shiny blue and onto the grass. Someone had just dumped paint all over it.

Tommy turned slowly toward the school and saw Daniel standing just inside

Story (continued)

the glass doors. Daniel waved, then walked down the hall. Tommy felt like someone had just hit him in the chest. And he felt mad. He'd tried hard to love Daniel and help him. Now this! He was FURIOUS! When he stomped into the room, Daniel was washing his hands. "You, you. . . how could you? Why?" Tommy demanded.

Daniel turned with a scowl on his face. "To teach you a lesson!" He pointed his finger at Tommy. "You think you're so wonderful! Well, I don't need a baby sitter and I don't need you in my face all the time! Just leave me alone!"

Tommy sank onto a desk, his legs suddenly weak. "You did do it all, didn't you?" He motioned at the room with one hand. "You broke the cassette player, the globe, ruined Setsuko's library book. Everything. You did it all."

"You don't have a shred of proof," Daniel boasted.

"If you could dump paint all over my bicycle, then you must have been the one to vandalize the school sign, too," Tommy guessed wildly. He was surprised when Daniel didn't deny it. "You did?" Tommy asked in amazement. "But why?" He jumped up and stepped toward Daniel. "You've hurt so many people, ruined so many things . . . and you knew how much I liked my bike!" Tommy was about to burst with anger. "I . . . I . . ." He clenched his hands and stared at his unrepentant friend.

"Sure, I did it all!" Daniel jeered. "Everything's my fault, anyway, so why not?" He laughed roughly. "It gives me something to do, and keeps you busy following me around!" Then he glared back at Tommy. "But leave me alone from now on! I don't need you for a friend anymore." His voice rose till he was yelling. "I don't need anybody!"

Then Tommy noticed the writing on the board just behind Daniel. It was the place Mr. Valentino always wrote the week's Scripture verse. The words "love for each other" seemed to leap out at him.

Tommy took a deep breath and read it through slowly. "Most important of all, continue to show deep love for each other, for love makes up for many of your faults." He sighed, took another deep breath, and looked back at Daniel. "God, please help me to show Daniel love," Tommy prayed silently. Then in a quiet voice he said, "I'm sorry you feel that way, Daniel, but I'll always be your friend, whether you need me or not. I forgive you for wrecking my bike." He turned and walked toward the door.

"Tommy!" Daniel's voice stopped him. "Tommy, you . . . uh, I . . .well . . . I mean I haven't even said I'm sorry, but you still forgive me?" Daniel finally choked out. Tommy just nodded. "Tommy, I don't know what to do!" Daniel's voice broke, then he began to cry. "Dad came back from a long business trip last night and they started again. I couldn't keep from listening." Daniel shook his head and continued in a dull voice. "Mom screamed at Dad that he didn't love her anymore and he said why should he? Then she said it wasn't fair that she had to stay home to take care of me all the time and he got to travel all over the place." Daniel gulped and Tommy moved closer to him. "I don't know when they stopped arguing. I put my head under the pillow when I heard something crash against the wall. It must have been the big black vase. It wasn't there this morning."

Neither boy realized that Mr. Valentino had been in the back of the classroom the whole time until he moved. When he wrapped his arms around Daniel, the boy began to sob even more. "It's okay, Daniel. I heard everything. You've got a true friend in Tommy, and I'm always here for you, too. We'll help you." Mr. Valentino's eyes were also a little damp when he smiled at Tommy over Daniel's head and nodded at the text on the board.

A few weeks later Mr. Valentino asked the class to stand and share some of their favorite Scripture verses that they'd learned so far that year. "My favorite is Ephesians 1:4." Rosa quoted the verse almost perfectly, "'Because of what God has done we are gifts that he delights in.'"

Daniel chose 1 Peter 4:8. Tommy said it under his breath along with Daniel. "Most important of all, continue to show deep love for each other, for love makes up for many of your faults."

When Daniel sat down he looked across at Tommy and smiled. Tommy grinned back and gave a thumbs up.

Daniel's parents were shaken when Mr. Valentino notified them about Daniel's behavior. They'd been so wrapped up in their own disagreements that neither of them had realized how deeply Daniel was hurting. They agreed to go to counseling together, and arranged for Daniel to see a counselor, too. His counselor helped him understand his parents' problems were not his fault. Daniel also began working after school with the custodian to pay for the damages he'd caused, including repairs to Tommy's bike.

Things still weren't perfect, but love really made up for many faults.

2 Discussion Time

Check understanding of the story and development of personal values.

- Why did Tommy and James decide to stick close to Daniel?
- What did the students of Knowlton Elementary see when they came to school one morning?
- What did Daniel do to Tommy's bike?
- How did Tommy react to Daniel messing up his bike?
- How did Daniel feel about Tommy forgiving him when he hadn't even said he was sorry?
- What kind of problems was Daniel having at home?
- Where did Tommy get the strength to be a loving friend to Daniel even though Daniel had many faults?

A Preview

Name ______________________

Write each word as your teacher says it.

1. rush
2. porch
3. neck
4. fresh
5. ranch
6. match
7. crash
8. sack
9. sandwich
10. kick
11. hatch
12. splash
13. teacher
14. switch
15. earth

Words with Consonant Digraphs

Lesson 10

Scripture

I Peter 4:8

61

3 Preview

Test for knowledge of the correct spellings of these words.

Customize Your List

On a separate piece of paper, additional words of your choice may be tested.

I will say the word once, use the word in a sentence, then say the word again. Write the word on the lines in the worktext.

Correct Immediately!

Let's correct our preview. I will write each word on the board. Put a dot under each letter on your preview as I spell the word out loud. If you spelled a word wrong, rewrite it correctly.

Take a minute to memorize...

Read the memory verse to the class twice. Have the class practice it with you two more times.

Day 1

Lesson 10

1.	rush	Daniel's father didn't **rush** home from his business trip.
2.	porch	Mrs. DeVore met him on the front **porch** when he got home.
3.	neck	She was so angry her face and **neck** were red.
4.	fresh	They started a **fresh** argument before he even came inside.
5.	ranch	Daniel wished he was far away on a **ranch** somewhere.
6.	match	His parents' shouting **match** seemed to go on and on.
7.	crash	Daniel stuck his head under the covers when he heard a **crash.**
8.	sack	The maid put the pieces of the black vase into a trash **sack.**
9.	sandwich	She made a **sandwich** for Daniel to take to school.
10.	kick	Daniel's angry, mixed-up feelings made him want to **kick** someone.
11.	hatch	He wanted an escape **hatch** for his feelings.
12.	splash	He chose to **splash** thick green paint all over Tommy's bicycle.
13.	teacher	Daniel was surprised that Tommy and his **teacher** forgave him.
14.	switch	Their love and friendship helped Daniel **switch** to better actions.
15.	earth	God loves each one of us on this **earth.**

Progress Chart

Students may record scores. (Reproducible master in Appendix B.)

Day 1

Lesson 10

4 Word Shapes

Help students form a correct image of whole words.

Look at each word and think about its shape. Now, write the word in the correct word shape boxes. You may check off each word as you use it.

(This lesson reviews consonant digraphs and introduces the **tch** spelling. The **tch** is usually used at the end of a word following a short vowel sound.)

In the word shape boxes, color the consonant digraph in each word. Circle the words that have a consonant cluster and digraph.

Words with Consonant Digraphs — Lesson 10

B Word Shapes Name ____________

Write each word in the correct word shape boxes. Next, in the word shape boxes, color the consonant digraph in each word. Circle the words that have a consonant cluster and digraph.

Word	Answer
1. crash	hatch
2. earth	porch
3. fresh	teacher
4. hatch	rush
5. kick	(crash)
6. match	(splash)
7. neck	(sandwich)
8. porch	(switch)
9. ranch	sack
10. rush	earth
11. sack	ranch
12. sandwich	match
13. splash	kick
14. switch	neck
15. teacher	(fresh)

62

Answers may vary for duplicate word shapes.

Be Prepared For Fun

Check these supply lists for **Fun Ways to Spell** presented **Day 2**. Purchase and/or gather needed items ahead of time!

General
- A Classmate
- Spelling List

Auditory
- Voice Recorder
- Spelling List

Visual
- a, c, d, e, e, f, h, h, i, k, k, l, m, n, o, p, r, s, s, t, u, w (written on upside-down cups)
- Spelling List

Tactile
- Art Paper (2 or 3 sheets per child)
- Magazines
- Glue Sticks
- Scissors
- Spelling List

C Hide and Seek

Name ____________________

Place an **X** on a coin for each word you spell correctly.

D Other Word Forms

Using the words below, follow the instructions given by your teacher.

crashed	refresh	matches	sacked	switched
crashes	hatched	matching	sacker	switching
crashing	hatches	rematch	sacking	teach
earthen	hatching	necks	sandwiched	teaches
earthly	kicked	porches	sandwiches	teaching
freshen	kicking	ranches	splashed	
freshly	kicks	rushes	splashes	
freshness	matched	rushing	splashing	

E Fun Ways to Spell

Initial the box of each activity you finish.

1. 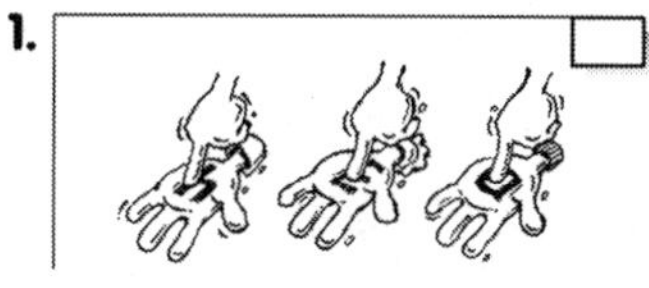
Spell your words in your classmate's hand.

3.
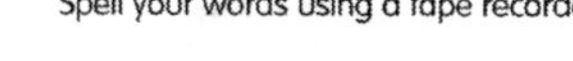
Spell your words using a tape recorder.

2. 

Spell your words with paper cups.

4. 
Spell your words with magazine clippings.

1 Hide and Seek

Reinforce correct spelling of current spelling words.

Write the words one at a time on the board. Use this activity for each word.

Say

- **Look** at the word.
- **Say** the word out loud.
- Let's **hide** (cover) the word.
- **Write** the word on your paper.
- Let's **seek** (uncover) the word.
- **Check** your spelling. If your word is spelled wrong, write the word correctly next to it.

2 Other Word Forms

This activity is optional. Have students unscramble these letters to write Other Word Forms:

seorphc	(porches)
igcahrsn	(crashing)
dahwsesnic	(sandwiches)
eesssrfhn	(freshness)

3 Fun Ways to Spell

Four activities are provided. Use one, two, three, or all of the activities. Have students initial the box for each activity they complete.

Options:

- assign activities to students according to their learning styles
- set up the activities in learning centers for the class to do throughout the day
- divide the class into four groups and assign one activity per group
- do one activity per day

General

To spell your words in your classmate's hand...
- Have your classmate sit next to you and hold his (or her) palm open in front of and facing both of you.
- Use your fingertip to write a spelling word in the palm of your classmate's hand.
- Have your classmate say each letter as you write it and then say the word you spelled.
- Next, have your classmate write a word in your palm.

Auditory

To spell your words using a voice recorder...
- Record yourself as you say and spell each word on your spelling list.
- Listen to your recording and check your spelling.

Visual

To spell your words with paper cups...
- Spell a word from your list by putting the cups in the right order.
- Check your spelling.

Tactile

To spell your words with magazine clippings...
- Cut the letters you need from old magazines.
- Glue the letters to your paper in the correct order.

1 Working with Words

Familiarize students with word meaning and usage.

Word Sort

Write the headings **ch**, **ck**, **sh**, **tch**, and **th** on the board. Say the words **path**, **black**, **catch**, **inch**, and **push**. Guide the students in putting these five words under the correct headings.

At the top of your page, write each spelling word under the correct consonant digraph heading.

Proofing

Write this sentence on the board: **theese socks not matck my shirt**. Ask the students to find the misspelled words. Demonstrate the mark used in proofreading to show that a word is misspelled. Ask the students if any words are missing. Draw the proofreading mark used to show that a word is missing. Have a volunteer find the letter that should be capitalized, and draw three lines under it.

You will be using the proofer's marks to show the errors in the paragraph at the bottom of your page. After proofing, write the misspelled words correctly on the lines.

Take a minute to memorize...

Read the memory verse to the class twice. Have the class practice it with you two more times.

Words with Consonant Digraphs — Lesson 10

F Working with Words — Name ____________

Word Sort

Write each spelling word under the correct consonant digraph heading.

ch	sh	tch
1. porch	5. crash	9. hatch
2. ranch	6. fresh	10. match
3. sandwich	7. rush	11. switch
4. teacher	8. splash	

Proofing

Use proofreader's marks to show the errors in the paragraph below. Write the nine misspelled words correctly on the lines.

(circle) word is misspelled — ^ word or words missing — ≡ capitalize letter

One day we decided play kickball at recess. Hal ate his sandwitch quickly and tossed his empty lunch sak in trash can. he ran outside with the ball and began to kitck it around, waiting for the rest of to finish lunch. The ground was damp the recent rain, and hal landed with a slpash when his foot a small puddle. The ball flew through the air and hit a dead limb on the old oak tree that stood the school. our teecher ran off the portch in a rusch when he saw limb fall to the erth with a krash and land on Hal.

1. sandwich	4. splash	7. rush
2. sack	5. teacher	8. earth
3. kick	6. porch	9. crash

Word Bank

crash	hatch	neck	rush	splash
earth	kick	porch	sack	switch
fresh	match	ranch	sandwich	teacher

64

G Dictation

Name ____________________

Listen and write the missing words and punctuation.

1. The fresh green paint spread across Tommy's bike.
2. Tommy felt a rush of shock in his chest.
3. Mom had to drive the old car after the crash.

Words with Consonant Digraphs

Lesson 10

H Proofreading

If a word is misspelled, fill in the oval by that word. If all the words are spelled correctly, fill in the oval by **no mistake**.

1. ○ bump ○ fresh ○ crash ● no mistake
2. ● erth ○ neck ○ front ○ no mistake
3. ○ porch ○ stamp ● hach ○ no mistake
4. ○ rush ● kik ○ young ○ no mistake
5. ○ splash ● macth ○ husband ○ no mistake
6. ● rantch ○ drank ○ grandfather ○ no mistake
7. ○ aunt ○ behind ● sak ○ no mistake
8. ● sanwhich ○ butter ○ address ○ no mistake
9. ○ spend ● teecher ○ string ○ no mistake

65

1 Dictation

Reinforce correct spelling by using current and previous words in context.

Listen as I read each sentence and then write the missing words and ending punctuation in your worktext. (Slowly read each sentence twice. Sentences are found in the student text to the left.)

2 Proofreading

Familiarize students with standardized test format and reinforce recognizing misspelled words.

Look at each set of words. If a word is misspelled, fill in the oval by that word. If all the words are spelled correctly, fill in the oval by **no mistake**.

Day 4

Lesson 10

3 Hide and Seek

Reinforce correct spelling of current spelling words. (A reproducible master is provided in Appendix A as shown on the inset page to the right.)
Write the words one at a time on the board. Use this activity for each word.

- **Look** at the word.
- **Say** the word out loud.
- Let's **hide** (cover) the word.
- **Write** the word on your paper.
- Let's **seek** (uncover) the word.
- **Check** your spelling. If your word is spelled wrong, write the word correctly next to it.

Check a coin for each word you spell correctly.

Other Word Forms

Sentence Fun

Circle the word that best completes each sentence. Write the word in the sentence.

1. There was a crashing sound during the storm. crashes (crashing)
2. The fire destroyed all her earthly goods. (earthly) earthen
3. The freshly baked bread smelled yummy! (freshly) freshen
4. Our class watched the little chick hatching. hatches (hatching)
5. The new girl kicks the soccer ball far. kicking (kicks)
6. Beth's new socks matched her T-shirt. (matched) matches
7. The water rushes through our pasture. rushing (rushes)
8. Tony put the cans in sacks to take to school. (sacks) sacking
9. The ball was sandwiched behind the cupboard. sandwiches (sandwiched)
10. They were splashing and didn't hear Mom call. splashed (splashing)
11. He can push switches to make his train run. switched (switches)
12. Mr. Valentino enjoys teaching his students. (teaching) teaches

Word Sort

Write each Other Word Form under the correct heading.

hatched porches teach rematch earthen kicked

One-syllable Words	Two-syllable Words
1. hatched	4. porches
2. teach	5. rematch
3. kicked	6. earthen

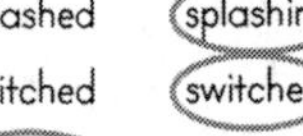

335

4 Other Word Forms

Have your students complete this activity to strengthen spelling ability and expand vocabulary.

1 Posttest

Test mastery of the spelling words.

I will say the word once, use the word in a sentence, then say the word again. Write the word on your paper.

1. ranch — Rosa brought pictures of her uncle's **ranch** to show her classmates.
2. switch — Kristin flipped the **switch**, but the tape player didn't work.
3. crash — The hanging ivy plant fell with a **crash**.
4. sack — Rosa's **sack** lunch was missing.
5. sandwich — Kristin shared part of her **sandwich** with Rosa.
6. porch — Many students stood on the covered school **porch** looking at the sign.
7. splash — One large **splash** of black spray paint covered several letters.
8. earth — Setsuko's library book about the **earth** was torn.
9. neck — Mr. Valentino rubbed his hand across the back of his **neck**.
10. hatch — What bad idea will Daniel **hatch**, or come up with, next?
11. rush — Tommy stopped playing catch with Stephen to **rush** after Daniel.
12. fresh — Lots of **fresh** green paint covered Tommy's bike.
13. kick — Tommy felt mad enough to **kick** Daniel.
14. match — God's love helped Tommy **match** Daniel's meanness with forgiveness.
15. teacher — Daniel's **teacher** gave him a hug.

Progress Chart

Students may record scores. (Reproducible master in Appendix B.)

Personal Dictionary

Students may add any words they have misspelled to their personal dictionaries for reference when writing. (Cover in Appendix B.)

Words with Consonant Digraphs

10

I Game Name ______________________

Complete the secret phrase by correctly spelling the words from this week's word list.

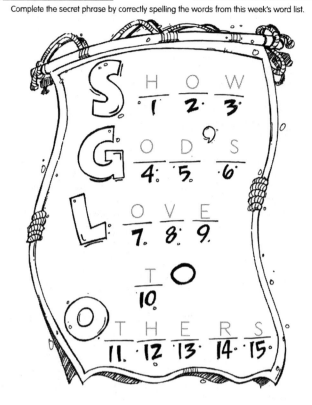

S H O W
1 2 3

G O D S
4 5 6

L O V E
7 8 9

T O
10

O T H E R S
11 12 13 14 15

Remember: Love can cover many flaws!

J Journaling

In your journal, make a list of people you know. Then write a prayer asking God to help you show deep love for each person on the list.

66

2 Game

Reinforce spelling skills and provide motivation and interest.

Materials

- game page (from student text)
- pencils (1 per child)
- game word list

Game Word List

Team A	Team B
1. crash (H)	1. porch (H)
2. earth (O)	2. ranch (O)
3. fresh (W)	3. rush (W)
4. hatch (O)	4. sack (O)
5. kick (D)	5. sandwich (D)
6. match (S)	6. splash (S)
7. neck (O)	7. switch (O)
8. porch (V)	8. teacher (V)
9. ranch (E)	9. crash (E)
10. rush (T)	10. earth (T)
11. sack (T)	11. fresh (T)
12. sandwich (H)	12. hatch (H)
13. splash (E)	13. kick (E)
14. switch (R)	14. match (R)
15. teacher (S)	15. neck (S)

Day 5

Lesson 10

How to Play:

- Divide the class into two teams.
- Have a student from team A choose a number from 1 to 15.
- Say the word that matches that number from the team's word list. (You may also wish to use the word in a sentence.)
- Have the student write the word on the board.
- If correct, have each member of team A write the given letter in the matching space on his/her game page.
- Alternate between teams A and B having the students choose a number of a blank space.
- The team to complete the secret phrase first is the winner.

Non-Competitive Option:

At the end of the game, say: "Class, I am proud of your efforts to spell the words correctly. If you had fun and tried your best, you are all winners!"

3 Journaling

Provide a meaningful reason for correct spelling through personal writing.

Review the story using discussion leads provided on the following page. Encourage students to apply the Scriptural value in their journaling.

Journaling (continued)

- What were some of the things Daniel did that were wrong? (Broke the tape player and tapes, tore Setsuko's library book, broke the globe, knocked down the hanging ivy plant, poked a hole in the wall, sprayed black paint on the school sign, and dumped army-green paint on Tommy's bike.)
- What do we call those kinds of actions? (Vandalism.)
- Do you think it would be easy to show love toward Daniel?
- Do you think Mr. Valentino was proud of Tommy? Why or why not? (Yes. Tommy controlled his anger and forgave Daniel. His true friendship helped Daniel want to change.)
- What does our Scripture say we are to do? ("Continue to show deep love for each other.")
- In your journal, make a list of people you know. Then write a prayer asking God to help you show deep love for each person on the list.

Take a minute to memorize...
Have the class say the memory verses from lessons 7, 8, 9, and 10 with you.

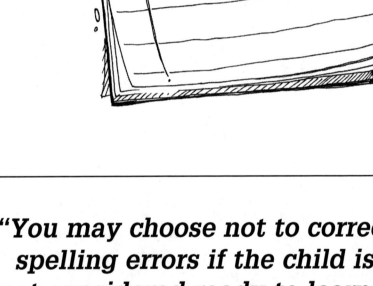

"You may choose not to correct spelling errors if the child is not considered ready to learn a spelling pattern or concept."*

*Lutz, Elaine. 1986. ERIC/RCS Report: Invented Spelling and Spelling Development. Language Arts, Vol. 63, No. 7, November: 742-744.

Special Abilities

Tony and Matthew learn to use their own special abilities to help each other.

"I didn't do well on this test, either." Tony put a big minus 15 at the top of his preview page in his worktext and slammed it shut before anyone could see it. "I'll never learn to spell these words. I'm not a great speller anyway, but all these words have silent letters in them. How can you spell a word when a bunch of its letters don't make any noise?"

"How'd ya do?" Stephen slid his spelling worktext into his desk. "I missed ten."

"Well, you did better than I did." Tony groaned. "Spelling is harder this year. I just can't remember where all those letters go."

Matthew stopped at Tony's desk on his way to the pencil sharpener. "You do okay on the preview?"

Tony tried to change the subject. "How many did you miss?"

"I missed one. I forgot the silent "gh" in "caught." Spelling is harder this year. I never used to miss any on the preview."

"Shhhhh." Mr. Valentino looked up from his desk and put his finger to his lips to remind the boys to be quiet.

Matthew continued on his way to the pencil sharpener. Tony breathed a sigh of relief. It was one thing for Stephen to know how bad he spelled—Stephen wasn't much better. Matthew was another story. He did well in all his subjects at school and he never even seemed to study.

"Arggh!" Tony took out a fresh piece of notebook paper and started to write each word he had missed three times. "This is going to take a long time," he muttered to himself as he peeked in his spelling book to check the spelling for "caught." "Who made up all these silly spellings anyway? Why can't "caught" just be c-o-t. That's the way it sounds!"

When Mr. Valentino finally said it was time for morning recess, Stephen and Tony gathered the stuff they needed to play "capture the flag" and hurried out the door to the playground. "Anyone who wants to play "capture the flag", meet us by the big pine tree," Tony called over his shoulder.

The game was well under way, but Tony was in jail. He glanced over at the swings and saw Matthew gliding slowly back and forth all by himself. "I wonder what's wrong with Matthew?" he mused. Stephen then tagged Tony, so he was out of jail and he quickly forgot Matthew in the excitement of trying to capture the flag of the other team.

It wasn't until lunch recess that Tony thought of Matthew again. He saw him sitting under the lone pine tree with a book. "Why isn't Matthew playing dodge ball?" he called over to Stephen.

Stephen shrugged his shoulders. "Beats me."

"He didn't play "capture the flag" this morning, either. Is he sick?" Tony threw the ball and hit Daniel on the foot. "You're out, Daniel. I got your foot."

"You did not!" Daniel screamed.

Mr. Valentino called Daniel over and talked quietly with him for a minute; then he blew the whistle for everyone to line up to go back inside.

Tony walked up and stood behind Matthew in the line. "You sick?"

"Nope," Matthew said quietly and looked down at his book.

"Good book?" Tony looked at the cover with the picture of young Daniel Boone holding his long rifle.

"Beth let me borrow it," Matthew said. "It's pretty good."

"Why aren't you playing with us at recess?"

Matthew looked down at the ground and scuffed the end of his leather shoes in the grass. "I just don't like 'capture the flag.'"

"Or dodge ball?" Tony wouldn't let the matter drop.

"It's not my favorite."

"What do you like? You don't like baseball or soccer. You don't want to play dodge ball or "capture the flag". How come?"

Matthew kicked at the tuft of grass. "I'm just not very good at sports and stuff. Nobody ever wants me on their team and I don't like it when I'm always picked last."

Tony nodded his head, realizing for the first time what his friend said was true. He'd always thought of Matthew as smart and had envied him for how easily he got his work done. Matthew always had time left over to do the special things Mr. Valentino had for them to do around the room. He'd never thought about how clumsy and awkward Matthew was at things that required physical coordination.

When they were all seated in the classroom again Mr. Valentino walked to the front of the classroom. "Get out your handwriting books and open them to lesson eleven. We're working on a Scripture verse this week about special abilities. We all have them, and God has given them to us so we can help each other. Raise your hand if you are good at 'capture the flag.'" Mr. Valentino looked around the room. "Now raise your hand if you think you are good at math." Tony noticed Tommy didn't raise his hand on that one. "Now raise your hand if spelling is something you do well," Mr. Valentino continued. Tony kept his hand quietly in his lap. He noticed that Stephen didn't raise his hand either. "Who is good at making things with their hands?" Katelynn slowly raised her hand and then whispered in a loud whisper for Setsuko to raise her hand, too. "Who is

Story (continued)

good at baseball?" Mr. Valentino asked.

After a few more questions Mr. Valentino said he had just one more. "Who thinks they are really good at every one of the things I just mentioned?" No one raised their hand. "We're all different," he continued, "and if we remember to help each other, we can make an awesome team. If you're good at something, it 's important for you to use your special abilities to help others who may need it."

Day 1

Lesson 11

"I don't think there is much I can do to help Matthew," Tony thought as he practiced writing in his handwriting worktext. "He's always been kind of clumsy."

The next morning at first recess Tony and Stephen carried out all the equipment for "capture the flag." Tony was a captain and quickly picked Stephen to be on his team. When it was his turn to pick again, he yelled Matthew's name and motioned with his arm for him to come over.

"Why did you pick him?" Stephen whispered in his ear.

Tony shrugged and continued to pick people for his team. When everyone was on a team, Tony called his team together for a strategy session. "Matthew, I want you to guard the flag on this side. Stephen, I want you to stand on the other side. Don't let your guard down. Beth is a good runner and she's not on our team today. She always seems to be able to sneak in when the guards are looking at something else."

"Thanks for picking me today," Matthew said later on the way back into the classroom. "You didn't have to do that, you know—just because of what Mr. Valentino said yesterday in handwriting."

"I know." Tony grinned. "But it wasn't just what Mr. Valentino said. It's what the Scriptures say. That text said to be sure to use our special abilities to help others. You 're a good guard. You kept Beth from getting our flag today!" Tony flung his arm across Matthew's shoulder.

"She's fast, too. I think we've found your special ability in "capture the flag." I bet you'd be a good catcher in baseball, too." Tony smiled at his friend.

"I'll have to think about dodgeball, though. You can't be great at everything, right?"

Later that afternoon when he was finished with his science, Matthew walked over to Tony's desk. "Tony, would you like some help with this week's spelling words? I know some good ways to remember all those silent letters. Here is a little chaw-lk board and a little piece of chaw-lk." Matthew pronounced the "l" in chalk and said the word with a deep Texas drawl. Tony laughed and nodded his head.

"How'd you know I was having a hard time in spelling, Matthew?"

Matthew raised his eyebrows and looked down at Tony's finished science paper and pointed to a few misspelled words. "Oh, it's not too hard to figure out. Besides, you didn't raise your hand yesterday when Mr. Valentino asked us to raise our hands if we thought we were good spellers."

"I guess we do each have our own special abilities. Thanks for using yours to help me." Tony smiled at his friend and picked up the piece of chalk. "Chalk. . .c-h-a-l-k. . .chalk," he wrote on the little chalkboard.

Matthew nodded his head and gave him a thumbs up.

2 Discussion Time

Check understanding of the story and development of personal values.

- Why do you think God doesn't just make us all good at everything?
- Why was Matthew reading a book during recess?
- How do you think Matthew felt when Stephen picked him for "capture the flag"?
- Why did Tony not want Matthew to know his score on the preview?
- How does Tony feel now that Matthew is helping him learn his spelling words?
- How do you feel when you help someone?
- Do you think God is happy when you feel that way?

A Preview Name ______________

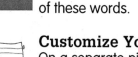

Write each word as your teacher says it.

1. bright
2. sight
3. half
4. caught
5. though
6. whole
7. clothes
8. sidewalk
9. knee
10. knot
11. neighbor
12. chalk
13. thumb
14. Wednesday
15. wrap

Words with Silent Consonants

Lesson 11

Scripture

I Peter 4:10

67

3 Preview

Test for knowledge of the correct spellings of these words.

Customize Your List

On a separate piece of paper, additional words of your choice may be tested.

I will say the word once, use the word in a sentence, then say the word again. Write the word on the lines in the worktext.

Correct Immediately!

Let's correct our preview. I will write each word on the board. Put a dot under each letter on your preview as I spell the word out loud. If you spelled a word wrong, rewrite it correctly.

Take a minute to memorize...

Read the memory verse to the class twice. Have the class practice it with you two more times.

Day 1

Lesson 11

1.	bright	It was a **bright**, sunny day.
2.	sight	Tony missed the word **sight** on his spelling preview.
3.	half	Tony missed more than **half** the words on the preview.
4.	caught	Matthew won't forget the silent letters in **caught**.
5.	though	Matthew is not very good at sports, **though**.
6.	whole	Matthew read *Daniel Boone* the **whole** recess.
7.	clothes	Matthew's **clothes** never get dirty during recess.
8.	sidewalk	The class lined up on the **sidewalk** to come back inside.
9.	knee	Tony put the spelling book on his **knee**.
10.	knot	There was a **knot** in Matthew's stomach.
11.	neighbor	It is good to help your **neighbor**.
12.	chalk	Matthew taught Tony how to spell **chalk**.
13.	thumb	Matthew raised his **thumb** in the thumbs-up signal.
14.	Wednesday	On **Wednesday** it's time for "Other Word Forms" in spelling.
15.	wrap	They will **wrap** up the spelling lesson with the posttest.

Progress Chart

Students may record scores. (Reproducible master in Appendix B.)

Day 1

Lesson 11

4 Word Shapes

Help students form a correct image of whole words.

Look at each word and think about its shape. Now, write the word in the correct word shape boxes. You may check off each word as you use it.

(A silent letter occurs when two letters spell the sound of only one letter or when two letters stand for a completely silent sound.)

In the word shape boxes, color the silent consonant or consonants in each word. Circle the word in which the digraph **wh** has the sound of **/h/**.

Words with Silent Consonants — Lesson 11

B Word Shapes Name ______

Write each word in the correct word shape boxes. Next, in the word shape boxes, color the silent consonant or consonants in each word. Circle the word in which the digraph **wh** has the sound of **/h/**.

	Word	Word Shape Answer
1.	bright	neighbor
2.	caught	sight
3.	chalk	bright
4.	clothes	though
5.	half	half
6.	knee	clothes
7.	knot	Wednesday
8.	neighbor	thumb
9.	sidewalk	chalk
10.	sight	whole (circled)
11.	though	caught
12.	thumb	wrap
13.	Wednesday	sidewalk
14.	whole	knee
15.	wrap	knot

68

Answers may vary for duplicate word shapes.

Be Prepared For Fun

Check these supply lists for **Fun Ways to Spell** presented **Day 2**. Purchase and/or gather needed items ahead of time!

General
- Markers
- Art Paper (2 or 3 sheets per child)
- Spelling List

Auditory
- Spelling List

Visual
- Letter Tiles a, b, c, d, d, e, e, f, g, h, h, i, k, l, m, n, o, p, r, s, t, u, w, y
- Spelling List

Tactile
- Paint Bags (tempera paint in plastic, resealable bags secured at top with heavy tape-1 per child)
- Spelling List

C Hide and Seek Name ____________________

Place an **X** on a coin for each word you spell correctly.

D Other Word Forms

Using the words below, follow the instructions given by your teacher.

although	clothing	knotted	thumbs
brighten	halftime	knotting	wholesome
brightest	halfway	neighborly	wholly
catch	halved	sidewalks	wrapped
catches	halves	sighted	wrapping
catching	knees	sights	wraps
chalky	knots	thumbed	

E Fun Ways to Spell

Initial the box of each activity you finish.

1. 
Spell your words with markers.

3. 

Spell your words while snapping.

2. 

Spell your words with letter tiles.

4. 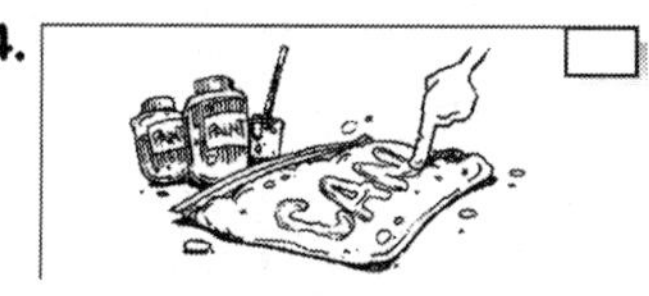
Spell your words with paint.

Words with Silent Consonants

Lesson 11

69

1 Hide and Seek

Reinforce correct spelling of current spelling words.

Write the words one at a time on the board. Use this activity for each word.

Say

- **Look** at the word.
- **Say** the word out loud.
- Let's **hide** (cover) the word.
- **Write** the word on your paper.
- Let's **seek** (uncover) the word.
- **Check** your spelling. If your word is spelled wrong, write the word correctly next to it.

2 Other Word Forms

This activity is optional. Have students write variations of this sentence using these Other Word Forms:

Can Tim wrap these gifts today?

wrapped, wrapping, wraps

3 Fun Ways to Spell

Four activities are provided. Use one, two, three, or all of the activities. Have students initial the box for each activity they complete.

Options:

- assign activities to students according to their learning styles
- set up the activities in learning centers for the class to do throughout the day
- divide the class into four groups and assign one activity per group
- do one activity per day

General

To spell your words with markers...
- Write a spelling word in thick, fat letters.
- Use other colored markers to decorate each letter with dots, flowers, stripes, etc.

Auditory

To spell your words while snapping...
- Look at a word on your spelling list.
- Close your eyes.
- Snap your fingers softly while you whisper the spelling of the word.
- Open your eyes and check your spelling.

Visual

To spell your words with letter tiles...
- Spell a word from your list by putting the tiles in the right order.
- Check your spelling.

Tactile

To spell your words with paint...
- Use your finger to write a spelling word on the paint bag.
- Check your spelling.
- Smooth out the paint and write another word.

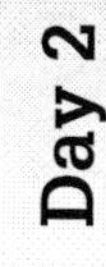

1 Working with Words

Familiarize students with word meaning and usage.

Spelling Clues

Sometimes words with silent letters can be difficult for students to spell. There are very few generalizations that apply to these words. You may like to write the following on the board to help students remember:
/ch/ can sometimes be spelled tch
/i-/ can sometimes be spelled igh
/j/ can sometimes be spelled dge
/m/ can sometimes be spelled mb
/n/ can sometimes be spelled kn
/r/ can sometimes be spelled wr
Write the words **high**, **tight**, **sight**, **night**, and **bright** on the board. Help students generalize that the sound of **/ī/** is sometimes spelled **igh**. Ask a volunteer to tell you which letters are not heard (**gh**). Next, write the words **knock**, **know**, and **knife**. Ask a volunteer which letter is silent in these words. Help students realize that words that begin with **/n/** sometimes have a silent **k** at the beginning.

Complete the top of your page by reading each clue.

Missing Letters

Write the consonant digraph for each spelling word.

Take a minute to memorize...

Read the memory verse to the class twice. Have the class practice it with you two more times.

Words with Silent Consonants — Lesson 11

F Working with Words Name ____________

Spelling Clues

Write the words in which you see the letter **l** but don't hear **/l/**.

1. chalk 2. half 3. sidewalk

Write the words in which you see the letter **k** but don't hear **/k/**.

4. knee 5. knot

Write the words in which you see the letter **w** but don't hear **/w/**.

6. whole 7. wrap

Write the words in which you see the letters **g** and **h** but don't hear **/g/** or **/h/**.

8. bright 9. neighbor 10. though
11. caught 12. sight

Which word has the consonant digraph **th** that is silent?

13. clothes

Write the word in which you see the letter **b**, but don't hear **/b/**.

14. thumb

Write the word in which you see the letter **d**, but don't hear **/d/**.

15. Wednesday

Missing Letters

Write the consonant digraph for these spelling words.

1. k n ot 2. w r ap 3. t h umb
4. k n ee 5. w h ole 6. t h ough

Word Bank

bright	clothes	knot	sight	Wednesday
caught	half	neighbor	though	whole
chalk	knee	sidewalk	thumb	wrap

70

G Dictation

Name ________________

Listen and write the missing words and punctuation.

1. Tony will write the word "caught" three times .
2. Mr. Valentino broke the chalk in half .
3. Matthew did not let the flag touch the sidewalk .

Words with Silent Consonants

Lesson 11

H Proofreading

If a word is misspelled, fill in the oval by that word. If all the words are spelled correctly, fill in the oval by **no mistake**.

1. ○ knot ○ earth ● brite ○ no mistake
2. ○ sight ○ hatch ● chaulk ○ no mistake
3. ● caut ○ kick ○ sack ○ no mistake
4. ● clothz ○ thumb ○ sandwich ○ no mistake
5. ○ whole ○ teacher ● haf ○ no mistake
6. ○ wrap ● knea ○ ranch ○ no mistake
7. ● negbor ○ sidewalk ○ match ○ no mistake
8. ○ ink ○ wind ○ though ● no mistake
9. ● Wensday ○ scrub ○ scream ○ no mistake

71

1 Dictation

Reinforce correct spelling by using current and previous words in context.

Listen as I read each sentence and then write the missing words and ending punctuation in your worktext. (Slowly read each sentence twice. Sentences are found in the student text to the left.)

2 Proofreading

Familiarize students with standardized test format and reinforce recognizing misspelled words.

Look at each set of words. If a word is misspelled, fill in the oval by that word. If all the words are spelled correctly, fill in the oval by **no mistake**.

3 Hide and Seek

Reinforce correct spelling of current spelling words. (A reproducible master is provided in Appendix A as shown on the inset page to the right.)
Write the words one at a time on the board. Use this activity for each word.

- **Look** at the word.
- **Say** the word out loud.
- Let's **hide** (cover) the word.
- **Write** the word on your paper.
- Let's **seek** (uncover) the word.
- **Check** your spelling. If your word is spelled wrong, write the word correctly next to it.

Lesson 11 — Other Word Forms

Hide and Seek

Check a coin for each word you spell correctly.

Other Word Forms

Suffixes

Choose the correct suffix to make a new word. Write the new word on the line.

1. bright + (est, ing) = brightest
2. catch + (ed, ing) = catching
3. halve + (s, er) = halves
4. sight + (ing, est) = sighting
5. chalk + (ly, y) = chalky
6. clothe + (s, est) = clothes
7. knot + (ty, ly) = knotty
8. wrap + (per, ly) = wrapper

Sentence Fun

Write the word that best completes each sentence.

1. Rosa is good at catching a ball.
2. My little brother gets knots in his shoestrings.
3. This is the brightest color of green I have seen.
4. Stephen likes to shovel snow off the sidewalks.
5. I need to buy more warm clothing for winter.
6. Mom is in her room wrapping gifts.
7. We sighted an eagle flying overhead.
8. When our car broke down, Dad thumbed a ride into town.
9. The people who live next door are kind and neighborly.
10. When we got halfway to school, I remembered my lunch at home.
11. Mom fixed a healthy breakfast of wholesome foods.
12. I was careful not to drop the candy wrapper on the ground.

Word Bank

brightest	clothing	knots	sidewalks	thumbed	wrapper
catching	halfway	neighborly	sighted	wholesome	wrapping

336

4 Other Word Forms

Have your students complete this activity to strengthen spelling ability and expand vocabulary.

1 Posttest

Test mastery of the spelling words.

I will say the word once, use the word in a sentence, then say the word again. Write the word on your paper.

1.	neighbor	Treat your **neighbor** just like you want to be treated.
2.	knot	There was a big **knot** in Tony's stomach after the preview.
3.	half	Tony didn't get **half** the words right.
4.	Wednesday	On **Wednesday** you will play "Hide and Seek" for spelling.
5.	caught	It seemed like Matthew never **caught** the ball.
6.	clothes	Matthew never tore his **clothes** during recess.
7.	sight	Matthew was out of **sight** for most of recess.
8.	sidewalk	They lined up on the **sidewalk** after recess.
9.	though	"I can help you remember those silent letters **though**," said Matthew.
10.	knee	Tony looked down at the tear on the **knee** of his pants.
11.	chalk	"Here is a piece of **chalk**," said Matthew.
12.	wrap	Let's **wrap** up our study time by praying.
13.	whole	Tony only missed one on the **whole** posttest.
14.	thumb	Matthew put his **thumb** up and smiled.
15.	bright	Tony's smile was **bright** and cheerful.

Progress Chart

Students may record scores. (Reproducible master in Appendix B.)

Personal Dictionary

Students may add any words they have misspelled to their personal dictionaries for reference when writing. (Cover in Appendix B.)

I Game Name ____________________

Glue on a piece of the puzzle-picture for each word you or your team spells correctly from this week's word list.

Remember: Use the gifts God has given you to bless someone else.

J Journaling

In your journal, write about how you can use one of your special abilities to help someone you know.

2 Game

Reinforce spelling skills and provide motivation and interest.

Materials

- game page (from student text)
- puzzle pieces (reproducible master in Appendix B, page 357)
- crayons
- scissors (1 per child)
- glue sticks (1 per child)
- game word list

Game Word List

1. bright
2. chalk
3. caught
4. clothes
5. half
6. knee
7. knot
8. neighbor
9. sidewalk
10. sight
11. though
12. thumb
13. Wednesday
14. whole
15. wrap

How to Play:

- Have the students color the puzzle picture, then carefully cut the picture apart along the dotted lines.
- Divide the class into two teams.
- Have a student from team A go to the board.
- Say the spelling word. (You may also wish to use the word in a sentence.)
- Have the student write the word on the board.
- If correct, instruct each member of team A to glue on one piece of his/her puzzle picture. (Note: If the word is misspelled, correct the spelling immediately.)
- Alternate between teams A and B.
- The team to complete its puzzle pictures first is the winner.

Non-Competitive Option:

At the end of the game, say: "Class, I am proud of your efforts to spell the words correctly. If you had fun and tried your best, you are all winners!"

3 Journaling

Provide a meaningful reason for correct spelling through personal writing.

Review the story using discussion leads provided on the following page. Encourage students to apply the Scriptural value in their journaling.

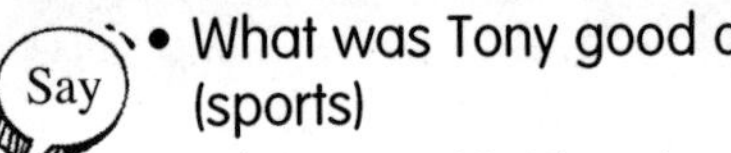

Journaling (continued)

- What was Tony good at? (sports)
- What was Matthew's special ability? (school work)
- How did they use their special abilities to help each other? (Tony helped Matthew in "Capture the Flag," and Matthew helped Tony learn to spell some spelling words.)
- What special abilities do you have? (Write responses on the board.)
- How could you use that ability to help someone else? (Brainstorm. Write responses on the board.)
- Write in your journal about how you can use one of your special abilities to help someone you know.

Take a minute to memorize...
Have the class say the memory verses from lessons 7, 8, 9 ,10, and 11 with you.

Invented spelling may be encouraged in journal writing and when writing first drafts. Spelling can be edited for finished work.

1 **Literature Connection**
Topic: Prayer
Theme Text: 1 Peter 3:12

Far Away Friends

Tommy learns that God is watching us and listening to all our prayers no matter where we are.

"Look at that one." Tommy jabbed his finger at the computer software catalog. "It's a racing program. You can choose what type of race car you want and how big its engine is."

James leaned in for a closer look. "This is awesome! You can even pick the conditions of the track."

Tommy jostled James' shoulder. "Hey, let me see, too!" James grinned as he moved a little and both boys hovered over the catalog.

"'Track conditions include wet, icy, and extreme heat,'" Tommy read aloud. "'For an even greater challenge, select oil and watch out!' Zzzzoooommm!" Tommy sped around his bedroom. "No! I've hit an oil spot!" He skidded back and forth violently. "Cr-r-r-r-a-a-sh!!" He landed in a heap on his bed.

James held his fist to his mouth like a microphone. "Ladies and gentlemen, car number 48, driven by the legendary Tommy Rawson, went out of control on the outside turn and has crashed. We now wait to see if Tommy is all right." Tommy took a few staggering steps. "He's out of the car and he's okay! Veteran Tommy Rawson has survived the third major crash of his career."

Tommy saluted and waved to the imaginary crowd while James clapped and whistled. "How much is that program, anyway?" Tommy plopped back on the floor by the open catalog.

"Probably more than you can come up with." James laughed. "Do you need joysticks to run the program or can you use the keyboard?"

"Hmmm." Tommy ran his finger along the text as he read. "'The keyboard will work to race against the computer, but you have to have joysticks to race against each other.'"

"Is your dad getting joysticks when he orders your new computer?" James turned the page to a whole new group of kid's software ads.

"I don't know." Tommy sighed. "I can't believe we're finally getting a computer. It seems like ages since I broke Daniel's monitor and Dad paid for it. It's taken all this time to save more money for our own computer."

"I bet you'll think twice before you throw a ball in the house again, huh?" James jabbed Tommy in the side.

"You bet!" Tommy held up his right hand. "I solemnly swear to never play ball indoors again! Anyway, now we'll have the computer when it's rainy outside." Tommy grinned. "Let's see if you can spend the night the weekend right after we get the computer, okay?"

"Yes!" James held up his hand for a high five and Tommy slapped it soundly.

"James!" Mrs. Rawson called from downstairs. "Your mother is here."

The boys planned their sleep-over as they headed downstairs. With both talking at the same time, it was hard for Mrs. Rawson and Mrs. Thomason to figure out what they were asking. When they understood, both mothers agreed. Tommy stood at the front door as James climbed into the car. James held his hand up in their special signal. Tommy returned the signal and waved as the Thomason's car drove away.

The next day Tommy bounded out of the car at school. "Bye, Mom!" he called as he rushed away to find James. He didn't even stop at his desk when he entered the room. "Guess what, James?" "Dad said he would order the computer today! And he's going to order that racing program and joysticks! Can you believe it?" Tommy hardly paused for breath. He didn't notice that James was slumped in his chair with a strange expression on his face. "Everything should get here in about two weeks, so you can sleep over on Saturday night about two weeks from now!"

Suddenly Tommy realized James didn't seem very excited. "What's wrong?" he asked.

"I won't be here in two weeks." James rubbed at a scratch mark on the top of his desk. "We're moving. Mom and Dad told me last night."

"Moving!" Tommy sat down hard on the desk next to James. "You can't!"

"Dad's company is transferring him to a new job. It's a better job, so Mom and Dad decided we should go." James' voice sounded flat and strange. "Dad's leaving tomorrow and Mom and I are leaving in three days."

Two days later Tommy sat staring at the peas on his plate. "How'd those get there?" he wondered silently. "I don't even like peas. I must not have been paying attention." He poked the pile with his fork. Shiny round peas tumbled across his plate into his mashed potatoes.

"Something bothering you, Son?" Dad questioned.

"I don't know," Tommy muttered, trying to catch the peas with his fork.

Dad watched him for a moment, then reached over. "Try this." He picked up Tommy's spoon and handed it to him. "I heard James is moving tomorrow?" Tommy nodded and mumbled "yes" around his mouthful of peas.

"You'll miss him." At Dad's quiet comment, tears gathered in Tommy's eyes, making the mountain of peas and mashed potatoes all blurry. All he could do was nod. "You know, Son, sometimes we feel so sad that we can't talk to other people. But God always understands. You can talk to God about how you feel, even when you don't know how to put it into words. God always listens."

James Thomason's last day at Knowlton Elementary School passed

Day 1 Review 12

Story Continued

much too quickly. Mr. Valentino surprised everyone with punch and oatmeal cookies after lunch.

"Well, James," Mr. Valentino waved a half-eaten cookie in the air. "Every time I taste an oatmeal cookie I'll remember they're your favorite."

"Yeah, and we'll all be glad you're not here so someone else gets some!" Daniel teased.

"Seriously, we'll all miss you, James." Mr. Valentino walked over to the cabinet and opened a drawer. "We want you to have something to remember your class by." He took a brightly wrapped package out of the drawer. Everyone watched as James tore the wrapping paper off to find a book about friends.

"Open it!" Kristin urged. "Open it up and look inside!"

Inside the front cover each of James' classmates had written a short message and signed their names.

"Thanks." James' voice sounded a little funny. He swallowed hard and said again, "Thank you all very much."

"Wherever you go, James, the Lord will be watching over you." Mr. Valentino placed his hand on James' shoulder. "We may be far apart, but God is always close to each of us, wherever we are. Remember our text?" He turned and wrote 1 Peter 3:12 on the board as the class repeated it together from memory. "The Lord is watching his children, listening to their prayers."

"Talk to God," Mr. Valentino urged. "God's always there for you."

After school, Tommy walked to James' car with him. The best friends were too choked up to say much, but James gave their special hand signal as the car drove away. Tommy returned it and sniffled loudly as he turned to get into his mom's car.

Tommy was quiet at school. He really missed James. He missed playing at recess with James. He missed talking to James. He missed sending special signals to James. He missed calling James on the phone. He missed looking across the room and knowing what James was thinking. He missed planning things with James. He missed James so much that it hurt. And he talked to God often about it.

He moped around at home, too, finding little that interested him. Mrs. Rawson wondered if he was coming down with something and talked about taking him to Dr. Cribner for a checkup. Mr. Rawson thought the arrival of the new computer would cheer him up. But when the new computer did arrive, it reminded Tommy that James was gone, and he wasn't coming to play the racing program or sleep over. Tommy let Lisa take his turns on the computer. He didn't seem to have any interest in anything.

A few days later Tommy wandered into the kitchen to get a drink. "Tommy!" his dad called from upstairs. Tommy gulped the rest of the water and went to find his dad. He found him seated in front of the glowing screen of the computer in the extra room. "Let me show you something, Son." Dad motioned to him to come closer. "You have an e-mail message."

"A what?" Tommy stared at the screen.

"An e-mail message." Dad chuckled. "You know, like a letter, except sent by computer instead of in the mail. It's from a friend of yours." Dad clicked a button on the keyboard and a note appeared on the screen.

"It's from James!" Tommy settled onto his dad's lap. "How did he know how to e-mail us?"

"I contacted his father and we worked it out." Mr. Rawson smiled as he stood and plopped Tommy into the chair. "I'll leave you alone so you can read your mail. Let me know when you want to write back and I'll show you how to do it." Tommy was totally focused on the screen before Dad even left the room.

"Hey, Tommy." Tommy read James' message aloud. "Isn't this e-mail stuff cool? My dad got a computer for us at home because of his new job. Is the racing program as awesome as it looked in the catalog? Have you crashed yet? Speaking of crashes, we almost did on the way up here. Mom was driving and it was raining really hard. A truck passed us loaded with smashed old cars. All of a sudden one of those smashed cars slid off the top and fell in the road in front of us. Mom has no idea how she missed it. We're all sure it was because God was watching over us."

A few minutes later Tommy bounced down the stairs into the kitchen. "Hey, Dad! Can you show me how to play the racing game? I need to know how it works so I can tell James all about it." His eyes sparkled with excitement. "And will you show me how to e-mail stuff? How often can you e-mail? Does it take very long to get there? How does it work?" He was still asking questions as his dad followed him back upstairs. Dad looked over his shoulder at Mom and winked, and they both smiled.

That night, Tommy snuggled under his covers and pulled the blanket up under his chin. "Thank you, God," he prayed silently. "Thank you for listening to my prayers about how lonely I was without James. Thank you for watching over him on the trip. Thank you for loving me and working everything out."

2 Discussion Time

Check understanding of the story and development of personal values.

- What was Tommy's family about to purchase?
- Why had it taken them so long to be able to buy a computer?
- What kind of software program did James and Tommy really like?
- What did the boys plan to do when the computer arrived?
- Why couldn't James sleep over that night after all?
- How did Tommy feel about James moving away?
- What did Tommy tell God in his prayers?
- Did God listen to Tommy's prayers?
- How did God watch over James?
- What happened that made Tommy feel better?

A Test-Words Name ______________________

Write each spelling word on the line as your teacher says it.

1. spread
2. sight
3. whole
4. crash
5. threw
6. sandwich
7. porch
8. rush
9. husband
10. strange
11. unhappy
12. supper

Review Lesson 12

B Test-Sentences

Write the sentences on the lines below, correcting each misspelled word, as well as all capitalization and punctuation errors. There are two misspelled words in each sentence.

the sidewak on our streat is badly cracked?

1. The sidewalk on our street is badly cracked.

Flip the swich if you need some brite light

2. Flip the switch if you need some bright light.

is your aunte riding with your granmother.

3. Is your aunt riding with your grandmother?

73

3 Test-Words

Test for knowledge of the correct spellings of these words.

I will say the word once, use the word in a sentence, then say the word again. Write the word on the lines in your worktext.

1. spread — The boys **spread** the catalog open on the floor.
2. sight — The **sight** of all the computer games was dazzling.
3. whole — The boys looked through the **whole** catalog together.
4. crash — Tommy and James pretended to **crash** their race cars.
5. threw — Tommy **threw** himself on his bed pretending to crash.
6. sandwich — The boys each ate a **sandwich** at Tommy's kitchen table.
7. porch — Tommy waved good-bye from the front **porch**.
8. rush — Tommy was in a **rush** to tell James about the computer and game.
9. husband — Mrs. Thomason's **husband**, James' dad, has a new job in another state.
10. strange — Tommy's stomach felt **strange** when he heard the news.
11. unhappy — He was very **unhappy** that James was moving.
12. supper — Tommy did not feel like eating any **supper**.

4 Test-Sentences

Reinforce recognizing misspelled words.

Read each sentence carefully. Write the sentences on the lines in your worktext, correcting each misspelled word, as well as all capitalization and punctuation errors. There are two misspelled words in each sentence.

Take a minute to memorize...

Read the memory verse to the class twice. Have the class practice it with you two more times.

Day 2

Review

12

1 Test-Dictation

Reinforce correct spelling by using current and previous words in context.

Listen as I read each sentence. Then write the missing words and ending punctuation in your worktext. (Slowly read each sentence twice. Sentences are found in the student text to the right. The words **ladder**, **scratch**, **sunny**, and **scrub** are found in this unit.)

2 Test-Proofreading

Familiarize students with standardized test format and reinforce recognizing misspelled words.

Look at each set of words. If a word is misspelled, fill in the oval by that word. If all the words are spelled correctly, fill in the oval by **no mistake**.

Review Lesson 12

C Test-Dictation Name ____________

Listen and write the missing words and punctuation.

1. The boys climbed the tall ladder .
2. My cat likes to scratch trees .
3. We play outside when the day is sunny .
4. They will scrub the deck of the big boat .

D Test-Proofreading

If a word is misspelled, fill in the oval by that word. If all the words are spelled correctly, fill in the oval by **no mistake**.

1. ● screem ○ lesson ○ bright ○ no mistake
2. ○ spring ○ husband ○ thumb ● no mistake
3. ○ porch ○ kick ○ straw ● no mistake
4. ○ million ○ knee ● streem ○ no mistake
5. ● suddin ○ classroom ○ fresh ○ no mistake
6. ○ drank ○ front ○ ranch ● no mistake
7. ○ neighbor ● yung ○ threw ○ no mistake
8. ○ chalk ○ ink ● macth ○ no mistake
9. ○ butter ● erth ○ half ○ no mistake

74

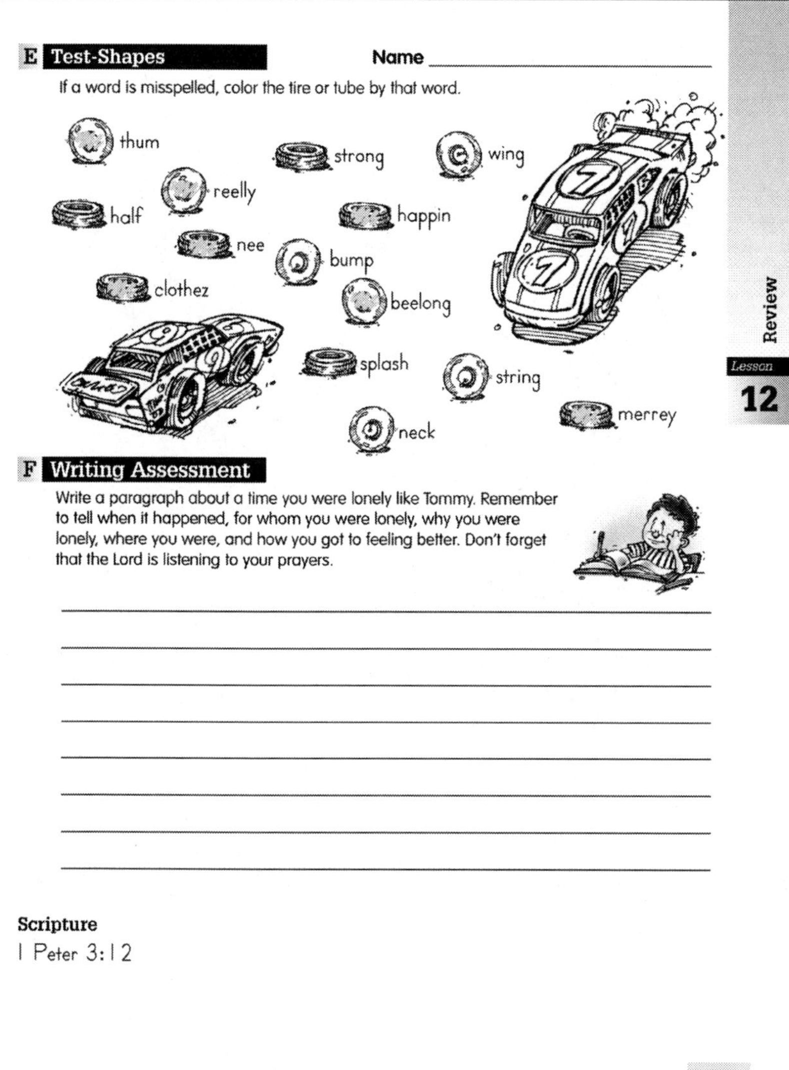

E Test-Shapes

Name ____________

If a word is misspelled, color the tire or tube by that word.

F Writing Assessment

Write a paragraph about a time you were lonely like Tommy. Remember to tell when it happened, for whom you were lonely, why you were lonely, where you were, and how you got to feeling better. Don't forget that the Lord is listening to your prayers.

Scripture

I Peter 3:12

Review Lesson 12

75

You may let parents and others know you are aware of children's invented spelling by stamping papers with "Unedited," "First Draft," "Sloppy Copy," or "Work in Progress."

1 Test-Shapes

Test mastery of words in this unit.

If a word is misspelled, color the object by that word.

2 Writing Assessment

Assess student's spelling, grammar, and composition skills through personal writing.

- Tommy's family was about to get the new computer they'd waited for since Tommy broke the DeVore's expensive monitor. How did Tommy feel about the new computer? (Very excited, glad, happy, etc.)
- Why were Tommy and James planning a sleep-over? (To play the car racing game on the new computer.)
- Why did James' family have to move? (His dad was transferred to a better job.)
- Have you ever had a very close friend that moved away?
- How did you feel?
- What did Mr. Valentino remind the classmates to do? Why? (Talk to God. Because no matter how far apart we are, God is always there.)
- Write a paragraph about a time you were lonely like Tommy. Remember to tell when it happened, for whom you were lonely, why you were lonely, where you were, and how you got to feeling better. Don't forget that the Lord is listening to your prayers.

1 Test-Sentences

Reinforce recognizing misspelled words.

Read each sentence carefully. Write the sentences on the lines in your worktext, correcting each misspelled word, as well as all capitalization and punctuation errors. There are two misspelled words in each sentence.

Review Lesson 12

G Test-Sentences Name ____________

Write the sentences on the lines below, correcting each misspelled word, as well as all capitalization and punctuation errors. There are two misspelled words in each sentence.

Put a stapm on the letter to your granfather

1. Put a stamp on the letter to your grandfather.

they sagn that tune in frunt of their class

2. They sang that tune in front of their class.

Our nayber bought a huge rantch.

3. Our neighbor bought a huge ranch.

H Test-Words

Write each spelling word on the line as your teacher says it.

1. Wednesday
2. ink
3. wrap
4. teacher
5. fresh
6. smell
7. classroom
8. kick
9. lesson
10. chalk
11. address
12. screen

76

2 Test-Words

Test for knowledge of the correct spellings of these words.

I will say the word once, use the word in a sentence, then say the word again. Write the word on the lines in your worktext.

1. Wednesday — **Wednesday** was James' last day at school.
2. ink — The students wrote their names in **ink** inside the book.
3. wrap — Kristin wanted to **wrap** the book for James.
4. teacher — Mr. Valentino is Tommy and James' **teacher**.
5. fresh — He baked **fresh** oatmeal cookies for the class.
6. smell — The **smell** of the cookies made the students feel hungry.
7. classroom — The **classroom** just wasn't the same without James.
8. kick — Tommy did not want to **kick** the ball at recess.
9. lesson — Mr. Valentino quoted the verse from their handwriting **lesson**.
10. chalk — He wrote the verse on the board with **chalk**.
11. address — Tommy's dad got James' e-mail **address**.
12. screen — Tommy was happy to read the message on the computer **screen**.

I **Test-Editing** Name ______________

If a word is spelled correctly, fill in the oval under **Correct**. If the word is misspelled, fill in the oval under **Incorrect**, and spell the word correctly on the blank.

	Correct	Incorrect	
1. skrap	○	●	scrap
2. straight	●	○	
3. buter	○	●	butter
4. milloin	○	●	million
5. rubber	●	○	
6. behind	●	○	
7. wind	●	○	
8. hach	○	●	hatch
9. sak	○	●	sack
10. caut	○	●	caught
11. knot	●	○	
12. tho	○	●	though

Review Lesson 12

77

3 Test-Editing

Reinforce recognizing and correcting misspelled words.

4 Action Game

Reinforce spelling skills and provide motivation and interest.

Materials

- one ***A Reason For Spelling***® book
- a bell (optional)
- small prizes (erasers, pencils, stickers)

How to Play:

- Seat the children in a circle.
- Give one student the ***A Reason For Spelling***® book.
- Have the students pass the book around the circle.
- When the teacher rings the bell (or says "stop"), have the child holding the book spell a word tested on days 1 through 4.
- If he spells it incorrectly, he remains in the circle; if he spells it correctly, he receives a prize and drops out of the game.
- Continue the game until every student has spelled a word correctly.

1 Game

Reinforce spelling skills and provide motivation and interest.

Materials

- game page (from student text)
- flat buttons, dry beans, pennies, or game discs (1 per child)
- game word list

Game Word List

Check off each word lightly in pencil as it is used.

Red (5 points)

1. neck
2. half
3. clothes
4. strong
5. merry
6. really
7. belong
8. bump
9. wing
10. string
11. splash

Blue (10 points)

1. scream
2. spring
3. straw
4. stream
5. sudden
6. drank
7. young
8. match
9. earth
10. thumb
11. knee

Yellow (15 points)

1. merrily
2. happiness
3. smelly
4. kicked
5. hatches
6. halfway
7. brightest
8. splashing
9. wholesome
10. sighted
11. teach

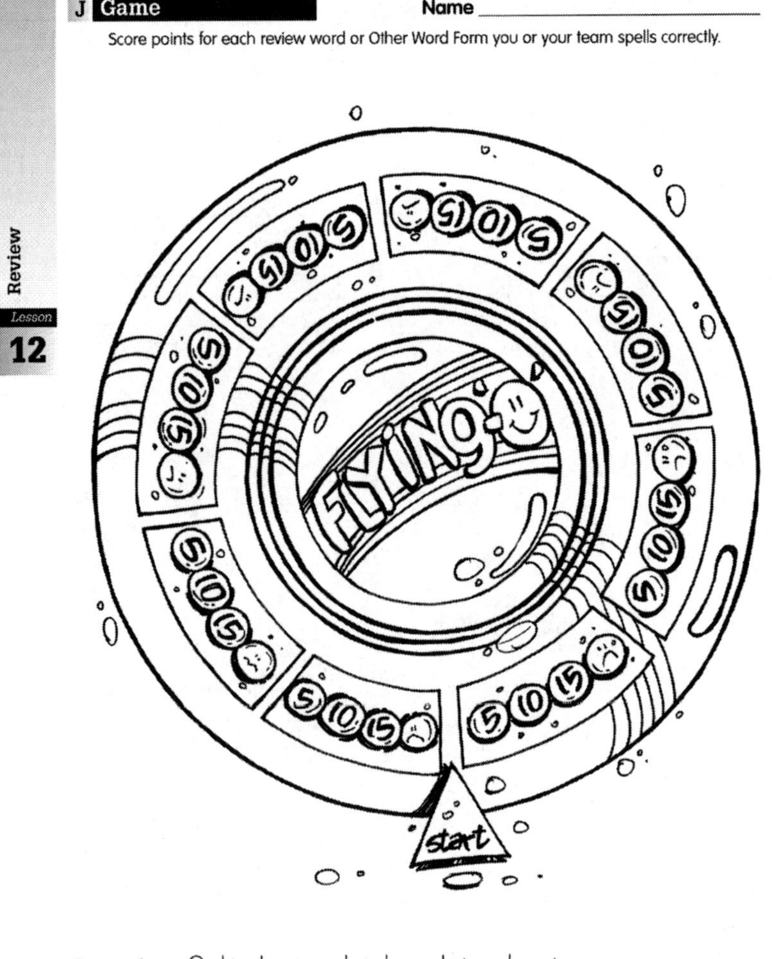
J Game
Name
Score points for each review word or Other Word Form you or your team spells correctly.
Review
Lesson
12
FLYING
start
Remember: God is always ready to hear what you have to say.

78

How to Play:

- Divide the class into two teams.
- Have each student place his/her game piece on Start.
- Inform the students of the following point system:
  Red list words = **5** points, **Blue** list words = **10** points
  Yellow list words = **15** points (these are Other Word Forms)
- Have a student from team A choose a color: red, blue, or yellow.
- Say a word from the correct color list. (You may also wish to use the word in a sentence.)
- Have the student write the word on the board.
- If correct, ask each member of team A to move his/her game piece forward (to the right and up, counter clockwise) to the corresponding color in the first section. Record the score. If the word is misspelled, have each member of that team move his/her game piece to the "sad face" in the first section.
- Alternate between teams A and B.
- The team with the highest score at the end of three rounds is the winner. (A round begins and ends at Start.)

Non-Competitive Option:

At the end of the game, say: "Class, I am proud of your efforts to spell the words correctly. If you had fun and tried your best, you are all winners!"

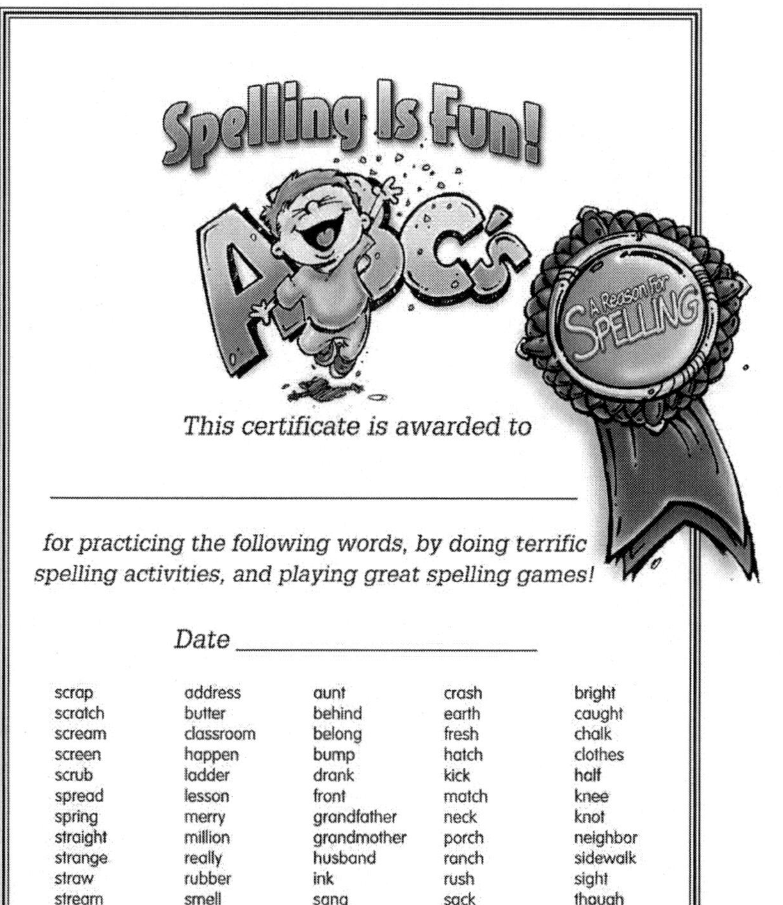

Spelling Is Fun!

ABC's

A Reason For SPELLING

This certificate is awarded to

____

for practicing the following words, by doing terrific spelling activities, and playing great spelling games!

Date ______________________

scrap	address	aunt	crash	bright
scratch	butter	behind	earth	caught
scream	classroom	belong	fresh	chalk
screen	happen	bump	hatch	clothes
scrub	ladder	drank	kick	half
spread	lesson	front	match	knee
spring	merry	grandfather	neck	knot
straight	million	grandmother	porch	neighbor
strange	really	husband	ranch	sidewalk
straw	rubber	ink	rush	sight
stream	smell	sang	sack	though
street	sudden	stamp	sandwich	thumb
string	sunny	wind	splash	Wednesday
strong	supper	wing	switch	whole
threw	unhappy	young	teacher	wrap

2 Certificate

Provide an opportunity for parents or guardians to encourage and assess their child's progress.

- Write your name on the first line.
- Write the date on the next line.
- Be sure to show your parents or guardian all the words you've practiced spelling.

Take a minute to memorize...
Have the class say the memory verses from lessons 7, 8, 9 ,10, 11, and 12 with you.

Day 5

Review 12

3 Letter

Provide the parent or guardian with the spelling word lists for the next unit.

Show your parents or guardian this letter that lists your spelling words for the next unit. Put it where you will remember to practice the words together.

Dear Parent,

We are about to begin a new spelling unit containing five weekly lessons. A set of fifteen words will be studied each week. All the words will be reviewed in the sixth week. Values based on the Scriptures listed below will be taught in each lesson.

Lesson 13	Lesson 14	Lesson 15	Lesson 16	Lesson 17
angel	asleep	careful	afraid	angry
cage	boss	copy	awake	busy
edge	certain	cover	date	carry
giraffe	circus	fork	eight	creek
huge	gas	kept	lady	deep
January	less	key	lay	February
jar	pass	October	made	field
jealous	race	queen	mail	heavy
jolly	save	quick	paper	honey
judge	sell	quiet	plane	leave
jug	seventh	quilt	sail	marry
juice	since	quite	shade	meal
July	soap	rack	table	mean
June	sorry	rake	wait	team
rage	sweet	track	weigh	twenty
1 Peter 3:4	1 Peter 3:8	1 John 1:7	1 Peter 3:9	Ephesians 3:17

1 **Literature Connection**
Topic: Being beautiful inside
Theme Text: 1 Peter 3:4

Beautiful Inside

At the nursing home, Rosa learns that how people look on the outside doesn't show what they're really like on the inside.

"The nursing home again?" Christopher Wright's eyebrows rose. "Those old people are. . .well, kinda creepy." He shrugged his shoulders.

"It's true that some of them are a little confused because of their age, but they're all people, just like us." Mr. Valentino rested his hand on Christopher's shoulder. "They can't do as much as they used to do and they can't go places, so we go to them! Now, let's make plans for our visit." He noticed Beth's hand waving to get his attention. "Question, Beth?"

"Are we going to make something to give them?" Beth brushed her blond hair behind her ear.

"Good point, Beth!" Mr. Valentino grabbed something off his desk and walked briskly over to a window. "We're going to design sun-catchers." He held up a rainbow made of brightly-colored transparent beads. Sunlight streaming through the window was split by the beads and shot colorful beams of light through the room.

"Oooh, that's beautiful!" Kristin exclaimed. "Are they hard to make? Can we make more than one?"

"Not very, and maybe." Mr. Valentino answered both Kristin's questions in one breath. "We'll have a short program, then visit with the people and give them the sun-catchers." Mr. Valentino turned to the board and wrote GROUP SONGS.

"Setsuko, will you play a piece on your violin?"

"Okay." Setsuko nodded shyly, and Mr. Valentino wrote VIOLIN SOLO on the board, followed by RECITE SCRIPTURES.

"We'll divide into groups to share some of the Scriptures we've learned," he explained. "Rosa, will you play a piano piece?"

"Uh, I guess so." As Rosa heard the words coming out of her own mouth, she cringed. "Why did I agree?" she thought. "I hate playing in front of a group!" Rosa had struggled to perform her piece at the piano recital last school year, but that was something she'd had to do. It was required when you took piano lessons from Mrs. Winston. She didn't have to do this, though, and she started to raise her hand to tell Mr. Valentino she'd changed her mind.

"This is great!" Her teacher slapped his hands together and stepped back to look at the list on the board. "I think our friends at the nursing home will enjoy this program a lot." Rosa dropped her hand back onto her lap and sighed.

"Okay, everyone, clear your desks," Mr. Valentino continued. "Stephen, please take this box and give each person a packet of red beads. Matthew, you may pass out the orange beads."

"Oh, well," Rosa muttered to herself as she crammed her notebook into her desk. "Most of those people can't hear very well, so maybe they won't care how I play!"

Later that evening Rosa lined up glasses in the dishwasher. "Dad, Mr. Valentino asked me to play a piano piece at the nursing home. What song do you think I should play?"

Mr. Vasquez swished a blue plate under the running water in the kitchen sink and handed it to Rosa. "Maybe one of those hymns you played last year. People often enjoy music more if they recognize it. If you play a familiar song, they can hum along or even think of the words."

"I think that book is in the piano bench." Rosa slid the last plate into the dishwasher. "I'll go see if I can still play any of those hymns."

Chipper, the chickaree, scurried up to perch on Rosa's shoulder as she began practicing. "One, two, three, four. One, two, three, four. One, two, Oops!" CRASH!! Rosa banged both hands onto the piano keyboard and a terrified Chipper took a flying leap to a nearby chair. "I'll never get this part right!" Rosa complained to the squirrel who had taken cover behind a throw pillow. Chipper peered through the tassel as Rosa started over again. "One, two, three, four."

When the vans pulled into the parking area at Pleasant Valley Retirement Center, Rosa was feeling a bit nervous. She clutched her piano book and filed into the building with her classmates. "Phew!" Christopher whispered. "It smells weird in here."

"You mean it stinks." Daniel held his nose as the students waited near the door while their teacher talked with the lady in charge. "Look at that man's hair. It's sticking straight up. And he doesn't have any teeth."

"Well, that lady's wearing a dress-up hat with pajamas." Rachel giggled.

"Ooh, and look at that lady." Kristin nudged Rosa with her elbow and nodded at an elderly lady in a wheelchair. The girls stared as an attendant pushed the lady down the hall to the meeting room. "I wonder what happened to her." Kristin shuddered. The lady looked normal on one side. But that made the other side seem even worse. Reddish purple scars covered the right side of her face and neck. The scars pulled her mouth into a twisted smile, and her eye drooped so much it was almost closed. Her right hand lay twisted in her lap, with angry-looking scars disappearing under her sleeve.

"She's enough to scare anyone," Rosa thought.

"Okay, gang." Mr. Valentino returned to the

Story (continued)

group of children. "Everybody ready? Have you all got your sun-catchers? Do you remember the order of the program?" He grinned. "Let's go share a little sunshine and happiness today. We're on!"

Mr. Valentino greeted the large group of elderly people gathered in the meeting room. As the children sang the first few songs, Rosa noticed many in the audience smiling and nodding. They clapped delightedly after each song. "I guess they really do enjoy having us here," Rosa thought. As they sang the next song, her gaze wandered around the room. She noticed the lady with the scars sitting quietly over to one side of the room. Although it was hard to tell if she was smiling, Rosa saw the fingers of her left hand tapping gently on the armrest of the wheelchair in time with the music.

Soon it was Rosa's turn. Her palms felt damp, and her stomach sick. Her breath came faster, and her head seemed to spin. She straightened her book on the piano, found the right keys, and with a deep breath began: "One, two, three, four." She counted in her head. "One, two, three, four." She was getting close to the hard spot in the piece. "One, two, Oops! Oh no, I messed up!" Rosa's face burned as she frantically found the right notes and continued the song. Finally it was over and Rosa scurried back to her place in the group. "I should have chosen a song no one knew," Rosa thought as she tried to hide behind Rachel. "Then no one would know for sure that I goofed."

After another group song, the children scattered around the room visiting with people. Rosa looked around for someone to give her sun-catcher to. Christopher looked a little uncomfortable as the lady he was talking to kept patting his head. Daniel stood back a couple of feet from a man who called him "laddie" in a very loud voice. Tommy laughed with a small man whose back was bent practically double. "Tommy knows how to talk to older people," Rosa muttered as she laid her music book down on the piano bench. "It must be because his grandma lives with him."

Then Rosa noticed no one was visiting the lady with the scars. She took a deep breath and walked across the room to stand in front of the lady's wheelchair. "Hi." Her voice sounded a little squeaky. "Uh, I'm Rosa Vasquez."

"Hello, dear." The lady's voice was quiet and gentle. "I'm Bessie Harper and I'm very pleased to meet you." She held out her left hand and Rosa awkwardly took it in her right hand. Bessie's skin felt cool, smooth, and extremely fragile. "Rosa," Mrs. Harper continued in her soft voice, "I want you to know how very much I enjoyed the hymn you played for us today. It has always been one of my favorites and now means more to me than ever. Thank you, Dear." The left side of Mrs. Harper's mouth curved into a smile and her left eye twinkled. Rosa smiled as Bessie squeezed her hand gently, and they began to visit.

As Mr. Valentino's class gathered at the front of the room again, Kristin slipped in beside Rosa. "I saw you talking to that lady with all the ugly scars. What's wrong with her, anyway?"

"Nothing," Rosa answered simply. "Her name's Bessie. Bessie Harper. She was a concert pianist and has performed all over the place, even in other countries. She's a really neat lady, Kristin. So nice! You should hear all the stuff that's happened in her life."

"But why does she have all those scars?" Kristin demanded as Mr. Valentino looked their way with a frown.

"Plane crash," Rosa whispered just as Beth's mom played the introduction to the last song of the program. "There is sunshine in my soul today," Rosa sang happily along with the group. "Oh, there's sunshine, blessed sunshine, when the peaceful, happy moments roll; When Jesus shows His smiling face, there is sunshine in my soul."

"We came to share sunshine and happiness with these people and they've shared sunshine and happiness with us as well," Rosa thought.

To end the program, the class repeated a final Scripture. "Be beautiful on the inside, in your hearts, with the lasting charm of a gentle and quiet spirit which is so precious to God." As Rosa said the words along with her classmates, she looked across the room at Bessie Harper. Sunlight spilling through the window highlighted those awful scars, but Rosa didn't notice them anymore. She realized Bessie was a beautiful person, truly beautiful on the inside, where it counts. When Mr. Valentino asked everyone to bow their heads for closing prayer, Rosa added her own silent prayer. "God, help me be a truly beautiful person inside—like Bessie."

2 Discussion Time

Check understanding of the story and development of personal values.

- Where was Mr. Valentino's class going?
- What did Mr. Valentino ask Rosa to do?
- What kind of song did Rosa choose to play and why?
- What did the students make to take to Pleasant Valley Nursing Home?
- Why did Rosa and Kristin notice the lady in the wheelchair?
- Did Rosa's piano piece go well?
- What had happened to the lady with all the scars?
- Where does I Peter 3:4 say that it is important to be beautiful?
- Think about it; are you truly beautiful where it counts, on the inside?

A **Preview** Name ______

Write each word as your teacher says it.

1. jar
2. edge
3. juice
4. huge
5. January
6. July
7. cage
8. jolly
9. giraffe
10. rage
11. June
12. angel
13. jug
14. jealous
15. judge

Words with /j/

Lesson 13

Scripture

I Peter 3:4

81

3 Preview

Test for knowledge of the correct spellings of these words.

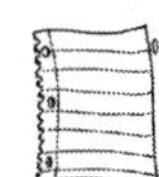

Customize Your List
On a separate piece of paper, additional words of your choice may be tested.

I will say the word once, use the word in a sentence, then say the word again. Write the word on the lines in the worktext.

Correct Immediately!
Let's correct our preview.

I will write each word on the board. Put a dot under each letter on your preview as I spell the word out loud. If you spelled a word wrong, rewrite it correctly.

Take a minute to memorize...
Read the memory verse to the class twice. Have the class practice it with you two more times.

Day 1

Lesson 13

1. jar — Did Stephen spill the **jar** of orange beads?
2. edge — One **edge** of the rainbow is red.
3. juice — Rosa put the **juice** glasses into the dishwasher one at a time.
4. huge — She thought agreeing to play a piano piece was a **huge** mistake.
5. January — **January** is one of the coldest months of the year.
6. July — Rosa's class brought a little **July** sunshine to the nursing home.
7. cage — Being indoors all the time is too much like being in a **cage**.
8. jolly — Many of the older people felt more **jolly** after their visit.
9. giraffe — One man who was tall and thin reminded Rosa of a **giraffe**.
10. rage — Another man frowned all the time as if he were in a **rage**.
11. June — That lady's first name is **June**.
12. angel — The children sang a song about an **angel**.
13. jug — The **jug** of apple juice is almost empty.
14. jealous — We shouldn't be **jealous** of the things other people can do well.
15. judge — Never **judge** people by what they look like.

Progress Chart
Students may record scores. (Reproducible master in Appendix B.)

4 Word Shapes

Help students form a correct image of whole words.

Look at each word and think about its shape. Now, write the word in the correct word shape boxes. You may check off each word as you use it.

(In many words, the sound of **/j/** is spelled with **j**, and it is often spelled this way when it is at the beginning of a word. The **/j/** sound can also be spelled with **g** when followed by **i**, **y**, or **e**. The spelling **dge** is only used at the end of a word.)

In the word shape boxes, color the letter or letters that spell the sound of **/j/** in each word. Circle the words in which **/j/** is spelled **dg**.

Words with /j/

Lesson 13

B Word Shapes Name ____________________

Write each word in the correct word shape boxes. Next, in the word shape boxes, color the letter or letters that spell the sound of **/j/** in each word. Circle the words in which **/j/** is spelled **dg**.

1. angel
2. cage
3. edge
4. giraffe
5. huge
6. January
7. jar
8. jealous
9. jolly
10. judge
11. jug
12. juice
13. July
14. June
15. rage

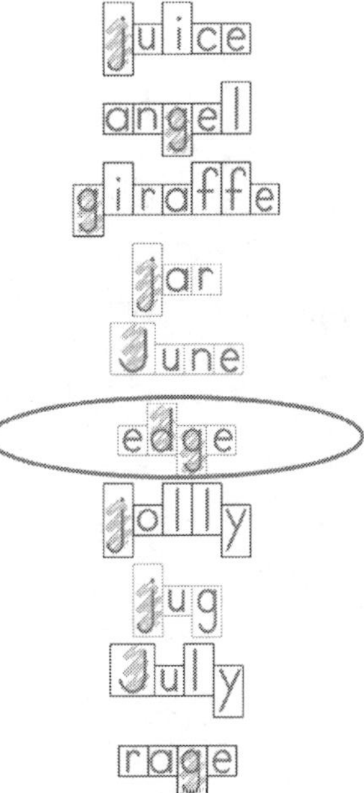

82

Answers may vary for duplicate word shapes.

Be Prepared For Fun

Check these supply lists for **Fun Ways to Spell** presented **Day 2**. Purchase and/or gather needed items ahead of time!

General
- Pencil
- 3 x 5 Cards (15 per child)
- Scissors
- Spelling List

Auditory
- Rhythm Instruments (two wooden spoons, two pan lids, maracas)
- Spelling List

Visual
- Letter Stencils
- Colored Pencils
- Art Paper (2 sheets per child)
- Spelling List

Tactile
- Play Dough
- Spelling List

C Hide and Seek

Name ____________________

Place an **X** on a coin for each word you spell correctly.

D Other Word Forms

Using the words below, follow the instructions given by your teacher.

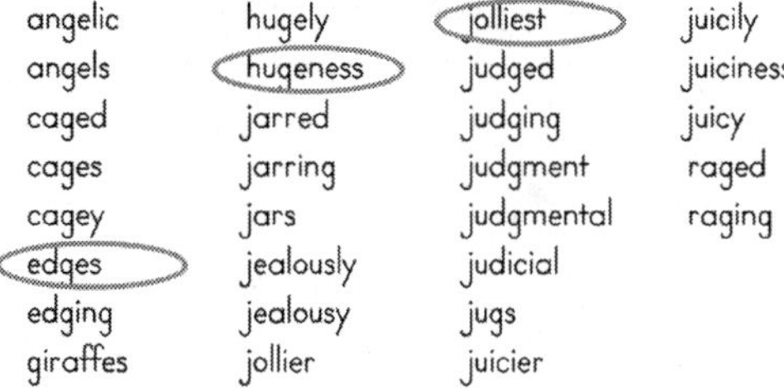

angelic	hugely	jolliest	juicily
angels	hugeness	judged	juiciness
caged	jarred	judging	juicy
cages	jarring	judgment	raged
cagey	jars	judgmental	raging
edges	jealously	judicial	
edging	jealousy	jugs	
giraffes	jollier	juicier	

E Fun Ways to Spell

Initial the box of each activity you finish.

1. 

Spell your words with puzzles.

3. 

Spell your words in rhythm.

2. 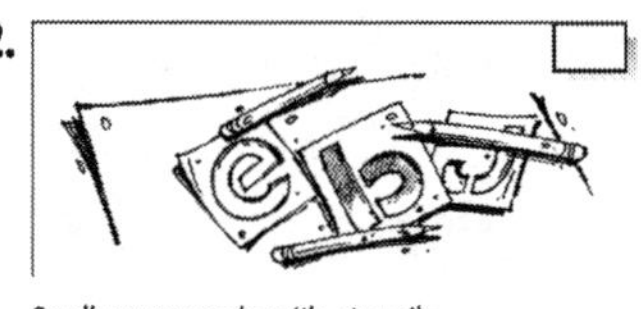

Spell your words with stencils.

4. 

Spell your words with play dough.

Words with /j/

Lesson 13

1 Hide and Seek

Reinforce correct spelling of current spelling words.

Write the words one at a time on the board. Use this activity for each word.

- **Look** at the word.
- **Say** the word out loud.
- Let's **hide** (cover) the word.
- **Write** the word on your paper.
- Let's **seek** (uncover) the word.
- **Check** your spelling. If your word is spelled wrong, write the word correctly next to it.

Day 2

Lesson 13

2 Other Word Forms

This activity is optional. Have students find and circle the Other Word Forms that are antonyms of the following:

smallness
saddest
middles

3 Fun Ways to Spell

Four activities are provided. Use one, two, three, or all of the activities. Have students initial the box for each activity they complete.

Options:

- assign activities to students according to their learning styles
- set up the activities in learning centers for the class to do throughout the day
- divide the class into four groups and assign one activity per group
- do one activity per day

General

To spell your words with puzzles...
- Write each word on a card.
- Cut each card into thirds using a straight cut.
- Mix your puzzle pieces.
- Put the puzzles together.
- Check your spelling.

Auditory

To spell your words in rhythm...
- Look at a word on your spelling list.
- Close your eyes.
- Play your rhythm instruments softly while you whisper the spelling of the word.
- Open your eyes and check your spelling.

Visual

To spell your words with stencils...
- Trace the outline of each letter of the spelling word.
- Color in the letters.

Tactile

To spell your words with play dough...
- Roll pieces of play dough into ropes.
- Use the ropes to make the letters of each word.
- Put them in the right order to spell each word.
- Check your spelling.

1 Working with Words

Familiarize students with word meaning and usage.

Rhyming Words

Say the words **moon** and **tune**. Ask students if these words rhyme. Write the words on the board. Explain to the students that although the words are spelled differently, they still rhyme because **oo** and **u-e** are both ways to spell the sound of **/ü/**.

Write the spelling word that rhymes with the given word. Remember a word may rhyme even when the spelling is different.

Clues

Read each clue. Find the spelling word that matches and write it on the line.

Dictionary Skills

Write the spelling word that would be the entry word for each definition.

Take a minute to memorize...

Read the memory verse to the class twice. Have the class practice it with you two more times.

Words with /j/ — Lesson 13

F Working with Words Name ____________

Rhyming Words

Write the spelling word or words that rhyme with the words below.

stage	holly	soon
1. cage	2. jolly	3. June
fudge	zealous	shrug
4. judge	5. jealous	6. jug
ledge	far	loose
7. edge	8. jar	9. juice

Clues

Write the spelling word that matches each clue.

1. first month — January
2. an African mammal — giraffe
3. seventh month — July
4. sixth month — June
5. envious — jealous
6. a small pitcher — jug
7. liquid from a fruit — juice
8. a heavenly messenger — angel
9. very large — huge
10. place for an animal — cage
11. a glass container — jar
12. full of high spirits — jolly
13. a public official — judge
14. violent anger — rage

Dictionary Skills

A dictionary entry word is followed by a definition. A definition tells what the word means. Write the spelling word that would be the entry word for each definition below.

1. cage — a container made of wires in which animals are kept
2. edge — the sharp side of a cutting tool

Word Bank

angel	giraffe	jar	judge	July
cage	huge	jealous	jug	June
edge	January	jolly	juice	rage

84

G Dictation

Name ____________________

Listen and write the missing words and punctuation.

1. Mom got out a jug of orange juice .

2. Rosa made a sun-catcher of a jolly giraffe .

3. Rosa learned not to judge people by how they look .

Words with /j/

Lesson 13

H Proofreading

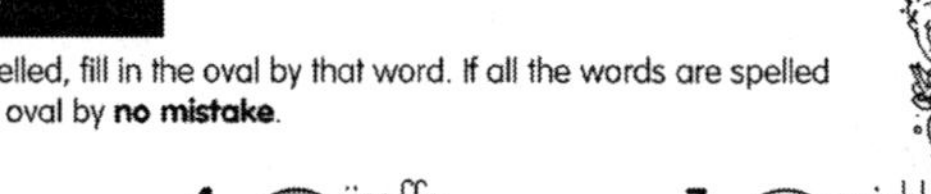

If a word is misspelled, fill in the oval by that word. If all the words are spelled correctly, fill in the oval by **no mistake**.

1. ○ huge ● aengle ○ bright ○ no mistake
2. ○ half ○ chalk ● caje ○ no mistake
3. ● edg ○ jar ○ jolly ○ no mistake
4. ● jiraffe ○ caught ○ clothes ○ no mistake
5. ○ jug ○ knee ● Janary ○ no mistake
6. ○ Wednesday ○ June ● jelous ○ no mistake
7. ○ neighbor ○ rage ● juge ○ no mistake
8. ● juce ○ neck ○ splash ○ no mistake
9. ○ knot ○ rush ● july ○ no mistake

85

1 Dictation

Reinforce correct spelling by using current and previous words in context.

Listen as I read each sentence and then write the missing words and ending punctuation in your worktext. (Slowly read each sentence twice. Sentences are found in the student text to the left.)

2 Proofreading

Familiarize students with standardized test format and reinforce recognizing misspelled words.

Look at each set of words. If a word is misspelled, fill in the oval by that word. If all the words are spelled correctly, fill in the oval by **no mistake**.

Day 4 / Day 5

Lesson 13

3 Hide and Seek

Reinforce correct spelling of current spelling words. (A reproducible master is provided in Appendix A as shown on the inset page to the right.)

Write the words one at a time on the board. Use this activity for each word.

- **Look** at the word.
- **Say** the word out loud.
- Let's **hide** (cover) the word.
- **Write** the word on your paper.
- Let's **seek** (uncover) the word.
- **Check** your spelling. If your word is spelled wrong, write the word correctly next to it.

4 Other Word Forms

Have your students complete this activity to strengthen spelling ability and expand vocabulary.

Hide and Seek

Check a coin for each word you spell correctly.

Other Word Forms

Suffixes

Choose the correct suffix to make a new word. Write the new word on the line.

1. cage + (ly,y) = cagey
2. jolly – y + (ier, en) = jollier
3. jar + (red, y) = jarred
4. angel + (es, s) = angels
5. edge + (s, en) = edges
6. huge + (ier, ness) = hugeness
7. rage + (d, ly) = raged
8. juice – e + (en, ier) = juicier
9. judge – e + (ing, er) = judging
10. jealous + (er, ly) = jealously

Hidden Words

Use the word bank to help you find and circle each of the words in the puzzle.

e	d	g	i	n	g	j	u	d	g	i	n	g
j	j	e	a	l	o	u	s	y	j	g	u	i
o	a	c	j	g	u	d	j	g	h	u	g	r
l	r	a	g	i	n	g	u	j	u	d	j	a
l	r	g	u	n	j	m	j	u	g	g	u	f
i	i	e	j	g	u	e	u	j	e	a	i	f
e	n	s	e	j	a	n	g	e	l	i	c	e
r	g	u	g	r	j	t	s	g	y	c	y	s

Word Bank

angelic, edging, hugely, jealousy, judging, jugs, raging, cages, giraffes, jarring, jollier, judgment, juicy

Other Word Forms

Lesson 13

337

1 Posttest

Test mastery of the spelling words.

I will say the word once, use the word in a sentence, then say the word again. Write the word on your paper.

1. June	There is no school in **June.**
2. July	Do you like to watch fireworks on the Fourth of **July**?
3. January	Mr. Valentino's class visited the nursing home in **January.**
4. jar	Stephen passed out orange beads from a big **jar** full of them.
5. giraffe	Rosa arranged her orange and yellow beads into the shape of a **giraffe.**
6. rage	When Rosa messed up, she banged the piano keys in **rage.**
7. cage	Chipper and Nipper didn't live in a **cage.**
8. jealous	Rosa was a little **jealous** of Tommy's ability to talk to older people.
9. jolly	The **jolly** man Daniel spoke to called him "laddie."
10. edge	Rosa sat nervously on the **edge** of the piano bench.
11. angel	There's an **angel** watching out for you.
12. juice	The children passed a glass of fruit **juice** to each person.
13. jug	A nurses aide filled each glass from a large **jug.**
14. huge	One lady had **huge** reddish–purple scars covering one side of her face.
15. judge	Rosa learned that you can't **judge** people by what they look like.

Progress Chart

Students may record scores. (Reproducible master in Appendix B.)

Personal Dictionary

Students may add any words they have misspelled to their personal dictionaries for reference when writing. (Cover in Appendix B.)

Words with /j/

Lesson 13

I Game Name ______________________

Mr. Valentino's class is visiting the people who live at the Pleasant Valley Retirement Home. Lead the way by moving one space for each word you or your team spells correctly from this week's word list.

Remember: God looks inside you to see who you really are.

J Journaling

In your journal, list as many character traits as you can think of that help to make a person beautiful inside. Circle a character trait that a friend has and write about how you see that good trait in his or her life.

86

2 Game

Reinforce spelling skills and provide motivation and interest.

Materials

- game page (from student text)
- flat buttons, dry beans, pennies, or game discs (1 per child)
- game word list

Game Word List

1. angel
2. cage
3. edge
4. giraffe
5. huge
6. January
7. jar
8. jealous
9. jolly
10. judge
11. jug
12. juice
13. July
14. June
15. rage

Day 5

Lesson 13

How to Play:

- Divide the class into two teams.
- Have each student place his/her game piece on Start.
- Have a student from team A go to the board.
- Say the spelling word. (You may also wish to use the word in a sentence.)
- Have the student write the word on the board.
- If correct, instruct each member of team A to move his/her game piece forward one space on the game board. (Note: If the word is misspelled, correct the spelling immediately.)
- Alternate between teams A and B.
- The team to reach the Pleasant Valley Retirement Home residents first is the winner.

Non-Competitive Option:

At the end of the game, say: "Class, I am proud of your efforts to spell the words correctly. If you had fun and tried your best, you are all winners!"

3 Journaling

Provide a meaningful reason for correct spelling through personal writing.

Review the story using discussion leads provided on the following page. Encourage students to apply the Scriptural value in their journaling.

Journaling (continued)

- Why do you think some of Rosa's classmates weren't very excited about going to the nursing home? (We are sometimes uncomfortable around people that look different.)
- How do you feel about visiting the people in a nursing home?
- Have you ever had a classmate that looked or acted different?
- How did your class treat that person? How did you treat him or her?
- Why was Rosa a little afraid to talk to Bessie Harper? (She looked different. She had large reddish-purple scars covering the right side of her face and neck. Her right hand was scarred and crippled as well.)
- What did Rosa discover about Bessie? (That she'd been a concert pianist. That she was a very interesting and nice lady.)
- What lesson did Rosa learn? (That you can't tell what people are like from their appearance.)
- What kind of character makes a person beautiful inside? (Character that is unselfish, patient, helpful, joyful, thoughtful, obedient, etc.)
- In your journal, list as many character traits as you can think of that help to make a person beautiful inside. Circle a character trait that a friend has, and write about how you see that good trait in his/her life.

Take a minute to memorize...
Have the class say the memory verse with you once.

Reading children's writing and letting them know what you think helps them learn how words are spelled.

1

Literature Connection

Topic: Loving others
Theme Text: 1 Peter 3:8

The Nicest Notes

Mr. Valentino helps his class see the good things in each other.

Mr. Valentino sat on the big table at the back of the classroom Tuesday morning, watching and listening as his students arrived. He heard Tony tell Stephen that his dad was going to take him to the mall after school. "But he'll probably call with some excuse about having to take his wife Merilee somewhere," Tony added as he plopped down at his desk, "or maybe his boss will make him work late again."

Stephen patted his friend's shoulder. "Well, I know he's done that before, but that doesn't mean it will happen again this time."

Icy rain slashed the windows behind Mr. Valentino. Cold air hit his feet as the classroom door opened and Beth and Katelynn hurried in. Beth hung up her coat and put her gloves on the shelf.

"Morning Beth!" Katelynn hung up her coat beside Beth's and followed her friend toward their desks. "Let's go over to my house after school today. I got some new clothes for my doll, Katie. My mom said she would take you home."

"Well, I don't know. My grandma is sick." Beth looked down. "We stopped at her house on the way to school this morning to check on her. Mom asked Mrs. Potter to stay with her all day in case she needed anything. I'm worried about Gram. She misses Grandpa so much since he died last year."

As Mr. Valentino continued to watch, Rachel followed Matthew into the classroom. Rachel's nose was red, her eyes swollen from crying. "What's wrong, Rache?" Matthew asked.

"Helen is tired all the time, now! She stays in bed a lot and keeps throwing up. She acts a lot like my Mommy did before she died of cancer."

Rachel wiped her eyes with the back of her hand. "I don't want her to have a new baby anymore. We can't even agree on a name!"

Mr. Valentino missed Matthew's reply because Daniel burst through the open door and stomped over to where Stephen and Tony were talking. "So, what's your problem today, Tony?" Daniel leaned against Tony's desk until it tipped sideways. Tony's books slid off and hit the floor with a crash.

"You're the problem!" Tony yelled in Daniel's face, and shoved him. Daniel tripped and landed on the floor, dropping his folder. Papers flew all around Tony's desk.

"These kids are so young, but they already have a lot of pain and sadness in their lives," Mr. Valentino thought as he got up to intervene. He glanced out the window and shivered as a gust of wind pinged ice crystals against the cold glass. Then he went quickly to where Daniel was sputtering on the floor.

"Tony pushed me down for no reason," Daniel complained.

"I see," Mr. Valentino said. "And did Tony throw his books on the floor first, Daniel?" He paused. "Are you certain that's how it happened?"

Daniel looked down, then quickly changed the subject. "I want to play basketball for recess today! We haven't played basketball for a long time."

"Let's play bombardment," Tony started stuffing books back into his desk. "That's a lot of fun."

The other children quickly gathered around and joined the discussion. Rosa wanted to play four-square, but Kristin wanted dodgeball. Tommy and Matthew insisted on "capture the flag." "No, let's play dare base!" Christopher countered. "We haven't played that in a long time."

"Can't we just have free time?" Sarah almost whispered. Setsuko stood behind her and nodded in agreement.

Just then the bell rang ending the lively discussion. The children made their way to their seats, and Daniel headed back toward the door to hang up his coat.

Mr. Valentino looked out at the playground, now covered with frozen rain and little crystals of ice. "Lord, please help me today," he prayed quietly as he walked to the front of the room. He looked at the story he'd chosen to help open a discussion on cultural differences, and to get Rachel to talk about her feelings about the new baby coming to her family. The story was about a happy African family that had just had a new baby.

He glanced at the Scripture verse he'd written on the board in spelling class the day before. "You should be like one big happy family, full of sympathy toward each other, loving one another with tender hearts and humble minds."

Then he thought about the conversations he'd overheard as his students were coming into the classroom. Somehow the sunny, warm African story didn't seem to fit in with the weather outside or the mood of his class. "This room is going to erupt with anger and frustration soon if I don't do something to defuse it," he thought.

Suddenly an idea popped into his head. He remembered something a friend had e-mailed him the night before. "Thank you, Lord," he thought to himself. Then he faced the class. "This morning we're going to do something different! I'd like all of you to get out a piece of paper and write down the name of everyone in the room. The order isn't important, but including everyone is." Mr. Valentino smiled at the surprised looks on the children's faces. "After you write every name, I want you to write the nicest thing you can say about every person in this room. Write just one thing—whatever you think is the most special thing

Story (continued)

about that person." The room quickly grew quiet as everyone began thoughtfully filling their notebook pages.

Mr. Valentino got out a stack of paper and wrote each student's name at the top of one.

Later, while Mrs. Morgan took his class to the gym for a game of "swim fish," Mr. Valentino looked at the papers filled out by his students. He started with Setsuko and made a list of what everyone especially liked about her. Then he compiled lists for all the other students and added his own thoughts at the bottom of each one. He smiled to himself as he thought of how these compliments would make his students feel.

Stretching his now tired arms above his head and leaning back in his chair, Mr. Valentino thought about the e-mail from his friend. It was a story by someone called "Sister Helen" about her junior-high class. They had done this same project many years ago. It had helped change the mood of her classroom that morning like she'd planned, but the busy, dedicated nun had forgotten the project after it was completed.

The story went on to tell of how that changed years later—the day one of her former students came back from Vietnam in a casket. His parents invited the faithful nun to their home after the funeral. There the parents pulled her aside and handed her a well-worn piece of paper that had been found in their son's billfold the day he'd been killed. As she unfolded it, Sister Helen was shocked to see that it was his "special qualities" list from the class project years before.

Many of the young man's former classmates were there to comfort his parents, and soon they were all talking about their lists, too! One girl pulled a worn, tattered copy out of her purse. Another said he still kept his in the top drawer of his desk. One girl confessed that she'd saved hers in her diary, and still looked at it regularly. Sister Helen was amazed at the impact those lists had in her students' lives.

Mr. Valentino stretched again, then stood up. "I know my kids are a lot younger than Sister Helen's, but they needed to feel special today," Mr. Valentino thought as he gathered the papers and folded them in half. "I want them to know that I love them, and that each of their classmates enjoys something special about them." He walked around the room, placing each student's sheet on their desk.

"What's this Mr. V?" Daniel snatched the paper from his desk as he walked in the room a few minutes later.

"Open it and see." Mr. Valentino smiled.

Daniel opened the paper and slowly read what was written there. A smile lit up the boy's usually sullen face. "Did you guys really write these nice things about me?" He looked around the room at his classmates. A few heads nodded, but almost everyone was deeply absorbed reading and rereading their own list.

Mr. Valentino continued to watch as Daniel carefully folded the piece of notebook paper and stuck it in the little zippered pocket of his backpack.

He looked down at Beth right in front of his desk as she giggled and looked over at Katelynn. "I know which one you wrote."

"You do?" Katelynn put down her own paper for a minute.

"Sure," Beth pointed to one of the things listed on her paper.

"You might be surprised." Katelynn said mysteriously.

Katelynn thought about her friend and all the things she liked about Beth. It had been hard to choose just which one she liked best. Daniel had been hard too—but for the opposite reason! There wasn't much she could find to like about Daniel. But she had come up with something that was true, and she really meant. She looked at the Scripture written on the board: "You should be like one big happy family, full of sympathy toward each other, loving one another with tender hearts and humble minds."

"Beth," she whispered across the isle, "I'm sorry your grandma is not feeling well. Do you want to see if my mom will take us over there after school instead of my house? Maybe we could make a list like this for her."

Mr. Valentino smiled down at the two girls in front of his desk. "Lord, you have such great ideas," he whispered to himself. And his eyes went once again to the text printed on the board. "You should be like one big happy family, full of sympathy. . ."

2 Discussion Time

Check understanding of the story and development of personal values.

- What was the weather like as Mr. Valentino's class was coming to school?
- What were some reasons the kids were upset when they came into the classroom?
- How did Mr. Valentino feel about the mood of his class? How do you know?
- What does 1 Peter 3:8 say?
- How did Mr. Valentino help his class "be like one big happy family, full of sympathy toward each other, loving one another with tender hearts and humble minds?"
- How do you think the class felt after they read the papers they found on their desks?
- What would you do with a list of nice things about you?

A Preview

Name ______________

Write each word as your teacher says it.

1. gas
2. boss
3. circus
4. certain
5. less
6. pass
7. race
8. seventh
9. since
10. sorry
11. sweet
12. soap
13. save
14. sell
15. asleep

Words with /s/

Lesson 14

Scripture
I Peter 3:8

87

3 Preview

Test for knowledge of the correct spellings of these words.

Customize Your List

On a separate piece of paper, additional words of your choice may be tested.

I will say the word once, use the word in a sentence, then say the word again. Write the word on the lines in the worktext.

Correct Immediately!

Let's correct our preview. I will write each word on the board. Put a dot under each letter on your preview as I spell the word out loud. If you spelled a word wrong, rewrite it correctly.

Take a minute to memorize...

Read the memory verse to the class twice. Have the class practice it with you two more times.

1.	gas	The school is heated with natural **gas.**
2.	boss	Mr. Vanetti's **boss** had turned the heat up too high.
3.	circus	The room was like a **circus** before the bell rang.
4.	certain	Beth was **certain** she knew what Katelynn had written about her.
5.	less	Kristin knew **less** about Sarah than she did about Rosa.
6.	pass	Everyone will **pass** this assignment.
7.	race	Making the lists was not a **race.**
8.	seventh	Daniel looked at the **seventh** thing on his list.
9.	since	Everyone felt better **since** they read their lists.
10.	sorry	Katelynn was **sorry** Beth's grandma was sick.
11.	sweet	Beth said **sweet** things about Katelynn.
12.	soap	"The **soap** you use smells nice," wrote Setsuko.
13.	save	Where would you **save** your list?
14.	sell	You can't **sell** your list.
15.	asleep	No one fell **asleep** while reading his list.

Progress Chart

Students may record scores. (Reproducible master in Appendix B.)

Day 1

Lesson 14

4 Word Shapes

Help students form a correct image of whole words.

Look at each word and think about its shape. Now, write the word in the correct word shape boxes. You may check off each word as you use it.

(In many words, the sound of **/s/** is spelled with **s**, and it is often spelled this way when it is at the beginning of a word. The **/s/** sound can also be spelled with **c** when followed by **i**, or **e**.

In the word shape boxes, color the letter or letters that spell the sound of **/s/** in each word. Circle the word in which **/s/** is spelled **s** and **c**.

Words with /s/ — Lesson 14

B Word Shapes Name ____________________

Write each word in the correct word shape boxes. Next, in the word shape boxes, color the letter or letters that spell the sound of **/s/** in each word. Circle the words in which **/s/** is spelled with both **s** and **c**.

Word	Word shape answer
1. asleep	sweet
2. boss	sorry
3. certain	asleep
4. circus	race
5. gas	save
6. less	certain
7. pass	gas
8. race	less
9. save	soap
10. sell	boss
11. seventh	(since)
12. since	(circus)
13. soap	sell
14. sorry	seventh
15. sweet	pass

88

Answers may vary for duplicate word shapes.

Be Prepared For Fun

Check these supply lists for **Fun Ways to Spell** presented **Day 2**. Purchase and/or gather needed items ahead of time!

General
- Chalk or Whiteboard Marker
- Chalkboard or Whiteboard (could be individual boards for each child)
- Spelling List

Auditory
- Box to Store Letters
- a, b, c, c, e, e, g, h, i, l, l, n, o, p, r, r, s, s, t, u, v, w, y (written on seasonal shapes like mittens or sleds)
- Spelling List

Visual
- Glitter Glue
- Art Paper (2 or 3 pieces per child)
- Spelling List

Tactile
- Thick Pile Carpet Squares
- Spelling List

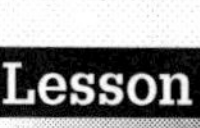

C Hide and Seek

Name ______________________

Place an **X** on a coin for each word you spell correctly.

D Other Word Forms

Using the words below, follow the instructions given by your teacher.

bossily	gassing	racism	sleeping
bossiness	lessen	saved	sleepy
bossing	lesser	saving	soapy
bossy	passable	savings	sorrier
certainly	passes	selling	sorriest
certainty	passing	sold	sorrow
circuses	raced	seven	sweeten
gases	racially	sleepily	sweetly
gasoline	racing	sleepiness	sweetness

E Fun Ways to Spell

Initial the box of each activity you finish.

1. 

Spell your words with chalk.

3. 

Spell your words out of the letter box.

2. 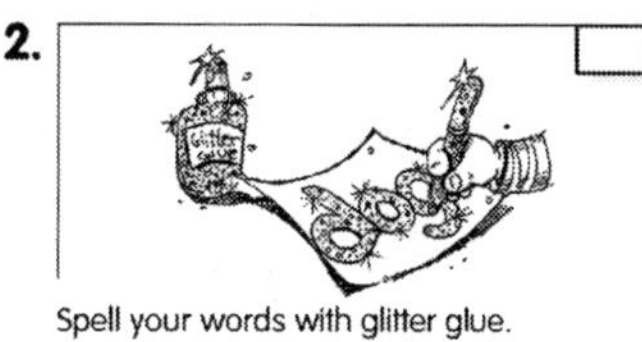

Spell your words with glitter glue.

4. 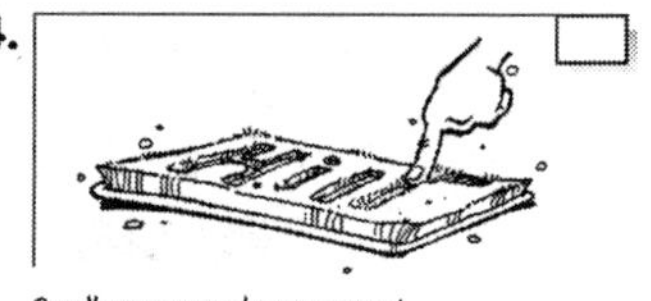

Spell your words on carpet.

Words with /s/

Lesson 14

89

1 Hide and Seek

Reinforce correct spelling of current spelling words.

Write the words one at a time on the board. Use this activity for each word.

- **Look** at the word.
- **Say** the word out loud.
- Let's **hide** (cover) the word.
- **Write** the word on your paper.
- Let's **seek** (uncover) the word.
- **Check** your spelling. If your word is spelled wrong, write the word correctly next to it.

2 Other Word Forms

This activity is optional. Have students write original sentences using these Other Word Forms:

bossy
raced
sold
seven

3 Fun Ways to Spell

Four activities are provided. Use one, two, three, or all of the activities. Have students initial the box for each activity they complete.

Day 2

Lesson 14

Options:

- assign activities to students according to their learning styles
- set up the activities in learning centers for the class to do throughout the day
- divide the class into four groups and assign one activity per group
- do one activity per day

General

To spell your words with chalk...
- Put your spelling list on your desk.
- Look at a word; then, walk to the chalkboard (or whiteboard).
- Write your spelling word on the chalkboard (or whiteboard).
- Return to your desk.
- Check your spelling.

Auditory

To spell your words out of the letter box...
- Spell a word from your list by putting the letters in the right order.
- Check your spelling.
- Spell your word out loud.

Visual

To spell your words with glitter glue...
- Write each of your spelling words on your paper.
- Check your spelling.

Tactile

To spell your words on carpet...
- Use your fingertip to write a spelling word on the carpet.
- Check your spelling.
- Smooth the word out with your hand and write another.

Day 3

Lesson 14

1 Working with Words

Familiarize students with word meaning and usage.

Sentence Clues

Complete the top of your page by reading the spelling clue.

ABC Order

Write the words **scent**, **school**, **sign**, and **science** on the board. Explain to the students that when words begin with the same letter, they need to look at the second letter in each word to put the words in alphabetical order. If the first two letters are the same, look at the third letter. Guide the students in putting these four words in alphabetical order.

Look at each set of words. Write them in alphabetical order on the lines.

Take a minute to memorize...

Read the memory verse to the class twice. Have the class practice it with you two more times.

Words with /s/ — Lesson 14

F Working with Words Name ____________

Spelling Clues

Words in which **c** has the sound of **/s/** usually have the letter **e**, **i**, or **y** following the **c**. Write the words in which **/s/** is spelled with **c**. Now, circle the vowel that comes after each **c** with the sound of **/s/**.

1. c(e)rtain 3. rac(e)
2. c(i)rcus 4. sinc(e)

ABC Order

Write the words from each group in alphabetical order.

less pass boss

1. boss 2. less 3. pass

asleep race gas

4. asleep 5. gas 6. race

Remember, when words begin with the same letter, look at the second letter to place the words in alphabetical order.

circus since certain

7. certain 8. circus 9. since

seventh sweet save

10. save 11. seventh 12. sweet

Remember, if the first two letters are the same, look at the third letter to put the words in alphabetical order.

sorry sell soap

13. sell 14. soap 15. sorry

Word Bank

certain	asleep	less	seventh	sorry
circus	boss	pass	sell	sweet
race	gas	save	soap	since

90

G Dictation

Name ______________________

Listen and write the missing words and punctuation.

1. Helen was asleep when Rachel left for school .

2. Mr. Valentino began to pass out the papers .

3. Daniel put the paper in his backpack to save it .

Words with /s/

Lesson 14

H Proofreading

If a word is misspelled, fill in the oval by that word. If all the words are spelled correctly, fill in the oval by **no mistake**.

1.	4.	7.
○ angel	○ race	● saop
● asleap	○ juice	○ jealous
○ boss	● gass	○ January
○ no mistake	○ no mistake	○ no mistake

2.	5.	8.
● certun	● sevinth	○ though
○ cage	○ save	○ sight
○ less	○ judge	● sorrie
○ no mistake	○ no mistake	○ no mistake

3.	6.	9.
○ July	○ giraffe	○ wrap
● circuss	● sinse	○ sweet
○ pass	○ sell	○ sidewalk
○ no mistake	○ no mistake	● no mistake

91

1 Dictation

Reinforce correct spelling by using current and previous words in context.

Listen as I read each sentence and then write the missing words and ending punctuation in your worktext. (Slowly read each sentence twice. Sentences are found in the student text to the left.)

2 Proofreading

Familiarize students with standardized test format and reinforce recognizing misspelled words.

Look at each set of words. If a word is misspelled, fill in the oval by that word. If all the words are spelled correctly, fill in the oval by **no mistake**.

Day 4 / Day 5

Lesson **14**

3 Hide and Seek

Reinforce correct spelling of current spelling words. (A reproducible master is provided in Appendix A as shown on the inset page to the right.)

Write the words one at a time on the board. Use this activity for each word.

- **Look** at the word.
- **Say** the word out loud.
- Let's **hide** (cover) the word.
- **Write** the word on your paper.
- Let's **seek** (uncover) the word.
- **Check** your spelling. If your word is spelled wrong, write the word correctly next to it.

Other Word Forms — Lesson 14

Hide and Seek

Check a coin for each word you spell correctly.

Other Word Forms

Spelling and Writing

Use each pair of words to write a sentence. Check your spelling.

1. gasoline, racing (Answers may vary)
2. soapy, sorriest (Answers may vary)
3. sleepy, passed (Answers may vary)
4. seven, bossing (Answers may vary)
5. savings, selling (Answers may vary)

Clues

Use the clues to write the words.

1. where clowns perform circuses
2. makes a car run gasoline
3. add more sugar sweeten
4. 1, 3, 5, ___, 9 seven
5. decrease lessen
6. tell others what to do bossy
7. money kept in a bank savings

Word Bank

bossy	gasoline	savings	sweeten
circuses	lessen	seven	

338

4 Other Word Forms

Have your students complete this activity to strengthen spelling ability and expand vocabulary.

1 Posttest

Test mastery of the spelling words.

I will say the word once, use the word in a sentence, then say the word again. Write the word on your paper.

1. boss — The principal is Mr. Valentino's **boss.**
2. asleep — Mr. Valentino was not **asleep.**
3. gas — Natural **gas** is the fuel for the school's heating system.
4. circus — The room was like a **circus** before the bell rang.
5. sorry — I'm **sorry** everyone is in a bad mood.
6. certain — Mr. Valentino was **certain** that his class needed an attitude adjustment.
7. less — The children were **less** than happy on Tuesday.
8. soap — "Use **soap** when you wash your hands for lunch," said Mr. Valentino.
9. race — There was a **race** to the door at recess.
10. pass — Everyone can **pass** this assignment.
11. save — Daniel will **save** his list in his backpack.
12. seventh — Katelynn's **seventh** thing was different than Beth's.
13. sell — You can't **sell** a list.
14. since — "Let's go to your grandma's **since** she is sick," suggested Katelynn.
15. sweet — "It was **sweet** of you to do this for us, Mr. Valentino," said Beth.

Progress Chart

Students may record scores. (Reproducible master in Appendix B.)

Personal Dictionary

Students may add any words they have misspelled to their personal dictionaries for reference when writing. (Cover in Appendix B.)

Words with /s/

Lesson 14

I Game Name ____________________

Mr. Valentino is passing out the lists of the special qualities his students wrote about each other. Lead the way by moving one space for each word you or your team spells correctly from this week's word list.

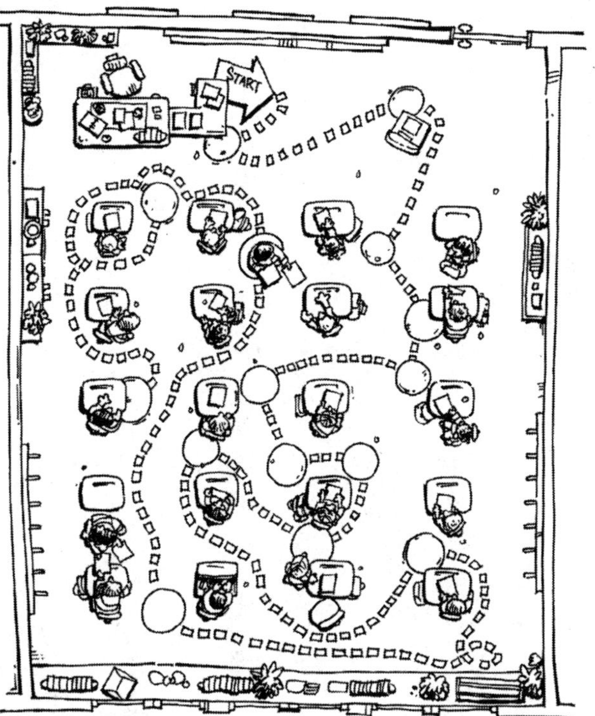

Remember: Getting along with each other is the result of walking with God.

J Journaling

In your journal, make a list of all the students in your class. Write the nicest thing you can say about each one.

92

2 Game

Reinforce spelling skills and provide motivation and interest.

Materials

- game page (from student text)
- flat buttons, dry beans, pennies, or game discs (1 per child)
- game word list

Game Word List

1. asleep
2. boss
3. certain
4. circus
5. gas
6. less
7. pass
8. race
9. save
10. seventh
11. sell
12. since
13. soap
14. sorry
15. sweet

How to Play:

- Divide the class into two teams.
- Have each student place his/her game piece on Start.
- Have a student from team A go to the board.
- Say the spelling word. (You may also wish to use the word in a sentence.)
- Have the student write the word on the board.
- If correct, instruct each member of team A to move his/her game piece forward one space on the game board. (Note: If the word is misspelled, correct the spelling immediately.)
- Alternate between teams A and B.
- The team to reach the last student's desk first is the winner.

Non-Competitive Option:

At the end of the game, say: "Class, I am proud of your efforts to spell the words correctly. If you had fun and tried your best, you are all winners!"

3 Journaling

Provide a meaningful reason for correct spelling through personal writing.

Review the story using discussion leads provided on the following page. Encourage students to apply the Scriptural value in their journaling.

Journaling (continued)

- What is the Scripture verse we have studied this week? (1 Peter 3:8)
- Why do you think God wants us to get along like a big happy family? (God knows, when we do nice things for others and forgive people who hurt us, we will be happiest.)
- What did Mr. Valentino do to help his students think of good things about each other? (Asked them to write down the nicest thing they could think of about each classmate.)
- At what age do you stop needing sympathetic words and kind things done for you? (Everyone needs love--always.)
- What did Beth and Katelynn decide to do after they read all the nice things that had been written about them? (They decided to do the same thing for Beth's grandma who was not feeling well.)
- How do you think Beth's grandma will feel when she reads her list of what the girls like about her? (happy, loved, content)
- Make a list in your journal of all the students in your class. Write the nicest thing you can say about each one.

"Students will learn how to spell and will learn the value of correct spelling, if they write often for authentic purposes."*

Take a minute to memorize...
Have the class say the memory verses from lessons 13 and 14 with you.

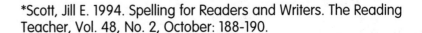

*Scott, Jill E. 1994. Spelling for Readers and Writers. The Reading Teacher, Vol. 48, No. 2, October: 188-190.

1 **Literature Connection**
Topic: Joy from God
Theme Text: 1 John 1:7

Joyful Light

Rachel learns that God can change her anger into joy.

"Time for breakfast." Vanessa leaned on the door frame of her step-sister's bedroom. "Mom says hurry 'cause we're running late this morning."

"Okay," Rachel and Rebecca said at the same time. The sisters' eyes met and they smiled. "We'll be. . ." both began, then burst into laughter. "Quit saying. . ." they started again at the same time, then fell on the bed and rolled with laughter. Thirteen-year-old Rebecca recovered first and finished the sentence alone. "Quit saying everything I say."

"Okay." Rachel sat up with a grin, then bent down to tie her shoelaces. "We'd better hurry. Helen doesn't have a fast-speed anymore. She's so tired all the time since she's been pregnant. I hope we have a boy, don't you?"

"Oh, I don't know." Rebecca ran a brush through her hair and checked the results in the mirror. "It might be fun to have five girls in our family."

Rachel winked at her sister as she walked toward the door. "You look marvelous, simply marvelous." Rebecca laughed and pretended to bow. "Let's go." The two girls followed the warm smell of breakfast downstairs.

David Jacobsen was already seated at the table with Vanessa, Natalie, and his wife, Helen, when the sisters trooped into the breakfast room. "Nice of you to join us." Father smiled warmly, then opened the Bible in his lap. "Our Scripture this morning is found in 1 John 1:7 and says 'If we are living in the light of God's presence. . . we have wonderful fellowship and joy with each other.' I want you to think about that text today and we will talk about what it means tonight at dinner. Let's bow our heads for prayer. . ."

Almost before the "amen" was out of his mouth, Helen was out the door and hurrying down the hall to the bathroom. "Mom said she was never this sick with Natalie and me," Vanessa said. "Maybe that means we're going to have a boy!"

Rachel sat quietly, memories of her mother's loosing battle with cancer flooding her mind. She remembered how sick the chemotherapy treatments had made her mommy. She quickly shook her head as if to rid herself of the sad thoughts. "I hope Helen will be okay," she thought. "I wonder if she'll be sick like this for the whole nine months. I'm not sure a baby brother is worth her feeling so bad."

Helen rejoined the family at the table looking pale and tired. "Pass the orange juice, please," she said quietly.

"I have to be in court this morning by eight-thirty, Helen, or I'd drive the girls to school for you." Mr. Jacobsen wiped his mouth with a napkin. "Maybe Tony's mom could come by and get them. They live just across the park."

"Grandma Miller takes Tony to school. And Mrs. Vanetti has already left for work." Rachel buttered her muffin and took a bite. "We wouldn't all fit in Grandma Miller's little car anyway."

"Stephen's mom could take us. They have a mini-van." Rachel said with her mouth full.

Helen nodded her head.

Mr. Jacobson stepped over to the phone. "Hello, Brad? This is David Jacobson. Could you do us a huge favor this morning? Yes. . ."

A few minutes later a horn beeped in the Jacobson's driveway. Helen opened the front door and ushered the four girls out. Mrs. Wilson rolled down the van window and waved. "Go back to bed, Helen, and take it easy. Be careful and don't push yourself so hard."

Helen waved her hand to acknowledge her neighbor's concern, then closed the door. "Oh, dear, I have that ultrasound scheduled this morning. That's the last thing I feel like doing." She walked over to the couch and picked up her quilt. "Maybe I'll feel better after resting awhile." She smiled and patted her growing stomach, then suddenly turned and rushed down the hall as another wave of nausea hit.

In the van, Vanessa and Natalie were chattering away about names for the baby. But Rachel was thinking about Helen. She pictured her on the front porch waving. "My mommy used to do that," Rachel thought. "She wanted to wave good-bye to us even when she was feeling awful after the treatments. Helen looked so much like her this morning holding her robe tightly around herself to keep out the cold. She looked so tired and pale. What if Helen dies like Mommy did? Helen does so many nice things for our family."

"I don't think we need a baby," Rachel blurted out.

The van was very quiet. Mrs. Wilson finally broke the silence. "A baby is very special, Rachel. I'm sorry that you feel that way." No one said anything else on the short trip to Knowlton Elementary. After dropping the children off, Mrs. Wilson drove straight home and made a quick phone call to the Jacobson law office before starting the breakfast dishes.

Later that afternoon Rachel looked up from a math problem she was working on and was surprised to see Mr. Valentino standing by her desk. "Gather your books, Rachel," he said. "Your father is here to pick you girls up early today. He's waiting out front."

Rachel wondered if something had happened to Helen as she loaded her backpack with

Story (continued)

the things she wanted to take home. When she opened the van door she found Natalie, Rebecca, and Vanessa all waiting inside. "What's going on? Is Helen okay? Why are we going home early?"

Mr. Jacobson turned around and smiled at his four daughters. "It's a surprise. You'll just have to wait and see."

They all knew their father well enough to know he couldn't be talked into changing his mind, so they rode in silence. When they arrived at the doctor's office, Mr. Jacobsen nodded to the receptionist and led his little tribe past a rack of magazines and then down to room six.

As he opened the door, the girls could see Helen lying on her back on a padded table. The nurse was standing over Helen's bare stomach, holding a black thing in her hand connected to a long, coiled cord. She gently moved her hand and adjusted a dial on the shelf behind her. She squeezed some clear toothpaste-like stuff onto Helen's stomach and moved the black thing around some more. Suddenly the room was filled with a very loud and fast "wha-whump, wha-whump, wha-whump."

Rachel jumped. "What's that noise? Is our baby dying?" Rachel looked up at her father for an explanation.

Father looked at Helen and smiled. Helen answered her questions. "No, Rachel, this is our baby's heartbeat. He's doing very well. I'm a bit bigger than I should be now, but our baby is doing just fine." Everyone started talking at once. Father counted the beats in 15 seconds and multiplied by 4. "One hundred forty beats a minute," he announced. "I think it will be a boy."

"I just want a healthy baby." Helen smiled up at her husband. The nurse wiped off the clear gel and Helen adjusted her clothes and sat up. Rachel looked at Helen's face. She was relieved to see the pink in her cheeks and a smile.

Helen looked down from her perch on the examining table. "The doctor says we're both doing fine! I'm hoping the nausea will quit soon. He says I'm well into the second trimester, so things should be smoothing out soon." Helen reached out and gave Rachel's arm a squeeze.

Helen slid off the table and led everyone back out through the waiting room and to the van while Mr. Jacobson talked to the receptionist and made a payment.

Rachel listened to the happy chatter of her family. Natalie was telling Helen how big the baby hamsters were getting at school. "Can we get one?" she heard Natalie plead. Rebecca and Vanessa were discussing baby names again. Rebecca was making a long list of possibilities in her notebook. Helen and Natalie joined their conversation, and added a few more names.

The afternoon sun filtered through the trees and into the van, making Helen's and Natalie's faces light up. Rachel thought of the text her father had read that morning at breakfast. "'If we are living in the light of God's presence, we have wonderful'. . .something. What was that word? And 'joy with each other.'" As she looked around the van, Rachel's heart was full of love for her father, her sisters, the new baby not yet born, and even for Helen. "God is changing my heart," she thought. "God is taking away the anger and exchanging it for joy!"

2 Discussion Time

Check understanding of the story and development of personal values.

- What did Helen do right after Father read the Scripture verse and prayed at the breakfast table?
- What is our Scripture verse this week?
- What happened after breakfast that helped Rachel begin to realize how much she needed and loved her step-mother Helen?
- Raise your hand if you think the kind things Helen has done for Rachel in the past have helped Rachel learn to love her.
- When Jesus is our friend it is easier to keep being kind to people even when they are not kind to us.

A Preview Name ______________

Write each word as your teacher says it.

1. copy
2. fork
3. careful
4. key
5. kept
6. quilt
7. cover
8. quiet
9. queen
10. October
11. track
12. quick
13. quite
14. rack
15. rake

Words with /k/ or /kw/

Lesson 15

Scripture
I John 1:7

93

3 Preview

Test for knowledge of the correct spellings of these words.

Customize Your List

On a separate piece of paper, additional words of your choice may be tested.

I will say the word once, use the word in a sentence, then say the word again. Write the word on the lines in the worktext.

Correct Immediately!

Let's correct our preview. I will write each word on the board. Put a dot under each letter on your preview as I spell the word out loud. If you spelled a word wrong, rewrite it correctly.

Take a minute to memorize...

Read the memory verse to the class twice. Have the class practice it with you two more times.

1.	copy	"I don't want you to **copy** what I say," warned Rebecca.
2.	fork	Rachel picked up her **fork** at the breakfast table.
3.	careful	"Be **careful** now that you are pregnant," suggested Mrs. Wilson.
4.	key	Stephen's mom turned the **key** and started the van.
5.	kept	Rachel **kept** her fears about Helen and the baby to herself.
6.	quilt	Helen picked up the **quilt** on the couch.
7.	cover	She will **cover** herself with the quilt and go back to sleep.
8.	quiet	It is easier for Helen to rest when it is **quiet.**
9.	queen	Helen has become **queen** of the Jacobson home.
10.	October	The baby will be five months old next **October.**
11.	track	Keep **track** of how long it will be until the baby is born.
12.	quick	Helen was no longer **quick.**
13.	quite	She is not **quite** over her nausea.
14.	rack	The magazines in the **rack** are for the patients to read.
15.	rake	Someone came to **rake** the yard.

Progress Chart

Students may record scores. (Reproducible master in Appendix B.)

Day 1

Lesson 15

4 Word Shapes

Help students form a correct image of whole words.

Look at each word and think about its shape. Now, write the word in the correct word shape boxes. You may check off each word as you use it.

(In many words, the sound of **/k/** is spelled with **k**, and it is often spelled this way when it is at the beginning or middle of a word. The **/k/** sound can also be spelled with **c** when followed by **a**, **o**, or **u**. The spelling **ck** occurs in the middle or at the end of a word. The letter **q** is always followed by **u** and usually has the sound of **/kw/**.)

In the word shape boxes, color the letter or letters that spell the sound of **/k/** or **/kw/** in each word.

Words with /k/ or /kw/ — Lesson 15

B Word Shapes Name ____________

Write each word in the correct word shape boxes. Next, in the word shape boxes, color the letter or letters that spell the sound of **/k/** or **/kw/** in each word.

Word	Answer
1. careful	rack
2. copy	rake
3. cover	quick
4. fork	cover
5. kept	copy
6. key	quiet
7. October	careful
8. queen	October
9. quick	quilt
10. quiet	queen
11. quilt	key
12. quite	track
13. rack	kept
14. rake	quite
15. track	fork

94

Answers may vary for duplicate word shapes.

Be Prepared For Fun

Check these supply lists for **Fun Ways to Spell** presented **Day 2**. Purchase and/or gather needed items ahead of time!

General
- Colored Pencils
- Art Paper (1 piece per child)
- Spelling List

Auditory
- A Classmate
- Spelling List

Visual
- Black Construction Paper (1 piece per child)
- Cotton Swabs (1 per child)
- Lemon Juice
- Spelling List

Tactile
- Pipe Cleaners (cut in an assortment of lengths)
- Spelling List

C Hide and Seek

Name ______________________

Place an **X** on a coin for each word you spell correctly.

D Other Word Forms

Using the words below, follow the instructions given by your teacher.

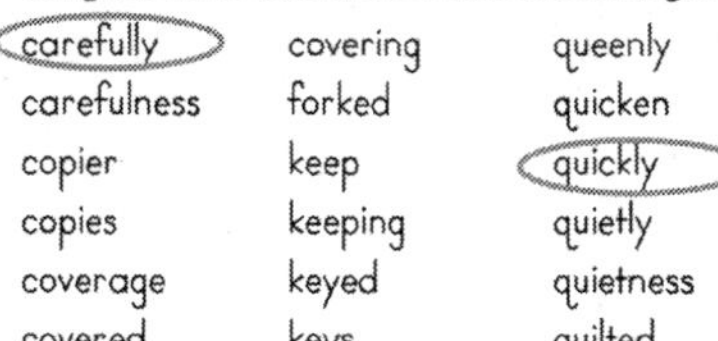

carefully	covering	queenly	racket
carefulness	forked	quicken	raked
copier	keep	quickly	raking
copies	keeping	quietly	tracked
coverage	keyed	quietness	tracking
covered	keys	quilted	tracks

E Fun Ways to Spell

Initial the box of each activity you finish.

1. 

Spell your words with pictures.

3. 
Spell your words out loud.

2. 

Spell your words with lemon juice.

4. 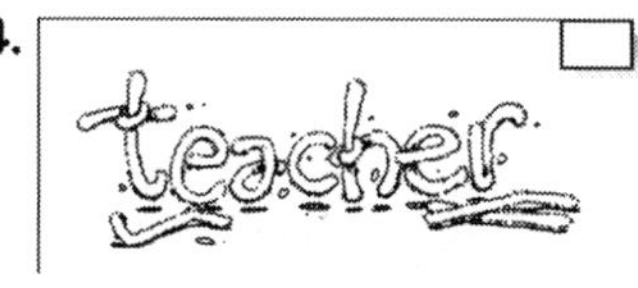

Spell your words with pipe cleaners.

Words with /k/ or /kw/

Lesson 15

95

1 Hide and Seek

Reinforce correct spelling of current spelling words.

Write the words one at a time on the board. Use this activity for each word.

Say

- **Look** at the word.
- **Say** the word out loud.
- Let's **hide** (cover) the word.
- **Write** the word on your paper.
- Let's **seek** (uncover) the word.
- **Check** your spelling. If your word is spelled wrong, write the word correctly next to it.

2 Other Word Forms

This activity is optional. Have students find and circle the Other Word Forms that are synonyms of the following:

footprints
cautiously
briskly

3 Fun Ways to Spell

Four activities are provided. Use one, two, three, or all of the activities. Have students initial the box for each activity they complete.

Options:

- assign activities to students according to their learning styles
- set up the activities in learning centers for the class to do throughout the day
- divide the class into four groups and assign one activity per group
- do one activity per day

General

To spell your words with pictures...

- Choose several words from your spelling list, and draw pictures that illustrate the meanings of those words.
- Write the correct spelling word beside each picture.
- Check your spelling.

Auditory

To spell your words out loud...

- Have a classmate read a spelling word from the list.
- Say a sentence with that spelling word to your classmate.
- Spell the spelling word you used in that sentence to your classmate.
- Ask your classmate to check your spelling.
- Do this with each word on your word list.

Visual

To spell your words with lemon juice...

- Dipping a cotton swab in lemon juice, write each of your spelling words on black construction paper.
- Check your spelling before your writing disappears!

Tactile

To spell your words with pipe cleaners...

- Choose a word from your spelling list.
- It may be a favorite word or a word you have trouble remembering how to spell.
- Shape the pipe cleaner to spell that word.

Day 3

Lesson 15

1 Working with Words

Familiarize students with word meaning and usage.

Crossword Puzzle

The sound of **/k/** can be spelled with a **c**, **ch**, **ck**, **k**, or **que**. When **c** has the **/k/** sound it is usually before **a**, **o**, or **u**. The **ck** is used at the end of a syllable or word. The sound of **/kw/** is spelled with **qu**. Draw a set of five boxes vertically on the board. Give this clue: **to do something fast**. Wait for the class to respond, then write the word **quick** in the boxes.

Say

Using the clues in your worktext, write each of the spelling words in the correct set of boxes.

Take a minute to memorize...

Read the memory verse to the class twice. Have the class practice it with you two more times.

Words with /k/ or /kw/

Lesson 15

F Working with Words Name ____________

Crossword Puzzle

Use the clues to write the words in the puzzle.

Across

2. a fall month
5. unlocks a door
6. used to eat with
9. a padded bed cover
10. a path used for trains
14. completely
15. calm and peaceful

Down

1. imitate
3. using caution
4. frame to put things on
7. took care of
8. fast, speedy
11. garden tool
12. to place something over
13. wife of a king

Word Bank

careful	fork	October	quiet	rack
copy	kept	queen	quilt	rake
cover	key	quick	quite	track

96

G Dictation Name ____________

Listen and write the missing words and punctuation.

1. Rebecca kept her quilt on a rack .
2. Rachel could hear the quick heartbeat of the baby .
3. Rachel was careful to copy the verse neatly .

Words with /k/ or /kw/

Lesson 15

H Proofreading

If a word is misspelled, fill in the oval by that word. If all the words are spelled correctly, fill in the oval by **no mistake**.

1.	4.	7.
○ certain	○ quick	○ since
● carefull	● kee	● queit
○ asleep	○ gas	○ soap
○ no mistake	○ no mistake	○ no mistake

2.	5.	8.
○ fork	○ seventh	○ race
○ June	○ quilt	○ rack
● copie	● october	○ sorry
○ no mistake	○ no mistake	● no mistake

3.	6.	9.
● cuver	● quean	○ jar
○ circus	○ quite	○ rage
○ kept	○ rake	● trak
○ no mistake	○ no mistake	○ no mistake

97

1 Dictation

Reinforce correct spelling by using current and previous words in context.

Listen as I read each sentence and then write the missing words and ending punctuation in your worktext. (Slowly read each sentence twice. Sentences are found in the student text to the left.)

2 Proofreading

Familiarize students with standardized test format and reinforce recognizing misspelled words.

Look at each set of words. If a word is misspelled, fill in the oval by that word. If all the words are spelled correctly, fill in the oval by **no mistake**.

3 Hide and Seek

Reinforce correct spelling of current spelling words. (A reproducible master is provided in Appendix A as shown on the inset page to the right.)
Write the words one at a time on the board. Use this activity for each word.

- **Look** at the word.
- **Say** the word out loud.
- Let's **hide** (cover) the word.
- **Write** the word on your paper.
- Let's **seek** (uncover) the word.
- **Check** your spelling. If your word is spelled wrong, write the word correctly next to it.

4 Other Word Forms

Have your students complete this activity to strengthen spelling ability and expand vocabulary.

1 Posttest

Test mastery of the spelling words.

I will say the word once, use the word in a sentence, then say the word again. Write the word on your paper.

Hide and Seek

Check a coin for each word you spell correctly.

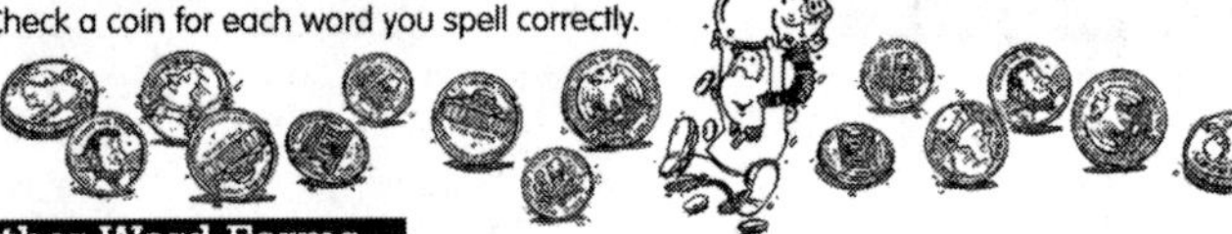

Other Word Forms

Suffixes

Circle the correct suffix.

1. Dave began track (ed, ness, ing) the bear.
2. The quiet (ness, ly, ed) of the forest was broken by a loud crash.
3. It seems like we have been rake (s, en, ing) leaves for a week!
4. Mom's new comforter is almost all quilt (y, et, ed).
5. In her new gown, Samantha looks queen (ly, ness, ing).
6. After the rain, Matthew track (ing, able, ed) up the floor.
7. I carried the lovely cake care (fulness, fully, ful).
8. We are copy (ing, es, iest) all the tax forms.
9. We are keep (able, ly, ing) Jenna's rabbit while she is gone.
10. Dad wanted us to come quick (ier, est, ly) to see the deer in the yard.
11. I cover (ed, ing, est) the hot dogs to keep them warm.
12. These three key (s, es, en) on my piano keep sticking.

Word Sort

Write each Other Word Form under the correct heading.

keyed copier queenly coverage racket forked

One-syllable Words	Two-syllable Words	Three-syllable Words
1. keyed	3. queenly	5. copier
2. forked	4. racket	6. coverage

Other Word Forms
Lesson 15

339

---

1. track — It is hard to keep **track** of how many weeks it will be before the baby is born.
2. October — The baby's birthday will not be in **October**.
3. quilt — The **quilt** was folded on the end of the couch.
4. cover — Helen wanted to curl up on the couch and **cover** herself with the quilt.
5. careful — "Be **careful** now that you are pregnant," suggested Father.
6. quiet — Rachel was **quiet** at the breakfast table.
7. fork — She played with the **fork** beside her plate.
8. quick — Mrs. Wilson made a **quick** phone call to Mr. Jacobson.
9. kept — The girls **kept** quiet on the way to the doctor's office.
10. key — Father parked the car and took the **key** out of the ignition.
11. rack — The **rack** in the office was full of magazines to read.
12. quite — It was **quite** exciting to hear the baby's heartbeat.
13. copy — "I would like a **copy** of the bill," said Father.
14. queen — Mother is the **queen** of the household.
15. rake — The girls will **rake** the leaves while Helen is so sick.

Progress Chart

Students may record scores. (Reproducible master in Appendix B.)

Personal Dictionary

Students may add any words they have misspelled to their personal dictionaries for reference when writing. (Cover in Appendix B.)

I Game Name ____________________

Fill in the secret phrase by correctly spelling the words from this week's word list.

G	O	D
1	2	3

C	A	N
4	5	6

G	I	V	E
7	8	9	10

U	S		J	O	Y
11	12		13	14	15

Remember: Walk in God's light and have great fellowship with others.

J Journaling

In your journal, make a list of at least 5 people with whom you have a wonderful time. Write a letter to one of them and tell them why you enjoy their company.

How to Play:

- Divide the class into two teams.
- Have a student from team A choose a number from 1 to 15.
- Say the word that matches that number from the team's word list. (You may also wish to use the word in a sentence.)
- Have the student write the word on the board.
- If correct, have each member of team A write the given letter in the matching space on his/her game page.
- Alternate between teams A and B having the students choose a number of a blank space.
- The team to complete the secret phrase first is the winner.

Non-Competitive Option:

At the end of the game, say: "Class, I am proud of your efforts to spell the words correctly. If you had fun and tried your best, you are all winners!"

2 Game

Reinforce spelling skills and provide motivation and interest.

Materials

- game page (from student text)
- pencils (1 per child)
- game word list

Game Word List

Team A	Team B
1. careful (G)	1. queen (G)
2. copy (O)	2. quick (O)
3. cover (D)	3. quiet (D)
4. fork (C)	4. quilt (C)
5. kept (A)	5. quite (A)
6. key (N)	6. rack (N)
7. October (G)	7. rake (G)
8. queen (I)	8. track (I)
9. quick (V)	9. careful (V)
10. quiet (E)	10. copy (E)
11. quilt (U)	11. cover (U)
12. quite (S)	12. fork (S)
13. rack (J)	13. kept (J)
14. rake (O)	14. key (O)
15. track (Y)	15. October (Y)

3 Journaling

Provide a meaningful reason for correct spelling through personal writing.

Review the story using discussion leads provided on the following page. Encourage students to apply the Scriptural value in their journaling.

Journaling (continued)

- Name three people with whom you have a wonderful time.
- Why do you like to be with these people? (Brainstorm. Make a list on the board.)
- What are some things people do that make you not want to be around them? (Brainstorm. Write responses on the board.)
- What helped Rachel realize she was learning to enjoy being around Helen? (She missed her when she wasn't there.)
- Why do you think it is easier to get along with others when Jesus is our friend? (Jesus gives us strength to keep being kind to others even when they aren't kind to us.)
- In your journal, make a list of at least five people with whom you have a wonderful time. Write a letter to one of them and tell them why you enjoy their company.

Take a minute to memorize...

Have the class say the memory verses from lessons 13, 14, and 15 with you.

"Reading may be the backbone of informal spelling instruction but writing is the lifeblood."*

*Scott, Jill E. 1994. Spelling for Readers and Writers. The Reading Teacher, Vol. 48, No. 2, October: 188-190.

1 **Literature Connection**
Topic: Kindness
Theme Text: 1 Peter 3:9

A Lesson in Kindness

Daniel sees God's blessing when he doesn't snap back at Christopher for falsely accusing him.

"Hold the door open a little wider, Cathy." Christopher and his sisters had just arrived at Knowlton Elementary School. "There, that's better." He moved carefully into the school followed by Kristin. Both twins carried boards the size of a pizza box in their arms. They moved slowly down the crowded hall.

"Thanks, Cathy," Kristin called to their little sister as the twins turned into the open door of their classroom. "See you after school."

"Hey, let me see your map." Stephen ran to see Christopher's project. "Cool! The way you did the ocean all around Hawaii makes it look almost real." He led the way across the room to an empty spot on the counter top. "Mr. Valentino said to put our salt/flour maps here. Wanna see mine?"

"Sure." Christopher eased the board onto the counter and straightened it carefully. "Didn't you do Texas?"

"Yep, sure as shootin', as they say in the Lone Star state." Stephen pointed to his map with pride.

"Wow! Texas covers lots of different kinds of country." Christopher waved his hand over Stephen's map as he admired the changing colors. "Look how it's really green over here and really dry and brown over there."

"Thanks." Stephen blew a speck of dust off Dallas. "My grandma helped me some," he added.

"Mom helped me figure out how to make the water look real." Christopher turned to look at the other state maps.

"Okay, everyone." Mr. Valentino's voice caught their attention. "Time for school to start." He greeted Rachel as she came into the classroom just then. "Good morning, Rachel. I think there's room for your map in the corner at the end of the counter." Mr. Valentino helped Rachel get Tennessee settled while the students went to their desks.

"You guys did a fantastic job with your map projects." Mr. Valentino's face creased in his familiar broad smile. "I'm proud of you. These maps look GOOD! The first three or four of you will give your oral reports today at social studies time, and I'll look over all these today." He waved his hand at the maps lining the sides of the room. "But to get the day started, let's stand and say the pledge of allegiance together."

Daniel yawned and peered up at the clock. Just about time for handwriting. He reached into his desk and pulled out his *A Reason for Handwriting*® worktext.

Mr. Valentino walked to the board. "We're going to practice a bit longer verse today. It's from 1 Peter again. Anyone want to volunteer to read it for us? Sarah, how about you?"

"'Don't repay evil for evil. Don't snap back at those who say unkind things about you . . . be kind to others, and God will bless us for it. 1 Peter 3:9.'" Sarah's voice was soft but clear.

"Thanks, Sarah." Mr. Valentino turned to write the text on the board. Daniel yawned again and blinked to focus on the words. "This may be one of the hardest bits of advice for us to follow." Mr. Valentino turned to look at the class seriously. "When someone's unkind, often our first response is to get even. Can you think of an example from Scriptures of this verse in action?"

For a moment the classroom was still, then Beth raised her hand. Mr. Valentino nodded in her direction. "Well, when Jesus was on trial just before they crucified Him, didn't they say all kinds of mean stuff about Him? You know, lies about how bad Jesus was? And He didn't say anything to get back at them."

"Good example, Beth." Mr. Valentino nodded. "In fact, a perfect example. Let's remember it and try to live it, too." He paused. "Now, be careful with your capital D's. They're tricky sometimes. And don't forget to dot all the i's and cross the t's."

Daniel turned to the correct page in his worktext, then took a sharp pencil from his desk. He carefully began the verse. "Don't repay evil for evil." "Well, at least capital D's are pretty easy for me," Daniel said to himself. "I practice them every time I write my name." He yawned again and his eyes wandered to the maps at the side of the room. He'd been up very late again trying to finish his map of Colorado. "My map isn't as good as a lot of those." He frowned. "Matthew's map of California is really good. His mountains are pointed and shaped just right. Mine look like globs stuck on a square."

Another yawn broke out and he paused to rub his eyes. "Of course, nobody helped me with my map at all. Dad hasn't gotten back from his business trip and Mother didn't even look at it." Even though Daniel was used to his parents lack of attention, it made him feel bad to remember how his mother had barely glanced at the project he'd struggled with. She'd only nodded and said, "Make sure you clean up that mess on the table before it dries."

With another deep sigh, Daniel started the last line of the Scripture.

Most of the students had already arrived the next morning when the twins entered their classroom. "My MAP!" Christopher wailed suddenly. Everyone in the room turned to stare. "My map! Mr. Valentino, someone broke my map!"

Mr. Valentino walked quickly across the room to see for himself. Sure enough, Hawaii was a mess. A big crack ran right through the island of Maui. Honolulu was chipped off Oahu, and Kauai was missing completely. He

Story (continued)

placed his hand on Christopher's shoulder. "I'm sorry about this, Christopher." He bent down and peered in the corner. "Here, I've found Kauai. It's not in too bad a shape. We'll glue it back on and patch up the other spots. I think we can make it look almost as good as new."

But Mr. Valentino's words rolled right over Christopher. Someone had broken his map! It was all right when he left school yesterday. He was sure, because he and Kristin had been the last ones in the room since their mom had been talking to Cathy's teacher. Who could have done it? Who had a chance? He'd worked so hard on it and had been so proud of the finished project. Angry tears stung his eyes. Who did it? He glanced around the room. Daniel!

"Daniel did it!" he blurted loudly before taking time to think. "Daniel was here after school yesterday." He rushed on before Mr. Valentino could stop him. "Everyone knows that Daniel has to help the custodian clean every afternoon and everyone knows that Daniel does mean things and likes to ruin other people's stuff. And . . .and . . ."

As Christopher sputtered to a halt, Mr. Valentino looked at him sternly. "Please go to your desk, Christopher. Now." His voice was very firm as he turned to face the shocked children. "It's almost time for school to start, so everyone please go to your desks."

Daniel had just come in and heard every word that Christopher said. He didn't understand until he saw Mr. Valentino holding the broken pieces of Hawaii. Suddenly he was deeply embarrassed. He wanted to turn around and go right back out the door. "How dare Christopher accuse me of breaking his stupid map?" Daniel fumed to himself as everyone settled at their desks. "That's not fair and he said it in front of everyone!" Daniel's breath came quickly and his fists clenched. "Boy, I'd love to tell him just what I think of him and his map. He's a liar! And he's mean! And I wish . . ."

Suddenly Daniel's eyes focused on the Scripture still written on the board. "Don't repay evil for evil. Don't snap back at those who say unkind things about you. . ." Daniel started praying, "Please help me, God," he begged silently. "Help me. It's so hard to keep from saying all the mean things I'm thinking about Christopher right now. Help me, God." Daniel's fists tightened as the battle raged inside him. "Everyone will believe Christopher because I've messed up before. I want to yell at everyone. Please help me to stay quiet."

Christopher slumped quietly in his seat. Why couldn't Daniel leave people alone? He glared across the room. "Daniel's done so many awful things. I thought he was getting over all that. Lately, he's been different, but I guess I was wrong." He glanced at the clock. It was time for school to start, but Mrs. Bentley had come in and was talking to Mr. Valentino. "I wish Daniel would've moved away instead of James," he thought. "It'd be a lot nicer around here without Daniel."

Mr. Valentino interrupted Christopher's thoughts. "Class, before we begin I think there's something you should all know." He paused and gazed solemnly around the room.

"Mrs. Bentley just told me that Mr. Noma came after school yesterday to pick up Setsuko's assignments. He needed an encyclopedia for Setsuko's project about Massachusetts. When he got it off the shelf, another book fell and knocked Christopher's map of Hawaii off the counter. Mr. Noma was extremely sorry and was going to call me to let me know what happened, but Mrs. Bentley told him she'd take care of it. But when she returned to the office, there was an urgent phone call and she forgot all about it. She just remembered and came to tell me what had happened."

Mr. Valentino paused for a long moment. The room was so quiet that you could have heard a pin drop—even on the carpet! "Now, let's begin our day." Mr. Valentino turned, but then paused as Christopher raised his hand. "Yes, Christopher?"

"Um, I wanted to tell Daniel. . .and everyone else. . . that I'm really sorry for saying he broke my map." His face was red and he felt awful as he turned to look at Daniel. "I'm really sorry."

Daniel could hardly believe his ears. Then he realized everyone was looking at him. "Uh, it's okay," he found himself smiling at Christopher. "I. . . uh . . . I'll help you fix it if you want."

"Thanks." Christopher looked very relieved. "I'd like that."

"We'll see what can be done later today." Mr. Valentino's familiar broad smile returned. He held his watch up and pointed at it. "But now, let's begin our day before it's gone."

"Thank you, God," Daniel prayed silently. "Thank you for helping me not say anything mean back to Christopher." He read the last few words on the board again. ". . .we are to be kind to others, and God will bless us for it."

Daniel smiled and added, "And thank you, God, for letting everyone know I didn't do anything wrong this time. Thank you for your blessing."

2 Discussion Time

Check understanding of the story and development of personal values.

- What projects were the students in Mr. Valentino's class bringing to school?
- Christopher's report and map were about which state?
- What happened to the map?
- Who did Christopher accuse of breaking his map?
- What did Daniel do when Christopher said he was the one who broke the map?
- Why was Daniel sleepy during school that day?
- Do you think most of the class believed Daniel had broken the map? Why or why not?
- How had Christopher's map really been broken?
- How did Christopher feel when he found out the truth?
- How did Daniel feel when everyone knew he hadn't done anything wrong?

A Preview Name ____________

Write each word as your teacher says it.

1. plane
2. table
3. made
4. wait
5. shade
6. date
7. paper
8. lady
9. mail
10. sail
11. afraid
12. awake
13. eight
14. weigh
15. lay

Scripture
I Peter 3:9

Words with /ā/ — Lesson 16

99

3 Preview

Test for knowledge of the correct spellings of these words.

Customize Your List

On a separate piece of paper, additional words of your choice may be tested.

I will say the word once, use the word in a sentence, then say the word again. Write the word on the lines in the worktext.

Correct Immediately!

Let's correct our preview. I will write each word on the board. Put a dot under each letter on your preview as I spell the word out loud. If you spelled a word wrong, rewrite it correctly.

Take a minute to memorize...

Read the memory verse to the class twice. Have the class practice it with you two more times.

Day 1 — Lesson 16

1.	plane	Dad used the **plane** to smooth the rough edges of the boards.
2.	table	Mom covered the **table** with plastic so the twins could work there.
3.	made	Christopher **made** a mixture of salt, water, and flour.
4.	wait	He had to **wait** for the map to dry before he could paint it.
5.	shade	He chose a medium **shade** of blue paint for the ocean.
6.	date	Christopher wrote his name and the **date** on the back of his map.
7.	paper	His **paper** told about Hawaiian leis, or necklaces of flowers.
8.	lady	A **lady** in Hawaii sent him some pictures.
9.	mail	The pictures came in the **mail** from the tourism office.
10.	sail	How long would it take to **sail** to Hawaii?
11.	afraid	Daniel was **afraid** his map wouldn't look very good.
12.	awake	He stayed **awake** very late trying to get it finished.
13.	eight	He painted more than **eight** rivers on his map of Colorado.
14.	weigh	All those mountains made the map **weigh** a lot.
15.	lay	Don't **lay** the blame for accidents on others, like Christopher did.

Progress Chart

Students may record scores. (Reproducible master in Appendix B.)

4 Word Shapes

Help students form a correct image of whole words.

Look at each word and think about its shape. Now, write the word in the correct word shape boxes. You may check off each word as you use it.

(In many words, the sound of **/ā/** is spelled with **a** at the end of a syllable, or with **a-consonant-e**, **ai**, **ay**, or occasionally **ei**.)

In the word shape boxes, color the letter or letters that spell the sound of **/ā/** in each word. Circle the words in which **/ā/** is spelled **ei**.

Words with /ā/ — Lesson 16

B Word Shapes Name ______________________

Write each word in the correct word shape boxes. Next, in the word shape boxes, color the letter or letters that spell the sound of **/ā/** in each word. Circle the words in which **/ā/** is spelled **ei**.

Word	Word shape
1. afraid	(eight)
2. awake	lay
3. date	mail
4. eight	date
5. lady	plane
6. lay	shade
7. made	awake
8. mail	(weigh)
9. paper	lady
10. plane	table
11. sail	wait
12. shade	paper
13. table	sail
14. wait	made
15. weigh	afraid

100

Answers may vary for duplicate word shapes.

Be Prepared For Fun

Check these supply lists for **Fun Ways to Spell** presented **Day 2**. Purchase and/or gather needed items ahead of time!

General
- A Classmate
- Spelling List

Auditory
- Voice Recorder
- Spelling List

Visual
- a, a, b, d, e, f, g, h, i, k, l, m, n, p, p, r, s, t, w, y (written on upside-down cups)
- Spelling List

Tactile
- Art Paper (2 or 3 sheets per child)
- Magazines
- Glue Sticks
- Scissors
- Spelling List

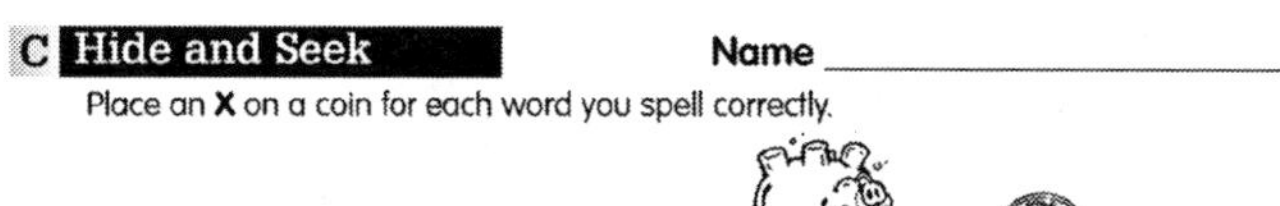

C Hide and Seek Name ______

Place an **X** on a coin for each word you spell correctly.

D Other Word Forms

Using the words below, follow the instructions given by your teacher.

awakened	ladies	making	sailor	waited
awakening	laid	papery	shaded	waiter
awoke	laying	planed	shading	waiting
dated	mailed	planer	shady	waitress
dates	mailing	planing	tabled	weight
dating	mails	sailed	tabletop	weightless
eighth	make	sailing	tableware	weighty

E Fun Ways to Spell

Initial the box of each activity you finish.

1. 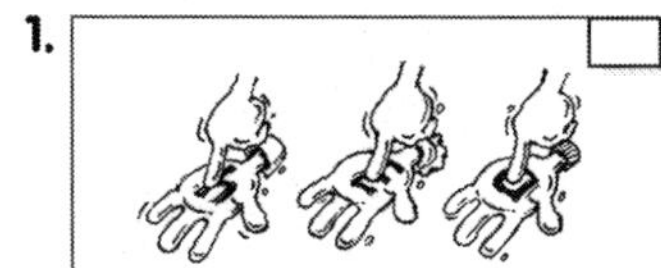
Spell your words in your classmate's hand.

3. 

Spell your words using a tape recorder.

2. 

Spell your words with paper cups.

4. 
Spell your words with magazine clippings.

Words with /ā/ Lesson 16

101

1 Hide and Seek

Reinforce correct spelling of current spelling words.

Write the words one at a time on the board. Use this activity for each word.

Say

- **Look** at the word.
- **Say** the word out loud.
- Let's **hide** (cover) the word.
- **Write** the word on your paper.
- Let's **seek** (uncover) the word.
- **Check** your spelling. If your word is spelled wrong, write the word correctly next to it.

2 Other Word Forms

This activity is optional. Have students unscramble these letters to write Other Word Forms:

tpotbale	(tabletop)
eidasl	(ladies)
deewaakn	(awakened)

3 Fun Ways to Spell

Four activities are provided. Use one, two, three, or all of the activities. Have students initial the box for each activity they complete.

Options:

- assign activities to students according to their learning styles
- set up the activities in learning centers for the class to do throughout the day
- divide the class into four groups and assign one activity per group
- do one activity per day

General

To spell your words in your classmate's hand...
- Have your classmate sit next to you and hold his (or her) palm open in front of and facing both of you.
- Use your fingertip to write a spelling word in the palm of your classmate's hand.
- Have your classmate say each letter as you write it and then say the word you spelled.
- Next, have your classmate write a word in your palm.

Auditory

To spell your words using a voice recorder...
- Record yourself as you say and spell each word on your spelling list.
- Listen to your recording and check your spelling.

Visual

To spell your words with paper cups...
- Spell a word from your list by putting the cups in the right order.
- Check your spelling.

Tactile

To spell your words with magazine clippings...
- Cut the letters you need from old magazines.
- Glue the letters to your paper in the correct order.

1 Working with Words

Familiarize students with word meaning and usage.

Sentence Fun

Write this incomplete sentence on the board:
We live in the state of __________.
Have a volunteer complete the sentence.

Choose the spelling word that best completes each sentence, and write it on the line.

Sentence Clues

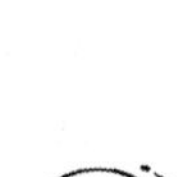

Write the spelling words that match the clues.

Take a minute to memorize...

Read the memory verse to the class twice. Have the class practice it with you two more times.

Day 3

Lesson 16

F Working with Words Name ____________

Words with /ā/ — Lesson 16

Sentence Fun

Write the correct spelling word on the line to complete each sentence.

1. A woman is called a _lady_.
2. A tree gives _shade_ from the sun.
3. The squares on a calendar mark the _date_.
4. To set something down is to _lay_ it down.
5. The opposite of asleep is _awake_.
6. Filled with fear means _afraid_.
7. We eat at the _table_.
8. You use a scale to see how much you _weigh_.
9. The number after seven is _eight_.
10. To send a letter is to _mail_ it.
11. Formed or prepared means _made_.
12. Ocean is to boat as air is to _plane_.
13. We write on _paper_.
14. Wind blows on the _sail_ to move a boat.
15. The opposite of hurry is _wait_.

Spelling Clues

Which words have the same spelling of /a/ as neighbor?

16. _eight_ 17. _weigh_

Write the spelling words that rhyme with state.

18. _date_ 19. _eight_ 20. _wait_

Word Bank

afraid	eight	made	plane	table
awake	lady	mail	sail	wait
date	lay	paper	shade	weigh

102

G Dictation Name ______________________

Listen and write the missing words and punctuation.

1. Stephen watched Christopher lay his map on the table .
2. Daniel is afraid Christopher will blame him .
3. Christopher made his paper plane sail across the room .

Words with /ā/ — Lesson 16

H Proofreading

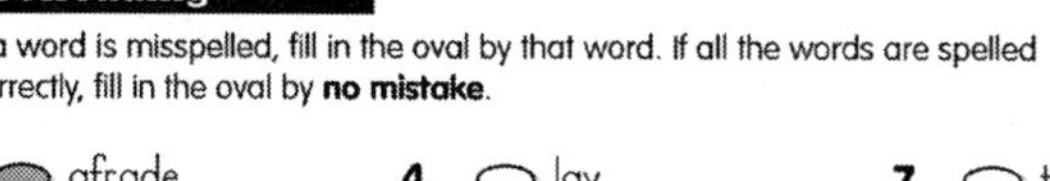

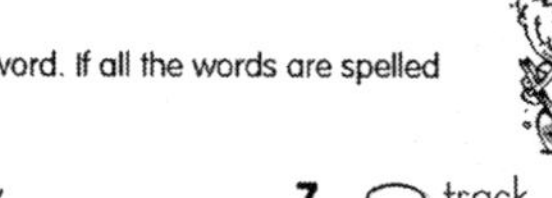

If a word is misspelled, fill in the oval by that word. If all the words are spelled correctly, fill in the oval by **no mistake**.

1.	4.	7.
● afrade	○ lay	○ track
○ awake	○ mail	● sial
○ careful	● ladie	○ weigh
○ no mistake	○ no mistake	○ no mistake

2.	5.	8.
○ copy	● maide	○ shade
○ cover	○ paper	○ sweet
● daet	○ queen	○ save
○ no mistake	○ no mistake	● no mistake

3.	6.	9.
● eite	● plaene	○ fork
○ key	○ wait	○ quilt
○ October	○ quiet	● tabel
○ no mistake	○ no mistake	○ no mistake

103

1 Dictation

Reinforce correct spelling by using current and previous words in context.

Listen as I read each sentence and then write the missing words and ending punctuation in your worktext. (Slowly read each sentence twice. Sentences are found in the student text to the left.)

2 Proofreading

Familiarize students with standardized test format and reinforce recognizing misspelled words.

Look at each set of words. If a word is misspelled, fill in the oval by that word. If all the words are spelled correctly, fill in the oval by **no mistake**.

Day 4 / Day 5

Lesson **16**

3 Hide and Seek

Reinforce correct spelling of current spelling words. (A reproducible master is provided in Appendix A as shown on the inset page to the right.)

Write the words one at a time on the board. Use this activity for each word.

- **Look** at the word.
- **Say** the word out loud.
- Let's **hide** (cover) the word.
- **Write** the word on your paper.
- Let's **seek** (uncover) the word.
- **Check** your spelling. If your word is spelled wrong, write the word correctly next to it.

4 Other Word Forms

Have your students complete this activity to strengthen spelling ability and expand vocabulary.

1 Posttest

Test mastery of the spelling words.

I will say the word once, use the word in a sentence, then say the word again. Write the word on your paper.

Other Word Forms — Lesson 16

Hide and Seek

Check a coin for each word you spell correctly.

Other Word Forms

Suffixes

When words end in silent **e**, drop the **e** when adding a suffix that begins with a vowel (rake + ed = raked). Add **-ed** or **-ing** to each word to make new words.

1. awaken + ed =	awakened	**8.** awaken + ing =	awakening
2. date + ed =	dated	**9.** date + ing =	dating
3. mail + ed =	mailed	**10.** mail + ing =	mailing
4. plane + ed =	planed	**11.** plane + ing =	planing
5. sail + ed =	sailed	**12.** sail + ing =	sailing
6. shade + ed =	shaded	**13.** shade + ing =	shading
7. wait + ed =	waited	**14.** wait + ing =	waiting

Clues

Use the clues to write the words.

1. to have placed — laid
2. under a tree it is — shady
3. women — ladies
4. comes before ninth — eighth
5. forming something — making
6. serious or important — weighty
7. wasp nests feel thin and — papery
8. person who works on a ship — sailor

Word Bank

eighth	laid	papery	shady
ladies	making	sailor	weighty

340

---

1. awake	It was hard for Daniel to stay **awake** during school.
2. made	He had **made** his salt/flour map all by himself.
3. table	All his mother said about it was to be sure to clean up the **table.**
4. paper	Each student wrote about their state on a piece of **paper.**
5. mail	Christopher got some information in the **mail** about Hawaii.
6. plane	Dad showed Christopher how to use a **plane** to smooth the wood.
7. weigh	Christopher's salt/flour map didn't **weigh** as much as Stephen's.
8. shade	Stephen had used a **shade** of brown to show the dry parts of Texas.
9. sail	Christopher's ocean looked almost real enough to **sail** on.
10. eight	Hawaii is made up of **eight** islands of different sizes.
11. date	March 18, 1959 is the **date** that Hawaii became our fiftieth state.
12. lay	The broken piece of Hawaii **lay** hidden in the corner.
13. wait	Christopher didn't **wait** to find out what really happened to his map.
14. afraid	Daniel was **afraid** everyone would believe that he'd broken the map.
15. lady	A **lady** called, and Mrs. Bentley forgot to tell Mr. Valentino what happened.

Progress Chart

Students may record scores. (Reproducible master in Appendix B.)

Personal Dictionary

Students may add any words they have misspelled to their personal dictionaries for reference when writing. (Cover in Appendix B.)

Words with /ā/

Lesson 16

I Game Name ______________________

Glue on a piece of the puzzle-picture for each word you or your team spells correctly from this week's word list.

Remember: God will bless you for being kind to the unkind.

J Journaling

Decide whether you are going to write from Christopher's or Daniel's view point. In your journal, write about what happened in this story as if you were Christopher or Daniel.

104

2 Game

Reinforce spelling skills and provide motivation and interest.

Materials

- game page (from student text)
- puzzle pieces (reproducible master in Appendix B, page 358)
- crayons
- scissors (1 per child)
- glue sticks (1 per child)
- game word list

Game Word List

1. afraid
2. awake
3. date
4. eight
5. lady
6. lay
7. made
8. mail
9. paper
10. plane
11. sail
12. shade
13. table
14. wait
15. weigh

Day 5

Lesson 16

How to Play:

- Have the students color the puzzle picture, then carefully cut the picture apart along the dotted lines.
- Divide the class into two teams.
- Have a student from team A go to the board.
- Say the spelling word. (You may also wish to use the word in a sentence.)
- Have the student write the word on the board.
- If correct, instruct each member of team A to glue on one piece of his/her puzzle picture. (Note: If the word is misspelled, correct the spelling immediately.)
- Alternate between teams A and B.
- The team to complete its puzzle pictures first is the winner.

Non-Competitive Option:

At the end of the game, say: "Class, I am proud of your efforts to spell the words correctly. If you had fun and tried your best, you are all winners!"

3 Journaling

Provide a meaningful reason for correct spelling through personal writing.

Review the story using discussion leads provided on the following page. Encourage students to apply the Scriptural value in their journaling.

Journaling (continued)

- Why do you think Christopher was so upset when his salt/flour map of Hawaii was broken? (He'd spent a lot of time on it and done a lot of work making the map.)
- Why didn't Daniel say anything when Christopher told everyone that Daniel had broken the map? (He wanted to, but he saw the Scripture Mr. Valentino had written on the board that said, "Don't snap back at those who say unkind things about you. . .")
- How did Jesus show us an example of this Scripture in action? (When Jesus was on trial, people told cruel lies about him, and He didn't say anything to get back at them.)
- Would you rather be Christopher or Daniel in this story? Why?
- Decide whether you are going to write from Christopher's or Daniel's view point. In your journal, write about what happened in this story as if you were Christopher or Daniel.

Take a minute to memorize...
Have the class say the memory verses from lessons 13, 14, 15, and 16 with you.

"The reason children learn to spell is to be able to write. The reason children learn to write is to provide themselves and others with things to read. The reason children learn to read is to be able to read what they and others have written. They all go together."*

*Harp, Bill. 1988. When the Principal Asks, "Why Are Your Kids Giving Each Other Spelling Tests?" Reading Teacher, Vol. 41, No. 7, March: 702-704.

1 **Literature Connection**
Topic: Trust in God
Theme Text: Ephesians 3:17

What's That Noise?

Setsuko conquers her fear of being home alone by trusting that God is with her.

"Okasan!" (ō kää sän - mother) Setsuko (set soo' kō) flopped onto her back and pulled the covers tighter around her chin. "OKASAN!" she called as loudly as she dared in the middle of the night. The miserable little girl relaxed slightly as she heard her mother's footsteps coming across the hall. Mrs. Noma reached for the lamp on Setsuko's bedside table. Click. The delicate china lamp flooded the room with soft light.

"What's wrong, Setsuko-chan (chän)?"Mrs. Noma sat on the side of Setsuko's bed and ran her hand over her daughter's forehead. "Atsui desu-yo! (a tsu' ē de sü yō - very hot!)"

Setsuko looked into her mother's face. Little worry lines crinkled the edges of her mother's eyes. "Okasan, I'm so c-cold and my head hurts."

"Your fever has gone up again, Setsuko-chan." When her mother stood to leave, Setsuko grabbed wildly at her arm. "It's all right, chiisai musume (chē ē sä ē mü sü mā - little daughter), I'm just going to get the thermometer to take your temperature."

Shivers kept running through Setsuko, making her teeth rattle against the glass thermometer as she waited for the minutes to tick by. Mrs. Noma held the thermometer near the lamp to check its reading. "102.6 degrees Fahrenheit. I'll give you some medicine, and you'll feel better when we get that fever down."

Setsuko obediently chewed the grape-flavored tablets and sipped the water her mother handed her. "Now rest, Setsuko-chan." Mrs. Noma turned out the light. Setsuko closed her eyes as she felt her mother sit down on the side of her bed. The gentle touch of her mother's hands stroking her hair soothed her, and she quickly fell asleep.

When Setsuko awoke, the sun was up, its weak rays struggling to warm the freezing winter air. Setsuko was glad she wasn't cold anymore. But although she didn't have the chills, her head still hurt.

"Ohayo (o hä yōō - good morning), Setsuko." Mrs. Noma entered the room, carrying a tray. "Breakfast in bed for you, young lady." She felt Setsuko's forehead and nodded. "Good. Your temperature's back down near normal, I think." She helped Setsuko to the bathroom and back to bed. By the time she was settled with the tray of hot cereal and orange juice, Setsuko felt almost too tired to eat. Only half the cereal was gone when Mother came in carrying another tray.

"Okasan!" Setsuko protested. "I can't eat any more than this."

Mrs. Noma chuckled. "You might have more of an appetite by lunch time." She moved the lamp and little china dog over to make room for the tray on the bedside table. Only then did she realize that her mother was dressed in one of the nice suits she wore to work.

"Okasan, are you going to work?" Setsuko's voice squeaked. "I don't feel like going to school."

"Don't worry, chiisai musume." Mrs. Noma smiled as she left the room. In a moment she was back, carrying the VCR and some videos. "You've had a relapse and will have to stay home a few more days." She set the TV on Setsuko's dresser. "But since I stayed home four days last week while you were sick, I can't take any more time off right now. Your father has those meetings that all the radiology staff are required to attend, so I've asked Andrea to check on you." She set up the VCR on a chair at Setsuko's bedside. "She'll be home all day writing a research paper on her computer."

Andrea and Rick Summers were college students who lived in the other side of the duplex that Setsuko lived in. "But, Okasan. . ." Setsuko started to protest.

"There's hot tomato soup in that thermos, a sandwich and grapes under the cover on this plate. . . Oh, and your water bottle is full, right here. Drink as much as you can. You can reach all these videos and books. Let's see, I'll bring your school work. I think your father put it in the living room." Setsuko, with wide, worried eyes, watched her mother arrange her school books nearby.

Mrs. Noma glanced at her watch. "I've got to go." She gave her daughter a warm hug. "I wish I didn't have to work today, Setsuko-chan, but you'll be fine. Don't worry." She pointed to a slip of paper on the bedside table under the cordless phone. "That's my work number, your father's work number, and Andrea's number. You can call any of us, Setsuko, and remember you can always talk to God, too. Let's ask God to be at home with you now."

The house seemed awfully quiet when the mini-van's sounds faded. Setsuko had never realized how much noise she made just breathing. She lay under the blankets, stiff as a board, eyes wide open, listening. What was that? She held her breath to hear it better. The strange clicking settled into a hum and she relaxed a little as she realized it was just the heating system coming on.

"Should I turn on a video?" Setsuko started to stretch her arms out, but stopped. Somehow, she felt safer all tucked under the covers. "If someone comes, I wouldn't be able to hear them with a video playing. What if someone does come? What would I do?" Scary thoughts swarmed through her head until she felt like screaming. "Maybe I should call Andrea and ask her to come over." She started to reach for the phone. "But mother said Andrea is busy with her

Story (continued)

school work. I'd better not bother her. She'll check on me when. . . what was that?"

Setsuko stared at the window and waited for the sound to come again. Thunk! "Wow, the wind sure has started blowing hard!" Thunk! "What is that? It must be small limbs or something hitting the house when the wind blows so hard." Setsuko jumped as she heard another sound. "Uh, oh. That's Chimi barking. I wonder what she's barking at? She sounds so fierce. Maybe someone is coming." She tried to burrow farther into her bed to make herself disappear, becoming more frightened every moment.

A creaking sound came from the front of the house. "What's that? It sounds like someone opening the front door! " Setsuko eyes opened wide with panic. "Oh, what do I do? Dear God, I'm so scared. Please be here with me. Help me to trust You to take care of me." Steps came closer down the hallway toward Setsuko's room.

"Oh, you're awake." Andrea Summer's long brown hair swung around her shoulders as she stepped into Setsuko's room with a smile. "And I was trying to be so quiet in case you were getting some sleep." Her laughter suddenly stilled as she noticed how Setsuko looked. "You okay, Setsuko? Are you feeling worse? Should I call a doctor?" She came over and sat on the side of the bed.

Setsuko shook her head. "No." She finally got her voice working. "No. I'm okay. I, uh, I just didn't know it was you." She shrugged.

"Oh, I see. You were afraid." Andrea patted Setsuko's hand. "I'm sorry, Setsuko. Your mother gave me a key so I could come in without you having to come unlock the door for me." Another series of loud, ferocious barks from the back yard began. Andrea walked over to look out the window. "Chimi's getting to be quite possessive of her back yard. She's got the Wiederman's cat up a tree. Of course, if that cat decided to challenge Chimi, I think the cat would win easily." She smiled at Setsuko.

Setsuko smiled back. "I thought maybe she was barking because someone was coming."

"Someone was." Andrea grinned and tickled Setsuko's ribs. "Wiederman's cat!"

"Stop! Stop!" Setsuko begged through her giggles.

"Okay." Andrea swung her hair back over her shoulders and straightened Setsuko's covers. "You don't feel like you have a temperature, but let's check anyway." She popped the thermometer into Setsuko's mouth. "Rick and I use the room just on the other side of your wall here to study." She walked over and knocked on the wall. "If you need anything at all, just knock like that and I'll come right over. And next time I come to check on you, I'll knock on the wall first so you'll know it's me coming in, okay?" She thumped three times on the wall. Setsuko nodded. Andrea looked over the things arranged around Setsuko's bed. "Looks like your mother fixed everything up." She took the thermometer out of Setsuko's mouth and checked it. "Still about a degree above normal. Do you need anything else?"

"Maybe a spoon to eat my soup." Setsuko pointed at the thermos.

"You could just drink it." Andrea grinned. "One spoon, coming up."

Setsuko heard her humming as she located a spoon in the kitchen and brought it back. "All right, young lady. Enjoy yourself." Andrea picked up her keys and walked to the door. "Remember, I'm just on the other side of that wall. I'll be working away like a slave while you're over here relaxing like a princess." With a wave, she was gone. Setsuko heard the front door open and close, but the silence didn't seem quite so empty this time.

Setsuko picked up a library book that looked interesting, but a few minutes later the book lay on the blankets and she was fast asleep.

The next morning Setsuko's temperature finally dropped back to normal and she felt a lot better. Mrs. Noma said she had to stay home at least one more day to make sure she didn't have another relapse. "You look like you feel much better today, Setsuko-chan." Mrs. Noma gave her a hug. "I hate to leave you again, but you don't seem as worried about staying home without your father or me as you were yesterday. Are you okay staying by yourself?"

"Well," Setsuko sat up in bed. "I'm not really alone, because Andrea's right next door and God is here always. It's okay, Okasan. Have a good day."

Setsuko watched a video and finished her book. "I'd better start on all this homework from the days I've been out of school. Let's see, Mr. Valentino's list says handwriting, pages 75 and 76 for this week. Looks like we're writing Ephesians 3:17." Setsuko ran her finger along the words as she read them aloud. "I pray that Christ will be more and more at home in your hearts, living within you as you trust in him."

Whshhhttt! "What was that noise!?" Setsuko clutched her handwriting book tightly in both hands for a moment, then thought, "God, you're here at home with me and in my heart just like this Scripture says. And I'm trusting in You." She opened her book and started writing.

2 Discussion Time

Check understanding of the story and development of personal values.

- Why did Setsuko call her mother in the middle of the night?
- Why couldn't Mrs. Noma stay home with Setsuko since she was sick?
- Who lived in the other half of the duplex in which Setsuko lived?
- What did Setsuko's mother leave by her bed?
- How did Setsuko feel when her mother left for work?
- Why was Chimi barking?
- What did Setsuko think when she heard footsteps coming down the hall?
- Why was Setsuko not so afraid to stay home by herself the next day?
- Think about it; is Christ at home in your heart?

A Preview Name ______________

Write each word as your teacher says it.

1. February
2. marry
3. honey
4. meal
5. heavy
6. field
7. twenty
8. leave
9. busy
10. creek
11. team
12. angry
13. carry
14. mean
15. deep

Scripture
Ephesians 3:17

Words with /ē/ Lesson 17

105

3 Preview

Test for knowledge of the correct spellings of these words.

Customize Your List

On a separate piece of paper, additional words of your choice may be tested.

I will say the word once, use the word in a sentence, then say the word again. Write the word on the lines in the worktext.

Correct Immediately!

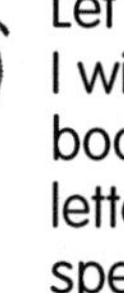

Let's correct our preview. I will write each word on the board. Put a dot under each letter on your preview as I spell the word out loud. If you spelled a word wrong, rewrite it correctly.

Take a minute to memorize...

Read the memory verse to the class twice. Have the class practice it with you two more times.

Day 1 Lesson 17

1. February — Andrea and Rick Summers were married in **February.**
2. marry — Women usually change their last name when they **marry.**
3. honey — Setsuko likes **honey** in her hot cereal.
4. meal — She didn't feel like eating her **meal** that morning though.
5. heavy — Setsuko's **heavy** quilt helped keep her warm.
6. field — The daisy pattern makes the quilt look like a **field** of flowers.
7. twenty — Mother has to leave for work in **twenty** minutes.
8. leave — She will **leave** some things for Setsuko to do.
9. busy — Watching videos, reading books, or doing homework will keep her **busy.**
10. creek — Setsuko likes the video about the things that live in a **creek.**
11. team — A **team** of scientists tells about frogs, fish, and other creatures.
12. angry — Chimi's barking sounded very **angry.**
13. carry — Setsuko was afraid someone might **carry** her away.
14. mean — What does "Christ will be more and more at home in your hearts" **mean**?
15. deep — Setsuko fell into a **deep,** peaceful sleep.

Progress Chart

Students may record scores. (Reproducible master in Appendix B.)

Day 1

Lesson 17

4 Word Shapes

Help students form a correct image of whole words.

Look at each word and think about its shape. Now, write the word in the correct word shape boxes. You may check off each word as you use it.

(In many words, the sound of **/ē/** is spelled with **ea**, **ee**, or **ie**. The spelling **ey**, or **y** can be used at the end of a word.)

In the word shape boxes, color the letter or letters that spell the sound of **/ē/** in each word. Circle the words which have more than one syllable.

B Word Shapes Name ____________________

Words with /ē/ — Lesson 17

Write each word in the correct word shape boxes. Next, in the word shape boxes, color the letter or letters that spell the sound of **/ē/** in each word. Circle the words with more than one syllable.

Word	Answer
1. angry	heavy (circled)
2. busy	mean
3. carry	February (circled)
4. creek	carry (circled)
5. deep	honey (circled)
6. February	busy (circled)
7. field	twenty (circled)
8. heavy	marry (circled)
9. honey	meal
10. leave	field
11. marry	angry (circled)
12. meal	team
13. mean	leave
14. team	creek
15. twenty	deep

106

Answers may vary for duplicate word shapes.

Be Prepared For Fun

Check these supply lists for **Fun Ways to Spell** presented **Day 2**. Purchase and/or gather needed items ahead of time!

General
- Markers
- Art Paper (2 or 3 sheets per child)
- Spelling List

Auditory
- Spelling List

Visual
- Letter Tiles a, b, c, d, e, e, F, f, g, h, i, l, k, l, m, n, o, p, r, r, s, t, t, u, v, w, y
- Spelling List

Tactile
- Paint Bags (tempera paint in plastic, resealable bags sealed again at top with heavy tape-1 per child)
- Spelling List

C Hide and Seek

Name ____________________

Place an **X** on a coin for each word you spell correctly.

D Other Word Forms

Using the words below, follow the instructions given by your teacher.

angrier	carrying	heaviness	marrying
angriest	deepen	honeys	mealy
angrily	deeply	leaving	meaning
busied	fielder	leavings	meaningful
busier	heavier	left	meanly
busiest	heaviest	married	meanness
carried	heavily	marries	teaming

E Fun Ways to Spell

Initial the box of each activity you finish.

1. 

Spell your words with markers.

3. SNAP
Spell your words while snapping.

2. 

Spell your words with letter tiles.

4. 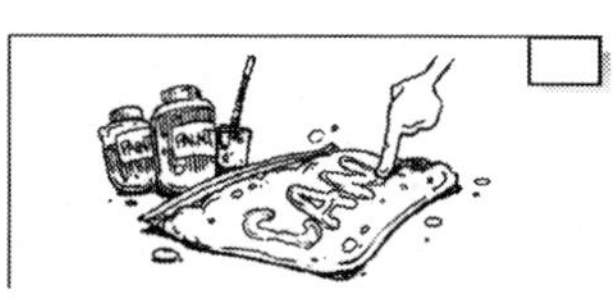
Spell your words with paint.

Words with /ē/

Lesson 17

107

1 Hide and Seek

Reinforce correct spelling of current spelling words.

Write the words one at a time on the board. Use this activity for each word.

Say

- **Look** at the word.
- **Say** the word out loud.
- Let's **hide** (cover) the word.
- **Write** the word on your paper.
- Let's **seek** (uncover) the word.
- **Check** your spelling. If your word is spelled wrong, write the word correctly next to it.

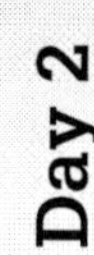

Day 2

Lesson 17

2 Other Word Forms

This activity is optional. Have students write variations of this sentence using these Other Word Forms:

This cardboard box is heavy.

heavier, heaviest

3 Fun Ways to Spell

Four activities are provided. Use one, two, three, or all of the activities. Have students initial the box for each activity they complete.

Options:

- assign activities to students according to their learning styles
- set up the activities in learning centers for the class to do throughout the day
- divide the class into four groups and assign one activity per group
- do one activity per day

General

To spell your words with markers...
- Write a spelling word in thick, fat letters.
- Use other colored markers to decorate each letter with dots, flowers, stripes, etc.

Auditory

To spell your words while snapping...
- Look at a word on your spelling list.
- Close your eyes.
- Snap your fingers softly while you whisper the spelling of the word.
- Open your eyes and check your spelling.

Visual

To spell your words with letter tiles...
- Spell a word from your list by putting the tiles in the right order.
- Check your spelling.

Tactile

To spell your words with paint...
- Use your finger to write a spelling word on the paint bag.
- Check your spelling.
- Smooth out the paint and write another word.

Day 3

Lesson 17

1 Working with Words

Familiarize students with word meaning and usage.

Proofing

Write the words **we, eat, these, green, receive, money, field**, and **only** on the board. Have volunteers underline the letter or letters that spell the sound of **/ē/** in each word. Explain that when the sound of **/ē/** is spelled with **ey**, or **y**, it comes at the end of the word. Now, write this sentence on the board: **sam went wading in creyk**. Ask the students to find the misspelled word. Demonstrate the mark used in proofreading to show that a word is misspelled. Next, ask the students if any words are missing. Draw the proofreading mark used to show that a word is missing. Now, have a volunteer find the letter that should be capitalized, and draw three lines under it.

At the top of your page, you will be using proofer's marks to show the errors in the paragraph. After proofing, write the misspelled words correctly on the lines.

Dictionary Skills

Write a sample sentence for each entry word.

Take a minute to memorize...

Read the memory verse to the class twice. Have the class practice it with you two more times.

Words with /ē/ — Lesson 17

F Working with Words Name ____________

Proofing

Use proofreader's marks to show the errors in the paragraph below. Write the misspelled words correctly on the lines.

○ word is misspelled	∧ word or words missing	≡ capitalize letter

The hevy, febuwary rains made creak very depe. The angree water rushed fast enough to cerry tree limbs and other rubbish. It kept a teem of twinty men bisy trying to rescue the calves were trapped the high corner of the feeld, then we all down to enjoy hot meel.

1. heavy	5. angry	9. busy
2. February	6. carry	10. field
3. creek	7. team	11. meal
4. deep	8. twenty	

Dictionary Skills

A dictionary definition tells what an entry word means. Sometimes a **sample sentence** comes after the definition. The entry word is in the sentence to help you understand the word meaning. Write a sample sentence for the entry words below.

mean. To matter: My friends mean a lot to me.
The sample sentence is: My friends mean a lot to me.

honey

1. (Answers will vary)

leave

2. (Answers will vary)

Word Bank

angry	creek	field	leave	mean
busy	deep	heavy	marry	team
carry	February	honey	meal	twenty

108

G Dictation Name ______________________

Listen and write the missing words and punctuation.

1. Setsuko was afraid for Mom to leave.
2. Mrs. Noma will carry a meal to Setsuko.
3. Setsuko lay awake for twenty minutes after Mom left.

Words with /ē/

Lesson 17

H Proofreading

If a word is misspelled, fill in the oval by that word. If all the words are spelled correctly, fill in the oval by **no mistake**.

1.	4.	7.
○ angry	○ made	● hevy
● buzy	● deap	○ twenty
○ afraid	○ plane	○ quick
○ no mistake	○ no mistake	○ no mistake

2.	5.	8.
○ date	● february	○ leave
○ eight	○ sail	○ marry
● cary	○ mean	○ wait
○ no mistake	○ no mistake	● no mistake

3.	6.	9.
● creke	○ team	○ meal
○ lady	● feild	○ mail
○ honey	○ table	○ paper
○ no mistake	○ no mistake	● no mistake

109

1 Dictation

Reinforce correct spelling by using current and previous words in context.

Listen as I read each sentence and then write the missing words and ending punctuation in your worktext. (Slowly read each sentence twice. Sentences are found in the student text to the left.)

2 Proofreading

Familiarize students with standardized test format and reinforce recognizing misspelled words.

Look at each set of words. If a word is misspelled, fill in the oval by that word. If all the words are spelled correctly, fill in the oval by **no mistake**.

3 Hide and Seek

Reinforce correct spelling of current spelling words. (A reproducible master is provided in Appendix A as shown on the inset page to the right.)
Write the words one at a time on the board. Use this activity for each word.

- **Look** at the word.
- **Say** the word out loud.
- Let's **hide** (cover) the word.
- **Write** the word on your paper.
- Let's **seek** (uncover) the word.
- **Check** your spelling. If your word is spelled wrong, write the word correctly next to it.

4 Other Word Forms

Have your students complete this activity to strengthen spelling ability and expand vocabulary.

1 Posttest

Test mastery of the spelling words.

I will say the word once, use the word in a sentence, then say the word again. Write the word on your paper.

Hide and Seek

Check a coin for each word you spell correctly.

Other Word Forms

Suffixes

When a base word ends with **y** after a consonant, change the **y** to **i** when adding the suffix (happy + ly = happily). Follow this rule to add the suffix to each word.

1. marry + ed =	married	7. busy + er =	busier
2. angry + er =	angrier	8. heavy + est =	heaviest
3. heavy + ness =	heaviness	9. busy + est =	busiest
4. angry + ly =	angrily	10. carry + ed =	carried
5. heavy + ly =	heavily	11. busy + ed =	busied
6. angry + est =	angriest	12. marry + es =	marries

Base Words

Write the base word for each Other Word Form.

1. teaming	team	12. busiest	busy
2. leaving	leave	13. carrying	carry
3. angrily	angry	14. fielder	field
4. deeply	deep	15. mealy	meal
5. heaviness	heavy	16. meanness	mean
6. angrier	angry	17. busier	busy
7. left	leave	18. marrying	marry
8. deepen	deep	19. busied	busy
9. heavily	heavy	20. angriest	angry
10. meaning	mean	21. carried	carry
11. married	marry	22. heaviest	heavy

Other Word Forms — Lesson 17 — 341

1. marry	Many people **marry** in the month of June.
2. February	People often get colds or flu in January and **February**.
3. honey	Mrs. Noma put **honey** in Setsuko's hot cereal.
4. leave	Setsuko didn't want her mother to **leave** her home alone.
5. meal	Mother left tomato soup for Setsuko's noon **meal**.
6. deep	Setsuko snuggled **deep** under her blankets to get warm.
7. busy	Andrea was **busy** writing a research paper for a college class.
8. twenty	The first **twenty** minutes passed slowly, like twenty hours.
9. angry	Chimi's barking made the Wiederman's cat **angry**.
10. heavy	Setsuko heard **heavy** footsteps coming down the hall.
11. mean	She was terrified that someone **mean** would come into the house.
12. team	Setsuko picked up a library book about a dog **team**.
13. field	The dogs pulled the sled over a snow-covered **field**.
14. carry	Dog sleds can **carry** a lot of weight.
15. creek	The sled broke through the ice covering the **creek**.

Progress Chart

Students may record scores. (Reproducible master in Appendix B.)

Personal Dictionary

Students may add any words they have misspelled to their personal dictionaries for reference when writing. (Cover in Appendix B.)

I **Game** Name ______________________

Andrea needs to check on Setsuko who is resting in her room. Lead the way by moving one space for each word you or your team spells correctly from this week's word list.

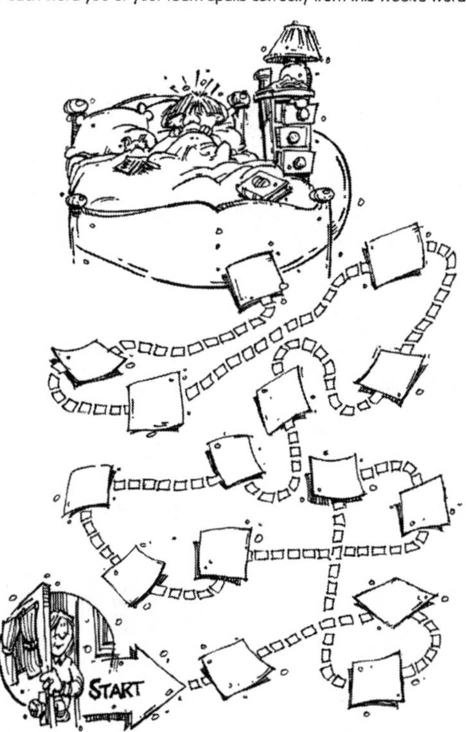

Remember: Allow Jesus to be your closest Friend. Trust Him always.

J **Journaling**

In your journal, write about a time when you were afraid. Tell how having Christ at home in your heart can help you when you're afraid.

110

How to Play:

- Divide the class into two teams.
- Have each student place his/her game piece on Start.
- Have a student from team A go to the board.
- Say the spelling word. (You may also wish to use the word in a sentence.)
- Have the student write the word on the board.
- If correct, instruct each member of team A to move his/her game piece forward one space on the game board. (Note: If the word is misspelled, correct the spelling immediately.)
- Alternate between teams A and B.
- The team to reach Setsuko first is the winner.

Non-Competitive Option:

At the end of the game, say: "Class, I am proud of your efforts to spell the words correctly. If you had fun and tried your best, you are all winners!"

2 Game

Reinforce spelling skills and provide motivation and interest.

Materials

- game page (from student text)
- flat buttons, dry beans, pennies, or game discs (1 per child)
- game word list

Game Word List

1. angry
2. busy
3. carry
4. creek
5. deep
6. February
7. field
8. heavy
9. honey
10. leave
11. marry
12. meal
13. mean
14. team
15. twenty

3 Journaling

Provide a meaningful reason for correct spelling through personal writing.

Review the story using discussion leads provided on the following page. Encourage students to apply the Scriptural value in their journaling.

Journaling (continued)

- Setsuko had been very sick and she got sick again, or relapsed.
- What kinds of things do you do when you're sick and have to stay in bed? (Watch videos, listen to tapes, sleep, take medicine, watch TV, look at books, etc.)
- Are there special foods that your mom fixes when you're sick?
- How would you feel if you had to stay at home alone all day?
- What ordinary noises did Setsuko hear that she thought were scary when she was all alone? (The heating system coming on, the wind blowing things outside, Chimi barking, the front door opening, and Andrea's footsteps.)
- What can you do when you're afraid? (Ask God to be with you, at home in your heart.)
- In your journal, write about a time when you were afraid. Tell how having Christ at home in your heart can help you when you're afraid.

Take a minute to memorize...
Have the class say the memory verses from lessons 13, 14, 15, 16, and 17 with you.

"Purposeful writing experiences are the key to cognitive growth in spelling"*

*Lutz, Elaine. 1986. ERIC/RCS Report: Invented Spelling and Spelling Development. Language Arts, Vol. 63, No. 7, November: 742-744.

1 **Literature Connection**
Topic: Obedience
Theme Text: Philippians 2:13

An Inside Job

Beth learns to ask God not only to help her be obedient, but to want to obey as well.

"Buzzzz! Buzzzz"! The dryer buzzer rang harshly from the next room. Mrs. Hill wiped her hands on the dish towel beside the kitchen sink and headed toward the noise. "Luke! Didn't I tell you to pick up these library books?" she asked as she passed the pile on the couch.

Luke lay sprawled across the family room floor. "Yeah. This is almost over." He nodded without looking away from the video he was watching.

Mom shoved the pile of books and papers out of the utility room doorway. The dryer was still buzzing loudly. "Beth!" she called over her shoulder. "You need to come pick up this school stuff as soon as you're done in the kitchen."

Beth scraped the bowl of crispy cereal and syrup into a pan, then patted it down with a spoon. "Okay," she called, "just a minute."

Luke turned off the TV as the credits scrolled down the screen, then headed to the couch to pick up his books. "Where are those ones about China? Beth would like the pictures in them." He quickly sorted through the pile of books. "Beth's class is doing a unit about China at school. . .oh, here it is!" He took the book into the kitchen where his sister was stacking dirty measuring cups and spoons in the sink. "Beth, look at this book I got at the library. It's all about China. Do you want to see some of the pictures?"

"Sure!" Beth nodded her head as she finished wiping off the counter.

Mom took the load of fresh-smelling clothes out of the dryer and put them on the counter. She pushed the button to start filling the washer with water, then turned and began carefully folding the warm clothes. After hanging up a couple of shirts, she picked up a stack of Beth's clothes and headed toward her daughter's room.

CRUNCH! Mom jumped at the sound and jerked her foot back, trying to peer over the pile of shirts, pajamas, and jeans she was carrying—but she lost her balance, and Beth's clothes flew out of her arms. She bent down and picked up a broken pair of chopsticks from the hall floor. "Oh, Beth," Mrs. Hill mumbled to herself as she gathered the scattered clothes. "What am I going to do with that girl?"

Mom refolded the clothes, then headed toward Beth's room. As she passed the family room, she saw Luke and Beth on the floor looking intently at an open book between them. "I'm happy you two are looking at a book together," Mom said quietly, "but isn't there something you should have done first? Luke?"

"I was supposed to put my library books away." Luke jumped up and headed upstairs with his stack of library books.

"And what about you, young lady?" she asked Beth.

Beth scuffed her toes in the soft carpet. "Put my school stuff away."

"Bethy, I need to show you something." Mom pulled the broken chopsticks out of her apron pocket.

"You broke my chopsticks!" Beth's eyes filled with tears. "Now I can't practice eating with them."

"I'm sorry, Bethy. They were right in the middle of the hallway and I couldn't see them over this tall stack of clothes, so I stepped right on them."

Beth hung her head, then went toward the hall to collect the rest of her things. Luke was standing at the foot of the stairs as she passed, holding the book on China. "Beth, how many people did you say lived in China?"

Beth looked at her brother. "Over one billion. There are five Chinese people for every one American."

"Wow! That's a lot of people!" Luke raised his eyebrows. "You're good at remembering all those facts, Beth."

"I know some more, too. Do you know what the largest man-made thing on earth is?" Luke shook his head. "It's over three thousand miles long and can be seen from space." Beth added, giving him a clue.

"Got me," Luke laughed. "What is it?"

"It's the Great Wall of China," Beth said proudly.

"Hey, I think there's a picture of it in one of my books." Luke sat down on the stairs to flip through the pages. "Here it is, Beth." Luke pointed to a picture of a huge wall meandering along part of China's northern border.

"Why don't we build a model of the Great Wall of China with our blocks, Luke?"

The two children soon had a huge wall stretching across Beth's room. They had used all the wooden blocks and plastic connecting sets that were in the toy box. They'd even used most of the books from Beth's bookcase. Beth gathered some miniature people and put them side by side across the width of the wall. "See, we made it the right size. Eight people can walk beside each other along the top of the real wall and eight people can walk side by side on our wall, too." Luke smiled.

"Oh! The Great Wall of China." Dad stuck his head in the door. "Longest structure on earth." He paused. "Speaking of China, does this happen to belong to you, Beth?" Dad held up a smashed Chinese paper hat.

Beth nodded slowly and picked at a piece of lint on her dark blue shirt. "Yes, it is. Why did you smash it, Dad?"

Story Continued

Mr. Hill knelt down and lifted Beth's chin. "I'm sorry I ruined your special hat, Bethy. I never saw it until it was too late. I was coming down the hall with my arms full of groceries, and it must have been sitting right in the way."

"Don't say it. I already know." Beth frowned. "If I'd only put my stuff away, then it wouldn't have gotten smashed." Beth wadded up the crushed hat and threw it in the trash. "Why can't I ever remember to do what I am supposed to do?" Beth mumbled to herself as she went to pick up the rest of her stuff.

The next morning Luke rushed into the kitchen. "Mom, have you seen my library books? I need to take all six back today so I can check out some more during our library time. I can find only five."

Mom looked up from the table, where she was arranging the silverware beside each plate. "Hmmm. . .I asked you to pick them up and put them in your room yesterday while I was doing the laundry. They were on the couch in the family room, remember?"

Luke nodded and went to look under the couch. He checked behind the couch and on the coffee table. The missing book was nowhere to be seen. "Why don't I do what I am supposed to do when I am supposed to do it?" He moaned and headed back upstairs to check his room again.

"Where are my crispy treats we made to take to school?" Beth plopped her backpack on the kitchen counter. "I can hardly wait to taste all the Chinese food today. Everyone is bringing something."

Mom smiled and handed Beth a pan covered with clear plastic wrap. "Go put this in the Expedition right now while we wait for Luke. Breakfast is almost ready."

After breakfast Mrs. Hill drove the children to Knowlton Elementary School. "Have a great day," she said as Beth and Luke climbed out of the new green sports utility vehicle. "Did you ever find that library book, Luke?"

"No," Luke replied. "I didn't."

"It's in my room, Luke. Remember we were looking at it so we'd know how to build the Great Wall of China?" Suddenly she stopped. "China! Where are my crispy treats, Mom? Did you get them? I think I left them on the dryer." Beth peeked through the glass of the Expedition to see if someone had put the dish in the back seat.

Mom shook her head. "No, I asked you to put it in the car while I finished getting breakfast ready."

"Oh no!" Beth groaned.

Mom motioned the children back into the car. Then she pulled out of the drop-off zone into a nearby parking space and turned off the engine.

She turned to look out her window so they couldn't see her frustration and anger. "Please help me, Lord," she prayed silently. Then she turned around to look at her two children. "You guys are not listening to me and it is becoming a big problem." Mom took a deep breath. "Beth, your chopsticks and hat got smashed yesterday and you don't have your crispy treats to share with your class. Luke, you couldn't find your library book this morning because you didn't put it away when I asked you to. You won't be able to check out any more books and there will be a fine for you to pay as well." She paused. "I love you both very much, but if you don't learn to obey, you will have problems your whole life. Learning to obey is something God tells us to do."

Beth looked out the window at the gray sky that was beginning to spit droplets of rain. She looked down at her hands. "I really do want to obey you, Mom. I just keep messing up. I wanted to look at Luke's China books and build the Great Wall of China. I get distracted doing other stuff. I don't plan to disobey you, it just happens."

Mom sighed. "Paul wrote something in the Scriptures that might help you. It's found in a letter he wrote to his friends in a city called Phillipi and says, 'God is at work within you, helping you want to obey him, and then helping you do what he wants.' Bethy, God is already helping you want to obey and that is the first step. If you ask God, I'm sure God will be delighted to help you."

"I think we better ask God right now before I forget again." Beth looked first at her mom, then her brother. "We aren't doing too well."

"Okay, you go first, Beth," Mom suggested.

The rain started falling harder on the Expedition as the Hill family bowed their heads to pray. "God," Beth said, "we need some help doing what You want. Amen."

Mom reached back and patted her kids' knees. "Go for it guys, or you'll be late. I'll run home and get someone's library book and a certain pan of Chinese treats." The two smiled and jumped out onto the wet pavement. Mrs. Hill watched her children make a dash for the front door of the school before starting the engine. "Thank you, God. I'm glad You are at work in our lives."

2 Discussion Time

Check understanding of the story and development of personal values.

- What mistake did the Hill children keep making?
- Did they do it on purpose?
- Why do you think it is important to learn to obey?
- What happened to some of Beth's things because she didn't obey?
- What do the Scriptures say God is willing to help you do?

A **Test-Words** Name ______________________

Write each spelling word on the line as your teacher says it.

1. table
2. jar
3. pass
4. twenty
5. heavy
6. cover
7. quiet
8. busy
9. eight
10. carry
11. lay
12. afraid

Review

Lesson **18**

B **Test-Sentences**

Write the sentences on the lines below, correcting each misspelled word, as well as all capitalization and punctuation errors. There are two misspelled words in each sentence.

please saev the sevinth seat for me?

1. Please save the seventh seat for me.

This sope has a very swete smell

2. This soap has a very sweet smell.

The kwean gave the little girl a gold kee.

3. The queen gave the little girl a gold key.

111

4 Test-Sentences

Reinforce recognizing misspelled words.

Say

Read each sentence carefully. Write the sentences on the lines in your worktext, correcting each misspelled word, as well as all capitalization and punctuation errors. There are two misspelled words in each sentence.

Take a minute to memorize...

Read the memory verse to the class twice. Have the class practice it with you two more times.

Day 1

Review

18

3 Test-Words

Test for knowledge of the correct spellings of these words.

I will say the word once, use the word in a sentence, then say the word again. Write the word on the lines in your worktext.

1.	table	Beth wiped the **table** with a cloth.
2.	jar	She put the **jar** of flowers in the middle of the table.
3.	pass	Beth will **pass** out the treats to her classmates.
4.	twenty	There were **twenty** crispy treat squares in the pan.
5.	heavy	The picture book about China was very **heavy**.
6.	cover	There was a beautiful picture on the **cover** of the book.
7.	quiet	Luke and Beth were **quiet** as they looked at the picture book.
8.	busy	Beth and Luke were **busy** building a wall of blocks.
9.	eight	As many as **eight** people can walk side by side on the Great Wall of China.
10.	carry	Mrs. Hill was trying to **carry** Beth's clothes to her room.
11.	lay	The chopsticks **lay** broken on the floor.
12.	afraid	"I'm **afraid** I stepped on these," said Mrs. Hill.

Day 2

Review

18

1 Test-Dictation

Reinforce correct spelling by using current and previous words in context.

Listen as I read each sentence. Then write the missing words and ending punctuation in your worktext. (Slowly read each sentence twice. Sentences are found in the student text to the right. The words **jolly**, **quilt**, **rake**, and **awake** are found in this unit.)

2 Test-Proofreading

Familiarize students with standardized test format and reinforce recognizing misspelled words.

Say

Look at each set of words. If a word is misspelled, fill in the oval by that word. If all the words are spelled correctly, fill in the oval by **no mistake**.

Review Lesson 18

C Test-Dictation Name ______________________

Listen and write the missing words and punctuation.

1. The man had a jolly laugh.
2. The quilt is red and yellow.
3. Can you rake these leaves for me?
4. I was awake very early this morning.

D Test-Proofreading

If a word is misspelled, fill in the oval by that word. If all the words are spelled correctly, fill in the oval by **no mistake**.

1. ○ race ● edje ○ asleep ○ no mistake
2. ● jellus ○ pass ○ paper ○ no mistake
3. ○ boss ○ certain ○ mean ● no mistake
4. ● sinse ○ eight ○ honey ○ no mistake
5. ○ fork ○ gas ○ shade ● no mistake
6. ○ mail ○ creek ● quik ○ no mistake
7. ○ rack ○ busy ○ February ● no mistake
8. ○ plane ○ field ○ key ● no mistake
9. ● deap ○ team ○ huge ○ no mistake

112

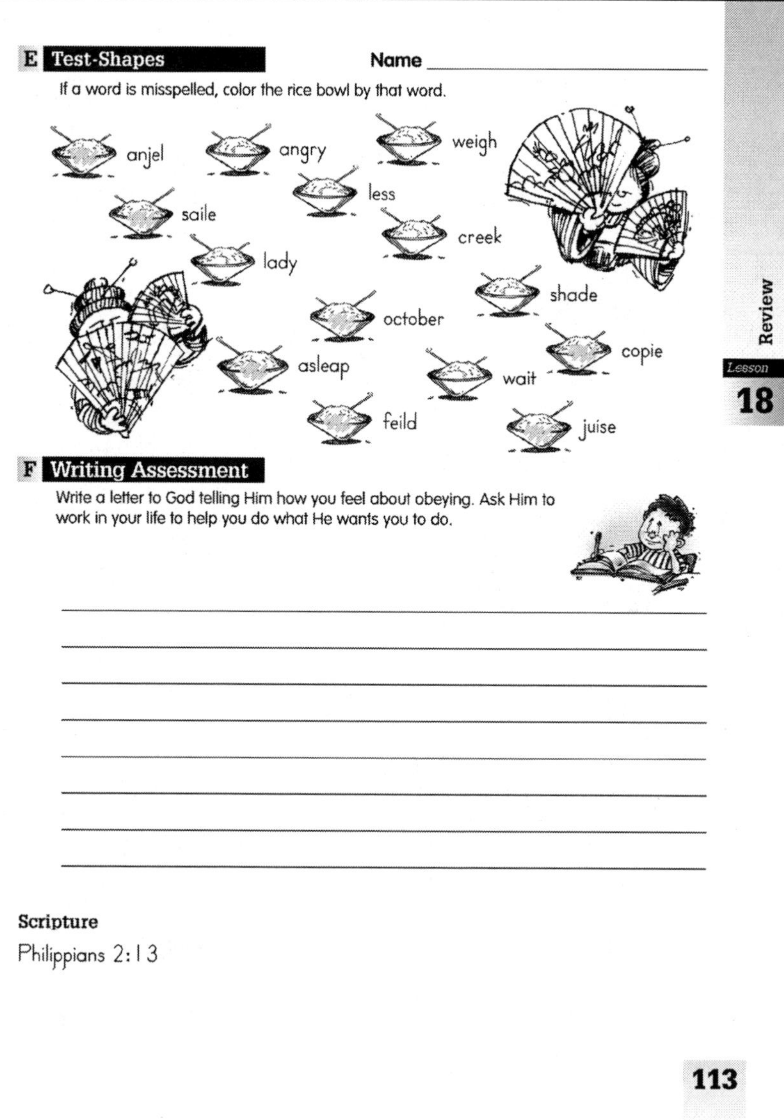

E **Test-Shapes** Name ____________________

If a word is misspelled, color the rice bowl by that word.

anjel
angry
weigh
saile
less
creek
lady
shade
october
copie
asleap
wait
feild
juise

Review

Lesson

18

F **Writing Assessment**

Write a letter to God telling Him how you feel about obeying. Ask Him to work in your life to help you do what He wants you to do.

Scripture

Philippians 2:13

113

1 Test-Shapes

Test mastery of words in this unit.

If a word is misspelled, color the object by that word.

2 Writing Assessment

Assess student's spelling, grammar, and composition skills through personal writing.

- Why did Beth keep disobeying her mom? (She didn't mean to disobey. She kept getting sidetracked and forgetting.)
- What happened when Beth didn't put her school things away? (Mom accidentally broke her chopsticks and Dad smashed her Chinese hat.)
- How did Beth feel about forgetting to do what her mom told her to do? (She cried. She was very frustrated.)
- Mrs. Hill said that the first step was wanting to obey God. God will even help you want to do that. What does our text say God will do next for you? (Help you do what He wants.)
- Write a letter to God telling Him how you feel about obeying. If you have had problems like Beth's, tell Him. Talk about how easy or hard it is for you to obey. Tell Him about someone you may have a hard time obeying. Finish by asking Him to work in your life to help you do what He wants you to do.

"Learning to write involves using real language in meaningful and developmentally appropriate ways."*

*Hoffman, Stevie and Nancy Knipping. 1988. Spelling Revisited: The Child's Way. Childhood Education, June: 284-287.

1 Test-Sentences

Reinforce recognizing misspelled words.

Read each sentence carefully. Write the sentences on the lines in your worktext, correcting each misspelled word, as well as all capitalization and punctuation errors. There are two misspelled words in each sentence.

G Test-Sentences Name ____________________

Write the sentences on the lines below, correcting each misspelled word, as well as all capitalization and punctuation errors. There are two misspelled words in each sentence.

Mom is serten the sirkus is coming to town.

1. Mom is certain the circus is coming to town.

my birthday is in januairy, not in july

2. My birthday is in January, not in July.

The jiraffe at the zoo is not in a caje.

3. The giraffe at the zoo is not in a cage.

H Test-Words

Write each spelling word on the line as your teacher says it.

1. leave
2. mail
3. paper
4. made
5. careful
6. kept
7. date
8. sorry
9. mean
10. huge
11. gas
12. meal

2 Test-Words

Test for knowledge of the correct spellings of these words.

I will say the word once, use the word in a sentence, then say the word again. Write the word on the lines in your worktext.

1. leave	"You shouldn't **leave** your things on the floor," she said.
2. mail	Mr. Hill brought the **mail** in with the groceries.
3. paper	Dad stepped on Beth's **paper** Chinese hat.
4. made	Beth had **made** the hat at school.
5. careful	Beth was not **careful** with her chopsticks and paper hat.
6. kept	Luke had not **kept** his library books together.
7. date	"This is the **date** the books are due," moaned Luke.
8. sorry	Beth was **sorry** she had not obeyed her mom.
9. mean	"I didn't **mean** to disobey," said Beth.
10. huge	Mrs. Hill gave each of her children a **huge** hug.
11. gas	Mrs. Hill stopped on the way to Knowlton Elementary to get **gas**.
12. meal	Beth and Luke should help clear the table after each **meal**.

I **Test-Editing** Name ____________

If a word is spelled correctly, fill in the oval under **Correct**. If the word is misspelled, fill in the oval under **Incorrect**, and spell the word correctly on the blank.

	Correct	Incorrect	
1. judg	○	●	judge
2. jug	●	○	
3. June	●	○	
4. raje	○	●	rage
5. race	●	○	
6. sel	○	●	sell
7. kwite	○	●	quite
8. trac	○	●	track
9. Febuary	○	●	February
10. honey	●	○	
11. marrie	○	●	marry
12. team	●	○	

Review Lesson 18

115

3 Test-Editing

Reinforce recognizing and correcting misspelled words.

4 Action Game

Reinforce spelling skills and provide motivation and interest.

Materials

- container with folded cards (1 per student) numbered consecutively
- chalk
- chalk board

How to Play:

- On the chalk board, write words tested on days 1 through 4 leaving out 2 to 3 key letters, and numbering them consecutively. (There should be as many words as there are students in your class.)
- Pass the container around the room having each student draw a number.
- Call each student to the board to fill in the missing letters of the word that coordinates with the number he/she drew.
- Have the class decide together if each word is spelled correctly.
- The game is over when every student has been to the board and all the words have been completed and checked.

1 Game

Reinforce spelling skills and provide motivation and interest.

Materials

- game page (from student text)
- flat buttons, dry beans, pennies, or game discs (1 per child)
- game word list

Game Word List

Check off each word lightly in pencil as it is used.

Red (5 points)

1. less
2. boss
3. rack
4. plane
5. deep
6. fork
7. asleep
8. copy
9. angry
10. creek
11. lady

Blue (10 points)

1. wait
2. field
3. sail
4. weigh
5. October
6. juice
7. edge
8. jealous
9. since
10. quick
11. angel

Yellow (15 points)

1. angelic
2. jarred
3. jolliest
4. circuses
5. gasoline
6. copies
7. quietly
8. angrier
9. marries
10. eighth
11. sailor

Day 5

Review

18

J Game Name ______________________

Score points for each review word or Other Word Form you or your team spells correctly.

Review

Lesson 18

Remember: God will help you desire to obey Him.

116

How to Play:

- Divide the class into two teams.
- Have each student place his/her game piece on Start.
- Inform the students of the following point system:
  Red list words = **5** points, **Blue** list words = **10** points
  Yellow list words = **15** points (these are Other Word Forms)
- Have a student from team A choose a color: red, blue, or yellow.
- Say a word from the correct color list. (You may also wish to use the word in a sentence.)
- Have the student write the word on the board.
- If correct, ask each member of team A to move his/her game piece forward (to the right, and up, counter clockwise) to the corresponding color in the first section. Record the score. If the word is misspelled, have each member of that team move his/her game piece to the "sad face" in the first section.
- Alternate between teams A and B.
- The team with the highest score at the end of three rounds is the winner. (A round begins and ends at Start.)

Non-Competitive Option:

At the end of the game, say: "Class, I am proud of your efforts to spell the words correctly. If you had fun and tried your best, you are all winners!"

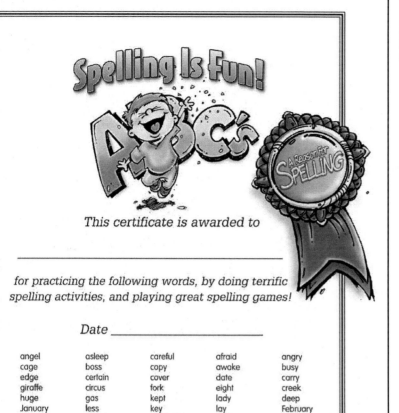

This certificate is awarded to

____

for practicing the following words, by doing terrific spelling activities, and playing great spelling games!

Date ________________________

angel	asleep	careful	afraid	angry
cage	boss	copy	awake	busy
edge	certain	cover	date	carry
giraffe	circus	fork	eight	creek
huge	gas	kept	lady	deep
January	less	key	lay	February
jar	pass	October	made	field
jealous	race	queen	mail	heavy
jolly	save	quick	paper	honey
judge	sell	quiet	plane	leave
jug	seventh	quilt	sail	marry
juice	since	quite	shade	meal
July	soap	rack	table	mean
June	sorry	rake	wait	team
rage	sweet	track	weigh	twenty

2 Certificate

Provide an opportunity for parents or guardians to encourage and assess their child's progress.

- Write your name on the first line.
- Write the date on the next line.
- Be sure to show your parents or guardian all the words you've practiced spelling.

Take a minute to memorize...

Have the class say the memory verses from lessons 13, 14, 15, 16, 17, and 18 with you.

3 Letter

Provide the parent or guardian with the spelling word lists for the next unit.

Show your parents or guardian this letter that lists your spelling words for the next unit. Put it where you will remember to practice the words together.

a reason for Spelling

Dear Parent,

We are about to begin a new spelling unit containing five weekly lessons. A set of fifteen words will be studied each week. All the words will be reviewed in the sixth week. Values based on the Scriptures listed below will be taught in each lesson.

Lesson 19	Lesson 20	Lesson 21	Lesson 22	Lesson 23
bicycle	ago	August	allow	airport
die	alone	autumn	amount	corner
fight	float	bought	anyhow	course
Friday	follow	brought	clown	floor
lie	goes	cause	crowd	fort
life	gold	daughter	doubt	fourth
nearby	open	fought	drown	horn
ripe	owe	hall	ground	order
shy	rode	paw	hour	pour
sign	rope	raw	loud	report
smile	sew	salt	mouse	score
tight	shown	song	mouth	sore
tiny	spoke	taught	plow	sport
wild	telephone	upon	power	storm
wipe	toast	wall	shout	wore
Philippians 1:11	Colossians 3:13	Colossians 3:14	James 3:17	Ephesians 4:2

1 **Literature Connection**
Topic: Doing good
Theme Text: Philippians 1:11

Eyes of a Leader

Stephen learns that his actions affect all those around him for good or bad.

"Time for handwriting class!" Mr. Valentino picked up the ***A Reason For Handwriting***® worktext sitting on his desk and thumbed through it until he came to lesson nineteen. "We're going to practice writing the letter 'k' today." He looked around the room at his class. "Some of you are not making your k's tall enough. Both upper and lower case k's should go all the way to the top of the space. Like this. . ." Mr. Valentino walked to the board and demonstrated the correct way to make a k in cursive.

"While we listen to this story tape I'm going to walk around the room looking for some bee-u-tee-full k's and other lovely looking letters in the day one section of your worktext."

Mr. Valentino smiled and punched the play button on the tape player, then picked up a bright blue marker and some snowflake stickers from the basket on the bookshelf. The music started to play and a voice announced the name of the story. Mr. V. walked up to Beth's desk and took a look at her paper. He continued down the row of desks, finding something good on each student's paper. He circled the best letters with his bright marker and put little blue snowflake stickers by them.

Mr. Valentino stood over Stephen's desk and watched him for a minute before he bent over and circled a nice "k" and the whole word "always."

"That's not my best word!" Stephen frowned. "This one is." Mr. Valentino put a finger across his lips and began to move to Matthew's desk. "But Mr. V." Stephen grabbed his teacher's sleeve and pulled. "Look at this word, 'May.' It's my best one!"

Mr. Valentino frowned at Stephen and motioned for him to be quiet again. "We are trying to hear a story, Stephen." As he turned to look at Matthew's work, Stephen kicked Tony's chair to get his attention. When Tony turned around Stephen rolled his eyes and frowned.

A few minutes before morning recess, Mr. Valentino came over to Stephen's desk and handed him his spelling test from Friday. "Stephen, I want you to rewrite these words as neatly as you did in handwriting this morning. I can barely read some of them. I can't tell if you spelled them correctly or not." He paused. "Before you go out for recess."

"What's wrong with them? Tony could read them. See? He's the one who graded my paper Friday. He said I didn't miss any." Stephen reached forward and tapped his friend on the shoulder. "What's this word, Tony?"

Tony turned around and looked at Stephen's paper. "Mean. No, I guess that's meal." Tony shrugged his shoulders.

Mr. Valentino raised his eyebrows and pointed to the paper. "Redo it, buddy. You can do much better than this."

Stephen rolled his eyes, grabbed the big notebook out of his desk and slammed it down beside the offensive spelling test. Tony turned around again. "Hurry up so you can play soccer," he whispered. "We need you as our goalie."

After recess Tommy trudged back into the classroom between Stephen and Tony. "Your favorite class comes next, Tommy." Stephen flung an arm across his friend's shoulders. "Multiplication tables! I'm on sixes now." A proud smile spread across Stephen's face.

"I finally start sevens today." Tony grinned. "I thought I was going to die before I ever passed my sixes. What are you on Tommy?" Stephen and Tony turned to look at Tommy.

"I'm still working on my threes. I almost passed yesterday. I got done in the right amount of time, but I missed one."

Stephen and Tony both rolled their eyes. "Seems like Mr. V. could give you a break, since math isn't your best subject," Stephen suggested.

Tommy just shrugged his shoulders and headed over to the counter to pick up the correct paper for the timed test given at the beginning of math class.

"Poor guy." Stephen whispered to Tony. "He works so hard at math. He studies those tables all the time. I think Mr. V should reward his hard work by letting him go on to the fours." Stephen headed over to get a drink before picking up his "sixes paper" off the counter at the back of the room.

"On your mark, get set, go!" Mr. Valentino started the stopwatch and 15 papers were simultaneously flipped over. Everyone started rapidly writing answers to multiplication problems.

"Stop." Mr. Valentino called a few minutes later.

"Yes!" Stephen said from his desk near the back of the room. "I finished my sixes today!"

Mr. Valentino gave Stephen the thumbs-up sign and smiled. "Way to go, Stephen. Let me check it for you quickly." Stephen watched expectantly as Mr. V. ran his finger down the paper. "What's this number, Stephen?"

Stephen quickly said, "Twenty-one."

"Sorry, buddy. That one should have been 28."

Stephen looked closer at his paper. "Oh! That's an eight, not a one. I was just in a hurry, Mr. V., I didn't make my eight very fat."

Mr. V shook his head. Stephen looked over at Tommy and rolled his eyes, but Tommy only frowned and said, " I didn't even finish my threes test today. I'm just not good at math."

Story (continued)

After the dismissal bell rang at the end of the day, Stephen, Tony, and Tommy walked to the door together. "Mr. V. is getting really picky. I can't believe he didn't let you pass your threes test yesterday when you only missed one, Tommy. And he made me rewrite my spelling test from last Friday before I could go out for recess this morning. If I had been there the whole game, I don't think we would have lost. I'm a better goalie than Beth."

"She's getting better, though," Tony countered. "If your dad helped her this spring like he helped me, I bet she could be as good as you by soccer season."

Stephen ignored the comment and started complaining again. "He didn't circle some of my best words in handwriting, either. I got only two stickers this morning."

"There's Grandma Miller." Tommy pointed to the little car pulling up to the curb. "You'd better get going, Tony."

"See you guys later," Tony said over his shoulder.

The next morning Mr. Valentino gathered the class around him. "We're going to do something a little different this morning. Mrs. Swanson is a 95-year-old lady who lives alone just a mile up the road from the school. She doesn't get out very often and she needs some help. We are going to shovel the snow from her driveway so she can have her groceries delivered and be able to walk to the main road to get her mail."

Stephen elbowed Tony in the ribs. "No soccer this recess," he whispered. Tony groaned, and even Tommy looked disappointed. Then Stephen turned to Daniel and whispered, "What is this, slave labor?"

Daniel cleared his throat to get the teacher's attention. "Is this slave labor or do we get paid for the work?"

"This is an assignment.," Mr. Valentino said, frowning slightly. "It's a lesson to help you better understand the text we're leaning this week in handwriting and spelling, Daniel." He paused. "Would you rather stay here in the office with Mrs. Bentley and do some Scriptural cross referencing on the subject?" Daniel quickly shook his head.

When the bell rang that afternoon for dismissal, Mr. Valentino asked Stephen to stay for a minute. After everyone had left the room, the teacher waved Stephen up to his desk. "Stephen, what's our Scripture verse this week?"

Stephen looked at the board where it was written and said, "'May you always be doing those good, kind things which show that you are a child of God, for this will bring much praise and glory to the Lord,' Philippians 1:11."

"Do you know what Mrs. Swanson told Mrs. Bentley today on the phone?" Stephen shook his head no. "Mrs. Swanson said no one had ever shoveled her driveway for free before in her entire life! And she's been around for almost a century. She couldn't believe we would do such a special thing for her just because we're God's children and that's what God wants us to do. How do you think God feels today?

"I think God is pretty glad about what we did."

"Stephen, do you know that the opposite of that text is true, too? When we do things that aren't good, we can start to ruin God's reputation." Mr. Valentino paused. "God has given us a special job of showing people what God is like by how we act."

"You're a leader, Stephen," he continued. "I've noticed that the last couple of days you roll your eyes every time you disagree with me. Now, Tony, Daniel, and Tommy are doing it too. Leaders have to be especially careful what they do because it can influence so many people. And your influence caused a lot of kids to not want to go over to Mrs. Swanson's this morning." He paused. "Can you see why I'm disappointed in your choices?"

Stephen hung his head. "I'm sorry, Mr. V. I want to do good, kind things like our text says. It was really fun this morning. I liked the hot chocolate and cookies Mrs. Swanson gave us, too. Do you think Jesus will forgive me?"

"Sure, Stephen. Just ask Him. One more thing before you go. I'd like you to do your best handwriting on this border sheet to give to Mrs. Swanson. I'm not sure she could read the one you handed in this morning very well."

Stephen gave a sheepish grin. "Yes, Sir," he smiled, looking Mr. Valentino right in the eye. "One beautiful border sheet coming up!"

2 Discussion Time

Check understanding of the story and development of personal values.

- How was Stephen disrespectful to Mr. Valentino?
- Who else started rolling their eyes in disgust?
- How did Stephen feel about helping Mrs. Swanson?
- How did Mrs. Swanson feel about the kind things the class did for her?
- What did Stephen learn about being a leader?
- Do your actions bring praise and glory to God?

A Preview Name ______

Write each word as your teacher says it.

1. tiny
2. wild
3. die
4. lie
5. smile
6. wipe
7. shy
8. fight
9. tight
10. nearby
11. life
12. ripe
13. Friday
14. sign
15. bicycle

Scripture

Philippians 1:11

Words with /ī/

Lesson 19

119

3 Preview

Test for knowledge of the correct spellings of these words.

Customize Your List

On a separate piece of paper, additional words of your choice may be tested.

I will say the word once, use the word in a sentence, then say the word again. Write the word on the lines in the worktext.

Correct Immediately!

Let's correct our preview. I will write each word on the board. Put a dot under each letter on your preview as I spell the word out loud. If you spelled a word wrong, rewrite it correctly.

Take a minute to memorize...

Read the memory verse to the class twice. Have the class practice it with you two more times.

Day 1

Lesson 19

1.	tiny	Mr. Valentino put **tiny** stickers by the *k*'s.
2.	wild	Tommy made a **wild** guess at some of the math problems.
3.	die	Tony thought he would **die** before he passed his sixes.
4.	lie	Stephen doesn't like to **lie** around at recess.
5.	smile	Stephen had a big **smile** on his face.
6.	wipe	You never see Stephen **wipe** out in soccer.
7.	shy	Stephen is not **shy.**
8.	fight	Stephen and Tony rarely **fight.**
9.	tight	Mr. V's class was on a **tight** schedule.
10.	nearby	Mrs. Swanson lives **nearby.**
11.	life	She has had a long **life.**
12.	ripe	Mrs. Swanson is the **ripe** old age of ninety-five.
13.	Friday	The class helped Mrs. Swanson on **Friday.**
14.	sign	Mr. Valentino gave Stephen the thumbs-up **sign.**
15.	bicycle	Tony often rides his **bicycle** in Mason Springs Park.

Progress Chart

Students may record scores. (Reproducible master in Appendix B.)

4 Word Shapes

Help students form a correct image of whole words.

Look at each word and think about its shape. Now, write the word in the correct word shape boxes. You may check off each word as you use it.

(In many words, the sound of /ī/ is spelled with **i** at the end of a syllable, or with **ie**, or **i-consonant-e**. It is sometimes spelled **y** at the end of a word.)

In the word shape boxes, color the letter or letters that spell the sound of /ī/ in each word. Circle the words which have the silent consonants **gh**.

Words with /ī/ — Lesson 19

B Word Shapes Name ____________

Write each word in the correct word shape boxes. Next, in the word shape boxes, color the letter or letters that spell the sound of /ī/ in each word. Circle the words which have the silent consonants **gh**.

Word	Answer
1. bicycle	die
2. die	sign
3. fight	bicycle
4. Friday	lie
5. lie	wild
6. life	shy
7. nearby	ripe
8. ripe	life
9. shy	fight (circled)
10. sign	nearby
11. smile	wipe
12. tight	smile
13. tiny	tight (circled)
14. wild	Friday
15. wipe	tiny

120

Answers may vary for duplicate word shapes.

Be Prepared For Fun

Check these supply lists for **Fun Ways to Spell** presented **Day 2**. Purchase and/or gather needed items ahead of time!

General
- Pencil
- 3 x 5 Cards (15 per child)
- Scissors
- Spelling List

Auditory
- Rhythm Instruments (two wooden spoons, two pan lids, maracas)
- Spelling List

Visual
- Letter Stencils
- Colored Pencils
- Art Paper (2 sheets per child)
- Spelling List

Tactile
- Play Dough
- Spelling List

C **Hide and Seek** Name ______________________

Place an **X** on a coin for each word you spell correctly.

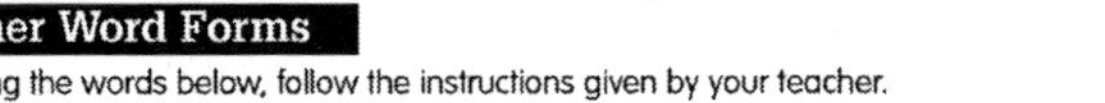

D **Other Word Forms**

Using the words below, follow the instructions given by your teacher.

bicycled	lay	ripen	signal	tiniest
bicycling	lied	ripened	signed	wilderness
bicyclist	lying	ripening	signing	wildly
died	lifeless	riper	smiled	wildness
dying	lifelike	ripest	smiling	wiped
fighter	lives	shied	tighten	wiper
fighting	near	shying	tightly	wiping
fought	nearly	shyly	tightness	
lain	nearness	shyness	tinier	

E **Fun Ways to Spell**

Initial the box of each activity you finish.

1. 
Spell your words with puzzles.

3. 
Spell your words in rhythm.

2. 
Spell your words with stencils.

4. 

Spell your words with play dough.

Words with /ī/

Lesson 19

121

1 Hide and Seek

Reinforce correct spelling of current spelling words.

Write the words one at a time on the board. Use this activity for each word.

- **Look** at the word.
- **Say** the word out loud.
- Let's **hide** (cover) the word.
- **Write** the word on your paper.
- Let's **seek** (uncover) the word.
- **Check** your spelling. If your word is spelled wrong, write the word correctly next to it.

2 Other Word Forms

This activity is optional. Have students find and circle the Other Word Forms that are antonyms of the following:

boldness
far
loosen

3 Fun Ways to Spell

Four activities are provided. Use one, two, three, or all of the activities. Have students initial the box for each activity they complete.

Day 2

Lesson 19

Options:

- assign activities to students according to their learning styles
- set up the activities in learning centers for the class to do throughout the day
- divide the class into four groups and assign one activity per group
- do one activity per day

General

To spell your words with puzzles...
- Write each word on a card.
- Cut each card into thirds using a straight cut.
- Mix your puzzle pieces.
- Put the puzzles together.
- Check your spelling.

Auditory

To spell your words in rhythm...
- Look at a word on your spelling list.
- Close your eyes.
- Play your rhythm instruments softly while you whisper the spelling of the word.
- Open your eyes and check your spelling.

Visual

To spell your words with stencils...
- Trace the outline of each letter of the spelling word.
- Color in the letters.

Tactile

To spell your words with play dough...
- Roll pieces of play dough into ropes.
- Use the ropes to make the letters of each word.
- Put them in the right order to spell each word.
- Check your spelling.

1 Working with Words

Familiarize students with word meaning and usage.

Day 3

Lesson 19

Secret Words

Draw four boxes vertically on the board. Explain to the students that an acrostic is an arrangement of words in which some of the letters, taken in order, spell a word or phrase. Give the students these clues:

1. **men wear this around their neck**
(Write the word **tie** across so **t** is in the first box.)
2. **number after five**
(Write the word **six** across so **i** is in the second box.)
3. **group of people who play a sport together**
(Write the word **team** across so **m** is in the third box.)
4. **color of a tomato**
(Write **red** across so **e** is in the fourth box.)

Ask students what word they see going down in the four boxes. (**time**)

The boxed letters in the acrostic complete a phrase from the Scripture verse for this week. Use the clues to write the words in the puzzle; then, write the boxed letters on the lines to find the secret phrase.

Take a minute to memorize...

Read the memory verse to the class twice. Have the class practice it with you two more times.

Words with /ī/ — Lesson 19

F Working with Words **Name** ______________________

Secret Words

Use the clues to write the words in the puzzle. Then write the boxed letters on the lines below and find the words from this week's Scripture.

		1. t	i	n	y		
	2. n	e	a	r	b	y	
		3. s	m	i	l	e	
	4. b	i	c	y	c	l	e
		5. s	h	y			
		6. l	i	e			
			7. l	i	f	e	
8. w	i	l	d				
			9. f	i	g	h	t
	10. s	i	g	n			
11. F	r	i	d	a	y		

1. very little
2. close to you
3. a happy look on your face
4. two-wheeled vehicle with pedals
5. bashful
6. not the truth
7. alive
8. not tame
9. battle
10. symbol
11. sixth day of the week

I a m a c h i l d o f G o d .

Word Bank

bicycle	Friday	nearby	sign	tiny
die	lie	ripe	smile	wild
fight	life	shy	tight	wipe

122

G Dictation Name ____________

Listen and write the missing words and punctuation.

1. Tony graded Stephen's paper on Friday .

2. Mr. Valentino gave Stephen a smile .

3. It was fun to shovel snow from the nearby sidewalk .

H Proofreading

If a word is misspelled, fill in the oval by that word. If all the words are spelled correctly, fill in the oval by **no mistake**.

1. ○ busy ○ awake ● bycycle ○ no mistake
2. ● fite ○ carry ○ creek ○ no mistake
3. ○ deep ● Fryday ○ weigh ○ no mistake
4. ○ February ● ly ○ shade ○ no mistake
5. ○ field ○ heavy ● nearbye ○ no mistake
6. ● sighn ○ die ○ life ○ no mistake
7. ○ ripe ● tite ○ shy ○ no mistake
8. ○ smile ○ mean ● tinie ○ no mistake
9. ○ marry ○ wipe ● wilde ○ no mistake

Words with /ī/ Lesson 19

123

1 Dictation

Reinforce correct spelling by using current and previous words in context.

Listen as I read each sentence and then write the missing words and ending punctuation in your worktext. (Slowly read each sentence twice. Sentences are found in the student text to the left.)

2 Proofreading

Familiarize students with standardized test format and reinforce recognizing misspelled words.

Look at each set of words. If a word is misspelled, fill in the oval by that word. If all the words are spelled correctly, fill in the oval by **no mistake**.

3 Hide and Seek

Reinforce correct spelling of current spelling words. (A reproducible master is provided in Appendix A as shown on the inset page to the right.)
Write the words one at a time on the board. Use this activity for each word.

- **Look** at the word.
- **Say** the word out loud.
- Let's **hide** (cover) the word.
- **Write** the word on your paper.
- Let's **seek** (uncover) the word.
- **Check** your spelling. If your word is spelled wrong, write the word correctly next to it.

4 Other Word Forms

Have your students complete this activity to strengthen spelling ability and expand vocabulary.

1 Posttest

Test mastery of the spelling words.

I will say the word once, use the word in a sentence, then say the word again. Write the word on your paper.

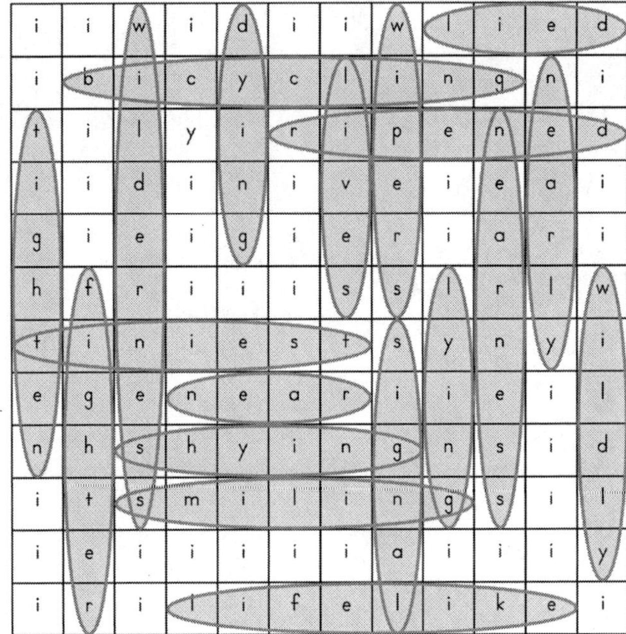

Other Word Forms

Lesson 19

Hide and Seek

Check a coin for each word you spell correctly.

Other Word Forms

Hidden Words

Use the word bank to help you find and circle each of the words in the puzzle.

i	i	w	i	d	i	i	w	l	i	e	d
i	b	i	c	y	c	l	i	n	g	n	i
t	i	l	y	i	r	i	p	e	n	e	d
i	i	d	i	n	i	v	e	i	e	a	i
g	i	e	i	g	i	e	r	i	a	r	i
h	f	r	i	i	i	s	s	l	r	l	w
t	i	n	i	e	s	t	s	y	n	y	i
e	g	e	n	e	a	r	i	i	e	i	l
n	h	s	h	y	i	n	g	n	s	i	d
i	t	s	m	i	l	i	n	g	s	i	l
i	e	i	i	i	i	i	a	i	i	i	y
i	r	i	l	i	f	e	l	i	k	e	i

Word Bank

bicycling, lied, lying, nearness, signal, tiniest, wipers, dying, lifelike, near, ripened, smiling, wilderness, fighter, lives, nearly, shying, tighten, wildly

342

1.	tiny	Stephen wanted more **tiny** snowflake stickers.
2.	die	"I'll **die** if I have to take this test again," wailed Stephen.
3.	shy	Stephen was not **shy** about what he wanted.
4.	wild	Stephen will play a **wild** game of soccer.
5.	fight	He will **fight** hard to get goals.
6.	sign	Stephen rolled his eyes as a **sign** of his displeasure.
7.	wipe	You must **wipe** that disrespectful look off your face.
8.	bicycle	No one rides his **bicycle** in the snow.
9.	nearby	Mrs. Swanson's house was **nearby.**
10.	Friday	They worked at Mrs. Swanson's on **Friday.**
11.	tight	The schedule was **tight,** but they finished on time.
12.	life	The class helped to make Mrs. Swanson's **life** easier.
13.	ripe	Mrs. Swanson may live to the **ripe** old age of one hundred.
14.	smile	Mrs. Swanson had a big **smile** on her face.
15.	lie	It wasn't a **lie** to say they had fun at Mrs. Swanson's.

Progress Chart

Students may record scores. (Reproducible master in Appendix B.)

Personal Dictionary

Students may add any words they have misspelled to their personal dictionaries for reference when writing. (Cover in Appendix B.)

I Game Name ______________________

Help Mr. Valentino's class shovel the snow from Mrs. Swanson's driveway. Move one space for each word you or your team spells correctly from this week's word list.

START

Remember: God gets great glory when you do what is right!

J Journaling

In your journal, make a list of kind things you could do to show respect for your elders.

2 Game

Reinforce spelling skills and provide motivation and interest.

Materials

- game page (from student text)
- flat buttons, dry beans, pennies, or game discs (1 per child)
- game word list

Game Word List

1. bicycle
2. die
3. fight
4. Friday
5. lie
6. life
7. nearby
8. ripe
9. shy
10. sign
11. smile
12. tight
13. tiny
14. wild
15. wipe

How to Play:

- Divide the class into two teams.
- Have each student place his/her game piece on Start.
- Have a student from team A go to the board.
- Say the spelling word. (You may also wish to use the word in a sentence.)
- Have the student write the word on the board.
- If correct, instruct each member of team A to move his/her game piece forward one space on the game board. (Note: If the word is misspelled, correct the spelling immediately.)
- Alternate between teams A and B.
- The team to reach Mrs. Swanson's front door first is the winner.

Non-Competitive Option:

At the end of the game, say: "Class, I am proud of your efforts to spell the words correctly. If you had fun and tried your best, you are all winners!"

3 Journaling

Provide a meaningful reason for correct spelling through personal writing.

Review the story using discussion leads provided on the following page. Encourage students to apply the Scriptural value in their journaling.

Journaling (continued)

- What kind of leader is safe to follow? (Someone who is a friend of God.)
- What are some things you have done to bring honor and glory to God's name and reputation? (Make a list on the board.)
- How have people demonstrated their appreciation for the kindness you've shown them?
- Raise your hand if you always get paid for the kind things you do.
- How do you feel when you are kind and respectful? (Write responses on the board.)
- In your journal, make a list of kind things you could do to show respect for your elders.

Take a minute to memorize...
Have the class say the memory verse with you once.

Encourage children to write and communicate their ideas.

1 Literature Connection

Topic: Forgiveness
Theme Text: Colossians 3:13

Cookie Crumbles and Grumbles

Kristin finds it hard to forgive her brother and sister—until she remembers the times she has been forgiven.

"One, two, and. . . one quarter." Kristin dusted the flour off her hands over the sink and replaced the lid on the large flour container. She leaned against the kitchen counter and read the next item on the recipe carefully. "One teaspoon baking soda. Baking soda." She read the labels on the ingredients Mom had placed on the counter for her to use. "Salt, vanilla, baking soda. That stuff in the yellow box is it. Now, which of these little spoons is one teaspoon? Not the yellow one. . . it says tablespoon. Ah, the blue one. One teaspoon of baking soda." Kristin carefully dipped the little blue spoon full of the white powder. She smoothed the top against the edge of the box to make sure it was an even teaspoon full like she'd seen her mom do.

Kristin felt very grown up. She was making cookies all by herself for the first time. Mrs. Wright had helped get the kitchen ready. She'd not only set out all the ingredients that Kristin would need, but had also set out the cookie tins, measuring cups, and spoons needed. Kristin had learned how to preheat the oven and had practiced setting the timer. Now, covered in a large apron, Kristin was on her own in the kitchen.

"There, now I need to stir all this dry stuff together and put the wet stuff in that other mixing bowl." Kristin stirred a little too enthusiastically and some of the white powdery mixture puffed out of the bowl. A few minutes later she found out that mixing the shortening and sugar in the other bowl took a lot of energy. Even though the shortening wasn't really cold, it took a lot of mixing to get the two kinds of sugar and shortening nice and creamy.

Kristin added a bit of extra vanilla when she continued to pour after the teaspoon she was holding over the mixing bowl was full. "Oh well, vanilla's good, right? Now, let's see, two eggs. How did Mom say to do this?" Kristin looked around at the things on the counter. "Oh, that's right, she said to break them into this little bowl first. I wonder why?" Crack. Smash. "Oops, maybe that's why." Kristin stared at the egg in the bowl. How was she supposed to get those little pieces of egg shell out of there? Picking up a spoon, she fished for pieces of egg shell.

Compared to that egg thing, the rolled oats, nuts, and chocolate chips were easy to add. Finally, the first batch of cookies were in the oven, and the kitchen was . . . well, a big mess! Kristin straightened her shoulders and got busy cleaning up. After all, she was doing this on her own. Soon the wonderful smell of baking cookies drifted through the whole house.

"Kistin, can I have a cookie?" Four-year-old Cory appeared in the kitchen doorway, looking hopeful.

"No, Cory." Kristin wiped the film of white flour off the counter. "These are for school. I'm supposed to take them tomorrow."

"Aren't there any extras at all?" Cory didn't give up easily.

"No, Cory!" Kristin dropped cookie dough onto another baking sheet. "I'm supposed to bring three dozen cookies and that's all of these."

"Are you sure?" Cory looked longingly through the oven window.

"I'm pretty sure." Kristin sighed. "But if there are enough extras, I'll give you one." BUZZZZ. "It's time to take out the first batch. Mom said to put this oven mitt on and open the oven door carefully. Whew! It's hot in there! Get back, Cory." Kristin repeated her mother's instructions aloud while she worked. "Now, I put on the other oven mitt and take out the cookie sheet. Set it on top of the stove and carefully set the next batch in to bake. Close the oven door, take off the mitts, and set the timer."

Cory sat at the table and watched Kristin scoop the golden brown cookies off the baking sheet with a spatula.

"Hey, Kristin, those smell yummy!" Cathy, Kristin's seven-year-old sister, reached for a cookie.

"Don't touch, Cathy!" Kristin waved the spatula at her. "You can't have any. These are for school tomorrow. I've got to be sure I have enough."

"Just a tiny little crumb?" Cathy's fingers inched closer again.

"No! No! and No!" Kristin propped her hands on her hips. "I know you. You'll eat a 'little crumb' and then another 'little crumb' and pretty soon there won't be one 'little crumb' left."

"Mmm-mmm, those cookies smell scrum-deli-icious!" Christopher came in from the garage.

"NO!" Kristin yelled.

"They don't?" Christopher gave his twin a puzzled look, then shrugged and started out the door.

"I mean no, you can't have one," Kristin said more calmly.

"Well, okay." Christopher shook his head. "But I thought they were for all the kids in Mr. Valentino's room."

"Aarrgh!" Kristin plunked the spatula down on the table. "They are, but you can't have one NOW."

"Did I ask for one now?" Christopher grinned and left the kitchen.

"Maybe not, but everyone else did," Kristin muttered after him as she glared at Cathy and Cory. Catching the hint, they quickly followed Christopher out.

Kristin was tired by the time she finally finished scooping the last cookie off the baking sheet. "Two, four, six. . ." She counted the cookies. "Sixteen, eighteen, twenty. . ." They really looked good. And

Story (continued)

smelled good, too. "Thirty-two, thirty- four, thirty-six, thirty-seven. One extra cookie."

"Sweetheart, you did a fantastic job." Mom came in and gave her girl a big squeeze. "I'm so proud of you. Your cookies look great and so does the kitchen."

"What shall I take them to school in, Mom?" Kristin returned her mom's hug.

"Let's see." Mrs. Wright opened a cupboard door. "I think they'll all fit in this large plastic container. We can line it with those fancy napkins and it should look very nice. But first, they need to cool completely. Why don't you take a break and then come put them in later."

A short time later, Kristin began placing cookies in the container. ". . . twenty-six, twenty-seven. . ." she counted. Then suddenly, she stopped. "Mom!" Kristin called. "There are only twenty-eight cookies here! Did you put some of them up or something?"

"No, sweetheart," Mrs. Wright called from the pantry. "They should all be there."

"But Mom, they're not!" Kristin wailed. "Someone ate my cookies! I'm supposed to have thirty-six and now I don't. Mom, what am I going to do?"

Mrs. Wright came and recounted the cookies. There were only twenty-eight. "Christopher, Cathy, Cory." Mrs. Wright called. "Please come to the kitchen." Pretty soon it was clear where the nine missing cookies had gone. Cathy insisted she'd heard Kristin say there were extra cookies, so she'd thought it would be okay to take one. Cory thought if Cathy could have one, then he could, too. But one thing led to another, and apparently the cookies were very good.

"I said there was one extra cookie. ONE!" Kristin practically shouted. She rushed out of the kitchen and down the hall to flop on her bed. Her cookies. The first ones she'd ever made all by herself. All of that work. She'd been so proud of them. And now she didn't have the cookies she'd promised to take to school tomorrow. What would Mr. Valentino think? Angry tears blurred her vision.

At the supper table Kristin managed to ignore Cathy and Cory. Mom explained that Dad would run to the store and get some more cookie ingredients after supper. Cathy and Cory would pay for all the ingredients out of their own money. Mom volunteered to make extra cookies after the kids were in bed so Kristin would have enough cookies to take to school.

"Thank you," Kristin said politely. She really did appreciate all the work her mom and dad were doing to help her, but she was still furious with Cathy and Cory. And it wouldn't be the same. Not really. The cookies wouldn't all be hers. Not ones she'd made all by herself.

Kristin remained icily silent as the sisters got ready for bed. "Kristin?" Cathy called softly across the dark room after they'd crawled into bed. "I'm really sorry. I mean, I'm really, really, really, REALLY sorry. Will you forgive me?" Kristin didn't answer.

The rich, warm smell of baking cookies wafted into the girls' room. "Kristin?" Cathy tried again. "Mom and Dad said Cory and I can't have any dessert for two weeks. And you know how much I like dessert." She paused, then finished in a very quiet voice. "But that's not why I'm sorry. I'm sorry because I ruined everything for you."

For a moment, Kristin lay there silent as a stone. "I won't forgive her. I won't! She knew better. She doesn't deserve to be forgiven." Her angry thoughts left little room for calmer thoughts, but they came crowding in just the same. "Setsuko forgave me when I said something mean that hurt her feelings. And Cathy forgave me when I broke her piggy bank. And I've done things I knew better than to do, too. How can I expect forgiveness if I won't forgive?"

Suddenly Kristin knew what she had to do. She took a deep breath. "Cathy? I forgive you. And Cory, too. I'll tell him in the morning."

"Thank you, Kristin." She could hear the relief in Cathy's voice. There was a long pause. "And Kristin? Your cookies really are good!" Cathy added. "Maybe next time you could bake a double batch!"

2 Discussion Time

Check understanding of the story and development of personal values.

- Why was Kristin making cookies?
- What kind of cookies did she make?
- How did her cookies turn out?
- What happened to some of her cookies?
- Why do you think it was hard for her to forgive Cathy and Cory?
- Why do the Scriptures say we must forgive others?

A Preview Name ____________

Write each word as your teacher says it.

1. shown
2. gold
3. open
4. float
5. goes
6. ago
7. toast
8. rode
9. alone
10. spoke
11. sew
12. telephone
13. rope
14. owe
15. follow

Words with /ō/

Lesson 20

Scripture
Colossians 3:13

125

3 Preview

Test for knowledge of the correct spellings of these words.

Customize Your List

On a separate piece of paper, additional words of your choice may be tested.

I will say the word once, use the word in a sentence, then say the word again. Write the word on the lines in the worktext.

Correct Immediately!

Let's correct our preview. I will write each word on the board. Put a dot under each letter on your preview as I spell the word out loud. If you spelled a word wrong, rewrite it correctly.

Take a minute to memorize...

Read the memory verse to the class twice. Have the class practice it with you two more times.

Day 1

Lesson 20

1.	shown	Mother has **shown** Kristin everything she'll need to use.
2.	gold	The flour is in that **gold** colored container.
3.	open	Please **open** the refrigerator to get out the eggs.
4.	float	The vanilla will **float** in the shortening and sugar.
5.	goes	The recipe tells what **goes** in the mixing bowl next.
6.	ago	How long **ago** did Kristin put the cookies in the oven?
7.	toast	Baking cookies smell better than **toast.**
8.	rode	Cory **rode** on Dad's shoulders.
9.	alone	Cathy and Cory ate some of the cookies when they were **alone** in the kitchen.
10.	spoke	Kristin **spoke** angrily to her sister and little brother.
11.	sew	Maybe Kristin will learn to **sew** next.
12.	telephone	Kristin will **telephone** Rosa to tell her what happened.
13.	rope	Cathy tried to **rope** Kristin into making more cookies next time.
14.	owe	We **owe** it to God to treat others kindly.
15.	follow	It is important to **follow** God's example and forgive others.

Progress Chart

Students may record scores. (Reproducible master in Appendix B.)

Day 1

Lesson 20

4 Word Shapes

Help students form a correct image of whole words.

Look at each word and think about its shape. Now, write the word in the correct word shape boxes. You may check off each word as you use it.

(In many words, the sound of **/ō/** is spelled with **o**, and it is often spelled this way when it is at the beginning of a word, or the end of a word or syllable. The **/ō/** sound can also be spelled with **o-e**, **oa**, **ow** and sometimes **ew**.)

In the word shape boxes, color the letter or letters that spell the sound of **/ō/** in each word.

Words with /ō/ — Lesson 20

B Word Shapes Name ____________________

Write each word in the correct word shape boxes. Next, in the word shape boxes, color the letter or letters that spell the sound of **/ō/** in each word.

Word	Answer
1. ago	owe
2. alone	spoke
3. float	ago
4. follow	telephone
5. goes	follow
6. gold	float
7. open	toast
8. owe	gold
9. rode	goes
10. rope	sew
11. sew	shown
12. shown	open
13. spoke	rode
14. telephone	rope
15. toast	alone

126

Answers may vary for duplicate word shapes.

Be Prepared For Fun

Check these supply lists for **Fun Ways to Spell** presented **Day 2**. Purchase and/or gather needed items ahead of time!

General
- Chalk or Whiteboard Marker
- Chalkboard or Whiteboard (could be individual boards for each child)
- Spelling List

Auditory
- Box to Store Letters
- a, d, e, e, e f, g, h, k, l, l, n, o, o, p, r, s, t, t, w (written on seasonal shapes like cardinals or pine trees)
- Spelling List

Visual
- Glitter Glue
- Art Paper (2 or 3 pieces per child)
- Spelling List

Tactile
- Thick Pile Carpet Squares
- Spelling List

C **Hide and Seek** Name ____________

Place an **X** on a coin for each word you spell correctly.

D **Other Word Forms**

Using the words below, follow the instructions given by your teacher.

floated	gone	openly	roping	speaking
floating	golden	openness	sewed	spoken
floats	loneliness	owed	sewing	telephoned
followed	lonely	owing	sewn	telephoning
follower	lonesome	ride	show	toasted
following	opened	rider	showed	toaster
go	opener	riding	showing	toasting
going	opening	roped	speak	

E **Fun Ways to Spell**

Initial the box of each activity you finish.

1. 

Spell your words with chalk.

3. 

Spell your words out of the letter box.

2. 

Spell your words with glitter glue.

4. 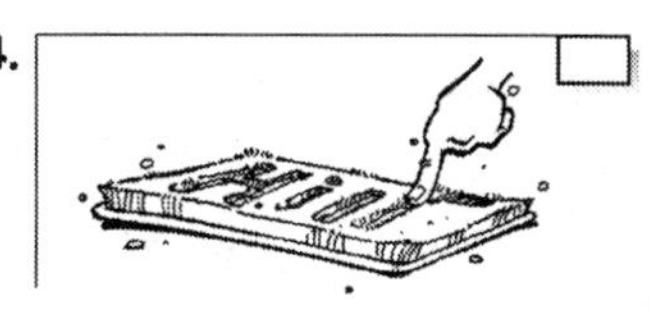

Spell your words on carpet.

Words with /ō/

Lesson 20

127

1 Hide and Seek

Reinforce correct spelling of current spelling words.

Write the words one at a time on the board. Use this activity for each word.

Say

- **Look** at the word.
- **Say** the word out loud.
- Let's **hide** (cover) the word.
- **Write** the word on your paper.
- Let's **seek** (uncover) the word.
- **Check** your spelling. If your word is spelled wrong, write the word correctly next to it.

2 Other Word Forms

This activity is optional. Have students write original sentences using these Other Word Forms:

floated
golden
speaking
telephoned

3 Fun Ways to Spell

Four activities are provided. Use one, two, three, or all of the activities. Have students initial the box for each activity they complete.

Options:

- assign activities to students according to their learning styles
- set up the activities in learning centers for the class to do throughout the day
- divide the class into four groups and assign one activity per group
- do one activity per day

General

To spell your words with chalk...
- Put your spelling list on your desk.
- Look at a word; then, walk to the chalkboard (or whiteboard).
- Write your spelling word on the chalkboard (or whiteboard).
- Return to your desk.
- Check your spelling.

Auditory

To spell your words out of the letter box...
- Spell a word from your list by putting the letters in the right order.
- Check your spelling.
- Spell your word out loud.

Visual

To spell your words with glitter glue...
- Write each of your spelling words on your paper.
- Check your spelling.

Tactile

To spell your words on carpet...
- Use your fingertip to write a spelling word on the carpet.
- Check your spelling.
- Smooth the word out with your hand and write another.

Day 3

Lesson 20

1 Working with Words

Familiarize students with word meaning and usage.

Spelling Clues

Recognizing that many words are made up of common letter patterns and/or smaller words can help students spell better. Write **finish** on the board. Have a volunteer circle the smaller words **fin**, and **in**. Now, write the word **elephant**. Have a volunteer circle the smaller word **ant**.

Find the spelling word that contains the smaller word and write it on the line.

Dictionary Skills

Write the number of the definition that matches the meaning of the bold word in each sentence.

Take a minute to memorize...

Read the memory verse to the class twice. Have the class practice it with you two more times.

Words with /ō/ — Lesson 20

F Working with Words Name ____________________

Spelling Clues

Write the correct spelling words on the lines.

1. The little word **phone** is in the bigger word telephone.
2. The little word **oat** is in the bigger word float.
3. The little word **low** is in the bigger word follow.
4. The little word **go** is in the bigger words ago and goes.
5. The little word **old** is in the bigger word gold.
6. The little word **pen** is in the bigger word open.
7. The little word **we** is in the bigger word owe.
8. The little word **rod** is in the bigger word rode.
9. The little word **own** is in the bigger word shown.
10. The little word **poke** is in the bigger word spoke.
11. The little word **one** is in the bigger word alone.
12. The little word **as** is in the bigger word toast.
13. Write the word in which /ō/ is spelled **ew.** sew
14. Write the word that rhymes with soap. rope

Dictionary Skills

Some dictionary entries have more than one meaning or definition. Read the entry word and its definitions. Write the number of the definition that matches the meaning of the bold word in each sentence.

rope **1.** strong cord made from twisted fiber **2.** to catch with a lasso

1. Father showed me how to **rope** a steer. 2
2. We watched a man making **rope** at the tractor show. 1

Word Bank

ago	follow	open	rope	spoke
alone	goes	owe	sew	telephone
float	gold	rode	shown	toast

128

G Dictation

Name ____________________

Listen and write the missing words and punctuation.

1. Kristin was careful to follow the recipe.
2. Mom had shown her what to do.
3. Open the oven and set the cookies on a rack.

Words with /ō/

Lesson 20

H Proofreading

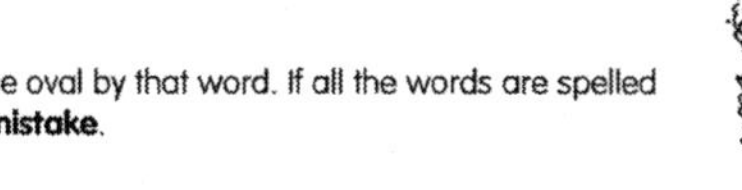

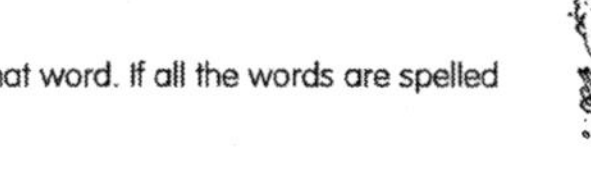

If a word is misspelled, fill in the oval by that word. If all the words are spelled correctly, fill in the oval by **no mistake**.

1. ○ bicycle ○ alone ● agoe ○ no mistake
2. ● flote ○ fight ○ Friday ○ no mistake
3. ● opin ○ follow ○ gold ○ no mistake
4. ○ owe ● goz ○ nearby ○ no mistake
5. ○ lie ○ sign ● roade ○ no mistake
6. ● roap ○ shown ○ wipe ○ no mistake
7. ○ sew ● telefone ○ tight ○ no mistake
8. ○ tiny ○ wild ● toste ○ no mistake
9. ○ spoke ○ twenty ○ meal ● no mistake

129

1 Dictation

Reinforce correct spelling by using current and previous words in context.

Listen as I read each sentence and then write the missing words and ending punctuation in your worktext. (Slowly read each sentence twice. Sentences are found in the student text to the left.)

2 Proofreading

Familiarize students with standardized test format and reinforce recognizing misspelled words.

Look at each set of words. If a word is misspelled, fill in the oval by that word. If all the words are spelled correctly, fill in the oval by **no mistake**.

Day 4

Lesson 20

3 Hide and Seek

Reinforce correct spelling of current spelling words. (A reproducible master is provided in Appendix A as shown on the inset page to the right.)
Write the words one at a time on the board. Use this activity for each word.

- **Look** at the word.
- **Say** the word out loud.
- Let's **hide** (cover) the word.
- **Write** the word on your paper.
- Let's **seek** (uncover) the word.
- **Check** your spelling. If your word is spelled wrong, write the word correctly next to it.

4 Other Word Forms

Have your students complete this activity to strengthen spelling ability and expand vocabulary.

1 Posttest

Test mastery of the spelling words.

I will say the word once, use the word in a sentence, then say the word again. Write the word on your paper.

Check a coin for each word you spell correctly.

Other Word Forms

Sentence Fun

Write the words that best complete each sentence.

1. The cowboy is good at riding his horse and roping calves.
2. Mom sewed the golden colored fabric to make my costume.
3. I dropped the bread into the opening on the toaster.
4. Rachel owed him an apology for speaking so crossly.
5. The lonely little puppy followed me around.
6. A snake floated past me, with only its head showing.
7. I telephoned my mom from school, but she was gone.

Code Words

Use the code to write each Other Word Form.

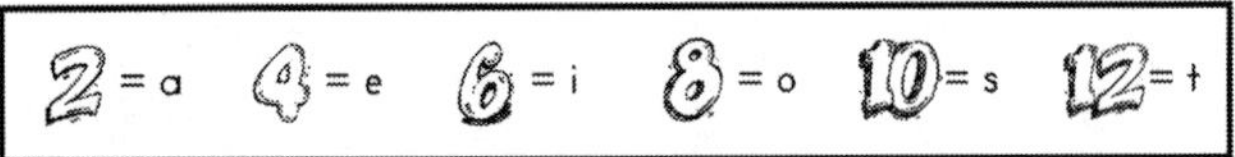

1. 10 p 8 k 4 n — spoken
2. 8 p 4 nly — openly
3. fl 8 2 12 6 ng — floating
4. l 8 n 4 10 8 m 4 — lonesome

Word Bank

floated, followed, golden, gone, lonely, opening, owed, riding, roping, sewed, showing, speaking, telephoned, toaster

Other Word Forms — Lesson 20 — 343

1.	telephone	The **telephone** is on the wall by the window.
2.	alone	Kristin was all **alone** in the kitchen making cookies.
3.	sew	Mother went into the other room to **sew**.
4.	follow	Kristin was very careful to **follow** the recipe directions.
5.	goes	What **goes** in the mixing bowl next?
6.	float	Kristin saw some pieces of shell **float** in the broken egg.
7.	shown	Mother had **shown** her just how to operate the oven.
8.	open	Kristin will **open** the oven door very carefully.
9.	gold	The freshly baked cookies were **gold** and brown.
10.	toast	Mother will **toast** cheese sandwiches for supper.
11.	rope	Christopher came in from jumping **rope**.
12.	rode	He **rode** to town with Dad to buy more cookie ingredients.
13.	owe	Cathy and Cory **owe** Dad money for the extra ingredients.
14.	ago	Kristin remembered breaking Cathy's piggy bank long **ago**.
15.	spoke	Finally she **spoke** the words, "Cathy? I forgive you."

Progress Chart

Students may record scores. (Reproducible master in Appendix B.)

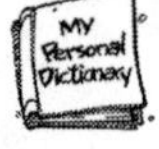

Personal Dictionary

Students may add any words they have misspelled to their personal dictionaries for reference when writing. (Cover in Appendix B.)

Words with /ō/

Lesson 20

I Game Name ______________________

Complete the secret phrase by correctly spelling the words from this week's word list.

Remember: Forgive others the way Jesus has forgiven you!

J Journaling

In your journal, write a paragraph about a time when you forgave someone.

130

2 Game

Reinforce spelling skills and provide motivation and interest.

Materials

- game page (from student text)
- pencils (1 per child)
- game word list

Game Word List

Team A	Team B
1. ago (D)	1. owe (D)
2. alone (O)	2. rode (O)
3. float (N)	3. rope (N)
4. follow (T)	4. shown (T)
5. goes (H)	5. spoke (H)
6. gold (O)	6. telephone (O)
7. open (L)	7. toast (L)
8. owe (D)	8. sew (D)
9. rode (G)	9. ago (G)
10. rope (R)	10. alone (R)
11. sew (U)	11. float (U)
12. shown (D)	12. follow (D)
13. spoke (G)	13. goes (G)
14. telephone (E)	14. gold (E)
15. toast (S)	15. open (S)

Day 5

Lesson 20

How to Play:

- Divide the class into two teams.
- Have a student from team A choose a number from 1 to 15.
- Say the word that matches that number from the team's word list. (You may also wish to use the word in a sentence.)
- Have the student write the word on the board.
- If correct, have each member of team A write the given letter in the matching space on his/her game page.
- Alternate between teams A and B having the students choose a number of a blank space.
- The team to complete the secret phrase first is the winner.

Non-Competitive Option:

At the end of the game, say: "Class, I am proud of your efforts to spell the words correctly. If you had fun and tried your best, you are all winners!"

3 Journaling

Provide a meaningful reason for correct spelling through personal writing.

Review the story using discussion leads provided on the following page. Encourage students to apply the Scriptural value in their journaling.

Journaling (continued)

- Kristin was making cookies to take to school. What was so special about these cookies? (It was the first time she'd made cookies all by herself.)
- Do you like to make things in the kitchen?
- Have you ever made cookies or some other food all by yourself?
- Why did Cathy say she'd taken a cookie? (She said she'd heard Kristin say there were extra cookies and she thought it would be okay to take one.)
- Was it all right for Cathy to take a cookie? (No.)
- What happened to Cathy and Cory because they took the cookies? (They had to pay for more ingredients and they couldn't have any dessert for two weeks.)
- How did Mom and Dad help Kristin? (Dad went to the store to get more ingredients and Mom made more cookies after the kids were in bed.)
- In your journal, write a paragraph about a time when you forgave someone.

Take a minute to memorize...
Have the class say the memory verses from lessons 19 and 20 with you.

Children learn more about writing every time they write independently.

Imperfect Harmony

Rachel and Daniel's argument turns out to be a waste of time. They learn that things aren't always the way we think they are.

"My dad says they're going to have soccer camp this summer at Mason Springs Park!" Daniel looked at Stephen excitedly. "Are you gonna go?"

"How much will it cost?" Stephen dug his hands down deep into his pockets. His mom and dad both worked, but they didn't have a lot of extra money. He'd love to go if it didn't cost too much.

"Well, Dad said volunteers from a bunch of churches are going to run the camp for all the kids in town. It won't cost anything!"

Rachel walked up to the group surrounding Daniel. "My mom said it was going to be a swim camp."

"Well, my dad is the chairperson of the committee, " Daniel raised his eyebrows, "so he should know!"

"Well, my mom is the secretary and she typed what everybody voted for last night on her computer." Rachel folded her arms across her chest and glared at Daniel. "I guess she should be able to read what she typed!"

Daniel rolled his eyes. "Maybe she typed the wrong thing. It's possible, you know."

"I don't think so. Helen was a secretary for years before she married my dad. She types very fast with no mistakes."

"Well, she made a mistake this time because my dad told me this morning what the city council is planning." Daniel's face wrinkled with an angry frown. "He said there was going to be a soccer camp this summer. He even said that Coach Larkin will be leading out and it'll be free!"

"Well, my mom was reading from the paper she typed this morning," Rachel shot back. "It said there would be swim camps this summer at the pool. But it will not be free. The council thought people would appreciate it more it they had to pay at least a small amount for each lesson."

"Tony, come over here." Daniel waved his arm wildly in the air as Tony walked into the classroom. "Isn't your mom's friend going to coach at a summer soccer camp?"

"Who? Coach Larkin?" Tony looked at Daniel. "I think so. I heard him talking with my mom about a soccer camp last night after practice. I think he wasn't sure he could do it all summer. He said he would tell the committee when he came back from his convention in New York next week."

"See, Rachel what'd I tell ya?" Daniel smirked. "Soccer camp this summer at Mason Springs Park!"

"He hasn't even said 'yes' yet, but you said your dad told you that Coach Larkin will be in charge! Maybe if Coach says 'no', there won't even be a soccer camp! Maybe you should get your facts straight before you go announcing what the city council is planning!" Rachel felt like hitting Daniel, but headed toward her desk instead.

Daniel ran his hand through his hair. "Rachel, just because your dad is a lawyer and your mom typed up what they talked about doesn't mean. . ."

Mr. Valentino interrupted the argument and asked everyone to take their seats. Rachel glared at Daniel as she stalked past him with her head held high.

"I can't believe him," Rachel said to Tony as she slid into her seat. "Just because his dad is the chairperson of the city council, Daniel thinks he knows everything. He can be so obnoxious! I know my mom told me it was a swim camp this summer! I'd like to hit him and knock some sense into his brain."

Tony smiled at her sympathetically as he pulled his notebook out of his desk.

Mr. Valentino walked over to Daniel's desk and stood beside it. "Daniel, did I hear you say there would be a soccer camp this summer?"

Daniel nodded his head and glanced at Rachel. "The churches around here are going to work with the city to plan stuff for us when school gets out. My dad said the city would let the kids use the equipment, and the churches would work together to make sure there were people to be counselors and lead out in soccer drills and games. Doesn't it sound fun?"

Mr. Valentino smiled and glanced over at Rachel and Tony, who were still whispering. "It does, Daniel. It also reminds me of the text we are studying this week." Mr. Valentino pointed to the board as he read. "'Most of all, let love guide your life, for then the whole church will stay together in perfect harmony.' Colossians 3:14. With all the churches working together on this project, I think it will make our town a nicer place to live. When people work together it helps them understand each other better and it will give you guys something fun to do all summer."

Mr. V. rubbed his hands together and smiled. "By the way, your China reports are due at the end of this week. I'll give you some time later this morning to work together in your groups and get your presentations ready."

Later that morning, Daniel, Tony, Rachel, and Rosa gathered around Tony's desk to work on their presentation. "Rachel, did you bring your Chinese jump rope?" Daniel asked.

Rachel shook her head 'no'. "I brought my set of jacks. Did you bring your yo-yo and backgammon game?"

"I brought the backgammon, but I already told you I don't have a yo-yo. Has

Story (continued)

your brain quit working today, Rachel?" Daniel shook his head and looked at the ceiling. "I brought my dragon kite and Frisbee too, just like we planned."

Tony held up a bright red and yellow yo-yo. "I have the yo-yo."

"Grandma Anderson let me borrow her badminton set." Rosa took two rackets and a shuttlecock out of the bag beside her desk. "We can borrow the volleyball and basketball here at the school for our report. I have the Chinese jump rope. I got it last Christmas in my stocking. It came with a little book that shows a bunch of different games you can play with it."

Rachel glared at Daniel. "See, my brain works fine. You're the one with some circuits fried. You probably can't remember the swim camp, just like you can't remember who's bringing a jump rope."

"I think that's all the Chinese games on our list," Tony interrupted, "except for table tennis and gymnastics. Does anyone know somebody with a ping pong table and some paddles? We can buy some balls easy enough."

"Don't ask Daniel. He'll forget," Rachel said.

"I didn't forget what I was supposed to bring, just what you were supposed to bring." Daniel shrugged his shoulders. "Why should I keep track of that?"

"Quit it, you two." Tony frowned. "We're supposed to be working together and having fun. Who has ping pong balls?"

"Not me." Daniel crossed his arms across his chest. "I'm already bringing most of the games."

"Rosa is bringing two things, and if she brings the basketball and volleyball, she'll have four. That's one more game than you, Daniel."

"Not if I bring the ping pong balls."

"My point exactly." Rachel smirked.

Tony just shook his head. "Now, who wants to make the poster with a list of all the games that come from China?"

"Someone else can make the poster," Daniel said. "I'm doing more than my share already."

"I'll make the poster," Rosa offered. "My dad has some neat letters that look like Chinese calligraphy on his computer. I'll get him to help me."

"I think Rachel should help you," Daniel pointed out. "Tony is going to do the talking for the report. I'm bringing most of the games. If you make the poster by yourself, what will Rachel do besides bring her jacks? Never mind. We'd better not let her do too much since her brain is on vacation. We need a good grade for this."

Rachel was about to give Daniel a hard kick with her foot when Mr. Valentino walked up behind her and asked the group how things were going. Tony said "fine," but Rachel got up and stalked off to the bathroom.

The next morning, before the first bell rang, Rachel walked quietly over to Daniel's desk. "Uh, Daniel. . . I was wrong yesterday. I talked to my mom last night and she said that there will be a soccer camp AND a swim camp this summer. There may even be a basketball camp and a gymnastics camp. It all depends on if they can find instructors. She just told me about the swim camp because she knew it would be something I'd like."

"I talked to my dad too. He said the same thing. There might be a swim camp or maybe a day camp where they play lots of different kinds of games. They're just planning right now." Daniel looked at the floor. "I'm sorry for what I said. . .and you have a good brain, too, Rachel."

"Thank you, Daniel. That's one of the nicer things you have said about me. You know, I think we should work on getting along, kind of like the churches are doing for us this summer. I think our class would like our report on Chinese games, that is, if we can quit fighting long enough to tell them about it. I'll help Rosa with the poster and I think I know an eighth grader who might come and show us some gymnastics techniques if we can bring a mat over from the gym."

"Yeah, you're right and I like your idea. I'll ask Mr. V. if we can have someone bring a mat over. Or maybe we could do our whole report in the gym." Daniel rubbed his hands together. "The kids might like to try some of the games and it would be easier there."

"I can't believe you said that, Daniel DeVore!" Rachel smiled. "Two nice things in a row. . . maybe working together is possible!"

2 Discussion Time

Check understanding of the story and development of personal values.

- What did Daniel say was going to happen at the day camp?
- What did Rachel say was going to happen?
- Who was right about the city council's plans?
- What could Rachel and Daniel have done to keep the fight from getting worse and worse as the day went on?
- What helped Rachel and Daniel realize they could work together on the Chinese project?
- Why does Jesus want us to live in harmony with each other?

A Preview Name ____________

Write each word as your teacher says it.

1. August
2. autumn
3. bought
4. brought
5. cause
6. wall
7. daughter
8. fought
9. hall
10. paw
11. raw
12. salt
13. taught
14. upon
15. song

Words with /ô/

Lesson 21

Scripture
Colossians 3:14

131

3 Preview

Test for knowledge of the correct spellings of these words.

Customize Your List
On a separate piece of paper, additional words of your choice may be tested.

I will say the word once, use the word in a sentence, then say the word again. Write the word on the lines in the worktext.

Correct Immediately!

Let's correct our preview. I will write each word on the board. Put a dot under each letter on your preview as I spell the word out loud. If you spelled a word wrong, rewrite it correctly.

Take a minute to memorize...
Read the memory verse to the class twice. Have the class practice it with you two more times.

Day 1

Lesson 21

1.	August	School started in **August** this year.
2.	autumn	It is usually late summer or **autumn** when school starts.
3.	bought	Daniel **bought** the ping pong balls.
4.	brought	Rosa **brought** her Chinese jump rope.
5.	cause	Misunderstandings are the **cause** of many fights.
6.	wall	Rachel and Daniel built a **wall** of misunderstanding.
7.	daughter	Rachel is Mr. Jacobson's **daughter**.
8.	fought	Daniel and Rachel **fought** all day long.
9.	hall	The door to the **hall** was open.
10.	paw	There was a picture of a **paw** in the spelling book.
11.	raw	Rachel's nerves were **raw** after fighting with Daniel.
12.	salt	An unkind answer is like pouring **salt** into a wound.
13.	taught	Mr. V. **taught** his class to work together.
14.	upon	Rachel realized she was wrong **upon** talking with her mom.
15.	song	There was a **song** in Rachel's heart after she talked to Daniel the next day.

Progress Chart
Students may record scores. (Reproducible master in Appendix B.)

Day 1

Lesson 21

4 Word Shapes

Help students form a correct image of whole words.

Look at each word and think about its shape. Now, write the word in the correct word shape boxes. You may check off each word as you use it.

(In some words **/ô/** is spelled with **a**, and it is often spelled this way when it is followed by **l** or **ll**. In some words **/ô/** is spelled with **aw**, **o**, **ou**, or **au**.)

In the word shape boxes, color the letter or letters that spell the sound of **/ô/** in each word. Circle the words which have the silent consonants **gh**.

Words with /ô/ — Lesson 21

B Word Shapes Name ____________

Write each word in the correct word shape boxes. Next, in the word shape boxes, color the letter or letters that spell the sound of **/ô/** in each word. Circle the words which have the silent consonants **gh**.

Word	Answer
1. August	fought (circled)
2. autumn	upon
3. bought	song
4. brought	August
5. cause	raw
6. daughter	bought (circled)
7. fought	paw
8. hall	brought (circled)
9. paw	salt
10. raw	daughter (circled)
11. salt	hall
12. song	cause
13. taught	wall
14. upon	autumn
15. wall	taught (circled)

132

Answers may vary for duplicate word shapes.

Be Prepared For Fun

Check these supply lists for **Fun Ways to Spell** presented **Day 2**. Purchase and/or gather needed items ahead of time!

General
- Colored Pencils
- Art Paper (1 piece per child)
- Spelling List

Auditory
- A Classmate
- Spelling List

Visual
- Black Construction Paper (1 piece per child)
- Cotton Swabs (1 per child)
- Lemon Juice
- Spelling List

Tactile
- Pipe Cleaners (cut in an assortment of lengths)
- Spelling List

C Hide and Seek

Name ______________________

Place an **X** on a coin for each word you spell correctly.

D Other Word Forms

Using the words below, follow the instructions given by your teacher.

bring	daughters	rawest	teach
(bringing)	fight	salted	teaching
buy	fighting	saltier	walled
buying	halls	saltiest	(walls)
caused	pawing	salty	
causes	paws	(singer)	
causing	rawer	singing	

E Fun Ways to Spell

Initial the box of each activity you finish.

1. 

Spell your words with pictures.

3. 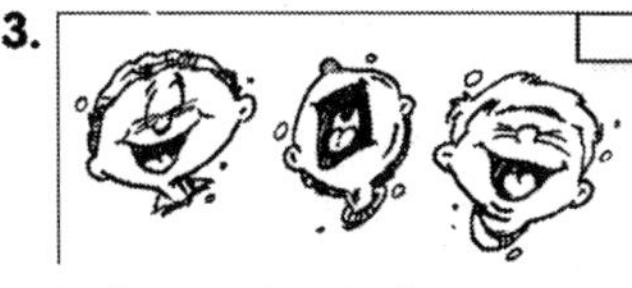
Spell your words out loud.

2. 

Spell your words with lemon juice.

4. 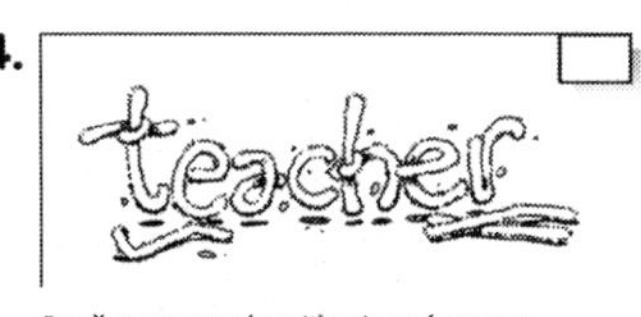

Spell your words with pipe cleaners.

Words with /ȯ/

Lesson 21

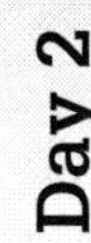

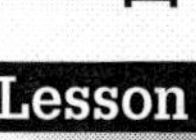

21

1 Hide and Seek

Reinforce correct spelling of current spelling words.

Write the words one at a time on the board. Use this activity for each word.

- **Look** at the word.
- **Say** the word out loud.
- Let's **hide** (cover) the word.
- **Write** the word on your paper.
- Let's **seek** (uncover) the word.
- **Check** your spelling. If your word is spelled wrong, write the word correctly next to it.

2 Other Word Forms

This activity is optional. Have students find and circle the Other Word Forms that are synonyms of the following:

vocalist
confines
carrying

3 Fun Ways to Spell

Four activities are provided. Use one, two, three, or all of the activities. Have students initial the box for each activity they complete.

Options:

- assign activities to students according to their learning styles
- set up the activities in learning centers for the class to do throughout the day
- divide the class into four groups and assign one activity per group
- do one activity per day

General

To spell your words with pictures...
- Choose several words from your spelling list and draw pictures that illustrate the meanings of those words.
- Write the correct spelling word beside each picture.
- Check your spelling.

Auditory

To spell your words out loud...
- Have a classmate read a spelling word from the list.
- Say a sentence with that spelling word to your classmate.
- Spell the spelling word you used in that sentence to your classmate.
- Ask your classmate to check your spelling.
- Do this with each word on your word list.

Visual

To spell your words with lemon juice...
- Dipping a cotton swab in lemon juice, write each of your spelling words on black construction paper.
- Check your spelling before your writing disappears!

Tactile

To spell your words with pipe cleaners...
- Choose a word from your spelling list.
- It may be a favorite word or a word you have trouble remembering how to spell.
- Shape the pipe cleaner to spell that word.

Day 3

Lesson 21

1 Working with Words

Familiarize students with word meaning and usage.

Word Sort

Write the headings **au**, **ou**, **a**, **aw**, and **o** on the board. Say the words **tall**, **caught**, **saw**, **thought**, and **dog**. Guide the students in putting these five words under the correct headings.

At the top of your page, write each spelling word under the correct heading.

ABC Order

Write the words **saw**, **sow**, **sew**, and **was** on the board. Explain to the students that when words begin with the same letter, they need to look at the second letter in each word to put the words in alphabetical order. If the first two letters are the same, look at the third letter. Guide the students in putting these four words in alphabetical order.

Look at each set of words. Write the words in alphabetical order on the lines.

Take a minute to memorize...

Read the memory verse to the class twice. Have the class practice it with you two more times.

Words with /ô/ — Lesson 21

F Working with Words Name ____________________

Word Sort

Write each spelling word under the correct heading.

au	ou	a
1. August	6. bought	9. hall
2. autumn	7. brought	10. salt
3. cause	8. fought	11. wall
4. daughter		
5. taught		

aw	o
12. paw	14. song
13. raw	15. upon

ABC Order

Write the words from each group in alphabetical order.

daughter cause brought

1. brought 2. cause 3. daughter

raw wall salt

4. raw 5. salt 6. wall

fought bought hall

7. bought 8. fought 9. hall

autumn August taught

10. August 11. autumn 12. taught

Word Bank

August	salt	taught	brought	hall
song	wall	bought	daughter	autumn
paw	upon	raw	fought	cause

134

G Dictation Name ______________________

Listen and write the missing words and punctuation.

1. The children fought over the games they brought .
2. The visitor taught them a song in Chinese .
3. The swim camp will begin in August .

H Proofreading

If a word is misspelled, fill in the oval by that word. If all the words are spelled correctly, fill in the oval by **no mistake**.

1. ○ paw ○ ago ● Awgust ○ no mistake	4. ○ fought ○ salt ● brouwt ○ no mistake	7. ○ upon ● hal ○ toast ○ no mistake
2. ● autum ○ float ○ goes ○ no mistake	5. ● cauze ○ song ○ rope ○ no mistake	8. ○ ripe ○ shy ● woll ○ no mistake
3. ○ open ● bowght ○ rode ○ no mistake	6. ● dawter ○ taught ○ telephone ○ no mistake	9. ○ life ● rauw ○ die ○ no mistake

Words with /ô/ Lesson 21

135

1 Dictation

Reinforce correct spelling by using current and previous words in context.

Listen as I read each sentence and then write the missing words and ending punctuation in your worktext. (Slowly read each sentence twice. Sentences are found in the student text to the left.)

2 Proofreading

Familiarize students with standardized test format and reinforce recognizing misspelled words.

Look at each set of words. If a word is misspelled, fill in the oval by that word. If all the words are spelled correctly, fill in the oval by **no mistake**.

3 Hide and Seek

Reinforce correct spelling of current spelling words. (A reproducible master is provided in Appendix A as shown on the inset page to the right.)

Write the words one at a time on the board. Use this activity for each word.

- **Look** at the word.
- **Say** the word out loud.
- Let's **hide** (cover) the word.
- **Write** the word on your paper.
- Let's **seek** (uncover) the word.
- **Check** your spelling. If your word is spelled wrong, write the word correctly next to it.

4 Other Word Forms

Have your students complete this activity to strengthen spelling ability and expand vocabulary.

1 Posttest

Test mastery of the spelling words.

I will say the word once, use the word in a sentence, then say the word again. Write the word on your paper.

Other Word Forms — Lesson 21

Hide and Seek

Check a coin for each word you spell correctly.

Other Word Forms

Spelling and Writing

Use each pair of words to write a sentence. Check your spelling.

1. causes, pawing (Answers may vary)
2. buying, daughters (Answers may vary)
3. walled, fighting (Answers may vary)

Clues

Use the clues to write the words.

1. a battle — fight
2. made something happen — caused
3. showing someone how — teaching
4. the feet of animals — paws
5. to take something with you — bring
6. long, narrow parts of a house — halls
7. divide the rooms in a house — walls
8. music made by a bird — singing
9. someone's girl children — daughters
10. to purchase — buy

Word Bank

bring	caused	fight	paws	teaching
buy	daughters	halls	singing	walls

344

1. August	The month of **August** is usually hot in China.
2. autumn	The leaves fall in the United States and China in **autumn.**
3. hall	The **hall** was quiet after the bell rang.
4. fought	Daniel and Rachel **fought.**
5. daughter	Rosa is Carlos Vasquez's **daughter.**
6. bought	Rosa hadn't **bought** a badminton game.
7. brought	Tony **brought** his yo-yo for the China report.
8. cause	Daniel was the **cause** of the next fight.
9. paw	The giant panda's **paw** is designed to hold things.
10. raw	The Chinese like to eat their vegetables almost **raw.**
11. salt	Chinese vegetable rice is lightly seasoned with **salt.**
12. song	They sang a Chinese **song.**
13. taught	You have been **taught** not to call people brainless.
14. upon	You will go to the next grade **upon** finishing this book.
15. wall	They hung the Chinese game poster on the **wall.**

Progress Chart

Students may record scores. (Reproducible master in Appendix B.)

Personal Dictionary

Students may add any words they have misspelled to their personal dictionaries for reference when writing. (Cover in Appendix B.)

Words with /ô/ Lesson 21

I **Game** Name ___________________________

Glue on a piece of the puzzle-picture for each word you or your team spells correctly from this week's word list.

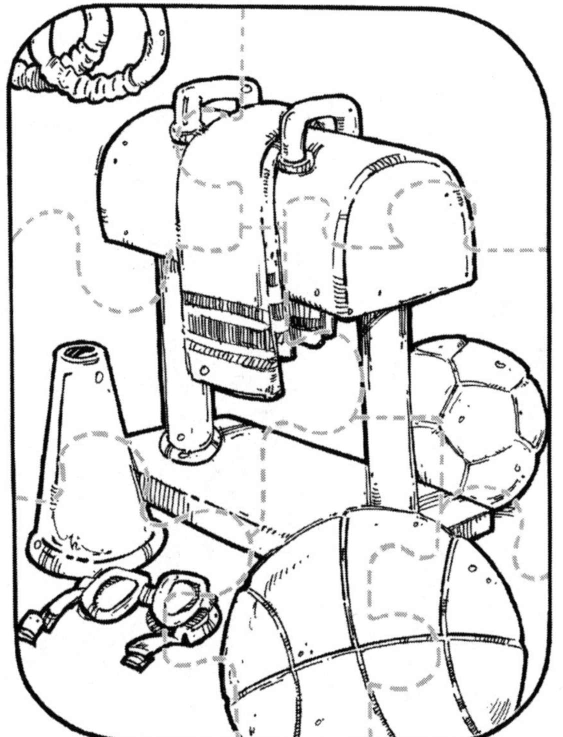

Remember: If you love God, do your best to get along with others.

J **Journaling**

In your journal, write about a time when you did not get along with someone. Finish by telling how you could have helped it not to happen.

136

2 Game

Reinforce spelling skills and provide motivation and interest.

Materials

- game page (from student text)
- puzzle pieces (reproducible master in Appendix B, page 359)
- crayons
- scissors (1 per child)
- glue sticks (1 per child)
- game word list

Game Word List

1. August
2. autumn
3. bought
4. brought
5. cause
6. daughter
7. fought
8. hall
9. paw
10. raw
11. salt
12. song
13. taught
14. upon
15. wall

Day 5 Lesson 21

How to Play:

- Have the students color the puzzle picture, then carefully cut the picture apart along the dotted lines.
- Divide the class into two teams.
- Have a student from team A go to the board.
- Say the spelling word. (You may also wish to use the word in a sentence.)
- Have the student write the word on the board.
- If correct, instruct each member of team A to glue on one piece of his/her puzzle picture. (Note: If the word is misspelled, correct the spelling immediately.)
- Alternate between teams A and B.
- The team to complete its puzzle pictures first is the winner.

Non-Competitive Option:

At the end of the game, say: "Class, I am proud of your efforts to spell the words correctly. If you had fun and tried your best, you are all winners!"

3 Journaling

Provide a meaningful reason for correct spelling through personal writing.

Review the story using discussion leads provided on the following page. Encourage students to apply the Scriptural value in their journaling.

Journaling (continued)

- How did the fight between Rachel and Daniel start? (Daniel said there would be a soccer camp in the summer. Rachel said the city council had voted to have a swim camp.)
- What else did Rachel and Daniel argue about? (Daniel said Rachel's mom is not a good secretary and that Rachel's brain doesn't work. Rachel said Daniel is a know-it-all because his dad is chairman of the city council. Rachel said Daniel forgets everything.)
- Who was right about the day camps planned for the summer? (They were both wrong. There was going to be a soccer camp and a swim camp.)
- What might Rachel have said to Daniel to stop the battle before it got started? (Nothing, or "I heard we might have a swim camp this summer.")
- What could Daniel have said to Rachel when she disagreed with him about the day camps that wouldn't have made her mad? ("Maybe I didn't understand right," or "I'll have to ask my dad.")
- What does our Scripture this week say about staying together in perfect harmony? ("Most of all, let love guide your life.")
- In your journal, write about a time when you did not get along with someone. Tell how you could have helped it not to happen.

Take a minute to memorize...
Have the class say the memory verses from lessons 19, 20, and 21 with you.

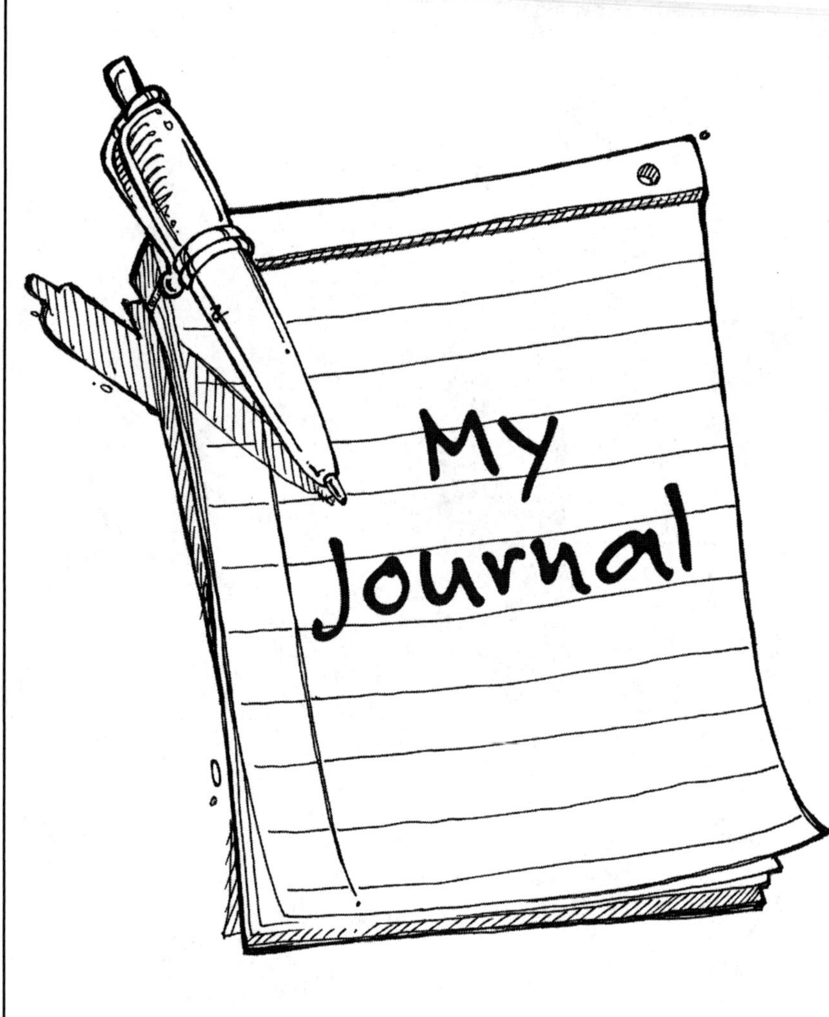

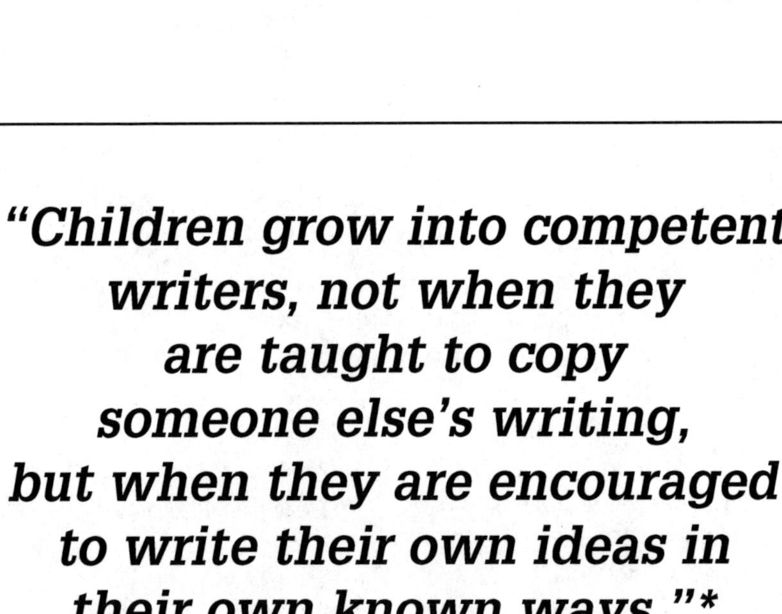

"Children grow into competent writers, not when they are taught to copy someone else's writing, but when they are encouraged to write their own ideas in their own known ways."*

*Hoffman, Stevie and Nancy Knipping. 1988. Spelling Revisited: The Child's Way. Childhood Education, June: 284-287.

1 **Literature Connection**
Topic: Courtesy
Theme Text: James 3:17

New from New York

Beth finds it difficult to be nice to a new girl in her class.

"Everyone ready? Okay. On your mark, get set. . . WAIT!" Mr. Valentino set the stopwatch down on his desk and walked over to talk with the school secretary, who was standing in the classroom doorway.

"I wonder what Mrs. Bentley wants?" Katelynn took a new eraser out of her desk and put it on the end of her pencil.

"I don't know." Beth twirled the multiplication test around on her desk. "She usually just says what she wants as soon as Mr. V. looks at her."

"Maybe we won't have to take this math test." Tommy grinned.

Beth twirled the paper around again. "Oh, we already have the tests, Tommy. They just take a couple of minutes. Are you on 'fours' yet?"

Before Tommy could answer, Mr. Valentino turned back to the class. "I have some exciting news!" he said. "We're getting a new student. She'll be here this afternoon, her name is Laney Ausherman, and she's from New York City. I hope each of you will help her feel comfortable and welcome." He walked back to the front of the classroom. "Okay, now let's take this test. On your mark, get set, GO!"

At lunchtime Laney was the main topic of conversation. Beth opened her sandwich and looked inside to see what kind it was. "I wonder where she's going to live?"

"I don't know. We'll have to ask her." Katelynn took a granola bar out of her sack. "Do you think she's been to the Statue of Liberty and up the Empire State building?"

"Probably," Beth said. "I wonder why she's moving here so near the end of the school year?"

"I heard my mom telling someone on the phone that Coach Larkin had just married a lady from New York who had a little girl." Katelynn said. "I think he went to a convention in New York City and saw her there or something." She opened a plastic container.

"He just saw her and married her?" Beth's eyebrows shot up.

"Oh, they knew each other from school or something," Katelynn shrugged. "Mom told whoever she was talking to that they'd been writing, but hadn't seen each other for a while. We can ask Laney when she gets here. I hope she's nice." She took a bite out of her granola bar. "Hey, maybe your mom will let her come to your slumber party this weekend. It will be fun to have another girl in our class. I want to know all about New York City. I've never been there, have you?"

"No, but Laney's mom might not let her come, you know. She doesn't even know us." Beth frowned. She wasn't sure she wanted a stranger at her slumber party. She'd been looking forward to it for a month. All the girls from her class were coming. Someone new might spoil all the fun.

"Well, Coach Larkin does." Katelynn didn't notice Beth's hesitation. "Didn't he coach your girls' soccer team last fall?"

"Well, er. . . yes he did, but. . ." Beth began, but stopped as Laney and her mom walked into the classroom behind Mrs. Bentley. Mr. Valentino smiled warmly and walked over to greet his new student and meet the new Mrs. Larkin.

"Look at her clothes," Katelynn whispered. "They're just like the ones I saw in the mall last week. They're really expensive. And look at her hair."

Beth made a face. "Do you like it?"

"What? Her clothes or her hair?"

"Either."

"Definitely not her hair, but the clothes are okay! Maybe that's the style in New York."

"Well, maybe." Beth frowned and got up to throw her lunch sack away. "But I don't like the style no matter where it comes from."

Katelynn went over to Mr. Valentino and pulled on his shirt sleeve. "Can Laney move her desk over by mine? I'd like her to sit by me."

Mr. Valentino smiled. "Sure, that would be great, Katelynn. You can help her learn how we do things here. Laney, this is Katelynn Hatasaki."

Katelynn smiled at the new girl, then moved the desks around and helped Laney put her things away. She showed her where the pencil sharpener was and pointed out the class schedule posted on the wall at the back of the room. "We get to go out for recess in a few minutes. Do you like to play 'four square'?"

Laney nodded her head and the two girls headed toward the door. Katelynn was so busy telling Laney who everyone was and why they were going to visit the retirement center the next day, she didn't notice Beth heading out the door in the opposite direction.

Katelynn led the way to the "four square" grid and called for Rosa and Rachel to come join them. Soon Setsuko, Sarah, and Kristin came over to play. Laney was good and everyone enjoyed hearing about what they played at recess in New York City.

It seemed only a few minutes passed before Mr. Valentino blew his whistle. "We line up at the back door when he does that." Katelynn grabbed the ball and the rest of the girls followed her to the back door of Knowlton Elementary School.

"I used to live in Dallas. I moved here two years ago when my dad married Helen. It was at the end of the year, too." Rachel

Story (continued)

smiled at Laney. "Helen is going to have a baby soon."

"My mom just married Edward Larkin. We live over by the park."

"We live across the street from the park. What side do you live on?" Rachel asked.

Laney shrugged her shoulders. "We live right across from the baseball diamonds."

"Oh, that's right up the street from me!" Rachel smiled warmly at Laney. "It will be fun to have a girl from our class near us. Tony and Stephen live across the park from us. They are those two boys at the head of the line." Tony and Stephen, overhearing the conversation, grinned and waved.

Katelynn turned around to look at Laney. "Have you ever been to the Statue of Liberty and to the top of the Empire State building?"

"Did you ride the subway to school or take one of those yellow taxis?" Rosa asked.

"Did you live by Central Park and shop at Macy's?" Kristin asked.

Beth walked up and stood at the end of the line. She heard all the friendly questions her classmates asked, but she didn't even try to hear Laney's answers. "I wonder why everyone is so impressed with her," Beth thought. "She has a different haircut and expensive clothes, but who cares that she lived in New York City. What's so great about New York? I wish she'd just go back there." Beth looked down at her scuffed tennis shoes.

Mr. Valentino held the door open for his students. When Beth shuffled past him, he said quietly, "Take a look at the text you wrote in handwriting this morning, Beth. I think it might apply to kids from New York, too." He smiled and let the door swing shut behind them.

Beth went straight to her desk and pulled out her handwriting worktext. She quickly found what she had written earlier that morning. "But the wisdom that comes from Heaven is first of all pure and full of quiet gentleness. Then it is peace-loving and courteous" James 3:17. She cringed and looked at the floor. It seemed like Mr. Valentino had read her mind! Had he noticed how rude she had been to Laney? Had he overheard her conversation with Katelynn? Beth's face turned red with shame. Suddenly she knew what she needed to do.

"Laney." Beth leaned across Katelynn's desk. "Do you think your mom would let you come to a slumber party at my house this weekend? I'm Beth Hill. Mr. Larkin knows who I am. He's my soccer coach. Have your mom talk to him if she's afraid to let you go to someone's house she doesn't know."

"It will be lots of fun!" Katelynn encouraged the new girl. "All the girls in our class are coming."

"Thank you, Beth." Laney smiled. "It sounds great. All of you are being so nice to me. I think living here is going to be more fun than I expected!"

2 Discussion Time

Check understanding of the story and development of personal values.

- How does Beth feel about a new girl coming?
- Was Beth courteous to Laney at first?
- How did Katelynn and the other girls treat the new girl?
- What did the girls do to help Laney feel welcome?
- What helped Beth decide to invite Laney to her slumber party?
- How do you think Beth felt after she invited Laney?

A **Preview** Name ____________

Write each word as your teacher says it.

1. hour
2. mouth
3. allow
4. amount
5. anyhow
6. clown
7. crowd
8. doubt
9. drown
10. ground
11. loud
12. mouse
13. plow
14. power
15. shout

Words with /ou/

Lesson 22

Scripture

James 3:17

137

3 Preview

Test for knowledge of the correct spellings of these words.

Customize Your List

On a separate piece of paper, additional words of your choice may be tested.

I will say the word once, use the word in a sentence, then say the word again. Write the word on the lines in the worktext.

Correct Immediately!

Let's correct our preview. I will write each word on the board. Put a dot under each letter on your preview as I spell the word out loud. If you spelled a word wrong, rewrite it correctly.

Take a minute to memorize...

Read the memory verse to the class twice. Have the class practice it with you two more times.

Day 1

Lesson 22

1.	hour	Laney came during lunch **hour**.
2.	mouth	Beth didn't open her **mouth** to greet Laney.
3.	allow	"I will **allow** Laney to sit by you, Katelynn," said Mr. V.
4.	amount	"My mother would never let me spend that **amount** of money on clothes."
5.	anyhow	Laney's mother won't let her come **anyhow**.
6.	clown	"She looks like a **clown** with that haircut," said Beth.
7.	crowd	There was a **crowd** of girls around Laney.
8.	doubt	I **doubt** Laney lives in the new apartment building in town.
9.	drown	Beth might **drown** in her sorrow.
10.	ground	Beth sat on the **ground** at the edge of the playground.
11.	loud	The laughter of the girls was **loud** and merry.
12.	mouse	There was a picture of a **mouse** in the spelling worktext.
13.	plow	The farmer used the **plow** to turn the soil.
14.	power	God can give us the **power** to make good choices.
15.	shout	Beth wanted to **shout** with frustration.

Progress Chart

Students may record scores. (Reproducible master in Appendix B.)

4 Word Shapes

Help students form a correct image of whole words.

Look at each word and think about its shape. Now, write the word in the correct word shape boxes. You may check off each word as you use it.

(A diphthong is two vowel sounds that are sounded together in the same syllable. In many words, the diphthong **/ou/** is spelled **ow** if it is at the end of a word or syllable, or comes before **l** or **n**. The **/ou/** sound is spelled **ou** everywhere else.)

In the word shape boxes, color the letters that spell the sound of **/ou/** in each word. Circle the words which begin with an **-r** or **-l** cluster.

B Word Shapes Name ____________

Words with /ou/ — Lesson 22

Write each word in the correct word shape boxes. Next, in the word shape boxes, color the letters that spell the sound of **/ou/** in each word. Circle the words which begin with an **-r** or **-l** cluster.

Word	Word shape
1. allow	anyhow
2. amount	doubt
3. anyhow	drown (circled)
4. clown	crowd (circled)
5. crowd	allow
6. doubt	ground (circled)
7. drown	hour
8. ground	clown (circled)
9. hour	plow (circled)
10. loud	amount
11. mouse	mouth
12. mouth	mouse
13. plow	power
14. power	shout
15. shout	loud

138

Answers may vary for duplicate word shapes.

Be Prepared For Fun

Check these supply lists for **Fun Ways to Spell** presented **Day 2**. Purchase and/or gather needed items ahead of time!

General
- A Classmate
- Spelling List

Auditory
- Voice Recorder
- Spelling List

Visual
- a, b, c, d, e, g, h, l, l, m, n, o, p, r, s, t, u, w, y (written on upside-down cups)
- Spelling List

Tactile
- Art Paper (2 or 3 sheets per child)
- Magazines
- Glue Sticks
- Scissors
- Spelling List

C Hide and Seek

Name ______________________

Place an **X** on a coin for each word you spell correctly.

D Other Word Forms

Using the words below, follow the instructions given by your teacher.

allowance	crowding	grounder	mouthful
allowed	crowds	groundless	powerful
allows	doubting	hourly	powerfully
amounted	doubtless	loudly	powerless
clowned	undoubtedly	loudness	shouted
clowning	drowned	mice	shouting
clowns	drowning	mouser	
crowded	grounded	mouthed	

Words with /ou/

Lesson 22

E Fun Ways to Spell

Initial the box of each activity you finish.

1. 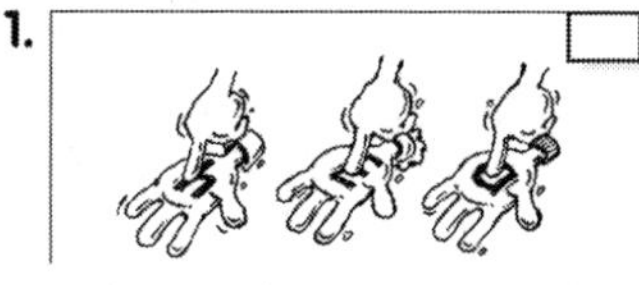

Spell your words in your classmate's hand.

3. 

Spell your words using a tape recorder.

2. 

Spell your words with paper cups.

4. 

Spell your words with magazine clippings.

139

1 Hide and Seek

Reinforce correct spelling of current spelling words.

Write the words one at a time on the board. Use this activity for each word.

Say

- **Look** at the word.
- **Say** the word out loud.
- Let's **hide** (cover) the word.
- **Write** the word on your paper.
- Let's **seek** (uncover) the word.
- **Check** your spelling. If your word is spelled wrong, write the word correctly next to it.

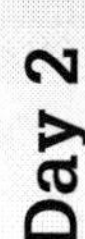

Day 2

Lesson 22

2 Other Word Forms

This activity is optional. Have students unscramble these letters to write Other Word Forms:

oyhurl	(hourly)
ltduesosb	(doubtless)
rpwoelfu	(powerful)

3 Fun Ways to Spell

Four activities are provided. Use one, two, three, or all of the activities. Have students initial the box for each activity they complete.

Options:

- assign activities to students according to their learning styles
- set up the activities in learning centers for the class to do throughout the day
- divide the class into four groups and assign one activity per group
- do one activity per day

General

To spell your words in your classmate's hand...
- Have your classmate sit next to you and hold his (or her) palm open in front of and facing both of you.
- Use your fingertip to write a spelling word in the palm of your classmate's hand.
- Have your classmate say each letter as you write it and then say the word you spelled.
- Next, have your classmate write a word in your palm.

Auditory

To spell your words using a voice recorder...
- Record yourself as you say and spell each word on your spelling list.
- Listen to your recording and check your spelling.

Visual

To spell your words with paper cups...
- Spell a word from your list by putting the cups in the right order.
- Check your spelling.

Tactile

To spell your words with magazine clippings...
- Cut the letters you need from old magazines.
- Glue the letters to your paper in the correct order.

1 Working with Words

Familiarize students with word meaning and usage.

Secret Code

Write **a b c d e f** and number the letters **1-6**. Next, write the numbers **6, 5, 5, 4** and draw a line over each one. Explain that each number you have written stands for a letter of the alphabet. Have a student write the matching letters on the lines to make the word **feed**.

Sometimes friends like to write notes in code to each other. Use the code at the top of your page to write your spelling words.

Dictionary Skills

Write the spelling word that would be the entry word for each definition.

Day 3

Lesson 22

F Working with Words Name ________________

Words with /ou/ Lesson 22

Secret Code

Katelynn and Beth like to write notes in code to each other. Use their code to write your spelling words.

a	b	c	d	e	f	g	h	i	j	k	l	m	n	o	p	q	r	s	t	u	v	w	x	y	z
1	2	3	4	5	6	7	8	9	10	11	12	13	14	15	16	17	18	19	20	21	22	23	24	25	26

1. a l l o w — 1 12 12 15 23
2. s h o u t — 19 8 15 21 20
3. c l o w n — 3 12 15 23 14
4. m o u s e — 13 15 21 19 5
5. p o w e r — 16 15 23 5 18
6. a m o u n t — 1 13 15 21 14 20
7. d o u b t — 4 15 21 2 20
8. h o u r — 8 15 21 18
9. m o u t h — 13 15 21 20 8
10. g r o u n d — 7 18 15 21 14 4
11. l o u d — 12 15 21 4
12. a n y h o w — 1 14 25 8 15 23
13. c r o w d — 3 18 15 23 4
14. p l o w — 16 12 15 23
15. d r o w n — 4 18 15 23 14

Dictionary Skills

Write the spelling word that would be the entry word for each definition below.

1. mouth — to say something by only moving your lips
2. allow — to let someone do something
3. amount — how much there is of something
4. ground — the surface of the earth
5. power — forms of energy such as electricity

Word Bank

allow	clown	drown	loud	plow
amount	crowd	ground	mouse	power
anyhow	doubt	hour	mouth	shout

140

Take a minute to memorize...

Read the memory verse to the class twice. Have the class practice it with you two more times.

G Dictation

Name ______________________

Listen and write the missing words and punctuation.

1. I doubt that he will allow us to skip the test .
2. Her daughter, Laney, will be here in an hour .
3. The loud shout brought a crowd to watch the game .

H Proofreading

If a word is misspelled, fill in the oval by that word. If all the words are spelled correctly, fill in the oval by **no mistake**.

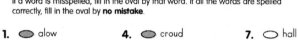

1. ● alow ○ pour ○ August ○ no mistake
2. ○ autumn ● amownt ○ hour ○ no mistake
3. ○ ground ○ bought ● inyhow ○ no mistake
4. ● croud ○ mouth ○ brought ○ no mistake
5. ○ plow ● dout ○ cause ○ no mistake
6. ● droun ○ shout ○ daughter ○ no mistake
7. ○ hall ● lowd ○ raw ○ no mistake
8. ○ wall ○ owe ● mowse ○ no mistake
9. ● powir ○ shown ○ song ○ no mistake

Words with /ou/ Lesson 22

141

1 Dictation

Reinforce correct spelling by using current and previous words in context.

Listen as I read each sentence and then write the missing words and ending punctuation in your worktext. (Slowly read each sentence twice. Sentences are found in the student text to the left.)

2 Proofreading

Familiarize students with standardized test format and reinforce recognizing misspelled words.

Look at each set of words. If a word is misspelled, fill in the oval by that word. If all the words are spelled correctly, fill in the oval by **no mistake**.

Day 4 Lesson 22

3 Hide and Seek

Reinforce correct spelling of current spelling words. (A reproducible master is provided in Appendix A as shown on the inset page to the right.)

Write the words one at a time on the board. Use this activity for each word.

- **Look** at the word.
- **Say** the word out loud.
- Let's **hide** (cover) the word.
- **Write** the word on your paper.
- Let's **seek** (uncover) the word.
- **Check** your spelling. If your word is spelled wrong, write the word correctly next to it.

4 Other Word Forms

Have your students complete this activity to strengthen spelling ability and expand vocabulary.

1 Posttest

Test mastery of the spelling words.

I will say the word once, use the word in a sentence, then say the word again. Write the word on your paper.

Hide and Seek

Check a coin for each word you spell correctly.

Other Word Forms

Riddles

Write the correct word in each riddle.

1. We like to act silly sometimes. Mom says we are clowning around.
2. He and his brother were yelling. They were both shouting.
3. My cat likes to catch mice. She is a good mouser.
4. My parents give me money each week. This is called an allowance.
5. The choir teacher sang the words with no sound. She mouthed the words.
6. The new vacuum cleans the carpet well. It is powerful.
7. There are a lot of people in the mall. It is too crowded.
8. I am not allowed to go anywhere fun. I am grounded for a week.
9. I am not sure whether to believe what he said. I am doubting that it is true.

Word Bank

allowance	crowded	grounded	mouthed	shouting
clowning	doubting	mouser	powerful	

Other Word Forms — Lesson 22 — 345

1.	allow	Will Laney's mom **allow** her to go to Beth's house?
2.	anyhow	"I don't want her to come to my house **anyhow**," said Beth.
3.	amount	What is the **amount** you spend on clothes?
4.	clown	The **clown** looked sad.
5.	crowd	There is always a **crowd** in New York.
6.	doubt	I **doubt** Laney will like it here at Knowlton Elementary.
7.	hour	We have an **hour** for lunch and recess.
8.	drown	Beth might **drown** in her own misery.
9.	ground	Beth sat by herself on the **ground** outside.
10.	loud	Their talking in line was **loud**.
11.	mouse	The book had a picture of a **mouse** in it.
12.	mouth	Guard what comes out of your **mouth** carefully.
13.	plow	Tommy will slowly **plow** through his multiplication tables.
14.	shout	Do not **shout** in the classroom.
15.	power	God gives us **power** to make good choices.

Progress Chart

Students may record scores. (Reproducible master in Appendix B.)

Personal Dictionary

Students may add any words they have misspelled to their personal dictionaries for reference when writing. (Cover in Appendix B.)

Words with /ou/

Lesson 22

I **Game** Name ____________________

Beth realizes she is not treating the new girl in school, Laney, the way Jesus says she should. Go with Beth as she invites Laney to her birthday slumber party. Move one space for each word you or your team spells correctly from this week's word list.

Start

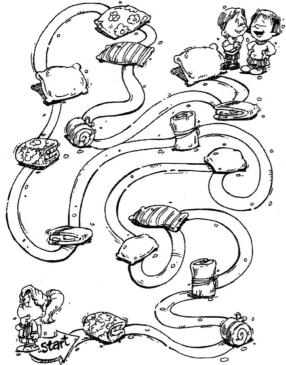

Remember: Plant yourself firmly in God's love. He will never fail you!

J **Journaling**

In your journal, make a list of at least five ways you could make a new member of your class feel welcome. Title your list.

142

2 Game

Reinforce spelling skills and provide motivation and interest.

Materials

- game page (from student text)
- flat buttons, dry beans, pennies, or game discs (1 per child)
- game word list

Game Word List

1. allow
2. amount
3. anyhow
4. clown
5. crowd
6. doubt
7. drown
8. ground
9. hour
10. loud
11. mouse
12. mouth
13. plow
14. power
15. shout

How to Play:

- Divide the class into two teams.
- Have each student place his/her game piece on Start.
- Have a student from team A go to the board.
- Say the spelling word. (You may also wish to use the word in a sentence.)
- Have the student write the word on the board.
- If correct, instruct each member of team A to move his/her game piece forward one space on the game board. (Note: If the word is misspelled, correct the spelling immediately.)
- Alternate between teams A and B.
- The team to reach Laney first is the winner.

Non-Competitive Option:

At the end of the game, say: "Class, I am proud of your efforts to spell the words correctly. If you had fun and tried your best, you are all winners!"

3 Journaling

Provide a meaningful reason for correct spelling through personal writing.

Review the story using discussion leads provided on the following page. Encourage students to apply the Scriptural value in their journaling.

Journaling (continued)

- How did Beth feel about having a new girl from New York City joining their class? (Not happy.)
- How did Katelynn feel? (She was excited about a new classmate.)
- What do you think Mr. V. noticed about Beth's actions that made him suggest she read her handwriting Scripture? (He might have overheard what she said about Laney to Katelynn, or the way she didn't play with Laney and the other girls at recess. She wasn't standing by Katelynn or her friends when they lined up.)
- Why do you think Beth was having such a hard time accepting the new girl? (She was jealous of how interested Katelynn was in getting to know her, of Laney's clothes and stylish hair cut, and of all the attention Laney was getting from all the girls.)
- The Scriptures say that wisdom that comes from heaven is pure and full of quiet gentleness. Then it is peace-loving and courteous. Raise your hand if you think Beth acted wisely at first.
- Stand by your desk if you think Beth made a wise choice when she asked Laney to her slumber party.
- In your journal, make a list of at least five ways you could make a new member of your class feel welcome. Title your list.

Take a minute to memorize...
Have the class say the memory verses from lessons 19, 20, 21, and 22 with you.

"Reading is not deciphering; writing is not copying."*

*Ferreiro, E., and Teberosky, A. 1979. Los sistemas de escritura en el desarrollo del nino. Mexico: Siglo Veintiuno Editores, (English translation, Literacy before schooling. Exeter, NH: Heinemann, 1982.)

1 **Literature Connection**
Topic: Patience
Theme Text: Ephesians 4:2

The Faults of Others

Christopher gets very upset about Daniel's fault of bossiness, then realizes one of his own faults is a lack of patience with Daniel.

"All right class, today's the day!" Mr. Valentino's broad smile was contagious. "Today we get our booth ready for the spring carnival." He walked briskly to the side of the room and waved his hand over the row of students seated at their desks. "This is group one." He moved along the front of the class room, pointing at each row in turn. "This row is group two, next row is group three, then four, and last row, group five. Each group will go to the gym separately during the day and work on our booth." Rosa waved her hand to get the teacher's attention. "Rosa?"

"How do we know what to do?" Rosa asked. "Are you going to go to the gym with each of the groups to show us what we're supposed to do?"

"Can't do that, Rosa." Mr. Valentino shook his head. "I'll be here in the classroom as usual today, but there'll be someone in the gym to show you what to do. Many parents have volunteered to help organize this carnival. Some of them will be there all day to help kids from each classroom get their booths ready. Another question, Beth?"

"My mom's helping today. She'll be there if we need help."

"Very good, Beth." Mr. Valentino smiled. "We couldn't do this without your mom and the others." He paused. "Now, every group will have a leader. The leader's job is to make sure that each person in the group gets a job to do, make sure the group is doing what the adults said should be done, and ask one of the adults for help if there are questions." Mr. Valentino held up three fingers and touched each one in turn as he listed the leader's responsibilities.

"Okay, I see several of you have questions." Mr. Valentino smiled at the hands waving in the air. "First, let me tell you who the group leaders are, and then I'll try to answer all these questions." An excited hum filled the room as Mr. Valentino turned to the board and made a list of the groups and their leaders.

"I'd sure like to be leader of our group," Christopher Wright thought as he leaned to his left to try to see past Mr. Valentino's back while the teacher was writing. Christopher's desk was in the last row, Group 5. Christopher glanced at the other kids in his row. "Setsuko, Rosa, Sarah, and Daniel. Except for maybe Rosa, I'd be the best leader for our group," Christopher assured himself. "Setsuko's too quiet, Sarah doesn't like to be in charge, and Daniel's much too bossy. Mr. Valentino's probably going to pick me."

"Okay, any questions?" Mr. Valentino stepped away from the board after he finished the list. There weren't nearly as many hands waving now. Everyone was looking at the list.

Christopher's eyes flew to the last line. Group 5 - Daniel. "Daniel! That's impossible!" Christopher thought. He couldn't believe his eyes. "Sure, Daniel's not as bad as he used to be, but Daniel for group leader?"

Christopher fretted about it all morning. Each time Mr. Valentino took a group over by the door and talked with them quietly a few minutes before sending them to the gym, Christopher's irritation grew. He was nibbling on his F-16 jet eraser, concentrating on his math, when a tap on his shoulder made him jump. "Come on, Christopher, Mr. Valentino said it's time for our group to go to the gym," Setsuko whispered.

"Remember, you are a team." Mr. Valentino spoke quietly to the five students who gathered by the classroom door. "We need each one of you to help get our booth ready." Mr. Valentino laid a hand on Daniel's shoulder. "Listen to your leader and work together."

"Wow!" Rosa exclaimed when they stepped into the gym. It was a beehive of noisy activity, with groups of students swarming over brightly colored, partially finished booths.

"You guys stay here by the door until I find out where our booth is," Daniel ordered.

"But. . ." Christopher's objection trailed off as Daniel headed for the nearest adult.

When Daniel returned, he pointed across the gym. "Come on, that's our spot right over there. Let's go." Daniel issued commands as the five classmates walked to their booth. "Christopher and Rosa, you two will put up the crepe paper streamer ceiling. Setsuko and Sarah, you will tape colored paper around the table and put the letters up."

"What. . ." Christopher's question ended before it began as Daniel continued talking.

"These are the streamers." He pointed to a stack against the wall when they arrived at their booth. "You're supposed to twist the blue and yellow together and then cut them the right length and tape one end to the wall and one end to that board that goes across the front of the booth. You put one up every four or five inches and that'll make a ceiling. Understand, Christopher? Rosa?"

"Of course," Christopher muttered. "There's nothing so hard about that."

"Got it!" Rosa picked up a roll of yellow crepe paper streamer. "Daniel, I don't see any scissors here. Can you get some for us?"

"Just get started twisting." Daniel wrote something on the clipboard he carried. "I'll bring some scissors to you after I get everyone else busy."

"Everyone else busy!" Christopher mimicked when

Story (continued)

Daniel moved away to talk to Setsuko and Sarah. "Why does he have to make it sound like he's in charge of the whole school?" He ripped open a package of blue streamers.

Rosa ignored his complaining. "Hand me the end of the blue and I'll hold this end of the blue and yellow together while you twist them together from that end, okay?"

Christopher handed the end of the streamer over and backed away, stretching the two colors out together. "And why does he need that silly clipboard, anyway?" He began turning his end over and over, twisting the two colors together.

Daniel returned a minute or two later with a pair of scissors. "No, that's not right!"

"You said to twist the two together." Christopher defended.

"But not so tight! It looks like you're trying to make a rope, or something!" Daniel plunked the clipboard and scissors down on the floor and grabbed Christopher's end of the streamers. "Like this, loosely, so that both the yellow and the blue show and look nice." Daniel unwound the streamers. "I thought everyone knew how to do this, it's so easy. NOW do you two understand?"

Christopher's face burned. Daniel could have shown them what to do in the first place. And what right did he have to try to make them feel stupid for not knowing how to twist crepe paper streamers? It wasn't like it was something everyone had to know to get along in life. He opened his mouth to tell Daniel just how he felt when he heard Rosa talking.

"Okay, we'll do it that way." She picked up the tape.

"Now make sure you remember to put a streamer up every five inches." Daniel reminded as Christopher moved the step stool over by the wall.

"Yes, master," Christopher mumbled under his breath as he held up his end of the streamer.

Rosa handed Christopher a piece of tape. "We'll use this ruler to measure and get it just right." Rosa pointed at a ruler on the floor by the stack of crepe paper rolls.

Daniel nodded. "You'd better use more tape than that. We don't want the streamers to come down during the carnival."

Christopher felt like a pot about to boil over. He wanted to yell at Daniel that just because he was the leader it didn't mean that they didn't know anything. They'd just gotten started. They would put more tape on each streamer after they got them twisted, measured, and placed. If they used a bunch of tape at first, it would be too hard to adjust the streamers to make them look even.

"We'll put plenty on before we're done." Rosa was still calm. She picked up the scissors as Christopher moved the step stool. Before long they got a routine going and the crepe paper ceiling began looking good.

Later that afternoon, back in the classroom, Christopher was still upset when he started handwriting practice. He quickly wrote a couple rows of "Be"s and started the next row, "patient."

"Be patient. Hmmm." Christopher flipped the page of his handwriting book and read the Scripture, Ephesians 4:2, silently to himself. "Be patient with each other, making allowance for each other's faults because of your love." He turned back to the first page of the lesson and wrote "p-a-t-i-e-n-t."

Suddenly Christopher stopped and stared at the back of Daniel's head in front of him. He tapped his F-16 jet eraser against his chin. "Patient," he thought. "Be patient with each other's faults. Patient." Rosa had been patient with Daniel's bossiness, but Christopher knew that he hadn't been. Daniel definitely had his faults, but not being patient was a fault, too—Christopher's very own fault!

He thought for a moment more, then quietly closed his eyes. "God, help me to be patient with others' faults," he prayed, "and thank you for being patient with my faults, too."

2 Discussion Time

Check understanding of the story and development of personal values.

- Why were the students working in the gym?
- What do you like best about school carnivals (or other activity)?
- How did Mr. Valentino divide the class into groups?
- Who was the leader of Christopher's group?
- Who else was in Group Five?
- What did Daniel tell Christopher and Rosa to do?
- Why did Christopher get upset at Daniel?
- How did Rosa react to Daniel's bossiness?

A Preview Name ____________

Write each word as your teacher says it.

1. storm
2. course
3. sore
4. report
5. order
6. fourth
7. floor
8. corner
9. wore
10. horn
11. fort
12. pour
13. score
14. airport
15. sport

Words with /ôr/

Lesson 23

Scripture
Ephesians 4:2

143

3 Preview

Test for knowledge of the correct spellings of these words.

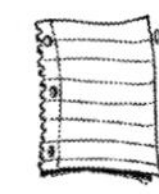

Customize Your List
On a separate piece of paper, additional words of your choice may be tested.

I will say the word once, use the word in a sentence, then say the word again. Write the word on the lines in the worktext.

Correct Immediately!

Let's correct our preview. I will write each word on the board. Put a dot under each letter on your preview as I spell the word out loud. If you spelled a word wrong, rewrite it correctly.

Take a minute to memorize...
Read the memory verse to the class twice. Have the class practice it with you two more times.

Day 1

Lesson 23

1.	storm	It's not supposed to **storm** on the day of the spring carnival.
2.	course	Of **course**, sometimes weather forecasts are wrong.
3.	sore	Setsuko's fingers got **sore** from cutting out the letters.
4.	report	Daniel will **report** their progress to Mr. Valentino.
5.	order	Sarah and Setsuko put the letters in the right **order**.
6.	fourth	The **fourth** streamer is a little crooked.
7.	floor	The tape is on the **floor** by the wall.
8.	corner	An eighth grader painted a backdrop in one **corner**.
9.	wore	He **wore** a big old paint shirt over his clothes.
10.	horn	He painted a **horn** on a mean looking bull.
11.	fort	Those old boards are for the front of the **fort** booth.
12.	pour	Someone will **pour** the bubble mixture into a large tub.
13.	score	The bigger the bubble you make, the higher your **score**.
14.	airport	You get to design and fly your own paper plane at the **airport** booth.
15.	sport	Christopher wasn't a very good **sport** about Daniel being his leader.

Progress Chart
Students may record scores. (Reproducible master in Appendix B.)

Day 1

Lesson

23

4 Word Shapes

Help students form a correct image of whole words.

Look at each word and think about its shape. Now, write the word in the correct word shape boxes. You may check off each word as you use it.

(In many words, the sound of **/ôr/** is spelled with **or** or **ore**. In a few words the sound of **/ôr/** is spelled **oor**, or **our** when it is at the end of a word or comes before a final consonant sound.

In the word shape boxes, color the letters that spell the sound of **/ôr/** in each word. Circle the words in which **/ôr/** is spelled **our**.

Words with /ôr/

Lesson 23

B Word Shapes Name ____________________

Write each word in the correct word shape boxes. Next, in the word shape boxes, color the letters that spell the sound of **/ôr/** in each word. Circle the words in which **/ôr/** is spelled **our**.

	Word	Answer
1.	airport	report
2.	corner	score
3.	course	airport
4.	floor	sport
5.	fort	(pour)
6.	fourth	storm
7.	horn	sore
8.	order	fort
9.	pour	(course)
10.	report	horn
11.	score	order
12.	sore	(fourth)
13.	sport	wore
14.	storm	floor
15.	wore	corner

144

Answers may vary for duplicate word shapes.

Be Prepared For Fun

Check these supply lists for **Fun Ways to Spell** presented **Day 2**. Purchase and/or gather needed items ahead of time!

General
- Markers
- Art Paper (2 or 3 sheets per child)
- Spelling List

Auditory
- Spelling List

Visual
- Letter Tiles a, c, d, e, f, h, i, l, m, n, o, o, p, r, r, s, t, u, w
- Spelling List

Tactile
- Paint Bags (tempera paint in plastic, resealable bags secured at top with heavy tape-1 per child)
- Spelling List

C Hide and Seek

Name ______________________

Place an **X** on a coin for each word you spell correctly.

D Other Word Forms

Using the words below, follow the instructions given by your teacher.

airports	four	scored	storming
cornered	horns	scores	stormy
corners	ordered	scoring	wear
coursed	ordering	sorely	wearing
coursing	orders	soreness	wears
floors	poured	sports	
flooring	pouring	sporty	
forts	pours	stormed	

E Fun Ways to Spell

Initial the box of each activity you finish.

1. 

Spell your words with markers.

2. Spell your words with letter tiles.

3. 

Spell your words while snapping.

4. 

Spell your words with paint.

Words with /ōr/

Lesson 23

145

1 Hide and Seek

Reinforce correct spelling of current spelling words.

Write the words one at a time on the board. Use this activity for each word.

- **Look** at the word.
- **Say** the word out loud.
- Let's **hide** (cover) the word.
- **Write** the word on your paper.
- Let's **seek** (uncover) the word.
- **Check** your spelling. If your word is spelled wrong, write the word correctly next to it.

2 Other Word Forms

This activity is optional. Have students write variations of this sentence using these Other Word Forms:

Did your team score any points?

scored, scoring, scores

3 Fun Ways to Spell

Four activities are provided. Use one, two, three, or all of the activities. Have students initial the box for each activity they complete.

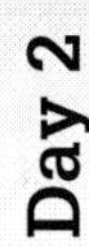

Day 2

Lesson 23

Options:

- assign activities to students according to their learning styles
- set up the activities in learning centers for the class to do throughout the day
- divide the class into four groups and assign one activity per group
- do one activity per day

General

To spell your words with markers...
- Write a spelling word in thick, fat letters.
- Use other colored markers to decorate each letter with dots, flowers, stripes, etc.

Auditory

To spell your words while snapping...
- Look at a word on your spelling list.
- Close your eyes.
- Snap your fingers softly while you whisper the spelling of the word.
- Open your eyes and check your spelling.

Visual

To spell your words with letter tiles...
- Spell a word from your list by putting the tiles in the right order.
- Check your spelling.

Tactile

To spell your words with paint...
- Use your finger to write a spelling word on the paint bag.
- Check your spelling.
- Smooth out the paint and write another word.

1 Working with Words

Familiarize students with word meaning and usage.

Complete the Word

Draw four boxes vertically on the board. Write **or** in each box. Explain to the students that the answer to each clue you give will have the letters **or** in it. Give the students these clues:

1. **a yellow vegetable** (Write the word **corn** across so **or** is in the first box.)
2. **a musical instrument** (Write the word **horn**, or **cornet** across so **or** is in the second box.)
3. **football is a game or** _____ (Write the word **sport** across so **or** is in the third box.)
4. **tool used for eating** (Write **fork** across so **or** is in the fourth box.)

Use the clues to write the words in the puzzle.

Take a minute to memorize...

Read the memory verse to the class twice. Have the class practice it with you two more times.

Words with /ôr/

Lesson 23

F Working with Words Name ______________________

Complete the Word

Fill in the missing letters to complete each word.

			1. c	o	r	n	e	r
			2. f	o	r	t		
	3. r	e	p	o	r	t		
			4. h	o	r	n		
5. a	i	r	p	o	r	t		
	6. f	l	o	o	r			
			7. s	o	r	e		
		8. s	p	o	r	t		
				9. o	r	d	e	r
		10. s	c	o	r	e		
			11. w	o	r	e		
		12. s	t	o	r	m		
			13. c	o	u	r	s	e
			14. p	o	u	r		
			15. f	o	u	r	t	h

1. place where two streets come together
2. an army post
3. write down the facts
4. hard bone on an animal's head
5. place to land airplanes
6. surface of room we walk on
7. painful
8. game played for fun
9. tell someone what to do
10. a record of points
11. had on clothes
12. wild weather
13. path to race on
14. to rain hard
15. comes before fifth

Word Bank

airport	floor	horn	report	sport
corner	fort	order	score	storm
course	fourth	pour	sore	wore

146

G Dictation Name ____________

Listen and write the missing words and punctuation.

1. Christopher thought he would forget to write his report .

2. He did not like Daniel to order him around .

3. The clown at the carnival wore a short , tight hat .

H Proofreading

If a word is misspelled, fill in the oval by that word. If all the words are spelled correctly, fill in the oval by **no mistake**.

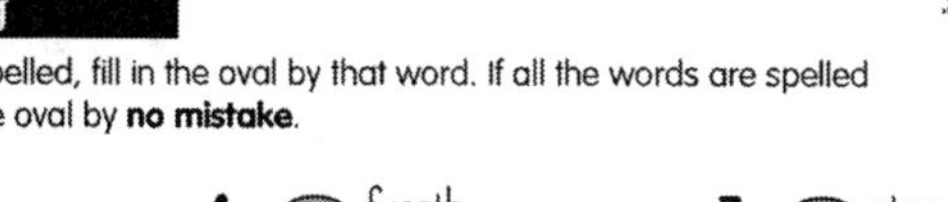

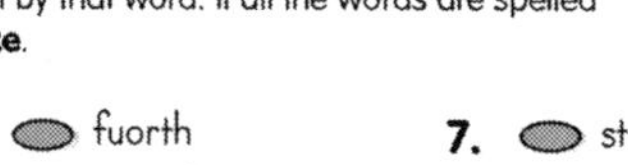

1.	4.	7.
○ allow	● fuorth	● storn
● areport	○ crowd	○ mouse
○ amount	○ horn	○ power
○ no mistake	○ no mistake	○ no mistake

2.	5.	8.
● corse	○ doubt	○ sport
○ wore	○ order	● repoort
○ anyhow	● scor	○ clown
○ no mistake	○ no mistake	○ no mistake

3.	6.	9.
○ fort	○ drown	● soare
○ clown	● cornir	○ pour
● flore	○ loud	○ mouth
○ no mistake	○ no mistake	○ no mistake

Words with /ôr/

Lesson 23

147

1 Dictation

Reinforce correct spelling by using current and previous words in context.

Listen as I read each sentence and then write the missing words and ending punctuation in your worktext. (Slowly read each sentence twice. Sentences are found in the student text to the left.)

2 Proofreading

Familiarize students with standardized test format and reinforce recognizing misspelled words.

Look at each set of words. If a word is misspelled, fill in the oval by that word. If all the words are spelled correctly, fill in the oval by **no mistake**.

Day 4 / Day 5

Lesson 23

3 Hide and Seek

Reinforce correct spelling of current spelling words. (A reproducible master is provided in Appendix A as shown on the inset page to the right.)
Write the words one at a time on the board. Use this activity for each word.

- **Look** at the word.
- **Say** the word out loud.
- Let's **hide** (cover) the word.
- **Write** the word on your paper.
- Let's **seek** (uncover) the word.
- **Check** your spelling. If your word is spelled wrong, write the word correctly next to it.

4 Other Word Forms

Have your students complete this activity to strengthen spelling ability and expand vocabulary.

1 Posttest

Test mastery of the spelling words.

I will say the word once, use the word in a sentence, then say the word again. Write the word on your paper.

Other Word Forms

Lesson 23

Hide and Seek

Check a coin for each word you spell correctly.

Other Word Forms

Scrambled Words

Use the sentence clues to help you unscramble the words. Write the unscrambled word in the sentence.

1. rofts — The children were building forts in the woods.
2. rescron — They wanted to use large posts for the corners.
3. rouf — The girls thought six sides would be better than four.
4. oderpert — One boy reported all the plans in a notebook.
5. redsor — They asked Tommy to give orders about how to build.
6. doingrer — The girls did not want a boy ordering them around.
7. sforlo — Even the floors shook when the thunder boomed.
8. mingstro — The children had to go inside when it began storming.
9. roudep — After the thunder and lightning, the rain poured down.
10. wainger — The children were outside wearing boots and raincoats.
11. prosts — The children were good sports.

Unscramble these Other Word Forms and write them on the lines.

1. ripstroa	airports	7. cginors	scoring
2. ringsuco	coursing	8. oprsty	sporty
3. rocess	scores	9. cdeorsu	coursed
4. rossense	soreness	10. shron	horns
5. deeloprrty	reportedly	11. aersw	wears
6. orlfogni	flooring	12. demorst	stormed

346

1. report	Each group leader will **report** to Mr. Valentino.
2. wore	Daniel **wore** an important look on his face.
3. order	Each group of students went to work in the gym in **order**.
4. fourth	The **fourth** group returned, so it was time for Christopher's group to go.
5. airport	The gym seemed as active as an **airport** terminal.
6. corner	Christopher's class worked on the booth in the **corner**.
7. horn	At one booth, a **horn** would blow if you hit the target with a ball.
8. fort	Another booth was being made to look like a **fort**.
9. score	There's a different **score** for each target you hit with a bean bag.
10. pour	An adult can **pour** the blue paint into your paint tray.
11. sport	Rosa was a good **sport** when Daniel bossed them around.
12. floor	"Don't forget to pick up the scraps off the **floor**," Daniel reminded.
13. course	Christopher thought, "Of **course** we won't forget!"
14. storm	His angry feelings stirred like a **storm** inside him.
15. sore	We shouldn't be **sore** losers like Christopher was when he wasn't leader.

Progress Chart

Students may record scores. (Reproducible master in Appendix B.)

Personal Dictionary

Students may add any words they have misspelled to their personal dictionaries for reference when writing. (Cover in Appendix B.)

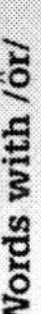

Words with /ôr/

Lesson **23**

I Game Name ____________________

Work patiently with Daniel to decorate for the school carnival. Move one space for each word you or your team spells correctly from this week's word list.

Remember: We can get all the patience we need from Jesus.

J Journaling

In your journal, write a pledge (like a promise) that you will try to be patient with your family, your friends, your classmates, and others.

148

2 Game

Reinforce spelling skills and provide motivation and interest.

Materials

- game page (from student text)
- flat buttons, dry beans, pennies, or game discs (1 per child)
- game word list

Game Word List

1. airport
2. corner
3. course
4. floor
5. fort
6. fourth
7. horn
8. order
9. pour
10. report
11. score
12. sore
13. sport
14. storm
15. wore

How to Play:

- Divide the class into two teams.
- Have each student place his/her game piece on Start.
- Have a student from team A go to the board.
- Say the spelling word. (You may also wish to use the word in a sentence.)
- Have the student write the word on the board.
- If correct, instruct each member of team A to move his/her game piece forward one space on the game board. (Note: If the word is misspelled, correct the spelling immediately.)
- Alternate between teams A and B.
- The team to reach Christopher and Rosa first is the winner.

Non-Competitive Option:

- At the end of the game, say: "Class, I am proud of your efforts to spell the words correctly. If you had fun and tried your best, you are all winners!"

3 Journaling

Provide a meaningful reason for correct spelling through personal writing.

Review the story using discussion leads provided on the following page. Encourage students to apply the Scriptural value in their journaling.

Journaling (continued)

- What kinds of projects have you worked on with a group of classmates?
- How did you feel if one of your group bossed everyone else around?
- If someone is doing something wrong, like being very bossy, is it okay for us to speak unkindly to them? Why? (No. Because being unkind to them doesn't help them do better and it makes us just as wrong as they are.)
- How was Rosa a good example? (She stayed calm when Daniel ordered them around and acted like they weren't doing a good job.)
- In your journal, write a pledge (like a promise) that you will try to be patient with your family, your friends, your classmates, and others. Ask God to help you keep that pledge.

Take a minute to memorize...
Have the class say the memory verses from lessons 19, 20, 21, 22, and 23 with you.

"When children read and write, they grow as spellers."*

*Wilde, Sandra. 1990. A Proposal for a New Spelling Curriculum. The Elementary School Journal, Vol. 90, No. 3, January: 275-289.

1 **Literature Connection**
Topic: Belonging to God
Theme Text: Ephesians 2:19

God's Family

The sign-man and his family, the Potters, find a place where they belong.

John Potter stepped up into the camper and quickly shut the door behind him. He rubbed his hands together and smiled at his wife. "I think it's getting warmer, Cheryl. The daffodil bulbs Harry Ellis planted are starting to pop up under the trees along the drive."

"That's wonderful!" Cheryl held a toy just out of Landon's reach so he would have to let go of the drawer handle and take a step to get it. "This camper seems so small when I have to spend the whole day cooped up inside it with the boys."

John glanced around. "Where's Harrison? Is he playing in the barn?"

"Grandma Ellis invited him into the house to make cookies this afternoon during Landon's nap. She stopped by earlier to give me a loaf of her wonderful homemade bread, and I think she could sense we were all about to pull each other's hair out."

"She's a delight, isn't she? I wish we could have known her husband, Harry. He sure kept this place in great shape. It's been easy to keep up with the chores and odd jobs this winter."

"And the farm sure beats that parking lot we stayed in the first week." Cheryl smiled and picked up Landon.

"Yes, it's worked out well for everyone. Grandma Ellis was worried about how she was going to catch up on all the work Harry used to take care of before he died."

Cheryl nodded. "She told me just this morning how nice things were looking again and how much safer she feels having us nearby, just in case there's an emergency." Landon wriggled out of her arms.

"Yes," John agreed as he reached over and tickled his son's bare tummy. "She told me once how isolated she feels out here on the farm without Harry."

"Well, I know how it feels to be uncomfortable with your surroundings. This camper is so tiny and crowded!" Cheryl laughed, then patted John's arm. "And I know it's tough on you, too, when you have to move the pickup after it's all leveled out and situated, not to mention how awkward it is to drive around with the camper on the back."

"I know." John stretched out his arms as Landon toddled his direction. "We can't keep using Grandma Ellis' car all the time, either. We need to find a place to rent or a small fixer-upper to buy. Then we'll have more space to live, and won't have to haul this camper around when we go someplace."

"We've saved quite a bit since you got that programming job, John," Cheryl hinted. "And we haven't had to spend much money living here."

"You're right." John grinned. "I'll call a realtor on my break tomorrow and we can go looking when I get off work." He picked Landon up and kissed his rosy cheek.

The Potter family spent every afternoon that week with a different realtor. They looked at small houses, apartments, duplexes, lots, dilapidated bungalows, old fixer- uppers, and even some modest mobile homes.

But they quickly realized they'd gotten used to country living, and no one was excited about moving back to town. Mom loved the pastures and woods she hiked through with Landon in the backpack. Dad loved the change of pace. The chores and outdoor work Grandma's farm required were refreshing after staring at a computer screen all day inside an office. Harrison loved Grandma's horses and had become great friends with Captain, her collie. He'd even named all the cows. The barn cats had become his special playmates, and Grandma had given him the long-haired black cat he called "Midnight." But most of the apartments and duplexes didn't even allow pets.

So the Potters began to look for small houses on a little land in the country—but it was difficult to find anything in their price range. After a particularly unsuccessful day with a pushy realtor who kept showing them things they couldn't afford, they finally headed back up Grandma's driveway.

"Well, that wasn't very encouraging," Dad sighed. Harrison and Mom just nodded their heads sadly. Landon, tired of being confined in his car seat, cried loudly as the truck rolled to a stop in front of Grandma's house.

Just then, Grandma popped out of the house, wiping her hands on her bright yellow apron. "I've got a hot pot of soup on the stove and I baked bread this morning. I'd love to have some company for supper." A smile spread across her wrinkled face. "I'm sure you're tired after another afternoon of house hunting." She waved at Landon, who had stopped crying long enough to see who was talking.

Dad smiled and nodded his head. "We'd be delighted, Grandma."

As the family sat down at the big kitchen table, Grandma sensed their somber mood. She listened quietly to their frustrations about available properties. She was sympathetic to Harrison's worries about Midnight if they rented an apartment. She patted Cheryl on the back and nodded as she shared her claustrophobic feelings of living in the small camper.

After everyone had eaten their fill of soup and fresh homemade bread, Grandma brought out big slices of her famous blueberry pie. Setting a piece down beside each plate, she gave them all clean forks.

Story Continued

"I can't tell you how much I've enjoyed having you here all winter," she said as they started eating dessert. "I've been thinking. There's that empty barn in the north pasture. Harry always talked about converting it into a guest house. The creek is close by, the woods are right behind it, and the pasture is in front. I think Harry even drew up some plans, and they're probably out in the workshop somewhere." She paused. "You know, if you could stand the camper for the summer, I think you kids could move in there by this fall."

Mr. Potter's eyes were suddenly wide open. Mom's forkful of blueberry pie had stopped halfway to her mouth. Suddenly, everyone was talking at once. Grandma's sparkling eyes reflected her huge smile as she took Dad to the shop to look for the plans. Mom took a pen out of her purse and did some quick figuring on a scrap of paper.

When Grandma unrolled the plans a few minutes later on the dining room table, the family could hardly contain their excitement. "Oh, this is so cute!" Mom traced the lines with her finger. The detailed plans had a materials list neatly printed on the back. "It's just what we've been looking for!"

Mr. Potter smiled. "We'd better talk about the price and do some checking on materials before we get too excited."

"Oh, I'm sure we can work that out," Grandma encouraged. "I'd love to have you nearby, so the land will be very reasonable. And you can use all those tools out in Harry's shop. My son-in-law is an electrician, and Mr. Schilling. . . I think you met him at the school the night you moved out here. . .he's a contractor and also knows plumbing. There are some other people that go to our church who have construction skills, too. I bet we can have you fixed up in no time at all."

A few weeks later, Mrs. Potter and the boys walked along a newly-graded and graveled road toward their "barn." Landon was still sleepy after waking up from his nap in the camper. Harrison had fallen asleep, too, and now he was rubbing his eyes as he trudged slowly behind. Mom smiled as the barn came into view. A fresh coat of light, brown paint set off the red door and shutters around the newly cut windows. It made their new home look warm and inviting. Mr. Jacobson was up on the roof securing the last of the red metal roofing panels. The sound of hammers and drills could be heard from inside as they approached.

Tears began to run down Mrs. Potter's face as she opened the door. "Why are you crying, Mom?" Harrison asked. "Did something break?"

"No, Harrison," she laughed. "These are tears of joy. I just can't believe all these unselfish people helping us get our house done so quickly. I've never seen people act so much like Jesus before."

Harrison looked around inside. A new wood stove sat on a hearth of beautifully-laid brick. The fresh pine floor gleamed in the light streaming from sparkling windows that Beth, Katelynn, and Laney were cleaning. Mr. Hill was connecting the wires to the ceiling fan in the kitchen. Mr. Schilling was under the kitchen sink hooking up the new garbage disposal. Mr. Hatasaki was drilling a hole in the exact same place on each kitchen cabinet door, with Janette Hill following close behind, attaching silver knobs to the white doors. Maria Vanetti was putting the final coat of paint on the walls in the living room. Mrs. Rawson was cleaning the mirror that had just been hung in the bathroom.

"Oh, my room is almost done!" Harrison danced around Mr. Larkin and his new wife Elisa, who were painting the walls navy blue. "Can I sleep here tonight?"

Mom put Landon down and watched him toddle over to the long table set up in the middle of the living room. Grandma Ellis and Mrs. DeVore were arranging the food everyone had brought. "You're just in time for dinner, Harrison." Grandma said. "And I'm glad you woke up, Landon."

Helen Jacobson knelt down so she could see Landon better. "Did you just wake up, little guy?" She picked him up and cuddled him over her protruding stomach. "We'll have a playmate for you soon," she whispered in his ear. "You won't be the youngest much longer."

"Can I hold him? Can I hold him?" Rachel eagerly held out her hands.

"Have you finished picking up all the trash and scraps outside?" Helen asked. Rachel nodded her head. "Then why don't you, Laney, and Rosa take Harrison and Landon down by the creek while we finish getting dinner ready? That would be a big help."

Rachel took the baby eagerly. "Harrison, do you want to go throw rocks in the creek with us?"

After the children left, Grandma Ellis came over to where Mrs. Potter was peeking into the master bedroom. "Well, Cheryl, what do you think?" Grandma gave her a squeeze.

"I can't believe all these people working on our home. You're like family, and less than nine months ago you didn't even know who we were."

"We are your family, Cheryl," Grandma smiled. "We're family because you belong to God's household with every other Christian. And helping each other is what family members are supposed to do."

2 Discussion Time

Check understanding of the story and development of personal values.

- Who are the members of your family?
- What is one thing your family has done together?
- How did you feel about what you did with your family?
- Raise your hand if you feel you're a part of God's very own family.
- Have you ever done something special with your "church family?"
- How did you feel about what you did with your "church family?"

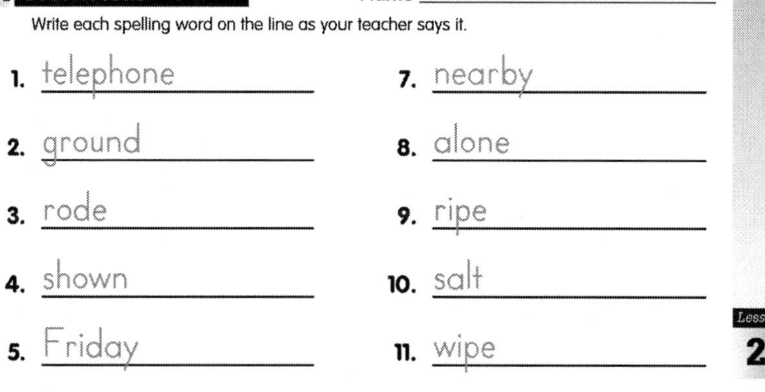

A Test-Words Name ____________________

Write each spelling word on the line as your teacher says it.

1.	telephone	7.	nearby
2.	ground	8.	alone
3.	rode	9.	ripe
4.	shown	10.	salt
5.	Friday	11.	wipe
6.	smile	12.	course

Review Lesson 24

B Test-Sentences

Write the sentences on the lines below, correcting each misspelled word, as well as all capitalization and punctuation errors. There are two misspelled words in each sentence.

The tiney petals will flote on the water.

1. The tiny petals will float on the water.

our teacher tawt us a silly saung.

2. Our teacher taught us a silly song.

There was a funny cloun at the cornir

3. There was a funny clown at the corner.

149

Day 1 Review 24

3 Test-Words

Test for knowledge of the correct spellings of these words.

I will say the word once, use the word in a sentence, then say the word again. Write the word on the lines in your worktext.

1. telephone — John Potter decided to **telephone** some realtors.
2. ground — The daffodils were breaking through the **ground**.
3. rode — The family **rode** in the realtor's van to look at the property.
4. shown — The realtors had **shown** them a lot of houses.
5. Friday — By **Friday**, the Potter family was tired of looking at properties.
6. smile — Grandma Ellis' **smile** was a welcome sight.
7. nearby — Grandma Ellis liked having the Potters **nearby**.
8. alone — She does not like being **alone**.
9. ripe — Grandma Ellis used the **ripe** blueberries to make a pie.
10. salt — She put in just the right amount of **salt**.
11. wipe — She always uses her yellow apron to **wipe** her hands.
12. course — Of **course**, lots of people were willing to help the Potters.

4 Test-Sentences

Reinforce recognizing misspelled words.

Read each sentence carefully. Write the sentences on the lines in your worktext, correcting each misspelled word, as well as all capitalization and punctuation errors. There are two misspelled words in each sentence.

Take a minute to memorize...

Read the memory verse to the class twice. Have the class practice it with you two more times.

Day 2

Review

24

1 Test-Dictation

Reinforce correct spelling by using current and previous words in context.

Listen as I read each sentence. Then write the missing words and ending punctuation in your worktext. (Slowly read each sentence twice. Sentences are found in the student text to the right. The words **toast**, **hall**, **wild**, and **owe** are found in this unit.)

2 Test-Proofreading

Familiarize students with standardized test format and reinforce recognizing misspelled words.

Look at each set of words. If a word is misspelled, fill in the oval by that word. If all the words are spelled correctly, fill in the oval by **no mistake**.

Review

Lesson 24

C Test-Dictation

Name ______

Listen and write the missing words and punctuation.

1. She drank milk with her toast .
2. I left my shoe in the hall .
3. The wild rabbit would not come near us .
4. Do I owe you seven or eight dollars ?

D Test-Proofreading

If a word is misspelled, fill in the oval by that word. If all the words are spelled correctly, fill in the oval by **no mistake**.

1. ○ die ○ score ○ upon ● no mistake
2. ● shye ○ taught ○ crowd ○ no mistake
3. ○ loud ○ shown ● sighn ○ no mistake
4. ○ gold ○ ground ○ wore ● no mistake
5. ○ mouse ● roap ○ float ○ no mistake
6. ● spoek ○ August ○ horn ○ no mistake
7. ○ bought ● autum ○ fourth ○ no mistake
8. ○ fought ○ report ○ order ● no mistake
9. ○ sew ● powir ○ anyhow ○ no mistake

150

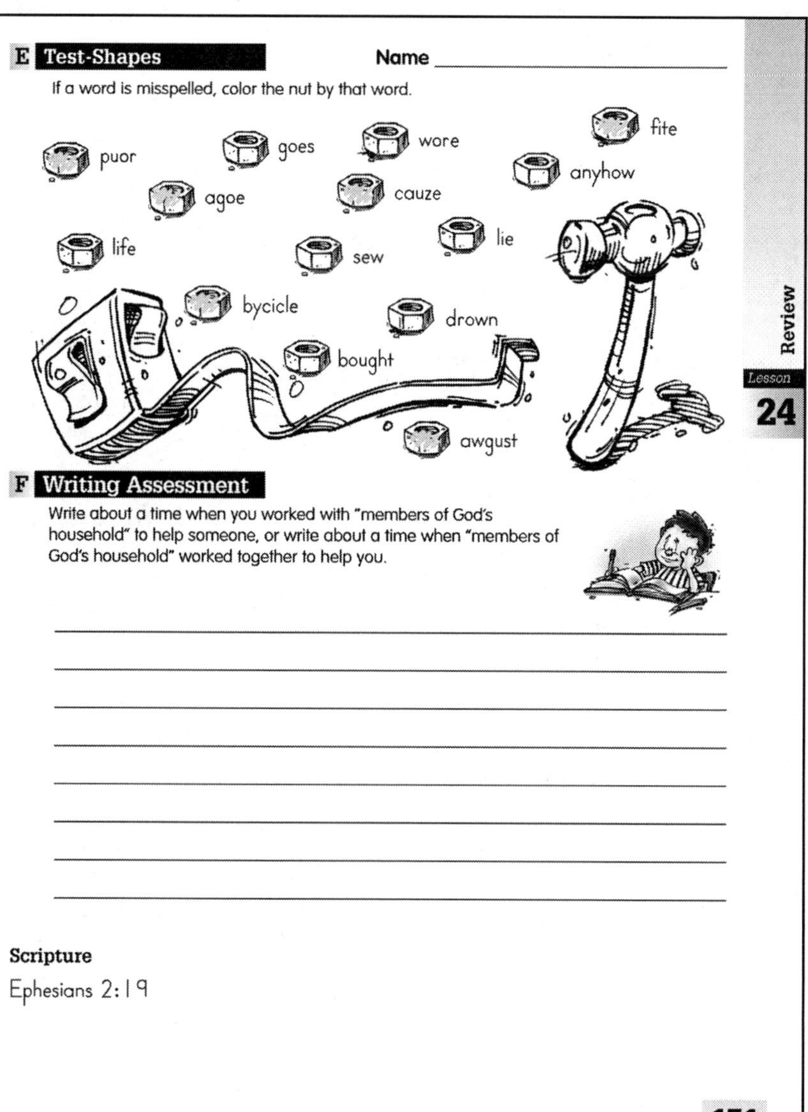

E Test-Shapes Name ____________

If a word is misspelled, color the nut by that word.

F Writing Assessment

Write about a time when you worked with "members of God's household" to help someone, or write about a time when "members of God's household" worked together to help you.

Scripture

Ephesians 2:19

Review Lesson 24

151

Command of oral language is the foundation for success in reading and writing.

1 Test-Shapes

Test mastery of words in this unit.

If a word is misspelled, color the object by that word.

2 Writing Assessment

Assess student's spelling, grammar, and composition skills through personal writing.

- How did the Potter family feel about living in the camper? (They were tired of living in such a small space.)
- What did they decide to do about it? (They decided to look for another place to live.)
- Where did they decide they wanted to live? (The country.)
- How did Grandma help them? (She sold them some land and a barn on her property.)
- What did the people from Grandma's church do? (They came and helped remodel the barn so the Potters could live in it.)
- Write about a time when you worked with "members of God's household" to help someone, or write about a time when "members of God's household" worked together to help you.

1 Test-Sentences

Reinforce recognizing misspelled words.

Read each sentence carefully. Write the sentences on the lines in your worktext, correcting each misspelled word, as well as all capitalization and punctuation errors. There are two misspelled words in each sentence.

Review Lesson 24

G Test-Sentences Name ____________

Write the sentences on the lines below, correcting each misspelled word, as well as all capitalization and punctuation errors. There are two misspelled words in each sentence.

did you oarder the forthe sandwich

1. Did you order the fourth sandwich?

Don't alow that mowse to come in here!

2. Don't allow that mouse to come in here!

she will meet her dawter at the aerport.

3. She will meet her daughter at the airport.

H Test-Words

Write each spelling word on the line as your teacher says it.

1.	floor	7.	open
2.	crowd	8.	wall
3.	amount	9.	doubt
4.	loud	10.	hour
5.	follow	11.	brought
6.	tight	12.	fort

152

2 Test-Words

Test for knowledge of the correct spellings of these words.

I will say the word once, use the word in a sentence, then say the word again. Write the word on the lines in your worktext.

1.	floor	The Potter's friends worked hard to put in a new pine **floor**.
2.	crowd	There was a great **crowd** of friends there to help.
3.	amount	Cheryl could not believe the **amount** of work they had done!
4.	loud	Mr. Hatasaki's drill made a **loud**, buzzing sound.
5.	follow	Mrs. Hill will **follow** with the cabinet knobs.
6.	tight	She will screw them on **tight**.
7.	open	Maria can **open** the gallon of paint.
8.	wall	Mr. Larkin and his wife were painting the **wall** navy blue.
9.	doubt	"I **doubt** this will need another coat of paint," said the coach.
10.	hour	"We'll be ready to eat in less than an **hour**," said Grandma Ellis.
11.	brought	Everyone **brought** food to the Potter's new home.
12.	fort	John Potter can build the boys a tree **fort**.

I **Test-Editing** Name ______________________

If a word is spelled correctly, fill in the oval under **Correct**. If the word is misspelled, fill in the oval under **Incorrect**, and spell the word correctly on the blank.

	Correct	Incorrect	
1. horn	●	○	
2. report	●	○	
3. skor	○	●	score
4. sor	○	●	sore
5. sport	●	○	
6. storm	●	○	
7. mowth	○	●	mouth
8. plow	●	○	
9. showt	○	●	shout
10. paw	●	○	
11. raw	●	○	
12. upon	●	○	

Review Lesson 24

153

3 Test-Editing

Reinforce recognizing and correcting misspelled words.

4 Action Game

Reinforce spelling skills and provide motivation and interest.

Materials

- one *A Reason For Spelling*® book
- audio player
- small prizes (erasers, pencils, stickers)
- additional books (one less than the total number of students)

How to Play:

- Place the books and the *A Reason For Spelling*® book in a circle around a table.
- Play music as the students march around the table.
- When you stop the music, each student must touch the book beside him/her.
- Have the student touching the *A Reason For Spelling*® book spell a review word.
- If he/she spells it incorrectly, have him/her march again; if he/she spells it correctly, give him/her a prize and have him/her return to his/her desk.
- Remove one book each time a student drops out and continue the game until every student has spelled a word correctly.

1 Game

Reinforce spelling skills and provide motivation and interest.

Materials

- game page (from student text)
- flat buttons, dry beans, pennies, or game discs (1 per child)
- game word list

Game Word List

Check off each word lightly in pencil as it is used.

Red (5 points)

1. die
2. shy
3. sign
4. gold
5. rope
6. spoke
7. ago
8. fight
9. lie
10. goes
11. life

Blue (10 points)

1. power
2. fought
3. autumn
4. bicycle
5. wore
6. anyhow
7. August
8. bought
9. cause
10. drown
11. pour

Yellow (15 points)

1. dying
2. lifeless
3. roping
4. gone
5. saltier
6. allowance
7. crowded
8. mouthful
9. powerless
10. flooring
11. groundless

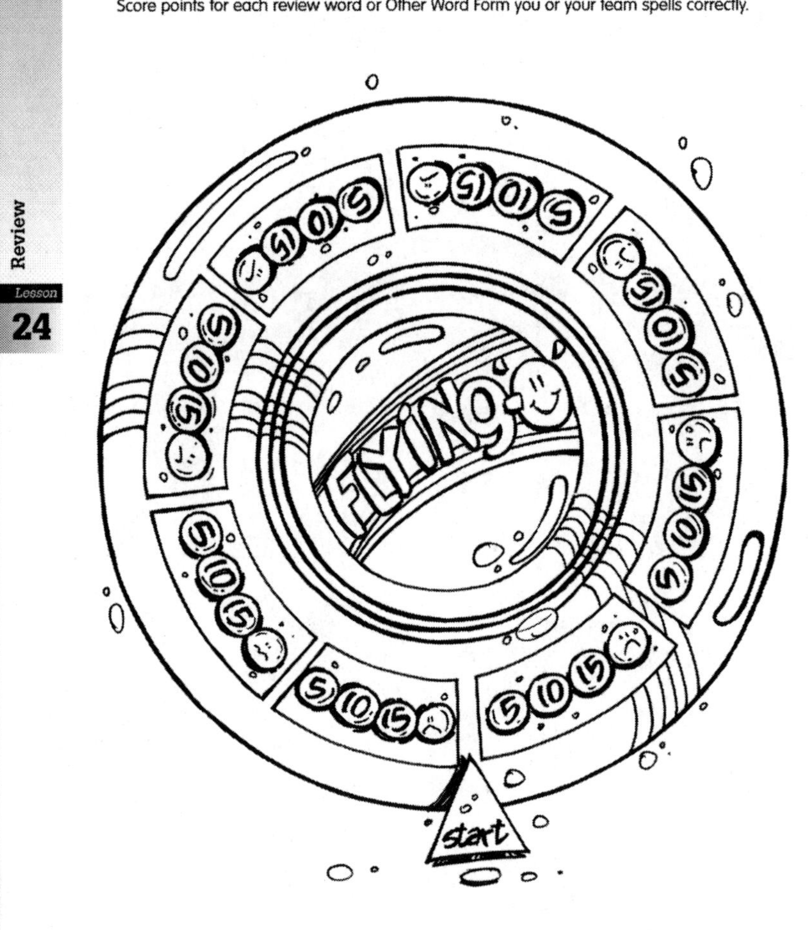
J Game
Name
Score points for each review word or Other Word Form you or your team spells correctly.
Review
Lesson
24
FLYING
start
Remember: When you know Jesus, you are a part of His family.
154

How to Play:

- Divide the class into two teams.
- Have each student place his/her game piece on Start.
- Inform the students of the following point system:
  Red list words = **5** points, **Blue** list words = **10** points
  Yellow list words = **15** points (these are Other Word Forms)
- Have a student from team A choose a color: red, blue, or yellow.
- Say a word from the correct color list. (You may also wish to use the word in a sentence.)
- Have the student write the word on the board.
- If correct, ask each member of team A to move his/her game piece forward (to the right and up, counter clockwise) to the corresponding color in the first section. Record the score. If the word is misspelled, have each member of that team move his/her game piece to the "sad face" in the first section.
- Alternate between teams A and B.
- The team with the highest score at the end of three rounds is the winner. (A round begins and ends at Start.)

Non-Competitive Option:

At the end of the game, say: "Class, I am proud of your efforts to spell the words correctly. If you had fun and tried your best, you are all winners!"

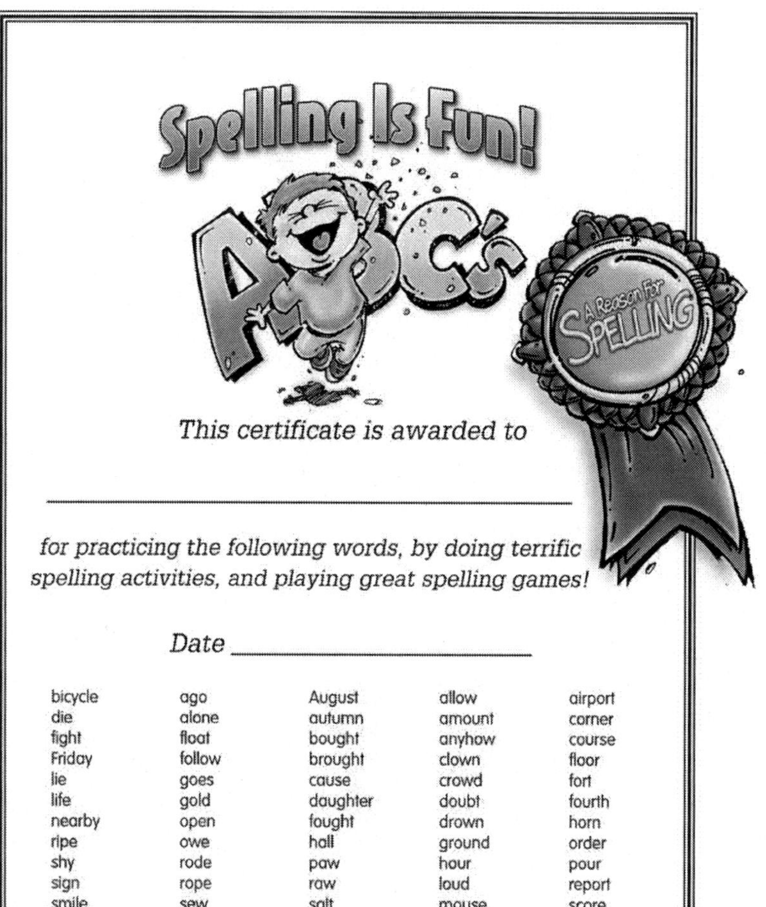

Spelling Is Fun!

ABC's

A Reason for SPELLING

This certificate is awarded to

____

for practicing the following words, by doing terrific spelling activities, and playing great spelling games!

Date ____________________

bicycle	ago	August	allow	airport
die	alone	autumn	amount	corner
fight	float	bought	anyhow	course
Friday	follow	brought	clown	floor
lie	goes	cause	crowd	fort
life	gold	daughter	doubt	fourth
nearby	open	fought	drown	horn
ripe	owe	hall	ground	order
shy	rode	paw	hour	pour
sign	rope	raw	loud	report
smile	sew	salt	mouse	score
tight	shown	song	mouth	sore
tiny	spoke	taught	plow	sport
wild	telephone	upon	power	storm
wipe	toast	wall	shout	wore

2 Certificate

Provide an opportunity for parents or guardians to encourage and assess their child's progress.

- Write your name on the first line.
- Write the date on the next line.
- Be sure to show your parents or guardian all the words you've practiced spelling.

Take a minute to memorize...
Have the class say the memory verses from lessons 19, 20, 21, 22, 23, and 24 with you.

3 Letter

Provide the parent or guardian with the spelling word lists for the next unit.

Show your parents or guardian this letter that lists your spelling words for the next unit. Put it where you will remember to practice the words together.

Day 5

Review 24

Dear Parent,

We are about to begin a new spelling unit containing five weekly lessons. A set of fifteen words will be studied each week. All the words will be reviewed in the sixth week. Values based on the Scriptures listed below will be taught in each lesson.

Lesson 25	Lesson 26	Lesson 27	Lesson 28	Lesson 29
alarm	center	able	burn	brook
apart	December	April	dirt	bushes
argue	dollar	bottle	early	cookie
army	driver	candle	earn	football
artist	forget	cattle	herd	good-bye
bark	hammer	eagle	hurry	hood
charge	later	handle	learn	hook
March	mirror	metal	person	neighborhood
mark	November	middle	return	notebook
market	remember	needle	Saturday	pulley
park	river	saddle	search	push
shark	silver	sprinkle	September	shook
sharp	sugar	squirrel	serve	wolf
smart	summer	travel	thirty	woman
start	wonder	turtle	worse	wool
Eph. 3:17-19	2 Thess. 3:5	James 4:11	Romans 15:5	1 Timothy 2:1

1 **Literature Connection**
Topic: God's love for us
Theme Text: Ephesians 3:17-19

Down Deep Roots

Rosa learns that being grounded in God's love helps us grow strong and true.

CRASH!! Rumble-umble-umble-ble. Rosa's eyes popped opened and she peered around her room. Total darkness. Suddenly, lightning jagged across the sky outside. Bright light highlighted the picture on the wall across from Rosa's bed. As the thunder rolled like huge boulders tumbling across the sky, and blackness again filled the room, Rosa eyes seemed to still see the picture's brilliant outline.

She turned her head toward the window just as another streak of lightning split the sky. The vivid light revealed trees tossing in the strong wind. The explosion of thunder was so close it seemed to rock the house. The spring storm the weatherman predicted had arrived with a vengeance! Rosa stuck her head under her covers. She could still hear the rain and feel the mighty blasts of thunder. The storm raged on, and eventually Rosa fell back to sleep.

"Come on, sleepy head." Maria tugged at Rosa's covers. "Time to get up."

Rosa opened blurry eyes to see sunshine streaming through the window. She blinked and looked up at her big sister. "Why'd you wake me up? It's not a school day, so I get to sleep late."

Maria laughed. "You did sleep late, lazy bones! Dad's got breakfast ready."

Rosa groaned and rolled over.

"Well, sleeping beauty, I know how to get you up." Maria threatened. "Just go back to sleep if you want, while I go find Nipper. She'll wake you up, all right!"

Rosa sat up quickly. "I'm up! I'm up!" She looked over at the clock on the wall. Nine o'clock!

"Well, hurry up, then." Maria turned to leave the room. "We're going over to the Andersons' right after breakfast. Dad wants to help Grandpa Anderson dig the holes for the new fruit trees he's planting in the orchard."

After breakfast, the Vasquez family walked down the country road to their neighbors' home. As they got close to the big white farm house on the hill, Rosa ran ahead around to the backyard. "Dad, look!" she screeched. "The tree!"

Mr. Vasquez gave a long whistle of surprise. The violent thunderstorm had brought down one of the huge trees at the edge of the Anderson's back yard. Its gigantic branches had barely missed the greenhouse, but it had taken a large limb out of a nearby tree as it fell across the garden.

"Quite a mess, Rafael." Grandpa Joe came out of the greenhouse, his thumbs tucked into his suspenders. "Reckon it'll take a bit of clearing up before Ruthie can get back to her gardening."

"Well, we'll get right on it, Joe." Dad leaned the posthole diggers against the garage. "I'll run home and get my chainsaw. We've got to get Grandma Ruth's garden back in shape or we'll miss out on all that good stuff she cooks and cans from it!"

Soon the roar of chainsaws reminded Rosa of last night's thunder. Grandpa Joe and Dad cut the tree into firewood-size pieces. Dad had to split the biggest pieces right in the garden before they were small enough to carry away. Carlos and Maria carried them to the woodpile by the back porch and stacked them neatly. Rosa and Grandma Ruth picked up branches and sticks and moved them to a clear spot with no trees nearby.

"What will you do with all this?" Rosa wondered aloud as she threw another armload of small branches onto the growing stack. "There's a lot more here than you'll ever need for kindling next winter."

Grandma Ruth chuckled and added her load to the pile that was already almost as tall as Rosa. "Well, Rosa, it's still cool in the evenings. I think a bonfire and hot dog roast would be a lot of fun, don't you?"

"Really?" Rosa squealed. "And marshmallows, too?"

"Of course!" Grandma Ruth acted surprised. "You can't have a bonfire without roasting marshmallows, can you?"

"Nope!" Rosa skipped along beside her "adopted" Grandma as they walked back to the muddy garden for another load.

By mid-afternoon, most of the mess was cleaned up. Grandma Anderson disappeared inside for a little while, then reappeared on the back porch flapping her apron to get everyone's attention. When Dad and Grandpa Joe looked up, she lifted her hand to her mouth over and over like she was eating and waved her arm for them to come inside. A huge grin spread over Dad's face and he rubbed his tummy with one work-gloved hand. Grandpa Joe chuckled and nodded so that Grandma Ruth could see they understood it was time to eat. It took only a few minutes for the chainsaws to chew their way through the last of the thick logs.

It seemed awfully quiet when the saws stopped. The last few loads Rosa carried felt heavier than the earlier ones. Even thirteen-year-old Carlos was carrying just one log at a time now. As they trooped wearily toward the house, Rosa dragged her feet in the grass, trying to scrape some of the thick mud off her boots. "Yuck!" She pointed to the clumps of mud attached to Carlos' and Maria's boots. "We've got half the garden on us! Oh, Carlos, you should see your face!"

"What?" Carlos rubbed a hand across his face, adding another streak of dirt. "What's wrong with it?"

"It sure looks awful." Maria sank down on the bottom step to take off her boots.

"My face?" Carlos

Story (continued)

frowned. "It can't be that bad!"

"Well, it is." Maria laughed. "But that's not what I was talking about. Look at that." She waved her hand toward the garden. "It looks horrible even after we've moved the tree!"

"Do you think anything will grow in it this year?" Rosa twisted her ankle sideways, holding on to the porch railing to keep her balance as she rubbed the side of her boot in the grass.

"Sure it will!" Grandpa Joe slapped his work gloves against his leg to knock the sawdust off. "With a few days of sunshine, all that thick mud will dry out. Then we can till the earth so it's nice and smooth again, ready for little plants and seeds. Grandma may have to replant some of her early stuff that got pretty well crushed, but it'll grow!" He tipped the brim of his hat back with one thumb. "Yes sir-ee, in a few weeks that piece of ground will be burstin' with growin' things, busy with bees checkin' out the blossoms and critters tryin' to get the good stuff before we do. After all, that's one of the ways our heavenly Father shows His deep love for us, by givin' us this earth that provides so much for us. Seed time and harvest have always come and always will. That's a special gift of our Father's love, don't you think?"

"But, Grandpa Joe, what if another big tree falls?" Rosa sat on a step and tugged at her left boot.

"Well. . ." Grandpa Joe took his hat off and scratched the back of his head. "Of course, that could happen, Rosita, but it's not very likely. Trees normally have a pretty incredible system of roots that hold them up. The root system goes down deep into the soil and spreads out as far underground as you see limbs and twigs on the top of the tree. Those roots tend to hold a tree firmly in place, unless somethin' goes wrong." Grandpa Joe thumped one of the freshly cut logs stacked neatly by the back porch. "This tree grew too near the edge of the hill. It's roots couldn't grow deep and wide in the earth, because there wasn't enough earth where it grew. That's why the storm brought it down."

"Anyone out here hungry, or should I just put the food away?" Grandma Ruth poked her head out the back door.

"We're coming!" Carlos exclaimed as everyone headed for the door at once.

That evening, another storm raged at the Vasquez home, but *indoors*!

"I did not!"

"You did, too!" Rosa yelled.

"Did NOT!"

"You did! On purpose, too! You're always pestering me!"

"Whoa!" Mr. Vasquez held his hands up as he entered the living room where the thunder was rumbling. "That's more than enough of that! Chipper's terrified and even Nipper ran to hide. What's going on?"

"Rosa says I took her Classics piano book and hid it so she couldn't practice. But I didn't, Dad. I don't know anything about it." Thirteen-year-old Carlos didn't look as grown up as he liked to think.

Rosa opened her mouth to tell Dad all about it, but he held up one hand. "Rosa, please go to your room. I'll be there in a moment." When his voice sounded like that, Rosa knew better than to say anything. "And Rosa, please look on your dresser."

It was there. The red piano book with the gold letters spelling "Classics" was on her dresser, right where she'd left it. Rosa flung herself onto her bed and curled into a ball. Her eyes burned and her cheeks felt hot. She wished Dad would forget about coming to her room. She wished Carlos would forget everything she'd yelled at him. She wished she could sneak out the window and up the hill to the Andersons' house. She wished she could relive the last few minutes of this day differently. She heard Dad come in and felt the side of the bed sink down a little as he sat beside her.

"You know, Rosita, I often pray that you and your brother and sister will be like trees." Rosa turned to look at her dad in surprise. He sighed and brushed her hair out of her face. "I want you to grow strong and true, to understand how very much God loves you and to love God in return. I want you to be like those other huge trees at Grandpa and Grandma Anderson's—the ones that didn't fall when the storm came. That's my prayer for you."

As Rosa snuggled into bed that night, she peered out the window. Tonight no thick clouds covered the sliver of moon and bright stars. Rosa smiled to herself and wriggled into a more comfortable position. She felt much better after telling Carlos and Dad that she was sorry. The storms were over.

"Eeek! Oh, Chipper, you startled me." Rosa scolded the small red squirrel as he settled himself. "Ouch!" she muttered as he scratched around making his bed to his liking. "You must think I'm a tree, or something."

It was Chipper's turn to be surprised when Rosa suddenly burst into giggles. "I guess I am sort of like a tree." She smiled, and then became more serious. "And I'm going to try to be like a strong tree with roots deep down in God's love, so I won't fall."

2 Discussion Time

Check understanding of the story and development of personal values.

- What damage did the spring storm do at the Anderson's home?
- What did the Vasquez family do about the fallen tree?
- Why was Rosa worried about Grandma Ruth's garden?
- Why did Grandpa Joe say the big tree had fallen?
- How does our Scripture verse say that we can be like a tree?

A Preview Name ____________

Write each word as your teacher says it.

1. shark
2. March
3. start
4. artist
5. park
6. sharp
7. army
8. bark
9. smart
10. alarm
11. apart
12. charge
13. market
14. mark
15. argue

Words with /är/

Lesson 25

Scripture
Ephesians 3:17–19

157

3 Preview

Test for knowledge of the correct spellings of these words.

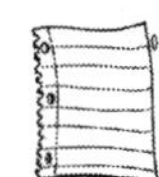

Customize Your List

On a separate piece of paper, additional words of your choice may be tested.

I will say the word once, use the word in a sentence, then say the word again. Write the word on the lines in the worktext.

Correct Immediately!

Let's correct our preview. I will write each word on the board. Put a dot under each letter on your preview as I spell the word out loud. If you spelled a word wrong, rewrite it correctly.

Take a minute to memorize...

Read the memory verse to the class twice. Have the class practice it with you two more times.

Day 1

Lesson 25

1.	shark	A **shark** grows new teeth all the time.
2.	March	**March** is said to come in like a lion and go out like a lamb.
3.	start	The weatherman said the storm would **start** that night.
4.	artist	An **artist** probably designed the map the weatherman uses on TV.
5.	park	Dad went to **park** the jeep in the garage before the storm came.
6.	sharp	Each **sharp** flash of lightning was followed by thunder rumbling loudly.
7.	army	The thunder sounded like an **army** fighting a war nearby.
8.	bark	Barkley and Digby always **bark** at the lightning and thunder.
9.	smart	They are **smart** enough to stay inside the barn during the storm.
10.	alarm	Maria threatened to use Nipper for an **alarm** clock to get Rosa up.
11.	apart	A big tree had fallen and broken **apart** as it hit the ground.
12.	charge	Rosa was in **charge** of stacking the small limbs, twigs, and bark.
13.	market	Grandma Ruth will get some more seeds at the **market**.
14.	mark	Grandpa Joe said that after a few days there wouldn't be a **mark** where the tree fell.
15.	argue	Rosa and Carlos started to **argue** about the missing piano book.

Progress Chart

Students may record scores. (Reproducible master in Appendix B.)

4 Word Shapes

Help students form a correct image of whole words.

Look at each word and think about its shape. Now, write the word in the correct word shape boxes. You may check off each word as you use it.

(In most words, the letters **ar** spell the sound of **/är/**, whether it is at the beginning, middle, or end of a word. There are very few exceptions.)

In the word shape boxes, color the letters that spell the sound of **/är/** in each word. Circle the words that have the digraph **ch** or **sh**.

B Word Shapes Name ____________________

Write each word in the correct word shape boxes. Next, in the word shape boxes, color the letters that spell the sound of **/är/** in each word. Circle the words that have the digraph **/ch/** or **/sh/**.

	Word	Answer
1.	alarm	market
2.	apart	smart
3.	argue	park
4.	army	apart
5.	artist	start
6.	bark	March (circled)
7.	charge	shark (circled)
8.	March	mark
9.	mark	sharp (circled)
10.	market	charge (circled)
11.	park	alarm
12.	shark	argue
13.	sharp	bark
14.	smart	artist
15.	start	army

Answers may vary for duplicate word shapes.

Be Prepared For Fun

Check these supply lists for **Fun Ways to Spell** presented **Day 2**. Purchase and/or gather needed items ahead of time!

General
- Pencil
- 3 x 5 Cards (15 per child)
- Scissors
- Spelling List

Auditory
- Rhythm Instruments (two wooden spoons, two pan lids, maracas)
- Spelling List

Visual
- Sidewalk Chalk
- Spelling List

Tactile
- Play Dough
- Spelling List

C Hide and Seek

Name ______________________

Place an **X** on a coin for each word you spell correctly.

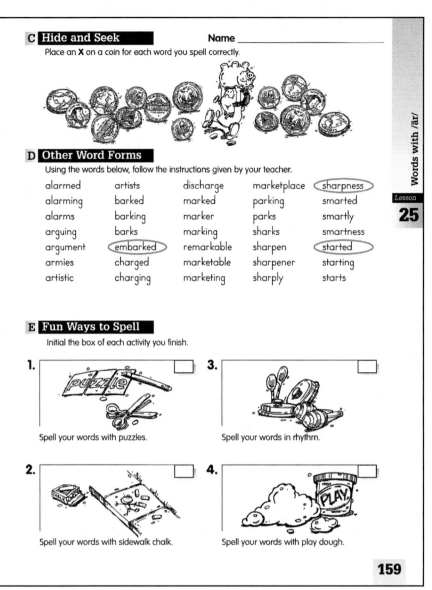

D Other Word Forms

Using the words below, follow the instructions given by your teacher.

alarmed	artists	discharge	marketplace	sharpness
alarming	barked	marked	parking	smarted
alarms	barking	marker	parks	smartly
arguing	barks	marking	sharks	smartness
argument	embarked	remarkable	sharpen	started
armies	charged	marketable	sharpener	starting
artistic	charging	marketing	sharply	starts

Words with /är/

Lesson 25

E Fun Ways to Spell

Initial the box of each activity you finish.

1\.

Spell your words with puzzles.

3\.

Spell your words in rhythm.

2\.

Spell your words with sidewalk chalk.

4\.

Spell your words with play dough.

159

1 Hide and Seek

Reinforce correct spelling of current spelling words.

Write the words one at a time on the board. Use this activity for each word.

- **Look** at the word.
- **Say** the word out loud.
- Let's **hide** (cover) the word.
- **Write** the word on your paper.
- Let's **seek** (uncover) the word.
- **Check** your spelling. If your word is spelled wrong, write the word correctly next to it.

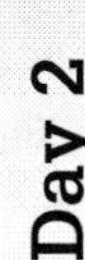

Day 2

Lesson 25

2 Other Word Forms

This activity is optional. Have students find and circle the Other Word Forms that are antonyms of the following:

dullness
ended
returned to port

3 Fun Ways to Spell

Four activities are provided. Use one, two, three, or all of the activities. Have students initial the box for each activity they complete.

Options:

- assign activities to students according to their learning styles
- set up the activities in learning centers for the class to do throughout the day
- divide the class into four groups and assign one activity per group
- do one activity per day

General

To spell your words with puzzles...
- Write each word on a card.
- Cut each card into thirds using a straight cut.
- Mix your puzzle pieces.
- Put the puzzles together.
- Check your spelling.

Auditory

To spell your words in rhythm...
- Look at a word on your spelling list.
- Close your eyes.
- Play your rhythm instruments softly while you whisper the spelling of the word.
- Open your eyes and check your spelling.

Visual

To spell your words with sidewalk chalk...
- Write each of your spelling words on the sidewalk (ball court or playground).
- Check your spelling.

Tactile

To spell your words with play dough...
- Roll pieces of play dough into ropes.
- Use the ropes to make the letters of each word.
- Put them in the right order to spell each word.
- Check your spelling.

1 Working with Words

Familiarize students with word meaning and usage.

Spelling Clues

Recognizing that many words are made up of common letter patterns and/or smaller words can help students spell better. Write **journal** on the board. Have a volunteer circle the smaller word **our**. Now, write the word **friend**. Have a volunteer circle the smaller word **end**.

Find the spelling word that contains the smaller word and write it on the line.

Dictionary Skills

Review your dictionary skills by using the entry word **bark** to tell about the dictionary parts.

Take a minute to memorize...

Read the memory verse to the class twice. Have the class practice it with you two more times.

Words with /är/ — Lesson 25

F Working with Words Name ____________

Spelling Clues

Write the correct spelling words on the lines.

1. The little word **arm** is in the bigger words alarm and army.
2. The little word **art** is in the bigger words apart, artist, smart, and start.
3. The little word **ark** is in the bigger words bark, mark, market, park, and shark.
4. The little word **harp** is in the bigger word sharp.
5. The little word **arch** is in the bigger word March.
6. Write the words which have the digraph **/ch/**. charge March
7. Write the words which have the digraph **/sh/**. shark sharp
8. Write the word in which /ū/ is spelled **ue**. argue

Dictionary Skills

Use the following information to tell about the dictionary parts below.

barge **base**

bark the hard covering on the outside of a tree: Birch bark is used for canoes.

1. entry word — bark
2. definition — the hard covering on the outside of a tree
3. guide words — barge base
4. sample sentence — Birch bark is used for canoes.

Word Bank

alarm	army	charge	market	sharp
apart	artist	March	park	smart
argue	bark	mark	shark	start

160

G Dictation

Name ______________________

Listen and write the missing words and punctuation.

1. The sharp sound of thunder made Rosa awake in alarm .

2. You can start to stack the wood by the porch .

3. Carlos and Rosa argued about a book .

Words with /är/

Lesson **25**

H Proofreading

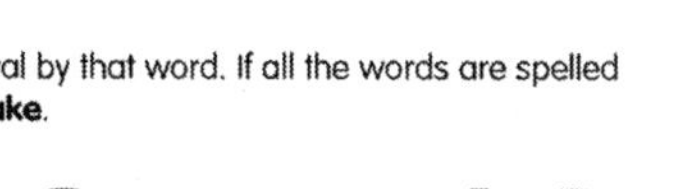

If a word is misspelled, fill in the oval by that word. If all the words are spelled correctly, fill in the oval by **no mistake**.

1. ○ alarm
   ● apatr
   ○ airport
   ○ no mistake

2. ○ army
   ○ course
   ○ floor
   ● no mistake

3. ○ bark
   ○ corner
   ● artest
   ○ no mistake

4. ● argu
   ○ bark
   ○ fourth
   ○ no mistake

5. ○ report
   ● charg
   ○ shark
   ○ no mistake

6. ○ sharp
   ● Martch
   ○ score
   ○ no mistake

7. ○ sore
   ○ start
   ● marck
   ○ no mistake

8. ● markit
   ○ storm
   ○ fort
   ○ no mistake

9. ○ life
   ● snart
   ○ loud
   ○ no mistake

161

1 Dictation

Reinforce correct spelling by using current and previous words in context.

Listen as I read each sentence and then write the missing words and ending punctuation in your worktext. (Slowly read each sentence twice. Sentences are found in the student text to the left.)

2 Proofreading

Familiarize students with standardized test format and reinforce recognizing misspelled words.

Look at each set of words. If a word is misspelled, fill in the oval by that word. If all the words are spelled correctly, fill in the oval by **no mistake**.

Day 4

Lesson **25**

3 Hide and Seek

Reinforce correct spelling of current spelling words. (A reproducible master is provided in Appendix A as shown on the inset page to the right.)
Write the words one at a time on the board. Use this activity for each word.

- **Look** at the word.
- **Say** the word out loud.
- Let's **hide** (cover) the word.
- **Write** the word on your paper.
- Let's **seek** (uncover) the word.
- **Check** your spelling. If your word is spelled wrong, write the word correctly next to it.

4 Other Word Forms

Have your students complete this activity to strengthen spelling ability and expand vocabulary.

1 Posttest

Test mastery of the spelling words.

I will say the word once, use the word in a sentence, then say the word again. Write the word on your paper.

Check a coin for each word you spell correctly.

Other Word Forms

Word Change

Use the clues to write the words in the puzzle.

1. very worried — alarmed
2. groups of soldiers — armies
3. very creative — artistic
4. quarrel — argument
5. set sail — embarked
6. send home — discharge
7. outstanding — remarkable
8. selling — marketing
9. ocean creatures — sharks
10. clearly — sharply
11. really stung — smarted
12. began — started

Word Bank

alarmed	armies	discharge	marketing	sharks	smarted
argument	artistic	embarked	remarkable	sharply	started

Other Word Forms
Lesson 25

347

1.	alarm	Instead of using an **alarm** clock, Rosa had Maria wake her.
2.	March	Many severe storms happen in **March**.
3.	park	After the big tree fell, the yard didn't look like a **park** anymore.
4.	army	Rosa and her family attacked the mess like a small **army**.
5.	apart	Dad and Grandpa Anderson cut **apart** the tree trunk.
6.	sharp	The **sharp** chain saws cut through the wood quickly.
7.	shark	Rosa thought the metal teeth on the chains were like the teeth of a **shark**.
8.	charge	Carlos likes to be in **charge** of stacking the logs.
9.	argue	Maria won't **argue** about where each log goes.
10.	bark	The garden was littered with limbs, twigs, and tree **bark**.
11.	start	Rosa will **start** a pile of wood for the bonfire.
12.	mark	Rosa's boots left a funny **mark** in the mud.
13.	market	Grandma Ruth's garden grew better food than you could buy at the **market**.
14.	artist	Isn't God a wonderful **artist** to have designed so many beautiful things?
15.	smart	It is **smart** to love God and grow strong and true in His love.

Progress Chart

Students may record scores. (Reproducible master in Appendix B.)

Personal Dictionary

Students may add any words they have misspelled to their personal dictionaries for reference when writing. (Cover in Appendix B.)

Words with /är/

Lesson 25

I Game Name ____________________

Help Rosa, Maria, and Carlos stack wood for Grandpa Joe and Grandma Ruth. Move one space for each word you or your team spells correctly from this week's word list.

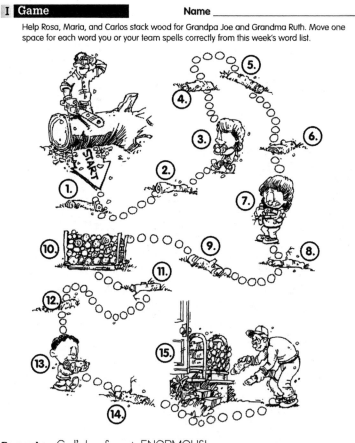

START 1. 2. 3. 4. 5. 6. 7. 8. 9. 10. 11. 12. 13. 14. 15.

Remember: God's love for us is ENORMOUS!

J Journaling

In your journal, write about what kind of tree you're like now and what kind of tree you want to be like.

162

2 Game

Reinforce spelling skills and provide motivation and interest.

Materials

- game page (from student text)
- flat buttons, dry beans, pennies, or game discs (1 per child)
- game word list

Game Word List

1. alarm
2. apart
3. argue
4. army
5. artist
6. bark
7. charge
8. March
9. mark
10. market
11. park
12. shark
13. sharp
14. smart
15. start

Day 5

Lesson 25

How to Play:

- Divide the class into two teams.
- Have each student place his/her game piece on Start.
- Have a student from team A go to the board.
- Say the spelling word. (You may also wish to use the word in a sentence.)
- Have the student write the word on the board.
- If correct, instruct each member of team A to move his/her game piece forward one space on the game board. (Note: If the word is misspelled, correct the spelling immediately.)
- Alternate between teams A and B.
- The team to reach the wood pile first is the winner.

Non-Competitive Option:

At the end of the game, say: "Class, I am proud of your efforts to spell the words correctly. If you had fun and tried your best, you are all winners!"

3 Journaling

Provide a meaningful reason for correct spelling through personal writing.

Review the story using discussion leads provided on the following page. Encourage students to apply the Scriptural value in their journaling.

Journaling (continued)

Say

- Have you ever helped clean up the mess a fallen tree can make?
- What keeps most trees from falling? (They have a large system of roots that grow down deep and anchor them.)
- Why did the tree fall across the Anderson's garden? (Because it grew too close to the edge of the hill and didn't have enough earth around it's roots to hold it up.)
- What was Rosa arguing with Carlos about? (She said he'd taken her piano book and he said he hadn't.)
- What prayer did Rosa's dad often pray for his children? (That they'd be like trees, growing strong and true, and understanding how much God loves them.)
- In your journal, write about what kind of tree you're like now and what kind of tree you want to be like.

Take a minute to memorize...
Have the class say the memory verse with you once.

Children will write like the authors they read.

Problems and Patience

Kristin realizes that grown-ups make mistakes, too, and learns to be patient with her mother's imperfections.

"Cathy." Mrs. Wright turned as her younger daughter passed the kitchen door. "Please let everyone know it's time for supper."

"Okay, Mom!" Cathy answered, then turned and yelled down the hall. "Hey, Christopher, Cory! It's time to eat!" Cathy's voice could be heard throughout the house. "And bring Kristin, too!" Mrs. Wright rolled her eyes and shook her head as she took the hot baking sheet out of the oven.

"Yummy-ummy!" Christopher came into the kitchen, flapping his half-wet hands in the air to dry. "I love those open-face sandwiches you make, Mom."

"Thank you, Son." Mrs. Wright placed a bowl of apple wedges on the table. "Perhaps next time you should dry your hands in the bathroom after you wash them."

"Oh. . .uh, okay." Christopher took his place at the table as Cory and Cathy came in. "Kristin said 'Just a minute,'" Cathy reported as she pulled her chair out.

"Thank you, Cathy." Mom set a glass of milk at Cory's place. "You know, I could have yelled for everyone to come myself. Next time, please go find everyone and tell them it's time to eat without yelling."

"Yes, Ma'am." Cathy looked sheepish.

Mrs. Wright glanced at the clock on the microwave. "What was Kristin doing, Cathy?"

"Oh, she was reading a new book she got from the library today, I think." Cathy reached to the table's center and pulled a napkin out of the basket just as Kristin arrived and slid into her chair.

"Kristin, do you think it's polite to keep us all waiting?" Mom rested a hand on Kristin's shoulder.

"Uh, no." Kristin fiddled with her fork. "I'm sorry."

Mom gave her shoulder a squeeze. "You're forgiven, Sweetie. Cory," Mom sat down and smiled at her youngest, "would you like to ask a blessing on our food this evening?"

Cory bowed his head. "Dear God, thank you for the sandwiches and the apples and the milk and cookies. Please keep Daddy safe and help him to come home real soon. Amen."

"When is Dad supposed to get back?" Christopher put some apples on his plate and passed the bowl to his twin.

Mom shrugged. "He wasn't sure how long it would take to get all his business settled in Miami. Maybe he'll know more when he calls tonight."

But that night, when Dad called, he still wasn't certain. Things weren't going very well and he wasn't sure when he'd be able to come home. Mom sat alone in the living room for a long time after the children were in bed.

The next morning, Treasure, the canary, greeted the sunlight streaking through the window with a merry song. "Mom," Christopher's voice reached the kitchen before he did. "I don't have any clean jeans to wear to school today. Are there any in the dryer?"

"No, Christopher!" Mrs. Wright slammed the box of cereal she was carrying down on the counter. "All the clean clothes are put away where they're supposed to be. Did you put all your jeans in the hamper so they could be washed?"

Christopher hung his head. "Uh, no. I. . .uh. . . I guess I didn't. . ."

"Well, then!" Mom's voice rose. "You'll just have to wear the same ones you wore yesterday, dirty or not, until you learn to do as you're told!" Christopher started to slink away. "And hurry! It's time for breakfast!"

Soon, Christopher was back, ready for breakfast along with Cathy and Cory. "Where's Kristin this time?" Mrs. Wright poured orange juice into glasses and set them on the table.

"She's almost finished with a chapter in her book. Maybe she's . . ." Cathy reached for a box of cereal and knocked her glass of orange juice over onto her lap. "Oh! Oh, no!"

"Cathy!" Mom grabbed a wash cloth and a bunch of paper towels. "Why can't you be more careful? What a mess!"

"I. . . I didn't mean to." Cathy looked up into her mother's stern face.

"Maybe not, but if you'd just be more careful, things like this wouldn't happen!" Mrs. Wright frowned. Quickly mopping up the worst of the mess, she rushed Cathy off. "Run change your clothes, Cathy. Fast!" Then she turned and caught sight of Cory. "Cory Tyler Wright! What do you think you're doing?"

Mom raced over and grabbed the box of cereal Cory was happily emptying on the table. Just as she turned to put the almost-empty box on the counter, Cory reached for his spoon buried somewhere under the mountain of cereal in front of him. Kristin came in just in time to see cereal cascading across the table, down Cory's legs, and across the shiny kitchen floor. "CORY!" Mom's shout startled everybody. Treasure stopped singing and hopped about nervously.

"Cory, don't touch anything else until I say!" Mrs. Wright wasn't shouting anymore, but her voice was cold and harsh. "Kristin, you knew better than to read when it was time to eat. Because you intentionally disobeyed you may not go to the hot dog roast with Rosa tonight. Christopher, you will put your dirty things in the hamper before you

Story (continued)

eat another bite. And Cathy," Mrs. Wright caught sight of her younger daughter hovering uncertainly in the doorway, "sit down and eat without making any more messes!"

Tears spilled down Cory's cheeks, and Kristin saw a suspicious sparkle in Cathy's eyes as her sister blinked rapidly before carefully picking up her glass. Kristin felt like a big, hot ball was stuck in her throat. She took a sip of orange juice and watched her mother stiffly sweeping up the spilled cereal.

"How could she yell at us like that? She didn't even ask me why I was late to breakfast or give me a chance to explain. I wasn't reading my book at all." Kristin shook her head as tears began to gather in her own eyes. "I was in the bathroom! Surely that's no reason to keep me from going to the Anderson's for the hot dog roast. How unfair!" The kitchen was unnaturally quiet as the children finished breakfast.

At recess that morning, Kristin told her best friend, Rosa, all about it. "Can you believe it, Rosa? She's not going to let me come to the hot dog roast and I didn't even do anything wrong!" Kristin pushed off the ground and sent her swing soaring.

Rosa trailed one foot in the dirt, turning her swing sideways. "Did you try to tell her that?"

"Are you kidding?" Kristin jerked the swing into a higher flight. "The way she acted this morning, I'd have been in big trouble just opening my mouth—no matter what I said!"

"Well, maybe something's bothering her." Rosa turned round and round, twisting the swing chain above her. "You know she doesn't usually get mad like that. Maybe you just need to be patient."

Kristin planted her feet, bringing her swing to a quick and dusty stop. "What?"

"You know, like that text we wrote this morning from Thessa . . . something or other. About understanding God's love and that patience comes from God." Rosa picked up her feet and let the chain unwind, twirling her in a fast spin. Kristin sat quietly, making marks in the dirt with the toe of her shoe. Rosa's swing slowed to a half spin and stopped. "Well?"

"I don't know." Kristin leaned back and let her hair almost touch the ground. "I've never thought of having to be patient with grown-ups. I mean, they're supposed to do everything right and be patient with us and stuff, aren't they?"

"I guess, usually." Rosa pushed off into a gentle glide. "But grown-ups are people, too. And Dad says everybody makes mistakes sometimes. Even the best people, like in the Scriptures. You know, like Abraham, and David, and Peter."

"And Solomon, even though he was so wise!" Kristin sat up and timed her swing so that it was gliding in time to Rosa's. "Maybe you're right."

"Mom, is there anything I can do to help you?" Mrs. Wright looked startled when Kristin came into the kitchen after school that afternoon.

"Well, you could tear apart some lettuce for the salad." She reached up on the shelf and got the clear glass bowl down. "Thank you, Sweetie."

Later, when the four children were gathered at the table, Mrs. Wright sat down and looked around. "Before we eat tonight, I need to ask each of you to forgive me." She sighed. "I'm so sorry for the way I acted and the things I said this morning at breakfast time. I was wrong."

"It's okay, Mom." Christopher grinned across the table at his mother. "I'm sorry I didn't put my dirty clothes where I was supposed to. I think I've learned my lesson."

Cory jumped out of his chair and ran around the table to fling his arms around his mother in a bear hug. "I love you," he said simply.

"I'm sorry I was so clumsy." Cathy looked down at her lap.

"Oh, Honey." Mom's voice broke. "I'm so sorry I made you feel clumsy and bad. That was wrong of me, Cathy. Accidents just happen and they're no one's fault at all. Okay, Honey?"

Cathy looked up with a small smile. "Okay."

"And Kristin." Mom settled Cory in one arm and reached out to Kristin with her free hand. "I realized later that Cathy didn't say you were reading. I'm sorry I jumped to conclusions and made decisions in anger without knowing the facts." She squeezed Kristin's hand. "Forgive me, Sweetie?"

Kristin swallowed the lump in her throat and squeezed back. "Yes. I love you, Mom."

Later that evening, Kristin pulled a crumpled piece of paper out of her jeans pocket as she got ready to go to the hot dog roast at the Andersons' farm. Quietly she read, "May the Lord bring you into an ever deeper understanding of the love of God and the patience that comes from Christ. II Thessalonians 3:5." Then she smiled. Rosa was right. Everyone makes mistakes sometimes, even grown-ups. But God is always ready to give us love and patience whenever we ask.

2 Discussion Time

Check understanding of the story and development of personal values.

- How was Mrs. Wright patient with the children at supper?
- Where was Mr. Wright?
- Why didn't Christopher have any clean jeans to wear to school?
- What accident did Cathy have at the breakfast table?
- When Cory spilled the cereal, what did Mom do?
- Why do you think she wasn't very patient at breakfast?
- Why couldn't Kristin go to the hot dog roast at the Anderson's?
- Do adults make mistakes sometimes, too?
- What did Kristin learn about her mother?

A Preview Name ____________

Write each word as your teacher says it.

1. wonder
2. driver
3. sugar
4. dollar
5. hammer
6. mirror
7. river
8. forget
9. later
10. summer
11. December
12. November
13. silver
14. center
15. remember

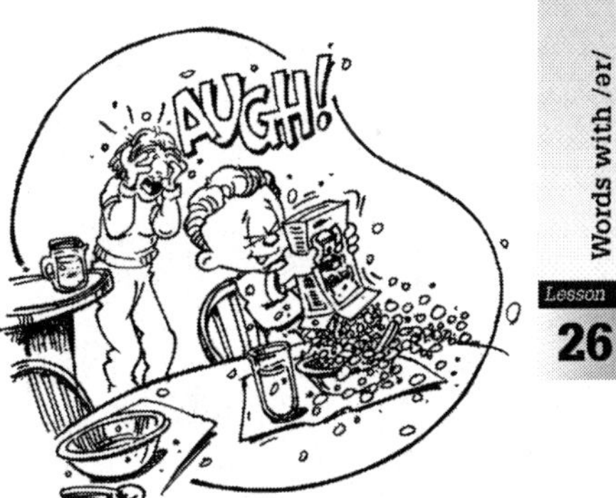

Words with /ər/

Lesson 26

Scripture

2 Thessalonians 3:5

163

3 Preview

Test for knowledge of the correct spellings of these words.

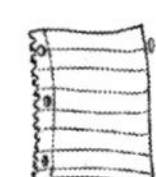

Customize Your List

On a separate piece of paper, additional words of your choice may be tested.

I will say the word once, use the word in a sentence, then say the word again. Write the word on the lines in the worktext.

Correct Immediately!

Let's correct our preview. I will write each word on the board. Put a dot under each letter on your preview as I spell the word out loud. If you spelled a word wrong, rewrite it correctly.

Take a minute to memorize...

Read the memory verse to the class twice. Have the class practice it with you two more times.

Day 1

Lesson 26

1.	wonder	I **wonder** when Dad will be back from his business trip.
2.	driver	A taxi **driver** will drive him from the airport.
3.	sugar	Cory likes cereal that's **sugar** frosted.
4.	dollar	That box of cereal cost a **dollar** more than this box.
5.	hammer	Kristin was reading a book about a **hammer**–head shark.
6.	mirror	She used a **mirror** to make sure her hair looked okay.
7.	river	Angry words can be like a mighty **river**; hard to stop.
8.	forget	Mrs. Wright's angry words were hard for Kristin to **forget**.
9.	later	A little **later** that day, Kristin told Rosa about her mother getting angry.
10.	summer	It was almost **summer** and the day was warm and sunny.
11.	December	The children enjoyed playing outdoors after the cold weather in **December**.
12.	November	It was very cold in **November**, too.
13.	silver	The swing set was painted with **silver** paint.
14.	center	Kristin chose the **center** swing.
15.	remember	Rosa helped Kristin **remember** that everybody makes mistakes sometimes.

Progress Chart

Students may record scores. (Reproducible master in Appendix B.)

Day 1

Lesson

26

4 Word Shapes

Help students form a correct image of whole words.

Look at each word and think about its shape. Now, write the word in the correct word shape boxes. You may check off each word as you use it.

(The sound of **/ər/** can be spelled with **ar**, **er**, **ir**, **or**, or **ur**. Because spellers cannot rely on a phonetic way of remembering the various spellings, this sound is often difficult.)

In the word shape boxes, color the letters that spell the sound of **/ər/** in each word.

Words with /ər/

Lesson 26

B Word Shapes Name ______________________

Write each word in the correct word shape boxes. Next, in the word shape boxes, color the letters that spell the sound of **/ər/** in each word.

	Word	Word shape
1.	center	sugar
2.	December	hammer
3.	dollar	remember
4.	driver	silver
5.	forget	December
6.	hammer	center
7.	later	mirror
8.	mirror	forget
9.	November	river
10.	remember	wonder
11.	river	summer
12.	silver	dollar
13.	sugar	November
14.	summer	later
15.	wonder	driver

164

Answers may vary for duplicate word shapes.

Be Prepared For Fun

Check these supply lists for **Fun Ways to Spell** presented **Day 2**. Purchase and/or gather needed items ahead of time!

General

- Chalk or Whiteboard Marker
- Chalkboard or Whiteboard (could be individual boards for each child)
- Spelling List

Auditory

- Box to Store Letters
- a, b, c, D, d, e, e, e, f, g, h, i, l, l, m, m, N, n, o, r, r, r, s, t, u, v, w (written on seasonal shapes like kites or clouds)
- Spelling List

Visual

- Glitter Glue
- Art Paper (2 or 3 pieces per child)
- Spelling List

Tactile

- Thick Pile Carpet Squares
- Spelling List

C 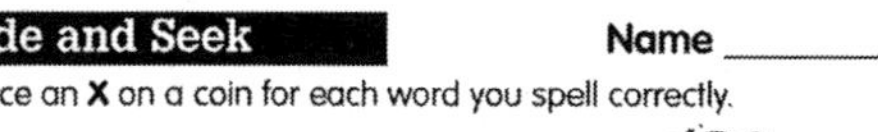

Hide and Seek

Name ______________________

Place an **X** on a coin for each word you spell correctly.

D

Other Word Forms

Using the words below, follow the instructions given by your teacher.

centered	drove	lately	remembered	sugaring
centering	forgetful	lateness	remembering	sugary
centers	forgetfulness	later	remembers	summery
dollars	hammered	latest	silvered	wondered
drive	hammering	mirrored	silvering	wonderful
driven	hammers	mirroring	silvery	wondering
driving	late	mirrors	sugared	wonders

E

Fun Ways to Spell

Initial the box of each activity you finish.

1. 

Spell your words with chalk.

3. 

Spell your words out of the letter box.

2. 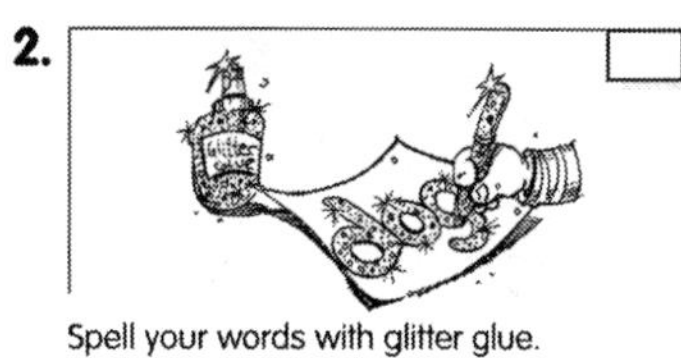

Spell your words with glitter glue.

4. 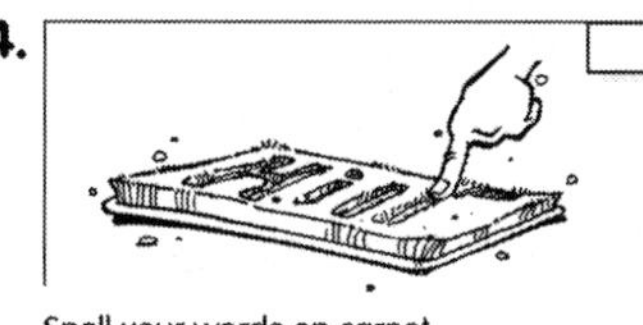

Spell your words on carpet.

Words with /ər/

Lesson 26

165

1 Hide and Seek

Reinforce correct spelling of current spelling words.

Write the words one at a time on the board. Use this activity for each word.

Say

- **Look** at the word.
- **Say** the word out loud.
- Let's **hide** (cover) the word.
- **Write** the word on your paper.
- Let's **seek** (uncover) the word.
- **Check** your spelling. If your word is spelled wrong, write the word correctly next to it.

2 Other Word Forms

This activity is optional. Have students write original sentences using these Other Word Forms:

hammering
centered
sugary
mirrors

3 Fun Ways to Spell

Four activities are provided. Use one, two, three, or all of the activities. Have students initial the box for each activity they complete.

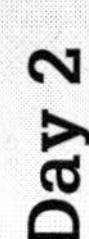

Options:

- assign activities to students according to their learning styles
- set up the activities in learning centers for the class to do throughout the day
- divide the class into four groups and assign one activity per group
- do one activity per day

General

To spell your words with chalk…
- Put your spelling list on your desk.
- Look at a word; then, walk to the chalkboard (or whiteboard).
- Write your spelling word on the chalkboard (or whiteboard).
- Return to your desk.
- Check your spelling.

Auditory

To spell your words out of the letter box...
- Spell a word from your list by putting the letters in the right order.
- Check your spelling.
- Spell your word out loud.

Visual

To spell your words with glitter glue…
- Write each of your spelling words on your paper.
- Check your spelling.

Tactile

To spell your words on carpet...
- Use your fingertip to write a spelling word on the carpet.
- Check your spelling.
- Smooth the word out with your hand and write another.

Day 3

Lesson 26

1 Working with Words

Familiarize students with word meaning and usage.

Syllables

Tell students that the words listed and explained in a dictionary are called entry words and that an entry word in the dictionary is often divided into syllables. Write the words **apple**, **hurry**, **after**, and **early** on the board. Explain that these are examples of entry words. Have a volunteer put a dot between the syllables.

Look at the first three items on your page and write how many syllables each word has. Write each spelling word on the line, putting a dot between the syllables.

Word Sort

Write the headings **er**, **ar**, **or**, and **ur** on the board. Say the words **color**, **occur**, **prefer**, and **onward**. Guide the students in putting these four words under the correct headings.

Write each spelling word under the correct heading.

Take a minute to memorize...

Read the memory verse to the class twice. Have the class practice it with you two more times.

Words with /ər/ — Lesson 26

F Working with Words Name ____________

Syllables

These are examples of entry words. Count how many syllables each word has and write the number on the line.

1. a•larm 2
2. shout 1
3. grand•fa•ther 3

Find each of the words below in the dictionary. Write them in syllables, putting a dot between the syllables.

1. center cen•ter
2. dollar dol•lar
3. hammer ham•mer
4. later la•ter
5. November No•vem•ber
6. river riv•er *or* ri•ver
7. sugar sug•ar *or* su•gar
8. wonder won•der
9. December De•cem•ber
10. driver driv•er *or* dri•ver
11. forget for•get
12. mirror mir•ror
13. remember re•mem•ber
14. silver sil•ver
15. summer sum•mer

Word Sort

Write each spelling word under the correct heading for the /ər/ spelling.

-er	-er	-ar
1. center	7. remember	12. dollar
2. December	8. river	13. sugar
3. driver	9. silver	
4. hammer	10. summer	-or
5. later	11. wonder	14. forget
6. November		15. mirror

Word Bank

center	driver	later	remember	sugar
December	forget	mirror	river	summer
dollar	hammer	November	silver	wonder

166

G Dictation Name ____________

Listen and write the missing words and punctuation.

1. Next time Christopher will remember to put his clothes away .
2. Let's put the silver spoon in the sugar bowl .
3. A river of cereal ran down the center of the table .

Words with /ər/

Lesson 26

H Proofreading

If a word is misspelled, fill in the oval by that word. If all the words are spelled correctly, fill in the oval by **no mistake**.

1. ○ driver ○ apart ● cinter ○ no mistake
2. ● Desember ○ artist ○ argue ○ no mistake
3. ○ charge ● dollor ○ March ○ no mistake
4. ○ smart ○ mark ● hamer ○ no mistake
5. ● ferget ○ market ○ remember ○ no mistake
6. ○ river ○ shark ● laeter ○ no mistake
7. ○ summer ● merer ○ silver ○ no mistake
8. ○ alarm ● november ○ start ○ no mistake
9. ○ horn ○ wonder ○ sugar ● no mistake

167

1 Dictation

Reinforce correct spelling by using current and previous words in context.

Listen as I read each sentence and then write the missing words and ending punctuation in your worktext. (Slowly read each sentence twice. Sentences are found in the student text to the left.)

2 Proofreading

Familiarize students with standardized test format and reinforce recognizing misspelled words.

Look at each set of words. If a word is misspelled, fill in the oval by that word. If all the words are spelled correctly, fill in the oval by **no mistake**.

Day 4

Lesson 26

3 Hide and Seek

Reinforce correct spelling of current spelling words. (A reproducible master is provided in Appendix A as shown on the inset page to the right.)
Write the words one at a time on the board. Use this activity for each word.

- **Look** at the word.
- **Say** the word out loud.
- Let's **hide** (cover) the word.
- **Write** the word on your paper.
- Let's **seek** (uncover) the word.
- **Check** your spelling. If your word is spelled wrong, write the word correctly next to it.

4 Other Word Forms

Have your students complete this activity to strengthen spelling ability and expand vocabulary.

1 Posttest

Test mastery of the spelling words.

I will say the word once, use the word in a sentence, then say the word again. Write the word on your paper.

Other Word Forms
Lesson
26

Hide and Seek

Check a coin for each word you spell correctly.

Other Word Forms

Suffixes

Circle the correct suffix.

1. Daniel center (ness, ing, ed) his picture on the paper.
2. The cookies are pretty and sugar (ing, ful, y).
3. Dad likes to keep up with the late (ness, est, ly) news.
4. Her face mirror (ing, ly, ed) her feelings.
5. Christopher got a go-cart that had not been drive (ing, ed, n) very much.
6. He never forget (ful, s, ting) to do his assignment.
7. I remember (ing, ed, ly) my homework when I got to school.
8. My birthday cake tasted wonder (ful, ly, ing).
9. Katelynn liked the angel with the silver (s, ing, y) wings.
10. This warm weather feels very summer (y, ful, s).
11. James earned several dollar (ing, ness, s) mowing lawns.
12. The woodpecker hammer (ed, ing, ly) on the house kept me awake.

Clues

Use the clues to write the Other Word Forms.

1. middles or	centers	**6.** motivated	driven
2. recently	lately	**7.** unmindful	forgetful
3. reflected	mirrored	**8.** recalling	remembering
4. touring	driving	**9.** shimmering	silvery
5. bank notes	dollars	**10.** pounding	hammering

Word Bank

centers	driven	forgetful	lately	remembering
dollars	driving	hammering	mirrored	silvery

348

1. November	Thanksgiving is a special holiday that comes each **November**.
2. December	What special holiday happens in **December**?
3. summer	The Wright family took a **summer** vacation to the mountains.
4. driver	Dad was the **driver** most of the time.
5. mirror	He used the rear view **mirror** to check for traffic.
6. dollar	Kristin had a **dollar** in her pocket.
7. center	Mom set the dish of apple wedges in the **center** of the table.
8. remember	Christopher didn't **remember** to put his dirty jeans in the hamper.
9. silver	Cory reached into the mound of cereal for his **silver** spoon.
10. river	Cereal poured over the edge of the table like a **river**.
11. sugar	There isn't very much **sugar** in some kinds of cereal.
12. wonder	I **wonder** why Kristin hasn't come to the table yet.
13. hammer	Kristin's heart began to **hammer** hard when her mother was upset.
14. forget	Don't **forget** to forgive others when they have wronged you.
15. later	A while **later** that day, Mom asked the children to forgive her.

Progress Chart

Students may record scores. (Reproducible master in Appendix B.)

Personal Dictionary

Students may add any words they have misspelled to their personal dictionaries for reference when writing. (Cover in Appendix B.)

Words with /ər/

Lesson 26

I Game Name ____________________

Glue on a piece of the puzzle-picture for each word you or your team spells correctly from this week's word list.

Christopher · Mom · Kristin

Remember: God can help you to learn patience.

J Journaling

In your journal, write a letter to your parents. Tell them what you really like about them and how much you love them.

168

2 Game

Reinforce spelling skills and provide motivation and interest.

Materials

- game page (from student text)
- puzzle pieces (reproducible master in Appendix B, page 360)
- crayons
- scissors (1 per child)
- glue sticks (1 per child)
- game word list

Game Word List

1. center
2. December
3. dollar
4. driver
5. forget
6. hammer
7. later
8. mirror
9. November
10. remember
11. river
12. silver
13. sugar
14. summer
15. wonder

Day 5

Lesson 26

How to Play:

- Have the students color the puzzle picture, then carefully cut the picture apart along the dotted lines.
- Divide the class into two teams.
- Have a student from team A go to the board.
- Say the spelling word. (You may also wish to use the word in a sentence.)
- Have the student write the word on the board.
- If correct, instruct each member of team A to glue on one piece of his/her puzzle picture. (Note: If the word is misspelled, correct the spelling immediately.)
- Alternate between teams A and B.
- The team to complete its puzzle pictures first is the winner.

Non-Competitive Option:

At the end of the game, say: "Class, I am proud of your efforts to spell the words correctly. If you had fun and tried your best, you are all winners!"

3 Journaling

Provide a meaningful reason for correct spelling through personal writing.

Review the story using discussion leads provided on the following page. Encourage students to apply the Scriptural value in their journaling.

Journaling (continued)

- What were some of the things the Wright children did that upset their mother? (Spilled cereal all over the place, forgot to put jeans in dirty clothes hamper, came late to breakfast, and spilled orange juice.)
- Does one of your parents have to be away on business trips occasionally?
- Mrs. Wright was frustrated that Mr. Wright wasn't coming home as soon as planned and she yelled at the children. How do you feel when your mom or dad yells at you?
- How can you be patient when your parent makes a mistake? (Remember that even moms and dads are people and all people make mistakes sometimes. Ask God to help you be patient and understanding.)
- In your journal, write a letter to your parents. Tell them what you really like about them and how much you love them.

Take a minute to memorize...
Have the class say the memory verses from lessons 25 and 26 with you.

"Anytime a child pays close attention to what's written, spelling awareness increases."*

*Scott, Jill E. 1994. Spelling for Readers and Writers. The Reading Teacher, Vol. 48, No. 2, October: 188-190.

1 **Literature Connection**
Topic: Criticism
Theme Text: James 4:11

Speak no Evil

Rosa is frustrated with her teacher, but finds that criticizing him doesn't help anything.

Late one afternoon, Rosa sat quietly looking out her bedroom window. A tiny sparrow landed on a nearby branch. He fluffed his feathers and hopped around as if preparing for some big event. Then he puffed out the black feathery bib that covered his little chest and begin to sing. Rosa grinned, enjoying the unexpected concert. Suddenly the little performer was startled by a rustling in the bright green leaves behind him, and he flew away with a whir of small wings. Onto the branch he'd just deserted sprang an inquisitive squirrel.

"Wouldn't you know!" Rosa chuckled. She reached down and tickled the red squirrel snoozing in her lap. "You and your kind are always causing trouble, Chipper." Rosa sighed. "I bet you'd love to be out there racing around the treetops like that squirrel." She smoothed a finger over Chipper's little round head. "I know I'd like to be outside if I could ever get this homework done!" She picked up her pencil and jabbed the eraser at a book open on her desk. "I don't know how to do this! I just keep getting mixed up." Rosa glared at the textbook while Chipper slept peacefully through her grumblings.

The next afternoon, as he drove the children home from school, Mr. Vasquez took a deep breath of the fresh spring air coming through his open window. "Sure is a beautiful day for a walk!" He turned into the driveway, then pulled the blue jeep slowly into the garage. "What do you think, troop? Shall we walk over to the Andersons' this afternoon? See how their garden's doing?"

"Let's go!" Carlos jumped out of the front seat.

"Well," Dad laughed, climbing out more slowly. "Let's get the piano practice and chores done first, Son."

"I'll practice first!" Maria called as she rushed into the house.

"Carlos?" Rosa tugged on her brother's arm as he began to follow their dad into the house. "Would you help me with my homework?"

"Trouble again?" Carlos' dark eyebrows rose in question, making Rosa feel stupid.

"Well, we've had a bunch of new stuff lately and it's hard!" Rosa defended herself. "Are you going to help me or not?"

"Okay, okay." Carlos held up both hands in surrender. "Let's go see what you need to do."

"Everybody ready to go?" Rosa jumped as Dad's voice broke the silence in her room a short time later. She glanced at the clock on her bedside table. "Five o'clock!" She said. "It can't be five already!"

Mr. Vasquez tapped the face of his wristwatch. "Well, my watch says five o'clock, too." He walked over and stood behind Rosa. "How's it coming, Rosita?"

"I've only got a few more questions to answer." Rosa jumped up and stretched. "I can finish them later tonight." She sat on the edge of her bed to put her sneakers on.

"Seems like you've had an awful lot of homework lately, Rosita." Dad turned Rosa's desk chair toward her and sat down. "Is there a problem?"

"A problem?" Rosa stiffly leaned over to pick up her other shoe. "What do you mean?"

"Well. . ." Mr. Vasquez rubbed his hand across the back of his neck. "You've never brought this much work home before. Are you upset about something? Are you having trouble with your classmates? Is there something that's bothering you and keeping you from really paying attention to your teacher? Are you . . .?"

"NO!" Rosa's exclamation surprised them both. But once she started talking, she couldn't seem to stop. She was so tired of having homework every night; tired of not really understanding what she was supposed to do; tired of having to ask Carlos or Maria to explain things to her; tired of feeling like she wasn't good enough.

"I do pay attention in class!" Her frustration bubbled over like an erupting volcano. "Mr. Valentino doesn't explain stuff very well. Oh, he talks a lot and tells us what to do, but not how to do it!" She couldn't seem to stop the hot words from spilling out. "He's not a very good teacher. I don't like him. I wish I could go to school somewhere else. He's not fair and doesn't care about all of us the same. He spends lots of time helping some of the kids and doesn't have any time for the rest of us." The angry words quickly tumbled over each other, followed by tears. "I'm not stupid! There's just a lot of new stuff that's really hard and I need someone to answer my questions! He never has time for me!" Rosa covered her face with her hands. "He doesn't have time for me," she repeated in a small voice as her dad sat down by her on the bed and folded her in a warm hug.

As soon as the words left her mouth, Rosa felt guilty. She knew Mr. Valentino didn't deserve such criticism, but she was angry and frustrated enough not to take any of it back. School work was usually pretty easy for her, but the few times she'd been confused and raised her hand to ask for help, it had seemed like the teacher would never get to her, and that he was ignoring her. She'd given up trying to get his attention.

Mr. Vasquez didn't break the silence for several

Lesson 27 Day 1

Story (continued)

minutes. Finally he gave her a squeeze and stood. "How about that walk now?" Rosa hopped up, relieved that Dad wasn't going to talk about it anymore.

The next school day was almost over, and the room was filled with activity as the children got ready to go home. Rosa grabbed her backpack and stuffed her notebook in the bag. She leaned over and reached for her math book just as a hand fell gently on her shoulder. Jumping up, she banged her head on the edge of her desk. "Uh, oh." Mr. Valentino touched the top of her head lightly. "Are you okay?" At her nod, he continued. "I'd like to talk with you for a few minutes after school. All right?" Rosa nodded again. Mr. Valentino smiled and turned to answer a question.

"I wonder what he wants to talk to me about." Rosa rubbed suddenly sweaty hands on her jeans. She took a few deep breaths, but that didn't seem to help her nervousness.

"See you tomorrow, Rosa," Kristin called as she followed her twin out the door. Rosa just waved. Too soon the classroom was empty, except for Mr. Valentino and Rosa. The teacher walked over and sat in Tony's chair at the desk next to Rosa's.

"Rosa," Mr. Valentino said, rubbing his hand through his hair, "I owe you an apology. Your dad called me last night and we had a nice, long talk." Rosa wanted to disappear, to vanish without a trace as Mr. Valentino continued quietly. "I want you to know that I appreciate you. Because you are a good student, both in your work and in the way you act, I'm afraid I've assumed that you didn't need my help. I'm sorry about that, Rosa."

Mr. Valentino leaned toward Rosa, his elbows on his knees. "I'd like for you to help me, to let me know when you need a question answered. Would you do that?" Rosa nodded.

"When you raise your hand with a question, I may not always be able to get to you right away, Rosa, but I will as soon as I can. You're important to me." Mr. Valentino's broad smile spread across his face. "I know it's frustrating to have to wait for an answer, but you're creative. I'm sure you can do other work or read a book while you're waiting. Just keep that hand up and I'll get there, sooner or later! I promise. Deal?" Mr. Valentino held out his hand.

"Deal." Rosa smiled back as she shook her teacher's hand to seal the deal.

"No homework tonight!" Rosa twirled in a circle as she entered her room that afternoon. "No homework tonight!" She tossed her backpack on the bed and twirled around again and again, finally collapsing in a dizzy heap on the bed herself. "Oops." She muttered as she rolled off the papers that had spilled out of the backpack. Sitting up, she gathered them together in a stack. The handwriting border sheet was a bit wrinkled. Rosa read it as she smoothed it with her hand.

"Dad!" Rosa called as she ran down the hall, border sheet in hand. "Dad, where are you?"

"Here, Rosita." Mr. Vasquez's voice led her to his office. Silently, she handed him the slightly rumpled border sheet. He read it aloud. "'Don't criticize and speak evil about each other. If you do you will be fighting against God's law of loving one another.'"

"I'm sorry I said all that mean stuff about Mr. Valentino." Rosa leaned against her dad's side as he sat in his desk chair. "I don't want to fight against God's law." She added in a little voice. "And I really didn't mean it all, anyway," she finished in a tiny voice.

Dad gave her a one-armed squeeze. "That's my girl. I think it's a lesson we all need to remem. . ." Suddenly, a small red streak dashed into the room, up Dad's leg, across the desk, and onto the windowsill. Once there, the little chickaree bounced back and forth in front of the open window, chattering squirrel insults at the top of her lungs. A surprised wild squirrel in the tree outside hurled them right back as loud as he could, then scampered away.

"Well!" Dad chuckled, "I guess Nipper still has a thing or two to learn about criticizing and speaking evil!"

2 Discussion Time

Check understanding of the story and development of personal values.

- What was Rosa having trouble getting done?
- Who did she ask to help her at home?
- Why do you think she talked about Mr. Valentino the way she did?
- How do you feel when you can't understand something new?
- How did Rosa feel when Mr. Valentino asked her to stay after school?
- What did Mr. Valentino ask Rosa to do whenever she needed help?
- What does James 4:11 say we're doing if we criticize others?

A Preview Name ____________

Write each word as your teacher says it.

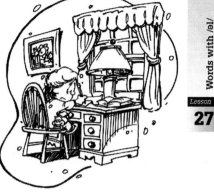

1. travel
2. eagle
3. able
4. April
5. cattle
6. sprinkle
7. candle
8. metal
9. saddle
10. squirrel
11. turtle
12. bottle
13. needle
14. middle
15. handle

Scripture
James 4:11

Words with /əl/
Lesson 27

169

3 Preview

Test for knowledge of the correct spellings of these words.

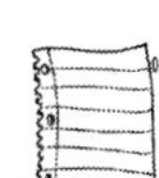

Customize Your List

On a separate piece of paper, additional words of your choice may be tested.

I will say the word once, use the word in a sentence, then say the word again. Write the word on the lines in the worktext.

Correct Immediately!

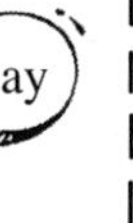

Let's correct our preview. I will write each word on the board. Put a dot under each letter on your preview as I spell the word out loud. If you spelled a word wrong, rewrite it correctly.

Take a minute to memorize...

Read the memory verse to the class twice. Have the class practice it with you two more times.

Day 1
Lesson 27

1.	travel	Do all birds **travel** north in the spring?
2.	eagle	The **eagle** does migrate every spring and fall.
3.	able	Birds are **able** to tell when it is time to fly north.
4.	April	**April** is a good time to be outdoors.
5.	cattle	The **cattle** enjoy the fresh spring grass.
6.	sprinkle	Rain will **sprinkle** the grass with water to help it grow.
7.	candle	There's a big **candle** in the windowsill.
8.	metal	It's in a Spanish-style black **metal** candle holder.
9.	saddle	The squirrel's fur was darker across its back, like a **saddle**.
10.	squirrel	The sparrow flew away when the **squirrel** startled it.
11.	turtle	Rosa seemed to be as slow as a **turtle** in getting her homework done.
12.	bottle	She had a **bottle** of water to drink while she worked.
13.	needle	Carlos' questions seemed to **needle** Rosa and make her feel stupid.
14.	middle	In the **middle** of talking about her teacher, Rosa knew she was wrong.
15.	handle	We need to **handle** our feelings without criticizing others.

Progress Chart

Students may record scores. (Reproducible master in Appendix B.)

4 Word Shapes

Help students form a correct image of whole words.

Say: Look at each word and think about its shape. Now, write the word in the correct word shape boxes. You may check off each word as you use it.

(In many words, the sound of **/əl/** is spelled with **le**, **al**, **el**, or **il**. Because spellers cannot rely on a phonetic way of remembering the various spellings, this sound is often difficult.)

In the word shape boxes, color the letters that spell the sound of **/əl/** in each word.

B Word Shapes Name ____________

Words with /əl/ — Lesson 27

Write each word in the correct word shape boxes. Next, in the word shape boxes, color the letters that spell the sound of **/əl/** in each word.

Word	Word shape
1. able	travel
2. April	needle
3. bottle	saddle
4. candle	squirrel
5. cattle	handle
6. eagle	sprinkle
7. handle	able
8. metal	cattle
9. middle	metal
10. needle	bottle
11. saddle	turtle
12. sprinkle	eagle
13. squirrel	middle
14. travel	April
15. turtle	candle

170

Answers may vary for duplicate word shapes.

Be Prepared For Fun

Check these supply lists for **Fun Ways to Spell** presented **Day 2**. Purchase and/or gather needed items ahead of time!

General
- Colored Pencils
- Art Paper (1 piece per child)
- Spelling List

Auditory
- A Classmate
- Spelling List

Visual
- Black Construction Paper (1 piece per child)
- Cotton Swabs (1 per child)
- Lemon Juice
- Spelling List

Tactile
- Pipe Cleaners (cut in an assortment of lengths)
- Spelling List

C Hide and Seek

Name ____________________

Place an **X** on a coin for each word you spell correctly.

D Other Word Forms

Using the words below, follow the instructions given by your teacher.

bottled	handled	saddled	traveling
bottling	handles	saddles	travels
candles	handling	saddling	turtleneck
(cattleman)	metallic	sprinkled	turtles
disable	needled	sprinkles	
(enable)	needles	sprinkling	
eaglet	needling	(traveled)	

E Fun Ways to Spell

Initial the box of each activity you finish.

1. 

Spell your words with pictures.

2. Spell your words with lemon juice.

3. 

Spell your words out loud.

4. 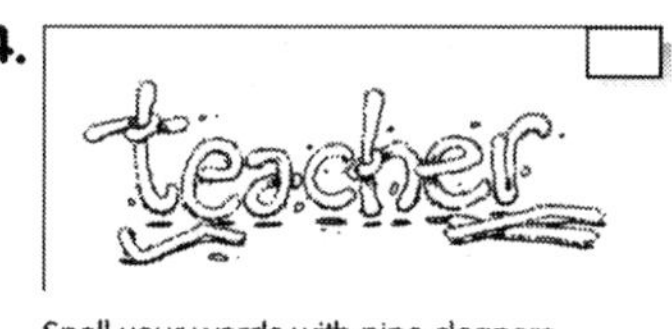

Spell your words with pipe cleaners.

Words with /əl/ Lesson 27

171

1 Hide and Seek

Reinforce correct spelling of current spelling words.

Write the words one at a time on the board. Use this activity for each word.

Say

- **Look** at the word.
- **Say** the word out loud.
- Let's **hide** (cover) the word.
- **Write** the word on your paper.
- Let's **seek** (uncover) the word.
- **Check** your spelling. If your word is spelled wrong, write the word correctly next to it.

2 Other Word Forms

This activity is optional. Have students find and circle the Other Word Forms that are synonyms of the following:

went abroad
make possible
cowboy

3 Fun Ways to Spell

Four activities are provided. Use one, two, three, or all of the activities. Have students initial the box for each activity they complete.

Lesson 27

Options:

- assign activities to students according to their learning styles
- set up the activities in learning centers for the class to do throughout the day
- divide the class into four groups and assign one activity per group
- do one activity per day

General

To spell your words with pictures...
- Choose several words from your spelling list and draw pictures that illustrate the meanings of those words.
- Write the correct spelling word beside each picture.
- Check your spelling.

Auditory

To spell your words out loud...
- Have a classmate read a spelling word from the list.
- Say a sentence with that spelling word to your classmate.
- Spell the spelling word you used in that sentence to your classmate.
- Ask your classmate to check your spelling.
- Do this with each word on your word list.

Visual

To spell your words with lemon juice...
- Dipping a cotton swab in lemon juice, write each of your spelling words on black construction paper.
- Check your spelling before your writing disappears!

Tactile

To spell your words with pipe cleaners...
- Choose a word from your spelling list.
- It may be a favorite word or a word you have trouble remembering how to spell.
- Shape the pipe cleaner to spell that word.

1 Working with Words

Familiarize students with word meaning and usage.

Sentence Fun

Write this incomplete sentence on the board: **I blew out the __ on my cake.** Have a volunteer complete the sentence.

Choose the spelling word that best completes each sentence, and write it on the line

Word Sort

Write the spelling words under the correct heading.

Take a minute to memorize...

Read the memory verse to the class twice. Have the class practice it with you two more times.

F Working with Words Name ______________________

Sentence Fun

Write the correct spelling word on the line to complete each sentence.

1. The candle gave very little light.
2. We should be able to come over.
3. We need to round up the cattle before dark.
4. The eagle circled over the lake.
5. A turtle does not walk very fast.
6. The needle in the compass points north.
7. It rained every afternoon in April.
8. The furry squirrel was not afraid of us.
9. At camp, I learned how to saddle a horse.
10. It is fun to travel to new places.
11. As we set up our tent, it began to sprinkle.
12. Rosa raised her hand during the middle of class.
13. He spilled the bottle of water on his homework.
14. The metal chest we dug up was very heavy.
15. The sign said not to handle the glass dishes.

Word Sort

Write the spelling words under the correct heading.

-el	-al	-il
1. squirrel	3. metal	4. April
2. travel		

Word Bank

able	candle	handle	needle	squirrel
April	cattle	metal	saddle	travel
bottle	eagle	middle	sprinkle	turtle

G Dictation Name ______________________

Listen and write the missing words and punctuation.

1. The bird flew away as a squirrel ran out on the branch .

2. The teacher will be able to help Rosa soon .

3. We wanted to travel in the middle of April .

Words with /əl/

Lesson 27

H Proofreading

If a word is misspelled, fill in the oval by that word. If all the words are spelled correctly, fill in the oval by **no mistake**.

1.	4.	7.
○ cattle	● candel	○ park
○ center	○ middle	○ turtle
● abel	○ later	● sprinckle
○ no mistake	○ no mistake	○ no mistake

2.	5.	8.
● Aprul	○ needle	● squirrle
○ December	○ mirror	○ driver
○ November	● eegle	○ bark
○ no mistake	○ no mistake	○ no mistake

3.	6.	9.
● botel	○ saddle	○ river
○ hammer	● metel	● travele
○ forget	○ sharp	○ summer
○ no mistake	○ no mistake	○ no mistake

173

1 Dictation

Reinforce correct spelling by using current and previous words in context.

Listen as I read each sentence and then write the missing words and ending punctuation in your worktext. (Slowly read each sentence twice. Sentences are found in the student text to the left.)

2 Proofreading

Familiarize students with standardized test format and reinforce recognizing misspelled words.

Look at each set of words. If a word is misspelled, fill in the oval by that word. If all the words are spelled correctly, fill in the oval by **no mistake**.

3 Hide and Seek

Reinforce correct spelling of current spelling words. (A reproducible master is provided in Appendix A as shown on the inset page to the right.)
Write the words one at a time on the board. Use this activity for each word.

- **Look** at the word.
- **Say** the word out loud.
- Let's **hide** (cover) the word.
- **Write** the word on your paper.
- Let's **seek** (uncover) the word.
- **Check** your spelling. If your word is spelled wrong, write the word correctly next to it.

Hide and Seek

Check a coin for each word you spell correctly.

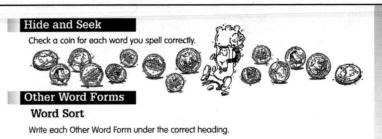

Other Word Forms

Word Sort

Write each Other Word Form under the correct heading.

cattlemen disable handled sprinkled turtleneck turtles

Two-syllable Words	Three-syllable Words
1. handled	4. disable
2. sprinkled	5. turtleneck
3. turtles	6. cattlemen

Guide Words

Pretend the words below are guide words on a dictionary page. Write the spelling words that would be found on each page.

both **disagree**
1. bottled 2. candles 3. cattleman 4. disable

eager **handwriting**
5. eaglet 6. enable 7. handling

message **reserve**
8. metallic 9. needles

sad **tusk**
10. saddled 11. sprinkling 12. traveling 13. turtleneck

Word Bank

disable candles metallic enable saddled turtleneck sprinkling
cattleman bottled handling eaglet needles traveling

349

Other Word Forms
Lesson 27

4 Other Word Forms

Have your students complete this activity to strengthen spelling ability and expand vocabulary.

1 Posttest

Test mastery of the spelling words.

I will say the word once, use the word in a sentence, then say the word again. Write the word on your paper.

1. sprinkle	Let's go for a walk before it begins to **sprinkle.**
2. cattle	There are **cattle** in the farms around Rosa's home.
3. April	Most birds build their nests in **April.**
4. travel	Some birds **travel** a long distance each spring and fall.
5. eagle	The sparrow strutted as proudly as if he were an **eagle.**
6. able	Rosa wasn't **able** to do her school work without help.
7. middle	She was stuck in the **middle** of the assignment.
8. needle	Her homework seemed as hard as looking for a **needle** in a haystack.
9. bottle	It isn't good to **bottle** up our feelings inside.
10. handle	Rosa didn't **handle** her feelings well when she talked about her teacher.
11. turtle	She wanted to hide like a **turtle** when Mr. Valentino asked to talk to her.
12. metal	She was so surprised, she bumped her head on the **metal** desk.
13. saddle	Dad's desk chair was covered in leather like a **saddle.**
14. squirrel	Nipper scolded the wild **squirrel** in the tree outside.
15. candle	She almost knocked the **candle** off the windowsill.

Progress Chart

Students may record scores. (Reproducible master in Appendix B.)

Personal Dictionary

Students may add any words they have misspelled to their personal dictionaries for reference when writing. (Cover in Appendix B.)

I Game Name ____________________

Complete the secret phrase by correctly spelling the words from this week's word list.

D O N ' T
1 2 3 4

S P E A K
5 6 7 8

E V I L
9 10 11

W O R D S
12 13 14 15

Remember: We are disobeying God when we say mean things about others.

J Journaling

Look at your classmates sitting on either side, in front of, and behind you. In your journal, write one or two compliments about each of these classmates. Share your compliments with them.

174

2 Game

Reinforce spelling skills and provide motivation and interest.

Materials

- game page (from student text)
- pencils (1 per child)
- game word list

Game Word List

Team A	Team A
1. able (O)	1. metal (O)
2. April (N)	2. middle (N)
3. bottle (')	3. needle (')
4. candle (T)	4. saddle (T)
5. cattle (P)	5. sprinkle (P)
6. eagle (E)	6. squirrel (E)
7. handle (A)	7. travel (A)
8. metal (K)	8. turtle (K)
9. middle (V)	9. able (V)
10. needle (I)	10. April (I)
11. saddle (L)	11. bottle (L)
12. sprinkle (O)	12. candle (O)
13. squirrel (R)	13. cattle (R)
14. travel (D)	14. eagle (D)
15. turtle (S)	15. handle (S)

How to Play:

- Divide the class into two teams.
- Have a student from team A choose a number from 1 to 15.
- Say the word that matches that number from the team's word list. (You may also wish to use the word in a sentence.)
- Have the student write the word on the board.
- If correct, have each member of team A write the given letter in the matching space on his/her game page.
- Alternate between teams A and B having the students choose a number of a blank space.
- The team to complete the secret phrase first is the winner.

Non-Competitive Option:

At the end of the game, say: "Class, I am proud of your efforts to spell the words correctly. If you had fun and tried your best, you are all winners!"

3 Journaling

Provide a meaningful reason for correct spelling through personal writing.

Review the story using discussion leads provided on the following page. Encourage students to apply the Scriptural value in their journaling.

Journaling (continued)

- Why was Rosa frustrated with her homework? (She had a lot of it and she didn't really understand how to do it.)
- Why did Rosa feel upset with Mr. Valentino? (She thought that he was ignoring her and spending all his time helping other kids.)
- Have you ever felt like Rosa did?
- What deal did Mr. Valentino make with Rosa? (That she'd keep her hand up if she had a question until he could get a chance to help her.)
- What did Rosa learn? (That it's wrong to criticize others.)
- Criticizing hurts. Compliments help. What is a compliment? (Telling others what we like, respect, or appreciate about them.)
- Look at your classmates sitting on either side, in front of, and behind you. In your journal, write one or two compliments about each of these classmates. Share your compliments with them.

Take a minute to memorize...
Have the class say the memory verses from lessons 25, 26, and 27 with you.

"Standard spelling is the result of writing and reading —not the way to it."*

*Scott, Jill E. 1994. Spelling for Readers and Writers. The Reading Teacher, Vol. 48, No. 2, October: 188-190.

1 **Literature Connection**
Topic: Getting along with others
Theme Text: Romans 15:5

Mountainous Problems

Tony is upset and embarrassed that his cousin will be in his classroom—until his attitude begins to change.

"Could you take Heather to school with you Thursday?" Marie Vanetti sat down beside her son Tony.

Tony picked up his *Earth* magazine from the end table and turned it over. "Look, Mama." He pointed to the title "Happy Hiking" on the back cover and read, "You might take any of the items pictured below with you on a hike. Use the clues to figure out what they are."

"Tony?" Mama said in her let's-stick-with-the-subject voice.

"But Mama," Tony groaned and looked up from the magazine. "It's bad enough that she's moving here this summer! Do I have to drag her along with me to school before she actually comes to stay?"

"Antonio Marcus Vanetti! You know it would make your cousin's move here easier if you would introduce her to your classmates and show her around the school." Maria Vanetti stood up and walked toward the kitchen.

"Well, she needs more than my help," Tony said. "She needs to spend a lot of time hiking or not eating or something. She's so fat, she waddles!"

Mama turned and looked at Tony's angry face. "Tony-O, do you only treat people nicely if they look good? I thought I taught you better than that."

"No, Mama." Tony looked down. "But she's huge and her hair is so red it almost glows in the dark! It's bad enough she's going to be in my class next year. Does she have to visit now? Maybe I should warn the kids about how much space to leave for her and stuff."

Mama tried not to smile at her son's obvious discomfort. "Maybe you could tell them how good she is at those tricky 3-D puzzles, and how well she plays the piano." Mama stepped into the kitchen to put the bread in the oven. As she opened the oven door she added, "Some people pay a lot of money to make their hair look the same color as your cousin's."

"Humpf! Maybe they won't come," Tony grumbled to himself. "Maybe they'll have a wreck. No, that wouldn't be good—she might get uglier. Maybe they'll spend so much time eating on the way down here they won't make it before school starts Thursday morning." Tony scowled.

"What did you say, Tony-O?" Mama asked from the kitchen.

"Nothing important, Mama." Tony groaned and looked at the magazine in his hand. He glanced at the first picture, then at the clue written underneath it. "'Don't blow this unless there's an emergency,'" he read to himself. "Well, this is an emergency. What do I blow?" He looked closely at the picture. It was a part of something shiny and silver. "Oh, a whistle," he said, writing the answer.

Tony continued the argument in his mind. "She's just so fat! I don't want anyone to know we're related. I don't even think Stephen will understand, and I can just hear Daniel now: 'Here are two chairs for you, Heather.' If she just wouldn't eat so much!" He looked down at the magazine in his hands again. The clue for picture number seven said, "Tremendous trekking when you don't forget this high-energy snack."

"Heather won't need any of this. She could live off her fat for a year," he mumbled as he stared at the magazine.

"What, Tony?" Mama called.

Tony looked at the picture again. "What's that hiking snack that's made from nuts, raisins, and M&Ms?"

"Gorp."

"Yeah, that's what it's called." Tony wrote the answer, then looked at the next clue. "'Every trail has its ups and downs. This can help you find your way,'" he read. "It must be some sort of map," he thought. "Well, my life will go downhill fast if I have to have Heather with me everywhere I go. No whistle is going to get me out of this!"

Tony threw the magazine down on the couch. "I've just got to think of a way to get out of this," he mumbled. "Maybe I'll get sick. She wouldn't want to visit without me. If she went without me, maybe no one would realize I was her cousin. I'm sure not fat, and I don't have red hair. How would anyone guess?"

Thursday came sooner than Tony thought possible. He trudged into the classroom just as the bell was ringing. Heather was right at his heels.

"Remember WWJD!" Mama had whispered in his ear when she'd left for work. What would Jesus do? Tony grabbed a chair from the back table and put it beside his desk. Mr. Valentino was already standing at the front of the class. He started talking before Tony had a chance to respond to the raised eyebrows and questioning looks of his classmates.

"This morning several of the girls are going to sing a song for us that they have been working on for a chapel program next week," Mr. Valentino announced. "Are you ready, Beth?"

"Well, we're ready, but Mom had to help Grandma this morning. She can't play the piano until next Monday. I don't think we can do it without the piano."

"I might be able to play it," Heather said brightly. "What's the song?"

"Good morning, Heather! Mrs. Bentley said you might visit us today." Mr. Valentino turned his attention to the red-headed girl. "Welcome to Knowlton Elementary." His eyes swept the classroom. "Heather and her family are moving here this summer," he continued. "She'll be part of your class next year when Mrs. Burton is your teacher."

"Tony is my cousin." Heather lifted her chin and smiled confidently. "What song are you guys singing?"

Story (continued)

Day 1

Lesson 28

Tony slouched down in his chair. "I can't believe she told everyone! So much for keeping it a secret!" he wailed silently. To Heather he whispered, "You really don't have to play for them, Cuz. Mrs. Hill will be here Monday to do it."

"We're going to sing 'Do Lord.'" Beth smiled at the new girl. "Do you know that song?"

Heather nodded and headed toward the piano. "She doesn't even have music," thought Tony. "She's gonna waddle up there and make a fool of us in the first five minutes. I can't believe this is happening to me." Tony grabbed the *Earth* magazine out of his backpack and slouched lower in his chair. He opened the magazine and pretended to be deeply absorbed in the last few pages. But no one was paying any attention to him. Everyone was watching Heather as she sat down at the piano and adjusted the bench. Suddenly several mouths dropped open as her fingers flew effortlessly across the keys. The melody of "Do Lord" could be heard clearly among the improvised notes. Beth, Katelynn, and Kristin started singing after the introduction. It was really very pretty. Even Daniel clapped as the four girls headed back towards their seats.

Just then, Stephen leaned forward and whispered, "Hey, Tony! You might be able to read *Happy Hiking* better if it were right-side up." Tony let out a sigh, and rotated the magazine right side up. He hadn't realized he was holding his breath. He looked back at his best friend with a sheepish grin on his face, but Heather sat back down before he could say anything to Stephen.

At recess time, much to Tony's relief, all the girls gathered around Heather and invited her to join them for Chinese jump rope. Tony watched her laugh and overheard the girls asking her where she was from and how she had learned to play the piano so well.

Stephen joined Tony and gave him a playful shove. "How come you don't play the piano as well as your cousin?" he teased.

Tony shrugged. "She is good, isn't she? I didn't even know she could play. I was too worried about her size."

"Well, she does kind of waddle, but look how good she is at Chinese jump rope! I can't do it that well and we practiced every day during our unit on China. Where did she learn to do that?" Stephen pointed to Heather's gracefully synchronized movements and watched her red hair bounce rhythmically.

Tony shrugged his shoulders. "I guess there's a lot I don't know about my cousin. Hey, can you help me with this?" Tony pulled out his magazine and turned to the back cover. "The clue says, 'Don't let the bad bugs bite. Here's a way to scare them off,'" he read as he pointed to what looked like a picture of some bright orange letters.

Stephen took the book and studied the picture carefully.

"Well, it hasn't been too bad so far," Tony thought while he waited. "Maybe having Heather around will be okay."

"Could be bug spray," Stephen finally answered, "Don't you use that when you go hiking? I think there's a brand called 'Off' or something. We have some at home."

"Yeah! I think you're right. Only three more to go. Look at these." While Stephen studied the rest of the pictures, Tony continued to watch his cousin.

"This must be one of those knives that has scissors." Stephen scratched his head. "But I can't get this last one either. The clue says, 'This sole saver will give you great traction action.' That's the hardest one. Jesus is the only soul saver I know. Maybe Mr. V. can figure it out. Those little black marks in the picture look like crosses, but what does that have to do with hiking?"

The two boys headed over to Mr. Valentino's supervision post by the big evergreen tree in the center of the playground.

"There's another kind of sole, Stephen," Mr. Valentino laughed as the boys explained their problem. "The one on the bottom of your shoe! Those little X's in the picture are for traction on the sole of a hiking boot. Traction keeps you on the path. It helps you not to slip and fall." He paused. "Now that I think of it, Jesus gives us a kind of traction, too, if we ask Him to be our friend. He helps us to make good choices. He keeps us from making mistakes and falling."

A group of girls walked with Heather towards the swings. "I like your hair, Heather. It is such a pretty color." Beth was saying. "Would you play for us at chapel? I don't think my mom even needs to come."

Tony remembered what Mama had whispered in his ear that morning. "What would Jesus do?" He smiled as he walked away from Mr. V. "I think God is giving me some soul traction right now as I'm learning about Heather. She's sure been full of surprises. I guess it's not really important what a person looks like. Maybe this wasn't such an emergency after all."

Tony looked at the last clue on the page. "Feeling all dried up? Thirsting for relief?" he read softly to himself. "Nope, not anymore!" he thought. "And when I do what Jesus would do, my problems don't seem like mountains anymore either."

Tony grinned, stuck the magazine in his pocket, and headed for the slide.

2 Discussion Time

Check understanding of the story and development of personal values.

- How does Tony feel about his cousin visiting Knowlton Elementary?
- Why does Tony think his classmates won't like Heather?
- How did Heather offer to help Beth?
- What else did Heather do that surprised Tony?
- Raise your hand if it's right to treat people nicely only if they look good.

A Preview Name ____________________

Write each word as your teacher says it.

1. September
2. person
3. worse
4. early
5. hurry
6. serve
7. dirt
8. thirty
9. burn
10. earn
11. Saturday
12. return
13. herd
14. learn
15. search

Words with /ûr/ or /ər/

Lesson 28

Scripture
Romans 15:5

175

3 Preview

Test for knowledge of the correct spellings of these words.

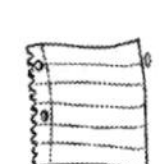

Customize Your List

On a separate piece of paper, additional words of your choice may be tested.

I will say the word once, use the word in a sentence, then say the word again. Write the word on the lines in the worktext.

Correct Immediately!

Let's correct our preview.

Say: I will write each word on the board. Put a dot under each letter on your preview as I spell the word out loud. If you spelled a word wrong, rewrite it correctly.

Take a minute to memorize...

Read the memory verse to the class twice. Have the class practice it with you two more times.

Day 1

Lesson 28

1.	September	Heather will come to Knowlton Elementary next **September**.
2.	person	Heather is an overweight **person**.
3.	worse	Tony didn't think things could be any **worse**.
4.	early	Thursday seemed to come **early** in the week.
5.	hurry	Tony was not in a **hurry** to get to school on Thursday.
6.	serve	When you **serve** others you are happier.
7.	dirt	The hiking trail was brown **dirt**.
8.	thirty	Maria Vanetti is about **thirty** years old.
9.	burn	Tony felt his face **burn** with embarrassment.
10.	earn	It was not hard for Heather to **earn** the respect of her classmates.
11.	Saturday	Heather will leave for home **Saturday** night.
12.	return	Heather will not **return** until next school year.
13.	herd	Mr. Valentino doesn't need to **herd** the class out to recess.
14.	learn	Tony needed to **learn** how to treat people nicely.
15.	search	You can **search** for something special in everyone you meet.

Progress Chart

Students may record scores. (Reproducible master in Appendix B.)

Day 1

Lesson

28

4 Word Shapes

Help students form a correct image of whole words.

Look at each word and think about its shape. Now, write the word in the correct word shape boxes. You may check off each word as you use it.

(The sound of **/ər/** can be spelled with **ar**, **er**, or **or**. The sound of **/ûr/** can be spelled with **ir**, **ear**, **er**, or **ur**. Because spellers cannot rely on a phonetic way of remembering the various spellings, this sound is often difficult.)

In the word shape boxes, color the letters that spell the sound of **/ər/** in each word.

Words with /ûr/ or /ər/

Lesson 28

B Word Shapes Name ____________________

Write each word in the correct word shape boxes. Next, in the word shape boxes, color the letters that spell the sound of **/ûr/** or **/ər/** in each word.

	Word	Answer
1.	burn	serve
2.	dirt	September
3.	early	return
4.	earn	thirty
5.	herd	Saturday
6.	hurry	early
7.	learn	search
8.	person	worse
9.	return	hurry
10.	Saturday	herd
11.	search	person
12.	September	dirt
13.	serve	learn
14.	thirty	burn
15.	worse	earn

176

Answers may vary for duplicate word shapes.

Be Prepared For Fun

Check these supply lists for **Fun Ways to Spell** presented **Day 2**. Purchase and/or gather needed items ahead of time!

General
- A Classmate
- Spelling List

Auditory
- Voice Recorder
- Spelling List

Visual
- a, a, b, c, d, e, e, e, h, i, l, m, n, o, p, r, r, S, s, t, t, u, v, w, y (written on upside-down cups)
- Spelling List

Tactile
- Art Paper (2 or 3 sheets per child)
- Magazines
- Glue Sticks
- Scissors
- Spelling List

C **Hide and Seek** Name ____________________

Place an **X** on a coin for each word you spell correctly.

D **Other Word Forms**

Using the words below, follow the instructions given by your teacher.

burned	earliest	hurries	returnable	servant
burning	earned	hurrying	returned	served
burnt	earning	learned	returning	serviceable
dirtier	earnings	learning	returns	serving
dirtiest	herded	learns	searched	worsen
dirty	herding	personable	searcher	worst
dirtying	herds	personal	searches	
earlier	hurried	personalize	searching	

E **Fun Ways to Spell**

Initial the box of each activity you finish.

1. 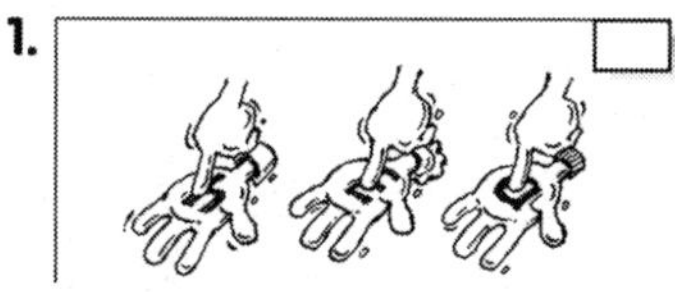

Spell your words in your classmate's hand.

3. 

Spell your words using a tape recorder.

2. 

Spell your words with paper cups.

4. 

Spell your words with magazine clippings.

Words with /ûr/ or /ər/ Lesson 28

177

1 Hide and Seek

Reinforce correct spelling of current spelling words.

Write the words one at a time on the board. Use this activity for each word.

- **Look** at the word.
- **Say** the word out loud.
- Let's **hide** (cover) the word.
- **Write** the word on your paper.
- Let's **seek** (uncover) the word.
- **Check** your spelling. If your word is spelled wrong, write the word correctly next to it.

2 Other Word Forms

This activity is optional. Have students unscramble these letters to write Other Word Forms:

neowrs	(worsen)
srteunr	(returns)
nniagers	(earnings)
eedlarn	(learned)

3 Fun Ways to Spell

Four activities are provided. Use one, two, three, or all of the activities. Have students initial the box for each activity they complete.

Day 2 Lesson 28

Options:

- assign activities to students according to their learning styles
- set up the activities in learning centers for the class to do throughout the day
- divide the class into four groups and assign one activity per group
- do one activity per day

General

To spell your words in your classmate's hand...
- Have your classmate sit next to you and hold his (or her) palm open in front of and facing both of you.
- Use your fingertip to write a spelling word in the palm of your classmate's hand.
- Have your classmate say each letter as you write it and then say the word you spelled.
- Next, have your classmate write a word in your palm.

Auditory

To spell your words using a voice recorder...
- Record yourself as you say and spell each word on your spelling list.
- Listen to your recording and check your spelling.

Visual

To spell your words with paper cups...
- Spell a word from your list by putting the cups in the right order.
- Check your spelling.

Tactile

To spell your words with magazine clippings...
- Cut the letters you need from old magazines.
- Glue the letters to your paper in the correct order.

1 Working with Words

Familiarize students with word meaning and usage.

Riddles in Rhyme

Say these riddles and have students complete each one with a rhyming word.

I found my cat, asleep on a __. I tried on the wig, but it was too __.

Read each of the riddles in your worktext. Write the spelling word that completes each rhyme.

Take a minute to memorize...

Read the memory verse to the class twice. Have the class practice it with you two more times.

F Working with Words Name ____________________

Riddles in Rhyme

Write the spelling word that completes each rhyme.

1. I am sure that he is hurt.
   He fell face down into the dirt.
2. I dropped my offering in the church,
   So my mother helped me search.
3. We cut each sandwich in a curve,
   And placed them on a plate to serve.
4. Matches! Candles! Can't she learn,
   To keep away from things that burn!
5. One day I always can remember.
   My birthday is the third of September.

6. Matthew, with the hair so curly,
   Always gets to school quite early.
7. To buy that game, my big concern,
   Is how much money I need to earn.
8. Around the tree the squirrels scurry.
   They must be in an awful hurry.

9. I think we'd better call the nurse.
   Before the patient gets much worse.
10. The cowboy could not hear a word,
    Surrounded by the noisy herd.

Word Bank

burn	earn	learn	Saturday	serve
dirt	herd	person	search	thirty
early	hurry	return	September	worse

G Dictation

Name ____________________

Listen and write the missing words and punctuation.

1. Tony had to learn a lesson about how to love other people.
2. What a person is like inside is more important than how he looks.
3. Tony was in no hurry to get to school early on Thursday.

Words with /ûr/ or /ər/

Lesson 28

H Proofreading

If a word is misspelled, fill in the oval by that word. If all the words are spelled correctly, fill in the oval by **no mistake**.

1. return / bern / able / no mistake
2. dert / April / bottle / no mistake
3. candle / erly / eagle / no mistake
4. earn / search / metal / no mistake
5. hird / sprinkle / travel / no mistake
6. hury / squirrel / September / no mistake
7. lern / serve / cattle / no mistake
8. thirty / persen / wonder / no mistake
9. silver / worse / saterday / no mistake

179

1 Dictation

Reinforce correct spelling by using current and previous words in context.

Listen as I read each sentence and then write the missing words and ending punctuation in your worktext. (Slowly read each sentence twice. Sentences are found in the student text to the left.)

2 Proofreading

Familiarize students with standardized test format and reinforce recognizing misspelled words.

Look at each set of words. If a word is misspelled, fill in the oval by that word. If all the words are spelled correctly, fill in the oval by **no mistake**.

Day 4

Lesson 28

3 Hide and Seek

Reinforce correct spelling of current spelling words. (A reproducible master is provided in Appendix A as shown on the inset page to the right.)
Write the words one at a time on the board. Use this activity for each word.

- **Look** at the word.
- **Say** the word out loud.
- Let's **hide** (cover) the word.
- **Write** the word on your paper.
- Let's **seek** (uncover) the word.
- **Check** your spelling. If your word is spelled wrong, write the word correctly next to it.

4 Other Word Forms

Have your students complete this activity to strengthen spelling ability and expand vocabulary.

1 Posttest

Test mastery of the spelling words.

I will say the word once, use the word in a sentence, then say the word again. Write the word on your paper.

Other Word Forms | Lesson 28

Hide and Seek

Check a coin for each word you spell correctly.

Other Word Forms

Suffixes

Change the **y** to **i** and add the suffix to each word to make a new word.

1. dirty + er = dirtier
2. hurry + ed = hurried
3. early + est = earliest

Add the suffix to each word to make a new word.

4. person + able = personable
5. return + able = returnable
6. service + able = serviceable
7. personal + ize = personalize

Add **-ed** and **-ing** to each word to make new words.

	+ed	+ing
8. burn	burned	burning
9. earn	earned	earning
10. herd	herded	herding
11. learn	learned	learning
12. search	searched	searching
13. return	returned	returning

Spelling and Writing

Use each pair of words to write a sentence. Check your spelling.

1. hurries, servant (Answers may vary)
2. dirty, searching (Answers may vary)

350

1.	thirty	Mr. Valentino was not **thirty** last year.
2.	herd	A **herd** of cattle is grazing beside the playground.
3.	September	Next **September**, Heather will join Mrs. Burton's class.
4.	person	Heather is a very talented **person**.
5.	earn	Heather will **earn** the respect of her classmates.
6.	serve	We should **serve** others as Jesus did.
7.	dirt	The **dirt** on the trail got on his hiking boots.
8.	burn	Tony knew his face would **burn** from embarrassment with Heather around.
9.	hurry	Tony wanted the day to **hurry** and get over.
10.	return	Heather will **return** to Knowlton Elementary next year.
11.	Saturday	Heather leaves for home **Saturday** night.
12.	worse	Tony thought things would be **worse** than they were.
13.	early	Heather is not going to leave town **early**.
14.	learn	What can we **learn** from Tony about how to treat others?
15.	search	Tony will **search** for the answers to the clues.

Progress Chart

Students may record scores. (Reproducible master in Appendix B.)

Personal Dictionary

Students may add any words they have misspelled to their personal dictionaries for reference when writing. (Cover in Appendix B.)

Words with /ûr/ or /ər/

Lesson 28

I Game Name ______________________

Tony learned to be proud of his cousin and treat her with kindness. Follow Tony to listen to Heather play the piano by moving one space for each word you or your team spells correctly from this week's word list.

Remember: Ask Jesus to put His attitude of love for others in your heart.

J Journaling

In your journal, write a paragraph about how you should treat people who are not beautiful on the outside.

180

2 Game

Reinforce spelling skills and provide motivation and interest.

Materials

- game page (from student text)
- flat buttons, dry beans, pennies, or game discs (1 per child)
- game word list

Game Word List

1. burn
2. dirt
3. early
4. earn
5. herd
6. hurry
7. learn
8. person
9. return
10. Saturday
11. search
12. September
13. serve
14. thirty
15. worse

Day 5

Lesson 28

How to Play:

- Divide the class into two teams.
- Have each student place his/her game piece on Start.
- Have a student from team A go to the board.
- Say the spelling word. (You may also wish to use the word in a sentence.)
- Have the student write the word on the board.
- If correct, instruct each member of team A to move his/her game piece forward one space on the game board. (Note: If the word is misspelled, correct the spelling immediately.)
- Alternate between teams A and B.
- The team to reach the piano first is the winner.

Non-Competitive Option:

At the end of the game, say: "Class, I am proud of your efforts to spell the words correctly. If you had fun and tried your best, you are all winners!"

3 Journaling

Provide a meaningful reason for correct spelling through personal writing.

Review the story using discussion leads provided on the following page. Encourage students to apply the Scriptural value in their journaling.

Journaling (continued)

- Why was Tony worried about Heather visiting his class? (He was embarrassed by how she looked.)
- What did Tony learn about Heather when she visited his class? (She could play the piano beautifully. Some people loved the color of her hair. She was cheerful and people liked to be around her. She was very coordinated.)
- What does WWJD stand for? (What would Jesus do?)
- How did Jesus help Tony discover his cousin's special abilities? (Tony's classmates accepted Heather even though she was overweight. Tony saw that there was more to Heather than just the way she looked. She could play the piano. She was cheerful, coordinated, and could play Chinese jump rope well.)
- Write a paragraph in your journal about how you should treat people who are not beautiful on the outside.

Take a minute to memorize...
Have the class say the memory verses from lessons 25, 26, 27, and 28 with you.

"Teaching a child to be a good speller involves both mental and verbal processes and needs to include the active participation of the child."*

*Downing, John, Robert M. Coughlin and Gene Rich. 1986. Children's Invented Spellings in the Classroom. The Elementary School Journal, Vol. 86: No. 3, January: 295-303.

1 **Literature Connection**
Topic: Prayer
Theme Text: 1 Timothy 2:1

Sarah's Sorrow

Sarah faces lots of problems because her mother is an alcoholic, but she believes God will answer her prayers for her mother.

"I pick Stephen!" Kristin pointed toward the group of boys and girls waiting to be chosen for soccer teams. Stephen walked over to stand by her.

"Rachel." Beth made the next choice for her team. One by one, names were called and the waiting group grew smaller and smaller.

Sarah Johansen wasn't surprised to be one of the last two or three kids chosen. She was used to being the last one picked for games at recess, the last one invited to be a part of other activities. "I'm just not very noticeable," she thought, looking at the ground as she waited to be chosen. "Invisible Sarah, that's me." She poked a clump of spring grass with the toe of her too-small sneaker. A flash of yellow appeared in the middle of the bright green. "I'm just like that dandelion. Nobody ever really sees me."

"Sarah." Beth made the final pick. Everyone rushed onto the field and the game began.

When school got out that afternoon, the halls quickly filled with kids. Sarah walked slowly, limping slightly in her too-small shoes. All the running she'd done during that soccer game had really made her feet sore. Sarah looked around for her mother's car as soon as she stepped out of the school building. The crumpled old car that had once been red wasn't there. Sarah felt a familiar cold, empty feeling inside.

"Momma didn't show up again?" Nellie, Sarah's big sister, walked up behind her.

Sarah shook her head and sank onto the curb to rest her feet and wait. "Maybe she's just late. Maybe something came up."

"Yeah, sure, something like another drink. . . or two or three!" Nellie shook her head angrily.

"Shhhh!" Sarah hissed and tugged on Nellie's sleeve.

Nellie ignored her. "She's always here on time if she isn't drinking." The thirteen-year-old's long, blond hair swung as she paced in front of Sarah. "She's a wonderful mother 'till she touches a bottle, then it's like we don't even have a mother!" She threw up her hands.

The sisters waited while other kids piled into waiting cars or pedaled away on their bikes. The minutes ticked by until the Johansen girls were the last two students left at Knowlton Elementary School.

"Nellie, Sarah? Can I give you a ride home?" Mrs. Bentley called from the sidewalk.

Sarah stood up quickly. "Yes, please, Ma'am. We'd really appreciate it." Mrs. Bentley didn't ask the girls for directions to their home. She didn't need to. Sarah remembered the first time the school secretary had offered them a ride. They'd been wondering what to do when their mother hadn't come to pick them up after school. They lived too far away to walk and knew of no one to call for help. Since then, Mrs. Bentley had been giving them a ride whenever they needed one. Lately, it had been more and more often.

The little gray house on Piney Street looked deserted. Nellie and Sarah thanked Mrs. Bentley politely for the ride. When the school secretary's car pulled away from the curb, Sarah's cold empty feeling grew worse. Without a word, Nellie pulled the house key out of her pocket and opened the squeaky front door. Both girls knew their mother wasn't home because the old car wasn't sitting out front. They also knew from experience that there was no way of guessing when she might come home.

Nellie tried to sound positive. "Let's do our homework, then I'll fix something for supper."

"Sure." Sarah nodded. "I don't have very much homework, so I can help you with supper." The girls settled at the kitchen table with the chipped Formica top. The old-fashioned clock on the kitchen wall sounded loud in the silence. Tick-Tock. Tick-Tock. Sarah's attention wandered from the book in front of her. "I sure am hungry," she thought. "Our lunches weren't very big. I wonder if Momma got any groceries today and when she'll come home." Her thoughts were interrupted by a loud growl from her stomach.

"Okay! I get the message!" Nellie laughed. "Let's fix supper now. I'm almost done with my history assignment and you're not working anyway." She playfully poked Sarah in the ribs as she walked by to open the refrigerator. A half-full bottle of ketchup was the only thing on one whole shelf in the door. The rest of the fridge was almost as empty. "Well. . ." Nellie gathered a few things from the cupboard and placed them on the counter. "Would you care to try 'Nellie's Surprise?'"

"Uh, okay, I guess." Sarah looked at the variety of ingredients Nellie had gathered on the counter. "Are you sure that stuff goes together and, um, tastes all right?"

"I guess we'll find out." Nellie shrugged. "We don't have a lot of choice. Momma got paid today so maybe there'll be more to eat tomorrow." Nellie got out a saucepan and slammed the cupboard door hard. "At least, if she doesn't spend it all on alcohol!"

Sarah washed her hands at the kitchen sink. "All right. What do I dump in first?"

The thrown-together meal really wasn't too bad.

Story (continued)

Between the two of them, they ate every bite before washing all their dishes and cleaning up the kitchen. Sarah swept the floor while Nellie started the washing machine so they'd have clean clothes to wear to school.

Later, Sarah turned over in her bed. The light from the kitchen shown down the short hall and into the small bedroom the sisters shared. Nellie was still up, finishing up her homework in the kitchen. Sarah sighed and thumped her pillow. "Why can't Momma be like other mothers and take care of us? If only she didn't drink! Then things would be better. Nellie wouldn't have to clean the house and cook and do everything. We'd have good food and clothes that fit if Momma didn't spend all that money on alcohol. If only things could be the way they used to be. . ."

Soundlessly, Sarah sat up and reached for the framed picture that sat on the small dresser between Nellie's bed and her own. Turning the frame so the soft light from the kitchen fell across it, Sarah looked at the photograph. The light wasn't really good enough to see the picture well, but Sarah could see it clearly in her mind. A man sat with his arm around a lovely young woman holding a baby, a little girl with blond braids perched on his knee. All of them smiling. The Johansen family as it used to be.

Tears rolled down Sarah's face. "Daddy, why did you leave? Momma, Momma. Where are you? Don't you know we need you? Don't you care about us at all? How can drinking alcohol be more important than your own little girls? Don't you see me, Momma? Am I 'Invisible Sarah' to my own mother, too?" Sarah cried herself to sleep hugging the picture.

Mrs. Johansen was there when the girls got up the next morning. Her eyes were red and she moved about slowly, like an old, old woman. Nellie got out the cereal and milk their mother had bought while Sarah got out bowls and spoons.

The girls knew from experience they needed to be as quiet as possible when their mother had been drinking and had a bad headache. No one said anything about the day before.

Later that day, at handwriting time, Mr. Valentino asked Rosa to read the Scripture for that week aloud. "Pray much for others," Rosa read clearly. "Plead for God's mercy upon them; give thanks for all He is going to do for them. 1 Timothy 2:1."

"Thank you, Rosa." Mr. Valentino smiled and nodded in her direction. "This Scripture not only tells us what to do when we see someone in need, it also promises that God will help them when we ask Him. It says that we should go ahead and give thanks knowing that God will help those we're praying earnestly for. So, I think we should get busy praying for others, don't you?" The teacher motioned to a piece of poster board on an easel in the front corner of the room. "Let's make a list of those we know of with special needs and then pray for them." Rachel waved her hand to get the teacher's attention. "Yes, Rachel?"

Rachel lowered her hand. "Helen. She's so tired all the time. I just want her to be okay and the baby, too."

Mr. Valentino was busy the next few minutes recording the names of those the children wanted to pray for. "I don't really know of anyone that's sick or hurt," Sarah thought. "But I do know my Momma needs help." She started to raise her hand, then jerked it back down. "If I ask the class to pray for my Momma, then they'll know she's an alcoholic."

"Sarah?" Mr. Valentino had seen her half-raised hand.

"Uh,. . . ah, that is . . .uh, my mother." Sarah almost whispered. Sarah was relieved when Mr. Valentino simply nodded with a smile and didn't ask any questions.

"Sarah's mother." Mr. Valentino repeated slowly as he added the words to the prayer list. He stepped back and looked at the list. "Remember, everyone, our verse says we should pray much for these special people, then give thanks for all God IS GOING to do for them."

As Sarah walked down the sidewalk after school, she noticed the bright yellow of a dandelion. It was blooming from a cracked place in the sidewalk where hundreds of feet passed by every day. Nobody noticed it as they rushed in or out of the building. It must have been stepped on lots of times, but it was still there and still blooming.

Sarah smiled down at the little yellow flower. "I'm still not very noticeable, either, and my life is pretty tough, too. But God has promised to listen to my prayers and to answer them, so I must be pretty important to God! I'll just keep talking to Him about Momma and trust Him to answer." And as she walked toward the car, Sarah's smile was as beautiful as a spring flower.

2 Discussion Time

Check understanding of the story and development of personal values.

- Why did Sarah's feet hurt after the soccer game?
- Why didn't Sarah's and Nellie's mother come to pick them up?
- How did the sisters get home when their mother didn't show up?
- Who fixed supper and washed clothes and cleaned the house?
- Why do you think they didn't have clothes that fit, very much food, or a nice car?
- How do you think Sarah felt about her mother's drinking problem?
- What has God promised to do when we pray for others?
- Can God help in any situation?

A Preview Name ____________

Write each word as your teacher says it.

1. football
2. shook
3. woman
4. neighborhood
5. good-bye
6. bushes
7. hood
8. push
9. hook
10. notebook
11. wolf
12. cookie
13. wool
14. brook
15. pulley

Words with /ú/

Lesson 29

Scripture

I Timothy 2:1

181

3 Preview

Test for knowledge of the correct spellings of these words.

Customize Your List

On a separate piece of paper, additional words of your choice may be tested.

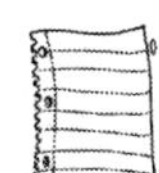

I will say the word once, use the word in a sentence, then say the word again. Write the word on the lines in the worktext.

Correct Immediately!

Let's correct our preview.

I will write each word on the board. Put a dot under each letter on your preview as I spell the word out loud. If you spelled a word wrong, rewrite it correctly.

Take a minute to memorize...

Read the memory verse to the class twice. Have the class practice it with you two more times.

Day 1

Lesson 29

1.	football	The game of soccer is called **football** in some countries.
2.	shook	Nellie **shook** her head when their mother didn't come to get them.
3.	woman	Their mother was a **woman** who sometimes drank a lot.
4.	neighborhood	Sarah's **neighborhood** isn't close to Knowlton Elementary School.
5.	good-bye	Mrs. Bentley waved **good-bye** as she drove away.
6.	bushes	The **bushes** by the door needed trimming.
7.	hood	The old car with the unpainted **hood** wasn't sitting out front.
8.	push	Nellie unlocked the door and used her foot to **push** it open.
9.	hook	There's a **hook** to latch the screen door.
10.	notebook	Sarah started to write in her **notebook**.
11.	wolf	Soon her stomach growled loudly like a **wolf**.
12.	cookie	Sarah had the last **cookie** in her lunch.
13.	wool	Since it's spring, Sarah doesn't need her **wool** coat that's too small.
14.	brook	People used to have to wash clothes in a tub or a **brook**.
15.	pulley	They sometimes used lines attached to a **pulley** to hang the wet clothes.

Progress Chart

Students may record scores. (Reproducible master in Appendix B.)

Day 1

Lesson 29

4 Word Shapes

Help students form a correct image of whole words.

Look at each word and think about its shape. Now, write the word in the correct word shape boxes. You may check off each word as you use it.

(In many words, the sound of **/ù/** is spelled with **oo**, or **u**. The **/ù/** sound is also spelled **o** in a few words.)

In the word shape boxes, color the letter or letters that spell the sound of **/ù/** in each word. Circle the compound words.

B Word Shapes Name ______

Words with /ù/ — Lesson 29

Write each word in the correct word shape boxes. Next, in the word shape boxes, color the letter or letters that spell the sound of /ù/ in each word. Circle the four compound words.

1. brook	cookie
2. bushes	notebook (circled)
3. cookie	brook
4. football	shook
5. good-bye	hook
6. hood	wolf
7. hook	pulley
8. neighborhood	bushes
9. notebook	wool
10. pulley	neighborhood (circled)
11. push	good-bye (circled)
12. shook	football (circled)
13. wolf	hood
14. woman	push
15. wool	woman

182

Answers may vary for duplicate word shapes.

Be Prepared For Fun

Check these supply lists for **Fun Ways to Spell** presented **Day 2**. Purchase and/or gather needed items ahead of time!

General
- Markers
- Art Paper (2 or 3 sheets per child)
- Spelling List

Auditory
- Spelling List

Visual
- Letter Tiles a, b, c, d, e, f, g, h, h, i, k, l, l, m, n, o, o, o, p, r, s, s, t, u, w, y
- Spelling List

Tactile
- Paint Bags (tempera paint in plastic, resealable bags secured at top with heavy tape-1 per child)
- Spelling List

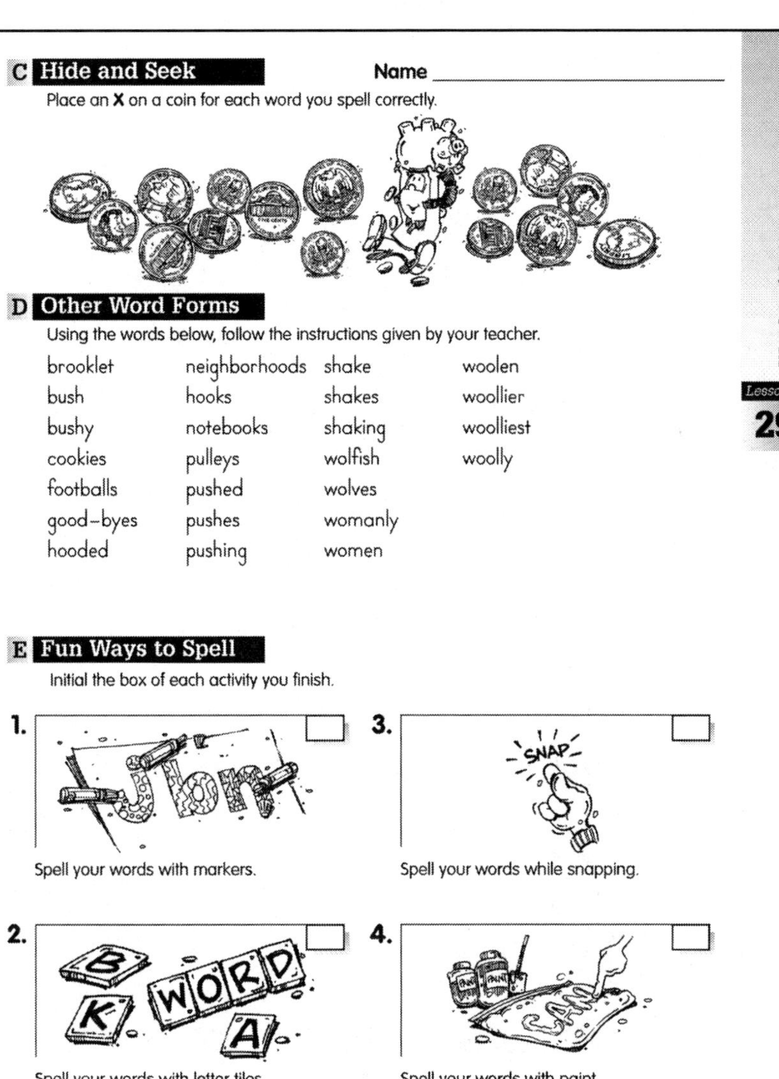

C **Hide and Seek** Name ______________________

Place an **X** on a coin for each word you spell correctly.

D **Other Word Forms**

Using the words below, follow the instructions given by your teacher.

brooklet	neighborhoods	shake	woolen
bush	hooks	shakes	woollier
bushy	notebooks	shaking	woolliest
cookies	pulleys	wolfish	woolly
footballs	pushed	wolves	
good-byes	pushes	womanly	
hooded	pushing	women	

E **Fun Ways to Spell**

Initial the box of each activity you finish.

1. Spell your words with markers.

3. SNAP Spell your words while snapping.

2. B WORD K A Spell your words with letter tiles.

4. Spell your words with paint.

Words with /ů/

Lesson 29

183

1 Hide and Seek

Reinforce correct spelling of current spelling words.

Write the words one at a time on the board. Use this activity for each word.

- **Look** at the word.
- **Say** the word out loud.
- Let's **hide** (cover) the word.
- **Write** the word on your paper.
- Let's **seek** (uncover) the word.
- **Check** your spelling. If your word is spelled wrong, write the word correctly next to it.

2 Other Word Forms

This activity is optional. Have students write variations of this sentence using these Other Word Forms:

They can push the stalled car off the road.

pushes, pushed, pushing

3 Fun Ways to Spell

Four activities are provided. Use one, two, three, or all of the activities. Have students initial the box for each activity they complete.

Options:

- assign activities to students according to their learning styles
- set up the activities in learning centers for the class to do throughout the day
- divide the class into four groups and assign one activity per group
- do one activity per day

General

To spell your words with markers...
- Write a spelling word in thick, fat letters.
- Use other colored markers to decorate each letter with dots, flowers, stripes, etc.

Auditory

To spell your words while snapping...
- Look at a word on your spelling list.
- Close your eyes.
- Snap your fingers softly while you whisper the spelling of the word.
- Open your eyes and check your spelling.

Visual

To spell your words with letter tiles...
- Spell a word from your list by putting the tiles in the right order.
- Check your spelling.

Tactile

To spell your words with paint...
- Use your finger to write a spelling word on the paint bag.
- Check your spelling.
- Smooth out the paint and write another word.

1 Working with Words

Familiarize students with word meaning and usage.

Missing Letters

Write the words **foot**, **cook**, and **bush** on the board. Have volunteers underline the letter or letters that spell the sound of **/ů/** in each word.

At the top of your page, write the missing letter or letters that spell the sound of **/ů/** in each spelling word.

Clues

Read each clue. Find the spelling word that is a synonym, and write it on the line. Remember, a synonym is a word that means the same or almost the same as another word.

Dictionary Skills

Write the number of the definition that matches the meaning of the bold word in each sentence.

Take a minute to memorize...

Read the memory verse to the class twice. Have the class practice it with you two more times.

Day 3

Lesson 29

F **Working with Words** Name ____________

Words with /ů/ — Lesson 29

Missing Letters

Fill in the missing letter or letters that spell the sound of /ů/.

1. h _o_ _o_ k	6. br _o_ _o_ k	11. w _o_ _o_ l
2. w _o_ man	7. p _u_ sh	12. neighborh _o_ _o_ d
3. b _u_ shes	8. w _o_ lf	13. g _o_ _o_ d-bye
4. sh _o_ _o_ k	9. p _u_ lley	14. f _o_ _o_ tball
5. c _o_ _o_ kie	10. h _o_ _o_ d	15. noteb _o_ _o_ k

Clues

Write the spelling word that matches each clue.

1. fastener or hook	8. winch or pulley
2. shove or push	9. community or neighborhood
3. sweet treat or cookie	10. stream or brook
4. shivered or shook	11. sheep fur or wool
5. shrubs or bushes	12. lady or woman
6. head gear or hood	13. ball game or football
7. farewell or good-bye	14. binder or notebook

Dictionary Skills

Some dictionary entries have more than one meaning or definition. Read the entry word and its definitions. Write the number of the definition that matches the meaning of the bold word in each sentence.

wolf 1. wild mammal related to a dog that hunts in a pack 2. to eat quickly and greedily

1. The hungry man began to **wolf** down his dinner. 2
2. The **wolf** chased a rabbit. 1

Word Bank

brook	football	hook	pulley	wolf
bushes	good-bye	neighborhood	push	woman
cookie	hood	notebook	shook	wool

184

G Dictation

Name ______________________

Listen and write the missing words and punctuation.

1. The children had to push aside the bushes to find their football .
2. She drove to Sarah's neighborhood and found the little gray house .
3. Sarah picked up her notebook and waved good-bye to Mrs. Bentley .

H Proofreading

If a word is misspelled, fill in the oval by that word. If all the words are spelled correctly, fill in the oval by **no mistake**.

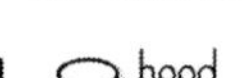

1.	4.	7.
○ hood	○ football	● notbook
● brooke	○ push	○ wool
○ burn	○ learn	○ Saturday
○ no mistake	● no mistake	○ no mistake

2.	5.	8.
● booshes	○ shook	○ serve
○ hook	○ person	● puley
○ dirt	● goodby	○ turtle
○ no mistake	○ no mistake	○ no mistake

3.	6.	9.
○ herd	● neborhood	○ middle
○ hurry	○ early	● wofl
● cooky	○ woman	○ search
○ no mistake	○ no mistake	○ no mistake

Words with /ʊ/

Lesson 29

185

1 Dictation

Reinforce correct spelling by using current and previous words in context.

Listen as I read each sentence and then write the missing words and ending punctuation in your worktext. (Slowly read each sentence twice. Sentences are found in the student text to the left.)

2 Proofreading

Familiarize students with standardized test format and reinforce recognizing misspelled words.

Look at each set of words. If a word is misspelled, fill in the oval by that word. If all the words are spelled correctly, fill in the oval by **no mistake**.

Day 4

Lesson 29

3 Hide and Seek

Reinforce correct spelling of current spelling words. (A reproducible master is provided in Appendix A as shown on the inset page to the right.)

Write the words one at a time on the board. Use this activity for each word.

- **Look** at the word.
- **Say** the word out loud.
- Let's **hide** (cover) the word.
- **Write** the word on your paper.
- Let's **seek** (uncover) the word.
- **Check** your spelling. If your word is spelled wrong, write the word correctly next to it.

4 Other Word Forms

Have your students complete this activity to strengthen spelling ability and expand vocabulary.

1 Posttest

Test mastery of the spelling words.

I will say the word once, use the word in a sentence, then say the word again. Write the word on your paper.

Hide and Seek

Check a coin for each word you spell correctly.

Other Word Forms

Word Sort

Use the clues to write the Other Word Forms.

Words with oo

1. where people live ___neighborhoods___
2. small stream ___brooklet___
3. pegs to hang things ___hooks___
4. made from sheep hair ___woolen___
5. lunch dessert ___cookies___
6. telling people farewell ___good-byes___
7. leather balls for games ___footballs___
8. coat with attached hat ___hooded___
9. folders to hold papers ___notebooks___

Words with u

10. small tree ___bush___
11. wheels and rope used to raise something ___pulleys___
12. shoving ___pushing___

Words with o

13. wild animals ___wolves___
14. ladylike ___womanly___

Word Bank

brooklet	cookies	good-byes	hooks	notebooks	pushing	womanly
bush	footballs	hooded	neighborhoods	pulleys	wolves	woolen

Other Word Forms
Lesson 29
351

1.	football	At recess, Sarah's class played soccer instead of **football**.
2.	woman	Mrs. Bentley was a kind **woman** who often gave the girls a ride.
3.	good-bye	She told the girls **good-bye** when she took them home.
4.	neighborhood	Sarah's house wasn't in a very wealthy **neighborhood**.
5.	bushes	The **bushes** around it were overgrown.
6.	brook	There is no **brook** on Brook Street.
7.	hood	The **hood** of their mother's car had a big dent in it.
8.	hook	Sarah hung her jacket on a **hook** in the closet.
9.	notebook	Nellie wrote the answers to her history assignment in her **notebook**.
10.	cookie	There wasn't a **cookie** left in the cupboard.
11.	shook	Nellie **shook** some salt into the food she was cooking.
12.	wolf	The sisters managed to **wolf** down all of their supper.
13.	wool	Sarah's old **wool** blanket was too hot on that warm evening.
14.	pulley	The word **pulley** rhymes with woolly.
15.	push	Mr. Valentino didn't **push** Sarah to tell everyone about her mother.

Progress Chart

Students may record scores. (Reproducible master in Appendix B.)

Personal Dictionary

Students may add any words they have misspelled to their personal dictionaries for reference when writing. (Cover in Appendix B.)

I Game Name ____________________

Join Mr. Valentino's class as they pray for God's mercy on the special people on their list. Move one space for each word you or your team spells correctly from this week's word list.

Prayer List:
Helen and baby
Tony's dad
Katelynn's neighbor
Sarah's mother

START

Remember: Spend a lot of time in prayer for other people!

J Journaling

In your journal, start a prayer list . Write the name of each person you are going to pray for and what he or she needs. You may add to your prayer list any time.

186

2 Game

Reinforce spelling skills and provide motivation and interest.

Materials

- game page (from student text)
- flat buttons, dry beans, pennies, or game discs (1 per child)
- game word list

Game Word List

1. brook
2. bushes
3. cookie
4. football
5. good-bye
6. hood
7. hook
8. neighborhood
9. notebook
10. pulley
11. push
12. shook
13. wolf
14. woman
15. wool

How to Play:

- Divide the class into two teams.
- Have each student place his/her game piece on Start.
- Have a student from team A go to the board.
- Say the spelling word. (You may also wish to use the word in a sentence.)
- Have the student write the word on the board.
- If correct, instruct each member of team A to move his/her game piece forward one space on the game board. (Note: If the word is misspelled, correct the spelling immediately.)
- Alternate between teams A and B.
- The team to reach the board first is the winner.

Non-Competitive Option:

At the end of the game, say: "Class, I am proud of your efforts to spell the words correctly. If you had fun and tried your best, you are all winners!"

3 Journaling

Provide a meaningful reason for correct spelling through personal writing.

Review the story using discussion leads provided on the following page. Encourage students to apply the Scriptural value in their journaling.

Journaling (continued)

- Why did Sarah think she was like the dandelion? (She didn't feel like anyone paid much attention to her.)
- What kind of problem did Sarah's mother have? (She was an alcoholic.)
- Was Sarah's mother drunk all the time? (No.)
- What kind of problems did her drinking cause? (She spent most of her money on alcohol so the family had little left to live on. When she was drinking, she didn't think of anything else, not even her children.)
- Did Sarah want anyone to know about her mother? Why? (No. She was embarrassed.)
- You may know someone with a drinking problem. Is any problem too hard for God to solve? (No.)
- What does God promise in our Scripture this week? (That when we pray for others, He is going to help.)
- Start a prayer list in your journal. Write down each person that you are going to pray for and what his or her needs are. You may add to your prayer list any time.

Take a minute to memorize...
Have the class say the memory verses from lessons 25, 26, 27, 28, and 29 with you.

"Mastering spelling is a complex intellectual achievement, not a low-order memory task."*

*Watson, Alan J. 1988. Developmental Spelling: A Word Categorizing Instructional Experiment. Journal of Educational Research, Vol. 82, No. 2, November/December: 82-88.

1 **Literature Connection**
Topic: Moderation
Theme Text: James 1:5

Clear Wisdom

Laney learns that what she eats affects how clearly she thinks.

"Six times one is six. Six times two is twelve. Six times three is eighteen. Six times four is twenty-four. Six times five is thirty. Six times six. . . Oh! I can never remember that one." Laney put the plastic lid on the leftover soup and headed for the pantry to get chips and desert for her lunch. "Thirty-six. Six times six is thirty-six. That rhymes. Six times seven is forty-two. Six times eight is forty-eight. Six times nine is fifty-four."

"Laney, you're doing very well." Mrs. Larkin smiled as she finished putting away some dishes. "I am proud of you. You know all your sixes now."

"I passed my fives yesterday. We never did timed tests in New York. I know my multiplication tables, but I'm not as fast as everyone here—except for Tommy. Math is hard for him." Laney filled a plastic baggy with corn chips, then grabbed three of her favorite dark chocolate candy bars and added them to her lunch before her mother turned around.

"Hurry and eat your breakfast, Laney. I'm going to run upstairs and see if Casey and Aunt Lorene still want to go shopping with me this morning over in Fayetteville. Lorene said she would help me pick out fabric for some new curtains in the living room. These things are so horrible." The new Mrs. Larkin fingered the dull brown draperies as she passed them on the way upstairs.

"Can I skip school and go with you, too?" Laney called after her as she filled her glass with chocolate milk. "Aunt Lorene and Casey will be going back to New York in just a few days. We might not see them again for a long time."

Elisa Larkin stopped on the stairs. "No, you need to pass your sixes today. You've already missed too much school because of our move here."

Laney groaned, then turned to pour chocolate milk on her Cocoa Puffs before taking a big bite of the chocolate eclair she'd found in the pantry.

"Look! It's froggy out there." Casey pointed out the car window half an hour later.

Laney leaned back in the plush seat of the big car and smiled before she turned toward her three-year-old cousin Casey. "Fooooooggy, Case. The river valley is foggy this morning." Laney reached over and tucked Casey's long brown hair behind her ear and tried not to giggle.

"Well, I can't see the horses through this white stuff. I want to see the baby horse." Casey squinted as she peered out her window trying to get a glimpse of the Arabian foal she had seen the day before.

"The fog will burn off by the time you come to pick me up from school this afternoon, Casey, and we can see the little foal then."

"Who's gonna burn it up?" Casey's forehead was furrowed with lines of worry. "Will the baby horse get burned, too?"

"No, Case. The water in the river is warmer than the air. When the warm air near the river hits cold air, it makes fog. As the air in the river valley heats up. . ."

"I thought Jesus made frogs." Casey interrupted with a frown.

"Fog, Case. Jesus created white fog and green frrrrrrogs that hop."

"Then He burns them up?" Casey still looked worried.

"No, when the sun warms the air up in the valley, the fog goes away. Look now. We're above the fog." Laney explained. "I think it looks like tired clouds down there in the valley."

Casey gazed thoughtfully out her window at the layer of fog in the river valley below. "The sun wakes up the tired clouds and they go up in the sky where they belong."

"Well, something like that." Laney smiled at her young cousin.

"Want some?" Casey held out a handful of brightly-colored candy.

"Sure." Laney made a colored bar graph with the M&Ms on the palm of her hand then popped a blue one into her mouth.

At lunch, Mr. Valentino told the class that since it had turned out to be a lovely spring day they were going to eat outside under the big pine tree on the playground. Rachel, Beth, and Laney sat together. "Oh, no!" Laney moaned. "I can't eat this soup without going back inside to warm it up in the microwave."

"It won't take long. I'll ask Mr. Valentino if I can go with you," Beth suggested.

Laney stood up and unwrapped one of her candy bars to eat while she waited. She was already on the second one by the time Beth came back with the needed permission.

When math class began Laney's head was beginning to hurt. She stared at the multiplication problems on the paper in front of her.

"On your mark. . . Get set. . . Go!" Mr. Valentino said from the front of the room.

Laney stared at the first problem. Six times one. She slowly wrote a six, then skipped down to the six times six. "That was twenty-six, I think." Her mind seemed sluggish and she had a hard time focusing on the numbers. She hadn't come close to completing the page when Mr. V. said to stop. "What's wrong with me?" she thought. "I knew all these this morning. I

Story Continued

guess I just need more practice."

The next morning Laney and her mom were once again in the kitchen. Laney looked up when Edward Larkin, Mom's new husband, walked in. "How are my girls this morning?" He smiled.

"Fine, except I just can't seem to pass my sixes," Laney complained. She set the stack of flashcards on the kitchen counter and poured herself a glass of chocolate milk.

"Where are the candy bars? I just bought a new package of them at the grocery store on Friday." Elisa poked her head out of the pantry.

Coach Larkin raised an eyebrow at his new stepdaughter. "Well, my little chocolate lover, do you have anything to say?"

Laney looked at the floor. "Casey and I ate some yesterday afternoon."

"What about the other four?"

"Well, I had one in my lunch on Monday."

"Laney Ausherman!" Mom frowned. "You ate four candy bars yesterday?"

Laney shifted her eyes and looked out across the street at the flowers blooming in Mason Springs Park. Slowly she nodded her head.

"Didn't you have chocolate milk and Cocoa Puffs for breakfast yesterday, too?" Coach Larkin grinned at the dark blond head below him. The head moved slightly up and down. He knelt down and lifted Laney's chin so her eyes would meet his. "Laney, just because we have special things for you to eat doesn't mean you need to eat them all at once. Was that timed test you took yesterday after lunch?" Laney nodded her head. "No wonder you didn't do well. Your mom was telling me how great you were doing yesterday morning. I really thought you'd pass. She said you knew all your sixes at breakfast." He paused. "You know, I bet your brain just fogged up after all those Cocoa Puffs, the chocolate milk, and three candy bars."

Laney just nodded her head again. She decided not to mention the chocolate eclair and M&Ms. "I don't know what happens to me," she said. "I just love chocolate. I don't know how to stop myself."

Elisa Larkin walked to the refrigerator and looked at the Scripture border sheet held on by magnets. "'If you really want to know what God wants you to do,'" she read, "'ask him and he will gladly tell you, for he is always ready to give wisdom to all who ask him.' Balance, Laney. Everything needs to be balanced. If you only ask, God will be delighted to help you quit fogging up your brain with chocolate. And I have a few ideas myself."

"Froggy?" Casey walked into the kitchen rubbing her eyes. "Did you say it's froggy outside again?"

"No, Case. We were talking about ways to keep from frogging. . . er, fogging up my brain." Laney laughed as she tucked a stray strand of hair behind her cousin's ear.

"Will the sun burn it off?" the little girl asked.

Mrs. Larkin smiled "No, but God's Son will help us keep our brains clear enough to make good choices. All we have to do is ask for wisdom."

2 Discussion Time

Check understanding of the story and development of personal values.

- What did Laney love to eat?
- What desserts did Laney have before math class?
- How did she do on her multiplication facts test after eating so many desserts?
- Why were her eating choices unwise?
- How can Laney make wiser choices in the future?

A Test-Words Name ______________________

Write each spelling word on the line as your teacher says it.

1.	woman	7.	dirt
2.	middle	8.	cattle
3.	mirror	9.	return
4.	river	10.	travel
5.	burn	11.	center
6.	early	12.	good-bye

Review

Lesson **30**

B Test-Sentences

Write the sentences on the lines below, correcting each misspelled word, as well as all capitalization and punctuation errors. There are two misspelled words in each sentence.

this sharck has hundreds of shapr teeth

1. This shark has hundreds of sharp teeth.

There are therty days in septimber

2. There are thirty days in September.

a small tertel sat by the quiet brooke,

3. A small turtle sat by the quiet brook.

187

3 Test-Words

Test for knowledge of the correct spellings of these words.

I will say the word once, use the word in a sentence, then say the word again. Write the word on the lines in your worktext.

1. woman — Aunt Lorene is a very kind **woman.**
2. middle — Casey's booster seat was in the **middle** of the back seat.
3. mirror — Casey could see herself in the rear view **mirror.**
4. river — "The **river** valley is foggy, not froggy!" laughed Laney.
5. burn — "The sun will **burn** off the fog," Laney told Casey.
6. early — The fog is often thick in the **early** morning.
7. dirt — Casey liked to see the foal paw the **dirt** in the pasture.
8. cattle — There were a few **cattle** in the pasture, too.
9. return — Casey and Aunt Lorene will **return** to New York soon.
10. travel — They will **travel** home by plane.
11. center — Laney arranged the candy in the **center** of her palm.
12. good-bye — Casey waved **good-bye** to Laney through the car window.

4 Test-Sentences

Reinforce recognizing misspelled words.

Read each sentence carefully. Write the sentences on the lines in your worktext, correcting each misspelled word, as well as all capitalization and punctuation errors. There are two misspelled words in each sentence.

Take a minute to memorize...

Read the memory verse to the class twice. Have the class practice it with you two more times.

Day 1

Review **30**

Day 2

Review 30

1 Test-Dictation

Reinforce correct spelling by using current and previous words in context.

Say

Listen as I read each sentence. Then write the missing words and ending punctuation in your worktext. (Slowly read each sentence twice. Sentences are found in the student text to the right. The words **market**, **serve**, **dollar**, and **summer** are found in this unit.)

2 Test-Proofreading

Familiarize students with standardized test format and reinforce recognizing misspelled words.

Look at each set of words. If a word is misspelled, fill in the oval by that word. If all the words are spelled correctly, fill in the oval by **no mistake**.

Review Lesson 30

C Test-Dictation

Name ______________________

Listen and write the missing words and punctuation.

1. Mom got that at the market .
2. Dad will serve on the board .
3. Can you make a cake that looks like a dollar bill ?
4. I saw an empty nest in that tree last summer .

D Test-Proofreading

If a word is misspelled, fill in the oval by that word. If all the words are spelled correctly, fill in the oval by **no mistake**.

1. ● Decimber ○ dollar ○ sugar ○ no mistake
2. ○ market ○ remember ● handel ○ no mistake
3. ○ March ○ center ○ wonder ● no mistake
4. ○ wolf ○ later ○ dirt ● no mistake
5. ○ sharp ● allarm ○ able ○ no mistake
6. ● botel ○ park ○ brook ○ no mistake
7. ○ summer ● silvir ○ worse ○ no mistake
8. ○ squirrel ○ football ○ good-bye ● no mistake
9. ○ river ○ argue ● mettal ○ no mistake

188

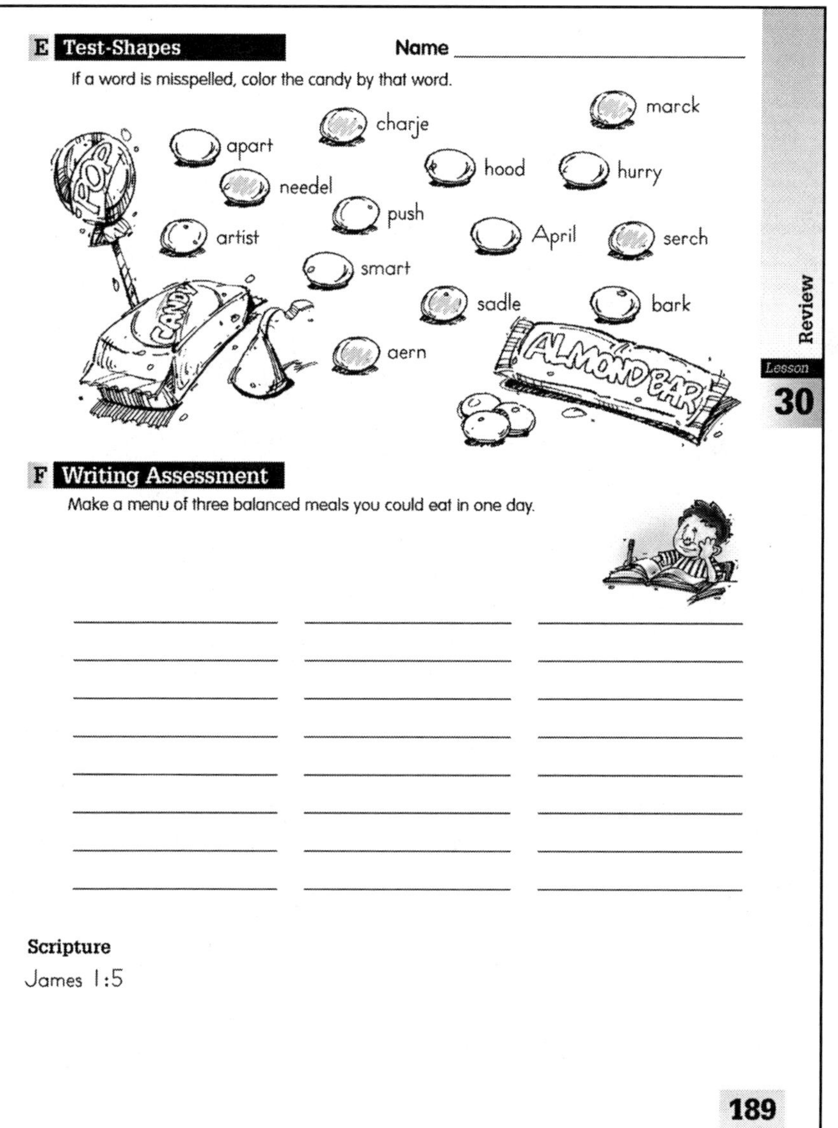

E Test-Shapes Name ______________________

If a word is misspelled, color the candy by that word.

Review

Lesson 30

F Writing Assessment

Make a menu of three balanced meals you could eat in one day.

Scripture

James 1:5

1 Test-Shapes

Test mastery of words in this unit.

If a word is misspelled, color the object by that word.

2 Writing Assessment

Assess student's spelling, grammar, and composition skills through personal writing.

- How was Laney's diet unbalanced? (She ate too much chocolate.)
- Why did Coach Larkin think Laney had not passed her multiplication facts? (She had fogged up her brain with too much chocolate.)
- Why is eating too much chocolate like fogging up your brain? (You can't see clearly when it is foggy. You can't think clearly when you eat a lot of sugar.)
- What Scripture verse did Laney's mom read from the border sheet on the refrigerator? (James 1:5)
- What did Laney's mom think would help Laney make better choices? (Asking God for help.)
- Make a menu of three balanced meals you could eat in one day.

"Spelling correctly is a courtesy to the reader."*

*Scott, Jill E. 1994. Spelling for Readers and Writers. The Reading Teacher, Vol. 48, No. 2, October: 188-190.

Day 4

Review

30

1 Test-Sentences

Reinforce recognizing misspelled words.

Read each sentence carefully. Write the sentences on the lines in your worktext, correcting each misspelled word, as well as all capitalization and punctuation errors. There are two misspelled words in each sentence.

G Test-Sentences Name ______

Write the sentences on the lines below, correcting each misspelled word, as well as all capitalization and punctuation errors. There are two misspelled words in each sentence.

does a wofl have fur or woul

1. Does a wolf have fur or wool?

the drievr can parck the bus over there

2. The driver can park the bus over there.

You will not find an eegel in the booshez?

3. You will not find an eagle in the bushes.

Review Lesson 30

H Test-Words

Write each spelling word on the line as your teacher says it.

1. learn
2. notebook
3. sprinkle
4. cookie
5. sugar
6. forget
7. start
8. able
9. shook
10. remember
11. Saturday
12. wonder

190

2 Test-Words

Test for knowledge of the correct spellings of these words.

I will say the word once, use the word in a sentence, then say the word again. Write the word on the lines in your worktext.

1. learn	Laney wants to **learn** her multiplication facts.
2. notebook	Laney wrote her assignments in her **notebook.**
3. sprinkle	Laney likes to **sprinkle** lots of sugar on her cereal.
4. cookie	Did Laney eat a **cookie** at breakfast, too?
5. sugar	Too much **sugar** made Laney's head ache.
6. forget	Laney hoped she would not **forget** what she'd studied.
7. start	Mr. Valentino gave the signal to **start** the timed test.
8. able	She thought she would be **able** to remember the answers.
9. shook	Laney **shook** her head in frustration.
10. remember	Laney could not **remember** the answers.
11. Saturday	Mrs. Larkin had seen the candy bars on **Saturday.**
12. wonder	She began to **wonder** what happened to all the candy bars.

I Test-Editing Name ______________

If a word is spelled correctly, fill in the oval under **Correct**. If the word is misspelled, fill in the oval under **Incorrect**, and spell the word correctly on the blank.

	Correct	Incorrect	
1. hammer	●	○	______
2. argew	○	●	argue
3. november	○	●	November
4. squirle	○	●	squirrel
5. candel	○	●	candle
6. army	●	○	______
7. purson	○	●	person
8. neyberhood	○	●	neighborhood
9. hook	●	○	______
10. pully	○	●	pulley
11. werse	○	●	worse
12. herd	●	○	______

Review Lesson 30

191

3 Test-Editing

Reinforce recognizing and correcting misspelled words.

4 Action Game

Reinforce spelling skills and provide motivation and interest.

Materials

- blindfold
- small prizes (erasers, pencils, stickers)

How to Play:

- Choose one student to be **IT** and blindfold him/her.
- Have the other students form a circle around **IT**, holding hands.
- Have the students circle around **IT**, and sing (to the tune of *London Bridge*): **Someone needs to spell a word, spell a word, spell a word. Someone needs to spell a word. It is you!**
- Instruct **IT** to point in any direction to choose a student to spell.
- Give the student to whom he/she points a word to spell tested on days 1 through 4.
- If he/she spells it correctly, give him/her a prize and have him/her return to his/her desk; if he/she spells it incorrectly, have him/her be **IT**.
- Continue playing until every student has spelled a word correctly.

1 Game

Reinforce spelling skills and provide motivation and interest.

Materials

- game page (from student text)
- flat buttons, dry beans, pennies, or game discs (1 per child)
- game word list

Game Word List

Check off each word lightly in pencil as it is used.

Red (5 points)

1. apart
2. artist
3. push
4. smart
5. April
6. mark
7. saddle
8. earn
9. hurry
10. later
11. bark

Blue (10 points)

1. needle
2. search
3. December
4. handle
5. charge
6. March
7. alarm
8. bottle
9. silver
10. football
11. metal

Yellow (15 points)

1. armies
2. marketplace
3. bottling
4. saddles
5. dirtiest
6. personal
7. servant
8. cookies
9. wolfish
10. woolly
11. wonderful

J **Game** Name ____________________

Score points for each review word or Other Word Form you or your team spells correctly.

Start

Remember: God has answers to your questions. Ask Him!

How to Play:

- Divide the class into two teams.
- Have each student place his/her game piece on Start.
- Inform the students of the following point system:
  Red list words = **5** points, **Blue** list words = **10** points
  Yellow list words = **15** points (these are Other Word Forms)
- Have a student from team A choose a color: red, blue, or yellow.
- Say a word from the correct color list. (You may also wish to use the word in a sentence.)
- Have the student write the word on the board.
- If correct, ask each member of team A to move his/her game piece forward (to the right and up, counter clockwise) to the corresponding color in the first section. Record the score. If the word is misspelled, have each member of that team move his/her game piece to the "sad face" in the first section.
- Alternate between teams A and B.
- The team with the highest score at the end of three rounds is the winner. (A round begins and ends at Start.)

Non-Competitive Option:

At the end of the game, say: "Class, I am proud of your efforts to spell the words correctly. If you had fun and tried your best, you are all winners!"

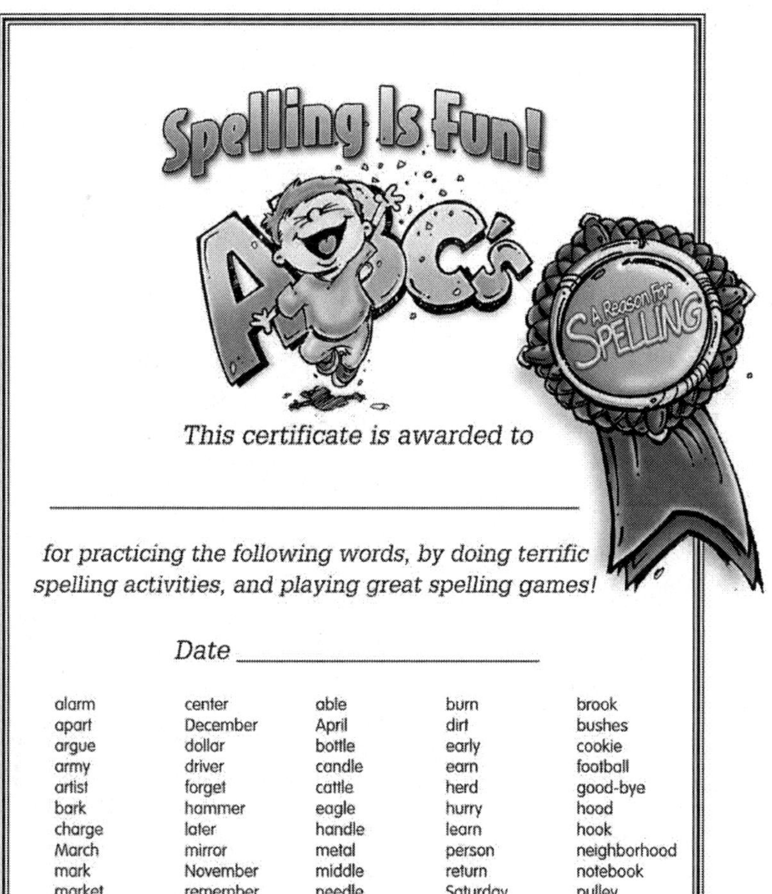

Spelling Is Fun!

This certificate is awarded to

____

for practicing the following words, by doing terrific spelling activities, and playing great spelling games!

Date ____________________

alarm	center	able	burn	brook
apart	December	April	dirt	bushes
argue	dollar	bottle	early	cookie
army	driver	candle	earn	football
artist	forget	cattle	herd	good-bye
bark	hammer	eagle	hurry	hood
charge	later	handle	learn	hook
March	mirror	metal	person	neighborhood
mark	November	middle	return	notebook
market	remember	needle	Saturday	pulley
park	river	saddle	search	push
shark	silver	sprinkle	September	shook
sharp	sugar	squirrel	serve	wolf
smart	summer	travel	thirty	woman
start	wonder	turtle	worse	wool

2 Certificate

Provide an opportunity for parents or guardians to encourage and assess their child's progress.

- Write your name on the first line.
- Write the date on the next line.
- Be sure to show your parents or guardian all the words you've practiced spelling.

Take a minute to memorize...

Have the class say the memory verses from lessons 25, 26, 27, 28, 29, and 30 with you.

3 Letter

Provide the parent or guardian with the spelling word lists for the next unit.

Show your parents or guardian this letter that lists your spelling words for the next unit. Put it where you will remember to practice the words together.

Dear Parent,

We are about to begin the last spelling unit of the year containing only one lesson. A set of fifteen words will be studied next week. All the words will be reviewed the following week. Values based on the Scripture listed below will be taught.

Lesson 31

boot	loose	suit
choose	moon	truth
drew	pool	Tuesday
flew	ruler	
fruit	shampoo	
group	smooth	

1 Peter 1:2

1 **Literature Connection**
Topic: Fear
Theme Text: 1 Peter 1:2

Freedom from Fear

Christopher learns to trust God when he is afraid.

"What are you reading?" Mr. Wright cocked his head at a funny angle trying to see the title of the book Christopher held.

Christopher laughed and tucked the book underneath the covers so his dad couldn't see it. "See if you can guess!"

"Well, let's see. . ." Dad sat down on the edge of the bed. "Because you are Christopher Wright, I'll bet it's a book about airplanes."

"Nope! You're wrong!" Christopher said, grinning from ear to ear. He pulled out the book and waved it in his dad's face. "See?"

"Whoa!" Mr. Wright grabbed the book so he could actually get a look at it. "Hmmm, spaceships. Well, I was close," he laughed. "They both fly." Dad began flipping through the pages. "Say, this space shuttle is really amazing."

"Look at this, Dad." Christopher took the book and quickly turned to a certain page. "Isn't that awesome?"

"It sure is." Mr. Wright studied the colorful two-page spread. "Absolutely awesome." Dad read the caption, "Supernova 1987A."

"The Hubble Space Telescope took that picture." Christopher adjusted his pillow more comfortably behind his back. "This book says a supernova is a star that exploded and can be a hundred million times brighter than our sun!" Christopher pointed at the picture. "That one exploded in February of 1987. Mr. Valentino said they did a Hubble servicing mission because something was wrong with the telescope's main mirror. They installed a new camera in the Hubble and it's working really well. Scientists are getting some great pictures of space!"

"You've been studying space for quite awhile at school now." Mr. Wright continued to slowly turn the pages. "Didn't you say something about a trip to a planetarium?"

"We're taking a field trip to the planetarium at the university over in Fayetteville." Christopher popped up so he was kneeling on his bed. "But guess what, Dad? We're also going to have a star party!"

"A star party!" Dad looked puzzled. "What's a star party?"

"Mr. Valentino said we all get to go to Beth's house one night because it's in the country away from the lights of town. He's going to have several telescopes set up and we'll get to see a bunch of different constellations and stuff!" Christopher bounced on his bed. "And we'll have hot chocolate to drink."

"Well, that sounds like a lot of fun." Mr. Wright closed the book and laid it on Christopher's desk. "But now it's getting late and you should get some sleep." Dad leaned over and gave Christopher a big hug before turning to leave the room. He paused at the door and flipped the light switch. "Sweet dreams, Son."

"DAD!" Christopher yelled before Mr. Wright had taken two steps down the hall.

"What do you need, Christopher?" Mr. Wright stepped back into the room with a concerned look on his face.

"You turned out the light." Christopher's eyes were wide. "And my night-light must be burned out, because it wasn't giving any light at all!"

"Okay, Son." Mr. Wright pulled the airplane-shaped night-light from the wall plug. "I'll go replace this bulb. Be back in a second." Dad left the overhead light on while he was gone. When he returned, he plugged in the night-light and came back to sit on the edge of Christopher's bed. "It's okay to use a night-light, Son, but you also need to remember the One you can trust in. Just talk to God when it's dark and you're afraid, all right?"

Christopher nodded and yawned at the same time. "Now, get some sleep. It's late." Dad chuckled and tucked the covers around Christopher, then left the room.

At school the next day Christopher watched in fascination as Mr. Valentino flashed some slides on the screen. "This is the galaxy M100. It's spiral-shaped like our own Milky Way galaxy." The slide revealed a brightly-colored object with two bright arms of stars whirling away from it. Several fainter arms of stars reached from the galaxy as well.

"This is one of the brightest members of the Virgo cluster of galaxies. It's in the constellation Coma Berenices and can be seen through some amateur telescopes." Mr. Valentino used his pointer to locate the constellations. "Look at how clearly the arms of this constellation can be seen. The M100 galaxy is tens of millions of light-years away and yet the Hubble Space Telescope can show us this detail! Isn't that incredible?"

"Now this is the Trifid nebula," he continued, clicking to the next slide. The reds, pinks, blues, and purples of the nebula stood out vividly against the black of space. "Doesn't that make you realize what an incredibly amazing God we have?" Mr. Valentino smiled as the slides continued. "And this is the Crab nebula."

As the image of the last slide faded, Mr. Valentino announced, "Our trip to the planetarium will be next Monday. The following Wednesday night we'll go to Beth's house for the star party. I'll send notes home with you today so your parents will know what to expect."

The days had raced by. Just before school was

Story (continued)

over for the day, Mr. Valentino reminded, "Make sure your parents get these notes about the party tomorrow night. You'll need to bring jackets because it can still be cool at night."

"Hey Christopher, wait up!" Christopher stopped walking and stepped to the side of the hall. "This party's going to be great, don't you think?" Tommy caught his friend and they joined the other kids heading for the outside door.

"Absolutely! I can't wait!" Christopher held up his hand for a high five. Tommy smacked it soundly with his hand.

"Beth said they're going to set up the telescopes on the hill across the valley from their house. Mr. Valentino found five people to bring their telescopes and help."

"Why do we need to be that far from Beth's house?" Christopher frowned. "Couldn't they just set up everything in their yard?"

"Because it needs to be really dark to see stuff through the telescopes better," Tommy explained patiently.

"You mean, there won't be any light at all?" Christopher's enthusiasm suddenly drained away.

"I don't know. Maybe to set up stuff, but not while we're looking at the stars." Tommy turned toward his mom's red sedan. "I gotta go. See you tomorrow!"

"Christopher, time to get up," Mom called as she poked her head in his door the next morning.

"I don't think I should go to school today," Christopher mumbled. "I think I'm getting sick."

Mrs. Wright crossed the room and placed her hand against his forehead. "You don't feel too warm. Does your tummy feel all right?"

"Um, yeah, I guess." Christopher grimaced. "I just don't feel too good."

Mom crossed her arms and looked down at Christopher with her I-won't-take-any-nonsense face. "Suppose you tell me just what's going on?"

"Well, the star party's tonight."

Christopher's answer confused his mother even more. "But you love learning about flight and space. It seems like you'd be anxious to go even if you were sick." She repeated her question. "What's going on?"

"It's really going to be dark!" Christopher exclaimed. "Really, really dark!"

"But you'll be right there with everyone else." Mom still didn't seem to understand.

"Mom!" Christopher practically wailed. "It's far away from the house! What if I have to go to the bathroom or something?"

"Well, just take a flashlight." Mrs. Wright turned toward the door. "Then, if you need to walk to the house, you'll have light."

"But, Mom, the kids will laugh at me if I take a flashlight. They'll think I'm stupid and call me names like 'fraidy cat' and stuff."

Mom returned and sat in the chair by Christopher's desk. "Oh, I see. You're afraid of the dark and you're worried about what the kids might think if they find out. Is that right?" When he nodded, she went on. "Do you remember the verse that goes like this, 'When I am afraid, I will trust in You. In God whose word I praise'?"

"Uh-huh." Christopher nodded. "It's on that Scripture song tape we have."

"That's right." Mom smiled. "Let's ask God right now to be with you tonight. You can always trust God, Son."

The star party was great fun! The sky was clear and cloudless, and the heavenly bodies the children spotted through the telescopes were fascinating. The hot chocolate was delicious, and everyone learned a lot and had fun.

And Christopher wasn't the only one with a flashlight!

The next day at school, Christopher smiled as he read the verse Mr. Valentino asked them to practice for handwriting. "May God bless you richly and grant you freedom from all anxiety and fear, I Peter 1:2," Christopher whispered to himself softly. "That's just what God did for me!" And smiling broadly, he carefully began writing the verse.

2 Discussion Time

Check understanding of the story and development of personal values.

- About what was Christopher reading?
- What special activities were Mr. Valentino's students going to do?
- Why didn't Christopher want to go to the star party?
- What is a star party?
- Have you ever been to one? If you have, tell about it.
- Did Christopher enjoy the star party?
- What promise did Christopher claim? (I Peter 1:2)

A Preview Name ______

Write each word as your teacher says it.

1. suit
2. fruit
3. flew
4. smooth
5. loose
6. pool
7. shampoo
8. ruler
9. Tuesday
10. drew
11. truth
12. boot
13. group
14. moon
15. choose

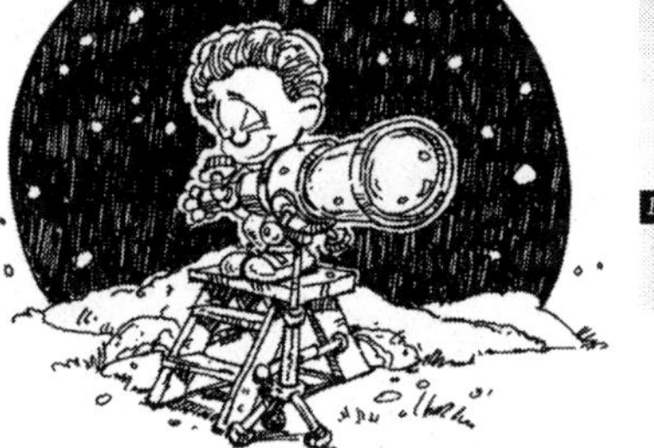

Words with /ü/

Lesson 31

Scripture
I Peter 1:2

195

3 Preview

Test for knowledge of the correct spellings of these words.

Customize Your List

On a separate piece of paper, additional words of your choice may be tested.

I will say the word once, use the word in a sentence, then say the word again. Write the word on the lines in the worktext.

Correct Immediately!

Let's correct our preview. I will write each word on the board. Put a dot under each letter on your preview as I spell the word out loud. If you spelled a word wrong, rewrite it correctly.

Take a minute to memorize...

Read the memory verse to the class twice. Have the class practice it with you two more times.

Day 1

Lesson 31

1.	suit	An astronaut's **suit** is designed especially for conditions in space.
2.	fruit	Astronauts' **fruit** and vegetables are fixed very differently from ours.
3.	flew	A rocket **flew** into space carrying the Hubble Space Telescope.
4.	smooth	Like an airplane, the space shuttle lands on a **smooth** runway.
5.	loose	It's booster rockets and fuel tank are cut **loose** after take off.
6.	pool	A supernova is an exploded star that looks like a bright **pool** of color.
7.	shampoo	Some supernovas look somewhat like spilled **shampoo.**
8.	ruler	Christopher uses a **ruler** to draw rockets and airplanes.
9.	Tuesday	On **Tuesday** Christopher realized it would be dark at the Star Party.
10.	drew	As the party **drew** nearer Christopher was more worried.
11.	truth	He finally told his mother the **truth,** that he was afraid of the dark.
12.	boot	Christopher dropped his flashlight when he retied his **boot** lace.
13.	group	The **group** of students got to see a lot of fascinating things.
14.	moon	They could see the craters on the surface of the moon.
15.	choose	We can **choose** to trust God to free us from our fears.

Progress Chart

Students may record scores. (Reproducible master in Appendix B.)

4 Word Shapes

Help students form a correct image of whole words.

Look at each word and think about its shape. Now, write the word in the correct word shape boxes. You may check off each word as you use it.

(In most words, the sound of **/ü/** is spelled with **oo**, or **u**. However, the sound of **/ü/** can also be spelled with **ew**, **ui**, **ou**, **u-consonant-e**, or **ue**.)

In the word shape boxes, color the letter or letters that spell the sound of **/ü/** in each word.

Day 1

Lesson 31

Words with /ü/ — Lesson 31

B Word Shapes Name ______________________

Write each word in the correct word shape boxes. Next, in the word shape boxes, color the letter or letters that spell the sound of **/ü/** in each word.

Word	Word shape
1. boot	boot
2. choose	loose
3. drew	pool
4. flew	shampoo
5. fruit	moon
6. group	suit
7. loose	truth
8. moon	Tuesday
9. pool	flew
10. ruler	drew
11. shampoo	smooth
12. smooth	choose
13. suit	ruler
14. truth	group
15. Tuesday	fruit

196

Answers may vary for duplicate word shapes.

Be Prepared For Fun

Check these supply lists for **Fun Ways to Spell** presented **Day 2**. Purchase and/or gather needed items ahead of time!

General
- Pencil
- 3 x 5 Cards (15 per child)
- Scissors
- Spelling List

Auditory
- Rhythm Instruments (two wooden spoons, two pan lids, maracas)
- Spelling List

Visual
- Sidewalk Chalk
- Spelling List

Tactile
- Play Dough
- Spelling List

C Hide and Seek Name ____________________

Place an **X** on a coin for each word you spell correctly.

D Other Word Forms

Using the words below, follow the instructions given by your teacher.

boots	fruits	pools	smoothness
choosing	grouped	ruled	suitable
chose	grouping	rules	suited
chosen	loosely	ruling	truthful
drawing	loosen	shampooed	truthfulness
drawn	looser	shampooing	
flies	loosest	smoothing	
flying	pooled	smoothly	

E Fun Ways to Spell

Initial the box of each activity you finish.

1. 

Spell your words with puzzles.

3. 
Spell your words in rhythm.

2. 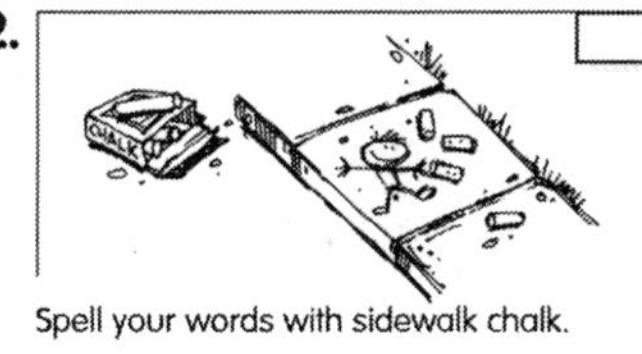
Spell your words with sidewalk chalk.

4. 

Spell your words with play dough.

Words with /ü/

Lesson 31

197

1 Hide and Seek

Reinforce correct spelling of current spelling words.

Write the words one at a time on the board. Use this activity for each word.

- **Look** at the word.
- **Say** the word out loud.
- Let's **hide** (cover) the word.
- **Write** the word on your paper.
- Let's **seek** (uncover) the word.
- **Check** your spelling. If your word is spelled wrong, write the word correctly next to it.

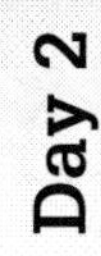

Day 2

Lesson 31

2 Other Word Forms

This activity is optional. Have students find and circle the Other Word Forms that are antonyms of the following:

dishonest
tighten
scattered

3 Fun Ways to Spell

Four activities are provided. Use one, two, three, or all of the activities. Have students initial the box for each activity they complete.

Options:

- assign activities to students according to their learning styles
- set up the activities in learning centers for the class to do throughout the day
- divide the class into four groups and assign one activity per group
- do one activity per day

General

To spell your words with puzzles...
- Write each word on a card.
- Cut each card into thirds using a straight cut.
- Mix your puzzle pieces.
- Put the puzzles together.
- Check your spelling.

Auditory

To spell your words in rhythm...
- Look at a word on your spelling list.
- Close your eyes.
- Play your rhythm instruments softly while you whisper the spelling of the word.
- Open your eyes and check your spelling.

Visual

To spell your words with sidewalk chalk...
- Write each of your spelling words on the sidewalk (ball court or playground).
- Check your spelling.

Tactile

To spell your words with play dough...
- Roll pieces of play dough into ropes.
- Use the ropes to make the letters of each word.
- Put them in the right order to spell each word.
- Check your spelling.

Day 3

Lesson

31

1 Working with Words

Familiarize students with word meaning and usage.

Complete the Word

Draw four boxes vertically on the board. Write **oo** in each box. Explain to the students that the answer to each clue you give will have the letters **oo** in it. Give the students these clues:

1. **something to read** (Write the word **book** across so **oo** is in the first box.)
2. **something used to sweep** (Write the word **broom** across so **oo** is in the second box.)
3. **to come right away** (Write the word **soon** across so **oo** is in the third box.)
4. **hoe, shovel, drill, saw** (Write **tools** across so **oo** is in the fourth box.)

Use the clues to write the words in the puzzle.

Take a minute to memorize...

Read the memory verse to the class twice. Have the class practice it with you two more times.

Words with /ū/

Lesson 31

F Working with Words

Name ______________________

Complete the Word

Fill in the missing letters to complete each word in the puzzle.

1. even
2. suds to wash hair
3. free
4. heavenly body
5. select
6. swimming hole
7. high shoe
8. sketched
9. soared
10. day of the week
11. matched outfit
12. apple, peach
13. crowd
14. fact
15. yardstick

1. smooth
2. shampoo
3. loose
4. moon
5. choose
6. pool
7. boot
8. drew
9. flew
10. Tuesday
11. suit
12. fruit
13. group
14. truth
15. ruler

Word Bank

boot	flew	loose	ruler	suit
choose	fruit	moon	shampoo	truth
drew	group	pool	smooth	Tuesday

198

G Dictation

Name ____________

Listen and write the missing words and punctuation.

1. The days flew by and soon it was Tuesday .

2. The group of thirty children gazed at the moon and stars .

3. God will take our fear away when we choose to trust Him .

Words with /ü/

Lesson 31

H Proofreading

If a word is misspelled, fill in the oval by that word. If all the words are spelled correctly, fill in the oval by **no mistake**.

1. ○ boot ● chooz ○ brook ○ no mistake
2. ○ drew ○ bushes ○ cookie ● no mistake
3. ● floo ○ good-bye ○ neighborhood ○ no mistake
4. ● froot ○ group ○ notebook ○ no mistake
5. ○ pulley ○ wolf ● loos ○ no mistake
6. ○ moon ○ return ○ needle ● no mistake
7. ● poole ○ ruler ○ shampoo ○ no mistake
8. ○ smooth ● siut ○ wool ○ no mistake
9. ○ truth ● Tuezday ○ woman ○ no mistake

199

1 Dictation

Reinforce correct spelling by using current and previous words in context.

Listen as I read each sentence and then write the missing words and ending punctuation in your worktext. (Slowly read each sentence twice. Sentences are found in the student text to the left.)

2 Proofreading

Familiarize students with standardized test format and reinforce recognizing misspelled words.

Look at each set of words. If a word is misspelled, fill in the oval by that word. If all the words are spelled correctly, fill in the oval by **no mistake**.

Day 4 / Day 5

Lesson **31**

3 Hide and Seek

Reinforce correct spelling of current spelling words. (A reproducible master is provided in Appendix A as shown on the inset page to the right.)

Write the words one at a time on the board. Use this activity for each word.

- **Look** at the word.
- **Say** the word out loud.
- Let's **hide** (cover) the word.
- **Write** the word on your paper.
- Let's **seek** (uncover) the word.
- **Check** your spelling. If your word is spelled wrong, write the word correctly next to it.

Hide and Seek

Check a coin for each word you spell correctly.

Other Word Forms

Other Word Forms Lesson 31

Sentence Fun

Write the word that best completes each sentence.

1. Dad likes to loosen his tie right after church.
2. Laney is always drawing a picture when she has free time.
3. I didn't have a costume suitable for the part in the play.
4. Tony had a hard time choosing which game to play.
5. Kristin shampooed her hair before the party.
6. My boots keep out the rain and snow.
7. People can trust us if we are always truthful.
8. Tommy waxed his skis until they slid smoothly.
9. The children grouped the shells by texture.
10. The vulture kept flying around the wounded sheep.
11. Daniel had a hard time remembering the rules of the game.
12. We all helped pick the ripe fruits from the orchard.
13. Stephen was the first player chosen for the soccer game.
14. We all pooled our money to buy Mother a birthday gift.
15. I tried to hold on, but my grip got looser as my hands tired.
16. There are always flies when we have a picinic.
17. The large jacket hung loosely from his shoulders.
18. The new hairstyle suited her perfectly.

Word Bank

boots	drawing	fruits	loosen	rules	suitable
choosing	flies	grouped	looser	shampooed	suited
chosen	flying	loosely	pooled	smoothly	truthful

352

4 Other Word Forms

Have your students complete this activity to strengthen spelling ability and expand vocabulary.

1 Posttest

Test mastery of the spelling words.

I will say the word once, use the word in a sentence, then say the word again. Write the word on your paper.

1.	flew	Christopher loved to learn about space and anything that **flew.**
2.	loose	A constellation is a **loose** group of stars given a name.
3.	boot	Is there a constellation that looks like a **boot**?
4.	ruler	We can't measure the vastness of space with a **ruler.**
5.	suit	Astronauts wear a special **suit** when they're in space.
6.	shampoo	I wonder if astronauts **shampoo** their hair in space.
7.	fruit	The Trifid Nebula is red, pink, and purple like ripe **fruit.**
8.	smooth	The arms of the M100 galaxy are bent in a **smooth** curve.
9.	pool	The night light's **pool** of soft light helped Christopher feel safe.
10.	Tuesday	Mr. Valentino sent notes home on **Tuesday** about the Star Party.
11.	drew	Mom finally **drew** out the real reason Christopher didn't want to go.
12.	truth	The **truth** was, Christopher was afraid of the dark.
13.	group	He was afraid someone in the **group** would make fun of him.
14.	choose	He had to **choose** to trust God for freedom from his fear.
15.	moon	The students saw the **moon** through the telescopes.

Progress Chart

Students may record scores. (Reproducible master in Appendix B.)

Personal Dictionary

Students may add any words they have misspelled to their personal dictionaries for reference when writing. (Cover in Appendix B.)

Words with /ü/

31

I Game Name ______________________

Join Christopher and his classmates at the Star Party. Move one space for each word you or your team spells correctly from this week's word list.

Remember: God has the power to free you from your fears!

J Journaling

In your journal, write a paragraph about a time when you were afraid.

200

2 Game

Reinforce spelling skills and provide motivation and interest.

Materials

- game page (from student text)
- flat buttons, dry beans, pennies, or game discs (1 per child)
- game word list

Game Word List

1. boot
2. choose
3. drew
4. flew
5. fruit
6. group
7. loose
8. moon
9. pool
10. ruler
11. shampoo
12. smooth
13. suit
14. truth
15. Tuesday

How to Play:

- Divide the class into two teams.
- Have each student place his/her game piece on Start.
- Have a student from team A go to the board.
- Read the spelling word. (You may also wish to use the word in a sentence.)
- Have the student write the word on the board.
- If correct, instruct each member of team A to move his/her game piece forward one space on the game board. (Note: If the word is misspelled, correct the spelling immediately.)
- Alternate between teams A and B.
- The team to reach the telescope first is the winner.

Non-Competitive Option:

At the end of the game, say: "Class, I am proud of your efforts to spell the words correctly. If you had fun and tried your best, you are all winners!"

3 Journaling

Provide a meaningful reason for correct spelling through personal writing.

Review the story using discussion leads provided on the following page. Encourage students to apply the Scriptural value in their journaling.

Journaling (continued)

- Christopher was fascinated by space and flying. Have you ever flown in a plane? Tell about your experiences. Do you like flying?
- Some people are afraid to fly, like Christopher was afraid of the dark. Have you ever been afraid in the dark? (Allow opportunity to describe experiences.)
- What other things are people sometimes afraid of? (Being alone, dogs, heights, snakes, the water, loud noises, storms, etc.)
- How can we manage our fears? (By trusting God to keep His promise. He promised to bless us and grant us freedom from all anxiety and fear.)
- In your journal, write a paragraph about a time when you were afraid.

Take a minute to memorize...
Have the class say the memory verse with you once.

1 **Literature Connection**
Topic: Joy fro m God
Theme Text: Colossians 2:7

Overflowing with Joy

Rachel finds real joy when her step-mother gives birth.

MONDAY MORNING

Hurry! Hurry! Hurry! I need to hurry! Helen. . .I mean Mom (I try to call her Mom now) has a doctor's appointment this afternoon after school. They check Mom and the baby every week instead of every month now. I need to put my tape player and headphones in my backpack and throw in a couple of those story tapes. Oh dear. Where did I put that set of tapes yesterday? Maybe they're under the bed. Helen says the baby could come any time now. I've decided I want a girl. It would be fun to have five girls in our family. Oh! Here they are; I put them in my desk. Now I will have something to listen to while they check Mom. I hope they let us hear the baby's heartbeat again. It sounds so loud and alive! Maybe the baby will be born today. I'd better hurry or I won't have time to eat much breakfast before school starts. I wish the baby would hurry and come. I want to see her!

MONDAY NIGHT

I'm lying in bed looking at the ceiling. It's hard to go to sleep when a baby is going to be born soon. Mom just tucked me in. "Rachel, you'd better get some sleep while you can," she said, rubbing her huge tummy and flipping off the light. "The baby may choose to be born in the middle of the night, or she might cry a lot and make it hard for you to sleep once we bring her home."

Mom is fine. I'm very thankful. She's been feeling much better than she did at first. At the doctor's office she sat on the table and swung her feet back and forth while she told Dr. Lang, "I'm just tired of being big and fat. It's hard to go to sleep because I can't get comfortable. Then when I finally do, the baby kicks and wakes me up." Dr. Lang just laughed. "That's normal. We worry when moms aren't getting bigger and babies don't move around."

Everybody got to hear the baby's heartbeat this afternoon. Even Father came. The doctor measured Mom. "Everything looks good. This baby is ready to be born." She winked at mom and helped her sit up.

I am so excited! Mom has a suitcase packed to take with her to the hospital. It's sitting by her bedroom door. She packed extra clothes and shampoo for herself, plus stuff for the baby. She wants to dress her up when we bring her home. This is so exciting. Vanessa, Rebecca, and Natalie think the baby will be a boy. We'll find out soon. Father doesn't care if it is a girl or a boy. "I'll be thankful for a healthy baby," he says.

TUESDAY MORNING

School will be done for the year this Friday! Mr. Valentino said our last Scripture to memorize is Colossians 2:7. We're practicing it for handwriting class right now. I already know it. It says, "Let your lives overflow with joy and thanksgiving for all he has done." I feel like I'm going to overflow with joy because school is out this Friday and soon we'll have a new baby. Maybe she'll come today!

TUESDAY NIGHT

I just helped Mom organize the cans in the pantry. Rebecca is cleaning the bathrooms. Natalie and Vanessa are helping Father clean the garage. Mom just asked me to dust the living room. I'm not sure why we're doing all this in the middle of the week. I wonder if we're going to have company or something.

Father just winked at me when I asked him about it. "Mom is nesting, Rache," he smiled. Natalie stopped sweeping and looked at him. "Is Mom helping the hamsters get a nest ready for their babies?" Father laughed and told her, "No, Natalie. Mom is getting the house ready for our baby."

Somehow I really don't think the baby will care if the garage is clean or if the cans are straight in the pantry. . . but they are!

WEDNESDAY MORNING

Rebecca is getting breakfast ready. Father walked in a few minutes ago rubbing his forehead. "Rachel, I need you to help Rebecca this morning," he said. "Set the table and make some peanut butter and jelly sandwiches for lunches."

Father looks worried. He keeps running his hand through his hair and rubbing his forehead.

Mom is walking slowly up and down the hall. "The contractions are starting." She smiles. "We'll have a baby soon!" She stops walking and talking when the muscles work to help the baby to be born. "It hurts some," she says when the contraction is over.

"The contractions don't come very often yet," Father explained as we ate. "They will be close together right before the baby comes. Contractions help the baby to be born."

All of us are very excited! "Can we stay home today?" I plead.

Father rubs his forehead and looks distracted. "This baby-being-born-business can take all day." He checks his watch and rubs his forehead again. "Everyone needs to go to school. You have some final tests that are important for you to take. Mrs. Larkin is coming to pick you up. I'll send someone to get you as soon as the baby is born."

Story Continued

WEDNESDAY NIGHT

I'm at Laney's house. Laney is already asleep. The baby has not come yet. I am having a hard time going to sleep. The clock on Laney's dresser says it is already 11 o'clock. Father promised we could come to the hospital just as soon as we have a baby. I wish the baby would hurry. I want to see what she looks like.

THURSDAY MORNING

Mrs. Larkin just woke me. up. She said she's taking me to the hospital now. She won't tell me if the baby is a girl or a boy. "You can see when you get to the hospital," she says as she zips my jacket.

Father meets me in the lobby of the hospital. He is holding Natalie who is almost asleep on his shoulder. Vanessa and Rachel look only half awake. The clock by the elevator says it's two o'clock in the morning. Father's eyes are red and he looks very tired. Maybe he has been crying. He has a funny look on his face. I hope Helen and the baby are okay.

We all walk into the birthing room. Mom is propped up in the hospital bed with lots of pillows. She is holding our baby sister in the yellow blanket that Grandma Jacobson knitted for her. Somebody else's baby is sleeping in one of those clear fish tanks on wheels beside Mom's bed. I walk over to read what is written on the blue card taped to the end. It says 'Jacobson boy.'

Father smiles down at me and says, "Surprise! We have twins." I gently touch the cheek of our baby boy. He is tiny. I wonder if he will be thankful for five sisters?

THURSDAY NIGHT

Grandma tucked me into bed tonight. I am thankful for our twins even if one of them is a boy. We didn't have to go to school today! Everyone was too tired. We got to pick up Mom and the twins from the hospital right after lunch. Grandma is here to help us. I am thankful I won't have to eat any more of Father's or Rebecca's breakfasts. They always give us cold cereal. Father says he and Mom knew we were going to have twins, but they wanted to surprise us. We were surprised all right. We have a boy and a girl. I am tired but the twins are crying. Mom was right. It is hard to sleep when babies cry.

FRIDAY MORNING

I guess I went to sleep last night. The sun is shining in my window. Today is the last day of school. We're going to clean our room and have a party. It should be fun. I will miss Mr. Valentino. He is fun. Mrs. Burton will be our teacher next year. I smell pancakes. Grandma Jacobson makes wonderful pancakes. She puts blueberries in them and lets me use all the syrup I want. I am thankful she is here.

FRIDAY NIGHT

We had a great party at school today. We got out early. Mr. Valentino gave us each a card when we left. He wrote a note telling me that he will miss me next year and I'm special. He let me show everyone pictures of the twins. They are too little to bring for "show and tell." He says our family might feel like the text we learned this week. "Let your lives overflow with joy and thanksgiving for all he has done." Mr. Valentino said there will be a party at the church for our babies next week. He called it a shower. Grandma gives the twins baths. They are too little for a shower. I hope they will be big enough for a shower next week because I love parties.

I got to hold Benjamin, and Rebecca held Leah during worship tonight. Mom is tired from having two babies at once. She is taking a nap. Grandma read us the Bible story of the twins Jacob and Esau. Our twins are sleeping. I know these babies will bring joy to our family. And I still can't believe we have two!

2 Discussion Time

Check understanding of the story and development of personal values.

- Why was Rachel excited at the beginning of the story?
- When was Knowlton Elementary going to dismiss for summer vacation?
- Did Rachel want their baby to be a boy or a girl?
- Why was the last day of school so exciting for Rachel?
- Why do you think a party for a new-born baby is called a shower?
- Tell about a baby shower to which you have been.
- How do you think Rachel felt as she held Benjamin during family worship?

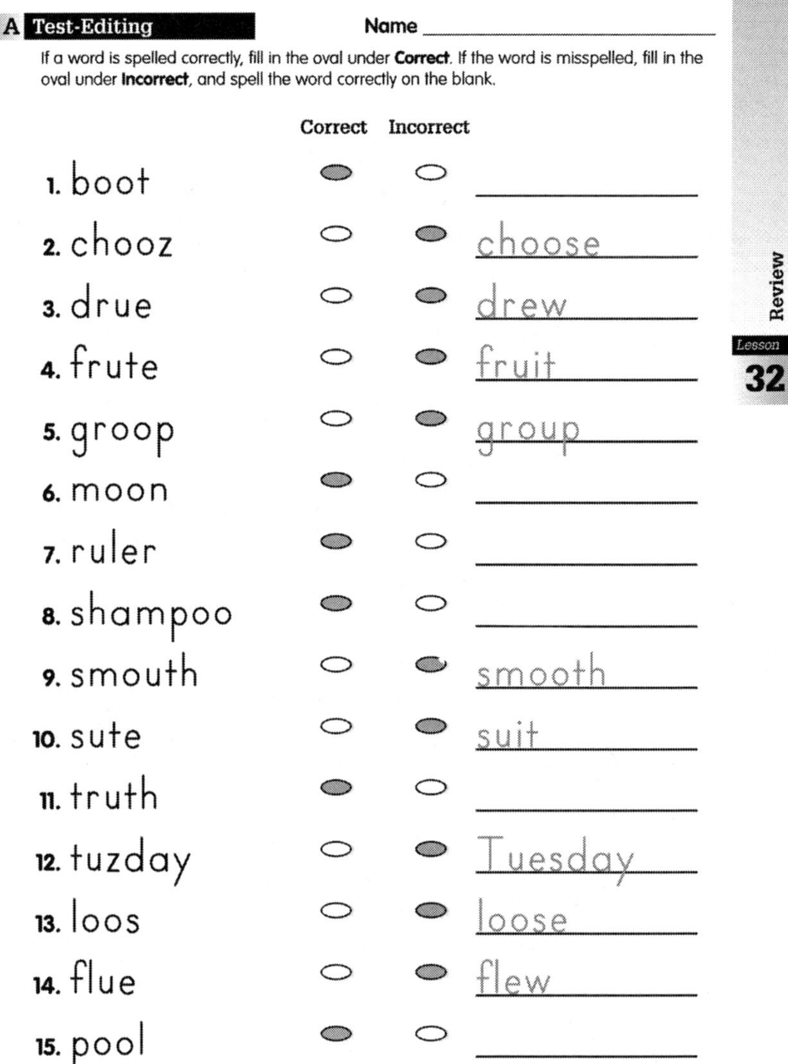

A Test-Editing Name ____________

If a word is spelled correctly, fill in the oval under **Correct**. If the word is misspelled, fill in the oval under **Incorrect**, and spell the word correctly on the blank.

	Correct	Incorrect	
1. boot	●	○	
2. chooz	○	●	choose
3. drue	○	●	drew
4. frute	○	●	fruit
5. groop	○	●	group
6. moon	●	○	
7. ruler	●	○	
8. shampoo	●	○	
9. smouth	○	●	smooth
10. sute	○	●	suit
11. truth	●	○	
12. tuzday	○	●	Tuesday
13. loos	○	●	loose
14. flue	○	●	flew
15. pool	●	○	

Review Lesson 32

201

Take a minute to memorize...

Read the memory verse to the class twice. Have the class practice it with you two more times.

Day 1

Review 32

3 Test-Editing

Reinforce recognizing and correcting misspelled words.

1 Game

Reinforce spelling skills and provide motivation and interest.

Materials

- game page (from student text)
- flat buttons, dry beans, pennies, or game discs (1 per child)
- game word list

Game Word List

Any spelling words from past units may be used in this game in addition to the lesson 31 words listed below.

1. boot
2. choose
3. drew
4. flew
5. fruit
6. group
7. loose
8. moon
9. pool
10. ruler
11. shampoo
12. smooth
13. suit
14. truth
15. Tuesday

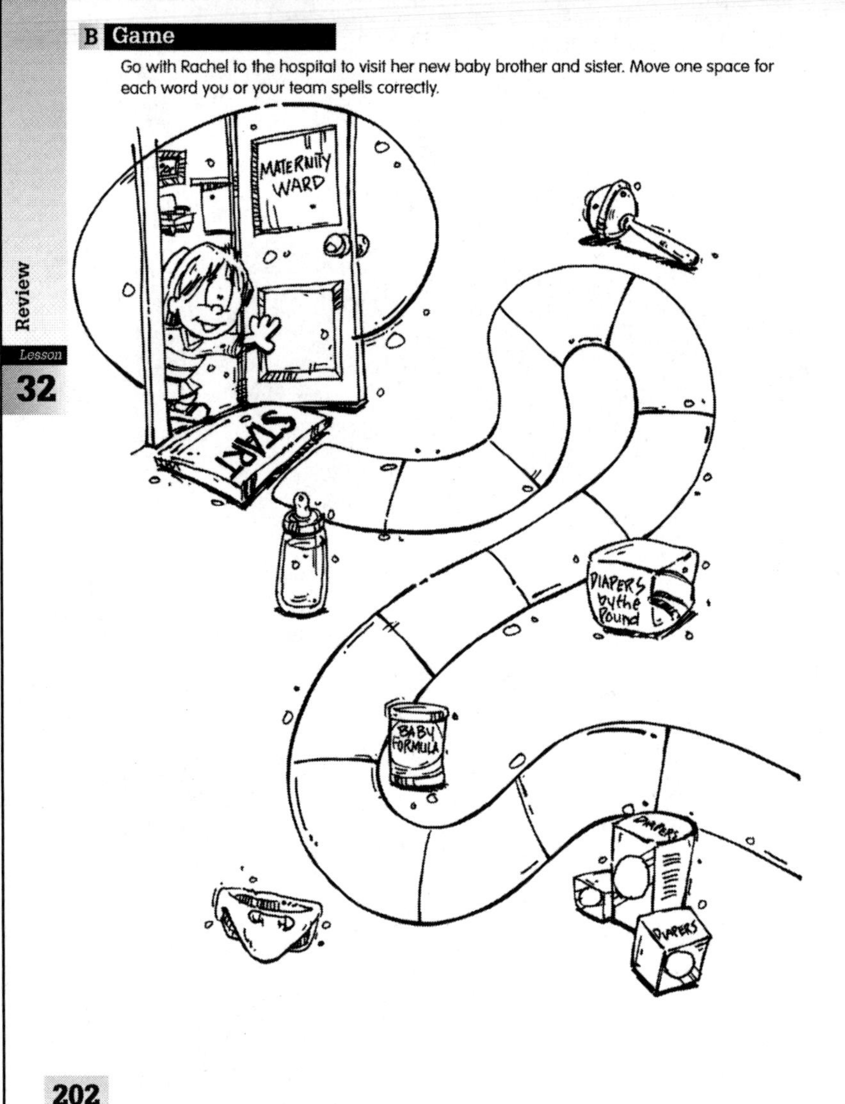

B Game
Go with Rachel to the hospital to visit her new baby brother and sister. Move one space for each word you or your team spells correctly.
MATERNITY WARD
START
DIAPERS by the Pound
BABY FORMULA
DIAPERS
Review
Lesson
32
202

How to Play:

- Divide the class into two teams, and decide which team will go first.
- Have each student place his/her game piece on Start.
- Have a student from team A go to the board.
- Say the spelling word. (You may also wish to use the word in a sentence.)
- Have the student write the word on the board.
- If correct, instruct each member of team A to move his/her game piece forward one space on the game board. (Note: If the word is misspelled, correct the spelling immediately.)
- Alternate between teams A and B.
- The team to reach Rachel's dad and the twins first is the winner.

Non-Competitive Option:

At the end of the game, say: "Class, I am proud of your efforts to spell the words correctly. If you had fun and tried your best, you are all winners!"

Name ______________________________

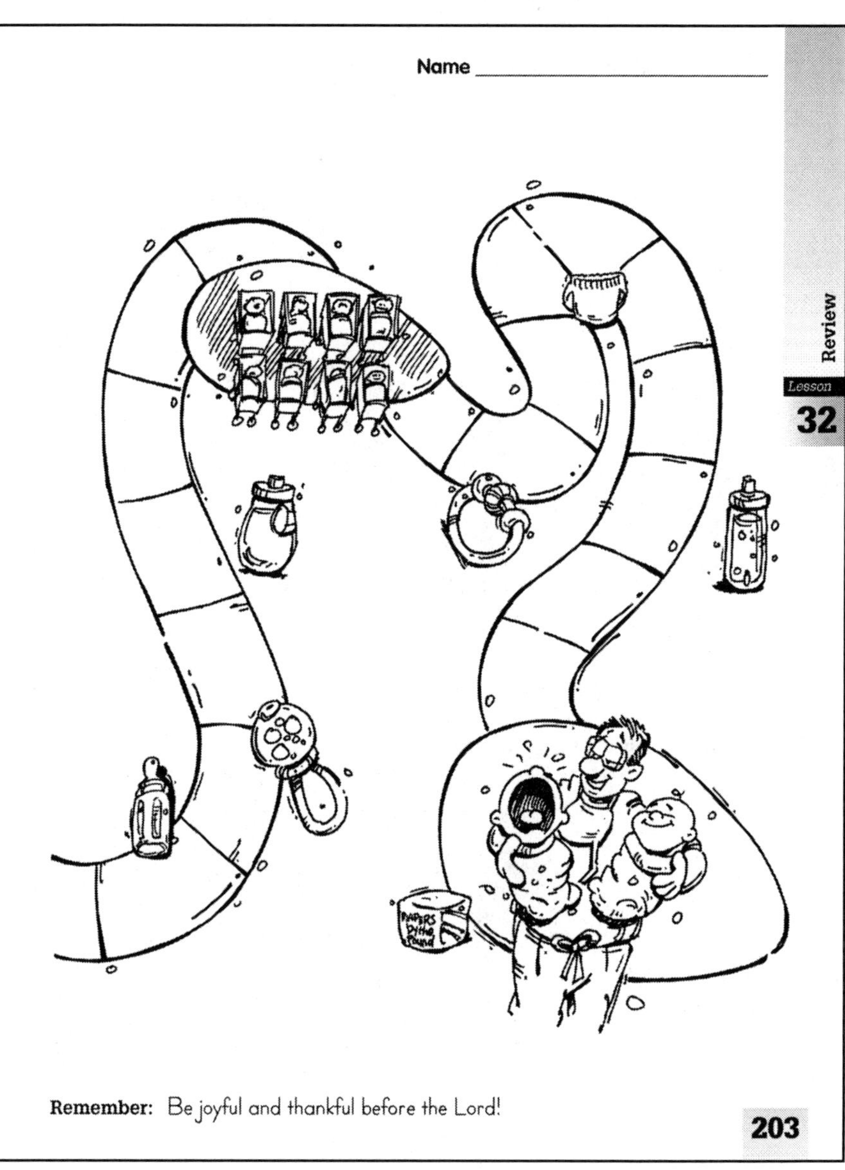

Remember: Be joyful and thankful before the Lord!

1 Writing Assessment

Assess student's spelling, grammar, and composition skills through personal writing.

- How do you think the Jacobson family felt as they listened to their baby's heartbeat? (Joyful. Excited.)
- How did Rachel feel about the coming summer vacation? (Happy. Excited.)
- How do you think Rachel felt when she found out their family had two babies? (Happy. Excited. Surprised.)
- How did Rachel feel about her grandmother coming? (Happy. Relieved. Thankful)
- How does Rachel feel about the baby shower for her new brother and sister? (Excited. Happy.)
- How was Rachel's life a lot like the scripture this week? (It was overflowing with joy and thanksgiving.)

Review Lesson 32

C Writing Assessment Name ____________________

Write a story about what you think the baby shower for the Jacobson twins might be like.

____

____

____

____

____

____

____

____

____

____

____

____

____

Scripture

Colossians 2:7

204

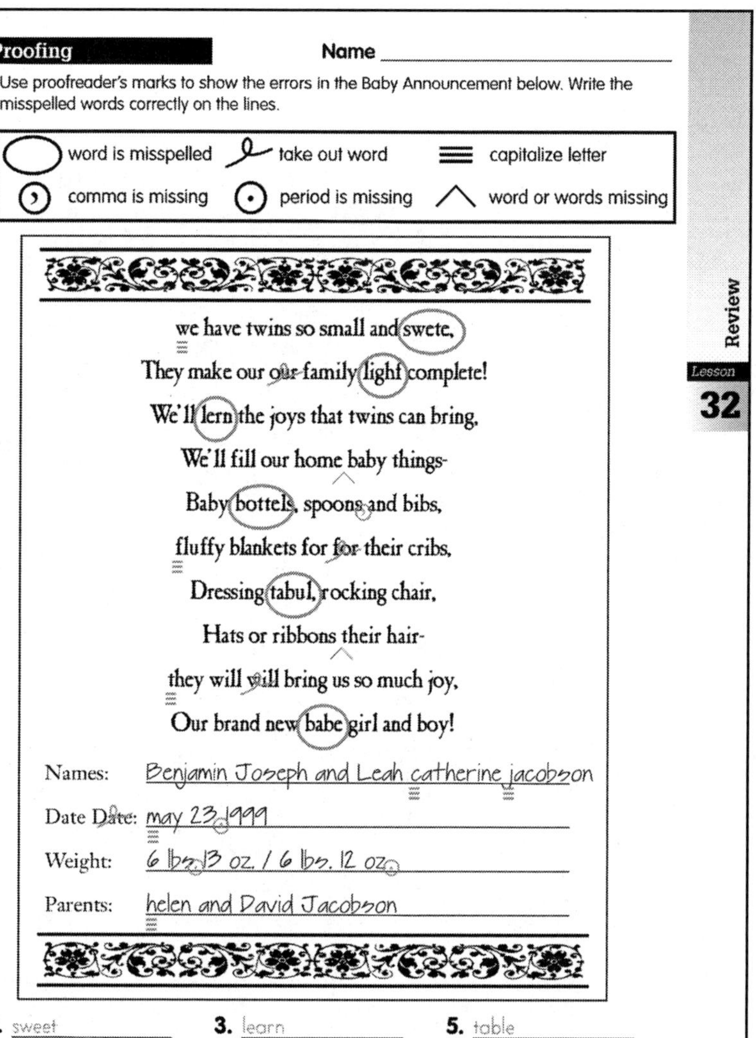

D Proofing Name ____________________

Use proofreader's marks to show the errors in the Baby Announcement below. Write the misspelled words correctly on the lines.

word is misspelled	take out word	capitalize letter
comma is missing	period is missing	word or words missing

we have twins so small and swete,
They make our our family light complete!
We'll lern the joys that twins can bring.
We'll fill our home baby things-
Baby bottels, spoons and bibs,
fluffy blankets for for their cribs,
Dressing tabul, rocking chair,
Hats or ribbons their hair-
they will will bring us so much joy,
Our brand new babe girl and boy!

Names: Benjamin Joseph and Leah catherine jacobson
Date Date: may 23 1999
Weight: 6 lbs 13 oz. / 6 lbs. 12 oz
Parents: helen and David Jacobson

1. sweet
2. life
3. learn
4. bottles
5. table
6. baby

205

Review

Lesson 32

3 Proofing

Reinforce recognizing capitalization, punctuation, and spelling errors.

Write this sentence on the board: **having too babies is are lot werk.** Ask the students to find the misspelled words. Demonstrate the mark used in proofreading to show that a word is misspelled. Now, ask the students if any words are missing. Draw the mark used to show that a word is missing. Continue by demonstrating the marks for letters that should be capitalized, missing punctuation, and extra words.

Say

You will be using proofer's marks to show the errors in the baby announcement in your worktext. After proofreading, write the misspelled words correctly on the lines.

Day 4

Review

2 Action Game

Reinforce spelling skills and provide motivation and interest.

Materials

- blindfold
- small prizes (erasers, pencils, stickers)

How to Play:

- Choose one student to be **IT** and blindfold him.
- Have the other students form a circle around **IT**, holding hands.
- Have the students circle around **IT**, and sing (to the tune of *London Bridge*):

  Someone needs to spell a word, spell a word, spell a word. Someone needs to spell a word. It is you!
- Instruct **IT** to point in any direction to choose a student to spell.
- Give the student to whom he points a word to spell from today's test.
- If he spells it correctly, give him a prize and have him return to his desk; if he spells it incorrectly, have him be **IT**.
- Continue playing until every student has spelled a word correctly.

1 Word Find

Familiarize students with word meaning and usage.

Wow, twins! Things will be pretty exciting and noisy around the Jacobson household for a while. Read the sentences. The words in bold print are hidden in the puzzle. Find each of these words and circle it in the puzzle. Words go across or down.

E Word Find

Name ____________________________

Find each of the bold words in the sentences below and circle them in the puzzle.

a	w	a	h	l	i	s	t	w	a	t	g	h
w	g	t	h	o	u	g	h	o	b	e	a	o
a	g	b	o	t	c	r	a	r	o	l	s	s
k	i	r	o	w	h	a	n	e	h	e	l	d
e	f	i	d	r	a	n	k	p	a	p	e	r
q	t	g	r	a	n	d	f	a	t	h	e	r
u	i	h	w	p	g	m	u	p	i	o	p	s
i	s	t	o	w	e	o	l	r	q	n	e	u
e	r	b	m	o	u	t	h	e	u	e	m	i
t	j	o	a	o	c	h	a	v	i	s	i	t
m	u	t	n	l	r	e	a	l	l	y	d	w
a	i	t	i	n	y	r	p	r	o	u	d	v
d	c	l	o	t	h	e	s	q	u	i	l	t
e	e	e	l	o	p	e	n	e	d	u	e	s

1. Mom made a **list** of things she would need for the baby.
2. We were eager to **visit** Mom in the hospital.
3. We called my **grandfather** and **grandmother** on the **telephone**.
4. Mom **held** a baby in her arms. It was **awake**.
5. The baby **opened** her **mouth** and gave a **loud** cry.
6. Father said it was time to **change** a diaper.
7. Benjamin was **asleep** even **though** Leah was not **quiet**.
8. Each baby **wore** a little **wool suit** with a **hood**.
9. The baby **clothes** looked so **tiny**.
10. A **woman** brought a **gift** in **really** pretty **paper**.
11. Grandma had **made** a **bright quilt** to **wrap** each baby in.
12. The babies woke up in the **middle** of the night.
13. Benjamin **drank** a **bottle** of **juice**.
14. We are **proud** of and **thankful** for our babies.

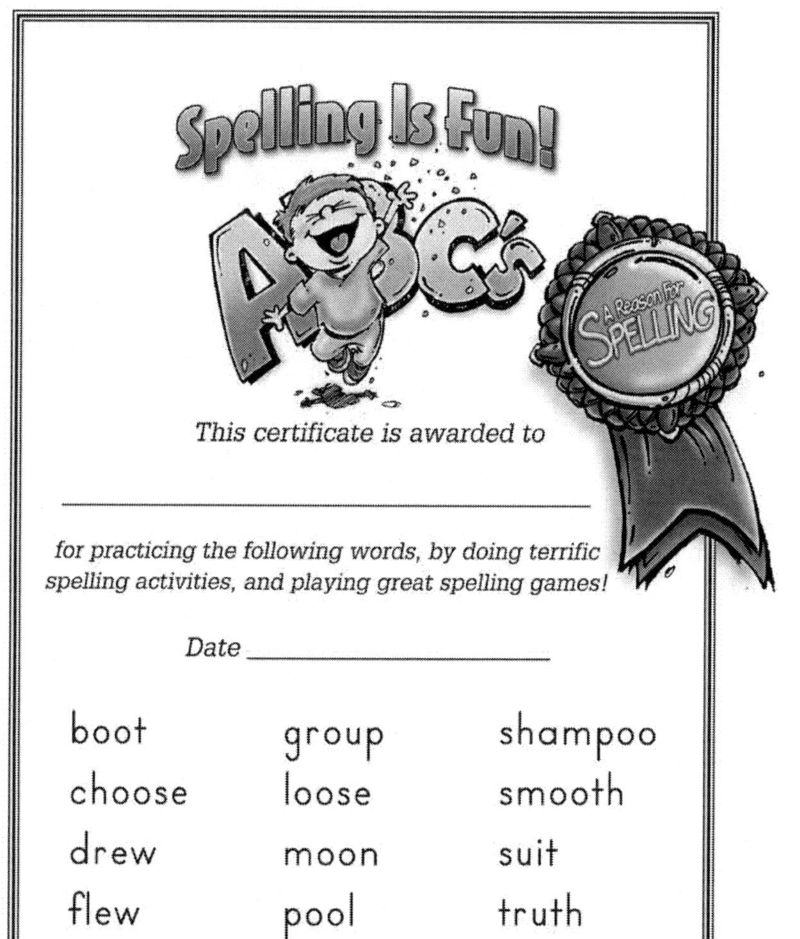

Spelling Is Fun!
ABC's
A Reason For SPELLING

This certificate is awarded to

for practicing the following words, by doing terrific spelling activities, and playing great spelling games!

Date

boot	group	shampoo
choose	loose	smooth
drew	moon	suit
flew	pool	truth
fruit	ruler	Tuesday

2 Certificate

Provide an opportunity for parents or guardians to encourage and assess their child's progress.

- Write your name on the first line.
- Write the date on the next line.
- Be sure to show your parents or guardian all the words you've practiced spelling.

Take a minute to memorize...
Have the class say the memory verses from lessons 31 and 32 with you.

The End

Please
Read this first!

Please Photocopy!

The following pages contain Black Line Masters for use with the **A Reason For Spelling**® Worktexts.

Photocopy privileges extend **ONLY** to the material in this section, and permission is granted only for those classrooms using **A Reason For Spelling**® Student Worktexts. Any other use of this material is expressly forbidden and all copyright laws apply.

Hide and Seek

Check a coin for each word you spell correctly.

Other Word Forms

Sentence Fun

Write the word that completes each sentence.

1.	When the telephone rings, she ____________ it.	answering	answers
2.	After swimming all day, he felt ____________.	chilling	chilly
3.	Sal and her mom picked ____________ on the hill.	berries	berrying
4.	Tom ____________ his head when he heard the noise.	lifted	lifting
5.	Meg ____________ things she wanted.	enlisted	listed
6.	It is hard to tell which cat is the ____________.	pickiest	picking
7.	The ____________ speaker told good stories.	visiting	visited
8.	The ____________ of the race cars were built strong.	bodily	bodies
9.	We will be ____________ over five chapters in math.	tests	tested
10.	My little sister is ____________ school this year.	begun	beginning
11.	The glass I was ____________ slipped from my hands.	holds	holding
12.	The ____________ have fluffy fur and curly tails.	puppy	puppies
13.	People are ____________ in many different ways.	gifts	gifted
14.	When I got to school, class had ____________.	begun	begin
15.	The air is ____________ than it was yesterday.	chillier	chilliest
16.	My cousin came as a ____________ to our class.	visited	visitor
17.	We had trouble ____________ the rocks.	lifting	lifts
18.	____________ strawberries with a friend is fun.	picked	picking
19.	Several kids brought ____________ to the party.	gifted	gifts
20.	We ____________ the zoo for our field trip.	visited	visiting

Hide and Seek

Check a coin for each word you spell correctly.

Other Word Forms

Clues

Use the clues to write the words.

1. glass to let light in ____________
2. baby sheep ____________
3. what a bee does ____________
4. wheat, rice, corn ____________
5. not eastern ____________
6. loud noise ____________
7. after eleventh ____________
8. desert plants ____________
9. breathing hard ____________
10. rigidly ____________

Hidden Words

Use the word bank to help you find and circle each of the words in the puzzle.

a	t	w	e	l	f	t	h	l	a	m	b	s
e	w	i	n	c	r	o	p	s	i	b	u	t
p	a	n	t	e	d	c	a	c	t	i	z	i
a	g	d	e	a	f	e	n	i	n	g	z	f
w	o	o	z	w	e	s	t	e	r	n	e	f
e	l	w	z	s	e	d	i	b	e	f	s	l
l	y	s	f	s	l	c	n	c	d	g	h	y
f	h	e	g	m	w	a	g	o	n	s	i	l

Word Bank

buzzes	crops	feel	panted	stiffly	wagons	windows
cacti	deafening	lambs	panting	twelfth	western	

Hide and Seek

Check a coin for each word you spell correctly.

Other Word Forms

Sentence Fun

Circle the word that completes each sentence.

1. He (change, changed, changing) into shorts for the bike race.
2. This is a very (cheese, cheesy, cheesiest) macaroni dinner.
3. Someone has been (bothers, bothered, bothering) the science projects.
4. You may get (shock, shocked, shocking) if you play with electricity.
5. We saw a (whales, whaled, whaling) ship.
6. I like my pie with (whips, whipped, whiplash) cream on it.
7. That wind from the (northern, northerly, northwest) is cold.
8. My dad is the (chairs, chairman, chairing) of the board.
9. These flies are very (bothered, bothersome, bothers).
10. I needed to (change, changing, exchange) the shirt for a new size.
11. The little chipmunk chattered in a (cheeky, cheeks, cheekiest) way.
12. (Thankfulness, Thankfully, Thankless), no one was hurt in the crash.

Spelling and Writing

Use each word in a sentence. Check your spelling.

1. cherries ______________________________

____

2. thirteenth ______________________________

____

Other Word Forms

Lesson 4

Hide and Seek

Check a coin for each word you spell correctly.

Other Word Forms

Prefixes and Suffixes

Choose the correct prefix or suffix to make a new word. Write the new word on the line.

1. flame + (ly, s) = ____________
2. glass + (y, ness) = ____________
3. flag + (ly, s) = ____________
4. close + (less, ly) = ____________
5. place + (s, ness) = ____________
6. sleeve + (less, ing) = ____________
7. flash + (ness, ing) = ____________
8. slice + (ly, s) = ____________
9. plain + (ing, s) = ____________
10. (ex, im) + plant = ____________
11. (dis, de) + close = ____________
12. (re, pre) + place = ____________
13. (in, dis) + please = ____________
14. (dis, ex) + plain = ____________

Rhyming Words

Write the Other Word Form that rhymes with each word below.

1. tagged ____________
2. sassy ____________
3. claiming ____________
4. dragging ____________
5. splashing ____________
6. sneezed ____________
7. hosing ____________
8. leaves ____________
9. canter ____________
10. basement ____________
11. shoved ____________
12. slanted ____________
13. dozed ____________
14. freezing ____________
15. icing ____________
16. vainly ____________

Word Bank

closed	flagging	glassy	plainly	pleased	slicing
closing	flaming	gloved	planted	pleasing	
flagged	flashing	placement	planter	sleeves	

Hide and Seek

Check a coin for each word you spell correctly.

Other Word Forms

Hidden Words

Use the word bank to help you find and circle each of the words in the puzzle.

r	e	d	n	e	s	p	s	t	n	e	p	s
p	p	i	k	s	k	i	p	p	e	n	n	d
g	r	a	b	b	i	n	g	s	k	i	g	e
g	r	a	y	r	n	i	s	h	p	r	s	l
i	z	s	p	e	n	d	i	n	g	e	p	l
d	c	p	r	a	y	e	r	f	u	l	l	y
b	r	e	a	k	s	k	a	t	d	y	i	e
r	o	l	y	i	c	r	c	o	s	s	k	p
e	s	l	e	n	i	p	r	o	u	d	l	y
a	s	i	r	g	s	k	a	t	i	n	g	s
d	i	n	f	i	n	g	y	c	r	a	s	r
e	n	g	u	n	b	r	o	k	e	n	s	e
d	g	s	l	b	r	e	n	g	n	i	p	l
c	r	o	s	s	r	e	s	m	n	t	e	l

Word Bank

breaded	breaking	crossing	prayerful	proudly	skinny	spending
breaks	crayons	grabbing	prayerfully	skating	spelling	unbroken

Hide and Seek

Check a coin for each word you spell correctly.

Other Word Forms

Code Words

Use the code to write each Other Word Form.

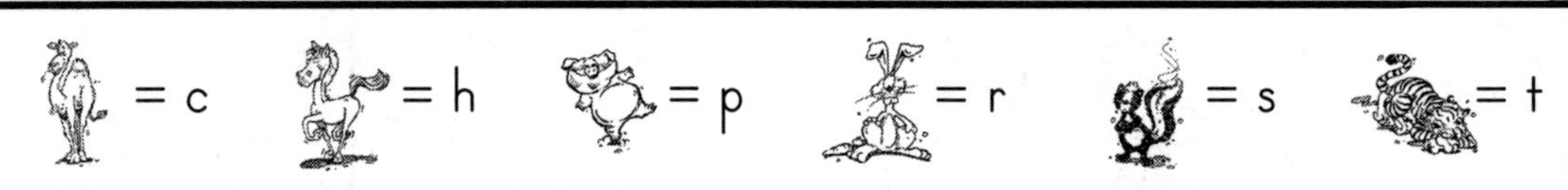

1. eamlined ____________________
2. eening ____________________
3. eading ____________________
4. atched ____________________
5. eams ____________________
6. ung ____________________
7. onger ____________________
8. ung ____________________
9. angest ____________________
10. ubber ____________________
11. owing ____________________

Hide and Seek

Check a coin for each word you spell correctly.

Other Word Forms

Secret Words

Use the clues to write the words in the puzzle. Then write the boxed letters on the lines below to find the words from this week's Scripture.

1. what your nose is used for
2. rooms in a school
3. the letter after u
4. happens quickly
5. the letter before g
6. what students are taught
7. soft and stretchy
8. person who has lots of money
9. spreading margarine on bread
10. sadly
11. what's going on
12. happily
13. what to write on envelopes

Secret Words: ___ ___ ___ ___ ___   ___ ___ ___ ___   ___ ___ ___ ___ ___ ___ ___ ___

Word Bank

addresses	classrooms	lessons	millionaire	smelling	unhappily
buttering	happening	merrily	rubbery	suddenly	

Hide and Seek

Check a coin for each word you spell correctly.

Other Word Forms

Scrambled Words

Use the sentence clues to help you unscramble the words. Write the unscrambled word in the sentence.

lobseng	**1.** The kitten ____________ to my aunts.
ginigsn	**2.** Tommy is ____________ at the top of his voice.
iwngdni	**3.** Grandmother is ____________ her yarn into a ball.
snorft	**4.** The ____________ of the cabinets are scratched.
egonury	**5.** Meg is ____________ than her sister.
bdempu	**6.** When it was dark, I ____________ my head.
kirnd	**7.** I am so hot, I need a ____________.
psastm	**8.** Tony played with the ____________ and got inky.
swing	**9.** The little bird tried its ____________.
ymbup	**10.** This road is rough and ____________.
strongyue	**11.** Grandpa tells stories about when he was a ____________.
tadspem	**12.** Beth was cold and ____________ her feet to warm them.
idwyn	**13.** On a ____________ day, my hat blew away.

Code Words

Use the code to write each Other Word Form.

3 = g	5 = n	7 = i

1. w 7 5 3 7 5 3 ____________

2. belo 5 3 7 5 3 s ____________

Hide and Seek

Check a coin for each word you spell correctly.

Other Word Forms

Sentence Fun

Circle the word that best completes each sentence. Write the word in the sentence.

1.	There was a ____________ sound during the storm.	crashes	crashing
2.	The fire destroyed all her ____________ goods.	earthly	earthen
3.	The ____________ baked bread smelled yummy!	freshly	freshen
4.	Our class watched the little chick ____________.	hatches	hatching
5.	The new girl ____________ the soccer ball far.	kicking	kicks
6.	Beth's new socks ____________ her T-shirt.	matched	matches
7.	The water ____________ through our pasture.	rushing	rushes
8.	Tony put the cans in ____________ to take to school.	sacks	sacking
9.	The ball was ____________ behind the cupboard.	sandwiches	sandwiched
10.	They were ____________ and didn't hear Mom call.	splashed	splashing
11.	He can push ____________ to make his train run.	switched	switches
12.	Mr. Valentino enjoys ____________ his students.	teaching	teaches

Word Sort

Write each Other Word Form under the correct heading.

hatched porches teach rematch earthen kicked

One-syllable Words	**Two-syllable Words**
1. ____________	**4.** ____________
2. ____________	**5.** ____________
3. ____________	**6.** ____________

Hide and Seek

Check a coin for each word you spell correctly.

Other Word Forms

Suffixes

Choose the correct suffix to make a new word. Write the new word on the line.

1. bright + (est, ing) = ____________
2. catch + (ed, ing) = ____________
3. halve + (s, er) = ____________
4. sight + (ing, est) = ____________
5. chalk + (ly, y) = ____________
6. clothe + (s, est) = ____________
7. knot + (ty, ly) = ____________
8. wrap + (per, ly) = ____________

Sentence Fun

Write the word that best completes each sentence.

1. Rosa is good at ____________ a ball.
2. My little brother gets ____________ in his shoestrings.
3. This is the ____________ color of green I have seen.
4. Stephen likes to shovel snow off the ____________.
5. I need to buy more warm ____________ for winter.
6. Mom is in her room ____________ gifts.
7. We ____________ an eagle flying overhead.
8. When our car broke down, Dad ____________ a ride into town.
9. The people who live next door are kind and ____________.
10. When we got ____________ to school, I remembered my lunch at home.
11. Mom fixed a healthy breakfast of ____________ foods.
12. I was careful not to drop the candy ____________ on the ground.

Word Bank

brightest	clothing	knots	sidewalks	thumbed	wrapper
catching	halfway	neighborly	sighted	wholesome	wrapping

Hide and Seek

Check a coin for each word you spell correctly.

Other Word Forms

Suffixes

Choose the correct suffix to make a new word. Write the new word on the line.

1. cage + (ly, y) = ____________

2. jolly – y + (ier, en) = ____________

3. jar + (red, y) = ____________

4. angel + (es, s) = ____________

5. edge + (s, en) = ____________

6. huge + (ier, ness) = ____________

7. rage + (d, ly) = ____________

8. juice – e + (en, ier) = ____________

9. judge – e + (ing, er) = ____________

10. jealous + (er, ly) = ____________

Hidden Words

Use the word bank to help you find and circle each of the words in the puzzle.

e	d	g	i	n	g	j	u	d	g	i	n	g
j	j	e	a	l	o	u	s	y	j	g	u	i
o	a	c	j	g	u	d	j	g	h	u	g	r
l	r	a	g	i	n	g	u	j	u	d	j	a
l	r	g	u	n	j	m	j	u	g	g	u	f
i	i	e	j	g	u	e	u	j	e	a	i	f
e	n	s	e	j	a	n	g	e	l	i	c	e
r	g	u	g	r	j	t	s	g	y	c	y	s

Word Bank

angelic, edging, hugely, jealousy, judging, jugs, raging
cages, giraffes, jarring, jollier, judgment, juicy

Other Word Forms

Lesson 14

Hide and Seek

Check a coin for each word you spell correctly.

Other Word Forms

Spelling and Writing

Use each pair of words to write a sentence. Check your spelling.

1. gasoline, racing ______________________________
____
2. soapy, sorriest ______________________________
____
3. sleepy, passed ______________________________
____
4. seven, bossing ______________________________
____
5. savings, selling ______________________________
____

Clues

Use the clues to write the words.

1. where clowns perform ______________
2. makes a car run ______________
3. add more sugar ______________
4. 1, 3, 5, ___, 9 ______________
5. decrease ______________
6. tell others what to do ______________
7. money kept in a bank ______________

Word Bank

bossy	gasoline	savings	sweeten
circuses	lessen	seven	

Hide and Seek

Check a coin for each word you spell correctly.

Other Word Forms

Suffixes

Circle the correct suffix.

1. Dave began track (ed, ness, ing) the bear.
2. The quiet (ness, ly, ed) of the forest was broken by a loud crash.
3. It seems like we have been rake (s, en, ing) leaves for a week!
4. Mom's new comforter is almost all quilt (y, et, ed).
5. In her new gown, Samantha looks queen (ly, ness, ing).
6. After the rain, Matthew track (ing, able, ed) up the floor.
7. I carried the lovely cake care (fulness, fully, ful).
8. We are copy (ing, es, iest) all the tax forms.
9. We are keep (able, ly, ing) Jenna's rabbit while she is gone.
10. Dad wanted us to come quick (ier, est, ly) to see the deer in the yard.
11. I cover (ed, ing, est) the hot dogs to keep them warm.
12. These three key (s, es, en) on my piano keep sticking.

Word Sort

Write each Other Word Form under the correct heading.

keyed copier queenly coverage racket forked

One-syllable Words	Two-syllable Words	Three-syllable Words
1. ______	3. ______	5. ______
2. ______	4. ______	6. ______

Hide and Seek

Check a coin for each word you spell correctly.

Other Word Forms

Suffixes

When words end in silent **e**, drop the **e** when adding a suffix that begins with a vowel (rake + ed = raked). Add **-ed** or **-ing** to each word to make new words.

1. awaken + ed = __________
2. date + ed = __________
3. mail + ed = __________
4. plane + ed = __________
5. sail + ed = __________
6. shade + ed = __________
7. wait + ed = __________
8. awaken + ing = __________
9. date + ing = __________
10. mail + ing = __________
11. plane + ing = __________
12. sail + ing = __________
13. shade + ing = __________
14. wait + ing = __________

Clues

Use the clues to write the words.

1. to have placed __________
2. under a tree it is __________
3. women __________
4. comes before ninth __________
5. forming something __________
6. serious or important __________
7. wasp nests feel thin and __________
8. person who works on a ship __________

Word Bank

eighth	laid	papery	shady
ladies	making	sailor	weighty

Hide and Seek

Check a coin for each word you spell correctly.

Other Word Forms

Suffixes

When a base word ends with **y** after a consonant, change the **y** to **i** when adding the suffix (happy + ly = happily). Follow this rule to add the suffix to each word.

1. marry + ed = ________________
2. angry + er = ________________
3. heavy + ness = ________________
4. angry + ly = ________________
5. heavy + ly = ________________
6. angry + est = ________________
7. busy + er = ________________
8. heavy + est = ________________
9. busy + est = ________________
10. carry + ed = ________________
11. busy + ed = ________________
12. marry + es = ________________

Base Words

Write the base word for each Other Word Form.

1. teaming ________________
2. leaving ________________
3. angrily ________________
4. deeply ________________
5. heaviness ________________
6. angrier ________________
7. left ________________
8. deepen ________________
9. heavily ________________
10. meaning ________________
11. married ________________
12. busiest ________________
13. carrying ________________
14. fielder ________________
15. mealy ________________
16. meanness ________________
17. busier ________________
18. marrying ________________
19. busied ________________
20. angriest ________________
21. carried ________________
22. heaviest ________________

Other Word Forms

Lesson 19

Hide and Seek

Check a coin for each word you spell correctly.

Other Word Forms

Hidden Words

Use the word bank to help you find and circle each of the words in the puzzle.

i	i	w	i	d	i	i	w	l	i	e	d
i	b	i	c	y	c	l	i	n	g	n	i
t	i	l	y	i	r	i	p	e	n	e	d
i	i	d	i	n	i	v	e	i	e	a	i
g	i	e	i	g	i	e	r	i	a	r	i
h	f	r	i	i	i	s	s	l	r	l	w
t	i	n	i	e	s	t	s	y	n	y	i
e	g	e	n	e	a	r	i	i	e	i	l
n	h	s	h	y	i	n	g	n	s	i	d
i	t	s	m	i	l	i	n	g	s	i	l
i	e	i	i	i	i	i	a	i	i	i	y
i	r	i	l	i	f	e	l	i	k	e	i

Word Bank

bicycling	lied	lying	nearness	signal	tiniest	wipers
dying	lifelike	near	ripened	smiling	wilderness	
fighter	lives	nearly	shying	tighten	wildly	

Hide and Seek

Check a coin for each word you spell correctly.

Other Word Forms

Sentence Fun

Write the words that best complete each sentence.

1. The cowboy is good at ____________ his horse and ____________ calves.
2. Mom ____________ the ____________ colored fabric to make my costume.
3. I dropped the bread into the ____________ on the ____________.
4. Rachel ____________ him an apology for ____________ so crossly.
5. The ____________ little puppy ____________ me around.
6. A snake ____________ past me, with only its head ____________.
7. I ____________ my mom from school, but she was ____________.

Code Words

Use the code to write each Other Word Form.

1. 10 p 8 k 4 n ____________
2. 8 p 4 nly ____________
3. fl 8 2 12 6 ng ____________
4. l 8 n 4 10 8 m 4 ____________

Word Bank

floated	golden	lonely	owed	roping	showing	telephoned
followed	gone	opening	riding	sewed	speaking	toaster

Hide and Seek

Check a coin for each word you spell correctly.

Other Word Forms

Spelling and Writing

Use each pair of words to write a sentence. Check your spelling.

1. causes, pawing ______________________________
2. buying, daughters ______________________________
3. walled, fighting ______________________________

Clues

Use the clues to write the words.

1. a battle ____________
2. made something happen ____________
3. showing someone how ____________
4. the feet of animals ____________
5. to take something with you ____________
6. long, narrow parts of a house ____________
7. divide the rooms in a house ____________
8. music made by a bird ____________
9. someone's girl children ____________
10. to purchase ____________

Word Bank

bring	caused	fight	paws	teaching
buy	daughters	halls	singing	walls

Hide and Seek

Check a coin for each word you spell correctly.

Other Word Forms

Riddles

Write the correct word in each riddle.

1. We like to act silly sometimes.
   Mom says we are ______________________ around.
2. He and his brother were yelling.
   They were both ______________________.
3. My cat likes to catch mice.
   She is a good ______________________.
4. My parents give me money each week.
   This is called an ______________________.
5. The choir teacher sang the words with no sound.
   She ______________________ the words.
6. The new vacuum cleans the carpet well.
   It is ______________________.
7. There are a lot of people in the mall.
   It is too ______________________.
8. I am not allowed to go anywhere fun.
   I am ______________________ for a week.
9. I am not sure whether to believe what he said.
   I am ______________________ that it is true.

Word Bank

allowance	crowded	grounded	mouthed	shouting
clowning	doubting	mouser	powerful	

Hide and Seek

Check a coin for each word you spell correctly.

Other Word Forms

Lesson 23

Other Word Forms

Scrambled Words

Use the sentence clues to help you unscramble the words. Write the unscrambled word in the sentence.

1. rofts The children were building ______________ in the woods.
2. rescron They wanted to use large posts for the ______________.
3. rouf The girls thought six sides would be better than ______________.
4. oderpert One boy ______________ all the plans in a notebook.
5. redsor They asked Tommy to give ______________ about how to build.
6. doingrer The girls did not want a boy ______________ them around.
7. sforlo Even the ______________ shook when the thunder boomed.
8. mingstro The children had to go inside when it began ______________.
9. roudep After the thunder and lightning, the rain ______________ down.
10. wainger The children were outside ______________ boots and raincoats.
11. prosts The children were good ______________.

Unscramble these Other Word Forms and write them on the lines.

1. ripstroa ______________	7. cginors ______________
2. ringsuco ______________	8. oprsty ______________
3. rocess ______________	9. cdeorsu ______________
4. rossense ______________	10. shron ______________
5. deeloprrty ______________	11. aersw ______________
6. orlfogni ______________	12. demorst ______________

Hide and Seek

Check a coin for each word you spell correctly.

Other Word Forms

Word Change

Use the clues to write the words in the puzzle.

			1.		a	r						
					2. a	r						
					3. a	r						
					4. a	r						
		5.			a	r						
6.					a	r						
		7.			a	r						
				8.	a	r						
			9.		a	r						
			10.		a	r						
			11.		a	r						
			12.		a	r						

1. very worried
2. groups of soldiers
3. very creative
4. quarrel
5. set sail
6. send home
7. outstanding
8. selling
9. ocean creatures
10. clearly
11. really stung
12. began

Other Word Forms

Lesson 25

Word Bank

alarmed	armies	discharge	marketing	sharks	smarted
argument	artistic	embarked	remarkable	sharply	started

Other Word Forms

Lesson **26**

Hide and Seek

Check a coin for each word you spell correctly.

Other Word Forms

Suffixes

Circle the correct suffix.

1. Daniel center (ness, ing, ed) his picture on the paper.
2. The cookies are pretty and sugar (ing, ful, y).
3. Dad likes to keep up with the late (ness, est, ly) news.
4. Her face mirror (ing, ly, ed) her feelings.
5. Christopher got a go-cart that had not been drive (ing, ed, n) very much.
6. He never forget (ful, s, ting) to do his assignment.
7. I remember (ing, ed, ly) my homework when I got to school.
8. My birthday cake tasted wonder (ful, ly, ing).
9. Katelynn liked the angel with the silver (s, ing, y) wings.
10. This warm weather feels very summer (y, ful, s).
11. James earned several dollar (ing, ness, s) mowing lawns.
12. The woodpecker hammer (ed, ing, ly) on the house kept me awake.

Clues

Use the clues to write the Other Word Forms.

1. middles or ____________
2. recently ____________
3. reflected ____________
4. touring ____________
5. bank notes ____________
6. motivated ____________
7. unmindful ____________
8. recalling ____________
9. shimmering ____________
10. pounding ____________

Word Bank

centers	driven	forgetful	lately	remembering
dollars	driving	hammering	mirrored	silvery

Hide and Seek

Check a coin for each word you spell correctly.

Other Word Forms

Word Sort

Write each Other Word Form under the correct heading.

cattlemen disable handled sprinkled turtleneck turtles

Two-syllable Words	Three-syllable Words
1. ______	4. ______
2. ______	5. ______
3. ______	6. ______

Guide Words

Pretend the words below are guide words on a dictionary page. Write the spelling words that would be found on each page.

both **disagree**

1. ______ 2. ______ 3. ______ 4. ______

eager **handwriting**

5. ______ 6. ______ 7. ______

message **reserve**

8. ______ 9. ______

sad **tusk**

10. ______ 11. ______ 12. ______ 13. ______

Word Bank

disable	candles	metallic	enable	saddled	turtleneck	sprinkling
cattleman	bottled	handling	eaglet	needles	traveling	

Hide and Seek

Check a coin for each word you spell correctly.

Other Word Forms

Suffixes

Change the **y** to **i** and add the suffix to each word to make a new word.

1. dirty + er = ________________

2. hurry + ed = ________________

3. early + est = ________________

Add the suffix to each word to make a new word.

4. person + able = ________________

5. return + able = ________________

6. service + able = ________________

7. personal + ize = ________________

Add **-ed** and **-ing** to each word to make new words.

	+ed	+ing
8. burn	________________	________________
9. earn	________________	________________
10. herd	________________	________________
11. learn	________________	________________
12. search	________________	________________
13. return	________________	________________

Spelling and Writing

Use each pair of words to write a sentence. Check your spelling.

1. hurries, servant ____

____

2. dirty, searching ____

____

Hide and Seek

Check a coin for each word you spell correctly.

Other Word Forms

Word Sort

Use the clues to write the Other Word Forms.

Words with oo

1. where people live ____________
2. small stream ____________
3. pegs to hang things ____________
4. made from sheep hair ____________
5. lunch dessert ____________
6. telling people farewell ____________
7. leather balls for games ____________
8. coat with attached hat ____________
9. folders to hold papers ____________

Words with u

10. small tree ____________
11. wheels and rope used to raise something ____________
12. shoving ____________

Words with o

13. wild animals ____________
14. ladylike ____________

Word Bank

brooklet	cookies	good-byes	hooks	notebooks	pushing	womanly
bush	footballs	hooded	neighborhoods	pulleys	wolves	woolen

Other Word Forms

Lesson 31

Hide and Seek

Check a coin for each word you spell correctly.

Other Word Forms

Sentence Fun

Write the word that best completes each sentence.

1. Dad likes to ________________ his tie right after church.
2. Laney is always ________________ a picture when she has free time.
3. I didn't have a costume ________________ for the part in the play.
4. Tony had a hard time ________________ which game to play.
5. Kristin ________________ her hair before the party.
6. My ________________ keep out the rain and snow.
7. People can trust us if we are always ________________.
8. Tommy waxed his skis until they slid ________________.
9. The children ________________ the shells by texture.
10. The vulture kept ________________ around the wounded sheep.
11. Daniel had a hard time remembering the ________________ of the game.
12. We all helped pick the ripe ________________ from the orchard.
13. Stephen was the first player ________________ for the soccer game.
14. We all ________________ our money to buy Mother a birthday gift.
15. I tried to hold on, but my grip got ________________ as my hands tired.
16. There are always ________________ when we have a picnic.
17. The large jacket hung ________________ from his shoulders.
18. The new hairstyle ________________ her perfectly.

Word Bank

boots	drawing	fruits	loosen	rules	suitable
choosing	flies	grouped	looser	shampooed	suited
chosen	flying	loosely	pooled	smoothly	truthful

Please
Read this first!

Please Photocopy!
The following pages contain Black Line Masters for use with the **A Reason For Spelling**® Worktexts.

Photocopy privileges extend **ONLY** to the material in this section, and permission is granted only for those classrooms using **A Reason For Spelling**® Student Worktexts. Any other use of this material is expressly forbidden and all copyright laws apply.

Appendix B

Level C

Spelling Progress Chart

Fill in the five lesson numbers for the unit in the first row of blocks. Use the first half of the column under each block to record the score for the Preview, and the second half of the column for the Posttest. To record the score, begin at the bottom of the column and color the blanks to show the number of words spelled correctly. Use one color for Preview and another for Posttest.

Words Spelled Correctly	Lesson Numbers									
	Preview	Posttest	Preview	Posttest	Preview	Posttest	Preview	Posttest	Preview	Posttest
15.										
14.										
13.										
12.										
11.										
10.										
9.										
8.										
7.										
6.										
5.										
4.										
3.										
2.										
1.										

Rubric for Scoring

You may wish to use this rubric at the end of each unit to track student progress.

	Standard	Usually	Sometimes	Not Yet
1.	Writes all letters correctly and legibly (upper and lower case)			
2.	Uses correct spelling on words from current and previous lessons			
3.	Writes a paragraph in response to a prompt			
4.	Uses appropriate punctuation			
5.	Uses capital letters correctly			
6.	Writes complete, coherent, and organized sentences			
7.	Includes descriptive language			
8.	Forms plurals correctly			
9.	Subjects and verbs agree			
10.	Uses a logical sequence of events			

my dictionary
bulb:(n)
bulge:(a)
bulldoz
bulletin:(n)

my journal
March 16

bright
thumb
Wednesday

12

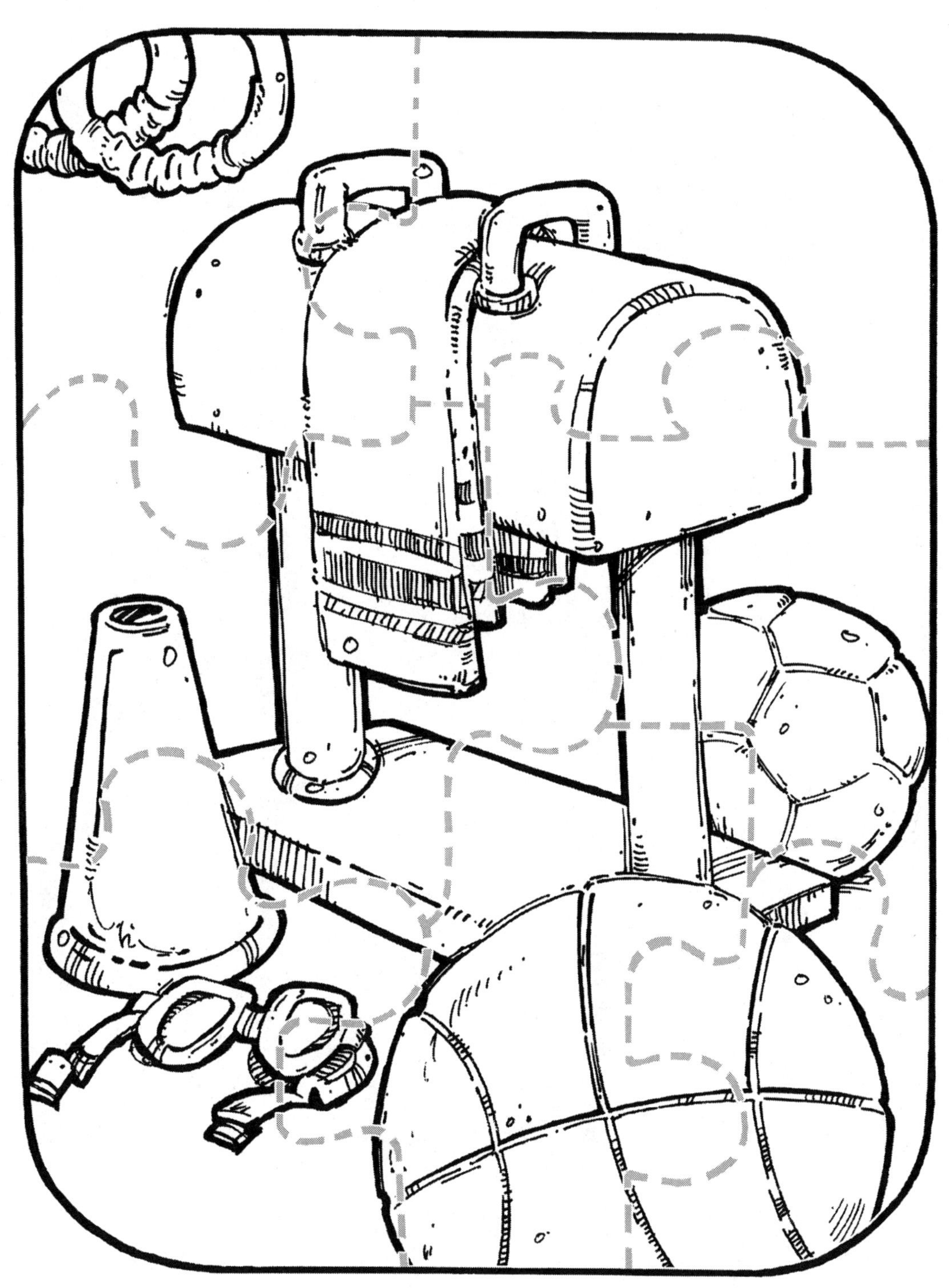

Christopher · Mom · Kristin

The End